SCAM

THE FIRST FOUR ISSUES!

BY ERICK LYLE

MICROCOSM PUBLISHING # 76081

ISBN # 978-1-934620-70-0

WWW.MICROCOSMPUBLISHING.COM

THERE WILL BE NO NEW LETTERS SECTION FOR THIS ANTHOLOGY. BUT, AS IT HAPPENS, I RECEIVED A TEXT MESSAGE FROM A KID NAMED BILLY IN MINOT, ND WHILE I WAS WORKING ON THIS INTRO. BILLY WRITES, "THE FIRST EVER HIT AND RUN GENERATOR PUNK SHOW IN THE HISTORY OF MINOT HAS JUST ENDED SUCCESSFULLY! IT WAS IN A HOSPITAL STAIRWELL! I'LL PUT IT UP ON YOUTUBE TOMORROW. THANKS, SCAM!"

TEXT MESSAGES, YOU TUBE... AND GENERATOR SHOWS! MANY THINGS HAVE CHANGED SINCE SCAM FIRST CAME OUT. HAPPILY, MANY HAVE STAYED THE SAME.

THE FIRST ISSUE OF SCAM CAME OUT ON JULY 6, 1991 AT A SHOW I HELPED SET UP IN MIAMI BEACH FOR THE BAY AREA BAND, FILTH. I WAS IN THE GROCERY STORE HERE IN BROOKLYN THE OTHER DAY AND THEY WERE PLAYING "SMELLS LIKE TEEN SPIRIT" OVER THE STORE'S PIPED IN RADIO STATION. THAT SONG, OF COURSE, WAS THE BIG HIT OF 1991, WHICH WAS ALSO THE YEAR THE FIRST GULF WAR STARTED AND — ACCORDING TO SONIC YOUTH — "THE YEAR THAT PUNK BROKE". I STOPPED AND REFLECTED THAT THIS WAR THAT I HAD PROTESTED IN ISSUE #1 HAS NOW BEEN GOING ON IN SOME FORM FOR LITERALLY MY ENTIRE ADULT LIFETIME AND "ALTERNATIVE" MUSIC HAS BEEN MUZAK THE WHOLE TIME. I THOUGHT ABOUT HOW SOME THINGS NEVER CHANGE. THEN I FILLED MY BAG WITH STOLEN GROCERIES AND WENT HOME.

1991 WAS A PIVOTAL YEAR. NEAR THE END OF THE PREVIOUS YEAR, GEORGE BUSH, SR. HAD ANNOUNCED THE DAWN OF THE "NEW WORLD ORDER". WHILE THIS PHRASE MOSTLY DESCRIBED AMERICAN IMPERIAL AMBITION ABROAD, IT ALSO SEEMED TO HERALD A MORE COMPUTERIZED AND CONTROLLED WORLD HERE AT HOME. IT WAS THIS NEW WORLD THAT SCAM SET OUT TO DESTROY. BY SNEAKING ACROSS THE BACKROADS OF AMERICA ON FREIGHT TRAINS, RIPPING OFF 10-15 COPIES OF EACH ISSUE AT KINKO'S IN EVERY TOWN AND USING STOLEN FEDEX NUMBERS TO SHIP THEM AHEAD TO THE NEXT DESTINATION. BY LEAVING SPRAY PAINTED MESSAGES ON BOXCARS AND UNDER BRIDGES CALLING OUT TO THE "SCAM PUNKS." BY NEVER WORKING, STEALING EVERYTHING. BY GLUING UP POSTERS AND STICKERS AND MAKING FAKE GREYHOUND TICKETS TO HELP FRIENDS GET TO THE WTO PROTESTS. BY LIVING IN SQUATS AND DOING ILLEGAL SHOWS IN THE STREETS AND DOING FOOD NOT BOMBS. AS A YOUNG PUNK AT THE TIME OF THE GULF WAR, I HAD FELT A SENSE OF ISOLATION. THERE WAS NO ONE PROTESTING IN SOUTH FLORIDA. BUT BY THE END OF THE DECADE I HAD FOUND MY PEOPLE WITH THIS ZINE.

SCAM CAME IN AT THE TAIL END OF THE GENERATION OF PUNKS AND ARTISTS THAT REVELED IN THE RUINS OF AMERICA'S DYING CITIES. THE RUINS WERE A KIND OF UTOPIA WHERE WE COULD BE FREE TO DREAM UP ANY LIFE WE WANTED. I SAT AROUND THE FT. LAUDERDALE PUNK HOUSE DRINKING STOLEN BEER, READING WORLD WAR III ILLUSTRATED AND DREAMING OF LIVING IN SQUATS LIKE THEY DID ON THE LOWER EAST SIDE. BUT WWIII ILLUSTRATED IS ALSO THE FIRST PLACE I READ THE WORD GENTRIFICATION. HOW WAS I TO KNOW THAT AS THE 1990'S PROGRESSED I WOULD BE FIGHTING FOR MY SPACE IN THE RUINS WITH THE YUPPIES OF THE BILL CLINTON GENERATION WHO NOW WANTED

TO RETURN TO THE CITIES AND TURN THE RUINS INTO LOFTS AND CAFES AND ORGANIC CHAIN GROCERY STORES? IRONICALLY, THE SURGING ECONOMY OF THE CLINTON ERA THAT HELPED CREATE THE WEALTH AND EXCESS THAT MADE "THE FANZINE REVOLUTION" AND FOOD NOT BOMBS POSSIBLE ALSO LED TO THE SHRINKING OF THE PUNK ROCK HOMELAND IN THE RUINS UNTIL SOON WE BECAME EXILES IN OUR OWN CITIES, PLACES NOW TURNED INTO UNRECOGNIZABLE ASSEMBLAGES OF THE VERY CHAIN STORES WE'D BEEN STEALING ALL OF OUR PHOTOCOPIES AND FOOD FROM.

TO ADD HUMILIATION TO OUR EXILE, IT IS NOT <u>FILTH</u>, BUT THEIR FORMER LABEL MATES, <u>GREEN DAY</u>, WHO LIKELY WILL BE INDUCTED INTO THE ROCK AND ROLL HALL OF FAME UPON ELIGIBILITY IN 2015. I DON'T TAKE THIS PERSONALLY IN THE WAY THAT, SAY, HUNTER S. THOMPSON WAS HAUNTED BY THE REEMERGENCE OF RICHARD NIXON IN 1968, BUT WHAT CAN I SAY? I SAW IT ALL COMING AND YOU READ IT HERE FIRST. THE SINCERE TRAGEDY HERE IS THAT IT HAS ALSO BECOME IMPOSSIBLE TO IMAGINE AN END TO THE WAR THAT BY THE TIME <u>GREEN DAY</u> TAKES THAT STAGE IN CLEVELAND TO ACCEPT THEIR AWARD WILL HAVE ENTERED ITS 24TH YEAR. WHEN I WAS 18 AND PUTTING OUT THE FIRST ISSUE OF THIS ZINE, I DID NOT YET UNDERSTAND THAT I HAD ENTERED INTO A LIFELONG BATTLE. FOR THAT REASON, IT MIGHT BE TEMPTING FOR SOME TO DISMISS THE EPHEMERAL MOMENTS OF FREEDOM DESCRIBED HEREIN. FOR THAT REASON, I WOULD ARGUE THAT THEY ARE EVEN MORE IMPORTANT.

THIS ANTHOLOGY COMPILES THE FIRST FOUR ISSUES OF <u>SCAM</u>, MOSTLY MY MIAMI YEARS. PURISTS WILL NOTE THAT I HAVE EDITED OUT SOME PAGES HERE AND THERE TO MAKE THE BOOK LESS BULKY AND TO LOWER THE COVER PRICE. IT SEEMS A MIRACLE TO ME THAT THE ACTUAL ZINE ORIGINALS USED TO MAKE THIS BOOK SURVIVED THE YEARS OF <u>SCAM</u> LIVING. EVERYTHING ELSE FROM THE MIAMI I WROTE ABOUT IS GONE, BUT SOMEHOW, EVEN AFTER YEARS CARRIED IN MY BAG ON FREIGHT TRAINS, HITCHHIKING TRIPS, BAND TOURS, AND EVEN TRIPS TO JAIL, THE WRITING IS STILL HERE.

THIS IS NO SMALL THING. I WAS CHASED OUT OF COUNTLESS COPY STORES OVER THE YEARS, ORIGINALS IN HAND, XEROXED PAGES FLYING BEHIND. I LOST MY BASS GUITAR AND ALL MY TAPES IN A BREAK-IN AT THE ZZ SQUAT, BUT SOMEHOW THE BAG MY ORIGINALS WERE IN WASN'T STOLEN. I ASKED IVY ABOUT IT THE OTHER DAY. SHE REMEMBERED A TIME WHEN HER MOM HAD BEEN EVICTED AND HAD PUT ALL THE STUFF IN HER HOUSE —— INCLUDING A BOX WITH THE ORIGINALS TO <u>SCAM #1</u> IN IT —— INTO STORAGE. INCREDIBLY, HER CAR WAS THEN STOLEN. THE KEYS TO THE STORAGE SPACE WERE ON THE FRONT SEAT AND THE THIEF, BEING FROM MIAMI AND A REAL PRO, OF COURSE, HEADED IMMEDIATELY TO THE STORAGE SPACE AND CLEANED THE PLACE OUT. THEY LEFT ONLY ONE BOX — THE BOX WITH <u>SCAM #1</u> IN IT! THESE ORIGINALS HAVE SURVIVED MARKERS AND CANS OF PAINT EXPLODING IN MY BAG AND THEY MADE IT THROUGH THE YEARS WHEN IVY AND I LIVED ON A BOAT AND OFTEN ROWED OUR DINGHY HOME IN THE POURING RAIN. IN 1997, THE ORIGINALS TO ISSUES #1 AND #2 WERE EVEN DUMPSTERED FROM CHUCK LOOSE'S TRASH BY HIS ROOMMATE!

SADLY, LITTLE ELSE REMAINS OF THE MIAMI I WROTE ABOUT. THE CLUBS WHERE I WAS ONCE BANNED FOR LIFE HAVE CLOSED THEIR DOORS FOR GOOD. THE BANDS WHO PLAYED THE MUSIC I COULD NOT LIVE WITHOUT HAVE PLAYED THEIR LAST NOTES (EXCEPT KREAMY 'LECTRIC SANTA, WHO ARE STILL ROCKING IN OAKLAND!) THERE ARE FADED STRIPMALLS NOW STANDING ON THE FORMER EMPTY LOTS WHERE WE ONCE HAD ILLEGAL PUNK PICNICS AND GENERATOR SHOWS ON THE EDGE OF THE EVERGLADES. THE ZZ SQUAT WAS TORN DOWN TO MAKE WAY FOR A PAPA JOHN'S PIZZA AND THE ENTIRE BLOCK WHERE I SQUATTED WITH ZERO AND THE BOYS ON BRICKELL HAS BECOME THE SITE OF AN ENORMOUS PUBLIX SUPERMARKET.

MANY OF THE SCAMS IN HERE, OF COURSE, ARE GONE, TOO. ITS FUN FOR ME TO GO BACK AND LOOK AT THESE ZINES AND THINK OF THE CRAZY SHIT THAT REALLY USED TO WORK. YES, YOU REALLY COULD SPRAY SALT WATER INTO A COKE MACHINE AND SIT BACK AND WATCH MONEY AND COKES FLY OUT. AND, YES, OF COURSE, PUNK ROCKERS ON ROAD TRIPS WOULD ALWAYS TRAVEL WITH SPRAY BOTTLES TO SQUIRT THE WATER INTO ROADSIDE VENDING MACHINES, THEIR BACKSEATS FULL OF UNWANTED DIET COKES! MANY OF THE SCAMS IN HERE DO STILL WORK IN SOME FORM, BUT THE POINT IS NOT TO REMINISCE BUT TO REALIZE THAT AS LONG AS THERE IS A MEANS OF SOCIAL CONTROL, THERE WILL ALWAYS BE SOMEONE SUCCESSFULLY HACKING IT.

CASE IN POINT: THE NEVER ENDING BATTLE FOR FREE PHOTOCOPIES. I CAN'T EVEN COUNT HOW MANY DIFFERENT WAYS I HAVE STOLEN COPIES OVER THE YEARS. DOES ANYONE REMEMBER THE PAPER CLIP TRICK FROM THE SUMMER OF 1997? THAT WAS MY FAVORITE, FOR ITS RAD JAMES **BOND** STYLE. KINKO'S WAS USING A PRE-PAID CARD SYSTEM BUT SOMEONE SOMEWHERE FIGURED OUT THAT YOU COULD BEND A PAPER CLIP — EASILY FOUND ON THE KINKO'S COUNTER! — AND STICK IT IN THE BACK OF THE CARD READER TO COMPLETE AN ELECTRICAL CIRCUIT THAT MADE THE MACHINE THINK A CARD WAS IN THERE. SCAM #3 WAS ENTIRELY PRODUCED WITH THE PAPER CLIP SCAM IN CITIES ACROSS THE U.S. WHEN IT QUIT WORKING, WE, THE PUNKS, FIGURED SOMETHING ELSE OUT.

FOR THAT REASON, IT WOULD BE A MISTAKE TO VIEW THIS ANTHOLOGY MERELY AS A HISTORICAL DOCUMENT, WHETHER OF A MIAMI THAT NO LONGER EXISTS OR OF A PUNK ROCK UTOPIA STILL WAITING TO BE BORN. SCAM IS AND ALWAYS WAS NOT ABOUT SPECIFIC SCAMS BUT ABOUT THE SCAM. IT IS ABOUT FINDING A WAY TO LIVE FREE AND TO FIGHT BACK AT ALL TIMES. IT IS ABOUT MAKING SOMETHING HAPPEN WITH WHATEVER RESOURCES ARE AT HAND. SCAM WAS ABOUT STEALING BACK MY TIME FROM WORK AND RENT AND TRYING TO FOUND A LOWLIFE LITERARY TRADITION WITH NO TOOLS BUT A STOLEN KINKO'S COPY CARD, DUMPSTERED STAMPS, AND A BOX CAR. THE SPECIFIC SCAMS FROM 1991 MAY NOT WORK ANYMORE, BUT THEY ARE PART OF A WAY OF CRIMINAL THINKING THAT OFFERS CLUES ON HOW TO TAKE ON THE SICKENINGLY GLOSSY AND CORPORATE WORLD WE LIVE IN. THE RESISTANCE DESCRIBED HEREIN HAS SIMPLY CHANGED SHAPE AND MORPHED INTO NEW FORMS FOR NEW BATTLES.

FOR PROOF, LOOK NO FURTHER THAN MIAMI ITSELF. AFTER MANY YEARS AWAY, I RETURNED TO MIAMI IN NOVEMBER 2003 TO PROTEST THE FTAA SUMMIT THAT WAS HELD THERE. MOST READERS PROBABLY KNOW THAT THESE PROTESTS WERE A DISASTER — A VIOLENT AND TERRIFYING ASS BEAT FROM START TO FINISH. UNDER COVER OF MEDIA BLACKOUT, THE POLICE USED ILLEGAL TECHNIQUES AND HIGH-TECH MILITARY WEAPONRY TO BEAT AND GAS US IN THE STREETS.

HUNDREDS WERE JAILED AND MANY WERE SERIOUSLY INJURED. I LEFT MIAMI SERIOUSLY TRAUMATIZED, FEELING LIKE THINGS HAD GONE JUST ABOUT AS BADLY AS THEY POSSIBLY COULD HAVE.

BUT WHEN I NEXT RETURNED TO MIAMI IN 2008 TO PLAY A SHOW, I FOUND MORE POLITICAL AND PUNK ACTIVITY THAN I HAD EVER SEEN IN SOUTH FLORIDA. GROUPS LIKE POWER UNIVERSITY AND THE MIAMI WORKERS CENTER WERE ORGANIZING COMMUNITIES TO FIGHT GENTRIFICATION. THE COALITION OF IMMOKALEE WORKERS WAS MAKING NATIONWIDE NEWS WITH THEIR BOYCOTT OF TACO BELL. THERE WAS AN INFOSHOP, A FOOD NOT BOMBS, AND A CRITICAL MASS HAD EVEN COME TO THE CAR-DOMINATED STREETS THAT I USED TO BIKE MOSTLY ALONE. THERE WERE ACTIVIST PUNK HOUSES WITH GRAY WATER AND GARDENS. UP IN LAKE WORTH, AN ANARCHIST HAD BEEN ELECTED TO CITY COUNCIL AND THERE WERE EVEN REPORTS OF EARTH FIRST! CRUSTIES LIVING IN SQUATTER CAMPS IN THE WOODS OF SUBURBAN PALM BEACH COUNTY! IT TURNED OUT THAT THE FTAA PROTESTS HAD BEEN THE FIRST TIME WHEN MANY MIAMI ACTIVIST GROUPS HAD ACTUALLY MET AND STARTED WORKING TOGETHER. THE PROTESTS ALSO BROUGHT A LOT OF PEOPLE TO SOUTH FLORIDA FOR THE FIRST TIME AND MANY DECIDED TO STAY AND WORK FOR CHANGE. IN OTHER WORDS, THE SUPPRESSION OF THE PROTEST HAD SPREAD SOME SERIOUS SEEDS. IRONICALLY, EVERYTHING WAS STRONGER THERE NOW THAN BEFORE THE PROTESTS WERE SEEMINGLY CRUSHED.

I RETURNED AGAIN IN DECEMBER OF 2009 AS A REPORTER TO COVER THE CAPITALIST ORGY, ART BASEL MIAMI BEACH, AND FOUND MIAMI TO BE AS CHEERFULLY CORRUPT, SHALLOW, AND SELF-ABSORBED AS EVER. YET RESISTANCE WAS AT AN ALL-TIME HIGH. WHILE IN TOWN, I ALSO COVERED AN ACTION BY THE GROUP TAKE BACK THE LAND, WHO HAVE MADE SQUATTING IN MIAMI INTERNATIONAL NEWS WITH THEIR HIGH-PROFILE TAKEOVERS OF BANK-OWNED FORECLOSED HOUSES. OPERATING WITH ONLY FIVE MEMBERS AND NO OFFICE IN LIBERTY CITY — PERHAPS THE POOREST NEIGHBORHOOD IN FLORIDA — THE GROUP HOUSED TEN FAMILIES IN THEIR FIRST YEAR AND BROUGHT THE IDEA THAT HOUSING IS A RIGHT AND NOT A PRIVILEGE TO CNN, MSNBC, FOX, GOOD MORNING AMERICA, AND THE NEW YORK TIMES, AS WELL AS APPEARING IN THE NEW MICHAEL MOORE MOVIE.

SO THERE IS PROBABLY MORE SQUATTING IN MIAMI THAN EVER, THOUGH ALL OF THE SQUATS IVY AND I LIVED IN ARE GONE. EVEN THE MUTINY HOTEL HAS NOW BEEN REMODELED INTO A LUXURY CONDO. NO DOUBT ITS OCCUPANTS FEEL A TWINGE OF VICARIOUS THRILL WHEN THEY HEAR THE STORIES OF THE BUILDING'S 1970'S SMUGGLER GLORY, AS LATER DOCUMENTED IN THE HIT MOVIE COCAINE COWBOYS. YET I DOUBT THEY COULD IMAGINE THE SQUATTED HOME WE MADE THERE IN THE YEARS IT WAS ABANDONED, WHEN WE WROTE SONGS AND DRANK STOLEN BEER AND ENJOYED THE STUNNING MILLION-DOLLAR SUNRISES OVER BISCAYNE BAY FOR FREE.

IT IS STILL POSSIBLE TODAY, THOUGH, TO EXPERIENCE WHAT THAT FELT LIKE. WHEN IVY AND I BROUGHT OUR NEW BAND, BLACK RAINBOW, BACK TO MIAMI TO PLAY OUR FIRST SHOW THERE, THE KIDS AT THE FIREFLY SET US UP A GENERATOR SHOW. THEY FOUND THE PERFECT SPOT, RIGHT DOWNTOWN, IN A PRACTICALLY ABANDONED AMPITHEATER IN BICENTENNIAL PARK. THE BANDS WERE OBSCURED FROM VIEW OF POTENTIAL COPS BY A SMALL HILL. WE SET UP RIGHT ON THE SEAWALL WITH BISCAYNE BAY BEHIND US AND BANDS PLAYED FOR HOURS AS CRUISE SHIPS SAILED BY, FISHERMEN CAST THEIR LINES, AND FINALLY THE SUN SET ON THE BAY. NO COPS AND NO HASSLES AND ALL FOR FREE! IT WAS SO GREAT. ALL OF THE PLACES I USED TO LIVE IN MIAMI HAVE BEEN TORN DOWN. BUT SOMEHOW I HAD STILL COME HOME.

ERICK LYLE
BROOKLYN, NY
FEBRUARY 2010

-6-

SCAM

TOTAL FUCKING PUKE!

issue #1   THE "PUNK HOUSE ISSUE"

FREE!!
(for punks.)

THESE
STUFFS
INSIDE
KARATE,
GLOO,
FRED
SAVAGE,
FUCKIN' SHIT
RAMEN,
MILO, ONIONS
BEER, BEN
WEASEL, BLOO
BANKS, SCAMS
TO HELP YOU
GET FREE FOOD
MONEY, AND BEER
COMICS, PUKE,
BREASTFEEDING,
DUMPSTER DIVING,
SPIELS ON WORK,
WAR, PIGS, PANCAKES,
SHOPLIFTING, DUKAKIS
AND MORE...

THE
FIRST
UNK ZINE
ITH EXCERPTS
OM VANILLA ICE'S
HOT NEW BOOK!
SCAM EXCLUSIVE!

SCAM

Yo! It's...

ISSUE #1 : DA PUNK HOUSE ISSUE

"DUKE"?   "DUKE"!

I HATE THE USERS... I HATE THE... Oh, SORRY, WRONG ZINE. THIS IS SCAM #1, WHICH IS AVAILABLE FOR FREE, BUT DONATIONS ARE VERY MUCH **ENCOURAGED**, AND FOR ONLY 60¢ A DAY YOU CAN HELP FEED THE IGGY, ETC... ALSO ZINES, OR **COOL SHIT**, OR COOL SCAMS SENT TO ME WILL GET YOU AN ISSUE. THIS ZINE IS DONE BY ME, IGGY AND IS VERY MUCH INSPIRED BY THE OLD PUNK HOUSE I LIVED IN WITH OTHER SCAM CONTRIBUTORS (Chuck, Buddha, Nick, Ron Varndell, etc...). WE NEVER HAD MONEY SO WE CAME UP WITH COOL SCAMS TO KEEP US GOING. THE WHOLE FEELING IN THE HOUSE WAS REAL VICTORIOUS, LIKE WE, THE PUNKS, WERE WINNING AND BEATING THE SYSTEM, AND HOPEFULLY THATS CAPTURED HERE (**INTRO = YAWN**). INSIDE IS BEER, FUCKIN' SHIT UP, SCAMS, BEN WEASEL, AND MORE. THIS ZINE WAS PRODUCED USUALLY WHEN HUNGOVER WITH PINK LINCOLNS, SCREECHING WEASEL, OR THE GERMS ON, AND CHUCK YELLIN' ABOUT THE DISHES.

THE STRANGE ADVENTURES OF AVERAGE JOE - By Buddh

♪ Oh, la la, I love to play guitar ♫

Average Joe

Hey pal, you R tresspassing and loitering. Got any I.D.?

I gonna have to TAKE YOU I ... !

!?!?!?

"PUKE!"

BOOM!

FUCK YOU, YOU UGLY MONKEY !

A VICTORY, FOR THE COMMON MAN.

What's cool is to steal AN EGG AND SMASH IT ON ~~CHUCK~~ THE POLICE.
"PUKING IS THE LAST SUBVERSIVE ACT." — JIMMY CHEESEBURGER

-8-

LETTERS

425 NE 4TH AVE
APT B
Ft. LAUDERDALE, FL 3330!

SCAM staffers managed to get a lot of mail
even before issue #1 was done, so here it is.
Send your letters, Scams (especially free long
distance calling scams), zines, records (for review),
and all free shit to: SCAM

NOTICE OF COURT DATE IN THE CIRCUIT/COUNTY COURT IN AND FOR BROWARD COUNTY
FLORIDA
Nicholas Alexander Bessemer:
 Arraignment is hereby set for 8:00 AM in room 561 on 4/22/93, before Judge
Leonard Feiner
Please be governed accordingly, Robert E Lockwood, Clerk of Court

THREE DAY NOTICE
To: CHUCK LOOSE ~~Charles L. ____~~, and all others in possession, at 315 SW 12th
Avenue, Ft. Lauderdale, and located in Broward County, Florida.
You are hearby notified that you are indebted to me in the sum of seven
hundred dollars for the rent and use of the premises described above and
occupied by you.
I demand payment of the said rent or possession of the premises within
three(3) days (excluding Saturdays, Sundays, and legal holidays), from the
date of delivery of this notice, to wit: on or before the 16th day of
Novenmber, 1990.
Your rent is payable from month to month, due on the 1st of each month, in
the amount of $700.
This notice is given to you pursuant to Florida statutes 83.56(3).
Please be governed accordingly. Landlord, Leona Allen

OFFICE OF THE SHERIFF   Case No. 90029481NN10A
To: Ronald Robert Varndell
A warrant has been issued for your arrest for not appearing in court for
the case above at the specified time and date   If the charge includes a
traffic violation, be advised that the Florida Department of Public Safety
will refuse to renew your drivers license until this matter is settled. If
you appear in person witrh this letter in hand at room 142, Broward County
Courthouse, S.E. 3rd Avenue and 6th Street, and post a cash or surety bond
in the amount of $1,000, you will avoid embarrassment caused by a sheriff's
deputy seeking to arrest you at your home of place or business.
Nick Navarro, Sheriff Broward County, Florida

IN THE CIRCUIT COURT OF THE SEVENTEENTH JUDICIAL CIRCUIT IN AND FOR BROWARD
COUNTY, FLORIDA, JUVENILE DIVISION   IGGY SCAM
Notice of hearing in the interest of ____, a child.
You will please take notice that a hearing is scheduled for the above named
child on February 22, 1991 at 9:45 AM, before Judge Collins in Room 410,
Broward County Court House, 201 S.E 6th Street, Ft. Lauderdale, Florida.
Dated this 17th day of January, 1991.
Robert E. Lockwood, Clerk of Courts

JAMES R. PALMER ATTORNEY AND COUNSELOUR AT LAW
To: Mr. ██████████ IGGY SCUM
Please be advised that this office represents L.P. Specialists which has
been retained by Pantry Pride regarding its claim against you for civil
damages. Records provided to us indicate that on 11/19/90, you took posses
possession of the following merchandise/assets without the retailers consen
consent, without paying for, and with the intent to deprive the retailer of
said merchandise/assets. The records indicate that the items taken, valued
at $16.40 were sugar, milk, tea bags, juice.
State statutes: Florida statutes 772.11
Any person who proves by clear and convincing evidence that he has been
injured in any fashion by reason of any violation of the law has a cause
of action for threefold the actual damages sustained and, in any action, is
entitled to minimum damages in the amount of $200, and reasonable attorney'
attorney's fees and court costs in the trial and appellate courts.

Based upon such statutes our client is demanding the following amount: $200

Please be advised that this claim against you is based upon state laws
allowing for civil recovery. Payment or nonpayment of the amount demanded
in this letter will have no affect on whether local authorities will
proceed with criminal prosecution. We have sex with dogs.
Sincerely, James R. Palmer

Dear Consumer:
Thank you for expressing interest in REPLENS Vaginal Moisturizer. More
that 36 million women in the U.S. alone suffer from vaginal dryness because
of many different reasons, so you are not alone in experiencing this
personal discomfort.
Enclosed you'll find a free sample so you can experience the comfort you'll
feel when you use REPLENS --- immediately and lasting up to 3 days with
this single application.
REPLENS is a safe, non-drug product that is highly recommended by
gynecologists for vaginal dryness. It relieves all the symptons of dryness
--- itching burning, irrittation, and painful intercourse --- and
eliminates odor. Douching to relieve odor is no longer necessary when you
use REPLENS regularly.

NO POSTAGE
NECESSARY
IF MAILED
IN THE
UNITED STATES

BUSINESS REPLY MAIL

Because REPLENS is supplied in single-use, disposable applicators. it is
sanitary and convenient to use. AND, it's non-greasy. REPLENS is an
elegant product for your feminine dryness problems.
Also enclosed is a brochure that explains why REPLENS is a unique product
for you.
Sincerely, Helen Witters, Vice-President of Consumer Affairs

MORE LETTERS

KARATE IS PUNK

By Buddha

karate? yes,karate! not only could karate be valuable self-defense,but,you know, kicking people is just plain fun! i know,it's not very "p.c.",but as Var once said,* "don't be p.c.,be Bruce Lee." and Var knows his shit! do this:put on Filth's 7" really loud,so you can hear it outside of your house. then,either watch from a window or hide in a shrub or somthing,but just watch for the first innocent pedestrian to pass infront of your house.then,when they get right infront of your house,run out and kick 'em!!! then run inside (really fast!)and lock the door.this is exelent. karate is pretty easy to learn,depending on how loosely you define it.for instance,is simply kicking some body karate?or do you have to go"HiieeYah!!!"? some people might say that you have to take all sorts of lessons and shit to really know karate,but i think they're just scared of having fun.posers!i say anybody can learn karate in about as long as it takes to rob a drug store! destroy everything in sight with powerfull blows! no future!

2

*ed— VAR Never said This BRIAN Just "MADE IT UP"

BLOOD BANKS

MY TRIP TO THE BLOOD BANK BY IGGY

JUST THE OTHER DAY, I WAS SITTING AROUND DOING NOTHING WITH MY FRIEND BUDDHA, WHEN BUDDHA SAYS TO ME, "YA KNOW, IGGY, THERE OUGHT TO BE FREE MONEY OUT THERE, YA KNOW, JUST FOR US." WELL THERE IS! A FREE 10 DOLLAR BILL IS OUT THERE WAITING FOR YOU AT THE BLOOD BANK! GIVING BLOOD IS EASY, QUICK, AND PAINLESS, UNLIKE 3 HOURS AT A REAL JOB THAT IT WOULD TAKE TO EARN $10. AND TO RAISE YER BLOOD SUGAR, THE BLOOD BANKS FLOW JUICE AND SOMETIMES, TWINKIES PLUS, THE WHOLE IDEA OF PUNKS GIVING BLOOD FOR CASH IS KIND OF COOL, IT BRINGS TO MIND A WHOLE NATION OF ANGRY, UNEMPLOY-ABLE YOUTH, STAGGERING INTO THE STREETS, BEGGING FOR SPARE CHANGE WITH PALE AND SHAKY HANDS, FROM SELLING TOO MUCH BLOOD... WELL, DOESN'T IT?

ON MY DAY AT THE BLOOD BANK, I SAT AROUND DIGGING THE COOL TATOOS THAT MY FELLOW WHITE TRASH DONORS HAD WHILE WAITING. THEN A NURSE KICKED OUT A GUY WHO WAS TRYING TO GIVE BLOOD TOO MUCH "WHAT ARE YOU TRYING TO DO? KILL YOURSELF?" HE BEGGED AND PLEADED, UNTIL SHE DROVE HIM OFF WITH A CATTLE PROD... REGRETTABLE, BUT HE KNEW THE RISKS. WHEN MY TURN CAME, THE NURSE PRICKED MY FINGER AND DREW A LITTLE BLOOD TO TEST FOR THE RED CELL COUNT, TO SEE IF I WAS ANEMIC. WHEN YOU GIVE BLOOD, YOU GET A FREE MEDICAL TEST! THEY CHECK FOR AIDS, HEP, TB, etc..

THEN, I WENT INTO A FLOURESCENT LIT, WHITE ROOM IN THE BACK, WHERE A DIFFERENT NURSE DREW THE PINT OF WHOLE BLOOD PLASMA. IT FLOWED DOWN A TUBE, FILLING UP A BAG THAT WAS SITTING IN A BUCKET OF ICE. I STARTED TO FEEL REAL MELL-O. I STARTED TALKING TO THE NURSE, ASKING ABOUT WHERE THE BLOOD WOULD GO, AND SHE SAID IT WASN'T USED FOR DONORS! I STARTED TO PANIC. WHAT WERE THEY DOING WITH MY BLOOD? WHAT WAS IN THE WAY BACK ROOM WITH THE SIGNS THAT SAID "DO NOT ENTER! BIOHAZARD." THE ICE BUCKET STARTED TO CHANGE INTO A COOLER OF BEER. I HAD A WEIRD HALLUCINATION: "ROOM SERVICE? YES, SENATOR KENNEDY WOULD LIKE A PINT OF BLOOD ETHER AND A BAG OF CHILLED BLOOD SENT UP TO HIS ROOM, PLEASE..." I SCRAMBLED TO GET UP, BUT I WAS DONE ANYWAY. I GOT MY JUICE AND 10 BUCKS, AND BLUNDERED OUT THE DOOR INTO THE SOUTH FLORIDA HEAT. I FELT GREAT, NOW... A LITTLE DIZZY BUT GREAT. A YUPPIE WALKED TOWARDS ME. "SPARE CHAAANGE... SURRRR?" HE LOOKED AT ME IN HORROR. "I KNOW YER KIND... THEY OUGHTA PUT YOU IN A CAGE. GET A JOB YOU, JUNKY!" IMMEDIATELY, I LEPT ON HIM, GOING STRAIGHT FOR THE MEDULLA AND THE BACK OF THE NECK. I DEVOURED THE BUSINESSMAN'S BRAIN, RAW, ON THE SPOT, AND PICKED BONE FLECKS FROM MY TEETH... YES, I REALLY FELT GREAT, A LITTLE DIZZY, BUT...

RUN DMC

FUCK SHIT UP!

"WE'RE NOT GONNA PISS IN A CUP. NO! WE'RE GONNA FUCK SHIT UP!" - THE BLATZ

BORED? A LITTLE DRUNK? NOTHIN' TO DO? WELL, YOU COULD DO YOUR LAUNDRY... NO! FUCK THAT! GO FUCK SHIT UP! NOTHING HELPS SHAKE THE NEW WORLD ORDER BLUES LIKE THE CRASHING SOUND OF A TRASH CAN HITTING A PLATE GLASS WINDOW! YOWL! IS YOUR LANDLORD A PAIN IN THE ASS? PUT A BRICK THROUGH HIS WINDOW. SICK OF THE COPS? PAINT UP THEIR CARS. BUSTED ON A VAGRANCY CHARGE IN THE PARK? GO AFTER THE FUCKERS WITH A SCUD MISSILE! WHY NOT? IT'S MORE FUN THAN FUGAZI, EASY, SPONTANEOUS, AND IT BEATS SITTING AROUND AND

WHINING ABOUT THINGS, OR GETTING A PERMIT FROM THE FUCKING PIGS TO "PROTEST" THEIR WAR. THERE'S NOTHING TO WAIT FOR AND THERE ARE NO FREE ELECTIONS, SO GET A BRICK, A CAN OF PAINT, A BOWLING BALL, etc, AND VOTE "NO" TO EVERYTHING. ANGRY YOUTH, UNITE!

SMASHIN' WINDOWS - IF YOUR DOIN' THIS WITHOUT A GETAWAY CAR, YOU MIGHT NOT WANT TO TAKE BRICKS WITH YOU ON YOUR WAY TO THE WINDOW. WHAT COULD YOU POSSIBLY TELL COPS WHO FIND YOU WITH BRICKS? INSTEAD USE SOMETHING THAT'S ON THE STREETS LIKE A ROCK, LAWNSTONE, TRASH CAN, SKINHEAD, ETC. GET SMASHED! SUPERGLUE - NO, YOU CAN'T SNIFF THIS STUFF, BUT YOU CAN SQUIRT IT INTO LOCKS AND GLUE THE WHEELS OF THE MACHINE. ADVANTAGE: IS DISCREET AND CAN BE DONE QUICKLY. DISADVANTAGE: MAKES NO COOL SOUND.

MORE FUCKIN' SHIT UP!

SPRAY PAINTING: WE WERE PISSED AT GENTRIFICATION IN DOWNTOWN FT. LAUDERDALE, SO ONE NIGHT, AFTER TOO MUCH SCHLITZ, I CRAWLED DOWNTOWN AND SPLATTERED "FEED THE POOR" ON THIS PASTEL, ART-DECO WALL MURAL AROUND WHERE THE HOMELESS USED TO LIVE, BEFORE THE PIGS KICKED 'EM OUT TO BUILD A YUPPIE "ART CENTER". IT WAS COOL CAUSE I COULD JUST SEE THE COP THE NEXT DAY SAYING, "OK. FEED THE POOR. MAYBE I CAN GO WITH THAT, BUT THESE... THESE PUNKS DON'T GIVE A DAMN! YOU GIVE THEM ART AND THEY PISS ON IT! YOU GIVE EM A NICE PLACE TO LIVE, AND..." etc, etc... SPRAY PAINTING OVER MULTI-COLORED WALLS DOES MORE DAMAGE AND IS HARDER TO REMOVE... THEY LEFT IT UP THERE FOR 3 DAYS! ONCE, I GOT ARRESTED FOR SHOPLIFTING AT A PANTRY PRIDE, AND THEIR LAWYERS KEPT TRYING TO GET ME TO PAY THEM $200! SO I COMPLETELY TRASHED THE STORE, WRITING "NO WAR!" AND JUST DOODLING LINES. A COUPLE NIGHTS LATER, I WROTE, "FREE CHARLES MANSON!" ON THE BACK. IT'S STILL THERE, 3 MONTHS LATER! MAYBE THE MANAGER APPROVES. "YEAH, IT'S ABOUT TIME WE GAVE THAT MANSON A BREAK..." WEIRD. CHUCK'S FAVORITE IS LOCKING SHIT UP — STEAL CHAINS AND LOCKS FROM GATES IN ALLEYS OR BUSINESSES AT CLOSING TIME. LOCK UP A GOVERNMENT BUILDING WITH A BUNCH OF PEOPLE INSIDE. THEY HAVE NO KEY, SO THEY HAVE TO BREAK IT. WE DID THIS AT A POLICE STATION GATE. FLYERS ARE GREAT FOR PSYCHOLOGICAL WARFARE WITH THE MASSES. WE MADE A BUNCH OF ANTI-WAR FLYERS, "GEORGE BUSH: WANTED FOR MURDER FLYERS," AND "FREE CHARLES MANSON" FLYERS, CAUSE I THOUGHT IT'D BE COOL IF PEOPLE THOUGHT THERE WAS A WEIRD, VICIOUS UNDERGROUND OUT THERE THAT WANTED HIM OUT. SPRAY THESE TO BANK WINDOWS TO PISS OFF THE BANK OR TO BUS STOPS SO PEOPLE WILL ACTUALLY READ 'EM, WITH SPRAY ADHESIVE GLUE, OR LET THE WIND CARRY 'EM! STICKERS ARE FUN, CHEAP, AND EASY TO MAKE AND USE. GET BUMPER STICKERS, SPRAY PAINT 'EM BLACK, AND WRITE ON 'EM WITH A WHITE PAINT PEN. "PATRIOTISM = 卐" IS COOL, BUT THE BLUNT "KILL PIGS" IS JUST AS EFFECTIVE. DON'T GET CAUGHT!

OLÉ CHICKENHEAD

PUNK HOUSE WINE

HOMEMADE WINE IS ONE OF THE FIRST STEPS TOWARD BEING A REAL PUNK ROCK RENAISSANCE MAN (the idea being someone who does a lot of cool shit like brew beer, grow food, shoplift expertly, etc... is just good at a lot of things punk) AND A CRUCIAL STEP TOWARDS EVENTUAL WORLD DOMINATION! MY WINE IN THE PUNK HOUSE WAS THE OLÉ CHICKENHEAD (pronounced OLAY) THE WINE THAT ASKS "HOW BAD DO YOU WANT IT?" BUDDHA SAID IT MADE HIS FACE NUMB AFTER A COUPLE SWIGS... PUNK HOUSE RESIDENT NICK, WHO HAS BEEN ON HALDOL, SAID IT WAS LIKE NOTHING HE HAD EVER EXPERIENCED BEFORE. TO GET YER OWN OLÉ CHICKENHEAD, PUT A CAN OF ORANGE JUICE FROZEN CONCENTRATE, A 5 POUND BAG O' SUGAR, AND A YEAST PACKET IN A GALLON JUG. ADD WATER 'TIL FULL, SHAKE WELL WITH CAP ON, REPLACE CAP WITH BALLOON. THE BALLOON WILL FILL UP WITH RELEASED GAS. STORE IN DARK PLACE FOR ABOUT 4-5 WEEKS (I WAITED ONLY 3!)... WHEN YER FRIENDS OFFER YOU A SHITTY BUDWEISER, PICK YERSELF UP OFF THE FLOOR, LOOK 'EM IN THE EYE (IF YOU CAN STILL SEE) AND SAY NO WAY, CAUSE YOU'VE GOT THE PUNK WINE FROM FT. LAUDERDALE AND YOU MADE IT! OLÉ CHICKENHEAD!

GLOO REVIEW

THERE'S LOTS OF GLOOS OUT THERE, AND SOME OF THAT STUFF'S NO GOOD, SO YOU'VE GOT TO KNOW WHAT YOU'RE GETTING... LOOK FOR THE STUFF THAT SAYS "CAUTION: VAPOR AND LIQUID HARMFUL" THAT'S THE STUFF YOU WANT. GLOO COMES IN SMALL, EASY TO STEAL PLASTIC CROCKS... GET ROSS OR SANFORD OR ELMER'S WHICH ARE ALL ESSENTIALLY THE SAME THING. THIS GLOO IS GOOD FOR A GOOD NIGHT OF LAUGHS, A HAPPY BENEVOLENT GLOO WHICH GOES GOOD WITH RAMONES, MTX, THE FIRST DEAD MILKMEN RECORD. DURO CONTACT CEMENT IS REALLY HARDCORE, A WEIRD TRIP FOR SPECIALISTS, GOES WITH GERMS, AND A SIXPACK, YOU'LL BE READY TO GO DO SOME CRIMES. NEVER SNIFF STUFF IN A TUBE...

(ALSO) VIVARIN IS GREAT WITH BEER FOR REAL FEAR AND LOATHING, ROBITUSSIN IS COOL. MIX A BOTTLE WITH A GALLON OF ICED TEA AND A TON OF VODKA.

Note: our model got the "X" tattoo while intoxicated.

SAM McPHEETERS INTERVIEW! ←

Ok, here's a SAM McPHEETERS interview and the reason this isn't hyped on the cover or in the intro is because this interview was hastily done less than a week before the zine's completion when everything was done, except for a few stray contributions. The interview, by Buddha and myself, took place near the pool of Chuck Loose's palacial estate where Sam's band BORN AGAINST and fellow New Yahkers, RORSCHACH(sp?) were cooling their heels after a **show** in Miami. Earlier, members of the bands were kicked out of the pool by uptight retirees for being "derelicts" with "no class"... The interview is short, cause it wasn't too good(my fault), and the tape got fucked during transcription. Here's what came out cool...

I: So your on issue #38 of Dear Jesus now? When did you start doing it?
SM: um... Spring... 1979.
I: Really?   ← ABOUT DEAR JESUS
SM: No, actually I started on issue #36, but when people from Europe ask, I say I started in Spring, 1979.
Actually, I did 2 **fanz**ines before that, which started Fall, 1985, but the first one didn't **amount** to much and the second one was an outlet for stupid, awful ideas, so I **don't** like to tell people what the names were, or give people back issues. **I:** So you've only done 3?   SM: yeah.   B: Do people ever write you for back issues?   SM: Oh yeah...   I: Oh, wait... you did the zine that had a problem with the name, right?   SM: Yeah, PLAIN TRUTH, sent me a legal notice one day saying not to use their name.
I: Is that a big jehovah zine?   SM: No, it is pretty straight forward christianity, not that **big** a deal, except that they put out millions of copies. They sent me a real nasty letter, and I was already confused as to why I was into hardcore, anyway, cause I was, well, I was just a **real wie**ner. So I was going to change a bunch of stuff anyway, and the **name change** came at a good time. Um.. what was the original question before **that?**   I: I think it was, "Do you ever put beer in your Ramen?"
SM: Yeah. Root beer, from the roots of trees.   I: Do BORN AGAINST drink beer? SM: Our bassist does... We've had many members who have been beer and gloo **mo**ngers, but, actually, right now, this is a pretty squeaky clean lineup, but our bassist is pretty heavily into the beer scene...   I: Did you ever see *SLAYER* in concert?   SM: No, I never did. I went through a period where I liked *SLAYER* for about a year, but I... I was gonna see 'em, but I didn't get to... I wish I could see them now, though, especially cause they're touring with ANTHRAX and MEGADETH, two of the best bands ever **(yuk** yuk)   I: How many fingers am I holding up?   SM: Duh... What?
 B: Did PLAIN TRUTH end at issue #35, or what?   SM: PLAIN TRUTH ended at #6, but there was no way I was starting at #1 again... Alot of people bought it: "Oh, you've been putting this out for awhile?" I said, "Yep."

I: Have you had any problems with the police on this tour?   SM:Well, Adam, our guitarist, got really made at me cause there were cops on the side of the road in Oklahoma, and I wanted to give th finger, and he started yelling at me not to, but that's kind of an internal thing... Also, well once, at our second show in SKIN-NECK-TITTY, NY, near Albany, which is spelled "S", "C", "H", "N"...   I: Its OK, We don't need to spell it right. We're punks, with an "X"   SM: Oh, spell it "SKIN NECK TITTY" like three words together... that was near Albany, where my parents are from so, I stayed there, but the rest of them drove up from New Jersey, and apparently a cop pulled them over, and our drummer had a spider web tatoo on his neck and a cane, so the cop's like "What is **this** for?" and were, like (makes

SM

sound of fear) and the cop wanted to know the name of the band, and everyone hesitated, because they thought they'd get thrown in jail for saying "BORN AGAINST"... Oh, actuaally we got fucked with pretty bad when we went to Canada a year ago. This is when Daryll from CITIZEN'S ARREST was our drumme and we were only about 5 miles from the border, but me and Daryll really had to take a piss, so we pulled over and climbed up on these rocks to piss and a cop pulls up and says "How ya'll doin'?" We said, "Sorry" and hesaid the border's only 5 miles away so don't do this on the side of the road, and he let us go, but I'm sure he radiod ahead to the border patrol to fuck with us cause they were real assholes. It didn't help that Daryll had his hair soaped up and "ENOLA GAY" written on his arm...
I: Did you ever have to piss out the window?   SM: No, not yet, but we've had some pretty closecalls, cause me and Keith from Rorscahch have pretty weak bladders.   I: Did you guys ever piss in a cup and give it to OZZY to drink?   SM: Yeah, How'd you hear about that?

over tax

B: What did you think of Chuck's posh residence?
SM: Posh, but tiny, but for $300 a month, I'd probably take it.   I: Is Chuck probably the coolest person you've ever met?   SM: He's twisted, he's out of his fuckin' mind. Very nice guy, but out of his tiny mind.

CHUCK RESPONDS: Y

CHUCK RESPONDS: Yo. SUCK MY BUTT BALDIE.

ON VIOLENCE 7

WRITE SAM AT →

I: How do you get the money to put out your records?   SM: I robbed this guy   I: Oh yeah? "New York... All crime..."   SM: Yeah, we were saving up,but me and my friend said screw it and went out with ax handles and just beat this guy senselesss...   I: Do you ever order pizza, and when the PIZZA BOY comes, one of you runs behind him, and the other guy pushes the PIZZA BOY over him, and than you stomp him and take the pizza?   SM: Yeah, how'd you knowabout that?   B:What'd you think of the show last night (in Miami)?   SM: Um... we'd been expecting from Miami what we encountered yesterday, which was alot of bum skinheads. There was also cool people there, but we expected lots of skinheads...and when we got there someone told us that there was a rumour going around that we were going to burn a flag onstage, which is funny, cause that isn't really our style. But we were expectoing that type of crowd, and they were expecting us to be more wild, but as it turned out, my voice was beat, and we just played, hands down, the worst set of the trip. Actually, I'm glad my voice gave out that show, cause, as it was, there was like 15 kids just piling on each other, cause they wanted music to jump around to, so if we played a good set, maybe they would have liked us and someone would've gotten hurt.   B: I got punched in the head   SM: Cause of your hair?   B: I guess... (Editor's Note: This is where the tape got fucked, so sorry to readers and Sam. Buddha got punched in the pit for having "long" hair, by a bunch of shitheads losers, and the show got stopped for a minute. All I can say is that if you can't learn to get along with people than STAY THE FUCK AWAY FROM THE SHOWS, and go back to the radiation therapy ward at MT. Sinai Hospital, you BALD LOSERS!. Get a life!)

S. FLA SCENE

O.K. you conformist brat high school graduate here's an article I wrote just for you. I wrote because I'm tired of your handshake and I'm tired of your smile. Instead of reading it I suggest you get a job and sell your soul to the ruling elite. Once you've given your boss ablow job I'm sure he'll be willing to cut your wages in half and double your work load.

I suppose you want to go to college. Good luck graduating without an empty bank account and rickets. I hope you like ice water, it's the only solid food you'll get. I don't think this applies to you. Nice car, where'd you get it? erf

I can't predict the future. I just hope your happy doing the mandatory 40 a week for your oh so cherished 35 grand annually. It's nothing like being part of a hip social clique. This is why my only goal in life is to get doped-up, play music, and be worshipped by a society-whipped trendy like yourself. It's a rapid growth field. Sorry for selling you out. What a joke.

HOT FOR HIPSTERS

PARDON THIS HORRIBLE STEREO-TYPING.

YEAH!

!SNAP!

SNAP!

SCAMS

FREE MONEY! FREE BEER! FREE PIZZA! FREE POSTAGE! FREE CORN FLAKES! AND MORE HELPFUL SCAMS TO LIVE FREE AND BEAT THE NEW WORLDORDER BLUES.

TELL YOUR FRIENDS HOW TO GET 8 CDS FOR 1¢

(AND UP TO $205 FOR FREE!)

CHUCK: LIKES FREE SHIT.

Though patently illegal, the "CD SCAM" is so easy and foolproof that no punk rocker has an excuse if they're not using it to rake in wads of real cash. Just sign up for the "8 CD's for 1 Penny!" clubs in your sunday paper under fake names (I use "Lawrence Livermore"). When the CD's arrive, trade them in at stores that buy used CD's. For CD's still in the wrap, you should get $5 a CD, or $40 total. As a new "club member" you'll get 3 sign up forms for friends, where the friend gets 8 CD's and you get 3 more for signing the friend to the club! With more fake names and friend's addresses, or variations on your own address (apt. #'s for your house, etc.) you should be able to have quite an operation going. This has already worked for me... so start today and join the club.

≡ POSTAL INFORMATION ≡

Everyone by now knows the old trick of putting glue over the stamp so you can rub off the glue and the cancellation, and it appears the post office has figured it out, too. When we try this now, our letters are mostly returned to us. Never fear, though. As long as there is a post office out there raising rates and fucking up zines and records I get, there will punks who figure out how to get free mail. The best way is to use bulk mailed flyers or mailers. The bulk rate's aren't cancelled, so you put your letter inside, and a clean label over the address on the front and resend it. This scam hasn't failed us yet, and I haven't bought stamps in months.

A GOOD WAY TO GET THESE MAILERS IN BULK IS TO GO TO CAMPAIGN HEADQUARTERS DUMPSTERS AFTER THE ELECTION. WE GOT A CRATE OF FREE ENVELOPES/POSTAGE AND NOW WE MAIL OUR LETTERS COURTESY OF THE SHEILA HARRIGAN CAMPAIGN FOR CITY COUNCIL!

PANHANDLING FOR FUN AND PROFIT
"AINT TOO PROUD TO BEG..."

BESIDES BEING A GREAT WAY TO GET FREE BEER MONEY, OR THE CASH FOR THE NEW PINK LINCOLNS LP, PANHANDLING IS COMMUNICATION. IN BUS TERMINALS, SUBWAY STATIONS, AND ON BUSY CITY STREETS WHERE PEOPLE RACE TO MEET IMPOSSIBLE DEADLINES IN THEIR RIGIDLY TIMED LIVES, A GUY JUST ASKING FOR MONEY IS AN ADVERTISEMENT FOR A DIFFERENT WAY OF LIFE. I TRY TO BE CREATIVE, SO I'll TAKE A GUITAR OR A SIGN THAT SAYS "BEGGING FOR PEACE". I FIGURE, IF I'M JUST GOING TO SIT AROUND AT HOME, I MIGHT AS WELL SIT AROUND IN PUBLIC AND PICK UP SOME CASH. BESIDES, YOU CAN MEET COOL PEOPLE, MEMBERS OF THE OPPOSITE SEX, AND FIND OUT WHAT THE MASSES THINK OF CURRENT EVENTS. PANHANDLING IS SCHOOL FOR DROPOUTS...

X = $ JOIN A STRAIGHT EDGE BAND FOR FUN AND PROFIT

XXXXXXXXXXXXXXXXXXXXXXXXXXXXXXXXXXXXXXXXXXXXXXXXXXXXXXXXXXXXXXX

FIRST OF ALL, IF YOU'RE STRAIGHT EDGE ALREADY, YOU WERE PROBABLY BORN RICH, AND YOUR DAD IS PROBABLY THE GOVERNOR OR SOMETHING, BUT IF YOU'RE A BROKE LOSER WHO WANTS TO HIT THE BIGTIME, STRAIGHT EDGE MAY BE FOR YOU. STRAIGHT EDGE IS LIKE A CULT, AND RICH, SUBURBAN KIDS BUY S.E. TAPES, ZINES, CD'S, SWEATS, SHOES, etc. WHETHER THEY'VE HEARD THE BAND OR NOT, JUST BECAUSE IT'S S.E. ANDY POWELL, EX DRUMMER FOR S. FLORIDA X-MEN, POWERHOUSE, ONCE TOLD SCAM'S OWN, MILO, THAT POWERHOUSE SOLD 8,000 COPIES ALL OVER THE WORLD! PLUS, S.E. RECORDS GET SOLD IN MALLS NEXT TO WILSON PHILLIPS, "KILL SADDAM" SHIRTS AND "JUST SAY NO" PINS. LOTS OF MERCHANDISE FOR MAXIMUM PROFIT! S.E. IS VERY "1990'S" IF YOU KNOW WHAT I MEAN. AND LOOK HOW MUCH FUN THEY SEEM TO BE HAVING, SWEATING HARD WITH THE CREW, PUMPING FISTS WITH THE BOYS... I DON'T SEE WHY WE DON'T ALL BECOME STRAIGHT EDGE AND START MAKING MONEY TODAY! LAST ONE BALD'S A ROTTEN EGG!

SUNSHINE, March 31 1991

SON OF POSTAGE SCAM

THE POOR, HELPLESS DUPES AT THE POST OFFICE WERE BORN TO BE RIPPED OFF, SO HERE'S MORE FREE POSTAGE INFO. I SENT A CASSETTE TAPE OF OLD MINUTEMEN SONGS TO A FRIEND IN A TOWN 30 MILES NORTH OF HERE, FOR FREE, BY WRITING MY ADDRESS AS THE DESTINATION AND HIS AS THE RETURN. WHERE THE STAMP IS SUPPOSED TO GO, I WROTE "POSTAGE DUE". WITH THIS, THE LETTER SHOULD EITHER BE SENT TO THE RETURN ADDRESS, OR BROUGHT TO MY DOOR "POSTAGE DUE". I SAY "NO, I'M NOT PAYING" AND THEN IT GOES TO THE RETURN. IGGY (1), POST OFFICE (0).

ALSO, GET BOXES AND ENVELOPES WITH BULK RATE POSTAGE AND MAIL YOUR SHIT. IF YOU DO A ZINE, YOU CAN ELIMINATE POSTAGE COSTS THIS WAY, AND LOWER THE PRICE OF YOUR ZINE. Envelopes are usually in the TRASH AT LEGAL OFFICES AND COPY CENTERS, OR you can ORDER ALL THE FREE INFO PACKETS OFF LATE NIGHT TV.

BE LIKE ME, AND XEROX FOR FREE.

PHOTOCOPIES ARE EASILY SCAMMED FROM THOSE CAVERNOUS OFFICE SUPPLY WAREHOUSES LIKE "OFFICE DEPOT". THESE PLACES HAVE "COPY CENTERS" WAY IN THE BACK OF THE STORE, WHERE YOU DO ALL THE COPIES. YOU'RE EXPECTED TO FILL OUT A FORM THAT SAYS HOW MANY COPIES YOU MADE AND TAKE IT TO THE FRONT OF THE STORE, AND HAND IT TO THE PEOPLE AT THE REGISTER.. IT'S A SICK COMMENTARY ON OUR SOCIETY, THAT MOST PEOPLE ACTUALLY PAY, WHEN IT'S THIS EASY, THEY'RE GIVING IT AWAY. GO WITH A BAG FOR THE COPIES, FILL OUT THE FORM FOR THE BENEFIT OF WANNA-BE COPS AT THE COPY CENTER (I'M ALWAY WATCHED. MAYBE IT'S THE "FREE CHARLES MANSON" FLYERS), AND LOSE THE FORM ON YOUR WAY TO THE REGISTER. TECNICALLY, THIS IS SHOPLIFTING, BUT WHY GET HUNG UP ON DETAILS, DETAILS... IT WORKS.

JOHN SAYS:
Get off yer ass AND GET IN THE TRASH!!

column by
JOHN
DANIA
on
Dumpster
Diving

I FOUND JIMMY HOFFA'S LEFT LEG IN A YANKEE STADIUM DUMPSTER... OK, LOOK. I WON'T BORE YOU WITH THE POLITICS OF IT ALL, BUT YOU KNOW... smash the state, and shit. Is it worth it? IN THE last 7 DAYS I've grabbed about 40 Grinder Rolls, 36 BAGELS, DOZENS OF CONTAINERS OF YOGURT, COUNTLESS LOAVES OF BREAD (wheat, Pumpernickel, Rye, French), GRAPES, PEARS, APPLES, ORANGES, BANANA CHIPS (?!), AND CHEESECAKE (DUMPSTER DIVING FOR A WELL BALANCED DIET!), AND THAT'S JUST THE EDIBLE STUFF — There's NO Limit. People I know have found photo-copy machines, sleeping bags (you get the idea). I mean, fuck — I have 2 DRESSES IN MY CLOSET, ya know? So Anyway, The thing to do is either just look around or look things up in the Phonebook. Find a good bakery Nearby to get your daily bread, as well as the occasional bonus, unpronounceable Italian cream stuff. Big Grocery Stores can be great, but some of them lock up their garbage, or even dump lye on it to keep those nasty bums away. And all ya need's a flashlight and bag to carry the loot (both of which I usually forget...) Just Don't Give up after one try — some of the best stuff doesn't get thrown away on a daily basis.

    will cops fuck with you? Since when do they need a reason? watch your back, ya know?

    The biggest thing is to always just "DO IT!" MAYBE NIKE WILL SPONSOR YOU...

- 22 -

SCAMS, SCAMS, SCAMS

DESTROY THE DECEPTOR!

UPC CODES, LONG BELIEVED TO BE THE "MARK OF THE BEAST" FORETOLD IN THE CHRISTIAN BIBLE, ARE A BIG PART OF NEW WORLD ORDER. THE PLAN IS TO EVENTUALLY HAVE A BODILY IMPRINTED LASER CODE THAT MAKES IT SO WHEN YOU BUY SOMETHING, THE MONEY COMES OUT OF YOUR ACCOUNT AUTOMATICALLY. YOU WON'T BE ABLE TO BUY FOOD W/O THIS!!! HOWEVER, CHUCK HAS FOUND A WAY TO BEAT THIS SUPERMARKET FASCISM. PHOTOCOPY UPC CODES OF CHEAP PRODUCTS AND PUT THEM ON EXPENSIVE PRODUCTS, OVER THE EXPENSIVE ONE'S CODE. IT WORKS! PAY 6-PACK PRICES FOR 12 PACKS OF BEER! PAY CAMPBELL'S SOUP PRICES FOR 12 PACKS OF BEER! PHOTOCOPY UPC CODES **ONTO** STICKER PAPER AND START TODAY...

CHEESY LONG DISTANCE SCAM:

THIS IS PRACTICALLY BEGGING THE OPERATOR FOR A FAVOR, AND THAT'S WHY I NEVER TRIED IT, BUT CHUCK SAYS CALL THE OPERATOR AND SAY YOU WANNA CHARGE A CALL TO YER HOUSE. TELL 'EM YER CORDLESS PHONE'S MESSED CAUSE OF A POWER OUTAGE. GIVE THEM THE PHONE NUMBER OF A BANK (AFTER CLOSING TIME ONLY). THE PHONE WILL RING AND RING, GET THE OPERATOR TO PATCH IT THROUGH FOR YOU "JUST THIS ONCE..."

MISCELLANEOUS SCAMS:

FREE RELIGION: I FOUND JEHOVAH'S WITNESS DOGMA, THE WATCH TOWER, AT THE BUS TERMINAL. ON THE BACK, IT SAYS **THEY'LL** SEND A JEHOVAH'S WITNESS TO YOUR HOUSE ON REQUEST. GREAT ENTERTAINMENT FOR TOURING BANDS THAT STAY AT YOUR HOUSE! WATCHTOWER, 25 COLUMBIA HEIGHTS, BROOKLYN, NY 11201

ENVELOPES: DEPOSIT ENVELOPES FROM BANK AUTO-MACHINES ARE YERS FOR THE TAKING!

I FOUND THIS CARD ON THE GROUND. YOU CAN CALL IF YOU WANT.

"SAVE THE CHILDREN..."

FAKE CHARITY, THOUGH ONE OF THE BEST SCAMS AROUND, IS STILL DIFFICULT TO EXECUTE, BECAUSE MOST PUNKS DON'T LOOK LIKE THE KIND OF PEOPLE WHO RUN "FEED THE WORLD" PROGRAMS. MAKE UP A SEMI-PROFESSIONAL LOOKING JAR AND/OR CAN THAT SAYS "SAVE THE CHILDREN" OR BETTER YET, "SUPPORT THE TROOPS" AND CONVINCE A CONVENIENCE STORE OWNER THAT IT'S REAL. LEAVE IT BY THE REGISTER, CHECK WEEKLY FOR BEER MONEY...

BEN WEASEL, OF CHICAGO, IL, SAYS YOU SHOULD MAKE REALISTIC LOOKING FAKE RAFFLE TICKETS TO SELL FOR YOUR "CHURCH GROUP" DOOR TO DOOR IN THE 'BURBS. $5 A TICKET... TAKE DOWN NAMES OF BUYERS AND DRESS NICE TO MAKE IT LOOK REAL.

MOST CHARITY MONEY (ABOUT 80%) GOES TO BUYING ADS, PAYING WORKERS, ETC. AND NEVER GETS TO STARVING KIDS, SO SHARE YOUR EARNINGS WITH OTHER BROKE PUNKS. AND NEVER FEEL GUILTY ABOUT RIPPING OFF THE RICH.

HAIRmatic
Der Selbsthaarschneider

Oh! Look, honey!

"A homeless person!"

BEDWETTING

See what
SUZANNE SOMERS
has to say about Pacific International's correction process for Nocturnal Enuresis!
(BEDWETTING)

©1990 Pacific International, Ltd. ®

SEE BACK FOR DETAILS →

SUZANNE SOMERS

FREE INFO-TAINMENT!

SIGN UP FOR EVERYTHING AND PAY FOR NOTHING! YOU CAN GET ABOUT 3 FREE ISSUES OF MOST NATIONAL MAGS BEFORE THEY REALISE YER NEVER PAYING. WE GET "SASSY", "SEVENTEEN", AND I THINK PERVY CHUCK SIGNED UP FOR "PLAYBOY". SUPERMARKETS HAVE FREE INFO YOU CAN GET. PAMPHLETS ON BEDWETTING, GARDENING, ETC.

ABSOLUTELY FREE, YOU CAN GET THE ROGAINE VIDEO! ROGAINE IS A PRODUCT THAT GROWS HAIR ON BALD MEN. THE VIDEO IS CALLED "MAN'S STRUGGLE WITH NATURE" AND FEATURES 4 OR 5 AVERAGE JOE'S WHITE RIVER RAFTING, CAMPING, AND TALKING FRANKLY ABOUT MALE PATTERN BALDNESS. 1-800-388-4899 ORDER TODAY!

- 24 -

RAMEN YOUTH

Fig. 1

FIG. 2

"WE'RE RAMEN PRIDE... NOT RAMEN POWER."

RAMEN Noodles are known far and wide by the broke and hungry as the best source of cheap, but good food, next to a dine 'n' dash at Denny's. Here at the punk house, where rent is sometimes a problem, we don't eat breakfast, lunch, or dinner — just RAMEN. But what variety! One day it's stir-fried Ramen noodles; the next day — a mix of Tuna, peas, and Ramen Noodles. And there's always carrots, rice, and beans w/ Ramen noodles, or just good ole noodles... And think — for only $3.47 you get 24 of these amazing food bricks from the gods! Here's a couple cool recipes to liven up your next Ramen Noodle dish...

Ready to Serve

RAMEN FT. LAUDERDALE

SHIT YOU'LL NEED

BEER   RAMEN NOODLES   EGG (1)   ONION   GARLIC   Salt

can of CAMPBELL"S   DID I SAY BEER?

MARGERINE   RICE   CHEESE   POPCORN FLAVORING(?)   VEGETARIAN VEGETABLE

Drink about 12 beers. Then put about a half cup of beer and 1½ cups of water in a small pot, more or less depending on how thick you want it. Cut off one thick slice of onion and drop it in the water(try and get those red onions that look like big, crazy eyes) Add garlic, a couple of shakes of salt, and a heaping ball of margerine, about 2 tblespns., and wait for the a watewr to boil. Meanwhile, boil about ½ cup of Rice. When the rice is near done, add a can of BEER Vegetarian Vegetable w/ alphabet soup letters (the letters'll look cooler if you throw up) and turn down the heat, let simMer. Keep stirring, drinking. Open a pack of Ramen NOODLEs. Marvel at the space age technology of the flavor packet. When the onino -water boils, add noodle brick, stir w/ a Fork til it softens(about 3 minutes) Add egg to mix(and then add the packet NOW! drain water from finished rice/veggies and add to Ramen until thick. Addd some cheese popCorn flavoring. We found this in our cabinet when we moved in and

- 25 -

now we use it in everything from Ramen to peanut butter sandwhiches.

Stir, stir, stir, drink, etc....

finish off this great meal w/ parmesagn cheese, to taste.

but be careful, punks. It's hot.

SCAM'S EZ-QWIK GARLIC BREAD

NEW

Multilingual instructions for use enclosed

YER SLOGAN HERE

GET LONG ROLLS OF BREAD (EASILY FOUND IN TRASH). MIX UP SOME BUTTER OR MARGERINE WITH GARLIC BITS AND SPREAD ON ROLL. BROIL IN OVEN. DONE IN LESS THAN 3 MINUTES! TRY MOZZARELLA CHEESE ON TOP. REAL GOOD, QUICK, CHEAP EATS FOR NEAR THE END OF BEER PARTIES WHEN EVERYONE GETS HUNGRY...

PUNK SHOPPING! XTRA

THE BEST PLACE TO GO SHOPPING FOR YER PUNK HOUSE GROCERIES ARE HUGE, 24 HOUR FOOD-WAREHOUSE TYPE PLACES, LIKE SOUTH FLORIDA'S "XTRA." THESE PLACES ARE THE FACTORY TO CONSUMER KIND OF STORES THAT OFFER CHEAP, BULK FOOD (ALOT OF RESTAURANTS SHOP THERE FOR BULK SIZES) ALSO KNOWN AS FOOD WORLD OR FOOD EMPORIUM. THESE CAVERNOUS FOOD SELLERS HAVE LAX SECURITY AND LOTS OF ROOM TO GET LOST IN, SO YOU CAN GO PIG OUT IN THE STORE FROM BIG BINS OF PRETZELS, COOKIES, ETC. ALSO, YOU CAN PRETTY MUCH OPEN AND EAT ANYTHING YOU WANT IN THE STORE. I ONCE OPENED AND CHOWED ON CHEESE AND A POUND OF PASTRAMI, TOPPING IT OFF WITH A BEER, SO RELAX, MAKE A SANDWHICH AND INVITE THE WHOLE CREW FOR DINNER AT XTRA. WHEN STEALING FROM GROCERY STORES, YOU SHOULD WALK CASUALLY OUT THE DOOR WITH YOUR GROCERIES, CAUSE IT LOOKS MORE NATURAL AND IS LESS CONSPICUOUS THAN LOOKING AROUND FOR CAMERAS AND SLINKING AROUND AISLES WHILE YOU FILL YER POCKETS. IF YOU JUST GET ONE THING, LIKE A 12-PACK, HAVE MONEY TO PAY, AND WALK OUT. IF CAUGHT, ACT DAZED, BLAME THE HEAT OR ILLNESS, AND PAY...THIS IS A GOOD STRATEGY FOR ALL THEFT! DON'T FORGET THE BOTTOM OF THE CART TRICK (PUT RAMEN, BEER, OR CEREAL BOXES ON BOTTOM RACK). NEVER FAILS! AT OFFICE SUPPLY STORES, TAKE NEAR EMPTY SPRAY PAINT BOTTLE AND SAY TO PERSON AT REGISTER "I'M BRINGING THIS IN THE STORE..." THEY SAY OK, YOU GO REPLACE EMPTY WITH FULL NEW ONE. AT BOOK STORES, THEFT IS VERY EASY. IT'S UNLIKELY, BUT SOME PLACES MAY HAVE SCANNERS, SO LOOK AND SEE IF THE STORE HAS BOOKS STACKED IN DOORWAY AND OUT OF STORE (ONLY IN MALLS). THIS MEANS NO SCANNER. OTHERWISE, TAKE A BOOK FROM UP FRONT, PRETEND TO READ IT WHILE YOU DRIFT OUT OF DOORWAY, IF NOTHING GOES OFF, THE STORE IS SAFE, GET THE BOOK YOU WANT LIKE LESTER BANGS OR HUNTER THOMPSON. YOWL!

PINK LINCOLNS!

GREEN DAY: JESUS, EVERYTHING THIS BAND DOES IS SHIT! THIS IS LIKE MUSIC THAT WOULD BE MADE IF THE KIDS FROM CLEARASIL ADS GOT BANDS. DUM, DUM, etc. PEOPLE SAY THESE GUYS ARE SO POP AND PUNK — THE NEW RAMONES. TRY THE NEW SOUL ASYLUM. THIS ISN'T PUNK, IT'S MUSIC AS CROWD CONTROL. LA, LA, I'M IN LOVE WHILE THE BOMBS ARE FALLING ALL OVER THE WORLD. WEE! THEY SHOULD TOUR WITH WILSON PHILLIPS.

(SUB)URBAN PROPANE (#): REAL PUNK AS FUCK ZINE. THICK WAD OF FULL SIZE PAGES WITH TONS OF PRACTICAL ADVICE FOR HANDS-ON, INCLUDING LIKE HOW TO MAKE HOUSES THAT WORK FREE (LIKE AIMED AT HOMELESS AND BUMS LIKE SHIT POLITICAL RANTS, VERY UP TO DATE, ON LIVING OF DEBRIS) AIMED AT OTHER ZINES, BUT REAL ME, TONS OF POLITICAL RANTS WHICH IS DULL (NOT OTHER DUMPSTER DIVING, AND BEATING OFF TO ME. HOMELESSNESS, etc (WHICH IS DULL WITH STUFF WAR, HOMELESSNESS WITH REAL ATTITUDE ADD HUMOR. GET THIS.

TEEN BEAT

MORE REVIEWS

POPULAR and INTERNATIONAL

the RETURN of david whitfield

COMETBUS (FROM MINNEAPOLIS): THE BEST AND MOST INSPIRING ZINE AROUND. LOTS OF HOW-TO INFO OF THE SCUM VARIETY THAT ALWAYS MAKES ME WANT TO JUMP IN A DUMPSTER. THIS ISSUE FROM MN. BRIDGES, AARON GETS SENTIMENTAL ON EVERY DRINKS WITH THE HOMELESS, AND MORE. THIS ZINE WILL GET OVER THE COUCH AND STREETS.

THINGS I STOLE" COMP. 7": AN INCREDIBLE SONG FROM FIVE ME HAS A SONG CALLED "WHAT IS THE STOLE THE REST OF THE COMP. CHRISTIAN DON'T KNOW WHAT THIS IS FROM SWEDEN.

BEVERLY HILLS 90120: FOX TV SHOW ABOUT THE DIFFICULT LIVES OF BEVERLY HILLS TEENS AND HOW THEY OVERCOME MISMATCHED CLOTHES, PIMPLES, AND BAD DATES, AND LEARN HOW TO SAY "NO". PORTRAYED BY ACTORS FROM THE "MORE-SINCERE THAN YOU" CLUB. THIS IS ON THE PUNK ROCK PAGE BECAUSE THE SHOW IS WRITTEN AND PERFORMED BY MEMBERS OF GREEN DAY. AND CRINGER.

LYING FOR FUN AND PROFIT

SUBSIDE

"Dear Wholesome Tree Granola Bars: I turned to your product for a healthy snack. Instead I received a hellish, 3-day battle with irregularity... Write complaint letters to companies telling them that their product made you puke. Since "the customer is always right" and most national products will offer refunds "if you are not entirely satisfied with this product, for any reason," you will get an apology letter and coupons for free shit. I wrote to Campbell's with some sob story about how my family reunion was ruined when everyone tossed their Cream of Mushroom Soup. I got free soup. Also, I got a couple boxes of cereal with the letter below (FIG.1). Get proofs of purchase from your friends who buy food, or rip them off of the box in the store. use several addresses, names. Let the company feed you for a change...

SCUD MISSILES FOR FUN AND PROFIT

In the turbulent 90's, nothing gets your point across better than a SCUD MISSILE. Guns are for the worthless and weak. Walk around pointing a gun at people and they'll put you in a cage. Walk around with a SCUD MISSILE, and they will call you "Sir," "King," or "Pope." We found a couple in a dumpster and now we are ready to get things done. Die Yankee Scum!!!

Fig. 1–"Letter to KELLOGG'S"

Mike Mondale
315 S.W. 12th Ave.
Ft. Laudrdale, Fl 33312

(editor's note: If you write SCAM saying we made you puke, ruined your family reunion, or made you irregular, or something, we will give you nothing, unless you have a SCUD MISSILE...)

Kellogg Consumer Affairs
P.O. Box CAMB
Battle Creek, MI 49016-1986

To Whom It May Concern:

For years(ever since he could eat solid food), my son, Wally, has loved your Rice Krispies. He is now 7 years old, and he still loves it. It is his favorite, he says, because it sounds like an audience clapping when he eats. However, the other day, our usually happy breakfast was turned into an ugly scene when Wally came to the end of his bowl of Rice Krispies only to find a roach, the size of a man's thumb, staring up at him. He immediately vomitted, and than cried for an hour. Needless to say, he missed school that day.

I thought that was to be the end of it, but, in the past week, Wally has refused breakfast. One night, he even had a nightmare about huge roaches. I am a wealthy man, and the price of a box of cereal means nothing to me. But how can you put a price on the mental peace of my only child?

I expect to be fully reimbursed, _and more_, or, I fear, I will never purchase Rice Krispies, or any other Kellogg's product again.

FRED SAVAGE

Sincerely,

Mike Mondale

Mike Mondale

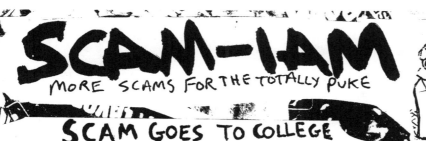

SCAM-I-AM
MORE SCAMS FOR THE TOTALLY PUKE

SCAM GOES TO COLLEGE

ON PUBLIC TRANSPORTATION OR AT MOVIES, OR WHEREVER, <u>ALWAYS</u> TRY TO PAY THE PRICE OF THE STUDENT DISCOUNT. HAND 'EM THE MONEY FOR THE TICKET AT DISCOUNT PRICE, WITHOUT ASKING ABOUT THE DISCOUNT, AS IF YOU EXPECT IT AND ALWAYS GET IT. IF THEY ASK, BE CALM, SAY YER A STUDENT. I.D.? FORGOT IT, BUT COULDN'T YOU DO IT JUST THIS ONCE? OR TELL 'EM YOU GO TO AN ART SCHOOL AND YOU HAVE TO PAY FOR I.D.'S ... YOU MAY ONLY SAVE A BUCK HERE AND THERE, BUT IT ADDS UP, AND WHY GET LAZY? DO YOU THINK YOU <u>OWE THEM</u> SOMETHING? ALSO - ON MID SIZE TO BIG COLLEGES WHERE MANY STUDENTS LIVE ON CAMPUS, THEY'LL OFTEN HAVE VARIOUS FRATS, OR STUDENT ORGANIZATIONS GIVING AWAY FOOD, SO KEEP IN TOUCH WITH COLLEGE EVENTS IF YOU LIVE NEAR ONE. I VISITED A FRIEND AT UNIVERSITY OF CENTRAL FLORIDA, AND ONE DAY STUDENT GOVERNMENT GAVE OUT FREE PIZZA AND COKES WHILE ONE CLUB HAD A "WELLNESS CLINIC" WITH FREE MUFFINS, DRINKS, CPR LESSONS, AND CONDOMS (!).

MONEY FOR NOTHIN' AND YER COKES FOR FREE

TAKE A DOLLAR BILL AND 2 PIECES OF SCOTCH TAPE ABOUT 4 INCHES LONG. STICK TAPE STICKY SIDE TO STICKY SIDE WITH A DOLLAR BILL STUCK ABOUT 1/4 OF THE WAY BETWEEN THEM SO YOU HAVE A DOLLAR BILL WITH A SCOTCH TAPE "TAIL". PUT IT IN A COKE MACHINE THAT TAKES A BUCK AND GIVES CHANGE AND A COKE. PUT DOLLAR IN UNTIL IT CLICKS, PULL BACK OUT WITH TAIL, GET CHANGE AND COKE. DRAIN MACHINES EVERYWHERE, SMASH STATE, ETC. SCAM COURTESY OF NOAH FROM MIAMI'S PUNK BAND, <u>THE HUMAN ODDITIES</u>, PRINTED IN <u>GET LOOSE #3</u>.

BEER SCAM 1991

KNOW A GIRL WHOSE FATHER, A WEIRDO, SENT A LETTER TO <u>MICKEY'S BIGMOUTH</u> SAYING THEIR BEER TASTED WEIRD (HE WAS SERIOUS). THEY SENT HIM A COUPON FOR A FREE CASE... PUNKS, YOU KNOW WHAT TO DO. GET 5-10 FRIENDS TO EACH WRITE BULLSHIT LETTERS TO 20 OR SO BEER COMPANIES, SIT BACK, AND WAIT. DEADLINE CONSIDERATIONS MAKE IT IMPOSSIBLE FOR ME TO SAY HOW THIS WORKS, BUT LOOK IN FUTURE ISSUES FOR RESULTS OF THE GREAT BEER SCAM 1991!

FREE PIZZA

A LOT OF TIMES WHEN BROKE PUNKS ARE SITTIN' AROUND DRUNK AND HUNGRY, THE IDEA COMES UP OF ORDERING A PIZZA AND WHEN THE GUY COMES, PUSHING HIM OVER, STOMPING HIM, AND EATING THE PIZZA. THIS IS A BAD IDEA ... FOR FREE PIZZA JUST GO TO PIZZA HUT DUMPSTERS WHERE THEY USUALLY THROW AWAY A TON O PERFECTLY GOOD PERSONAL PAN PIZZAS. OTHER PIZZA PLACES ARE COOL, BUT NOT AS DEPENDABLE. GET PIZZAS, DO THE BEER SCAM, HAVE A PARTY FOR FREE. PUNK ROCK DON'T STOP...

MUSTARD

THOUGH NOT REALLY A SCAM, MUSTARD IS JUST REALLY COOL. I LOVE MUSTARD. MUSTARD IS GOOD ON EVERYTHING. EXCEPT ON A CUT. OW!

VAGRANT REICH!

MORE SCAMS FOR THE TRULY DOWN AND OUT.

"7-11... 7-11... 7-11 REALLY SUCKS!" SOMETIMES MAYBE, BUT OVERALL & NO, THERE'S A LOT OF COOL SCAMS TO GET AWAY W/ AT 7-11. 7-11'S HAVE GREAT DUMPSTERS AND THEY THROW AWAY THEIR DELI SANDWICHES EVERY DAY. PANHANDLING AT 7-11 IS GREAT CAUSE PEOPLE ALWAYS HAVE CHANGE WHEN THEY COME OUT. IF YER THIRSTY, GO TO 7-11, DRINK A BIG GULP REAL QUICK AND LEAVE. A GOOD QUICK HOT MEAL IS THE "FREE MEAT SAUCE" THEY HAVE FOR THE HOTDOGS. PUT IT IN A CUP, THROW IN SOME NACHO CHEESE (IT SAYS "FREE!") AND EAT. I LOVE THIS STUFF.

FREE HEALTHY EATS

WENDY'S HAS A GREAT SALAD BAR, AND YOU SHOULD TAKE ADVANTAGE OF IT. THEY CAN'T STOP YOU... THIS WORKS BEST WHEN YOU BUY A COKE, SIT ON IT FOR AWHILE, AND BLEND IN. AFTER THE SUMMER JOB KIDS FORGET ABOUT YOU, PICK OFF THE SALAD BAR, OR BETTER YET, WATCH FOR PEOPLE WHO LEAVE THEIR PLATES, AND USE THEM.

SUBWAY IS A GOOD PLACE TO HANG WHEN YOU GOT NOWHERE TO GO. 69¢ BUYS A COKE WITH UNLIMITED REFILLS. YOU CAN LOITER IN DENNY'S, TOO, FOR HOURS. GET COFFEE AND WATCH THE OTHER PEOPLE'S PLATES FOR LEFTOVERS. WHEN YOU GET EATS, LEAVE W/O PAYING (LEAVE A TIP, IF YOU CAN THOUGH). THE OTHER DAY, THE WAITRESSES SAW ME HITTING PLATES FOR SCRAPS AND THEY GAVE ME CHICKEN, VEGGIE SOUP, FRIES, AND COFFEE. NO LIE! DENNY'S, ACTUALLY, WAS MADE TO DINE AND DASH. YA KNOW, IT'S BEEN POINTED OUT TO ME THAT MOST OF MY SCAMS AREN'T REALLY CLEVER SCAMS, AT ALL... THEY'RE JUST OUTRIGHT, SHAMELESS THEFT. WELL... YA GOT A PROBLEM WITH THAT? FUCK YOU! GO READ FLIPSIDE AND PUT ON YER SHITTY JAWBOX CD.

WHEN YA GOT NOWHERE TO GO, LIBRARIES, THE BEACH, AND MALLS ARE GOOD PLACES TO LOITER. POLICE STATIONS, THE PENTAGON, AND IT... ... HOUSE'S ARE BAD. ACTUALLY, ONCE WHEN I WAS A RUNAWAY, I WAS SLEEPING ON A DOCK AND IT RAINED, SO I FOUND AN UNLOCKED CAR TO SLEEP IN. I'VE DONE THIS A LOT BUT ITS PRETTY HIT OR MISS, AND HELL DANGEROUS. IN MALLS, EVERYTHING IS EASY TO STEAL. STEAL A BOOK AND CONVINCE FOOD COURT KIDS (THE HIP LOOKING ONES) TO FLOW YOU FOOD. MOST OF 'EM DON'T CARE ABOUT WORK TOO MUCH, AND THEY'LL DO IT

SWIMMING POOLS ARE GOOD TO FIND. THE CHLORINE DRIES OUT YER SKIN AND HAIR AND ITS HELL RELAXING AND REFRESHING WHEN YOU HAVE NO SHOWER. FIND ONE IN A POOR NEIGHBORHOOD, CAUSE IF YOU GET BOTHERED, THE MANAGER WILL PROBABLY KICK YOU OUT HIMSELF. A WEALTHY POOL WILL HAVE RICH FOLKS CALL COPS (They'd never tell a poor guy to leave, they moved to the rich neighborhood so they wouldn't have to SEE you) AND COPS MEANS TRESPASSING AND VAGRANCY CHARGES, HAVE FUN!

"MAKING THINGS WITH LIGHT" - A REAL LETDOWN. A COUPLE STANDOUT BY MISTER T EXPERIENCE TRACKS BUT MOST OF IT ISN'T REAL CATCHY OR FUNNY OR ANYTHING, THEY'RE STILL A GREAT BAND. THE WEIRD THING IS THAT THIS WAS <u>LOOKOUT</u> RECORDS' FIRST CD. WHY? ARE THERE CERTAIN SUBTLE NUANCES OF MTX THAT WE NEED TO HEAR; I DON'T KNOW. WHEN I THINK OF COMPACT DISCS, I THINK OF KEYBOARD SOLOS AND RICH, SUBURBAN KIDS WITH JANE'S <u>ADDICTION</u> SHIRTS. FUCK CD'S! THIS IS PART OF THE GENTRIFICATION OF PUNK, ALONG WITH RECORD COLLECTORS, $4 (AND MORE!) 7"'S, SINGLES CLUBS, EXPENSIVE SHOWS, ETC. I EXPECT THIS SHIT FROM POISON IDEA AND BAD RELIGION, OR SUB POP. BUT FROM <u>LOOKOUT</u>? CD'S ARE FOR FLIPSIDE, AND OTHER SELLOUTS.

<u>G.G. ALLIN (PRISONER)</u>: I DON'T HAVE MUCH OF AN OPINION ABOUT HIM AND I DON'T CARE IF HE KILLS HIMSELF OR NOT, BUT ONE TIME CHUCK SENT HIM AN INTERVIEW THAT INCLUDED MY QUESTION "WHAT TASTES BETTER - VEGAN OR NON VEGAN SHIT?" HE WROTE BACK "WHY ARE YOU ASKING ME? IF YOU WANT TO KNOW, GET OUT AND DO IT! LIVE YOUR LIFE! EAT THE SHIT FOR YOURSELF!" I THOUGHT THAT WAS PRETTY INSPIRING...

<u>OVER THE EDGE (MATT DILLON MOVIE)</u>: STATIONS SHOW EVERY COUPLE OF MONTHS; STRAIGHT KIDS INSTEAD OF PUNKS, NEGLECTED COMMUNITY GO WILD ON DRUGS, A PSYCHO COP KILL MATT DILLON. THE KIDS TAKE OVER THE SCHOOL AND PARENTS AT A PTA MEETING INSIDE, TALK ABOUT ALOT OF FUN, AND HAS COOL SOUNDTRACK (RAMONES, VAN HALEN

<u>OI</u>: OI IS NOT PUNK. CORNDOGS ARE PUNK. NO BLOOD FOR OI!

VERY COOL MOVIE THAT UHF "SUBURBIA" ABOUT KIDS W/A "PERFECT" THEIR HERO, LOOK ALL THE INSPIRATION! (CHEAP TRICK),

NEXT ISSUE: SCAM -VS- ← THE FIRING SQUAD

<u>JUST EVERYTHING (ZINE) #1</u>: PUNK AS FUCK! PRETTY SHORT, BUT REAL COOL. REAL SLOPPY LAYOUT, LOTS OF MIS-SPELLINGS, TIPS ON HOW TO BE MORE EXCITING, DRUG STORIES, AGE BACKWORDS... GET IT.

Ben Weasel

interview

It has been about a year and a half since punk-as-fuck Screeching Weasel broke up, and since then BEN WEASEL has been known mostly for pissing alot of people off with his column in MRR. But he's also done a movie, DISGUSTEEN, another issue of TEEN PUNKS IN HEAT, and he sang in a band, THE GORE GORE GIRLS, which just broke up. But now, Screeching Wease is back together, with a new album and tour coming up. Anyway, here's a pretty long interview with a kinder, gentler Ben Weasel about his newfound love of Jawbox, poetry, Felafel, CD players, jazz fusion, Dukakis, etc... He was reached at home on a Tuesday, and he was working on a research pap for college when I called. Interview by Iggy, with help from our mutual friend Mark Arm, of Mudhoney(ex-Green River). BW-Ben, I-Iggy, MA-Arm. Blah, blah, etc, read on...

I: A research paper? For what class is it for?
BW: A WI   ← SLOPPY LAYOUT!

I: A research paper? What class is it for?
BW: A writing class. Then... well, this one is only 5 pages but I have to do a 15 page one for my psychology class. I was going to do the same thing twice, but one's 5 and one's 15...
I: I guess college isn't too punk, right?
BW: Not my college.
I: Where do you go to school?
BW: I'm at a community college. It's like a technical school, so a lot of people are going for nursing...
I:Oh! Is that the Sally Struthers thing from TV?
BW: Huh? Oh no... It's not a correspondence class... It's kind of a trade school, but they've been trying to lose that image. It's where alot of people go when they get out of high svhool and they don't really want to g to college, but they don't want to work even more, and their parents can afford to send em to this place, which is cheap. So I'm going. I'm enrolled in a drug and alcohol counseling program.
I: What--- receiving or giving?
BW: (laughs) I already received; now I would be giving. But I don't know if that's what I'm going to end up doing. I figure that the classes I'm taking now, I can apply them to whatever I decide to do in college.
I: Is that the goal, to get in some kind of writing gig?
BW: Well, yeah, that's what I'd really like to do. I wouldn't want to actually go to writing school, though. This class is just for credit. order to get a degree in journalism, you have to learn all that crap abou newspapers...
I: yeah, the pyramid lead!
BW:Yeah I would never write for a newspaper. So anyway...
I: So you still live with your parents?
BW: Yeah, I'm going to be here for another month, and then with my girlfriend for a couple weeeks, then I'm going on tour. And then, I'm going to live with her for good.
I: Are your parents cool about answering the phone for Ben "Weasel", an punk rock, all that shit?
BW: Oh, yeah. They're cool about it. My mom was in the movie I made.
I: Did she get killed in it?

BW: No, she didn't. She was one of the few people who didn't. She played an angry mom harassing her punk rock kid, who was played by my guitarist, Dan... But hey! SCREECHING WEASEL got back together!
I: Yeah, I heard that.
BW: Well, where did you hear that from? **← BEN WEASEL INT. CONT**
I: I heard that from Chris in Tampa.
BW: Oh, yeah... We got back together and we're touring this summer. We're going to record an album in San Francisco. It was kind of like--- we were going to do the South cause we do real well there, and its alot of fun, but we wanted to record an album on tour, and we found a really good, cheap studio in San Francisco. We're going to spend about a week out there recording and hanging out with the BLATZ and THE GARGOYLES.
I: Do you got alot of new songs already, or do you have alot of shit just laying around?
BW: Oh no... it's all new songs, except... Well, we're recording an album and an EP. The EP will have "I wanna Be a Homosexual" on it, re-recorded, and the album will have "Kamala's Too Nice" and "Fathead", which we did before. But all those songs--- most people don't even have them. The album'll have 16 tunes with 2 that have been heard before.
I: Any GORE GORE GIRLS songs on there?
BW: Um... We're still talking about it. If there are it'll only be the first one ("Nightbreed") and the last one ("Jennifer Blowdryer") from the tape I sent you.
I: How did it happen that this got back together, and who is in it now?
BW: I don't know... Like John(guitar) never says what's on his mind. Apparently, he wasn't too happy with the band breaking up to begin with, but when I talked to him then, he was just like "yeah, that's cool. We should break up." But when we originally broke up, it was because the drummer, Brian, had quit once and I talked him into staying. Then he was talking about quitting again so I said, "If you're gonna quit, then quit." He goes, "Ok. I quit." I say, fine. He says, "By the way, Dan(bass in S.W.) wants to quit, too, but he's afraid to say anything." I'm like, Ok, the band's over. It turns out that Dan never wanted to quit. Brian made that up. So, Dan and John had been talking about getting together, then the Gore Gore Girls broke up, and John said, "let's go do some Screeching Weasel stuff," and Dan was sittin' there in the bar, too, so I said "If were gonna do it, let's make it a band, cause I want to go on tour and suff. So Dan used to play bass, and we moved him to guitar, so him and John both play guitar now. We got a new guy, Dave, who plays bass, and a guy named "Clam" who plays drums.
I: Clam Weasel...
BW: Well his real name's Dan, but we've got two Dan's so he has to be Clam He used to drum for IVY LEAGUE.
I: Oh God... Well, I don't want to say anything...
BW: Well, I didn't really like the band either but he's a great drummer and a cool guy. Plus, he's really, really, into it. That's the difference between the way the band is and the way it was two years ago. Everyone's totally into it. Before, I would show them a song, and it would be like, "Oh no... another one of Ben's songs,"and they'd sit around the practice space with all these mopey looks on their face. Now we're really psyched.
I: That's good. You guys play out yet at all?
BW: No, we play Madison(WI) on the 18th and Milwaukee on the 26th and Chicago on June 9th (laughs)... Bad Religion's playing in the city that night.
I: Gee, should make alot of money that night.
BW: Well, they're charging $14.50 and we're charging $5, so I think we'll be abe to hold our own against them.
I: Oh! I thought you meant you were playing with them.
BW: Oh no. God, no... The whole point of doing the show is as a tour benefit for us, so we have money to tour and record an album. We'd make 100 bucks if we played with them...

MORE BEN WEASEL INTERVIEW LATER IN THIS ISSUE

I: What music have you listened to today?
BW: None.   I: What about yesterday?   BW: None.
I: Well, what are you listening to at all?
BW: I just got the new MR. T EXPERIENCE album and 7" and I've listened to that about 800 times. It's real good.
I: Didn't get it on CD, did you?   BW: (laughs) No, I got the album. I've been listening to THE QUEERS. The Queers are the best punk band in the country right now.
I: Where are they from?   BW: Boston. Also, I've been listening to TEENAGE HEAD.   I: Did you ever see that shitty Michael J. Fox movie, THE CLASS OF '84? They're in it?   BW: Yeah, they're playing a real good tune in there, too... I've been listening to them, and of course, THE DICKIES, and THE RAMONES. Uh, I got this new SEWER TROUT record that I haven't listened to yet, but they're always good.   I: What's your favorite MTX song?   BW: It would be one of the new ones, really. I always liked "Danny Partridge" or "Song about a girl who went shopping," but I think now, my favorite MTX song is "Last Time I Listened to You" off of the 7" or "Parasite" off of the album. I: Are the Parasites any good? I ordered their record. It seems like they're on some neo-Ramones trip...   BW: Oh yeah! I heard them once. We did a radio show there(in New Jersey) and their drummer was our sound guy. He played a tape of them for us, and they're real good, but I haven't heard the records.
I: When's the last time you sniffed GLOO?   BW: I never did in my life. I: (disbelief) No way! Hmmm... Do you know anyone who died from inhaling the coolant, freon?   BW: (laughs) No! But, I DID do that! I was probably 15. It was when I was in drug rehab. I was sitting in the corner, cause they put you in the chair in the corner, when you're bad, and the chair was next to the air conditioner...
I: Well, MTX is real cool on GLOO, that's why I bring it up. BW: Well, I hear that stuff is really bad for your brain...
I: It is!
BW: ...and I've got enough problems with my brain without making it any worse. In fact, What a segue! That's the name of the new album. "My Brain Hurts." I don't know if anyone'll put it out. We're still looking for a record label.
I: Wait... so you're giving drug rehab now?!?   BW: No, I'm just in school for it...   I: Is this some kind of Narcotics Anonymous trip, or... BW: No, no, no, no... In fact, I'm totally against that kind of stuff. But I will say that there are alot of people who need help. If I went into that field, I'd work at some place that's somewhat cool and treats people like human beings.
I: What about beer?   BW: Well, beer is the worst of em all, and I drink beer, so I can't really say too much, but it really is the worst...

WEASEL GRUB

I:Do you ever put beer in your RAMEN?   BW: No. I don't eat it as a soup, either. I: Yeah! Do you stir fry it?   BW: No, I cook it in the water, but I drain it. Alot of people eat it as soup. I: You should try it stir-fried some time. It's real Ft. Lauderdale.   BW: Well, If you're looking for cheap eats, you should make your own pizza because you can do that real cheap.
I: I don't know. We just get it out of the trash. We're... uh... fuckin' scum.   BW: Yeah. I: I got a bag of like 30 pizzas in the trash last noght at Pizza Hut.   BW: Yecch! I
don't think I'd really like something out of the dumpster.   I: Well (referring to the list), That's one of the questions on here(never refer to the
the list). "Have you ever eaten out of the trash?"   BW: Not that I can remember...   I: It's got kind of a bad social stigma, but...   BW: well, as long as I can afford to pay for food, I'll avoid that, just because you can never tell...   I: Our motto is "Get off of your ass and get in the trash!" (actually Nobody I know EVER says that).   BW: Well, I'm real picky about what I eat.   I: Do you ever buy Felafel?   BW: I don't even know what that is...

ORSON WEASEL : BEN'S MOVIE "DISGUSTEEN"

I: What's the movie, DISGUSTEEN, about?   BW: Basically, its about a bunch of punk rockers that are vampires, and kill people. The new movie, uh... I don't even know what that's about, cause it doesn't exist yet.   I: It gets written as it goes along?   BW: Yeah, well, I've got to have something done in a few weeks, cause I got more people than I need who are going to be in it, which is cool, because this time I have more people who are willing to give 100% and do insane things.   I: Are there any well-known punks who get killed in Disgusteen, like anyone that writes for MRR?   BW: The only person is Doug Ward who writes the scene reports (Chicago).   He gets run over by a car and set on fire.   I: Do you hink the movie is really worth $25?   BW: Uh... It depends. If you're just some punk rocker who is not really into movies and all that, well, no. But if you're into underground movies, then, yeah, because people do underground films that are like 20 minutes on film for $35, and mine is 55 minutes on video. It's cheesy as hell, but the people who've bought it thought it was entertaining. Put it this way: If you're poor, I wouldn't recommend saving up for it. If you've got the money, yeah, it's worth it. I:That's cool... Do you own a gun? BW: No.

NO BLOOD FOR MONEY

I: What waas the inspiration for "I Want to Be a Homosexual"?   BW: When I was with Roadkill, we were gonna put out a SLOPPY SECONDS record called "I Don't Want to Be a Homosexual" and I had told Bruce le Bruce of JD's(?) about it and he said we should do the I want to...   I: What was the inspiration for "March of the Lawnmowers"?   BW: I used to live in the suburbs and cut the grass all the time... I don't think most of my songs have alot of inspiration.   I: Do you think "THE KURDS" is a good name for a band?   BW: well... you'd have to add something to it...   I: like JIMMY AND THE KURDS ?   BW: or the FILTHY KURDS, or something. You'd have to put something in front of it...   I: Do you ever give blood for money? BW:(laughs) Huh? No.   I: really?   BW: Nah... We almost did in Tuscon cause the record store we were at was right next door to one of those places, but I figured we were eating so badly at the time, that if we started giving blood, it'd be real unhealthy. I'd do it but they don't pay enough. You only get like $10.   I: Yeah, but they give you a free meal of Twinkies and Orange Juice, which is hell punk...   BW: Yeah, I'd do that if I needed money, but I heard the first time you go, you have to sit there and wait for like 3 hours, and I don't have the patience. That's why I never applied for welfare. You spend as much time at a welfare office as you would at a job...   I: How many times have you been arrested?   BW: only once. When I was 14 for truancy.

SCAM COLUMNIST "DUKE" RIDES IN A TANK.

Scam, slayings linked
JACKSON, Miss. —A connection between a Louisiana prison scam and the 1987 slayings of Mississippi Judge Vincent Sherry and his wife, Margaret, has been made in an indictment that points to a reputed hit man as the suspect.
The Sherrys were ...ot to death in their ... 4, 1987. He w...

WE DIDN'T DO IT, I SWEAR!

I: Once you told me you did a spoken word show where you just talked about stupid shit you did when you were a kid... What were some of the stupid things? BW: Well, it depends-- stupid now as compared to then. I didn't think it was stupid, then, an even now, I don't think it was stupid. Things like... Well, behind my house was one gigantic field, and then they started building houses there. The company that started building houses went bankrupt, so there was like 3 houses where there should have been like 100. There was this huge hill of dirt. Gigantic. We used to go back there and spend, literally, all day scavenging for wood. Then we'd start a fire an sit on this kid's roof who lived right behind there and watch all

the fire engines come. I: Right on, man! We still do that! BW: We used to to steal everyone's mailbox on the block, but we'd steal everyone's but ours. That was pretty stupid. We'd go peep in windows when we were 12 to see someone's mom walking around naked. I: Yeah, I knew a guy here who knew all of the houses, but he was like 25... BW: Yeah, I think there comes a time when you have to give that up, if for nothing else but legal reasons. We did all the stuff that kids do, though, throw rocks through windows...

After that the "interview" degenerated into mindless talk about baseball, with Ben admitting to being a huge Cubs fan (Mark Arm digs the Mariners) and talk about who'll take the AL West, etc. Very unpunk. Ben mentioned that in San Francisco, he will try to convince Lawrence Livermore to put out h the new LP on LOOKOUT! so stay tuned. Anything else? Uh... He thinks "Swingin' singles" clubs are the biggest scam around, a trip for suburban losers(cause that's all who can afford it). The clubs have no money for releases so they get it all up front, before the records exist. Ben Weasel on the Dwarves: "I booked em once and they were slow and heavy, and had long hair, so either they ggot real cool and decided to play punk, or, more likely, they're just playing around with some gimmick, and no one will give a shit about em a year from now the same way that no one cares about GWAR now, except the heavy metal people." Watch for Screeching Weasel in a town near you, get the new vinyl, rah, rah, etc. Enough.

(FILLER: by IGGY
ONE TIME RON VARNDELL AND ME WERE WALKING HOME, REAL LATE AT NIGHT. WE WERE PISSING ON THIS WALL AND I YELLED "COPS!" AND RON PISSED ALL OVER HIMSELF.

- 36 -

"FEAR AND LOATHING IN YBOR CITY."

CHRIS ARROWS COLUMN

TAMPA MAIN EVENT

ASSIN
ASSIN

I live in a trailer and there's another trailer and they sit on an e in White Trash, Central Florida. It is lovely. However, I don't t to talk about that. What I want to talk about is what happened sterday. My girlfriend wanted to go shopping and, me being the patron- ing guy that I am, said "sure." So we went to a place in Ybor City ere a friend of ours, Billy, got a spud gun (a gun that shoots potato eces). Anyway, we get there and go in and look around. Never mind the ame of the shop, but their "motto" was "Whimsical Creations." Very over- riced pieces of useless shit. Very impractical items of stupidity. This is hen they had 1 small table with cheap, affordable, cool shit. This is here the spud guns were. The spud guns were a tad cheesy and unim- pressive, so I browsed around somemore. I didn't get too far into my crap perusing before I noticed 2 women talking in the middle of the shop. One was a 45-ish year old woman who looked well dressed and well kept. Facing her, but with her back to me, was a younger girl with a big, frilly, ballerina-type thing. It looked like a mini-dress with a five foot diameter. Topping off this ensemble was an army fatigue that was cut off at the shoulders. She had pretty hair.

I wandered around the store a bit, and then I looked back at them. At this point, she was facing me. She had the face of an angel. It didn't take long before I realized that she had a baby hanging off of her big, beautiful breast. Time froze for a moment. When I was sure I had memorized her "bosom", I went back to pretending I was looking at stuff. I thought, "Shit! This is great! She's got her things pulled out in pub- lic and I'm in the same room. How cool." Then, I thought,"Even though, this isn't California, it's natural to breast feed, and it is good for th the baby, and all. This isn't a filthy thing! It's a really fantastic, wonderful, beautiful part of this thing called life. However, I became instantly jealous of that goddamn baby. I looked up at her beautiful cild-like face and she was staring back at me with a very deliberate, smile-like stare. Fuck. Anyway, to make a short story shorter, my girl- friend bought 2 guns that were transparent fishes that shoot sparks, for $3 a piece. We paid(the mother was the cashier after she put her off- spring away), and we left. I've seen females breast feed in public before but they've just never smiled at me like that while they were doing it. Everybody was a winner. Me, the baby, the girl made a sale, my girl- friend got fish guns, and life was great. As we were getting into the car, I told my girlfriend about the weening I had witnessed. She said, "Did she have big tits?" I said, "...uh... Not really." Then we went to go get ice cream.

Sat Feb

WRESTLIN

Record Reviews

by BUDDHA

"Can You Break Through?" (V/A Skean Records comp. LP) - NO! I can't break through, and I don't want anymore shitty fucking records! After sitting through an entire LP of dark, moody, experimental shit and one quite dissapointing GreenDay song, with your last hope being a GO! song, finding out that the GO! song just goes "GREG!" makes me feel used. (B) (Address: Fuck you if you want to buy this!)

Poison Idea 2x7" - I should be shot for paying the 7.99 or whatever I was stupid enough to pay for this. One really good song that's on the "Feel..." LP, and 3 shitty, shitty covers. I feel beaten. I'm not even gonna tell how to buy this. Fuk

Volkswhale 7" - Weird shit. Like taking a lot of acid and locking yourselfe in the refrigerator. MRR wouldn't review it because it's got keyboards and stuff, but I highly recomend it! ($3 ppd, from David Schall, P.O. Box 2143, Stow, OH 44224) (B)

Blatz/Filth split LP - This is a great record. Blatz might win but only by a little. Both bands play rad fucking punk, with Batz being more upbeat and snotty, with Filth more heavy and "dirgy!". This is very good. Two thumbs up! (Lookout!) (B)

Straight Youth 7" - A.S.E. parody 7" that might be kind of funny if it wasn't made by ex-powerhouse (a serious S.E. band last year when S.E. was cool.) members. (4½ Fingers) (B)

⑤

"The Texas Chain Saw Massacre."
   Here are the horrible facts of "the case of the century", as told by Judge Robert H. Gollman, before whom Gein stood trial. What drove this reclu~~s~~ ~~tion, fratricide, grave-robbing~~

FUCK YOU!
STILL MORE REVIEWS
"KILL FOR GONZO!"

"Gripping study . . . for true-crime addicts."
—*Publishers Weekly*

S (THE KICK TO THE GROIN):
DEFINITELY SCAM'S MOST RUTHLESS AND EFFECTIVE MOVE. BEWARE THE HANDSHAKE THAT CONCEALS A FIST...

CONSPIRACY THEORIES: NOTHING LIVENS UP A BAD PARTY LIKE A WEIRD DRUNK SITTING ALONE IN THE CORNER, MUMBLING ALOUD ABOUT BRAIN EATING MILLIONAIRES AND BLACK MARKET KIDNEYS... EVERYBODY KNOWS THAT TEDDY KENNEDY USED HIS POWER TO COVER UP DETAILS OF CHAPPAQUIDDICK, BUT WHO WOULD BELIEVE THAT THE REAL REASON HE TOOK THAT GIRL OFF OF THE BRIDGE, WAS BECAUSE HE WANTED TO SNACK ON HER MEDULLA? I WOULD! WHY NOT?!? CONSPIRACY THEORIES OFFER HOURS OF ENTERTAINMENT. OUR CURRENT FAVORITE IS A STORY ABOUT RESEARCH INTO SATANIC CULTS THAT LINKS AMERICA'S TOP BUSINESS, POLITICAL, ACADEMIC, AND ENTERTAINMENT LEADERS IN A SUPERSECRET ORGANIZATION OF TWISTED DEVIL WORSHIPPORS WHO DRINK BLOOD FOR POWER. IN THIS WORLD, IS IT SO HARD TO BELIEVE THAT LEE IACOCCA DRINKS BLOOD WITH NORMAN SCHWARZKOPF BY THE LIGHT OF THE FULL MOON? OR THAT WEALTH, WHISKEY, AND INBREEDING HAVE TURNED THE REMAINING (KENNEDY)ES INTO INHUMAN MONSTERS WITH A TASTE FOR YOUNG WOMEN'S BRAINS? HOW 'BOUT THIS ONE? THERE'S A SECRET BLACK MARKET WHERE THE RICH AND FAMOUS BUY BLACK KIDS AND EAT THEM AS A DELICACY AT POWER LUNCHES. JOHN SUNUNU CLAMBERS INTO THE STREETS OF D.C. TO HAND PICK KIDS, WHICH HE BUYS, AND, UNABLE TO CONTAIN HIMSELF, EATS ON THE SPOT. MY FRIEND WAS PICKED UP BY BEAUTIFUL, ORIENTAL WOMEN AT A BAR. THEY TOOK HIM TO A DRUG PARTY IN A PENTHOUSE SUITE. HE AWOKE 2 DAYS LATER WITH NO WALLET AND A SEARING PAIN IN HIS GROIN. ONE OF HIS KIDNEYS HAD BEEN REMOVED! GEORGE BRETT ATE 6 FETUSES AND WON THE BATTING TITLE! THE MOON LANDING WAS FAKED! THE MAYOR OF FT. LAUDERDALE HAS STRING WARTS ALL OVER HIS BACK...

SCAM READER WHO KNEW TOO MUCH"

WELCOME TO FORT LAUDERDALE BEACH

Greater Ft. Lauderdal

from chuck, iggy, milo, tony, & mike

PUNK HOUSE

TOTAL FUCKIN! PUKE!

FT. LAUDERDALE SCENE REPORT

THE GATES OF HELL *OPENED?*

Unlike some cities that are known for their wind, bridges, or Buffa wings, Ft. Lauderdale is, unfortunately famous for its cops. When the FOX TV show "COPS" originally went on the air, it was filmed with Ft. Lauderdale police. It was the brownshirts in the Broward County Sheriff organization, led by brainless, PR-mad sheriff Nick Navarro, that busted the 2 LIVE CREW in nearby Hollywood, FL. And no South Florida resident can ever forget Navarro and Geraldo Rivera tossing kilos of seize cocaine into a furnace on live TV, primetime, while chanting "Burn, Baby, Burn!"

Until recently, Ft. Lauderdale was the well-known "spring Break cap't of the world, but the local pigs' relentless hassling of visiting tourist along with cops, raiding springbreak clubs like the Button South, new stone age laws against driving back and forth on the strip, and open container laws have single-handedly destroyed the local tourist trade. Add to this the fact that outgoing Mayor, Bob Cox IS A NATIONALLY RECOGNIZE

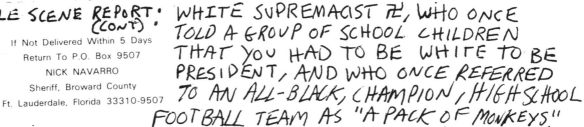

If Not Delivered Within 5 Days
Return To P.O. Box 9507
NICK NAVARRO
Sheriff, Broward County
Ft. Lauderdale, Florida 33310-9507

WHITE SUPREMACIST 己, WHO ONCE TOLD A GROUP OF SCHOOL CHILDREN THAT YOU HAD TO BE WHITE TO BE PRESIDENT, AND WHO ONCE REFERRED TO AN ALL-BLACK, CHAMPION, HIGH SCHOOL FOOTBALL TEAM AS "A PACK OF MONKEYS" THE RAPID GENTRIFICATION DOWNTOWN, AND THE POLICE ATTACKS ON THE HOMELESS, THE MINORITIES, AND CHUCK, AND YOU HAVE A PRETTY BACKWARDS TOWN.

Anyways, FUN IN Ft. Lauderdale is what you can get away with, and Getting away with IT STARTS AT THE WEST SIDE MARKET" ON THE CORNER OF 11ᵗʰ AND LAS OLAS. PUNK ROCKER, BUDDHA, SAYS "YOU CAN GET A MOUNTAIN DEW, AND, LIKE A CAKE FOR 89¢." THE GUY BEHIND THE CORNER CALLS ME "DUDE" AND SELLS ME BEER, HE KNOWS I'M A "WEST SIDE PUNK..."

THERE'S NO DENNY'S AROUND, WHICH IS OK WITH ME. YOU EVER NOTICE HOW OPPRESSIVE SOME PEOPLE ARE ABOUT DENNY'S, AND DENNY'S AT 2AM, COFFEE, AND BEING "PUNK"? AS FAR AS I'M CONCERNED, IF YOU DON'T LIKE BEER OR ED GEIN, ITS COOL, BUT SOME PEOPLE CAN NEVER UNDERSTAND WHY YOU DON'T WANT TO TROOP DOWN TO A FUCKING WAL'S W/10 PEOPLE IN THE MIDDLE OF THE NIGHT TO GIGGLE AT THE WAITRESSES AND ORDER FRENCH FRIES. ANYWAY, THERE'S A DAYBREAK INN UP ON 15ᵗʰ WHICH IS LIKE A POSER DENNY'S, ONLY WORSE. WE WENT THERE TO GET CHEESEBURGERS ONE NIGHT, AND A GEEK WHO LOOKED LIKE JEB BUSH TOLD US THEY CLOSED AT 9:00PM, CAUSING BUDDHA TO SNEER, "GUESS THAT'S WHY THEY CALL IT THE DAYBREAK INN..."

DOWNTOWN, ITS A SHORT WALK TO THE LIBRARY, WHICH IS A PRETTY COOL WAY TO WASTE TIME. THEY DON'T HAVE THE ED GEIN BOOK BUT

Scientists are afraid that they have opened the gates to hell. A geological group who drilled a hole about 14.4 kilometers deep (about 9 miles) in the crust of the earth, are saying that they heard human screams. Screams have been heard from the condemned souls from earth's deepest hole. Terrified scientists are afraid they have let loose the evil powers of hell up to the earth's surface.

"The information we are gathering is so surprising, that we are sincerely afraid of what we might find down there," stated Mr. Azzacov, the manager of the project to drill a 14.4 kilometer hole in remote Siberia.

The geologists were dumbfounded. After they had drilled several kilometers through the earth's crust, the drill bit suddenly began to rotate wildly. "There is only one explanation – that the deep center of the earth is hollow," the surprised Azzacov explained. The second surprise was the high temperature they discovered in the earth's center. "The calculations indicate the given temperature was about 1,100 degrees Celsius, or over 2,000 degrees Fahrenheit," Dr. Azzacov points out. "This is far more than we expected. It seems almost like an inferno of fire is brutally going on in the center of the earth."

"The last discovery was nevertheless the most shocking to our ears, so much so that the scientists are afraid to continue the project. We tried to listen to the earth's movements at certain intervals with super-sensitive microphones, which were let down through the hole. What we heard, turned those logically thinking scientists into a trembling ruins. It was sometimes a weak, but high pitched sound which we thought to be coming from our own equipment," explained Dr. Azzacov. "But after some adjustments we comprehended that indeed the sound came from the earth's interior. We could hardly believe our own ears. We heard a human voice, screaming in pain. Even though one voice was discernible, we could hear thousands, perhaps millions, in the background, of suffering souls screaming. After this ghastly discovery, about half of the scientists quit because of fear. Hopefully, that which is down there will stay there," Dr. Azzacov added.

Translated from *AMMENUSASTIA*, a newspaper published in Finland.

MORE FT. LAUDERDALE SCENE REPORT;

IT'S STILL A PRETTY COOL PLACE TO WASTE TIME. YOU CAN GO OUTSIDE ON THE ROOF AND LOOK OUT OVER BEAUTIFUL DOWNTOWN FT. LAUDERDALE, WHICH IS KIND OF, UH, INSPIRING, I GUESS. ALSO, THEY HAVE A COMPUTERIZED CARD CATALOG, SO YOU CAN LOOK UP BOOKS ON ANUS, FECES, JOHN WAYNE GACY, THE PENIS, ETC, AND GET A COMPUTER PRINT OUT TO LEAVE FOR THE NEXT GUY. I'M 18 YEARS OLD AND I STILL THINK THAT'S PRETTY FUNNY...

ALSO, REAL NEAR OUR HOUSE IS CLARK'S OUT OF TOWN BOOKS, WHICH AT FIRST GLANCE IS REAL COOL, BUT REALLY IS RUN BY A BUNCH OF KID HATING, NEO-FASCISTS. THEY DON'T HAVE THE ED GEIN BOOK, EITHER, BUT THEY DO HAVE ALL KINDS OF COOL BOOKS ON BLOWING SHIT UP OR GETTING FAKE I.D.'S, AS WELL AS WORLD WAR III ILLUSTRATED, ANARCHY MAGAZINE, AND COOL CIA CONSPIRACY BOOKS. HOWEVER, EVERY TIME I GO IN THERE I'M WATCHED AT ALL TIMES. ALSO, THE BOOKS ALL COST $10 OR $20, WHICH IS RIDICULOUS, CAUSE THE PEOPLE WHO USUALLY WANT TO BLOW SHIT UP, DON'T USUALLY HAVE THE CASH. TO TOP IT ALL OFF, BOOKS ARE SEALED IN SHRINKWRAP SO YOU REALLY CAN'T BROWSE AT ALL. FUCK THESE PEOPLE. IF YOU GO THERE, STEAL FROM THEM.

MOVIN' UP U.S. 1 TO SEARS TOWN, YOU FIND A REAL OLD 1950'S SEARS WHERE IGGY PAYS THE PHONE BILL AND CHUCK STEALS HIS GOOFY PANTS. NEXT DOOR IS ALL BOOKS AND RECORDS WHICH IS WHERE I SELL MY CD'S FOR THE CD SCAM. A LITTLE OVERPRICED, BUT OK. THEY HAVE SHELVES AND SHELVES OF USED BOOKS, INCLUDING SOME REAL FINDS LIKE GEORGE HAYDUKE'S "GETTING EVEN, Pt. II" AND THE CONFRONTATIONAL "BLACK POWER" BY STOKELY CARMICHAL. I GOT A GREAT BOOK CALLED "CRIME AND JUVENILE DELINQUANCY" WHICH IS A REAL DRAMATIC SHOCKER FROM THE 60'S: "BARELY 13, HIS LIFE WAS ALMOST OVER, THIS WAS BILLY'S FOURTH APPEARANCE IN COURT, AND HE ALREADY HAD THE EARMARKS OF A FUTURE CRIMINAL..." THEY ALSO SELL RECORDS HERE AND CHUCK FOUND THE INFAMOUS COLLECTOR FAVORITE "GOD PUNISHES THE EAT" BY THE EAT (from Miami). THIS WAS ONCE FEATURED IN MRR'S COLLECTOR NERD COLUMN, AND, VALUED AT OVER $150 (CHUCK BOUGHT IT FOR $3 (IT'S A COOL RECORD. CHUCK'LL TAPE IT FOR YA). NEXT DOOR TO ALL BOOKS IS A PLACE THAT CLAIMS TO HAVE THE BEST ISRAELI FOOD IN TOWN. WHY NOT?!?

AROUND THE CORNER, DOWN SUNRISE, THERE'S A THRIFT SHOP, DICKER 'N' DICKER WHERE I LIKE TO HAMMER ON THE PIANO AND CHUCK GETS HAWAIIN SHIRTS (CHUCK CHANGES CLOTHES ALOT, VERY UNPUNK). THESE PEOPLE ARE PRETTY MEAN TO US KIDS, WHICH IS LIKE I SAID, THE FT. LAUDERDALE ATTITUDE FROM TOP TO BOTTOM.

TONIGHT CHUCK AND I WALKED UP AND DOWN SUNRISE HITTING DUMPSTERS, BUT NO LUCK. GREAT DOUGHNUTS AT MR. DONUT, BUT MOSTLY LETTUCE AND COKE CUPS AT RALLY BURGER AND SUBWAY, AND CHAINED AND LOCKED DUMPSTERS(!) AT LITTLE CAESER'S, McDONALD'S, BURGER KING, AND HOT DOG HEAVEN. I CAN'T BELIEVE PEOPLE LOCK UP THEIR TRASH. FUCK 'EM, THEY'RE ALL POSERS, ANYWAYS, ALL THE GOOD TRASH IS ON 17th Street (McDonald's and PIZZA HUT FOR QUANTITY, DOUGHBOY'S PIZZA FOR AWESOME QUALITY).

UP ON THE FAMOUS FT. LAUDERDALE BEACH, IDIOCY IS THE RULE. STONED METALHEADS AND STEROID CRAZY JOCKS CRUISE THE FAMOUS A1A STRIP LOOKING FOR "CHICKS". THERE'S A BUNCH OF REAL DEPRESSING "PARTY" PLACES LIKE "THE WORLD FAMOUS CANDY STORE" AND "PENRODS ON THE BEACH" WHERE JARHEADED DRUNKS FLABBY SALESMEN GAWK AT WET T-SHIRT CONTESTS. THERE'S A BAR, "SUMMER'S ON THE BEACH", WHERE I SAW A REAL VIOLENT D.R.I. SHOW 2 YEARS AGO, AND A REAL DEPRESSING CIRCLE JERKS SHOW 2 DAYS BEFORE I MOVED TO LAUDERDALE IN OCTOBER. FOR THE RECORD, WE GO ON A1A ALL THE TIME AND WE NEVER SEE VANILLA ICE...

8. OCTOPUS

Staff photo/JOHN CURRY

Artist Russell Rand paints over the graffiti that mars his artwork on many Brickell Avenue buildings.

FT. LAUDERDALE SCENE REPORT CONTINUES...

Downtown graffiti mars streetside art

By TERRY NEAL
Staff Writer

FORT LAUDERDALE — As an artist, Russell Rand has done a lot of hollering about freedom of expression and artistic integrity.

Now he's hollering about a graffiti artist who has freely expressed himself with spray paint over Rand's work.

Last year, Rand told city officials he wanted to "play jazz visually" on 7,000 square feet of boarded-up storefront property on Brickell Avenue, south of Southeast Second Street.

At first, officials said no. But he continued to hound them. In the end, his persistence won them over.

From January to March, Rand spent 125 hours of his free time splashing and brushing, dripping and splattering. When he was finished he stepped back from his massive canvas and liked what he saw.

"It definitely looks better," said Rand, a Broward County government lab technician by day, a self-described "performing artist" by night. "And everybody seems to like it. They come by and say, 'Hey, that looks pretty good.'"

But just days after he finished his work, someone armed with a can of black spray paint embellished Rand's art with another brand of expression — graffiti.

Feed the Poor.
Cure AIDS Now.
No More War.

"I guess he's making his point, but he's killing me," said Rand, his voice rising, arms flailing. "Hey, I'm all for feeding the poor and no more war and curing AIDS, but this isn't the way to do it."

On a recent weekday, Rand came out to paint over the graffiti. He sported paint-splattered garments, nearly blending in with the rainbow colored backround.

It's almost become a game. The graffiti artist sprays. Rand brushes and splashes over it. And so on.

"Russell goes right out there and fixes it up, he's been great about that," said Steve Tilbrook, an administrative assistant in the city's Riverwalk office.

Rand's dripping artwork is also displayed on the facade of Broward Art Guild in the 200 block of South Andrews Avenue.

Across the street from the newly painted buildings on Brickell Avenue, Neil Sterling, who runs the family-owned Sterling's Mens and Boys store, said he likes Rand's work.

"I love it," Sterling said. "I think it brightens the entire block. It's great."

Great maybe, but city officials hope it's only temporary.

The city wants to redevelop boarded-up buildings into an entertainment district of bars and restaurants. The city is expecting to open proposals from developers on May 31.

"WE CAN'T HELP IT IF WE'RE FROM LAUDERDALE" — THE FT. LAUDERDALE SCENE REPORT MARCHES AHEAD...

COME BACK WEST ON LAS OLAS BLVD. AND CHECK OUT THE GENTRIFIED YUPPIE CAFE STRIP. ONE ART GALLERY CLAIMS TO SELL STUFF IN A NEW MEXICAN MOTIF AND THERE'S AN ART DECO, TURQUOISE DOG IN THE WINDOW, HOWLIN' AT THE MOON. YUPPIE SHIT...
ON LAS OLAS IS THE CHEMIST SHOP, WHICH CLAIMS TO BE THE "WORLD'S MOST UNUSUAL DRUG STORE." EITHER WAY, CHUCK IS THE RESIDENT LINE COOK THERE. ONE DAY, I WORKED, AS A FAVOR, AT THE SODA JERK POSITION, AND I SCAMMED 4 HUGE HAMBURGER PATTIES W/ BUNS, LETTUCE AND CHEESE. I COOKED 'EM UP AT HOME W/ BEER, BUTTER, GARLIC, BBQ SAUCE AND ONIONS. I LOVE CHEESEBURGERS...

ON LAS OLAS, THERE'S THE PANTRY PRIDE, A LONG TIME SYMBOL OF OPRESSION TO THE FT. LAUDERDALE NATIVES. WHEN I FIRST MOVED HERE, I LIVED IN CHUCK'S OLD APARTMENT W/ NO ELECTRICITY OR MONEY — ALONE EXCEPT FOR HUGE ROACHES THE SIZE OF A MAN'S THUMB. EVERY MORNING IT WAS A SHORT WALK TO THE PANTRY PRIDE WHERE I'D START MY DAY BY STEALING A 12 PACK OF MOUNTAIN DEW AND SOME SOUP, BEER, OR A DELI SANDWHICH (ALWAYS SALAMI, PROVOLONE, ONIONS, MUSTARD ON RYE). ANYWAY, I GOT CAUGHT THERE ONCE AFTER I WAS 2 OR 3 HUNDRED BUCKS AHEAD, AND ARRESTED. NOW, THEIR LAWYERS SEND ME BULLSHIT EXTORTION LETTERS DEMANDING $200 IN "COMPENSATION" FOR THE $16 WORTH OF STUFF THEY CAUGHT ME WITH. SO, I IGNORE THE LETTERS AND GO OUT EVERY ONCE IN AWHILE TO FUCK THE PLACE UP W/ SPRAY PAINT. I THINK IT'D BE PRETTY FUNNY TO JUST KEEP ATTACKING THIS SAME SUPERMARKET, MAKE IT A RITUAL, AND PUZZLE THE FUCK OUT OF STOREOWNERS. "WHY US?!? WHY WOULD SOMEONE WRITE "FREE CHARLES MANSON!" ON OUR WALL?" FOR THE RECORD, PANTRY PRIDE HAS A PRETTY GOOD DUMPSTER WHERE ME, CHUCK, AND JOHN DANIA GET TONS 'O' BREAD FOR OUR HOMEMADE GARLIC BREAD HABIT.

FT. LAUDERDALE ÜBER ALLES!

NOW YOU'RE WORKING YOUR WAY BACK DOWNTOWN, WHICH IS FILLED WITH HUGE BUILDINGS THAT BLOCK OUT THE SUN AND HAVE SMOOTH WALLS, PERFECT FOR GLUING FLYERS TO. ALSO THERE'S A COUPLE COOL CONSTRUCTION SIGHTS WHERE YOU CAN HANG OUT AND GET COOL CHAIRS OR OTHER HOME IMPROVEMENT ITEMS. EVERY ONCE IN A WHILE, CHUCK WILL FIND SOMETHING ON THE GROUND HERE AND PUT IT IN HIS MOUTH.

A "PERFORMING ARTS CENTER" WAS BUILT NEAR OUR HOUSE TO GENTRIFY OUR NEIGHBORHOOD, AND DRIVE THE PREDOMINATELY BLACK POPULATION AWAY TO BE REPLACED BY YUPPIES, WHO HAVE MORE OF AN APPRECIATION FOR THE MAYOR'S DOWNTOWN ART. THIS NEW CENTER HAS POLICE ATTACKING THE HOMELESS AND DRIVING THEM FROM THE DOWNTOWN AREA, CAUSE ITS TOO MUCH OF A DOWNER TO LOOK OUT THE LIMO WINDOW ON THE WAY TO THE OPERA AND SEE A BUM, OR, A... A... NEGRO! NICK AND I STARTED A SHORT LIVED "FOOD NOT BOMBS" WHICH FED THE DOWNTOWN HOMELESS REHEATED DUMPSTER PIZZAS AND BIG MACS, UNFORTUNATELY, WE ALL MOVED OUT OF LAUDERDALE BEFORE IT COULD GET GOING. NOW, WITH THE TROOPS COMING HOME, THE TIME IS RIPE FOR DEVELOPERS TO SELL THIS PHONY DOWNTOWN ART AND RIVERWALK SCAM, WHERE COUPLES CAN WALK ARM AND ARM AND SEE THE MANY SHOPS AND CAFES... " THE POOR ARE OUT, AND THE 50'S ARE IN ...

ANYWAY, DOWNTOWN ALSO HAS THE FT. LAUDERDALE CHAMBER OF COMMERCE, WHICH I THINK IS UNUSED. THIS IS FAMOUS, KIND OF, CAUSE ELVIS HAD AN OBSCURE B-SIDE CALLED "THE FT. LAUDERDALE CHAMBER OF COMMERCE." I SAW ELVIS ON A1A, BUT NO VANILLA ICE. DOWNTOWN ALSO FEATURES THE COUNTY COURTHOUSE, WHERE I WENT ONCE (30 HOURS COMMUNITY SERVICE WHICH I NEVER DID) THE PEOPLE INSIDE ALL PRETTY MUCH DESERVE TO BE LIT ON FIRE, BUT THE REAL STORY IS THE HOT DOG VENDORS OUTSIDE. MY ACTUAL DREAM IN LIFE FOR MANY YEARS, BESIDES BREWING

SON, IF YOU ACCEPT CHRIST, YOU HAVE *EVERYTHING* TO GAIN AND NOTHING TO LOSE. BUT TO REJECT HIM — YOU HAVE *NOTHING* TO GAIN AND **EVERYTHING** TO LOSE! — *PLEASE* READ THIS CAREFULLY!

YE MUST BE BORN AGAIN

OK!

2500 YEARS FROM TONIGHT, YOU WILL REMEMBER THIS MEETING!

CHICK TRACTS ARE FOUND ON LAUDERDALE STREETS.

THOSE DAMN CRITICS!

MORE REVIEWS

40-OUNCERS (BEER):

PUNK AS FUCK! AS BUDDHA SAYS, QUARTS and 40's ARE A NECESSARY part of the Ft. Lauderdale image we have to live up to. Weird, SLOPPY DRUNKS with big heavy bottles... DRINKING QUARTS OF MAGNUM MAKES ME WANT TO GET A BIG, ORANGE MOHAWK AND SIT AROUND CUSSING IN A RIDICULOUS ENGLISH ACCENT ABOUT BEING "ON THE DOLE...", or GO LIVE IN A CHURCH WITH CHAVO AND ROBO... TOTALLY PUKE! (I)

DUMPSTER PANCAKES:

LATELY, NICK AND I HAVE FOUND THE MOTHERLODE OF BREAKFAST IN A McDONALD'S DUMPSTER — About 50 McMUFFINS with SAUSAGE/ BACON/HAM, etc. But, ALSO, TONS OF "HOTCAKES". DUMPSTER PANCAKES ARE A WEIRD PHENOMENA — they're HARD TO REHEAT. I FINALLY FOUND THEY'RE GOOD COLD, WITH MARGERINE ON 'EM. It's ALL WE EAT NOW, CAUSE WE'RE BROKE, McWEIRD... (I)

CHUCK'S ZINE— GET LOOSE #1 (W/FILTH, LOVE GODZ, COOL SHIT):

CHUCK'S WAR, YOU'RE ONE OF THEM, YOU SAY YOU'RE CHUCK'S FRIEND BUT YOU'RE ONE OF THEM... Neer, neh neh-nuh-neh, neer, nuh, nuh, neer, nuh, nuh... (I)

SNIFFIN' GLUE (PUNK ACTIVITY):

RUBBER CEMENT IS COOL AND REAL EASY TO STEAL, but get Elmer's cause I GOT A WEIRD BRAND LAST TIME AND I GOT A BAD HEADACHE. "EVIL DEAD, II" IS A GOOD MOVIE ON INHALENTS, but I USUALLY WATCH CLUB-MTV AND LISTEN TO THE RAMONES AND BLACK FLAG - NEVER CRINGER. (I)

OMAR (scenemaster):

OMAR'S COOL. WE GOT A LETTER FROM HIM TODAY. HE'S DOING A ZINE CALLED IVY LEAGUE (sloppy layout) AND HE WORKS IN A HEALTH FOOD STORE. WRITE OMAR AT 115 25 SW 12¼ Ct, MIAMI, F OMAR SPELLED BACKWARDS IS RAMO. (I) 33186

MY OWN BEER, WAS TO BECOME A HOTDOG VENDOR, AND BE MY OWN MAN. BUT — YOU HAVE TO GET THOUSANDS OF DOLLARS OF INSURANCE AND LICENSES. I ASKED ONE OF THE DUDES IF THE PIGS EVER CHECKED, AND RIGHT THEN A SHERIFF CAME AND CHECKED... OH WELL,

THE PARK BY OUR HOUSE IS WHERE THEY HAVE "ART FESTIVALS" AND "WELCOME HOME MURDERERS" RALLIES. CHUCK, NICK, KATLEEN, AND JOHN GOT ARRESTED AND ROUGHED UP BY FT. LAUDERDALE'S FINEST THERE, ONE NIGHT, FOR WALKING THROUGH THE OPEN PARK AT 11:00 PM. THEY ALL GOT OFF WITH FINES AND COMMUNITY HOURS... WHAT THEY DID WRONG IS STILL UNCERTAIN, BUT...

OVER THE HILL, WEST, PAST I-95 IS THE JUVENILE DETENTION CENTER. YIKES! DON'T GO THERE!

ANYWHERE ELSE YOU GO, YOU'RE GONNA NEED A BUS. BUS STOPS ARE EVERYWHERE, BUT, BUSES, HOWEVER, JUST DON'T RUN ON TIME. ONE TIME, I WENT TO CATCH THE 2:40 AT 2:10. BY 4:00, I WAS HELL PISSED. THEN THE BUS CAME AND WENT — THE GUY DROVE RIGHT BY ME, WHILE I WAVED FRANTICALLY, THROTTLING THE BUS STOP SIGN AND SCREAMING. THE BUS DRIVER ACTUALLY LOOKED AT ME AND MIMICKED MY GESTURE, THE FINAL NAIL, AS IF TO SAY "I SEE YOU. FUCK YOU!" BUS DRIVERS ARE ALMOST AS BAD AS COPS. I GUESS YER PRETTY PUNK WHEN THE BUS WON'T EVEN STOP FOR YOU...

I USED TO RIDE THE BUS TO MY SHITTY FAST FOOD JOBS, WHICH IS DRAINING CAUSE THE BUSES RUN SO LONG, KIND OF A KAFKA BUREAUCRATIC, WARTIME AMERICA THING, AND THE BUSES ARE LIKE HOLDING CELLS ON WHEELS, WITH EVERYONE PILED ON TOP OF EACH OTHER. MY FIRST LAUDERDALE JOB WAS AT A TURKEY PLACE IN THE BROWARD MALL. THE BROWARD MALL HAS A WALDENBOOKS WHERE I STOLE "KILLER CLOWN: THE JOHN WAYNE GACY STORY." MY OTHER JOB WAS AT A "NATHAN'S FAMOUS" IN SAWGRASS MILLS, WHICH CLAIMS TO BE THE WORLD'S LARGEST MALL. IT'S THE FUTURE OF ALIENATING SUPER MALLS AT THE END OF THE CENTURY AND IT HAS BIG TV SETS HANGING FROM THE CEILINGS, PLAYING THE NATIONAL ANTHEM, MESSAGES TO REMIND US TO RECYCLE, ODES TO THE TROOPS AND ANTI-GUN MESSAGES, PRETTY CREEPY. ALSO, BOOTHS SELLING "PEACE ☮" SHIRTS AND "KILL SADDAM" T-SHIRTS, WHICH PROVES PEACE AND WAR ARE JUST PRODUCTS LIKE EVERYTHING ELSE...

The "BORN TO LOSE" SCENE REPORT CONTINUES...

NOT POLICE IN LAUDERDALE. THEY NEVER GET CAUGHT.

THE END OF THE SCENE REPORT...

ON MY WAY TO THESE EX-JOBS, THE BUS WENT THROUGH PITIFUL PLANTATION, FL. ONE DAY, ME AND BUDDHA ARE GONNA GET A SCUD MISSILE AND TAKE OVER PLANTATION. NAME IT SOMETHING REAL COOL LIKE "FUCK" OR "NEW CHINA" OR "SHITZ" (with a Z!) THEN WE'LL GET REAL RICH IN THE ARMS TRADE AND BECOME IRAQI TERRORISTS. THEN WE'LL RETIRE TO SOMETHING EASY LIKE BLACK MARKET KIDNEYS OR MAIL ORDER BRIDE SCAMS. I MEAN I WENT THROUGH PLANTATION EVERYDAY AND IT'S NOTHING! ITS OURS FOR THE TAKING!

BUT UNTIL THEN, WE'LL BUY OUR BREWS WITH THE DUDES AT WEST SIDE, AND ~~SORRA~~ STILL TRY TO STICK IT TO THE GREEDHEADS HERE IN GOOD OLE FT. LAUDERDALE. IF YOU'RE EVER IN TOWN, DROP BY AND WE'LL SET YA US WITH SOME RAMEN AND SOME OLE CHICKENHEAD AND TELL 'EM IGGY SENT YA...

IGGY'S COMIC

Photo © Steve Granitz/Retna Ltd.

Dancing is one of the things that I do best.

<u>FLIPSIDE</u> (EVERY ISSUE): "... while its true that our FEAR records collect dust while HELMET BLASTS FROM THE CD PLAYER ..." THAT QUOTE SAYS IT ALL. FUCK THESE GUYS. OUT WITH THE OLD AND IN WITH THE NEW. EVERY ISSUE IS NOW FILLED WITH MAJOR LABEL INTERVIEWS, ADS, AND WANNA-BES THAT DRINK WITH AL. CHECK OUT THE LETTER SECTION AND READ AL'S COPOUT — "WE'RE NOT SELLING OUT, WE'RE BUYING IN..." THERE'S NOTHING <u>IN</u> THERE FOR PUNKS. GUESS I'M NOT "WITH IT". CHECK OUT THE "POSITIVE ALTERNATIVE SCENE REPORT" WITH RAVES FOR PUNK HEROES FAITH NO MORE AND MEGADETH (GRRR!). "...THEN OZZY CAME ON STAGE AND DID WAR PIGS! WE ALL SPIT IN A CUP AND GAVE IT TO OZZY TO DRINK, BUT THE BOUNCERS HIT US WITH FLASHLIGHTS!" SCENARIO #1: BAR ROOM ROCK UBER ALLES! All THE L.A. BANDS FINALLY GET SIGNED, AND THE PUNK WORLD IS FORCED TO ADMIT THAT STEPPENWOLF WAS THE FIRST PUNK BAND. THE BANDS PROVE THEY AREN'T SELLOUTS BY DRESSING UP IN WEIRD COSTUMES, DRINKING WITH JOHNNY ANUS, AND SHOVELLING BULLSHIT DOWN EACH OTHER'S THROATS ABOUT ATTITUDE, WHILE GETTING BOMBED IN PAY TO PLAY CLUBS. SCENARIO #2: ONE OF THE NEXT ISSUES HAS JANE'S ADDICTION OR SONIC YOUTH ON THE COVER, AND A LITTLE BLURB FROM AL ABOUT HOW THEY'RE "BROADENING THEIR SCOPE." All THE PAGES GO GLOSSY. BUT KRK STILL SNIFFS GLUE AND LISTENS TO THE RAMONES, SO ITS PUNK. RIGHT? FUCK FLIPSIDE. I'M NOT A STEPPING STONE.

SCAM READER SURVEY. CLIP 'N' SAVE. SEND.

TOTALLY PUKE! — MORE REVIEWS FOR YOU

SCAM REVIEW STAFF?

PUKE! A BUNCH OF NAKED SPEED FREAKS BARFING INTO A MIKE ABOUT FUCKING SHIT UP. IT'S CHEAPER THAN THE BEER. MY BAND WILL BE CALLED SCHLITZ... THE BLATZ 7": TOTAL

3M SPRAY ADHESIVE GLUE: THE SHIT FOR PUTTING UP FLYERS THAT CAN'T BE REMOVED. YOU CAN'T SNIFF IT THOUGH, 'CAUSE WHEN YOU SPRAY IT, YOU FEEL SICK IF YOU'RE JUST IN THE SAME ROOM. THE CAN LISTS PRACTICAL USES AND SIDE EFFECTS. I MADE A FLYER THAT SAID "GEORGE BUSH WANTED FOR MURDER" AND ONE THAT SAID "FREE CHARLES MANSON." AND PUT 'EM UP ALL OVER FLORIDA WHILE I WAS HITCHING.

MORE REVIEWS

SEVENTEEN MAGAZINE (MAY 1991):

"Thanks a million for putting Richard Grieco on the cover of your February valentine issue! My heart almost burst when I saw him! When I read "If looks could kill," I was thrilled to find out that he owns a garden of roses, which he loves. I found it amazing that a guy who wears a leather jacket and rides a motorcycle likes pure nature and poetry. I think he is sooo romantic! Now any time I see roses I'll think of him. Thanks again. SEVENTEEN, you couldn't have done a better job! move on to bigger things, This is a great zine that helps chicks adjust, get dudes for the prom. Makes me want to eat a handful of PROZAC and go dancing. WEEEEEE!

CARS:

Cars aren't very punk. Roller skates are punk. YOWL!!! Your supposed to get a car to be free and independant, but you end up working all of the time to pay for repairs insurance, DUI, etc.

Lost in a sea of bills and stress, you notice you're always at work, or on the way to or from; you're trapped in line with all the other losers, choking on exhaust and waiting for green lights that will never come(the government controls the lights). Eventually, a broken man, you will be found getting loaded with rednecks and telling racist stories around the Vend-a-Bait machine... "I don't think chick's, should be firefighters. Yawn...

1-900-SEX CONFESSION #'s: I've had sex with every member of Gorilla Biscuits. Call me...

SCHLITZ (Beer):

It takes about a half hour of panhandling to get six of these babies. Asr great American beer since 1849? Why not?!? At least its cheap and it doe
goeat American beer since 1849? Why not?!? At least its cheap and it doe
AAArgh! Fuckin' typewriter! At least its cheap and doesn't come from
Milwaukee. Drink Schlitz and smash cops, drink Schlitz and puke on Gorilla
Biscuits, drink Schlitz and throw the empties on the neighbor's lawn, etc.
Schlitz is cool. That's no bull-Schlitz. Arrg.

REVIEWS

"ICE BY ICE: VANILLA ICE IN HIS OWN WORDS" by VANILLA ICE-- YO!

CONFESSIONS OF A KILLER: TED BUNDY IN HIS OWN WORDS-- Done in an interview style with Bundy. Really interesting, as Bundy was a pretty intelligent guy. For trivia buffs: Ted's favorite beer was Mickey's Big Mouth, and Ted said if he had it all to do over again, he would be a lumberjack (I guess he likes working with an axe)... Kind of a fun book to take with you onto the bus. Essential.

IN SEARCH OF (TV SHOW): Ya know, TV just hasn'y been anything since they took this classic off the air. Great soundtrack, cool shows in search of UFO's, King Tut, Lost civilizations, psychic stuff, haunted houses, etc. Hosted by Leonard Nimoy, whose probably a pretty cool guy. Call your UHF station and demand the return of this broadcast legend...

BEVERLY HILLS 90120 (TV SHOW): I don't want to understate how brilliant this show is. The one actor who looks like Richard Marx (Billy Joe from Green Day) is really good. He plays the smart older brother who gives advice. He's pretty smart. Its tough moving from Minnesota to Beverly Hills. Really. Its hard to fit in. THere's a lot of pressure to drive uncool cars or go too far on a date, but you've just got to remember to be yourself...

"ON MY OWN" by Brooke Shields: Almost as educational as BEVERLY HILLS 90120. Brooke has lots of advice for young women just out on their own. Study habits, beauty tips, the ever-present "How to say 'NO' on a date", etc. In a drunken stupor, I gave this book to Var from NO IDEA, cause he was having trouble color coordinating his clothes. Blues AND reds?!? Get in the CENTURY, baby...

DANNY BONADUCE (AMAZING CELEBRITY): This guy is really amazing. He's now more famous for smoking crack, than for being on the Partridge Family. More shameless than Mayor Barry, Bonaduce blunders into the 90's. A couple months ago the WEEKLY WORLDS NEWS had him marrying a girl he just met in a midnight ceremony, where Danny called the priest out of the phone book (she wouldn't go to bed with him, until they were married). Now, Danny Partridge was arrested for smoking crack and beating up a transvestite prostitute, when the hooker wouldn't screw Danny a second time. The last true punk...

"SCORE!": DANNY, HIS NEW WIFE, AND AN 8 BALL...

DEDICATION

To all the friends and students of Bruce Lee

INDEPENDENCE DAY, 1991

I'VE NOW FINISHED EVERYTHING FOR THE ZINE, AND I'M LOOKING IT OVER AND WRITING THIS IN, OF ALL PLACES, MY PARENT'S HOUSE, WHERE I HAVEN'T EVEN SET FOOT IN 9 MONTHS... THE WEIRD THING IS THAT WITH MY DRUNK MOM AND STEPFATHER, THE PROTOTYPE "RACIST, SEXIST CHILDBEATING BASTARD" THIS ZINE WOULD HAVE BEEN IMPOSSIBLE TO MAKE HERE. A YEAR AGO, WHILE LIVING HERE, ALL I DID WAS WORK AND DRINK, WORK AND DRINK, etc... IT TOOK THE SHOCK TO MY SYSTEM OF HAVING TO LEAVE, WITH NOWHERE TO GO, TO BRING ME BACK TO LIFE.

FIRST, BEING HOMELESS, AND THEN MOVING TO THE PUNK HOUSE GAVE ME WHOLE NEW INSPIRATION AND FORCED ME TO LIVE DIFFERENTLY. AFTER A WHILE, THOUGH, EVEN THE CREATIVE, VICTORIOUS PUNK HOUSE ATMOSPHERE BEGAN TO STALE, AS I HAD TO WORK TO PAY BILLS, AND WORK JUST REALLY KILLS ME. IT WAS HARD TO CONVINCE MYSELF THAT BY WORKING AND PAYING RENT, I WAS ANY DIFFERENT FROM MY PARENTS, EVEN IF I'M A "PUNK"...

SO, FOR VARIOUS REASONS (alot my fault) THE PUNK HOUSE DIDN'T WORK OUT, AND I'VE SPENT THE LAST TWO MONTHS LIVING ANYWHERE I CAN. I REALLY FEEL ALIVE AGAIN. SOON, I'M MOVING INTO A CONDEMNED HOUSE IN MIAMI, FOR GOOD, AND I HOPE TO HITCH HIKE ALOT OF THE SUMMER... ANYWAY THE POINT I'M STRUGGLING TO MAKE IS THAT, IN A COUNTRY WHERE INDEPENDENCE IS A **LIE**, MAYBE TRUE FREEDOM CAN BE FOUND (CRAWLING AROUND THE EDGES OF SOCIETY, NOT WORKING, PAYING TAXES, SETTLING DOWN, ETC. INDEPENDENCE IS FREEDOM FROM YOUR LIFESTYLE AND FORCING YOURSELF TO TAKE A NEW PATH... SO LONG. HERE'S A COMIC BY CHUCK!

SCAM

THE MUTINY IN MIAMI ISSUE!

ISSUE #2 5/91 ~ 6/93 WRITIN'

PROUDLY UNEMPLOYED SINCE FEBRUARY 7, 1991

INSIDE: SHLITZ, CROWBARS

AND BOXING IN THE STREETS!!!

SCAM #2 YEA!

I HAVE TO..
IT'S MY
DESTINY...

THEFT

Was the first one just an illusion? Even if it was real, is it over? No, says the author.

SCAM IS AN UNDER THE COVERS WAY PAST YER BEDTIME FLASHLIGHT READIN' PUNK FANZINE!

OK, I USED TO LIVE IN A GREAT PUNK HOUSE IN FT. LAUDERDALE, ABOUT 20 MILES NORTH OF MIAMI, WHERE WE USED TO DRINK ALOT OF BEER AND GO OUT AND BREAK STUFF AND LISTEN TO SCREECHING WEASEL, ETC., ETC. WHEN IT BROKE UP IN MAY '91, I DECIDED TO MOVE TO MIAMI AND SQUAT. I NEVER REALLY HUNG OUT DOWN THERE, BUT I FIGURED, WELL IT'S A HUGE TOWN, SO THERE'LL BE A MILLION ABANDONED BUILDINGS, AND I'LL JUST LIVE IN ONE, AND THEN, YA KNOW, SCAM THE ELECTRICITY, OR WHATEVER, AND IT'LL BE JUST LIKE THE PUNK HOUSE, ONLY WITHOUT RENT AND CHUCK LOOSE ON MY ASS ALL THE TIME ABOUT THE FUGGIN' DISHES... I'M NOT SURE WHAT I WAS THINKIN' BUT I DO KNOW THAT IF MY DREAMS HADN'T BEEN SO BIG AND CRAZY, I NEVER WOULD'VE BOTHERED TO STICK WITH 'EM, AND GET AS FAR AS I DID... IT WAS A GREAT VISION.

IT'S BEEN WELL OVER 2 YEARS SINCE SCAM #1 CAME OUT, AND PEOPLE GAVE ME ALOT OF SHIT ABOUT IT TAKING SO LONG. ONE FRIEND OF MINE EVEN THREATENED TO PUT IT OUT HIMSELF, USING LETTERS I'D SENT HIM! THE 2 YEARS I SPENT WORRYING ABOUT "NOT GETTING ANYTHING DONE", THOUGH, WERE 2 YEARS WHERE ME AND MY FRIEND, IVY, HAD ONE OF THE BIGGEST CITIES IN THE COUNTRY, BASICALLY, AS OUR PERSONAL PLAYGROUND. WE ATE AT THE FINEST RESTAURANTS, SWAM IN THE POOLS AT THE FINEST HOTELS, WE RODE THEIR FREIGHT TRAINS, USED THEIR CALLING CARDS FOR FREE LONG DISTANCE CALLS, AND TOOK WHAT WE WANTED FROM THEIR STORES. WE MADE BEAUTIFUL HOMES IN THEIR ABANDONED BUILDINGS WITH THEIR TRASH AS FURNITURE. OBVIOUSLY, THERE WERE ALOT OF TOUGH TIMES, TOO, BUT THEY WERE ON MY OWN TIME, YA KNOW? AND I LEARNED ALOT BECAUSE OF IT, AND THEN SUDDENLY, WE GOT PRETTY MUCH WHAT WE THOUGHT WE ALWAYS WANTED,... AND THEN IT WAS TIME TO MOVE ON.

SO THIS IS A BIG PILE OF TWO YEAR'S WORTH O' STORIES OF MIAMI SQUATTIN' AND OTHER TRAVELLIN' AND SCAMMIN', ETC. PRETTY COMPREHENSIVE. THE ONLY THING MISSING, I THINK, IS A PAGE OF SCAM SCRATCH 'N' SNIFF STICKERS, SO, AS YOU READ ALONG, YOU CAN SMELL THE CUBAN COFFEE, AND THE RICE AND BLACK BEANS AND MY FEET AND THE SHLITZ AND THE SPRAY PAINT AND THE VELVET CREME DUMPSTER, AND, UH... IVY. WELL, MAYBE NEXT TIME.

Get-rich-quick scheme
In Jacksonville, Michael Wayne Critzer, 37, pleaded guilty to putting a phony night deposit box outside a bank and collecting $140,000 in cash and checks. Critzer disabled the bank's night depository and posted a note directing depositors to the five-foot, 350-pound homemade box, which had the same stone finish as the bank.

wealthy.
2. Polarize public opinion by targeting the powerful and the
1. Instill fear in the general population.

2. Are you a danger to yourself or to the community?

3. Will you show up for your court hearing?

4. Are you a runaway risk?

5. If released to home will you obey your parents?

6. Will you abide by all of the rules and regulations, including a curfew your community youth leader sets for you?

REMEMBER TO: DID YOU

Droppin' some shit that's D-O-P-E
So fuck the P-O-L-I-C-E
And any motherfucker that disagrees

PICTURED ABOVE: THE VIEW FROM MY BALCONY IN THE MUTINY! - BISCAYNE BAY, THE ANCHORAGE AND POINTS BEYOND...

IF YOU'RE WRITING AN ARTICLE ABOUT ZINES, OR "THE ZINE REVOLUTION", OR SOME SUCH SHIT — PLEASE, LEAVE ME OUT OF IT, OK?

YOU CAN ORDER SCAM #2 FROM

**BLACKLIST MAILORDER
475 VALENCIA
SAN FRANCISCO, CA 94103**
IT COSTS $1.50 POSTAGE PAID

SCAM PRIEST/LAWYER/SECRETARY/MAIL GUY, **JOHN DANIA**, EVIDENTLY FEARING FOR HIS LIFE, AND TIRED OF LOOKING OUT FOR THE OLE SNAKE-IN-THE-MAILBOX-THING AND LETTERBOMBS, HAS RESIGNED AS HEAD OF SCAM MAIL, AND LEFT DANIA FOR "THE ISLANDS." HE IS CURRENTLY A MISSING PERSON. THE NEW GUY IS EMIL. HE ONLY HAS 4½ FINGERS (SEE PHOTO TO LEFT). YOU CAN SEND LETTERS AND STUFF TO ME, THROUGH HIM, AT **4787 S.W. 154th AVENUE, MIAMI, FL 33185**, BUT DON'T ORDER THE ZINE FROM THAT ADDRESS, OR YOU MAY NEVER GET IT. YOU CAN ALSO ORDER THE CHICKENHEAD 7" FROM EMIL. ITS ONLY A BUCK. WHEN I FIRST STARTED GETTING MAIL AT EMIL'S, HIS MOM WONDERED WHY I GOT SO MANY LETTERS FROM FOOD COMPANIES. EMIL TOLD HER ABOUT THE COMPLAINING-TO-THE-COMPANY-FOR-FREE-FOOD SCAM. SHE WAS SO IMPRESSED, SHE WROTE A LETTER TO ZAGNUT CANDY BARS RIGHT AWAY! SCAM — THE ZINE FOR THE WHOLE FAMILY...

THIS ZINE IS DEDICATED TO THE GREATEST FIGHTER OF ALL TIME:
← **MUHAAMED ALI!!!**

LETTERS

WHAT SCAM READERS ARE SAYING:

HEY IGGY — THANKS FOR THE ZINE. I REALLY LIKED IT. BUT, I TRIED TO MAKE THE OLE CHICKENHEAD WINE, AND I'M NOT SURE I MADE IT RIGHT. IT MADE ME AND MY FRIENDS PUKE!
(YOU DID IT RIGHT. — ed)
— M. YODER
ALLIANCE, OHIO

SCAM — I LOVED YOUR ZINE, EXCEPT ONE THING. I MADE THE RAMEN ACCORDING TO YOUR RECIPE AND I THREW UP! IT WAS DISGUSTING! GOOD ZINE, BAD RAMEN.
(TOTAL FUCKING PUKE! — ed)
— BEANSPROUT
COLORADO SPRINGS, CO

SCAM SELLS OUT

SCAM #1, THE PUNKHOUSE ISSUE, IS NO LONGER AVAILABLE. THE ORIGINALS ARE PRETTY SHREDDED, AFTER BEING ON 3 BAND TOURS, COUNTLESS HITCH HIKING TRIPS, A COUPLE FREIGHT TRAINS, AND SUFFERING ONE POLICE CONFISCATION, BE A COUPLE DRAMATIC CHASES FROM OFFICE DEPOT, AND 428 ISSUES. IF I CHANGE MY MIND, I'LL LET YA KNOW.

WHY SCAM IS NO LONGER FREE, EXCEPT IN SOUTH FLORIDA

THE FIRST ZINE WAS FREE TO PROVE THAT THE FREE POSTAGE AND XEROXING SCAMS WORK. NOW, AFTER HUNDREDS OF LETTERS THAT SAY ONLY, "SEND ME YOUR FREE ZINE." I DON'T CARE WHAT YOU THINK OF MY SCAMS. CHARGING FOR IT WILL WEED THOSE ORDERS OUT. THE REASON I GOT BLACKLIST TO DO THE MAILORDER IS BECAUSE I'M TRAVELLING AROUND THIS YEAR, EVEN AS I FINISH THIS ISSUE, AND I DON'T WANT TO GET WAY BEHIND ON ORDERS, OR ASK A FRIEND TO TAKE CARE OF IT. I'M KINDA BUMMED ABOUT CHARGING AND THE BLACKLIST THING — IT MAKES IT LESS PERSONAL — BUT ITS THE ONLY WAY TO KEEP THIS FROM BECOMING A JOB. I SHOULD MENTION SOMEWHERE IN HERE THAT IF YOU WRITE ME, MY RESPONSE WILL PROBABLY BE IN A BULK RATE MAILER TO SCAM POSTAGE. IT'LL LOOK LIKE SOME COMPANY'S JUNK MAIL, BUT WILL REALLY BE A LETTER SO DON'T THROW IT OUT!

ABOUT THE SCAM

IN THIS ISSUE, THE SCAMS AREN'T SEPARATED FROM THE NARRATIVE.— THEY'RE A PART OF THE WRITING, SO YOU CAN SEE HOW THEY FIT IN MY LIFE, SO ITS LESS LIKE A CHECKLIST OF THINGS TO TRY. I THINK ALOT OF PEOPLE WHO WRITE ME, MISS THE POINT ABOUT SCAMS. I'M NOT INTO GREEDILY AQUIRING ALOT OF CRAP, OR MONEY TO SPEND ON CRAP. SCAMMIN' IS A MEANS TO AN END. I WANT TO LIVE SIMPLY, SO WITH A COUPLE, EASY, EFFECTIVE SCAMS, I ALWAYS HAVE LIKE 20 BUCKS ON ME, BUT I NEVER BUY MUCH ANYWAY. JUST WHAT I NEED TO GET BY. SCAMMIN' ALLOWS ME THE FREEDOM TO LIVE LIKE I PLEASE — TO HAVE ALL THE TIME IN THE WORLD TO SWIM AND LAY AROUND IN THE SHADE, DRINKIN' ICED TEA, TO STEAL DA SHLITZ AND SPRAYPAINT THE WALLS, TO RIDE MY BIKE ALL OVER TOWN TIL SUNRISE, TO READ, WRITE, BE IN A BAND, TRAVEL, WHATEVER. THE REAL SCAM IS JUST DOING WHAT YOU WANT TO DO, WHENEVER, NO MATTER WHAT — JUST LIVING YOUR LIFE.
THIS ZINE IS DIVIDED INTO 6 DIFFERENT PARTS, SO YOU CAN PRETEND ITS 6 DIFFERENT ZINES. BOOK REPORTS DUE AT END OF SEMESTER.

I'VE NEVER SEEN A ZINE FROM MIAMI, WHERE THE EDITORS ACTUALLY LIKED MIAMI, BUT I LOVE MIAMI. I LOVE BILLBOARDS IN SPANISH AND HANGIN' OUT DOWNTOWN AND DRINKIN' ON THE STREETS AND HOPPIN' THE METRORAIL. I LOVE COCONUTS, RIGHT OFF THE TREE AND NUDE SWIMMIN' AT SUNRISE AT THE MATHESON HAMMOCKS, IN THE CLOSED OFF PART WHERE YER NOT SUPPOSED TO GO. MIAMI'S GOT NATURAL BEAUTY AND BIG CITY STYLE ALL IN ONE, AND IT HAS WEIRD, SINISTER UNDERGROUNDS, MIDNIGHT PLANES AND INTERNATIONAL DRUG DEALIN', AND CRAZY ISLAND RELIGIONS, AND LATIN AMERICAN EXILES, STOCKPILIN' WEAPONS AND CASH AND WAITIN' FOR A CHANCE TO RETURN HOME AND SEIZE POWER. YEAH, MIAMI ALWAYS SEEMED LIKE THE KIND OF PLACE WHERE, IF YOU KNEW THE RIGHT PEOPLE, YOU COULD SEE BOXING MATCHES WHERE THE LOSER HAS TO DIE, IF YA KNOW WHAT I MEAN. EVEN AFTER 2 YEARS OF ON AND OFF LIVING THERE, IT REMAINS A BIG MYSTERY TO ME. BUT I STILL LOVE IT.

BUT... IT WASN'T ALWAYS THAT WAY...

MOVIN' TO MIAMI

EL PAN DE LA MUERTE

Legs Are you glad you were born?

Richard I have my doubts.

Por J.T.C.

WHEN I FIRST WENT TO LIVE IN MIAMI, I WAS TERRIFIED. IT WAS AT THE END OF A LONG WEEK, THE LAST WEEK OF THE FT. LAUDERDALE PUNK HOUSE, AND I HAD BEEN ON AN 8 OR 9 DAY DRINKING BINGE / COUNTDOWN TO RUIN. I HAD SPENT THE ENTIRE $120 I'D SAVED UP TO START MY POST-PUNKHOUSE LIFE WITH, ON BEER DOWN AT THE OLE WESTSIDE MARKET. ONE BY ONE, MY ROOMMATES PACKED UP THEIR STUFF AND LEFT, AND THEN, FINALLY THERE I WAS, 2 DAYS AFTER THE RENT WAS UP, SITTIN' THERE IN A BIG EMPTY HOUSE DRINKIN' BEER, LISTENIN' TO PUNK TAPES, AND WAITIN' FOR WHATEVER WAS GONNA HAPPEN TO ME TO FUCKIN' HAPPEN. A MONTH BEFORE, KNOWING THE PUNKHOUSE WAS ENDING, ME AND PUNKHOUSER, NICK, HAD DECIDED TO SQUAT IN MIAMI, AND HAD ASKED AROUND AT A SHOW TO SEE IF ANYONE KNEW OF A GOOD PLACE. THIS GIRL, IVY, SAID THAT THERE WERE NOT ONE, BUT TWO ABANDONED HOUSES RIGHT NEXT DOOR TO HER AND SHE'D BEEN IN 'EM, SO WE SHOULD LIVE THERE. IT SOUNDED GREAT, SO WE GAVE HER OUR # (SHE HAD NO PHONE) AND DIDN'T LOOK FOR ANYTHING ELSE. A MONTH LATER, SHE STILL HADN'T CALLED, AND NICK WAS GETTIN' HIS OWN PLACE ON MIAMI BEACH. THINGS WERE BAD, YES. BUT AT LEAST I HAD BEER AND MUSIC. BUT THEN, BELIEVE IT OR NOT, RIGHT IN THE MIDDLE OF THE DK'S "KILL THE POOR" THE TAPE PLAYER SHUTS OFF, AND I CAN'T FIGURE OUT WHAT'S WRONG WITH IT, BUT THEN I REALIZE EVERYTHING'S OFF! I RACE OUTSIDE AND SEE THE FLORIDA POWER AND LIGHT GUY TURNIN' OFF THE POWER! I DON'T KNOW... I WAS DRUNK. I DON'T KNOW WHAT I SAID TO THE MAN. MAYBE I SCARED THE MAN. BUT I GOT HIM TO TURN IT BACK ON, FOR ONE MORE DAY, AND WENT BACK INSIDE TO DRINK. THERE, THAT NIGHT, THE LAST NIGHT, I GOT THE COLLECT CALL FROM IVY, AND DIRECTIONS TO MY NEW HOME. IN MIAMI.
THE NEXT DAY I WOKE UP AND CHECKED THE PHONE. OFF. SHE'D CALLED JUST IN TIME. I GOT JOHN DANIA TO COME OVER AND GET MOST OF MY STUFF, LIKE MY HUGE BOX OF SHEILA HARRIGAN BULK MAILERS AND MY MATTRESS W/ THE BIG BROWN DURO RUBBER CEMENT STAIN ON IT, AND TAKE IT TO HIS HOUSE. I GOT MY GUITAR AND RADIO AND A BIG PILE OF OTHER STUFF ON THE TRI-RAIL, SOMEHOW, AND HEADED SOUTH TO MYSTERIOUS MIAMI. WHEN I CAME DOWN THE ESCALATOR AT THE BRICKELL METRORAIL, PENNILESS AND INSANE, THERE WAS IVY WAITIN'

Hijos, este santo varón está implorándole al Dios del cielo que entre en ese pan . . .

Es lo que llamamos transubstanciación.

Hocus Pocus Domi Nocus

¿Qué está diciendo?

SANTERIA CHURCHES AND STREET GANGS:
BEAT 'EM OR JOIN 'EM?
'MOVIN' TO MIAMI' CONTINUED

FOR ME AND SMILING. I HAD THE TERMINAL SWEATS FROM LUGGING ALL THAT STUFF AROUND IN 90° WEATHER WITH NO BEER FOR THE FIRST TIME IN WEEKS. GOOD GOD, I THOUGHT. WHAT IS SHE SMILING ABOUT? **CAN'T SHE SEE THAT I'M ABOUT TO DIE?!?**

SHE TOOK ME ON A TOUR OF MY NEW NEIGHBORHOOD. AROUND THE CORNER WAS THE TREE WHERE, THE NIGHT BEFORE, THE SANTERIA PEOPLE HAD TIED UP SOME POOR MAN AND SET FIRE TO HIM!!! JESUS, WHAT HAD I GOTTEN MYSELF INTO?!? I KNEW ONE THING FOR SURE, AND THAT WAS THAT I DIDN'T WANT TO GET TIED TO A TREE AND SET ON FIRE! FUK. BUT IVY MANAGED TO CONVINCE ME THAT THEY DIDN'T JUST GO AROUND DOING THIS TO ANYBODY, THAT IT MUST HAVE BEEN A REAL SERIOUS INTERNAL THING. I JUST KINDA STARED AT THE TREE FOR AWHILE IN DISBELIEF 'TIL SHE DRAGGED ME ON DOWN THE STREET. OK, I SAID. HOW 'BOUT DUMPSTERS FOR FOOD? ARE THERE ANY GOOD ONES? SHE WASN'T SURE, SO WE WENT TO CHECK WOOLEY'S DUMPSTER. I OPENED THE LID AND IT WAS ENTIRELY FULL OF COCKROACHES!!! I THOUGHT I WAS HALLUCINATING. THE D.T.'S! BUT IVY CALMED ME DOWN AND LED ME AWAY. THERE, THERE, IGGY. IT'S OK. THE COCKROACHES CAN'T GET YOU NOW...

THEN SHE TOOK ME TO SEE MY NEW HOUSE. IT WAS THE CLASSIC, LITTLE HAVANA STYLE BOX/HOUSE WITH ONE BEDROOM, A KITCHEN AND A LIVING ROOM. THE WOMAN WHO'D LIVED THERE BEFORE WAS CRAZY. SHE STAYED UP NIGHTS, SCREAMING AT HER DOGS AND BANGING ON BIG POTS. ONE NIGHT, THEY TOOK HER AWAY FOR GOOD, AND THE HOUSE WAS LEFT FULL OF CLOTHES, DISHES, A BED, AND IT EVEN STILL HAD RUNNING WATER! IVY SHOWED ME HOW TO CRAWL IN THE SIDE WINDOW AND GAVE ME A SAINT LAZARUS CANDLE AND I LOOKED AROUND AND TESTED THE BED AND SHE SAID, THIS IS IT, AND I FLUSHED THE TOILET A COUPLE TIMES AND LOOKED AT MY DIM REFLECTION IN THE BATHROOM MIRROR AND SIGHED. YEP. THIS IS IT. WELL, IT WAS A NICE LITTLE HOUSE, AND IT WAS ALREADY FURNISHED. I COULD EVEN USE THE BATHROOM... YES, I COULD REALLY DO WELL HERE, AFTER ALL, I THOUGHT. I COULD WORK ON SCAMMIN' THE ELECTRICITY, AND THEN, IF I COULD JUST STAY AWAY FROM THE SANTERIA PEOPLE, I WOULD BE ABLE TO FINISH MY ZINE HERE. IVY SAYS, OH YEAH, THERE'S **ONE** PROBLEM... THERE'S THIS STREET GANG THAT LIVES HERE! SHE'S TRIED TO GET THEM TO LEAVE, BUT THEY WOULDN'T. SHE SAID SHE'D KEEP TALKING TO HER SISTERS ABOUT IT. OH YEAH, HER SISTERS WERE IN THE GANG.

THAT NIGHT, I MET THE GANG LEADER, ZERO. WELL, I THOUGHT. MAYBE HE HAS SOME GOOD SCAMS. ZERO SAID, "WELL, YA KNOW, I HIT A STORE, YA KNOW, I GOT MY GUN, AND THEN, I GET MY WINE AND MY SMOKES AND I DO ALLRIGHT." MAYBE NOT. I TRIED TO SLEEP IN THE LIVING ROOM WITH MY BASS GUITAR TIED TO MY ARM BY THE STRAP, WHILE ZERO FOUGHT WITH AND THEN MADE UP, AT LENGTH, WITH HIS GIRLFRIEND. TWO OTHER GANG MEMBERS, SLEEPING ON THE BEDROOM FLOOR, BEGGED TO BE ALOUD TO MAKE UP WITH HER, TOO. IT WAS PRETTY BAD, YES.

THE NEXT MORNING I WENT DOWNTOWN TO EXPLORE THE NEW CITY, BUT I GUESS THE SHOCK OF BEING HOMELESS AND MY POOR HEALTH HAD REALLY MESSED ME UP. I STOOD THERE IN THE SEA OF PEOPLE, STRUCK DUMB BY THE SPECTACLE OF IT ALL. I COULDN'T EVEN MAKE UP MY MIND WHICH WAY TO WALK, OR WHY. AND ALL THOSE TALL BUILDINGS! WHAT IF ONE OF THEM FELL OVER?!? WOULD I BE ABLE TO GET OUT OF THE WAY? I WASN'T SURE... IVY CAME HOME FROM SCHOOL AND WE HUNG OUT IN HER HOUSE, WITH HER MOM SCREAMIN' AT HER, AND HER YOUTH GANG SISTERS FIGHTING AND MOSQUITOS AND STRAY CATS ALL OVER AND IVY JUST SITS THERE DRAWIN', BUT I'M SO DEPRESSED I CAN'T EVEN BELIEVE IT. MEN SET ON FIRE, ARMED ROBBERS FOR ROOM MATES... AND ALL THIS POVERTY AND FIGHTING. IT FELT LIKE THE BLEAKEST PLACE I'D EVER BEEN IN MY LIFE, MIAMI DID. IT FELT LIKE I HAD ENTERED SUCH A COMPLETELY ALIEN WORLD, THAT I EVEN WROTE A LETTER TO JOHN DANIA, EVEN THOUGH HE WAS ONLY 20 MILES AWAY AND I COULD EASILY TAKE 2 BUSSES TO HIS HOUSE. I WAS THAT DISTANT. HOW I MISSED FT. LAUDERDALE WHERE THE DUMPSTERS WERE FILLED TO THE RIM WITH PIZZA AND I KNEW EVERY ALLEY...

BUT, AFTER A COUPLE DAYS, I DEVELOPED A ROUTINE, AND FELT MORE LIKE MY OLE **SCAMMIN'** SELF. IT TURNED OUT THAT ZERO DIDN'T STAY IN THE HOUSE EVERY NIGHT, AND THE BED WAS COMFORTABLE AND I SLEPT GOOD. I'D WAKE UP AND SWIM IN THIS APARTMENT COMPLEX'S POOL DOWN THE STREET, THEN HEAD OVER TO THE 7-11 TO PANHANDLE A BIT. THE FIRST DAY I WAS THERE, A CRAZY BUM GUY CAME

UP TO ME AND SAID "EXCUSE ME, SIR. ARE FAMILIAR WITH THE WORKS OF... VAN HALEN?!?" "I WAS! HE TOLD ME NOT TO ASK FOR "SPARE CHANGE" BUT TO ASK FOR A WHOLE BUCK, CUZ YOU GET MORE MONEY THAT WAY. HE DEMONSTRATED BY YELLING, "HEY GIVE THIS KID A BUCK!" UNTIL THE MANAGER CHASED US AWAY. I DIDN'T GET MY MONEY, BUT IT WAS FUN. I USUALLY ONLY DID IT FOR 15 MINUTES ANYWAYS— JUST TIL I GOT $1.95 FOR A MIAMI HERALD, A USA TODAY, AND A BIGGIE COKE AND 25¢ REFILL AT WENDY'S. T WENDY'S I'D SCAM THE SALAD BAR AND READ. I THOUGHT THE SPANISH COMICS IN EL HERALD, THE SPANISH LANGUAGE HALF OF THE HERALD WERE REAL COOL, AND I'D TRY AND SEE IF I COULD FIGURE OUT WHAT THEY MEANT. I GUESS I LOOKED ALL RAGGED AND STUDIOUS, CUZ WHEN I'D TABLE DIVE, PEOPLE WOULD ALWAYS COME UP TO ME AND GIVE ME MONEY. I MADE 10-15 BUCKS A WEEK.

AND THEN THERE WAS HANGIN' OUT AT IVY'S, AFTER SHE GOT OUT ❤ SCHOOL. THERE WERE 6 HOUSES THERE ON THE LOT, 3 ABANDONED, AND YOU'D OPEN A GATE AND WALK DOWN A PATH WHERE, WAY BACK IN THE CORNER, IN THE BACK, NESTLED THERE IN THE TREES AND TALL GRASS AND SHADE, WAS IVY'S PLACE. THERE WAS A CRAZY TRASHPILE OUT FRONT THAT USUALLY INCLUDED MOST OF IVY'S STUFF, WHEN HER SISTERS WERE ORDERED TO CLEAN THE HOUSE, AS WELL AS TIRES, BEAT UP CHAIRS, AND AN ENTIRE TOILET, SERVING AS THE JUNKYARD THRONE. STRAY CATS WERE EVERYWHERE AND IVY KNEW ALL THEIR NAMES. YES, THAT HOUSE WAS NOTORIOUS ON THE LOT. LATE RENT, COPS CALLED TO BREAK UP FIGHTS BETWEEN IVY'S MOM AND HER BOYFRIEND, GANG KIDS ALL AROUND... BUT IT COULD BE TRULY LOVELY IN THE MIDDLE OF ALL THAT CRAZINESS, LIKE WHEN IVY WANTED TO MAKE COFFEE TO CHEER ME UP ON A RAINY DAY, BUT THE CITY HAD SHUT OFF THEIR WATER, SO SHE USED RAINWATER. AND IT WAS A GREAT MOMENT WHEN WE GOT ~~OUR~~ MY FIRST MIAMI COCONUT AND SMASHED IT OPEN WITH A HAMMER FOR THE MILK INSIDE. FUK. THIS WAS BETTER THAN DUMPSTERS... IT WAS NATURE! THEN, ONE NIGHT, THE COPS ARRESTED ZERO, CUZ HE HAD SHOT SOMEONE WHILE TRYING TO ROB THE MALAGA RESTAURANT ON 8th STREET. WELL, I WASN'T HAPPY THAT HE GOT ARRESTED, BUT THE HOUSE WAS ALL MINE NOW... AND SO WE LIVED HAPPILY EVER AFTER THERE IN EAST LITTLE HAVANA... RIGHT? NAH, BEFORE I EVEN GOT TO APPRECIATE ANY OF THIS, TRAGEDY STRUCK. I CAME BACK TO SHOW NICK MY PROUD HOME, AFTER A WEEKEND AT HIS PLACE, AND IT HAD BURNED DOWN! THE SEARCH WAS ON FOR A NEW HOUSE. GUESS NOTHIN'S EVER EASY, HUH?

STUFF TO DRINK IN MIAMI + MIAMI SODA REVIEWS ↓

COCO FRIO IS TOTAL MIAMI STYLE. DURING THE LONG, HOT SUMMER, ALL THE COOL OLD GUYS GO TO THE SIDE OF THE ROAD TO SELL IT. ITS JUST A COCONUT WITH A HOLE PUNCHED IN AND A STRAW TO STICK IN IT. THAT'S ALL. CAFE CUBANO or CUBAN COFFEE IS THICK, BLACK SYRUP THAT IS TOTALLY STRONG, AND CHEAP AND AVAILABLE ANYWHERE. ONE SHOT = ONE CUP OF AMERICAN COFFEE AND IS ONLY 25¢ USUALLY. 5 SHOTS AT ONCE IS A "COLADA" USUALLY BETWEEN 60¢ AND 90¢. ANY HIGHER IN PRICE IS PROBABLY POSER CORAL GABLES SH*T! WATER: ALL THE CUBAN RESTAURANTS HAVE BIG ORANGE COOLERS IN THE STREET COUNTER WINDOWS, FULL OF FREE ICE WATER! PRETTY RELIEVIN SOMETIMES, BUT I DON'T KNOW... FREE WATER? SOUNDS KIND OF COMMUNIST!. ¡COMMUNISTA! MIAMI HAS A LOT OF GREAT LOCAL SODAS, WHICH WILL BE RATED HERE BY 1) TASTE 2) LEVEL OF OBSCURITY 3) AESTHETICS. IRON BEER: THIS IS THE BEST BY TASTE. ITS NOT A BEER. ITS A PEPPERY KIND OF LICORICE SODA WITH A BIG STRONGARM AS THE LOGO. I LIKE IT SO MUCH THAT I WROTE THE COMPANY BEGGING TO TOUR THEIR PLANT OVER IN HIALEAH. ITS PRETTY MAJOR LABEL — I'VE SEEN FUCKING DIET IRONBEER AS FAR NORTH AS DELRAY BEACH — BUT THEY'RE STILL PRETTY ACCESSIBLE TO THEIR FANS CUZ THEIR PHONE #'S RIGHT ON THE LABEL! GIVE 'EM A CALL AT (305) 592-4366. MATERVA TASTES OK, BUT I CAN'T EVEN REMEMBER WHAT IT TASTES LIKE, AND THE CAN DOESN'T GIVE YOU ANY REASON TO WANNA FIND OUT. LAME. IF YOU INSIST ON GETTING IT, AT LEAST GO TO SOME TINY STORE LIKE ZUGAMI'S ON FLAGLER AND 22 AND REACH WAY BACK ON THE SHELF FOR A DUSTY, FADED LABEL BOTTLE. GEORGE "THE CHAMPION" PRINCE SODA: IS THE CHAMPION HERE. IT TASTES AWESOME, KINDA CREAMY FRUITY AND IT HAS A PORTRAIT ON THE CAN OF GEORGE "THE CHAMPION" PRINCE, WHO'S ALL CHARLES ATLAS LOOKIN'. WHO THE HELL IS THIS GUY? WHO CARES? HE'S GOT A GREAT SODA AND YOU CAN ONLY FIND IT ON LEAP YEARS, WHEN THE MOON IS FULL, IN A HANDFUL OF LITTLE HAITI MARKETS. WATERMELON SODA: OK, I KNOW YER THINKIN' "WATERMELON SODA?! THAT IS LIKE... PORK SHERBERT!" BUT IT RULES AND STAINS YER TONGUE RED. THEY EARN BONUS POINTS FOR PROMOTING RACIAL HARMONY ON THE CAN, W/ PICTURES OF A LITTLE WHITE GIRL AND LITTLE BLACK GIRL ENJOYING BIG ❤ MELONS, CUZ ALL FOLKS LIKE WATERMELON, YES... MALTA HATUEY HAS AN INDIAN ON THE LABEL, BUT IS TERRIBLE! ITS THIS THICK BLACK MIAMI RIVER SLUDGE THAT'S LIKE MALT LIQUOUR W/ NO ALCOHOL. WHY? BUT IT HAS DEFINATE STYLE POINTS. ITS NAMED AFTER THIS CUBAN INDIAN, HATUEY, WHO WOULDN'T TURN CHRISTIAN WHEN THE SPANISH MISSIONARIES CAME, SO THEY WERE GONNA BURN HIM AT THE STAKE. THEY SAY, HERE'S YER LAST CHANCE TO GO TO HEAVEN. LEGEND HAS IT THAT HATUEY SAID, "WILL THERE BE MORE MEN LIKE YOU THERE?" THEY SAY, OF COURSE. HE SAYS, THEN BURN ME, YA PIGS! YO, HATUEY! YOU THINK HE'D DO BETTER THAN TO HAVE THIS STUFF NAMED AFTER HIM. ALSO, ALL THE DIFFERENT VARIETIES HAVE DIFFERENT BOTTLE CAPS, AND THE "I ❤ MALTA", WHITE WRITING ON RED, IS THE COOLEST CAP AROUND. I SENT ONE TO A GIRL ONCE BUT SHE DIDN'T ❤ MALTA, SHE DIDN'T ❤ ME, SHE DIDN'T ❤ NUTTIN' (THE SYMBOL IS A POOR DRAWING OF A HEART, OK). ITS TOTALLY THE RAREST CAP TO FIND, TOO, EVEN IN STORES. ONE TIME I WALKED, INCH BY INCH UP S.W. 8th STREET, LOOKIN ON THE GROUND FOR IT AND FINALLY, AFTER AN HOUR OR SO AND A MILLION "MALTA GOYA" AND "MALTA EL SOL" I FOUND ONE, ALL RUSTY, BUT PROUD.

IT WAS A GREAT DAY...

SCAM HABLA ESPAÑOL

YO! SCAM SPEAKS SPANISH, AND IF YER GONNA COME TO MIAMI, SO SHOULD YOU. MIAMI HAS A HUGE LATIN POPULATION AND MOST SIGN, BILLBOARDS, AND CONVERSATIONS ARE IN ESPAÑOL, AS WELL AS HALF The MIAMI HERALD. SO, AS A PUBLIC SERVICE, SCAM BRINGS YOU PHRASES IN SPANISH That YOU, The SCAM PUNX, WILL NEED TO SURVIVE IN MIAMI. REMEMBER TO ROLL THOSE "R"S. VIVA LA SCAM!

1. BEER = CERVEZA pronounced "SIR-BAY-

2. EXCUSE ME, SIR/MISS, DO YOU HAVE ANY SPARE CHANGE? = ¿PERMISO, SEÑOR/SEÑORITA, TIENE CAMBIO?

3. IS THE RIOTING OVER? = ¿Ya se termino desorden?

4. PLEASE, DO NOT SHOOT ME, OFFICER. = POR FAVOR, NO ME DES PARE, SEÑOR POLICIA.

5. LET GO OF HER. = DEJA LA IR. (DAY LA EAR")

6. I HAVE A GUN. = YO TENGO UNA PISTOLA.

7. DO YOU SELL ROBITUSSIN? = ¿USTED VENDE ROBITUSSIN

8. I HAVE A CROWBAR = YO TENGO CRUZETA

HERE'S 4 PHRASES YOU MAY HEAR IN MIAMI.

1. GET A JOB = COJE UN TRABAJO (J's sound like "H". CO-HAY UN TRABA

2. HEY FAGGOT = OYE MARICON

3. I'M CALLING The POLICE = ESTOY llamando la Policia (ll = "y" sound

4. I HAVE A GUN = (see above)

Other words of interest

ENEMA = LAVADO
DUMPSTER = BASURERO
JAIL = CARCEL
DEATH = MUERTE

OLAFO

¡COJE UN TRABAJO, MARICON.

¿CERVEZA? ¿POR FAVOR?

Browne

BUS STOP

SHIT FACE DRUNK

PUKE

© 1991 by King Features Syndicate, Inc. World rights reserved.

Lamento informarles que la presentación de las dos de la tarde ha sido cancelada

CHRIS BROWNE

"PUKE" IS THE SAME L ANY LANGUAGE.

FOR LOVE AND ORANGES!!!

SOME MIAMI HISTORY, BITS... (AND TRIVIA) ... WITH A SPECIAL GUEST APPEARANCE BY MUHAMMAD ALI!

A HUNDRED YEARS AGO, WHAT IS NOW MIAMI WAS JUST A MESS OF IMPENETRABLE SWAMP, MANGROVE AND COCONUT TREES, AND MOSQUITOS DOWN AT THE SOUTH END OF WHAT FLORIDA SPORTSMAN, L.B. LIVES CALLED, "A FILTHY, DOOMED PENINSULA." HENRY FLAGLER BUILT HIS FLORIDA EAST COAST RAILROAD AS FAR SOUTH AS WEST PALM BEACH, THEN SAID, FUCK THIS! NO MAS! THERE WERE A FEW SETTLERS IN WHAT ARE NOW THE COCONUT GROVE AND BRICKELL AREAS OF MIAMI, AND THEIR MAIL WAS CARRIED DOWN THE TREACHEROUS COAST, ON FOOT, BY THE LEGENDARY "BAREFOOT MAILMAN." ONE OF THE INHABITANTS OF THE AREA ALONG THE MIAMI RIVER WAS THE TOUGH AND CRAZY, YOUNG WIDOW, JULIA TUTTLE, WHO HAD MOVED TO THE SWAMP FROM CLEVELAND, DETERMINED THAT A GREAT CITY WOULD ONE DAY RISE THERE. SHE KNEW THAT THE RAILROAD WOULD HAVE TO BE EXTENDED TO SOUTH FLORIDA, FIRST, THOUGH. THEN, AS FATE WOULD HAVE IT, THERE WAS A TERRIBLE FREEZE ONE WINTER, RUINING ORANGE CROPS AS FAR SOUTH AS WEST PALM. AS THE STORY GOES, MISS TUTTLE SMUGLY SENT AN UNFROZEN ORANGE BLOSSOM TO FLAGLER TO SHOW THAT THE FREEZE HAD NOT GO NEAR AS FAR SOUTH AS THE FUTURE MIAMI. FLAGLER VISITED HER TO CHECK IT OUT, AND THEN DECIDED TO BUILD HIS RAILROAD SOUTH TO MIAMI. HMM... I ALWAYS THOUGHT THERE HAD TO BE MORE TO THAT STORY, LIKE HE MUST HAVE BEEN IN LOVE WITH HER. AH YES... LOVE — THE REAL REASON MEN BUILD RAILROADS, LEAD COMMUNIST REVOLUTIONS, SHOOT REAGAN, ETC... HE LOVED HER, SO HE SHOWED OFF A BIT BY BUILDING A RAILROAD TO HER HOUSE. WELL, IT TURNS OUT, THE PART THAT'S OFTEN LEFT OUT OF THIS STORY IS THE HUGE TRACTS OF LAND THAT TUTTLE GAVE FLAGLER TO BUILD A CITY ON. SO HE WAS IN LOVE, BUT WITH MONEY. LAME. NO ROMANCE AT ALL, HE WAS JUST THE FIRST OF MANY SWINE DEVELOPERS TO COME MAKE A FORTUNE TURNING A NATURAL PARADISE INTO A STRING OF HOTELS...

PEOPLE HAVE ALWAYS THOUGHT KINDA BIG IN MIAMI. LIKE THE TIME WHEN THAT FREAK **CRISTO**, THE "ARTIST," SURROUNDED THE ISLANDS IN BISCAYNE BAY WITH FLOATING, PINK PLASTIC. ONLY IN MIAMI. SHEESH. IN THE BOOM PERIOD, FOLLOWING MIAMI'S INCORPORATION IN 1896, IT WAS NO DIFFERENT. CARL FISHER, AN APPARENT MANIAC, TURNED AN ISLAND OF DENSE MANGROVES INTO MIAMI BEACH, JACKIE GLEASON'S "FUN AND SUN CAPITOL OF THE WORLD" BY PUMPING THE BEACH SAND BY THE TON OUT OF THE BOTTOM OF BISCAYNE BAY. NOW, SOUTH BEACH IS SUCH A DISGUSTING YUPPIE/TOURIST MESS THAT I WISH THERE WAS A WAY TO PUT IT BACK! FUCK! DON'T DO US ANY MORE FAVORS, CARL! CORAL GABLES, ON THE SOUTHWEST BORDER OF MIAMI WAS CREATED BY GEORGE MERRICK TO BE A RICH NAZI PLAYLAND WITH A SPANISH THEME — CORAL BUILDINGS, OLD SPAIN ARCHITECTURE, SPANISH STREET NAMES, WEEKLY RECREATIONS OF GREAT MOMENTS FROM THE INQUISITION, ETC. WHO KNOWS HOW FAR THESE MEN WOULD HAVE GONE IF THE GREAT HURRICANE OF 1926 HADN'T RUINED EVERYTHING?!!

MIAMI BEACH HAS ALWAYS HAD THE REPUTATION OF A BIG, RETIREMENT COMMUNITY, BUT OVER IN MIAMI QUITE A FEW HAVE BEEN RETIRED, TOO. TWO CUBAN PRESIDENTS, **GERARDO MACHADO** AND **CARLOS PRIO**, FLED CRUMBLING DICTATORSHIPS ON MIDNIGHT PLANES FROM **HAVANA**, IN ORDER TO SAVE THEIR LIVES. IN MIAMI, THEY WATCHED AND WAITED FOR A CHANCE TO RETURN HOME TO POWER, BUT IT NEVER CAME. TODAY, THEY'RE BOTH BURIED IN MIAMI'S WOODLAWN CEMETARY. WHEN AL CAPONE MOVED TO MIAMI, HE CALLED IT "THE GARDEN OF AMERICA" AND SAID HE LIKED IT SO MUCH THAT HE'D RECOMMEND IT TO HIS FRIENDS. THEN OLE "SCARFACE" GOT BAGGED BY THE I.R.S. FOR TAX EVASION AND WENT UP THE RIVER. WHEN HE GOT OUT OF ALCATRAZ, HE WAS POWERLESS AND HIS BRAIN WAS RAVAGED BY SYPHILIS. HE LIVED OUT HIS LAST YEARS, MEEKLY, ON PALM ISLAND, IN THE BAY, NEVER KNOWING HIS FORMER GREATNESS.

TWO OF MY GREATEST HEROS ALSO SPENT SOME NOTEWORTHY TIME IN MIAMI. IN NOVEMBER OF 1955, PLAGUED BY DEATH THREATS AND THE SECRET POLICE, THE YOUNG **FIDEL CASTRO** LEFT CUBA FOR A FUNDRAISING SPEAKING TOUR OF THE U.S. HE RENTED THE OLD FLAGLER THEATER AND TOLD A GROUP OF CUBAN EXILES "THE FRUIT OF LIBERTY IS NOT BEGGED... IT IS WON WITH THE BLADE OF THE MACHETE!" YO FIDEL! IN FEBRUARY OF 1966, THE GREATEST FIGHTER OF ALL TIME, **MUHAMMAD ALI** LEARNED HE WOULD BE DRAFTED TO FIGHT IN VIETNAM. ALI REFUSED TO GO, TELLING REPORTERS IN TRUE ALI-STYLE, "KEEP ASKING ME, NO MATTER HOW LONG, ON THE WAR IN VIETNAM, I SING THIS SONG/ I AIN'T GOT NO QUARREL WITH THE VIET-CONG!" A COUPLE YEARS LATER, WHILE THE CONTROVERSY STILL RAGED ABOUT HIS DRAFT RESISTANCE, ALI WAS PICKED UP IN MIAMI, CUZ HE HAD A WARRANT OUT FOR AN OLD TRAFFIC VIOLATION. HE DID 7 DAYS IN THE DADE COUNTY JAIL. HEY, I'VE BEEN IN THAT JAIL, TOO! GOSH... MAYBE IF I EVER GET TO MEET 'EM, I CAN GET HIM TO AUTOGRAPH MY PROPERTY SLIP...

A WHOLE MESS 'O STOOPIT CELEBRITIES LIVE IN MIAMI THESE DAYS, BUT NOW THAT THEY'VE MADE IT BIG, THEY DON'T HANG AROUND MY SQUATS ANYMORE. OUT ON **STAR ISLAND**, JUST OFF THE MCCARTHUR CAUSEWAY (NAMED AFTER THE GENERAL) BETWEEN MIAMI AND MIAMI BEACH, YOU'LL FIND THE HOMES OF DON JOHNSON, JULIO IGLESIAS, AND **VANILLA ICE**. ONE TIME, KATHLEEN AND THEY WENT OVER THERE AND THE GUARD SAID, "WHO DJA WANNA SEE?" AND THEY SAID, "BOBBY VAN WINKLE" (ICE'S REAL NAME). TO THEIR SURPRISE, THE GUARD LET 'EM ON. THEY DROVE AROUND IN A CIRCLE, LOOKIN' FOR A CLUE TO WHERE HE LIVED, UNTIL THEY ASKED THIS OLD MAN WHERE TO FIND VAN WINKLE'S PLACE. THE MAN SAID, "THIS IS IT HERE... BUT BOBBY IS ON TOUR NOW IN JAPAN." IT WAS VANILLA ICE'S DAD! HE SAID TRY BACK IN A COUPLE MONTHS. THEY SHOULDA KIDNAPPED HIM AND MADE HIM ROB BANKS! OH WELL...

AS FOR PUNK ROCK HISTORY, THERE USED TO BE SHOWS BACK IN 1980 AT THE **POLISH-AMERICAN CLUB** ON N.W. 22ND AVE., WHICH LOCALS WILL NOTE AS BEING RIGHT ACROSS THE STREET FROM LOCAL LEGEND SCOTT BALDWIN'S (EX- POWERHOUSE, TRI-RAILS, CHICKENHEAD, INHOUSE MASSACRE, CANADIANS, CARTER) HOUSE. THE **PINK LINCOLNS** HAVE A GREAT SONG CALLED "MIAMI," BUT THEY'RE FROM STOOPIT TAMPA. THE BEST RECORD EVER FROM MIAMI IS PROBABLY "**COMMUNIST RADIO**" BY **THE EAT**. THE COVER OF THIS 7" "GOD PUNISHES THE EAT" FEATURED A LIGHTNING BOLT, PRESUMABLY FROM GOD, STRIKING THE DOWNTOWN MIAMI SKYLINE. THEY GOT MAIL AT 2600 TRAPP AVENUE IN THE GROVE, BUT I WACKED BY THERE AND DIDN'T SEE ANY SIGNS OF AGING PUNKS. BUT THEY STILL PLAY OUT LIKE TWICE A YEAR AND CHUCK SAYS THEY'RE REAL FAT AND COOL.

"I HATE WHAT YOU STAND FOR AND I THINK YOU KNOW WHY.
I DON'T WANNA WORK ALL MY LIFE, GO TO FLORIDA AND DIE!"
— SCREECHING WEASEL ← FLORIDA IN SONG

"There are still some drivers who feel guilty when they turn down a 'thumb bum' on the highway, yet there is no reason to feel any obligation toward these moochers.

• Hitchhiking is illegal throughout the United States.
• It's a good idea to cut your hair short if you want to pick up ride
• Knapsacks are hideously uncomfortable.

SCAM'S THOUGHTS ON

HOW NOT TO DRAW THUMBS ↓

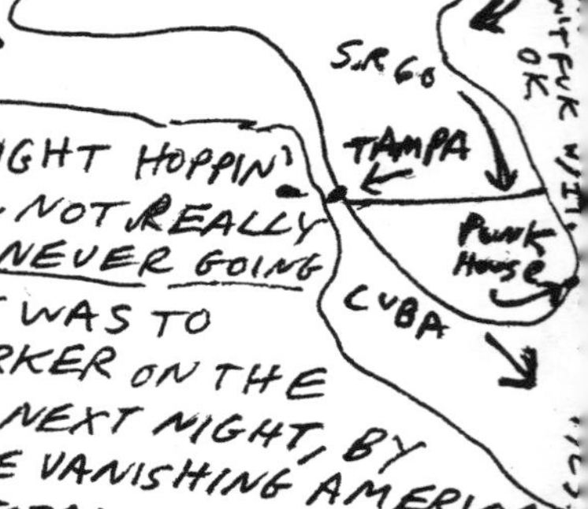

HOW NOT TO HITCHHIKE
OR... MY FIRST HITCHIN' TRIP

FIG 1-A: FLORIDA
DON'T FUK WITH OK
S.R. 60
TAMPA
PUNK HOUSE
CUBA

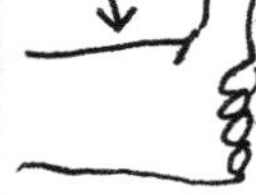

MY FIRST HITCH HIKING TRIP WAS SUPPOSED TO BE MY FIRST FREIGHT HOPPIN' TRIP. I WAS MOVIN' OUT OF THE OLE LAUDERDALE PUNK HOUSE, NOT REALLY BECAUSE I WANTED TO, BUT BECAUSE I HAD NO MONEY AND WAS NEVER GOING TO WORK AGAIN, SO I WAS GONNA BECOME A HOBO. THE NIGHT BEFORE I WAS TO LEAVE, I WENT TO THE MINI CSX YARD IN LAUDERDALE AND CONVINCED A WORKER ON THE TRAINS TO TELL ME WHEN A TRAIN WOULD BE LEAVING TOWARDS TAMPA THE NEXT NIGHT, BY TELLING HIM I WAS A COLLEGE JOURNALIST WRITING AN ARTICLE ON "THE VANISHING AMERICAN HOBO." I CAME BACK WHEN HE TOLD ME TO, TOTALLY PREPARED, OR AT LEAST, TOTALLY DRUNK. CHUCK LOOSE, WHO WAS ALSO REAL DRUNK CAME WITH ME TO HELP CARRY MY STUFF. THERE WAS A LITTLE DRAMA WHEN CHUCK FELL ASLEEP ON THE TRACKS, BUT I WOKE HIM UP AND OTHER THAN THAT, THINGS WENT SMOOTH AND, SURE ENOUGH, A NORTHBOUND CAME ROLLIN' BY RIGHT ON TIME. "ISN'T THERE SUPPOSED TO BE AN OPEN BOXCAR?" I ASKED CHUCK. HE WAS ASLEEP AGAIN. I HELPLESSLY WATCHED MY TRAIN GO BY WITH NO IDEA HOW TO RIDE IT, AND WOKE CHUCK UP AND WENT BACK TO THE PUNK HOUSE. IT LOOKED LIKE MY CAREER AS A HOBO HAD GONE THE WAY OF MY CAREER AS A WINEMAKER AND MY SHORT CAREER AS A VICIOUS, DRUNK, PROFESSIONAL SKATEBOARDER...

BUT, I STILL HAD TO LEAVE. SO AT ABOUT MIDNIGHT, I GATHERED UP MY LAST BEERS AND MY SIGN THAT SAID, "TAMPA" AND HEADED FOR THE HIGHWAY. SOON, A CAR STOPPED AND I WAS ALL "ALLRIGHT MAN! YER MY FIRST RIDE EVER! WANNA BEER? I'M A HOBO!" IT WAS A GUY WHO LIVED IN DELRAY ON HIS WAY BACK FROM A HEAT GAME. HE DROPPED ME IN DELRAY AND THERE WERE FEW CARS OUT ON I-95, BUT THEN, I GOT A RIDE FROM RICK, THE PALM BEACH POST DELIVERY GUY. I HAD A GREAT TIME WITH THIS GUY. HE SMOKED HIS POT AND I DRANK MY BEER AND WE TALKED ABOUT CONSPIRACY THEORIES AND THE BULLSHIT GULF WAR AND YELLED A LOT—STUFF LIKE "STICK IT TO THE GREEDHEADS!" AND "DEATH TO THE SWINE!" THE HIGHLIGHT OF OUR RIDE TOGETHER WAS WHEN WE BOTH PISSED ON THE DOOR OF THE BURT REYNOLDS RANCH IN WEST PALM BEACH, WHEN HE HAD TO PUT THE POST IN THE MACHINES THERE. RICK LET ME OUT IN JUPITER AT LIKE 4:00 A.M., AND SAID I WAS AT A GOOD SPOT WHERE TRUCKERS WOULD BE AND I'D GET A RIDE. IT DIDN'T OCCUR TO ME THAT I DIDN'T EVEN KNOW HOW TO GET TO TAMPA, OR WHAT ROADS TO TAKE. WHO CARES?

THIS WAS FUN!!! (FUK THE LAW)

BUT, AFTER AWHILE, I WAS PRETTY BUMMED, WHEN NO TRUCKS WOULD STOP FOR ME. I STARTED THROWING ROCKS AT CARS THAT PASSED ME. FUCK THEM. I FINALLY PASSED OUT ON A BENCH BY A "SHADES OF YOGURT" IN A JUPITER STRIP MALL, AND WOKE UP WITH THE PALM BEACH SHERIFF IN MY FACE! "GET A MOVE ON, KID. YER BAD FOR BUSINESS!" KID? IT'S "HOBO" TO YOU, BUDDY!!!

NOW THERE WAS NO TURNING BACK. I GOT A RIDE FROM TWO GUYS IN A TRUCK WHO SAID, "WHERE ARE YA GOIN'?" "TAMPA! "WE'RE GOIN' ~~NICE~~ TO DAYTONA." OK, UM... SOUNDS GOOD. I'M GOIN', UM... UP AND THEN... OVER! I WENT TO SLEEP IN THE BACK OF THEIR TRUCK AND THEY WOKE ME UP AT VERO BEACH AND SAID, "HEY, UH... YOU MIGHT WANT TO GET OUT HERE AND TAKE STATE ROAD 60. IT GOES STRAIGHT TO TAMPA." I WAS SUSPICIOUS, BUT IT WAS THEIR TRUCK, SO I GOT OUT. AT A GAS STATION, I CHECKED A MAP AND THEY WERE RIGHT, THOUGH. 60 WAS THE WAY. GUSH.

AND SO, HERE WAS MY FIRST INNOCENT ENCOUNTER WITH STATE ROAD 60, A ROAD WHOSE NAME WOULD ONE DAY BE SYNONOMOUS IN MY MIND WITH ROMANCE AND DANGER, A ROAD THAT I WOULD COME TO KNOW LIKE THE BACK OF MY HAND. A NICE TRUCKER TOOK ME TO LAKE WALES AND TOLD ME ABOUT DRIVIN' 60 LATE AT NIGHT AND HAVIN' TO SCREECH ON THE BRAKES, CUZ OF ALLIGATORS IN THE ROAD! IN LAKE WALES, I SCAMMED A COKE AT SUBWAY AND CONSIDERED, KEROUAC-STYLE WHAT LIFE MUST BE LIKE IN THIS HOPELESS LITTLE BURG, AND DECIDED THAT THE GIRL BEHIND THE COUNTER WAS PROBABLY THE-PRETTIEST-GIRL-IN-LAKE-WALES. THEN I WAS OFF TO THE OPEN ROAD...

-GGY, THE PROPHET AND YOU!
HITCHIN' SPIELIN' CONTINUIN'

I GOT A RIDE WITH A GUY IN A SPEED METAL BAND WHO HAD ACTUALLY SEEN THE NK LINCOLNS PLAY THE WEEK BEFORE. HE DROPPED ME IN BARTOW, RIGHT NEXT TO THE PROPHET. THE PROPHET WAS A MIDDLE AGED BLACK GUY IN A WHITE AND BLUE SILK KINDA ADVATION GOWN, STANDING BY A SIGN THAT SAID "THE PROPHET." I RAN UP TO HIM. "IS IT RUE?!? ARE YOU THE PROPHET?" YEAH. THERE WAS A MOTORCYCLE PARKED NEXT TO HIM. S THAT YOUR CYCLE?" YEAH. THAT'S HOW I GET AROUND. I DIDN'T KNOW WHAT TO SAY TO THE OPHET, SO I TOLD HIM ABOUT MY TRIP, AND HE SAID, "WELL, LET ME SAY A PRAYER FOR YOU, MY OD MAN." AND GRIPPED MY SHOULDER AND BOWED HIS HEAD. I SHRUGGED AND BOWED MY HEAD, TOO. GOOD LORD, LET THIS FINE YOUNG MAN HAVE A SAFE TRIP ON THE ROAD. GOOD LORD, DO NOT T THIS MAN STAND BY THE SIDE OF THE ROAD TOO LONG. PLEASE HELP THIS TRAVELLER TO GET RIDE VERY QUICKLY. AMEN." THAT'S IT? "THAT'S IT." I SAID GOODBYE AND TURNED TO WALK NAY AND THEN SAW THE SIGN ACROSS THE STREET AT HARDEE'S: "3 HAMBURGERS FOR A BUCK" FOR A BUCK?!? I WAS STARVING, THANK YOU, PROPHET!!!

A COUPLE RIDES LATER, I ARRIVED AT MY DESTINATION, WHICH WAS NOT TAMPA, BUT, ACTUALLY EARBY CLEARWATER. I SHOWED UP AT MY FRIEND'S WORK ALL WIDE EYED AND WEIRD FROM THE OAD, TOTALLY EXCITED. HE COULDN'T BELIEVE THAT I'D MADE IT. NEITHER COULD I! I HAD A GREAT TIME THAT WEEKEND THERE. SO GREAT THAT I LOST MY SHOES AT A PARTY. I HITCHED HCK BAREFOOT, AND WALKED INTO LAUDERDALE A GRIZZLED VETERAN OF FLORIDA'S BACKROADS. ND IT TURNED OUT THAT BUDDHA SAID I COULD LIVE IN HIS ROOM, AND NICK HAD AN D PAIR OF CONVERSE FOR ME... I HAD A HOME AGAIN, WITH BEERS AND A BED AND A LACE TO REST MY OLE THUMB, FOR ANOTHER MONTH OR SO AT LEAST...

THE FEARLESS (AND DRUNK) TOMATO PIRATES OF STATE ROAD 60!

AFTER I MOVED OUT OF THE PUNK HOUSE FOR GOOD, I STARTED HITCHIN' ALOT, WHEN I WASN'T LOOKING FOR SQUATS, JUST FOR THE FUN OF IT. GRADUALLY, I LEARNED A COUPLE IMPORTANT HITCHIN' RULES LIKE 1) DON'T THROW STUFF AT CARS 2) KNOW WHERE YER GOIN' AND 3) TRY TO ITCH IN THE DAY, CUZ CARS CAN'T SEE YOU AT NIGHT (AT NIGHT, IT'S BETTER TO ASK FOR RIDES T TRUCKSTOPS, GAS STATIONS, ETC.)

ON MY WAY BACK FROM TAMPA ONCE, IT WAS GETTIN' LATE IN LAKE WALES AND I WAS ETTIN' NERVOUS W/ 4 HOURS OF ROAD AHEAD AND ONLY 2 HOURS OF SUNLIGHT. BUT, FINALLY, A LUE VAN PULLED OVER, AND I HEAR ALL KINDS OF CRAZY LAUGHIN' COME OUT THE DOOR WHEN IT PENS AND THIS KINDA REDNECK GUY GETS OUT THE PASSENGER SIDE, AND HE'S GOT THIS RED UST ON THE BEARD AROUND HIS MOUTH AND HE SAYS, "YER NOT WEIRD, ARE YA?" UH... O. "OK." HE SLIDES OPEN THE VAN DOOR AND MOTIONS TO GET IN, AND SAYS "BE CAREFUL HERE YA SIT." I CRAWL IN AND THE INSIDE OF THE VAN IS FULL OF PILES AND PILES OF OMATOES!!! "IF YOU SMOOSH ANY, YOU'VE BOUGHT 'EM!" YELLS THE DRIVER AS HE PEELS OUT, ND JACKS THE VAN UP TO 80 M.P.H.

STATE ROAD 60 IS STATISTICALLY THE MOST UNSAFE ROAD IN THE STATE, WITH THE IGHEST ACCIDENT RATE AND THE 47 MILE STRETCH BETWEEN LAKE WALES AND YEEHAW VNCTION IS THE WORST PART, WITH NO CITIES, 2 LANES, NO SHOULDERS, NO LIGHTS, AND IN 1OST PLACES - NO GUARDRAIL, JUST DITCHES AND ALLIGATORS. THE VAN WAS GOIN' 80 ASILY, AND THE DRIVER WAS BLINDLY JERKING IT AROUND AND PASSING SLOWER VEHICLES WITHOUT LOOKING TO SEE IF CARS WERE COMING IN THE WESTBOUND LANE. THE PASSENGER OOKS AROUND AT ME AND SAYS, "WASSA MATTER WITH YOU, KID? YOU LOOK CRAZY! YOU DRINK BEER?" H...BEER. YES. PLEASE. "WHAT YOU REALLY WANT IS SOME OF THIS!" SAYS THE DRIVER, FFERING ME A WIDE MOUTHED, UNLABELED JAR FULL OF A CLOUDY, FOUL SMELLING LIQUID. WE MADE IT OURSELVES!!!" UH... NO THANKS. "SUIT YOURSELF!" HE POURS HIMSELF AND THE ASSENGER A DRINK, THEY WERE MIXING IT WITH TOMATO JUICE. UM... SAY, HY DO YOU GUYS HAVE ALL THESE TOMATOES ANYWAYS?

AS IF WE HEARD MORTAR SHELLS, WE CUSS MORE IN OUR ZINE, CUT DOWN ON THE HALF TONES | TOMATO PIRATE FLAG DRAWN BY K.C. EZ-1 decide a minute or a mile after passing you to come back and offer a lift. For this reason, avoid shouting pleas or obscenities or making similar gestures to motorists who fail to stop. They may come back, unless your roadside manners have turned them off.

toughest states for hitchhikers, but there are still some w attempt to evade the law by making their pitch from roadsi service stations and cafés."

MY LIFE WITH THE TOMATO PIRATES VOLUME II

THE DRIVER SAYS, "WELL, WHAT WE CAN'T SELL, WE EAT!!" HA HA HA HA! THE FRONT SEAT OF THE VAN ERUPTS IN LAUGHTER. THE PASSENGER LEANS BACK, ALL CONFIDENTIAL STYLE, SAYS "WELL, SEE, THESE HERE ARE UNLICENSED AND UNINSPECTED TOMATOES. WE'RE TRYIN' TO SELL 'EM TO RESTAURANTS, AND SINCE WE'RE CHEAPER THA A LEGITIMATE FRUITSELLER, WE DO ALLRIGHT." NOW, I UNDERSTOOD. THEY WERE TOMATO PIRATES, BARRELLING DOWN THE SWAMPY BACKROADS & CENTRAL FLORIDA, ALL DRUNK AND CRAZY WITH A VAN FULL OF BLACKMARKET PRODUCE! YO!!! THINGS WERE LOOKING GOOD. I WENT TO WORK ON MY 2nd BEER, THE PASSENGER PLAYED HIS HARMONICA, AND TH DRIVER BEAT ON' BURNED THE OLE VAN UP, 70, 80, 90, GO!

THEN, ALLASUDDEN, WE PULL OVER. UH OH. WHAT IF THEY'VE FLIPPED OUT AND THE WANT ME TO WALK THE PLANK, FOR SOME REASON, OUT HERE IN NO MAN'S LAND?!? BUT ITS OK. THE DRIVER JUST STICKS HIS HEAD OUT THE WINDOW AND BLASTS A STREAM OF FOAMY RED PUKE. ONCE, TWICE, THREE TIMES. "UGH", HE GURGLED, AS HE WIPED HIS FACE ON HIS SLEEVE AND POURED A FRESH BEER INTO HIS CUP OF TOMATOE JUICE/LIQUID. THE PASSENGER SAYS "YER DRUNK." THE DRIVER SAYS "YER UGLY!" HA HA HA HA HA!!!

ON WE DRIVE TO YEEHAW JUNCTION, WHICH IS A COUPLE TRUCKSTOPS AT THE INTERSECTIO OF S.R. 60 AND U.S. 441. WE STOPPED AT A RESTAURANT TO SEE IF THEY COULD SELL SOME TOMATOES. THE DRIVER, THE ONE WHO PUKED, COMBED HIS HAIR BACK, ALL GREASY AND PUT ON H FLIP FLOPS AND SAID, "I'LL TAKE CARE OF THIS. I'M NORMAL LOOKIN'." "FUK YOU" MUMBLE THE PASSENGER. A TRUCK DRIVER CAME OUT OF THE RESTAURANT AND WALKED TO HIS TRUCK. "LOOK AT THAT DUMB REDNECK," SAYS THE PASSENGER. "HEY!" HE YELLS. "HEY, YOU FUCKIN REDNECK!" THE TRUCKER COMES OVER, "WHAT?" THE PASSENGER SAYS "WHATCHA GOT I THAT TRUCK, HUH?" TRUCKER SAYS, "SAND." "SAND?!? YOU CAN'T EAT SAND YELLS THE PASSENGER. "WHAT YOU NEED IS TOMATOES!!!" HE SAYS, WILDLY WAVIN A FIST AT THE TRUCKER. THE TRUCKER KINDA RUNS AWAY AND THE DRIVER'S BACK "NO LUCK. FUCK 'EM." "YEAH. BUNCH OF FUCKIN' REDNECKS!!!" HA HA HA HA !!

WE MADE GOOD TIME AND SOON WE WERE AT VERO BEACH AND I-95, WHERE MY LIFE WITH TH TOMATO PIRATES WAS TO COME TO AN END. THEY WERE HEADIN' NORTH, TOWARDS COCOA BEACH AND MOR BEER AND TRUCKSTOPS AND FIGHTING AND ADVENTURE AND I WAS STANDIN' ON 95 SOUTH, STILL BUZZIN' AND WAITIN' FOR WHATEVER WOULD COME ALONG NEXT...

WHAT THE HELL'S THE DEAL WITH FUCKIN' OPA-LOCKA?
A BRIEF HISTORY OF DADE COUNTY'S WEIRDEST TOWN

OPA-LOCKA'S FUCKIN' WEIRD. ITS A CITY IN THE NORTHWEST METROPOLITAN MIAM AREA, SOME 120 BLOCKS FROM DOWNTOWN MIAMI. ITS BASICALLY A GHETTO, WIT A LOT OF INDUSTRIAL AND WAREHOUSE BUILDINGS, TOO - YA KNOW, STUFF THAT NO ONE E WANTS. WHAT'S WEIRD IS THE CITY'S INEXPLICABLE ARABIAN THEME. THE CITY STREETS ARE NAME 'ALI BABA WAY", "SHARAZAD AVE", "BAGHDAD AVE", "CAIRO AU ETC. AND THE CITY HALL HAS ARABIAN-STYLE MINARETS ON THE ROOF! GOLD MINARETS THE GHETTO! THE STORY IS THAT IN THE BOOM DAYS OF THE 20'S, FLORIDA AVIATOR/MILL GLEN CURTISS WANTED TO CREATE A RESORT CITY TO RIVAL MERRICK'S CORAL GABL AND FISHER'S MIAMI BEACH, SO HE DECIDED ON THE ARABIAN THEMELAND. SHEESH! WHA WERE THESE GUYS ON? I ALWAYS FIGURED THEY MUST HAVE BEEN DOIN' A LOT OF COKE OR SOMETHIN'. BUT, REALLY, IT WAS JUST MONEY THAT THEY WANTED. STILL THERE'S A LITTL CHARM IN TAKIN' A BIG EMPTY SPACE AND DOIN' SOME TOTALLY CRAZY CREATIVE THING WITH IT. THAT'S WHY I SQUAT. ANYWAYS, THEY HAD BIG PLANS FOR OPA-LOCKA. THEY MON THE ARCHITECTURE STRICTLY TO CREATE THE MIDDLE EASTERN LOOK. IT WAS TO BE A B STOP ON THE RAILROAD. THEN, THE HURRICANE OF 1926 WIPED 'EM OUT. CURTISS DIE NEARLY BROKE AND OPA-LOCKA WENT UNFINISHED. IN THE 40'S, ARMY BASES WERE BUILT WHICH WERE TURNED INTO LOW INCOME HOUSING AFTER THE WAR. IT BECAME A DUMPING GROUND FOR JUNKYARDS, STORAGE SPACE, ETC. BY THE 70'S, THE MINARETS ANC HALL WERE PRETTY TRASHED, BUT THEY WERE RECENTLY REFURBISHED. YOU CAN SEE TH OPA-LOCKA TRAIN STATION FROM THE TRI-RAIL. ITS COVERED WITH GRAFFITTI, HAS NU DOORS OR WINDOWS AND IS FULL OF TREES. NO TRAINS STOP IN OPA-LOCKA THESE DAYS, BUT THE WHOLE CRAZY PLACE REMAINS AS SOME SORT OF LONELY MECCA FOR THE DOOMED.

UM... A MINARET IS, YA KNOW, THE POINTY SHAPED THING ON TOP OF A BUILDING IN BAGDAD LOOKS LIKE ⌂ or um ⌂ or ⌂ FUK IT, LOOK IT UP

ROAD KILL RECIPES!

PUKE!

DELICIOUS!

TASTY!

BORN 2 LOSE!

LUTZ 64 mi.

SO YER HITCHIN' AROUND AND YOU LOOK DOWN UD FIND A HUGE, BLOODY, BUG-EATEN ARMADILLO, JITH ITS EYES MASHED INTO ITS INTESTINES. EWWW. JOULD YOU DARE TOUCH IT? WOULD YOU EAT IT?!? YES!!! EVERY TRUE, EXPERIENCED ROAD WARRIOR NOWS THAT THE BEST EATS ON THE ROAD COME RIGHT FF THE ROAD. HERE ARE A FEW OF MY FAVORITE LL TIME ROAD-TRIP LUNCH RECIPES FOR YOU. SCAM: THE TASTE THAT'LL RUN YOU OVER.

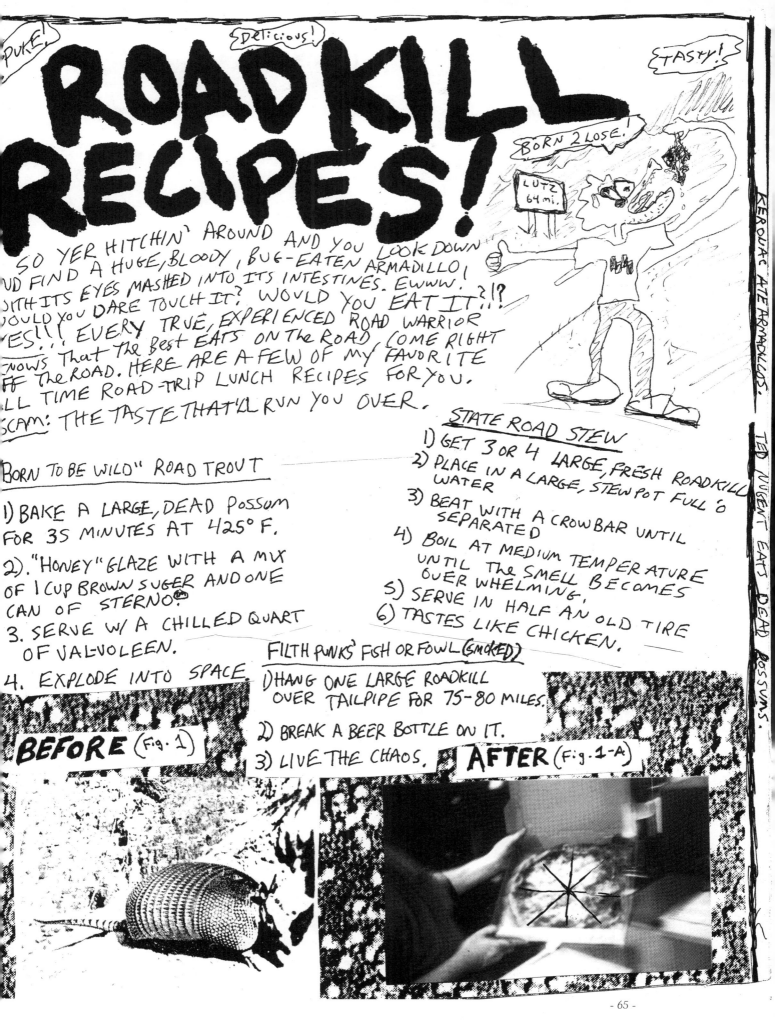

"BORN TO BE WILD" ROAD TROUT

1) BAKE A LARGE, DEAD POSSUM FOR 35 MINUTES AT 425° F.

2) "HONEY" GLAZE WITH A MIX OF 1 CUP BROWN SUGER AND ONE CAN OF STERNO®

3. SERVE W/ A CHILLED QUART OF VAL-VOLEEN.

4. EXPLODE INTO SPACE

STATE ROAD STEW

1) GET 3 OR 4 LARGE, FRESH ROADKILL

2) PLACE IN A LARGE, STEW POT FULL 'O WATER

3) BEAT WITH A CROWBAR UNTIL SEPARATED

4) BOIL AT MEDIUM TEMPERATURE UNTIL THE SMELL BECOMES OVER WHELMING,

5) SERVE IN HALF AN OLD TIRE

6) TASTES LIKE CHICKEN.

FILTH PUNKS' FISH OR FOWL (SMOKED)

1) HANG ONE LARGE ROADKILL OVER TAILPIPE FOR 75-80 MILES.

2) BREAK A BEER BOTTLE ON IT.

3) LIVE THE CHAOS.

BEFORE (Fig. 1)

AFTER (Fig. 1-A)

KEROUAC ATE ARMADILLOS. TED NUGENT EATS DEAD POSSUMS.

¡FREE MALANGA!

or
why i love miami even tho it sucks

el cop, miami

free pedro navaja

Miami is part of Latin America. It's not the South, but but South in the global sense. Local politics works like a Latin American regime, complete with right wing government sponsored terrorism by morons like Alpha 66 and Jorg Jorge Mas Canosa (self-appointed multi-millionaire Prez-in-Exile of Cuba asshole), monsters fed by hatred and reality-free nostalgia. We bury the dictators here and the word exile is used loosely. The truth is that most of Miami's Latins are not so driven by greed.

Latins comehere from the Third World, which refers to countries that have been turned into ghettos. The word ghetto comes from Nazi Germany and it implies genocide: neighborhoods of Jews and Gypsies, minorities stamped by language, poverty, starvation, disease, yellow and blue stars, pink triangles. I come from a little island colony of the USA called Puerto Rico which has the nation's worst enviromental pollution, the most cancer, the most sterilization, astronomical unemployment and welfare, etfuckingcetera. Try Colombia, Panama, Dominican Republic, Peru, Mexico; it's no wonder people get out and never want to go back.

FREE PATATo Y MENARK

santa bárbara.

Latins bring their religion to Miami. Like the colors of our skin which come from the "mixing of races" (Africans are referred to by continent so that Senegalese=Bambara= Eritrean, but that's something else), our religions bring together European, African, and native elements.Look at rooster, snakes, and other non-Christian symbols on the Jesus candles they sell at Latin supermarkets.

The most popular religion in Latin Miami (apart from Catholicism) is Santeria. Santeria is based on Yoruba traditions from what is now Nigeria. Although very few santeros speak conversation Yoruba, the only European elements in the litany are the images of saints associated with African deities, which is the source for the popular name Santeria. Light-skinned and white Latins devote themselves to this African religion, while most African Americans are Protestant. Weird.

Santeria (nanigo, lucumi, palo monte, etc.) is essentially from Cuba, so it's strong in Miami and New York. You can see it in the Yellow Pages under "religious organizations". But Miami's very strange, so the Santeria can also be a little funny. For instance, there was the babalawo (high priest) who held divination ceremonies to know whether or not his drug deals were sanctified by the spirits. The spirits gave him a green light to deal with a new cocaine importer who turned out to be a DEA agent. Our glorious Miami Herald played it up by speculating about ex-DEA spirits, but there was never any mention of the spirits sending this clown to prison.

A few months ago a judge ruled that animal sacrifice during religious ceremonies was legal. A Babalawo comemierda (translation impossible) invited the tv news to watch him cut animals up for 6 o' clock. The next day a babalawo named Pichardo of the Church of the Lucumi Babalu Aye held a news conference dressed in a three-piece suit to condemn the actions of the babalawo comemierda. Credentials were challenged and, eventually, the babalawo comemierda apologized. Some sort of order was re-established. Needless to say, this sort of thing doesn't happen in Cuba.

FREE CHUCHO "JESUS"

The news and —on a very disturbing note— animal rights protesters failed to mention that babalawos are expert butchers (like Kosher butchers) and the animals are eaten. Alarms go off in my head when I hear "savage, cruel, primitive religion"; I never heard shit about that on 10.12. The truth is that Santeria is beautiful, happy religion based community and love. Live clean.

P.S.: I also feel obligated to mention that Miami-style bass is bad as fuck.

E L
MACHETE
AKA "FLINT."

shangó alayé

ah ah ah, malanga murió

SQUATS THAT FAILED

AFTER MY LITTLE HAVANA HOUSE BURNED DOWN, I WAS PRETTY HEARTBROKE. I TRIED TO MOVE INTO THE ABANDONED HOUSE NEXT DOOR, BUT IVY'S MOM WOULDN'T LET ME, CUZ THAT'S WHERE SHE WAS GONNA LET HER CREEPY BOYFRIEND LIVE. SO I SPENT THE LAST MONTHS OF '91 AND THE FIRST MONTH OF '92, EITHER STAYIN' AT NICK'S, HITCHIN' AROUND FLORIDA, OR LOOKIN' FOR A NEW SQUAT.

ONE OF THE FIRST PLACES I TRIED WAS A 2-STORY APARTMENT HOUSE ON 11TH AND MICHIGAN ON SOUTH BEACH. IT WAS A GREAT LOOKIN' PLACE, BUT MIAMI BEACH WAS TERRIBLE. THE PLACE HAD SUCH A VICIOUS FEEL TO IT, WITH ALL THE FISTFIGHTS OUT FRONT OF THE BARS AND DRUNK FOREIGNERS. AND THE COPS WERE EVERYWHERE. ME AND NICK GOT STOPPED ALL THE TIME, AND I'D BEEN PUSHED OVER AND KICKED BY ONE ONCE IN THE 7-11 PARKING LOT ON 5TH AND ALTON. I WAS PRETTY WORRIED ABOUT 'EM. I WAS AFRAID THEY'D FIND ME IN THE BUILDING AND JUST BEAT ME TO DEATH WITH FLASHLIGHTS OR SOMETHIN'. WHEN I WAS WALKIN' ON WASHINGTON AVE. AND I'D SEE ALL THAT EMPTY BLACK OF THE NIGHT AND OCEAN OUT THERE, JUST BEYOND THE DRUNKEN YELLING AND THE NEON, IT ALWAYS FELT LIKE I WAS IN SOME GODLESS ABANDONED ZONE AT THE VERY EDGE OF THE WORLD. IT WAS A HARD PLACE TO SURVIVE, TOO, WITH NO GOOD FOOD DUMPSTERS, AND THE DENNY'S WITH THE "ONE REFILL ONLY" POLICY (FOR LOCAL SCUMBAGS, NOT TOURISTS WITH CREDIT CARDS). TO TOP IT OFF, THERE WERE SOME KIND OF PAINT FUMES IN THE BUILDING THAT WERE MAKING ME REAL SICK. I WALKED AROUND THE WHOLE FILTHY, DOOMED ISLAND ~~EVERY NIGHT~~ EVERY NIGHT, WEAK AND WEIRD, FEELING ABOUT AS DESPERATE AND DISCONNECTED AS YOU CAN GET. AH, ALIENATION... YES, ALOT OF PEOPLE THROW THAT WORD AROUND, BUT THIS WAS IT. IT GOT SO BAD, THAT I ALMOST MADE FLYERS TO PUT UP THAT SAID, "BASICALLY, "I HATE YOU AND I HOPE A HURRICANE COMES AND DESTROYS THIS TOWN OR YOUR BELOVED COPS COME AND PUT YOU IN A HOLE!" I HATE THIS PLACE!!! " I REACHED BOTTOM ONE DAY WHEN I WAS AT THE SoBe PUBLIC POOL (WHICH WAS FREE BACK THEN). I'D SWIM THERE AND TAKE A GOOD, HOT SHOWER IN THE LOCKER ROOM EVERY MORNING. ONE DAY, AFTER MY SHOWER, I WAS... UM... MASTURBATING IN A TOILET STALL, WHEN ALL THESE OLD JEWISH GUYS CAME IN TO SHOWER AND STARTED SINGING REAL LOUD: "DOSHE BELLSH URR RING KING... FAW MEEN MY GAL! DOSHE BIRDSH URR SHING KING... FAW MEEN MY GAL!" OI VEY! I COULDN'T EVEN BEAT OFF! FUK THIS TOWN! I COULDN'T LIVE THERE ANYMORE. THAT WAS IT. SHEESH...

AFTER THE CHRISTMAS HOLIDAY, I CAME DOWN FROM MY MOM'S PLACE, WITH MY NEW CROWBAR, READY TO FIND A PLACE. A GUY ON THE METRO RAIL SAID, "NOW THAT'S A CROWBAR!" YEA! I WAS EXCITED CUZ I WAS GOING TO MEET IVY WHO WAS NOW GOING TO TRY AND MOVE INTO A SQUAT WITH ME, CUZ SHE WAS SICK OF HER MOM'S PLACE. WITH MY CROWBAR AND HER EXTENSIVE KNOWLEDGE OF THE STREETS OF MIAMI, HOW COULD WE LOSE? BUT THERE WERE STILL THINGS WE HADN'T THOUGHT OF. ONE DAY, NOAH VAIL WAS DRIVING US AROUND TO LOOK FOR A PLACE IN HIS DAD'S NEW CAR. WE FOUND A COOL HOUSE ON THE CORNER OF PLAZA STREET AND U.S. 1, ACROSS FROM THE MIAMI SUBS, ON THE POOR SIDE OF THE GROVE. IT WAS GREAT, AND ALREADY OPEN TOO! WE COULD JUST PUT ON OUR OWN LOCK AND WE'D BE ALL SET... WHEN I WALKED OUT, 3 COPS, WHO WERE WATCHING US WHILE EATING LUNCH AT MIAMI SUBS, WERE COMIN' OVER TO US. THEY WENT THROUGH THE CAR. "WHAT'S THE CROWBAR FOR?" NOAH GOES, "UH... ITS THEIRS!" I GO, "UH... I FOUND IT! AND... I'M TRYING TO SELL IT? WANNA BUY IT?" THE COP GOES, "YEAH... I KNOW WHY YOU WERE HERE." I GULP. "YOU WERE OUT ON A NICE AFTERNOON TAKIN' DADDY'S NEW CAR DOWN TO THE CRACK HOUSE!" CRACK HOUSE?!? "WELL, SINCE YER CLEAN I'M LETTIN' YA GO, BUT IF I EVER SEE YA OVER HERE AGAIN, I'LL BUST YA." HOW WERE WE GONNA USE THE CROWBAR TO SMOKE CRACK? I HAD TO LAUGH. YEAH, ALL THESE FAILED SQUATS WEREN'T REALLY FAILURES, CUZ WE LEARNED ALOT. THE HOUSE WAS IN A BAD NEIGHBORHOOD, KINDA, AND ALREADY OPEN, SO IT WAS A CRACK HOUSE.

THE NEXT PLACE THAT ME AND IVY TRIED WAS A QUAINT, LITTLE CORAL AND WOOD HOUSE ON THE CORNER OF S.W. 80TH STREET AND S.W. 72ND AVE. IT WAS REAL OLD. YOUNG FIDEL TOLD ME THAT HE WAS PRETTY SURE IT WAS A REGISTERED CITY HISTORICAL SIGHT. WE KICKED DOWN THE "FOR SALE" SIGN AND I HAPPILY USED A HAMMER TO RIP THE FLIMSY LOCK OFF THE DOOR (THIS, I BELIEVE, IS ONE OF THE MOST FUN AND SATISFYING THINGS YOU CAN DO). WE HAD HIGH HOPES FOR THE PLACE, CUZ IT HAD GREAT LOCATION. IT WAS RIGHT BY DADELAND MALL, WHERE YOU CAN GET MONEY OUT OF THE FOUNTAINS, OR TABLE DIVE PILES AND PILES OF FOOD THAT THE KENDALL RICH FUKS LEAVE BEHIND AT THE FOOD COURT. THE X-TRA 24 HOUR SUPERMARKET WAS NEARBY WITH ITS BULK BINS AND THE INFAMOUS BOOKSTOP (NOW BARNES AND NOBLE) WAS A BLOCK AWAY ON KENDALL DRIVE. I'D STEAL 3 OR 4 BOOKS AND STOP IN AT FRESHEN'S YOGURT WHERE EMIL WORKED, FOR FREE YOGURT. THE EASY-TO-HOP DADELAND SOUTH METRO RAIL WAS THERE, CLOSE BY, AND, TO TOP IT OFF, THERE WAS AN APARTMENT COMPLEX, WITH A POOL, AND AN UNLOCKED SORT-OF "CLUBHOUSE" BUILDING, WITH A HOT SHOWER, A REFRIGERATOR, AND COFFEE MAKER, JUST ACROSS THE STREET. WE WERE SET!!)

WE SPENT A DAY, OR SO CLEANING THE PLACE OUT. ONE DAY, WHEN IVY HAD GONE TO DADELAND TO STEAL SOMETHING, TWO WELL DRESSED MEN PULLED UP IN A SPORTS CAR. OH SHIT! I WAS AFRAID IT WAS SOME OWNER OR UNDERCOVER COPS. I SAID, "HI. I'M CLEANIN' THE OLE PLACE OUT." ONE GUY SAYS, "OH, WE'RE JUST LOOKIN' AROUND," AND THEY WALK BEHIND THE HOUSE. I GO BACK TO SWEEPING, BUT THEN, DECIDE THAT I'D BETTER GO FORCE A CONFRONTATION, FIND OUT JUST WHAT THESE GUYS WANT. I WALK AROUND THE CORNER OF THE HOUSE, AND THE TWO GUYS ARE STANDING THERE WITH THEIR PANTS DOWN, ONE FIRMLY GRIPPING THE OTHER'S PENIS! WHOOPS! I MUMBLE, "SORRY," AND GO BACK TO THE FRONT AND SWEEP, AND A COUPLE MINUTES LATER THEY GET IN THEIR CAR AND LEAVE. I WAS KINDA RELIEVED, CUZ IT WASN'T THE LAW, BUT I WAS A LITTLE WORRIED THAT MAYBE ALOT OF PEOPLE USED MY NEW NEW BACK YARD FOR SEX, AND THERE'D ALWAYS BE STRANGERS FUCKING BACK THERE. THAT'D BE JUST MY LUCK.

THE NEXT DAY (THIS IS ANOTHER GRAPHIC STORY, SO BE WARNED, OR, IN MIAMI, "AVISO") WE WERE AT THE SQUAT AND I HAD TO "SQUAT" OR GET LOOSE, SO TO SPEAK, AND THERE WAS NO TOILET WITHIN A MILE, SO I TOOK OUR TOILET PAPER AND ADJOURNED TO THE SIDE YARD TO DO THE DOO. THIS MANIAC WHO LIVES IN THE NEAREST HOUSE, ABOUT A FOOTBALL FIELD AWAY, SOMEHOW SEES ME THROUGH THE TREES AND OVERGROWN LOT AND STARTS YELLING FOR ME TO STOP? HOW? I YELL, "I'M TAKING A SHIT!!! GO AWAY!!!" TO NO AVAIL. I RUN INTO THE HOUSE TO WIPE, AND THEN DECIDE TO GO INGRATIATE MYSELF TO THE MAN AND APOLOGIZE PROFUSELY, IN ORDER TO KEEP HIM FROM GETTING NEAR ENOUGH TO OUR HOUSE TO SEE THAT IT WAS OPEN. BUT THE GUY WON'T EVEN LET ME SAY A WORD. HE'S STANDING THERE WITH SEVERAL BIG, VICIOUS DOGS, AND JUST KEEPS SAYIN', "THE POLICE ARE ON THEIR WAY." FINE. SO I GET IVY, AND WE LEAVE, ONLY TO BE STOPPED BY THE COPS DOWN THE STREET. IT WAS THE BRUTAL, ROVING FREE AGENTS FROM THE METRO-DADE POLICE! BUT THE TRUE STORY ABOUT SHIT SEEMED TO DRAW UNUSUAL EMPATHY FROM THE PIGS, WHO SEEMED TO BE REMEMBERING THE TIMES WHEN THEY WERE YOUNG AND WERE JUST MOVING INTO THIS KILLER SQUAT, ONLY TO GET CAUGHT WHILE SHITTING IN THE YARD. THEY LET US GO AND DIDN'T EVEN CHECK THE HOUSE AT ALL. STILL, THIS DOG LOVING MANIAC WAS A PROBLEM. WHY COULDN'T HE MIND HIS OWN BUSINESS? I STAYED THERE A COUPLE NIGHTS, AND CAME BACK ONE DAY TO FIND A NEW LOCK ON THE DOOR. I RIPPED IT OFF, FOR FUN, BUT IT WAS CLEAR I COULDN'T STAY THERE ANYMORE.

THE WORD ON THE STREETS!
WHAT PEOPLE ARE SAYIN' ON THE STREETS OF SOUTH FLORIDA

IN WEST PALM BEACH, IF SOMEONE SAYS THEY WENT TO "45TH STREET" OR IF YOU SAY SOMEONE IS REALLY "45TH STREET", YER REFERRING TO THE MENTAL HEALTH HOSPITAL THAT'S ON 45A STREET, SO THAT MEANS THEY'RE CRAZY OR JUST GOT OUT OF THE HOSPITAL, ANYWAYS. IF YOU SPEND THE NIGHT IN "THE GUN CLUB" THEN YOU'VE SPENT A NIGHT IN JAIL, CUZ THE COUNTY JAIL IS ON GUN CLUB ROAD. IF SOMEONE SAYS THEY'VE "BEEN WORKIN' THE SIGN" THEY'VE BEEN STANDIN' BY THE SIDE OF THE ROAD WITH A "WILL WORK FOR FOOD" SIGN. IN OVERTOWN, "CHESTER" IS AN INSULT FOR WHITE PEOPLE. ALSO, IN OVERTOWN, ALL THE DRUGS COME IN LITTLE MANILLA ENVELOPES THAT ARE STAMPED WITH THE SELLER'S NAME, LIKE A NAME BRAND, SO YOU KNOW WHO TO GO TO. YOU FIND ALOT OF DIME BAGS ON THE GROUND IN O-TOWN, SOME EVEN FULL OF POT! IN COCONUT GROVE, THE PRICE OF A STOLEN BIKE IS ALWAYS 8 BUCKS. NEVER MORE, NEVER LESS... RAFAEL SAYS ON CALLE OCHO, YOU MAY GET FREE FOOD BY WALKING INTO THE CAFETERIA AND SAYING, "CASTRO VA A CAERR!" IT MEANS, "CASTRO WILL FALL!"

ONE TIME I WAS RIDIN' MY BIKE OVER IN LITTLE HAVANA, OVER BY THE ORANGE BOWL, AND I SAW THIS GANG DRINKIN' BEER AND GAMBLING IN FRONT OF AN ABANDONED HOUSE. IT WAS LIKE NINE IN THE MORNING...

Growin' up Crazy in Miami by Ivy AKA GIRL

Lenny's shotgun

MERCURY   Pearl

MUTTS!

stinky guava tree

HELL BABY

    When I was 8, or 9, me and my mom and my sisters lived in Goulds, which is
southwest of Miami. Its real cheap to li ve there, so we had this huge plot of
land, and a two-story house with a real   big porch, surrounded by all kinds
of trees--- bamboo, mango, guava. It was our own forest! We had these two mutts
named Pearl and Mercury, and we'd always go runnin' around, adventuring in the
woods, with them. Our mom would buy us Barbie dolls and stuff, but we'd never
play with them. We'd just hang out in our forest, and the dogs would chew up

all the dolls she bought. Finally, she got so mad, that she took one of the chewed
up Barbie heads and tacked it up to the front door with a sign that said, "Beware
of children!!!" One time, when I was alone in our forest, I found one of those
wood stakes with the red ribbon tied to it , that hT
wood stakes with the red ribbon tied to it, that the phone company use to mark
underground phone lines. I got very sad, cause I thought it was someone's grave.
I took flowers to it, once a week, for over a year.
    We also lived with Lenny, the drunk, nudist, inventor. He was my dad's best
friend. Before my dad died, Lenny promised him that he'd raise us if anything
ever happened to him. Lenny was always   drunk, and always nude, but he was
never mean. He would just get drunk, puke, and pass out in this old bathtub in
the backyard. In the backyard, there was also this guava tree that stunk so bad.
It was just the shittiest tree! We'd always have to run past it, it smelled so bad.
One time, Lenny got out of the bathtub and roared, "I'M FINALLY GONNA GET RID OF
THAT SMELLY FUCKIN' TREE!!!" He got his gun --- he was naked--- and shot down the
guava tree and we all stood around and cheered.
    Lenny always used to tell us about his inventions. He said that he'd invented
The Most Comfortable Bed In The World. It used magnets. Lenny said that your body
had both positive and negative properties, and he could make a bed that had the same
properties as you, so that it repelled you, and you just hovered over it, on air. He
tried to sell the idea to Levitt's Furniture, but it never went anywhere.
    Lenny was 6'4, with crazy, red hair, and big, blue eyes. He would terrify my
friends by making them scream. He'd yell, "Scream like this! RAAARGH!!!" and they'd
try to do it, and he'd go, "No, no! Like this! RAAARGH!" Then he'd sit back and say,
"See? I have perfect pitch. " Then he'd play the guitar. He'd play for hours, but
he only knew two songs: the one that goes,"Stop! Hey! What's that sound? Everybody
look what's goin' down." and Margueritaville. Lenny had a big scar running up the
center of his chest from a   car accident . He said that he'd already died 3 times,
and come back. He would gather us all around and yell, "Hey, kids, you wanna hear
about smuggling?" and he'd tell us all about how he'd died three times, smuggled
millions of tons of marijauna into the U.S. and had killed 54 people. These days,
he's a shrimper in the Coconut Grove marina, and he still says 54 . Never more, or
less. I'll always remember Lenny's great advice. He said, "Listen up, kiddies!
Never brush your teeth. The toothpaste is bad for ya!" Lenny had three teeth...
    Then, my mom and Lenny got arrested in an undercover drug bust. She had been
joking with the DEA agents before the arrest. She said, "This is where I launder MY
money," and she threw their cash in the washing machine. Then the police came in.
One of them had a jacket with missing letters on it, so she said, "What the hell is
this? The 'LICE' are raiding my house ?!?" In court, when they played back the tape
that they made with the hidden microphone, the judge started laughing so hard, he had
to duck down, behind his bench until he composed himself. Since he thougth my mom,
was so funny, she only got one year in the Women's Detention Center.

GROWIN' UP IVY CONTINUED

My sisters and I got taken away by the state and put in a foster home, called the Florida Baptist Children's Home. Within the first two weeks of my being there, I became a christian and was baptised. My mom came to see it with all her cellmates, since the jail would let you go to church. I remember waving to her, and all these fancy chruch people staring at her, cause she had a jail uniform on.

I hated the foster home. I was there for almost 5 years. I would just runaway all the time. I would just split. When I was 10, me and 4 other kids had this plan to runaway. We said, as soonas the bell rings, lets ditch school and go to Dadeland Mall. We ditched and hid our books in this bush, and got to Dadeland just when it was opening for the day. We went in and stole about 15 bucks out of the fountains, and Iwent into Rite-Aid drug store, where my shoplifting career began. I stole a bunch of lighters.

We decided to get on the Metro-Rail and go to downtown Miami, to just get as far away from the home as we could. In downtown, we visited one of the other runaway girls mom. She lived in the old hotel that had the historic Coppertone sign on it. It was a real old Miami landmark, but recently, they tore it down. It was a rundown, shitty, drug motel. Her mom bought us McDonald's dinner, and then, we went on the Metro-rail to Okeechobee, the last stop, in Hiahleah.

It was getting dark. With our money, we bought a 2-liter bottle of coke, a loaf of bread, a pound of meat and a pound of cheese. We were all pretty excited, like, "Yeah, we made it now!" We found blankets and went to this roof to camp out. We were running around, celebrating, and playing with our lighters. Then, we came down from the roof, and found this golf cart. We wanted to hot-wire it, but, right then, a cop drove by, so we hid under it, and rolled up paper, and pretended to smoke it. We passesd it around, saying, "Oh man, I'm so stoned..." Then we went to the convenience store. It was really late by now. I lit a trash can on fire with my lighter and the cops came and got us. Our punishment at the home was to stay up all night, digging holes in the garden...

I THINK THEREFORE I SCAM — SHIT TO DO AT THE UNIVERSITY OF MIAMI

THERE'S ALWAYS FREE COFFEE IN A COLLEGE SOMEWHERE. AT U.OF M., CHECK OUT THE PHILOSOPHY FACULTY LOUNGE, ON THE 5TH OR 6TH FLOOR OF THE BUILDING NEAR THE LIBRARY (I'M BEIN' KIND OF VAGUE SO YA DON'T RUIN MY COFFEE SCAM, OK?). HERE'S WHAT YOU GET — COUCHES, PILES OF PHILOSOPHY BOOKS AND COFFEE." I THINK, THEREFORE I SCAM" —IGGY. (COLLEGE STUDENTS ARE SUPPOSED TO BE SMART, RIGHT?) HOW COME NO ONE EVER EATS THE COCONUTS THAT COME FROM THE TREES LININ' THE CAMPUS SIDEWALKS? IT TAKES A LITTLE WORK TO GET 'EM DOWN, BUT WELL WORTH IT. REMEMBER, ONLY THE BROWN ONES! THERE ARE LOTS OF WALLS, TRASHCANS, BILLBOARDS, ETC. AT U.M. FEEL FREE TO WRITE ON THEM WITH A PERMANENT MARKER. I ALWAYS WRITE "DROP OUT!" ON THE A.T.M. MACHINE. THE UNIVERSITY HAS RARELY SEEN CAMPUS SECURITY, AND NO REAL COPS, SO ITS A KINDA SANCTUARY FROM THE EVIL CORAL GABLES' PIGS. MAKES FOR GOOD DRINKIN' SPOTS...THE LIBRARY IS PRETTY GOOD, BUT, TECHNICALLY, NOT OPEN TO NON-STUDENTS. I SPENT A WHOLE AFTERNOON TRYIN' TO SNEAK INTO THE BACK OF THE LIBRARY, IN THE SERVICE AREA, AND EVEN GOT A PILE OF POSTAGE STAMPS OUT OF A DESK, BUT KEPT GETTING CAUGHT, CUZ THE SERVICE ELEVATOR NEEDS A KEY. BOY, DID I FEEL DUMB WHEN I JUST WALKED RIGHT IN THE FRONT DOOR AND TOLD THE GUY I LOST MY I.D. THIS ALWAYS WORKS. ITS USUALLY THE SAME OLD GUY, AND HE GETS REAL EXASPERATED, BUT HE LETS YOU IN. I MEAN, ITS A LIBRARY, YA KNOW—NOT A FUCKIN' ROCK CONCERT. SHEESH... THE STUDENT ACTIVITY CENTER HAS EVERYTHING YOU NEED — A STOVE, A SHOWER, EVEN A PIANO! THE STOVE IS UP THE STAIRS, FIRST DOOR ON RIGHT. THE SHOWER IS IN THE SWIM TEAM LOCKER ROOM. ON A SCAM WEIRD-PLACE-TO-TAKE-A-SHOWER- SCALE OF 1-10, ITS LIKE 6. WATER'S WARM, BUT YOU MAY HAVE TO BATTLE WITH SWIMMER GUYS FOR SPACE. THE PIANOS UPSTAIRS. I'VE GONE THERE AND TRIED TO PLAY THE THING FOR HOURS, 'TIL SOME REAL FRAZZLED, WIDE-EYED GUY FROM THE NEARBY SCHOOL PAPER WOULD STAGGER OVER TO ME. "PLEASE...STOP...PLEASE!. THE RADIO STATION IS UPSTAIRS, TOO. BUG THE D.J.'S TO PLAY BLACK FLAG. THEY'VE GOT X-RAY SPECS, ON CART, TOO. ME AND IVY GOT HANNAH, THE D.J., TO LET US ON THE AIR ONE TIME, AND WE PLAYED "WILD IN THE STREETS" FOR THE THEN RIOTING CITY OF L.A. AND "RISE ABOVE" FOR CHUCK LOOSE, WHO WAS HAVIN' A BAD MONTH. THERE IS, I THINK, STILL A PUNK WHO WORKS AT THE STATION. HE HAS A MOHAWK AND HIS NAME IS AXEL. U. OF M. IS A GREAT PLACE TO STEAL FURNITURE FOR YOUR SQUAT, AND IT EVEN HAS "UNIVERSITY OF MIAMI" WRITTEN ON IT. IS A BONUS FOR U.O.FM. ATHLETICS FANS... WHEN IN DOUBT, RIDE YOUR BIKE IN THE HALLS. THEY HATE THAT!!!

LIBERTY CITY WEEKEND

FTER THE HOUSE BY DADELAND, WITH THE PSYCHOTIC NEIGHBOR AND HIS DOGS, WE DECIDED THAT WE OULD TRY A POORER NEIGHBORHOOD WHERE THE NEIGHBORS WOULDN'T CARE SO MUCH. WELL, NEIGHBOR-OODS IN MIAMI DON'T GET ANY POORER THAN LIBERTY CITY. LIBERTY CITY IS FAMOUS FOR THE RIOTING THAT AS OCCURRED THERE. SEE, IN MIAMI, EVERY COUPLE YEARS, FOR NO APPARENT REASON, A WHITE COP URDERS A BLACK MAN. THEN, WHEN THE COP IS, OF COURSE, ACQUITTED, THE POOR, BLACK SECTIONS OF TOWN, KE LIBERTY CITY AND OVERTOWN ERUPT IN VICIOUS RIOTING. WE DECIDED TO START LOOKING HERE. WE TOOK THE METRORAIL TO THE MARTIN LUTHER KING, JR. PLAZA STOP AROUND 10:00 P.M. ON A FRIDAY NIGHT ND DECIDED TO JUST WALK AROUND AND SEE WHAT WE COULD FIND TO SLEEP IN, CONFIDANT THAT NO COPS WOULD TOP US FROM BRAKING IN AT NIGHT. OK ... THIS ISN'T A "HOW TO" LOOK AT SQUATTING, CUZ GOIN' INTO E CITY'S HARSHEST GHETTO, LATE ON A WEEKEND, WITH NOWHERE TO GO IS PROBABLY A BAD IDEA, ANYWAY OU ANALYZE IT. BUT THESE EARLY DAYS IN MIAMI WERE INNOCENT ONES, YES, AND WE WERE CONFIDANT THAT E WERE RIGHT, YA KNOW? LIKE, WE NEED A HOME, EVERYONE NEEDS A HOME ... SO IF WE GET OUT AND OOK, THINGS'LL FALL INTO PLACE.

JUST 5 MINUTES AFTER WE GOT OFF THE RAIL, THINGS STARTED DOIN' JUST THAT. THE FIRST PERSON WE SAW IN BERTY CITY CAME WALKIN' BY — THIS 8 YEAR OLD, BLACK KID, NATHANIAL. WE SAY, WELL, WHAT THE HELL, ND ASK HIM IF HE KNOWS OF ANY ABANDONED HOUSES AROUND, AND HE DOESN'T REALLY THINK ITS STRANGE, CUZ YA SEE, HE'S ALL INNOCENT, TOO, AND HE DOES KNOW WHERE A PLACE IS, AND SAYS HE'LL SHOW US IF WE GO TO THE STORE WITH HIM, FIRST, CUZ HIS MOM NEEDED SOMETHIN' BUT THE STORE'S FAR AWAY TO GO ALONE. AT THE STORE, WE START TO REALIZE THAT OUR PRESENCE HERE IN LIBERTY CITY IS PRETTY UNUSUAL, CUZ EVERYONE DOES A DOUBLE TAKE WHEN WE WALK UP. BUT NO ONE IS THREATENING, SO ITS COOL SO FAR. NATHANIAL LIVES WITH HIS MOM, BROTHER, AND SISTER. HE TELLS US, IN THESE PROJECT BUILDINGS ABOUT A LOCK FROM WHERE WE MET HIM, AND THAT'S WHERE OUR NEW HOME IS, TOO. THE PLACE HE SHOWS US IS AN BANDONED, OPEN APARTMENT WITHIN AN UNABANDONED PROJECT. ITS A LITTLE SKETCHY, BUT WE FIGURE T'LL DO FOR THE NIGHT, AND WE CAN LOOK FOR A BETTER PLACE TOMORROW. NOW, WE NEEDED CANDLES, ND OBVIOUSLY, THERE'S NO 24 HOUR SUPERMARKET AROUND CUZ THERE AIN'T TOO MANY NICE THINGS, ON THE OOR SIDE 'O TOWN, BUT THERE IS A GREAT LITTLE STORE ON 27TH AVE, AND ABOUT 58TH CALLED HATTIE AND OPEEP'S. IT WAS ONE ROOM WITH ALL THE STUFF YER EVER GONNA NEED, AND ITS ALL BEHIND THE OUNTER ON SHELVES — RAZOR BLADES AND SHOESTRINGS AND HAIR GREASE AND 10¢ CANDLES! SO WE GET BUNCH OF CANDLES AND WALK TO THE PROJECTS AND THERE ON TOP OF THE PROJECT TRASH PILE, LAY WO PERFECTLY GOOD MATTRESSES! THE ROOM WAS CONCRETE COLD, AND UGLY, BUT NOW WE FELT A LOT MORE SECURE. WE DIDN'T HAVE A HOME, BUT WE HAD TONIGHT, WITH BEDS AND CANDLES, BUYIN' TIME, FOR SLEEP AND DREAMS, BEYOND THE BLEAK ...

AND IT WAS PRETTY BLEAK, WAKIN' UP WITH A DIRTY, COLD, GREY LIGHT ALL OVER EVERYTHING — DUSTY BARBWIRED WINDOWS KEEPIN' OUT THE MORNING. BUT THERE WERE STILL KIDS LAUGHIN' AND PLAYIN' OUTSIDE, SOUNDS OF SUNNY SATURDAY, SO IT SEEMED ALLRIGHT. WE EMERGED FROM THE APARTMENT, AND NATHANIAL AND HIS FRIENDS STOPPED PLAYIN' FOOTBALL TO CROWD AROUND US IN WONDER, LIKE WE WERE ALIENS COMIN' OUT THE U.F.O. IVY SAID, THEY LOOKED AT US LIKE OUR PRESENCE THERE, AS WHITE PEOPLE, COULD ONLY MEAN THAT SOMETHING BAD WAS HAPPENING, CUZ WHITE PEOPLE ARE COPS AND LAND-LORDS ... BUT NATHANIAL'S PRETTY EXCITED, CUZ WE'RE HIS FRIENDS, SO HE'S THE GUARDIAN OF THE SECRET OF THE MYSTERIOUS PEOPLE, SO HE STARTS EXPLAINING AND WE HANG OUT AND TALK FOR A WHILE AND ANSWER QUESTIONS AND GET OUR FIRST DAYLIGHT LOOK AT THE OUTSIDE OF THE PROJECT. AT FIRST, YOU CAN TELL SOMETHING'S HORRIBLY WRONG, BUT YA CAN'T QUITE PLACE IT, AND THEN YOU REALIZE ITS THE TREES! THE TREES HAD ALL THEIR LIMBS SAWED OFF, SO THEY WERE JUST TWISTED BODIES REACHIN' AT THE SKY WITH SEVERED ARMS, AND NO LEAVES AND NO GREEN. IT WAS HIDEOUS TO LOOK AT. YOU CAN SEE, ITS NOT JUST A MATTER OF POOR PEOPLE NOT HAVIN' THE MONEY FOR NICE THINGS, CUZ THIS WAS A DELIBERATE AND CRUEL DECISION TO MAKE THEIR HOMES UGLY AND SHITTY (ABOUT A YEAR LATER, IT WAS EXPLAINED TO ME THAT THIS IS DONE SO COPS CAN SEE INTO THE PROJECTS BETTER, NO VEGETATION TO HIDE IN). I IMAGINED EVERY MORNIN', GETTIN' UP AND LOOKIN' OUT THE WINDOW, BARBWIRE FOR BREAKFAST, AND SEEIN' THE MEN COME CUT DOWN YOUR TREES ... IT WAS VERY BITTER-SWEET, THESE TOUGH KIDS PLAYIN' IN ALL THIS UGLY, BUT BEIN' LIKE THOSE TREES, TRYIN' TO GROW HERE AND GETTIN' ALL CUT BACK. I DIDN'T KNOW IF THEY'D MAKE IT. OR IF WE WOULD, EITHER ...

WE LEFT TO LOOK FOR A NEW HOUSE, WALKIN' ON 54TH EAST, MORE TOWARDS THE HEART OF LIBERTY CITY. AROUND 22nd AVE, WE MET ANOTHER LARGE GROUP OF KIDS, ON BIKES, NONE OLDER THAN 10 or 11. THEY WERE ALSO PRETTY SHOCKED TO SEE US IN THEIR NEIGHBORHOOD. IN FACT,

THEY CALLED US NAMES AND THREATENED US! BUT WE STOPPED AND TALKED TO 'EM ABOUT IT FOR AWHILE, AND THEN THEY WERE MORE CURIOUS THAN MEAN, LIKE NATHANIAL AND HIS FRIENDS. FINALLY, THE LOUDEST, COCKIEST KID STEPPED FORWARD AND SAID HE'D SHOW ME A PLACE WE COULD LIVE. ON THE WAY THERE HE TOLD ME NOT TO TAKE THE INSULTS TOO SERIOUSLY. HIS MOM WAS BLACK AND HIS DAD WAS WHITE, AND THE KIDS CALLED HIM "CRACKER", TOO, BUT HE BEAT A BUNCH OF EM UP, AND NOW THEY LEAVE HIM ALONE. WE GOT TO ANOTHER ABANDONED SECTION 8 BUILDING. THIS ONE WAS AN ENTIRE HOUSE. THE KID SAID THE HOUSE WAS USUALLY OPEN, AND IT HAD ELECTRICITY AND WATER, AND THE LANDLADY ONLY CAME AROUND ONCE A WEEK, TO GET RENT. HOWEVER, WHEN SHE CAME, SHE CAME WITH A COP, SO NO ONE SHOT HER TO GET ALL THE RENT. THE DOOR NOW, WAS LOCKED, THOUGH. I WAS ABOUT TO TURN AND LEAVE, BUT THE KID SAID, "WHERE YA GOIN'? LET'S GO IN IT!" AND HE STARTS THROWIN' HIMSELF AGAINST THE DOOR. ONE CRACK, TWO CRACKS... AND "WATCH THIS!" SMASH! THE DOOR FLIES OPEN! I MUST ADMIT I STARTED LAUGHIN', I BET THIS NEVER HAPPENED TO KEROVAC...OK. THE HOUSE IS REAL NICE. THE KID'S PRETTY EXCITED. "YOU SHOULD GET YOUR STUFF AND MOVE IN NOW! THE LANDLADY'S NEVER HERE AND NO ONE ELSE WILL CARE!" THE ONLY PROBLEM, HE ADDS, MATTER-OF-FACTLY, IS THAT "IF YOU LIVE AROUND HERE, YOU'LL PROBABLY GET SHOT!" IT WAS PRETTY DEPRESSING, IN A WAY, CUZ HE SAW IT AS THIS BIG GAME: IF THEY FUCK WITH YOU, BEAT 'EM UP. WHEN THEY GET A GUN, YOU GET A BIGGER ONE... THE WAY HE SHOWED OFF BY YELLIN' AT US AND THEN BY KNOCKIN' DOWN THE DOOR, I COULD TOTALLY SEE HIM SHOOTIN' SOMEONE JUST TO PROVE HE'S NO WIMP. BACK WHERE I'D LEFT IVY, WITH THE YOUNGER KIDS, THINGS WERE MORE MELLOW. THEY WERE ALL SITTIN' AROUND DRAWIN' PICTURES IN IVY'S NOTEBOOK, WHILE SHE PUT A BAND-AID ON THIS GIRL'S BLOODY KNEE... AND JUST A COUPLE MINUTES BEFORE THEY WERE CALLIN' US "CRACKER!" WE HUNG OUT THERE, DRAWIN' AND TALKIN' FOR MOST OF THE AFTERNOON, AND WHEN WE WERE FINALLY WALKIN' AWAY, THIS OLDER GIRL CAME RUNNIN' OUT OF HER HOUSE WITH A SANDWICH FOR US! JUST A PIECE OF BALOGNA ON WHITE BREAD... MAN, THAT WAS QUITE A GESTURE. I'VE NEVER HAD PEOPLE SO POOR TRY TO GIVE ME SOMETHING, LOOKIN' AT THE SANDWICH, I DIDN'T KNOW WHETHER TO EAT IT, OR PRAY TO IT...

WE KEPT ON WALKIN' AND LOOKIN'. ONE THING I NOTICED IS THAT IN LIBERTY CITY, THE CULTURE KINDA REVOLVES AROUND THE CORNER STORE. THERE WAS THE OLD GUY, TRASHCAN FIRE SCENE OVER BY HATTIE 'N' BO PEEP'S AND THE LOUD, BASS THUMPIN' BLOCK PARTY SCENE AT THE MARKET NATHANIAL TOOK US TO. BUT, THE COOLEST PLACE WAS CHARLIE'S, THAT HAD A JUKEBOX OUTSIDE, BLASTIN' BLUES RECORDS ON VOLUME 1,000 THAT YOU COULD HEAR FOR A COUPLE' BLOCKS! PLUS, THEY ALL HAD REAL CHEAP STUFF LIKE THE 25¢ HONEYBUN AND THE 4 RITZ COKES FOR A BUCK. THIS IS A MEASURE OF A REGION'S POVERTY, CUZ OVERTOWN ONLY OFFERS 3 RITZ COKES FOR A BUCK! ANYWAY, WE FINALLY FOUND A GREAT HOUSE, AFTER PASSING DOZENS OF BURNED OUT, WIDE OPEN LOOKIN' CRACK HOUSES, BUT THE WOMAN NEXT DOOR CAME OUT AND YELLED AT US. SHE CALMED DOWN WHEN WE TALKED TO HER AND I ALMOST THOUGHT SHE'D LET US LIVE THERE, BUT NO LUCK. SHE SAID IF IT'D BEEN NIGHT TIME, SHE JUST WOULD'VE SHOT AT US! THEN WE STARTED HEADIN' UP 17TH AVE TO WALK BACK ON 62, BUT A MAN CAME RUNNIN' AFTER US, YELLIN' "NO! DON'T GO DOWN THERE!" HE EXPLAINED TO US THAT WE WERE SURELY HEADED TO OUR DEATH IF WE WENT DOWN THAT STREET! SHIT. WE MULLED IT OVER AT THIS RESTAURANT RIGHT BY THE METRORAIL (BROWN'S? I'M NOT SURE...) WHERE THEY HAD 50¢ COFFEE AND TOTAL FREE REFILLS — THE COOLEST COFFEE DEAL IN MIAMI I'VE EVER SEEN. IT SEEMED LIKE THERE WAS REALLY NO PLACE WE COULD GO WHERE WE WEREN'T JUST ABOUT TO GET SHOT, AND WE THOUGHT THAT WE'D GIVE UP RICH STORES TO SCAM IN FAVOR OF ANONYMITY, BUT, INSTEAD, WE COULDN'T WALK ONE BLOCK WITHOUT A BUNCH OF STARTLED AND AMAZED, BUT, FRIENDLY, LOCAL PEOPLE COMIN' UP TO ASK US WHY WE WERE THERE. AND, I DON'T KNOW WHAT I'D SAY TO A COP WHO STOPPED ME THERE... YES IT LOOKED LIKE DISASTER WAITING TO STRIKE DESPIT OUR BEAUTIFUL WEEKEND... THAT NIGHT, WE LISTENED TO GUNSHOTS AND BURNED 10¢ CANDLES AND DECIDED TO LEAVE IN THE MORNING. WHEN I GOT UP I WENT TO USE THE PHONE AND CAME BACK TO FIND SOME GUY SMOKING CRACK, TALKIN' TO IVY! SHE HAD WOKE UP WITH HIM SITTIN' ON THE BED! WELL, HE WAS HARMLESS, IT TURNED OUT BUT IT WAS PRETTY CREEPY. WE GOT OUR STUFF AND LEFT, AND THERE WERE THE MEN FROM THE CITY, CUTTIN' DOWN THE TREES OUT FRONT...

THE DRAWINGS ABOVE ARE BY THE KIDS IN LIBERTY CITY

LOOKING BACK, THE WHOLE TRIP TO LIBERTY CITY SEEMS DOOMED AND CRAZY, BUT WE WENT THERE LIKE WE WENT EVERYWHERE THEN (AND LIKE WE MOSTLY, STILL DO): WITH NO POSSESSIONS, AND THEREFORE NO FEAR AND NO DEFENSES. IT COULD HAVE BEEN DISASTROUS. INSTEAD, IT WAS KINDA INSPIRING. NOW, I RIDE THROUGH THERE ON MY BIKE, AND PEOPLE YELL AND EVEN THROW ROCKS AT ME, AND I'M AFRAID, REALLY, TO GO THERE, AND WON'T GO NEAR IT AT NIGHT. ITS REALLY SAD. I MEAN PART OF ME SAYS, "WELL, FUCK IT, WHY GET SHOT?" AND "THEY DON'T WANT YOU IN THEIR NEIGHBORHOOD." BUT, YES, REALLY ITS SAD, CUZ THE FEAR, I KNOW IT MEANS THAT THE MEAN OLE MEN OF SOCIETY HAVE MANAGED TO ~~SLOW~~ SLOWLY SAW A LIMB OR TWO OFF OF ME...

BACK TO BRICKELL!
DO NOT PASS GO.... DO NOT COLLECT $200... BUT DON'T REALLY MIND IT...

WE WENT BACK TO BRICKELL, AND WENT TO WORK, LOOKING FOR A NEW PLACE RIGHT AWAY. THE FIRST NIGHT, WE WALKED AROUND, FEELIN' KIND OF OBNOXIOUS, AND STOLE A HUGE FLAG FROM THE FONTANA DE TREVI RESTAURANT ON CORAL WAY. THEN, WE GOT CHASED BY BIG MEN FROM THE RESTAURANT, EVEN AFTER WE HAD DROPPED THE FLAG! THEY STARTED TO FOLLOW US AROUND IN A CAMARO, SO WE DITCHED 'EM AND HID UNDER THE WQBA RADIO DUMPSTER FOR 3 HOURS! WELL, IT WAS WARM AND DRY... BUT, NOT MUCH OF A SQUAT, THOUGH, MAYBE IF WE FIXED IT UP A LITTLE, YA KNOW, PUT A COUPLE PUNK STICKERS ON IT...

BUT, THE NEXT DAY, AS LUCK WOULD HAVE IT, I WAS EATIN' COOKIES OUT OF THE BULK BIN AT WOOLEY'S AND A GUY NOTICED ME, AND BOUGHT ME LUNCH. WHEN I TOLD HIM OF ME AND IVY'S SEARCH FOR A HOME, HE SUGGESTED THE VERY NEWLY ABANDONED, GREY APARTMENT BUILDINGS, RIGHT AROUND THE CORNER, ALSO ON CORAL WAY. I DON'T KNOW HOW WE'D MISSED 'EM! THEY HAD EVERYTHING — TWO STORIES, A BED, RUNNING WATER, NICE, WOOD PANEL FLOORS — AND LEMME SEE, THAT'S NO MONEY DOWN, WITH NO DEPOSIT, NO FIRST AND LAST MONTH'S RENT? YO! I'LL TAKE IT!

IVY DECIDED TO STAY AT HER MOM'S, SINCE IT WAS ONLY A COUPLE BLOCKS AWAY, BUT I WASTED NO TIME IN MOVING IN TO THE GREY APARTMENTS. I LIVED IN ONE APARTMENT ON THE TOP FLOOR, AND, IT TURNED OUT, A SAD, SILENT LOOKING, OLD MAN, WHO WAS A SORT-OF CARETAKER, LIVED, LIKE ME, WITH NO ELECTRICITY, IN THE OTHER BUILDING. I'D SIT IN THE FRONT ROOM, BY THE WINDOW, AND SPEND HOURS PICKING THROUGH ALL THE BOXES OF CRAZY PICTURES AND PAPERS (MOSTLY IN ~~ESPRY~~ ESPAÑOL) THAT HAD BEEN LEFT BY WHOEVER LIVED THERE BEFORE, OCCASIONALLY, THE THIN, OLD MAN ACROSS THE WAY WOULD LEAVE HIS APARTMENT AND WALK ACROSS THE STREET, TO THE LIQUOR STORE, AND RETURN TO HIS EMPTY BUILDING WITH A FULL BOTTLE. I WORRIED ABOUT WHAT WOULD HAPPEN IF HE CAUGHT ME, BUT ONE DAY, HE WALKED IN ON ME WHILE I WAS WRITING A LETTER, AND I JUST KINDA STAMMERED, "I...UH...LIVE HERE NOW... UH...OK?" HE JUST KINDA SIGHED AND NODDED, NO SOUND, AND WALKED OUT THE DOOR AND ACROSS THE STREET TO THE LIQUOR STORE...

AND SO I HAD A PLACE, AND WE WERE BACK IN EAST LITTLE HAVANA, WITH ITS LONG, LAZY SUNDAY AFTERNOONS, ROOSTERS CALLIN' OUT, AND TENNIS SHOES STRUNG UP OVER THE POWER LINES. THE BRICKELL METRORAIL BROUGHT IN THE INVADING ARMY EVERYDAY, BY THE TRAIN LOAD — THE BUSINESS MEN AND WOMEN WHO WORKED THE BURGEONING BRICKELL FINANCIAL DISTRICT. THEY'D STOMP THROUGH OUR TINY, THIRD WORLD NEIGHBORHOOD, HECTIC AND CRAZED, LOOKIN' AT THEIR WATCHES, AND RUNNIN' FOR TRAINS. BUT WE'D JUST SIT IN FRONT OF OUR FLOPPY OLE HOUSES, OR ON THE STREET CORNER, AND LAUGH AT 'EM. YES, IT WAS A MELLOW LIFE THERE IN THE SHADOWS OF THEIR SKYSCRAPERS, WITH THE SUN SETTIN' EVERY NIGHT ON GOOD FRIENDS AND A GOOD NEIGHBORHOOD, ALL DRAWN TOGETHER UNDER A CLOUD OF THE SMELL OF BLACK BEANS AND RICE AND DINNERTIME, COMIN' FROM EVERY OPEN WINDOW...

BRICKELL LIFE INVOLVED A GREAT CAST OF CHARACTERS. UP AT 7-11, THERE WAS SHOESHINE, THE KING OF THE BUMS, WHO BEGGED UP BEER CASH THERE. HE WAS OLD SCHOOL - A GENTLEMAN, ALL CRAZY AND FULL 'O LIFE. WHEN HE FELT LIKE IT, HE WAS KNOWN TO STORM UP AND DOWN THE NEIGHBORHOOD, FULL ON NAKED, EXCEPT HIS BOOTS AND BIG, RED BEARD, SINGIN' AND YELLIN', ALL DRUNK AND HAVIN' THE TIME OF HIS LIFE. THERE WAS PHILADELPHIA, WHO WAS IMMORTALIZED BY A PORTRAIT OF HIM WITH HIS OUTSTRETCHED HAND, ON A WALL ON S.W. 7TH STREET, BY THE GUY WHO PAINTS SHADOW PORTRAITS ALL OVER MIAMI AND SOUTH BEACH. RICHARD, THE BUM POET, WAS A GREAT GUY WHO ~~AND~~ WANDERED BY OCCASIONALLY, STOPPING FOR A BEER AND A QUICK DISCUSSION OF POLITICS...

BUT THE REAL CENTER OF ACTION WAS DOWN AT THE BRICKELL METRORAIL. HERE, YOU COULD USUALLY FIND H.E.L.L., THE LATIN METALHEAD WITH THE PENTAGRAM NECKLACE AND LEATHER JACKET. H.E.L.L. STOOD FOR HUGO EDUARDO LOPEZ LEAL. HIS PARENTS DIDN'T SPEAK ENGLISH, SO THEY DIDN'T REALIZE THAT THE NAME THEY GAVE HIM WAS AN ANAGRAM FOR SATAN'S HOME. I GUESS IT WOULD HAVE BEEN HARDER TO COME UP WITH A NAME THAT SPELLED THE ESPAÑOL "INFERNO"... LESLIE, THE HIPPIE GIRL, WAS USUALLY AROUND, TOO. SHE LIVED IN THE COOLEST HOUSE IN THE NEIGHBORHOOD. IT HAD BEEN THE ORIGINAL MIAMI HIGH SCHOOL BACK IN THE '20s. THERE WAS BLISS, THE NEIGHBORHOOD TRANSVESTITE KID. AND THERE WAS THE CLUMSY, DRUNK YOUTH GANG, THE B.O.B. (BOYZ ON BRICKELL, WHO ALSO HAD A FEMALE CHAPTER, THE S.O.B. (SISTERS ON BRICKELL) WHOSE MEMBERS INCLUDED IVY'S SISTERS. UNLIKE ZERO'S OLD CREW, THESE GUYS WERE PRETTY HARMLESS. THEY JUST DRANK BEER AN LISTENED TO LOUD DANCE MUSIC UNTIL THE METRORAIL CLOSED. SEEMING TO HOLD THIS ALL TOGETHER WAS SOTOMAYOR, THE METRORAIL GUARD, WHO WAS KIND OF THE EYES AND EARS OF THE HOOD. HE ALWAYS HAD A MESSAGE FOR YA THAT SOMEONE ELSE HAD LEFT WITH HIM, OR KNEW HOW TO FIND WHO YOU WERE LOOKING FOR. HE WAS A REBORN CHRISTIAN. HE'D LET US ALL ON THE RAIL FOR FREE AND CALL AFTER US "VIA CON DIOS" BUT, FOR A CHRISTIAN COP HE WAS A PRETTY LIKABLE GUY WHO COMMANDED ALOT OF RESPECT THERE IN BRICKELL, WHICH IS PROBABLY WHY THE B.O.B. NEVER GOT INTO SERIOUS CRIME. THEY WOULD'VE BEEN ASHAMED TO FACE HIM...

ME AND IVY SPENT OUR DAYS DOWNTOWN, EITHER AT THE LIBRARY OR ON THE STREETS, ~~AND~~ ~~ARCADE~~ IT WAS ONLY A SHORT WALK OF 10 MINUTES FROM BRICKELL, OVER THE MIAMI RIVER. AT NIGHT, WE'D DRINK A FEW BEERS UP ON THE CORNER BY 7-11, WITH SHOESHINE, AND WAIT FOR TH CHURCH VAN TO SHOW UP WITH THE FREE SOUP. OR WE'D HANG OUT IN THE PARK BY THE FIRE STATION WITH HELL AND LESLIE. OR WE'D BUY 10¢ COOKIES WITH FOOD STAMPS AT WOOLEY'S, 'TIL WE HAD BEER MONEY (AND WHILE I BOUGHT A 6, IVY USUALLY MADE OFF WITH A BIG OLE BOTTLE OF WINE). AND WE'D SIT IN THE BREEZE BY THE BAY, THE FREE AIR CONDITIONING, AND DRINK AND TALK ALL NIGHT. SOMETIMES WE'D JUST SIT BY THE METRORAIL AND SEE WHO OR WHAT HAPPENED TO COME ALONG. IT WAS SPRING IN LITTLE HAVANA, AND THE DAYS WERE MILD, THE NIGHTS WERE COOL AND I WENT TO SLEEP IN MY FREE APARTMENT EVERY NIGHT WITH A SMILE ON MY FACE...

THE POINT HERE IS THAT WE WERE PART OF A GOOD NEIGHBORHOOD. IT SEEMS LIKE SO MANY PUNKS MOVE INTO A NEW CITY OR PART OF TOWN AND JUST FIND OUT WHERE THE COOL CAFES ARE AND WHERE THE PUNK SHOWS ARE - JUST WHERE THEY CAN HANG OUT WITH OTHER PUNKS - AND DON'T REALLY SEE THEMSELVES AS PART OF THE COMMUNITY. I'M KINDA SICK OF HOW COOL ~~AND~~ ALOT OF PEOPLE THINK IT IS TO SAY "I'M FROM THE HARDEST STREETS OF OAKLAND", OR WHATEVER. MOST OF THE TIME ITS NOT REALLY EXACTLY TRUE. IF YOU GET OUT AND MEET PEOPLE, YOU MIGHT FIND YOU DON'T HAVE TO WASTE ALL YOUR ENERGY SCOWLIN' AND BEING TOUGH AND PUNK LOOKIN'.

OF COURSE, NOT EVERYONE IN THE COMMUNITY WAS GLAD TO HAVE US AROUND. THE MANAGER OF THE WOOLEY'S SUPERMARKET HATED US. HE THOUGHT WE WERE STEALING FROM HIM. OF COURSE WE WERE! HE JUST NEVER CAUGHT US. BUT HE DID CATCH US PANHANDLING INFRONT OF HIS STORE ONE TIME, SO HE'D ALWAYS SEE US AND YELL AT US. WE'D GO IN THE STORE AND HE'D FOLLOW US AROUND IN THE STORE, YELLING AT US. HE WAS FUNNY. AND REAL SHORT. WE CALLED HIM "EL POQUITO HOMBRE" (THE LITTLE MAN). THEN THERE WAS THE MANAGER OF THIS APARTMENT COMPLEX WHO KICKED ME OUT OF HIS POOL. I HAD JUST FINISHED SWIMMING AND WAS WASHING MY SHEETS AND BLANKETS IN THE COMPLEX'S LAUNDRY ROOM, WHEN HE RAN UP, SCREAMING AT ME IN SPANISH. I JUST KIND OF STARED AT HIM. THEN, HE TRIED TO PULL MY LAUNDRY OUT OF THE WASH AND THROW IT AT ME, BUT HE PULLED OUT THIS BIG HEAVY BLANKET AND JUST GOT WATER ALL OVER HIMSELF. HE KEPT YELLIN', ALL SOAKED NOW. I FINALLY JUST WALKED AWAY. I COULD NEVER FIGURE OUT WHY ~~THESE~~ PEOPLE GOT SO UPSET ABOUT SOME- ONE USING THEIR POOL, OR TABLE DIVIN' OR WHATEVER. THEY JUST START SCREAMING AT YOU AND YER PRETTY CALM ABOUT IT, AND THAT MAKES 'EM MORE UPSET. THEY'RE LIKE DOGS, THAT ARE CHAINED UP AND START BARKIN' HYSTERICALLY WHEN YOU WALK BY - LIKE ITS ALL REFLEX. THEY DON'T KNOW WHY THEY THINK YOU SHOULDN'T BE ABLE TO USE THE POOL, OR WHY THEY CARE. THEY JUST KNOW THE RULES...

ANYWAYS, OUR ARCHENEMY WAS IRONFACED MARTA MIERDA OF THE BRICKELL WENDY'S SALAD BAR PATROL. IVY AND I WOULD DRINK COKES AND PLOT STRATEGY AT WENDY'S AND MARTA WOULD RACE US TO THE HALF-EATEN BURGERS THAT PEOPLE LEFT BEHIND. I GUESS WE BEAT MARTA TO THE BAKED POTATO ONE TOO MANY TIMES, CUZ SHE COMPLAINED TO THE HEAD MANAGER, WHO THEN DECREED THAT THERE WOULD BE NO MORE REFILLS ON COKES DUE TO "NEW POLICY". I SEE... SO, I WENT IN THE TOILET AND TOOK A SHIT IN MY BIGGIE COKE CUP AND TURNED IT UPSIDE DOWN ON THE TABLE AND WE WENT OUTSIDE TO WATCH MARTA RUSH OVER TO GET IT. THE LOOK ON HER FACE WAS CLASSIC. IT WAS THE SHIT HEARD 'ROUND THE WORLD. IN AN HOUR, THE WHOLE HOOD KNEW ABOUT IT. WHEN YA GET THE TURD ON THE TABLE, YER THROUGH IN THIS TOWN. SO LONG, MARTA!

THE SHIT LIST (A SHORT LIST OF PLACES WHERE I'M "BANNED FOR LIFE")

3 separate Denny's!

The DENNY'S ON U.S.1, N.E. 2nd, AND on Coral Way (for table diving). BILTMORE HOTEL in Coral Gables. WASHINGTON SQUARE on South Beach for sneaking behind bar to steal pitchers of beer at Foryou show. POGUIES PIZZA on S.W. 7th AND 1st Ave for bein' scummy! We fucked up their new paint job. The next night, The fuckers. DADELAND MALL FOR TABLE DIVIN' AT Food Court. BRICKELL WENDY'S FOR SHITTING ON TABLE. YET Records for blatantly stealin' MRR, AND A putting obnoxious notes on the ad board about CEITGS and LOAD. ENTIRE CITY OF PLANTATION FOR FAILED 1991 COUP ATTEMPT. I can usually still go in all these places, though.

SCAM GUIDE TO DOWNTOWN MIAMI

FIRST OFF, YOU GOTTA MAKE SURE YOU GET SOME CAFE CUBANO. CACIQUE'S CORNER, AT THE DOWNTOWN BUS TERMINAL IS A GREAT SPOT, EVEN THOUGH THEY RAISED THE PRICE OF A COUPLA 2 BITS, TO 90¢. DRINK IT UNDER THE METRORAIL ND WATCH SAPS RUN FOR THE TRAIN, AND TAP INTO THE POWER OF **THE THIRD RAIL**! ON HE SOUTHWEST CORNER OF GOVERNMENT CENTER IS THIS HUGE, LAME SCULPTURE THAT'S SUPPOSED TO BE BROKEN BOWL, SURROUNDED BY ORANGE PEELS, WITH A FOUNTAIN IN THE CENTER. THE IS FEET TALL OKEN BOWL PIECES" ARE ACTUALLY SLIDES! RUN UP 'EM FULL SPEED, FLIP IN MID AIR, SLIDE WN! THE ORANGE PEEL IN THE CENTER OF THE FOUNTAIN IS A GOOD SPOT TO RELAX FOR A WHILE ND WATCH THOSE BIG, CRAZY BLACK BIRDS THAT FLY AROUND THE POINT AT THE TOP OF THE COURT OUSE. ITS THE ONLY BUILDING THEY FLY AROUND! MAYBE THEY'RE THE DOOMED SOULS OF BAD JUDGES, EINCARNATED! SORRY... ITS THE CUBANO TALKIN'... NOW, YOU CAN WAIT, OR RUN BACK FOR MORE COFFEE, 'D HEAD FOR THE ROOFTOPS. I NEVER MADE ONTO THE TOP O THE COURTHOUSE, CUZ THE TOP FLOORS ARE LLED WITH HUGE PIPES AND EXPOSED WIRES, AND THE ONLY WAY UP IS A LADDER! BUT ONE TIME, I AS GOIN' TO THE BATHROOM ON THE 33rd FLOOR, AND, I COULDN'T RESIST, I SCOOPED UP MY TURD AND VE IT A TOSS OUT DA WINDOW! COULDN'T WAIT TO SEE THE HEADLINES: "HUMAN FECES FALLS FROM URTHOUSE!" ACROSS THE STREET FROM THE WENDY'S ON N.E. 3RD AVE. IS A BUILDING WITH A SHOWER ON HEIR ROOF. I WAS GONNA TAKE ONE, BUT A MAN CAME AND SAID I HAD TO LEAVE. I WISH HE HAD CAUGHT ME J THE SHOWER... THE GUSMAN ART BUILDING HAS GARGOYLES ON THEIR ROOF, BUT YOU CAN'T SEE 'EM FROM THE REET AT ALL. SO WHY ARE THESE NICE STATUES UP THERE? WHAT ARE THEY DOIN' UP THERE?!? HERE'S ANOTHER SHOWER, AND A WHOLE LITTLE APARTMENT, ON THE TOP FLOOR OF A BUILDING ON E. 2ND STREET, ACROSS FROM THE RESTAURANT WITH ALL THE FLAMES PAINTED ON IT, AND THE OOF ACCESS IS ONE OF THOSE COOL, SECRET SPY STYLE HATCHES. NICK SMOKED POT W A BUM ON THE OOF OF THE MIAMI ARENA ONCE... THE WENDY'S SALAD BAR IS ONE OF THE LONGEST LASTING FREE OD SCAMS IN MIAMI. GOIN, GRAB A SALAD PLATE OFF A TABLE, AND EAT, EAT, EAT! YOU MIGHT BE ABLE TABLE DIVE AT BAYSIDE. YOU MIGHT FIND CHANGE IN THEIR FOUNTAIN. BIG DEAL. DON'T GO NEAR AYSIDE. JUST DON'T. A CRAZY PLACE TO EAT IS THE MANOLO Y RENE CAFE, THE ONLY 24 HOUR CAFE U DOWNTOWN. ITS PRETTY OPPRESSIVE. THE PLACE IS SO SMALL THAT THE GUY MAKES YER FOOD AND THEN AS NOWHERE TO GO, SO HE JUST STANDS OVER YOU WHILE YOU EAT! AND THE FOOD... THEY'RE THE LY PEOPLE THAT I'VE SEEN LITERALLY TRANSLATE "HOT DOG" INTO "PERRO CALIENTE" ON THEIR ENU, SO ITS PROBABLY REALLY DOG MEAT... THE RESTAURANTS INSIDE GOVERNMENT CENTER WILL USUALLY VE YOU FOOD WHEN THEY CLOSE. IF YOU GET SOME, GO DOWN THE ESCALATOR AND SHARE SOME WITH EITH, THE ONE LEGGED GUY (NOT TO BE CONFUSED W/THE ONE ARMED GUY), KEITH'S PRETTY TOUGH. THE METRO- OVER'S PRETTY COOL. EASY TO HOP (BUT ONLY 10¢), AIR CONDITIONED, HAS A GOOD VIEW ABOVE DOWNTOWN. GOOD ACE TO HAVE A PICNIC. OR PLAY PUNK ROCK. WHEN I PLAYED DRUMS IN THE FUNYUNS' JUNIOR AUXILIARY QUAD, ME AND STEVE WOULD PLAY ON THE METROMOVER, WITH A SNARE AND HIS GUITAR AND PORTABLE AMP. E WERE PRETTY POLITE ABOUT IT, LIKE WE'D PLAY A SONG AND A BUNCH OF PEOPLE'D GET ON, AND WE'D Y "ANYBODY MIND IF WE PLAY ANOTHER SONG?" AND SOME GUY WOULD GO, "UH... I KINDA MIND..." "OH ELL. OUT ON THE STREETS, WE WEREN'T SO POLITE, USING MAILBOXES AND PARKING METERS FOR PERCUSSION MAKING UP A SONG CALLED "WE'RE GONNA ROB THIS BANK!" IN FRONT OF A BANK, AND GETTIN' THE OT FROM THE MAN WHEN WE ROCKED THE COURTHOUSE STEPS... THE M-MOVER IS ALSO THE EASIEST AY ONTO THE METRORAIL FREE, CUZ THE GUARD IS ALMOST NEVER THERE AT THE BACK WHERE THE OVER LETS YOU OFF, AND IF HE IS, YER W/A BUNCH OF PEOPLE SO HOP ANYWAYS!

WELL, I'M PROBABLY A LITTLE OFF ON THE EXACT LOCATIONS OF THESE PLACES. AND I'M LEAVING LOT OF COOL STUFF OUT, LIKE THE KRISHNAS, AND THE BLACK MUSLIMS, AND DOWNTOWN AT DAWN HEN THE CITY COMES TO LIFE, AND THE FLAGLER STREET GRILL PEOPLE WHO HAND OUT THE "HOT FUDGE NDAE" FLYERS, AND McCRORY'S, BUT LIKE THE SONG SAYS, "ITS BETTER THAN T.V. AND THERE'S A HOLE LOT TO SEE, WHEN YER HANGIN' DOWNTOWN" SO GET DOWN THERE AND GET SOME CUBANO ND CHECK IT OUT FOR YOURSELF. IF YOU GET BORED, YOU CAN ALWAYS WALK UP TO VERTOWN AND LOOK FOR DRUGS ON THE GROUND.

THE LAST TEMPTATION OF IGGY SCAM

A COMPLICATED LOVE TRIANGLE, BETWEEN A MAN, A WOMAN, AND A BOXCAR...

LIFE, THE GOOD LIFE, IN BRICKELL CREPT ALONG FINE, UNTIL ONE DAY, SOMETHING WEIRD HAPPENED. ON ONE OF THOSE LONG WEEKENDS, WHEN IVY WAS UP IN BOCA SINGIN' AT TRI-RAILS PRACTICE, I KINDA MOVED INTO LESLIE, THE HIPPIE GIRL'S, HOUSE. IT HAPPENED PRETTY SUDDENLY. WE WALKED TOGETHER ON A SLOW SUNDAY NIGHT, EATING ORANGES AND SMELLING THE GREAT COOKING THERE IN THE NEIGHBORHOOD. WE DECIDED TO TRY AND SNEAK INTO THE CLOSED JOSÉ MARTI PUBLIC POOL. WE HOPPED A BUNCH OF FENCES, AND I WAS IMPRESSED AT HOW SHE WAS WAY BETTER AT HOPPING HUGE FENCES THEN ME. I GUESS IT WAS KIND OF ROMANTIC. WE WENT BACK TO HER HOUSE, AND ... UH, I WAS MOVIN' IN.

IT WAS ALL RIGHT AT FIRST. SHE TOOK ME ON A LATE NIGHT TOUR OF CREEPY SIMPSON PARK, SHOWED ME A HIDDEN TUNNEL UNDER A BRICKELL AVENUE BANK'S FOUNTAIN, AND MADE ME WALK ON THE UNCOMPLETED TRACKS OF THE NEW BRICKELL METROMOVER, WHICH WAS LIKE WALKING A CONCRETE PLANK, THAT WAS TILTED AT A 30° ANGLE, 30 FEET OFF THE GROUND, FOR 100 YARDS! IT WAS CRAZY, BUT SHE WAS RIGHT — NOW WE COULD SAY WE WERE THE FIRST PEOPLE ON IT.

HER, ME, AND IVY STARTED HANGIN' OUT A LOT. SOMETIMES WE'D GO TO JUMP ON THE TRAMPOLINE IN THE BACK YARD OF THIS HIPPY FAMILY'S HOUSE DOWN THE STREET. THESE PEOPLE ALSO HAD A GREAT OLD MIAMI HOUSE, TWO STORIES 'O CREAKIN' WOOD. WHEN YOU WENT INSIDE, YOU'D NOTICE THAT THERE WERE BEES EVERYWHERE! THEY LIVED IN THE WALLS! ONE TIME THEY'D CALLED AN EXTERMINATOR, BUT HE'D SAID THAT THE HOUSE WAS SO OLD THAT THE HONEYCOMBS WERE THE ONLY THINGS THAT KEPT THE WALLS TOGETHER! IT WAS BEES-VS.- TERMITES, SO THEY JUST DECIDED TO LIVE WITH IT ... SOMETIMES WE'D GO TO WOOLEY'S TO GET GINGER AND HONEY AND CINNAMMON FOR TEA AND TO GET YELLED AT BY EL POQUITO HOMBRE FOR AWHILE. AND SOMETIMES WE'D GO VISIT THE PEOPLE WHO LIVED IN THE BOXCARS.

BY THE MIAMI RIVER, WHERE MIAMI AVENUE CROSSES INTO DOWNTOWN, THERE'S A HUGE EXPANSE OF WEEDED THROUGH PARKING LOT WHICH ENDS WITH A 4-STORY WALL OF BOXCARS. PEOPLE LIVE IN 'EM! YOU'D SEE THEM, MOSTLY AT DUSK, DRIFTING FACELESSLY ACROSS THE SHADOWY LOT, INTO THE WEEDS AND OUTTA SIGHT. BUT, THEN, SOMETIMES THEY'RE OUT THERE PLAYIN' IN BROAD DAYLIGHT IN WATER FROM A HOSE. I HAD GONE DOWN THERE ONE NIGHT, AND THEY'D SENT A REPRESENTATIVE TO TALK TO ME. HE ASKED ME QUESTIONS ABOUT MYSELF IN BROKEN ENGLISH. PRETTY FRIENDLY. YOU WOULD BE, TOO, IF YOU WERE RAISED BY BOXCARS! SO, ME AND IVY AND LESLIE WENT DOWN TO TRY AND COMMUNICATE FURTHER WITH THIS BRAVE AND MYSTERIOUS RACE OF MEN. LESLIE HAD A CAMERA AND TOOK A PICTURE OF ME AND IVY AND T.P.W.L.I.T.B.C. BY THEIR CAMPFIRE. T.P.W.L.I.T.B.C. POSED, HOLDING UP A NEWSPAPER FRONT PAGE, WITH A PICTURE OF THE CUBAN FLAG ON IT AND POINTED TO IT, SAYING "NUMERO UNO!" IT WAS GOOD TO KNOW THAT NOW THAT I WAS LIVING IN LUXURY, AT LEAST SOME PEOPLE STILL HAD CRAZY HOMES...

BUT, IT WASN'T TOO LONG BEFORE MY NEW LIFE WITH LESLIE BEGAN TO SOUR. THERE WASN'T MUCH LEFT TO EXPLORE, AND IT TURNED OUT THAT WE REALLY DIDN'T HAVE ANYTHING IN COMMON. SHE TRIED TO TAKE ME TO THE PLANETARIUM TO SEE A LASER LIGHT SHOW! OH NO! IGGY, WHAT HAPPENED TO YOU?!? I WAS TRYING TO WRITE ISSUE #2, AND IT JUST WASN'T WORKING, AND I WAS GETTING FRUSTRATED, WITH THE ONE- YEAR ANNIVERSARY OF ISSUE #1'S RELEASE RAPIDLY APPROACHING. IT HAD BEEN A YEAR, AND I HAD NO AWESOME SQUAT, NO SCAMMED ELECTRICITY, NO... NO VICTORY! IT WAS CRAZY. HERE I WAS LIVIN' IN THE OLD MIAMI HIGH, WITH FREE FOOD, HOT SHOWERS AND EVEN A WARM BED, WITH A GIRL IN IT, BUT I WASN'T HAPPY. I WAS BORED AND LAZY. BRING BACK THE DIRT, THE BUSSES! WHERE'S MY DUMPSTER? I WANNA LIVE! I'D LAY NEXT TO HER IN BED AND THINK ABOUT T.P.W.L.I.T.B.C. MAN, IN A BOXCAR ALL YOU'D NEED WOULD BE

PICTURED ABOVE: THE PEOPLE WHO LIVE IN THE BOXCARS, HANGIN' IN THE BOXCAR ANNEX — THEIR FLOPPY OLE D.I.Y. HOUSE BY THE BOXCARS

A KEROSENE LAMP AND A MATTRESS AND YOU'D BE SET!

I KNEW THIS WOULDN'T GO ON MUCH LONGER. THE GIRL'S MOM HATED ME, AND LESLIE WAS MOVING TO CANADA TO GO TO COLLEGE IN A COUPLE WEEKS ANYWAYS. BUT I WANTED OUT. FINALLY, I KNEW WHAT TO DO. ONE SATURDAY MORNING, I BORROWED THE AXE FROM THE TOOLSHED AND MARCHED OFF IN BROAD DAYLIGHT TOWARDS THE MIAMI RIVER AND MY NEW HOME... THE BOXCARS! I WAS GONNA SPLIT ONE OF THE BOXCARS RIGHT OPEN AND THEN I WAS GONNA LIVE IN IT! THERE WAS NO STOPPIN' ME! I RESISTED THE TEMPTATION TO WANDER AROUND DOWNTOWN WITH THE AXE, AND, INSTEAD, PICKED OUT A NICE, BLUE BOXCAR AND WENT TO WORK.

I RAISED THE AXE HIGH AND... CLUNK! NOT EVEN A SCRATCH! I TRIED AGAIN, AND AGAIN, BARELY SCRATCHIN' AND IN NO WAY DENTIN' THE HUGE BOXCAR. A REPRESENTATIVE OF T.P.W.L.I.T.B.C. CAME OUT TO WATCH ME. AGAIN, NO LUCK. HE SHOOK HIS HEAD SLOWLY AND SADLY AND MOTIONED FOR ME TO COME BACK INTO THE ROWS WITH HIM. HE SHOWED ME THAT THE BOXCARS THEY LIVED IN WERE ALREADY OPENED BEFORE THEY EVER LIVED IN 'EM. HE WAS EXCITED THAT I WANTED TO LIVE WITH THEM, BUT THERE WERE NO MORE OPENINGS. BUT, HE SAID, THEY WERE GOOD TO SLEEP ON TOP OF. NO, NO. I COULN'T LIVE ON A BOXCAR. BAD FORM. THANKS ANYWAYS. I WALKED BACK TO LESLIE'S IN DEFEAT. OF COURSE, I THOUGHT. THE BOXCARS ARE MADE TO STAY TOGETHER IF THE TRAIN THEY'RE ON SOMEHOW DERAILS AT 80 M.P.H. NO AXE WAS GONNA GET ONE OF THESE OPEN. I WAS STUCK.

Dolor de Vida.
THE PAIN OF LIFE!!

HERE IT WAS AGAIN - CERTAIN DOOM. IVY'S MOM WAS GETTING EVICTED, AND LESLIE WAS LEAVING FOR COLLEGE IN CANADA. ON THE SAME DAY. ME AND IVY WOULD BOTH BE HOMELESS. I HAD A COUPLE DAYS WARNING, SO I WENT INTO RIGOROUS HOMELESS TRAINING, ON A DIET OF STALE BREAD AND PEPSI. YES, I HAVE TASTED POVERTY, AND EVEN FOUND IT SOMEWHAT AGREEABLE... ANYWAY, THE FATEFUL DAY CAME. ONE MINUTE, ME AND IVY WERE SAYING OUR GOODBYES TO LESLIE, AND, THE NEXT, WE WERE TRUDGING DOWN TO THE METRORAIL, WITH ALL OF OUR STUFF. AS LUCK WOULD HAVE IT, THE GRAY APARTMENTS WERE BOARDED UP THAT DAY, TOO, SO THERE WAS NO GOING THERE. IVY'S MOM HAD LEFT A NUMBER OF A FRIEND THAT SHE HOPED SHE'D BE ABLE TO STAY WITH, AND THEN, HADN'T BEEN HEARD FROM SINCE. WE HAD NOWHERE TO GO, AND NO IDEA WHAT TO DO, SO WE JUST SPRAWLED OUT IN THE MIDDLE OF THE RUSH HOUR METRORAIL TRAFFIC, AND PEOPLE, WISELY, GAVE US A WIDE BERTH. ONLY H.E.L.L. DARED SPEAK TO US. WE TOLD HIM OUR STORY AND HE THOUGHT IT' OVER FOR A MINUTE, THEN PRODUCED A BOTTLE OF POWERFUL, PINK PILLS FROM OUT OF HIS IRON MAIDEN JACKET. HE GENEROUSLY POURED 28 OF THE PILLS INTO MY HAND, WISHED US LUCK, AND WENT HOME. THANKS, H.E.L.L.

WE GOT A SHOPPING CART. IT WAS A BIG MOMENT FOR US, OUR FIRST CART. IF YOU'RE BUMMED OUT THAT YOUR MOHAWK AND PIERCINGS AREN'T ALL THAT SHOCKING THESE DAYS, YOU SHOULD GET A SHOPPING CART AND PUSH ALL YOUR STUFF AROUND IN IT. PEOPLE MOVE OUTTA YOUR WAY.

WE PUSHED OUR CART TO IVY'S MOM'S FRIEND'S HOUSE TO SEE IF IVY COULD FIND HER MOM. AFTER A LOT OF KNOCKING THE DOOR OPENED A CRACK, AND THIS MEAN, FAT LADY GROWLED, "YOUR MOM'S NOT HERE!" AND SHUT THE DOOR. AFTER MORE KNOCKING, WE GOT HER TO TELL US THAT IVY'S MOM HAD 1) HAD HER CAR, WITH MOST OF HER STUFF IN IT, STOLEN, AND, 2) HAD BEEN BITTEN BY A VERY RARE AND POISONOUS SPIDER AND HAD HAD TO GO TO THE HOSPITAL! FUK! TALK ABOUT BORN TO LOSE! IVY ASKED IF THE MEAN, FAT LADY COULD SPARE ANY BLANKETS, CAUSE WE HAD TO SLEEP ON THE STREETS TONIGHT, BUT SHE SLAMMED THE DOOR ON US. THINGS WERE GETTING WORSE AND WORSE. WE PUSHED OUR CART UP TO WOOLEY'S AND IVY WATCHED IT, OUTSIDE, WHILE I WENT IN TO CHANGE A FOODSTAMP FOR MONEY FOR THE PAYPHONE. WHEN I CAME OUT, SHE WAS CRYING! SHE SAID THAT THE POQUITO HOMBRE HAD COME OUT AND YELLED AT HER. I RAN BACK IN THE STORE AND SHOUTED AT HIM, "HEY! WHAT THE FUCK DID YOU DO TO HER?!? "...ETC., AND WE STARTED YELLIN' IN EACH OTHER'S FACES, WHILE THE WHOLE STORE STOPPED IN SHOCKED SILENCE TO WATCH. HE TOLD ME TO LEAVE THE STORE. I THREW A SHOPPING CART AT HIM. IT WAS AN UGLY SCENE. THE SUN HAD NOW SET ON LITTLE HAVANA, AND WE SLOWLY PUSHED OUR CART DOWN CORAL WAY IN THE DARK, WITH IVY SNIFFLIN', THE CART RATTLIN', AND THE LITTLE OLD LADIES IN THE NEIGHBORHOOD CROSSIN' THEMSELVES AND MUTTERIN' AS WE ROLLED BY.

AH... THINGS WERE BAD. ON 8TH STREET, THEY CALL IT "DOLOR DE VIDA" - THE PAIN OF LIFE. WE PUSHED OUR CART 'TIL WE GOT TO A SALVATION ARMY CLOTHING DROP BOX THAT WAS OPEN WITH CLOTHES SPILLIN' OUT. WE STARTED TO HALFHEARTEDLY PICK THROUGH THE CLOTHES, BUT THEN I SAID, "HEY! LET'S SLEEP IN THIS!" IT WAS PRETTY FUNNY, LIKE MY OLD JOKE WHERE I'D POINT TO A "MYSTERY BOX" ON THE SIDE OF THE ROAD AND SAY, "HEY, I KNEW A GUY WHO LIVED IN ONE OF THOSE FOR 6 MONTHS!" WELL, THE OLD JOKE ABOUT DOLOR DE VIDA, THAT IVY SAYS, IS YA GOT TO WALLOW IN IT. LIKE - ITS 100° AND YER WALKING 10 MILES WITH 100 POUNDS OF STUFF? PUT ON A SWEATER AND SUCK ON ROCKS! SO WE SLEPT IN THE DROP BOX. IT WAS COMFY, LIKE A BIG LAUNDRY HAMPER AND IT WORKED. IN THE MORNING, WE WOKE UP WITH NEW FREEDOM, THE KIND NORMALLY ONLY ENJOYED BY PEOPLE WHO TALK TO THEMSELVES AT BUS STOPS. WE WERE ON THE OTHER SIDE... WE SWAM, DRANK BEER, AND STAYED UP THE NEXT NIGHT ON HELL'S PILLS.

THE NEXT DAY, WE WERE WALKING TO DOWNTOWN IN THE MORNING WHEN THE PEOPLE WHO LIVE IN THE BOX CARS WAVED US OVER AND GAVE US A BOX OF ASSORTED HOLIDAY COOKIES. CRAZY FROM THE PILLS, WE TOOK 'EM WITHOUT QUESTION AND TRIED TO GIVE THE COOKIES TO BUSINESSMEN. I: WANT A COOKIE? B: (BLANK STARE) I: SURE YA DON'T WANT A HOLIDAY COOKIE? B: WHAT'S THE HOLIDAY? I: ENEMA DAY, SAP! (HURLS COOKIE AT BASE OF NAZI'S SKULL!) THEN, DOWNTOWN, THERE WAS A SMALL PARADE GOING ON. WE FILED IN AT THE END OF THE PARADE AND YELLED "FREE COOKIES!" AND TOSSED 'EM OUT. PEOPLE WOULD LUNGE AND FLAIL AND LEAP TO CATCH 'EM, BUT THE COOKIES USUALLY CRASHED IN FRONT OF THEM. I EVEN WHIZZED A COUPLE BY THIS SURLY LOOKIN' COP'S HEAD! WE HAD GONE FROM TOTAL BUMS TO THE STARS OF A DOWNTOWN MIAMI PARADE IN JUST A COUPLE MINUTES! IT WAS ANOTHER PUNK ROCK SUCCESS STORY! AH... IF ONLY THE PEOPLE WHO LIVED IN THE BOXCARS COULD SEE US NOW!

Pt. 2: THE 22 HOUSE

THE 22 HOUSE, A 2-STORY, ABANDONED BUILDING, ON THE CORNER OF S.W. 22nd STREET AND S.W. 22nd AVE, WAS OUR FIRST REAL SQUAT SUCCESS STORY. I LIVED THERE WITH IVY AND ROBW FOR A COUPLE MONTHS. IT WAS A GOOD HOME WITH LOTS OF CRAZINESS, ALL GUIDED BY THE MYSTERIOUS... "POWER OF 22".

LIKE, ONE TIME, I FOUND A NEARLY BRAND NEW PAIR OF SHOES IN THE MEDIAN OF
DOUGLAS ROAD. THEY WERE SIZE ELEVEN. TWO ELEVENS EQUALS... 22!!!
IT WAS THE POWER OF 22! NEED I SAY MORE?

← ↗ THE 22. HOUSE

FROM THE FIRST NIGHT, IT WAS CRAZY. WE WERE WALKING AROUND, TALKING ABOUT HOW WE NEEDED MATTRESSES, AND WE TURN A CORNER, AND THERE'S 2 HUGE MATTRESSES, PERFECTLY GOOD, ON A TRASH PILE! YO! 22! WE PUT THE MATTRESSES ON OUR BACKS AND RAN THROUGH 4:00 AM STREETS WITH THEM, SO WE CAN GET BACK WITHOUT MEETING ANY COPS. FUCK THE LAW! A COUPLE NIGHTS LATER, ME AND ROBIN FOUND AN ENORMOUS COUCH AND PUSHED IT ACROSS TOWN ON A SHOPPING CART, AND DRAGGED IT UP THE STAIRS. THEN, ON THE WEEKEND OF THE COCONUT GROVE BED RACES, WE WALKED AROUND WITH A SHOPPING CART, FINDING ALL KINDS OF AMAZING TRASH PILES IN THE UPPER CLASS 'HOODS BETWEEN 22 AND THE GROVE. AFTER A COUPLE HOURS, WE HAD ALL THE STUFF OUR SQUAT NEEDED — FORKS, SPOONS, CUPS, A COOLER, A SIGN THAT SAID "THIS HOME PROTECTED BY ROLLINS" AND A BLUE HORSE-ON-A-STICK NAMED MILO. WE RODE MILO AROUND THE AFTERMATH OF THE BED RACES AND GOT A TON 'O FREE FOOD THAT THE VENDORS WERE THROWING OUT, AND THEN WENT TO CELEBRATE OUR NEW HOME BY SWIMMING IN THE 22 HOUSE FOUNTAINS. THE 22 FOUNTAINS WEREN'T ACTUALLY IN 22. THEY WERE INSIDE THE MAYFAIR MALL. WE PARKED OUR SHOPPING CART AND DOVE IN! IT WAS A GREAT SWIM, LOOKIN' UP THROUGH THE WATER AT THE FOUNTAINS AND THE GAWKING SHOPPERS AS YOU SWAM UNDER 'EM, THEN WE DECIDED TO RELAX IN THE 22 JACUZZI. THE 22 JACUZZI IS ACTUALLY LOCATED INSIDE THE MAYFAIR HOTEL. GO TO THE 2ND LEVEL OF THE MALL AND LOOK FOR THE SPIRAL STAIRCASE THAT'S BLOCKED FROM MALL ACCESS BY A SLITTED WOOD PANEL. DISCREETLY SQUEEZE AROUND THE PANEL AND YOU'RE IN. TELL 'EM IGGY SENT YA... THEN WE USED THE 22 PHONE TO CALL FRIENDS IN CALIFORNIA TO TELL 'EM ABOUT OUR GREAT, NEW HOME. THE 22 PHONE, FREE FOR PUNKS, IS RIGHT THERE AT THE BAR. OH, DIAL '9' TO GET OUT...

I GUESS I SHOULD TELL MORE ABOUT WHAT LIFE WAS LIKE INSIDE OF THE 22 HOUSE.

WE DIDN'T HAVE ELECTRICITY, AIR CONDITIONING, OR RUNNING WATER, BUT WE DID HAVE PLENTY OF LOVE, CANDLES, AND CHEAP WINE...
THE FIRST THING WAS TO PUT ON OUR OWN LOCK. THAT GUY, ERNST, FROM JACK ACID, PICKED THE OLD LOCK FOR US, AND WE STOLE A NEW ONE TO PUT ON THE IRON GATE IN ONE OF THE DOORWAYS IN THE ALLEY. WE NAILED A SWINGING BOARD IN THE DOORWAY THERE, SO YOU'D UNLOCK THE GATE AND SWING THE BOARD OVER AND LOCK THE DOOR AND SQUEEZE IN. THE BOTTOM FLOOR WAS LIKE ONE HUGE ROOM WITH NO WALLS AND A LOT OF DUST AND PIGEONS. WE LEFT THIS EMPTY, AND LIVED MORE HIDDEN ON THE 2ND FLOOR. UP THE RICKETY STEPS, DUCKIN' THROUGH THE WRECKED DOORWAY, DOWN THE NARROW, DARK HALLWAY, PAST THE MYSTERIOUS, FADED "NO VALUES" AND "MY WAR" GRAFFITI (HAD PUNKS LIVED HERE BEFORE?) THROUGH THE HOLE WRECKED IN THE WALL, IN THE TWO BACK ROOMS. IN THE FIRST ROOM, THERE WAS OUR COUCH, THE D.I.Y. CARD PLAYIN' TABLE (WOOD ON STACKED MILK CRATES), THE BOOK SHELVES FULL OF BOOKS AND ZINES, THE CHAIRS STOLEN FROM THE UNIVERSITY OF MIAMI, AND THE "WINDOW" — A CRACK BETWEEN THE BOARDS WHERE THE SUN LEAKED IN. IN THE

SHIT 2 DOO ...

1) Destroy!
2) Get stuff for squat: ~~lock, lock,~~ lock, rug, mattress, hammer, nails for screen, drapes, #10 wire, circuit breaker, soap, table, trashcan + trashbags, shelves/furniture etc
3) ~~Talk to Victoria 'bout Xeroxing at her place~~
4) ~~Get blank tapes~~
5) ~~See if outdoor plugs work by Frenchy's/Put show together~~
6) ~~Get lock and take off wood door~~
0) ~~Go to the beach, Get Food Stamps~~

New Shit 2 DOO!
1) Annihilate This week.
2) ~~Get Lock~~
3) ~~Remove Door (wooden)~~
4) ⊘ Do Zines
5) ~~Get Hammer~~/Put up Screen
6) Look for Mattresses
7) Get more milk crates
8) Do July 8th Flyers
9) Socks
10) Shoes
11) Test Plugs by Frenchy's/Do show
12) Blank tapes
13) TRY BOLT CUTTERS OUT
14) TRY Coke Machine Scam
15) ~~Get New Spray paint~~
16) ~~Headphones for walkman~~
17) Circuit Breaker/screwdriver/#10 wire etc
(8) Table for Rooftop
(9) Get Mail
20) ~~Get new tires~~ ~~Practice of Mom's~~ ~~(if I get tires)~~
21) Dress for Success
22) Fly to Geneva for Accords
23) EAT MORE FIBER
MUST EAT MORE DAMN FIBER

ABOVE: 22 ERA "THINGS TO DO" LIST.
BELOW: THE 22 PISSBUCKET©

NO DUMPING
POLICE ORDER   MAX. FINE $500.⁰⁰

THE PISS BUCKET, PORTRAIT OF THE ARTIST AS A YOUNG FREAK, AN ODE TO CISCO, ETC... LIFE IN 22 CONTINUED... ↓

NEXT ROOM WAS OUR MATTRESSES, CLOTHES, TOOLS, AND PILES OF USELESS DUMPSTERED SHIT. THIS ROOM WAS WALLPAPERED WITH BUS SCHEDULES OF THE CITY OF MIAMI. I WAS OBSESSED WITH GETTING EVERYONE OF 'EM, AND I'D JUST STAND BACK AND LOOK AT 'EM IN DISBELIEF, ALL THOSE BUSSES GOIN' INTO EVERY CORNER OF MIAMI, AND BEYOND, TO CRAZY PLACES LIKE GOULDS AND OPA-LOCKA. MY FAVORITE WAS WHEN THE #36 BUS AND THE #54 CAME OUT WITH A SPLIT SCHEDULE ON RED PAPER. THERE WERE ONLY 1,000 MADE!

IN THE CLOSET, IN THE ADJOINING HALL, WAS THE MIGHTY 22 HOUSE PISS BUCKET. THE PISS BUCKET© WAS A BUCKET WITH A TOILET SEAT THAT WE WENT TO THE BATHROOM IN. TO KEEP IT FRESH, WE POURED LYSOL AND AMMONIA IN IT, AND CHANGED ITS WATER, AND POLISHED IT, AND TALKED SOOTHINGLY TO IT, AND LIT CANDLES FOR IT, AND STUFF. AND IF YOU THREW A PENNY IN IT AND MADE A WISH, IT WOULD INVARIABLY COME TRUE. LONG LIVE THE PISS BUCKET! THESE DAYS, NOW THAT THE PUNK SQUAT THING IS REAL BIG, YOU SEE KIDS TAKING THEIR PISS BUCKETS ON THE BUS AND STUFF, OR AT THE SHOW WITH SHINY, NEW PISS BUCKETS THAT THEIR MOMS BOUGHT FOR 'EM, BUT, IN THOSE DAYS, THERE WAS NO GLAMOUR IN IT, I CAN TELL YOU. STILL, WE DID HAVE A CANDLE BY THE 22 HOUSE PISS BUCKET, SO YOU COULD RELAX AND RELIEVE YOURSELF BY CANDLELIGHT. AFTER ALL, WE WERE NOT SAVAGES.

THE 22 HOUSE WAS MY FIRST HOME IN MIAMI, AS IN MY PLACE, A PLACE I WANTED TO BE, AND NOT SOMEONE'S COUCH OR FLOOR. I'D GET DRUNK AT MY FRIEND, SIR ROBERT, THE CRAZED, PUNKROCK GENIUS OF COCONUT GROVE HOUSE AND HE'D SAY, "YOU CAN CRASH HERE IF YOU WANT," BUT, MORE OFTEN THAN NOT, I'D WALK 30 BLOCKS TO 22, DRUNK, TO BE HOME. STILL, THERE WERE A COUPLE DISCOMFORTS. FIRST, THERE WERE THE MOSQUITOS THAT CAME IN GREAT SWARMS, LIKE A BLACK FOG, EVERY NIGHT, NO DOUBT TRYING TO GET DRUNK OFF THE CISCO IN OUR BLOOD. WE TRIED ALL MANNER OF ELABORATE SCHEMES TO GET RID OF 'EM, FROM NAILING UP SCREENS OVER THE "WINDOW", TO MAKING IVY DRESS UP IN A BIG MOSQUITO SUIT TO TRY AND LEAD THEM AWAY. OK. I MADE THAT UP. ANYWAY, IT TURNED OUT BURNING A LITTLE CITRANELLA SCARED 'EM OFF, SO THAT WAS SOLVED. BUT THE FLORIDA SUMMERTIME HEAT WAS RELENTLESS. WE SLEPT AND WALKED AROUND NUDE, OR NEXT TO IT, TO COOL OFF. HMM... LOOKING BACK, I GUESS A BUNCH OF NAKED, SMELLY KIDS, HANGIN' OUT IN AN ABANDONED BUILDING SEEMS KINDA WEIRD, BUT IT WAS FUN, TRUST ME. ONE TIME, I WAS COLLATING (THAT'S A BIG WORD THAT ZINE EDITORS THROW AROUND) 50 COPIES OF SCAM #1, RUNNING ALL ACROSS THE ROOM, BENDING AND STOOPING FOR PAGES, ETC. AFTER ABOUT 5, I WAS DRENCHED WITH SWEAT, SO I DID THE OTHER 45 TOTALLY NUDE, WONDERIN' WHAT WOULD HAPPEN IF THE COPS RAIDED THE PLACE AT THAT VERY MOMENT TO FIND THIS TOTAL FREAK, SWEATIN', NUDE, IN A PILE OF PAGES SAYIN' "FUCK SHIT UP!" LIKE, WHAT WOULD THEY CHARGE ME WITH.

I GUESS THE LIVING CONDITIONS OF 22 WERE A LITTLE PRIMITIVE BUT YOU HAVE TO LEARN TO LAUGH A LITTLE TO GET BY, YA KNOW I MEAN, PEOPLE ALWAYS TREAT SQUATTING LIKE IT HAS TO BE THIS SERIOUS, POLITICAL STATEMENT, AND ARE ALWAYS MAKING CLENCHED FISTS AND GOIN' ON ABOUT "THE STRUGGLE" THIS AND "THE STRUGGLE" THAT, BUT I REFUSE TO BE SOMBER AND DRAMATIC ABOUT IT, OR EVEN TO TRY AND MAKE IT SEEM TO BE MORE DIFFICULT THAN IT ACTUALLY WAS, FOR MY OWN GLORY. WE WERE HAVING FUN. THE 22 HOUSE DAYS WERE DAYS OF COOL SWIMMING POOLS AND BLACK BEANS AND RICE, AND GOOD, LOCAL PUNK SHOWS, AND THE GOLDEN AGE OF CISCO, WHEN THE WORDS "LIQUID CRACK" STILL CAPTURED A MAN'S IMAGINATION... IT WAS EXCITING TO LIVE ALL GANG-STYLE IN A PLACE THAT EVERYONE CARED FOR AND WORKED TOGETHER ON. IVY AND ROBIN DREW BIG PICTURES ON THE WALLS. ROBIN BROUGHT HOME A BRAVE PLANT THAT WE STRUGGLED TO KEEP ALIVE. WE PLAYED CARDS BY CANDLELIGHT AND NURSED PIGEONS WITH BROKEN WINGS BACK TO HEALTH AND SWEATED AND SIPPED CISCO AND THINGS WERE GOOD. IT WASN'T LIKE SOME STUPID, CRUSTY BAND'S RECORD COVER WITH US THROWING BOTTLES AT THE COPS ALL THE TIME. IT WAS ABOUT HOUSING. WE NEEDED IT. WE TOOK IT. WE HAD NO ILLUSIONS ABOUT THE 3 OF US TAKING ON THE CITY OF MIAMI POLICE FORCE, SO WE WERE STEALTHY, VIET-CONG STYLE. I THINK THAT WHOLE "FIGHTING THE COPS" THING TENDS TO MAKE YOU WORRY TOO MUCH ABOUT COPS, ANYWAYS — MAKES YOU SEE THEM AS HAVING ALL THE POWER AND YOURSELF WITH NONE. WELL, IT SEEMS LIKE PEOPLE ARE ALWAYS READY TO GET IN LINE TO TELL YOU YOUR DREAMS WON'T COME TRUE, BUT YOU WON'T HEAR IT FROM ME. WHAT I LEARNED FROM SEEING 22 GROW INTO A HAPPY HOME, IN THE DEPTHS OF AN ABANDONED BUILDING, IS THAT YOU REALLY CAN DO ANYTHING.

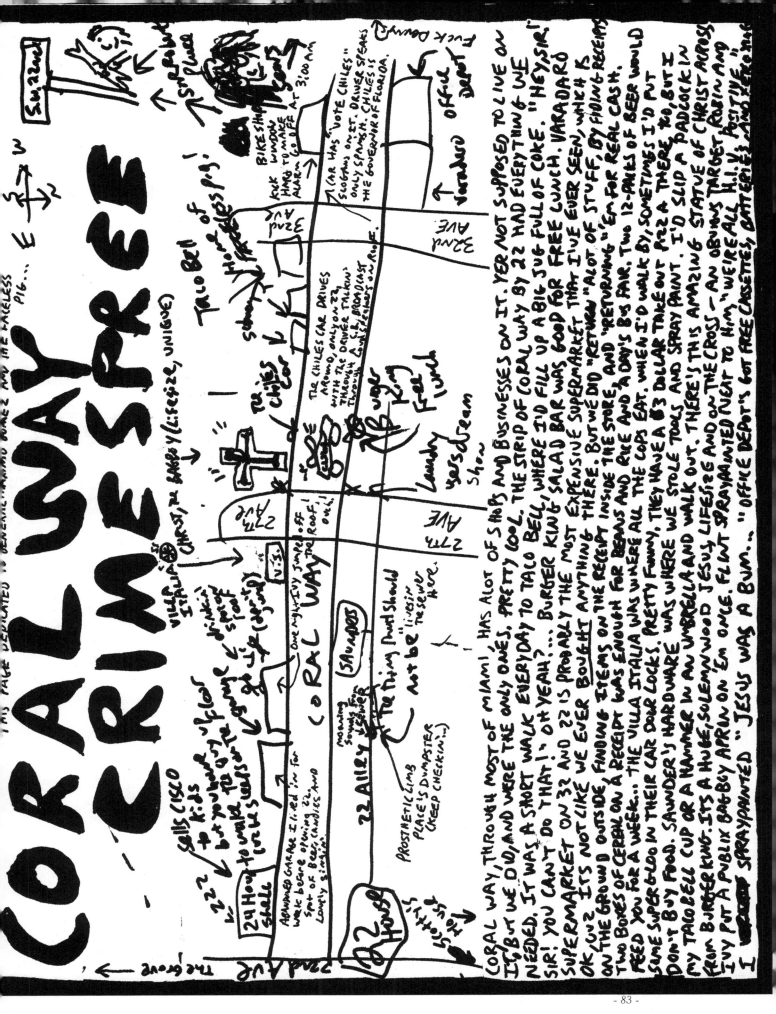

CORAL WAY CRIME SPREE

THIS PAGE DEDICATED TO GENERAL TOMMAND GOMEZ AND THE FACELESS PIG... E → W

Labels around the map:

SW 22nd

↑ STREETLIGHT PLACE
↑ STREETLIGHT PLACE

SELLS CISCO + KIDS ↓ BUT YOU WANT TO GO TO A GAY BAR FOR DRINKS ↓ (IN THIS WALK SW TINY SLOWLY)

24 HOUR STORE

ABANDONED GARAGE I LIVED IN FOR A WEEK BEFORE OPENING 22 LONELY SIMBAD.

VILLA ITALIA — CHRIST, THE BARGY (LIFESIZE, UNIQUE)

TACO BELL

ONE NIGHT IVY JUMPED OFF ROOF! OW!

V.S.

CORAL WAY

SAUNDERS

22 ALLEY

MORNING SONGS FOR SEWER

THE THING PANT SHOULD NOT BE "LIVE" IN TRESEVE HERE.

PROSTHETIC LIMB PLACE'S DUMPSTER (KEEP CHECKIN')

R2 HOUSE

S. 1 HOUSE

↑ SUBWAY

BIKE SHOP

KICK WINDOW HARD TO MAKE ALARM GO OFF AT 3:00 AM

32nd AVE

27th AVE

CAR HAS "VOTE CHILES" SLOGANS ON IT. DRIVER SPEAKS ONLY SPANISH. CHILES IS THE GOVERNOR OF FLORIDA.

THE CHILES CAR DRIVES AROUND, ONLY ON 22, WITH THE DRIVER TALKIN' THROUGH A P.A. BROADCAST THROUGH 4 OR 5 SPEAKERS ON ROOF.

BURGER KING FREE LUNCH

LAUNDRY 35¢/DREAM SHOW

FUCK DONNIE

FUCK DONNIE

← VARADARO

← OFFICE DEPOT

CORAL WAY, THROUGH MOST OF MIAMI, HAS ALOT OF SHOPS AND BUSINESSES ON IT, BUT WE DID, AND WERE THE ONLY ONES. PRETTY COOL. THE STRIP OF CORAL WAY BY 22 HAD EVERYTHING WE NEEDED. IT WAS A SHORT WALK EVERYDAY TO TACO BELL, WHERE I'D FILL UP A BIG JUG FULL OF COKE. "HEY SIR! YOU CAN'T DO THAT!" OH YEAH?... BURGER KING! SALAD BAR WAS GOOD FOR FREE LUNCH. VARADARO SUPERMARKET ON 32 AND 22 IS PROBALY THE MOST EXPENSIVE SUPERMARKET THAT I'VE EVER SEEN, WHICH IS OK, CUZ IT'S NOT LIKE WE EVER BOUGHT ANYTHING THERE. BUT WE DID "RETURN" ALOT OF STUFF, BY FINDING RECEIPTS ON THE GROUND OUTSIDE, FINDING ITEMS ON THE RECEIPT INSIDE THE STORE, AND "RETURNING" 'EM FOR REAL CASH. TWO BOXES OF CEREAL ON A RECEIPT WAS ENOUGH FOR BEANS AND RICE AND A DAY'S BUS FARE. TWO 12-PACKS OF BEER WOULD FEED YOU FOR A WEEK... THE VILLA ITALIA WAS WHERE ALL THE COPS EAT. WHEN I'D WALK BY, SOMETIMES I'D PUT SOME SUPER-GLUE IN THEIR CAR DOOR LOCKS. PRETTY FUNNY. THEY HAVE A $3 DOLLAR TAKE OUT PIZZA THERE TOO, BUT I DON'T BUY FOOD. SAUNDER'S HARDWARE WAS WHERE WE STOLE TOOLS AND SPRAY PAINT. I'D SLIP A PADLOCK IN MY TACO BELL CUP OR A HAMMER IN AN UMBRELLA AND WALK OUT. THERE'S THIS AMAZING STATUE OF CHRIST ACROSS FROM BURGER KING. IT'S A HUGE, SOLEMN/WOOD JESUS, LIFESIZE AND ON THE CROSS—AN OBVIOUS TARGET. ROBIN AND I PUT A PUBLIX BAG-BOY APRON ON 'EM ONCE. FLINT SPRAYPAINTED NEAR TO HIM, "WE'RE ALL H.I.V. POSITIVE." I ████ SPRAYPAINTED "JESUS WAS A BUM..." OFFICE DEPOT'S GOT FREE CASSETTES, BATTERIES, AND XEROXING.

I HATE THE USERS!

THE STORY OF THE 22 HOUSE BAND

SO, THINGS WERE GOOD. WE WERE CRIMINALS WITH A GREAT HIDEOUT. WE DECIDED TO PAY TRIBUTE TO THE "POWER OF 22" BY CARVING "22" IN OUR ARMS WITH A RAZOR, AND BY STARTING A BAND TOGETHER. IVY WOULD SING, ROBIN WOULD PLAY BASS, I WOULD PLAY DRUMS AND, MY DRINKING PARTNER, ANDY POWELL WOULD PLAY GUITAR. ANDY COULD BE IN OUR BAND, CAUSE HE WAS THE ONLY PERSON WHO DIDN'T ACTUALLY LIVE IN 22 WHO HAD DARED TO STAY THE NIGHT THERE. HE WAS ALSO THE ONLY ONE WHO COULD ACTUALLY PLAY AN INSTRUMENT. OUR BAND WAS CALLED **THE USERS**.

WE WENT TO WORK ON THE USERS RIGHT AWAY. ROBIN MADE GREAT PATCHES THAT SAID, "I HATE THE USERS!" ON 'EM. I MADE A COUPLE USERS T-SHIRTS WITH BLANK, WHITE T-SHIRTS AND MAGIC MARKERS. WE DRANK A LOT OF BEER AND CISCO AND TAGGED "THE USERS" ON THE METRORAIL, AND DID EXTENSIVE GRAFFITTI ON THE ALLEY BEHIND SAUNDER'S HARDWARE. BEIN' IN THIS BAND WAS FUN. NOW, WE JUST NEEDED TO BORROW EQUIPMENT AND WRITE SONGS...

FINALLY, WE WERE ABLE TO SNEAK PRACTICE TIME AT THE END OF TRI-RAIL'S PRACTICES. IT WAS SO EXCITING WHEN OUR SONGS CAME TOGETHER. WE WERE BETTER THAN THE CLASH! WE WERE BETTER THAN BLACK FLAG! WE WERE THE USERS, DAMMIT! WE HAD 3 SONGS.

THE FIRST SONG WAS "I HATE THE USERS!" IT WAS ABOUT CHUCK LOOSE. HE HATED THE USERS. WELL, FINE. THE 2nd SONG, I NEVER KNEW THE TITLE OF, WE CALLED IT THE FIRST SONG. THE THIRD SONG WAS A COVER OF "WILD IN THE STREETS", AN OLDIE, BY A LESSER BAND. WE SANG IT LOUD AND PROUD FROM OUR DRINKIN' SPOT, THE ROOF ACROSS THE STREET FROM 22. OUR DREAM WAS TO BE THE FIRST PUNK BAND TO PLAY AT THE LAVENDERIA (LAUNDRY MAT) ON THE CORNER OF S.W. 27th AVENUE AND CORAL WAY.

FINALLY, WE GOT TO PLAY AT THE JACK ACID/CHICKENHEAD/TRI-RAILS SHOW IN GAINESVILLE. ROBIN WAS SO FUCKED UP, SHE FORGOT TO TURN ON HER AMP. I WAS SO DRUNK THAT I COULDN'T KEEP UP AND THE SONGS JUST GOT PROGRESSIVELY SLOWER ~~AS THEY~~ LIKE, DURING THEM! ANDY KEPT PLAYING HUSKER DÜ SONGS, DURING AND BETWEEN OUR SONGS. "WILD IN THE STREETS" CAME OUT OK. THE CROWD WAS SILENT WHEN WE WERE THROUGH, OBVIOUSLY STUNNED BY OUR BRILLIANCE.

THE NEXT DAY, IN MIAMI, AT THE PUNK ROCK PICNIC, OUR SHOW WAS MORE SMOOTH, WE PLAYED ALL THE SONGS. A REVIEW OF THE SHOW APPEARED IN A NOW FOR-GOTTEN LOCAL ZINE: "THE USERS WERE GOOD, BUT 3 SONGS WAS ALL I COULD TAKE." WELL, THAT ZINE WAS GOOD, BUT OBVIOUSLY ONE ISSUE WAS ALL I COULD TAKE. AFTER THAT, WE KIND OF FELL APART. ROBIN WENT SOLO, ANDY WENT KRISHNA.

← IVY JOINED THE STONE TEMPLE PILOTS, AND I HOPELESSLY TRIED TO KEEP THE NAME OF THE BAND ALIVE, TO KEEP THE BEER AND PILL MONEY ROLLIN' IN. STILL, WE HAVE A C.D COMING OUT THIS MONTH OF RARE UNRELEASED TRACKS. VIVA LA USERS!

THE LYRICS TO "I HATE THE USERS"

I HATE THE USERS, (AND THEY HATE ME — LOCK 'EM UP IN JAIL AND THROW AWAY THE KEY (2x) SNIFFIN' GLUE HAS WRECKED THEIR BRAINS, THEY BUY CHEAP WINE WITH MY SPARE CHANGE (2x) ON THE METRORAIL, THEY PLAY BLACK FLAG AND SHOOT UP SMACK AND PISS ON THE FLAG

I HATE THE USERS (2x)

THEY SIT NEXT TO ME ON THE BUS, THEY'RE ALL COVERED WITH SHIT AND PUSS THEY SPRAY PAINT ON THE WALLS AT SCHOOL, THEY THINK CHARLES MANSON'S COOL!

WHAT ABOUT POLITICS?

ANARCHY | PORNOGRAPHY | HOMOSEXUALITY

LITTLE HAITI, CHURCHILL'S, THE STUN GUNS AND YOU!

Inappropriate d... personal hygiene. Some chil... may be rejected because they dress oddly, bathe infrequently, pick their noses in public or have other unacceptable habits.

LITTLE HAITI

One of the greatest things about livin' in 22 was wakin' up on the days when there was a show, especially if my band or Ivy's band was playin'. ~~It was a good vacation~~ It was a good vacation to lay around til late afternoon, and then take the 9 or 10 bus up from downtown and walk around Little Haiti til people started to show up at the show. I enjoyed the whole combination of wakin' up in an abandoned building, takin' the bus, appreciating someone else's neighborhood, and then going to the show feeling kinda more connected to everything around me. It seemed very honest, like I wanted to live in the city and see how things were there, and this was it.

I'd buy a 50¢ George "The Champion" Prince soda at Neptune Bros. and walk around checkin' out voodoo dolls in botanicas and the old Lemon City post office. One time, me and John Dania and Ghislaine walked around lookin' for a place they could get dinner at. We went into a restaurant and asked for a menu and the man there kind of shrugged and motioned us into the kitchen where he pointed at several large pots on the stove. "We got this, we got some of this, we got some that, this and that." They ordered this and that, over rice.

The coolest thing would be leaving the show to walk around for a minute and turning a corner and seeing this huge political demonstration goin' on like two blocks from Churchill's with the streets all blocked off and people cookin' up food and drummin' and dancin' and givin' speeches somewhere in there "U.S. Out of Haiti.", sayin' the CIA started the coup there, demanding political exile for the refugees rotting at the Navy bases in Guantonomo Bay. It was a brave neighborhood all bustin' out with a Friday night block party revolution! YO! People, especially the "professional" bands that played Churchill's, would always put it down and say it was in a shitty neighborhood, but this just wasn't true, and these crazy demonstrations were a good example of that. It IS one of the poorest neighborhoods in one of the poorest cities in the U.S., but when you walk around there, you won't be threatened by an army of malt liquour thugs all spillin' out of alleys. There's no sound of gunshots. There's probably the only 24 hour laundromat with no security guard in the whole city right there on 2nd ave. Little Haiti's a tough, tight knit community, way down there on the bottom of Miami, and the U.S., and just about everybody's political totem pole, all proud and defiant and out in the streets.

After a while, I'd head over to the show. When I say the show, I mean Churchill's Hideaway, cuz that's where all the shows were then, or all the good ones, anyways. Churchill's was this total dive bar that let kids in. At first, they only booked punk bands on Friday the 13th, but I guess, after a couple Chickenhead shows, no one else would play there, and the punks took over! There were other shows, like Washington Square on Miami Beach was where all the "pro" style L7's and Dwarves and Mighty Bosstones would play, and where all the old school Miami Hardcore kids went to scowl and sneer and pay 13 bucks to get beat up by the vicious bouncers. But the Churchill's bands couldn't get shows at any of those places anyway, or when we did, like when Kreamy 'Lectric Santa played the Blue Marlin Sports Bar, or when Chickenhead played the Junkyard, the OWNERS of the clubs wanted to beat us up!!! Fuk! Well, we didn't want those shows anyways. We didn't want "independant management" or to be part of the "scene". We just wanted to have fun. Plus, Churchill's shows were always free.

Churchill's was what every brave little strugglin' scene needs: a place where the bands that can't play can, uh, try to or, at least, yell all smart ass and spit and throw shit at each other. Bands sprang up outta nowhere, like The Tri-Rails, who played their first show without a guitarist. And '77 style Start, whose drummer, Dori, couldn't really play, but would kinda crazy flail at the drums, then top it off by screaming at the top of her lungs at the end of the song. And Crawl --slow, heavy Crawl (now called Cavity) who as of this writing have managed to tour and put out a record without playing a single note-- just feedback and drums and yellin' and pain all Crawlin' along.

SORRY NO POLITICS DOOD.

It was a total trash and burn style attack on old school Miami. Anything could happen at a Churchill's show. Where else could you see a band like The Tri-Rails, with bassist, Timmy all nude, and guitarist Doug the Slug dressed like Barbara Bush and Kathleen standin' on her head and Ivy havin' to read the lyrics outta her notebook? Where else could you see Chuck Loose drive his motorcycle up onto the stage? And what about Kreamy 'Lectric Santa? They had 3 singers, a violin, AND a rapper! Yo!

And there was the truly drunk and unpredictable STUN GUNS, The Stun Guns, led by singer/ guitarist Paul Enema played some of the greatest shows I ever saw. On one Friday the 13th, they were so drunk that they could barely stand, but still knocked out some great, two guitar punk, while the bar erupted into a huge trash fight, with balls of paper and cups and beer flyin' all over and Paul Enema's so drunk, he's laughin' and drops his guitar and uses the mike stand to support himself and just sings, and even the dumb, fat English guy who runs the place is walking around smiling, handing out flyers to wad up and throw at ole Enema. I went home and I could not sleep! Man, the STUN GUNS had it all. Besides great songs, they had personality. Paul Enema was the closest thing that Miami had to a punk rock hero. Like, I was in Gainesville once, and all these girls were like "Yer from Miami? Do you know Paul Enema?" He had good lines like you'd go "Hey Paul, you guys playin' tonight?" and say "I hope not." And he wrote cool lyrics like in their song "Hitman" where he says "I've got a briefcase full 'o blues" and in "Hiroshima" where Paul warns "Don't hang around if you can't take it". Paul was also a hero, cuz he was 25, still lived with his mom, and spent all day drinking beer and watching "The Godfather" on video. Guitarist Marky Awesome was totally into Johnny Thunders right down to the cigarette danglin' from his mouth while he played those crazy leads. He also wrote their song "Rockslinger" which started off "I could rock before I could walk". During the week, he worked at a toy store. Bassist, George Kelly was the total bachelor guy, with a fridge full of old taco bell nachos and his fellow bums all passed out drunk on his floor in a pile of comics and newspaper clippings from the Miami Dolphins' Perfect Season. And drummer, Andy, was the youngest, sort of a loser-in-training, drinking a lot of Cisco, sleeping on people's floors, and hanging out with me. Yes, the STUN GUNS were the true trash, well on their way to 30, goin' nowhere fast, but at Churchill's, they were heroes. Actually, everybody was, kinda.

Well, eventually, the guy who ran the place wanted money, which we didn't have, and he wouldn't let underage kids in anymore, so that was the end of it. We had great shows there from August '91 to July '92, and ya know, except K.L.S. and Harry Pussy, not one of the lame alternative bands on the Live at Churchill's CD, would ever be caught dead at one of our shows. Even the HUMAN ODDITIES, who got their start as goofy kids at Churchill's, were were above us now, in the glamorous Miami Music Scene. God, ya know, it used to be that a band had to go country or something to sell out, but now even punk bands are full of young business-men. Sheesh.

Now, I see that Churchill's has started an all ages night, run by the old school. I went to check out a show there and the old Miami tension was back. The singer of the band on stage was all muscle-bound, flexin' and Hardcore, and I yelled, "Put yer shirt back on. man!!! " and all these people looked at me nervously, like, uh oh, that guy's talkin' shit" and cleared away from me. A little later, I went up between songs and gave the singer these boxing gloves that me and Ivy had found and he seemed real offended and said, "I used to be a boxer!" Great. It was pretty depressing. I also went to the AVAIL show. Every once in awhile, someone books an out of town band at Churchill's hoping that the owner won't be around and the kids can get in. Then you get there, and he's checking I.D.'s at the door and there's like 50 kids out front who can't get in. So the AVAIL show got moved to the Cavity wherehouse, and turned out real good with all these people crammed in this tiny spot, and somehow, a keg. I liked AVAIL. They had this guy with them who just kinda jumped around and did flips while the band played, kinda neat, like goin' to the circus or something.

So, I guess the days of great shows at Churchill's are over. But there's still shows in Little Haiti, and I rode my bike by one a couple days before I left Miami. It was crazy. The streets were all blocked off and totally filled with people. The crowd was gathered around 4 or 5 drummers who were standing on a small raised platform in front of a restaurant. Presently, there was no music, and one of the drummers was yellin' into a microphone, givin' an impassioned speech about the evils in our society, and how we could all unite and fight together, and rise above, and beat the cops, or whatever. He went on and on, and the crowd got more and more restles until a couple wise guys started yellin' at em, somethin' in creole, probably "Yeah, yeah, enough already. Shut up and play!" I guess some things are the same everywhere. The drummer guy kinda shook his head and laughed and leaped on his drums, and the crowd roared, and started dancin' and jumpin' and all 54th Ave jerked around like a big, crazy snake. There was all kinds of laughin' and singin' and even free food, and totally helpless lookin' cops. It was a great show...

CHURCHILL'S WAS...

THESE STRIPES DRAWN BY IVY →

55TH AND 2nd NOT 53rd AND 3rd.

CHURCHILL'S WAS THE FUNYONS PLAYING A COUPLE SONGS ONSTAGE THEN DECIDING TO GO PLAY OUTSIDE AT THE PARKING LOT "SINCE EVERYONE WAS LEAVING ANYWAYS..."

CHURCHILL'S WAS KILLER KANE PLAYING ENDLESS FEEDBACK TO A NEAR EMPTY BAR FOR NEARLY 45 MINUTES 'TIL THE CRAZY OLD BRITISH BARMAID YELLED,

"TURN OFF THAT BLOODY NOISE!!!"

CHURCHILL'S WAS JOAQUIN, THE HOMELESS GUY OUTSIDE, WHO WOULD DRAW PICTURES OF PEOPLE FOR SPARE CHANGE, ONLY HE DREW YOU SO WEIRD AND WRONG AND TERRIFYING, THAT YOU'D END UP PAYING HIM NOT TO DRAW YOU...

CHURCHILL'S WAS BUYING THE $1.98 6 PACKS OF MEISTERBRAU AT THE SABAL PALM SUPERMARKET, THAT SELLS TO ANYBODY, AND SNEAKING YER OWN BEER INTO THE BAR...

CHURCHILL'S WAS WAKING UP THE NEXT DAY WITH THE "CHURCHILL'S HANGOVER" FROM ALL THAT MEISTERBRAU AND FINDING THE WEIRD PICTURE THAT JOAQUIN DREW OF YOU IN YOUR POCKET AND REALIZING HE WAS DRAWING YOU LAST NIGHT AS YOU'D LOOK NOW!!!

CHURCHILL'S WAS SILVIO SINGIN' "BLITZKRIEG BOP" IN SPANISH ON STAGE WITH CHICKENHEAD. CHURCHILL'S WAS DRINKIN' IN THE PARKING LOT AT THE NEW YEAR'S EVE TRASH MONKEY'S REUNION, AND SEEIN' THIS WOMAN AT THE BOTANICA ACROSS THE STREET MAKE THIS HUGE, SMOKY FIRE IN THE DOORWAY RIGHT AT MIDNIGHT...

CHURCHILL'S WAS GETTING THERE LATE AND SEEING PEOPLE RUNNIN' FROM THE CLUB WITH THEIR HAND OF THEIR OVER THEIR EARS, AND KNOWING THAT CRAWL MUST BE PLAYING.

CHURCHILL'S WAS GETTING REAL DRUNK AND HUNGRY AND STEALING AND EATING LIKE 10 BAGS OF CHIPS FROM THE RACK BY THE SOUNDBOARD.

CHURCHILL'S WAS ABSOLUTELY NO ONE KNOWING HOW TO RUN THE SOUNDBOARD. THE "CHURCHILL'S SOUND" WAS FROM SIR ROBERT TRYING...

CHURCHILL'S WAS NOT REALLY CARING THAT YOU SAW THE SAME BANDS EVERY WEEK, AND NOT NOTICING THAT THE SAME PEOPLE WERE IN ALL THE BANDS...

THE TRI-RAILS
← WERE...
Left to Right
Timmy-BASS
Scotty-DRUMS
IVY - BASS SINGIN'
KATHLEEN SINGIN'
DOUG THE
SLUG - GUITAR

THINGS WERE SO GOOD SOMETIMES, livin' in 22, That I couldn't sleep. Like one Night right when we moved in, me and Ivy, were hangin' out, AND PEOPLE KEPT GIVING US STUFF. LIKE YET RECORDS GAVE ME THE NEW MISTER T EXPERIENCE RECORD, OR AT LEAST THEY DIDN'T TRY AND STOP ME WHEN I WALKED OUT THE DOOR WITH IT. THEN, WE WERE CHECKIN' TABLES AT THE BLUE SKY COMIDA POR LIBRE, WHEN SOME GUY BOUGHT IVY A HUGE MEAL. BLACK BEANS. RICE. PLANTANOS. WANT AN IRONBEER WITH THAT? YO! THEN, WE WERE BUMMIN' A QUARTER FOR THE PAYPHONE, AND SOME OTHER GUY GIVES US A 5 DOLLAR BILL! SO WE GO TO ALLEN'S PHARMACY/CAFE ACROSS THE STREET FOR COFFEE. WE GOT A LITTLE MONEY, WAITER. RELAX. KEY LIME PIE AND COFFEE AND A MILKSHAKE THE PLACE CLOSES AT 10:00, BUT THEY DON'T ASK US TO LEAVE. THEY LOCK EVERYONE ELSE OUT, AND THE COOL OLD WAITER GUY— HE'S WORKED THERE FOR 30 YEARS, HE SAYS— HE KEEPS THE REFILLS COMIN'. MORE COFFEE? JUST FOR US.

WE TAKE THE LAST #40 BUS, AND DECIDE TO WALK AROUND ALL NIGHT. DOWN ON 8TH STREET, I GET A BIG GULP OF COFFEE FOR A FOODSTAMP AT 7-11, AND WE DECIDE TO CHECK OUT THE SCENE AT VELVET CREME. THEY MAKE ALL THE VELVET CREME DONUTS IN MIAMI THERE AT THE LITTLE HAVANA V.C., AND THE ONE VELVET CREME TRUCK COMES AND LOADS UP AROUND ONE OR TWO, AND THE DRIVER DRINKS A BUNCH OF COLADAS AND DELIVERS TO CONVENIENCE STORES ALL NIGHT. FOR SOME REASON, THERE'S ALWAYS A BUNCH OF BOXES OF DONUTS LEFTOVER AND YOU CAN TAKE 'EM AND SNEAK IN THE SIDE DOOR WITH YOUR 7-11 COFFEE AND WATCH THE OLD CUBAN GUYS ARGUE AND LAUGH AND SMOKE CIGARS ALL NIGHT. THERE'S SOME PRETTY HEATED DEBATE AND DRAMATIC ORATORY THERE AT THE V.C. 'ROUND 3:30, YES... IF ONLY I KNEW WHAT THEY WERE SAYIN'... SO, WE WATCH THE MEN LOAD THE TRUCK AND WAIT FOR THE LEFTOVERS, BUT THEN A GUY WHO WORKS THERE SEES US AND COMES OVER AND SAYS SOMETHING IN SPANISH AND GIVES US 3 BOXES OF DONUTS! 36 FREE DONUTS. WE SIT INSIDE AND EAT A COUPLE AND THEN HE COMES OVER, AND GIVES US 2 MORE BOXES, AND 2 DOLLARS. WE'RE PRETTY STOKED, BUT DECIDE TO LEAVE QUICKLY BEFORE HE CAN GIVE US ANYMORE...

WE HEAD DOWN CALLE OCHO TOWARDS IVY'S MOM'S PLACE, STOPPIN' TO SAY HI TO THE HOOKERS ON 33rd. WANNA DONUT? "NO THANKS, HONEY. BUT CAN YOU SPARE A CIGARETTE?" OF COURSE. IVY GIVES 'ER A SMOKE AND WE WALK 'TIL WE DECIDE TO FUCK UP THE ARMY RECRUITER'S OFFICE JUST OFF 27TH. HAD TO WAIT A WHILE FOR

UP ALL NIGHT STORIES 🌐
SCAM IS A 24 HOUR FANZINE

[LAYOUT SMASHOUT]

THE STREET TO CLEAR CUZ ONE GUY KEPT TROLLIN' BY, LEERIN' AT US, AND TURNIN' AROUND. HEY! WE'RE NOT GONNA HAVE SEX WITH YOU, GUY, SO GET LOST SO WE CAN TRASH THIS GOVERNMENT BUILDING! SHEESH! SOON, THE COAST IS CLEAR, SO I SPRAY PAINT ALL OVER IT AND HIDE THE PAINT IN ONE OF THE DONUT BOXES, AND WE LEAVE. YES, WE DO MORE BEFORE 9:00 AM THAN MOST PEOPLE DO ALL DAY... IVY DECIDES TO CRASH AT HER MOM'S, BUT I'M TOO WIRED, SO I HEAD DOWNTOWN. ON THE WAY, I DO A "SCAM PUNKS IN LITTLE HAVANA" GRAFFITI WITH THE SCAM PUNK GUY DRINKIN' A 64 OZ. COLADA. THEN, ON THE BRIDGE WHERE 12TH AVE. GOES OVER THE MIAMI RIVER, I FOUND A LADDER THAT GOES ALL THE WAY DOWN TO A PLATFORM ON THE WATER, WHERE YOU CAN SIT WITH YER FEET IN THE WATER AND SEE THE WHOLE DOWNTOWN SKYLINE RISIN' OUTTA THE RIVER. JUST DON'T LEAVE YER FEET IN THE WATER TOO LONG.

I WALKED ON TO DOWNTOWN, SINGIN' A BIT. THE CITY WAS MINE. IT WAS THAT MAGIC TIME, THE FOUR-SOMETHIN', NO-MAN'S LAND BETWEEN WHEN THE BARS CLOSE AND WHEN THE MIAMI HERALD TRUCKS SNEAK OUT TO CHANGE THE HEADLINES. THERE WAS NO ONE OUT BUT ME AND A BUNCH OF STRAY DOGS, WHO WERE ON A MISSION, ALL RUNNIN' AND PANTIN' BY ME, NO TIME TO TALK, NO. WHO DO STRAY DOGS ANSWER TO? NO ONE !!!

I TOOK MY TIME WALKIN', WRITIN' ON OVERTOWN WALLS, POKIN' IN TRASH PILES, AND GOT TO THE DOWNTOWN BUS TERMINAL JUST WHEN CAGIQUE'S CORNER OPENED. I BOUGHT A COLADA AND SAT AGAINST A WALL WATCHIN' THE BUSSES START THEIR DAILY CIRCLIN' AND THE SLEEPIN' MASSES STUMBLIN' OUT IN A MUDDY, GRAY LIGHT. THEY LOOKED PRETTY BEAT.

I GOT ANOTHER COFFEE. WELL I STILL HAD ALL THESE DONUTS TO DEAL WITH... SO I MADE A HUGE SIGN THAT SAID, "TELL ME A JOKE AND I'LL GIVE YOU A DONUT!" AND SAT BETWEEN THE TERMINAL AND THE METRORAIL. A BUM GUY CAME UP, ALL HESITANT, "UH... SAY, MAN... LEMME GET ONE OF THEM DONUTS OFF YA." WELL, ORDINARILY, I'D JUST GIVE THIS GUY A DONUT, AND MAKE THE WORKERS TELL JOKES, BUT OUT OF PRINCIPAL, I SAY, "NO, YA GOTTA TELL A JOKE." HE LOOKED PRETTY PAINED. "HOW 'BOUT A DIRTY JOKE?" WELL, OK, I'LL BITE. "OK. MY BROTHER WAS ON A BICYCLE, AND HE... HE... FELL OVER IN A MUD PUDDLE!" HUH? "A MUD PUDDLE, SEE? A DIRTY JOKE..." SHEESH. HERE'S YER DONUT, GUY. GET LOST...

WELL, AFTER THAT, CAN YOU BELIEVE I SAT FOR TWO HOURS AND NOT ONE PERSON TOLD ME A JOKE? THEY MOSTLY WALKED BY AND IGNORED ME. SOME STOPPED, READ THE SIGN, AND THEN IGNORED ME! I GUESS SOME THINGS ARE SO FAR OUT OF PEOPLE'S EVERYDAY LIVES, THAT THEY SEE IT, BUT IT DOESN'T REGISTER IN THEIR MINDS. LIKE, "OH THERE'S A GUY WALKIN' DOWN THE STREET IN A BANANA SUIT. OH, I'M LATE FOR WORK." I LEFT THE SIGN AS A REMINDER OF HOW MUCH LIFE COULD BE AND WALKED AROUND GIVING AWAY THE DONUTS TO MY FELLOW BUMS...

I WAITED FOR THE #8 BUS, RIGHT BY THE "SCAM PUNKS WAITIN' FOR THE #8 BUS" GRAFFITI, AND THEN PICKED UP MY MTX RECORD FROM IVY'S MOM'S PLACE AND WALKED BACK TO 22, READY TO SLEEP. BUT WHEN I GOT THERE, I COULD SEE THAT SOMEONE ELSE HAD BEEN IN THERE! DID SOMEONE BREAK IN?!? IVY WAS AT HER MOM'S AND ROBIN WAS STAYIN' AT TONY'S... DID SOME OWNER PERSON COME IN?!?

I RAN UP THE STAIRS TO OUR ROOM, AND THERE WERE PLANTS THERE ON THE WINDOWSILL AND A NEW SHELF AND AND PILES OF WEIRD STUFF, LIKE DUMPSTERED SECURITY GUARD UNIFORMS... THERE WAS A NOTE. ROBIN AND TONY HAD STOPPED BY TO BEAUTIFY THE PLACE! AND I WAS THINKIN' MAYBE 22 HAD A LIFE OF ITS OWN, AND WAS GOIN' ABOUT BEAUTIFYIN' ITSELF... I FELL BACKWARDS ON THE SMILIN' AND BOUNCIN'... AH, THE POWER OF 22... FUCK SLEEP! I GOT UP INSTEAD, AND WENT SWIMMIN' AND TOOK THE #22 BUS TO SCOTTY'S TO TRY FOR ANOTHER 24 HOURS AWAKE...

WHILE I'S WRITIN' THIS UTRILLO AND HIS FRIENDS WENT TO THROW ROTTEN AVOCADOS AT BANKS AND THEY BROKE A WINDOW AND HAD TO RUN AWAY FAST

I ALWAYS TELL PEOPLE THAT SCAM IS A "PUNK ROCK FANZINE." BUT I REALLY DON'T WRITE ABOUT MUSIC TOO MUCH. STILL, MUSIC, WAS A HUGE PART OF OUR LIVES. BOTH IVY AND I WERE IN BANDS. EVERYTHING WAS ALWAYS TOTALLY CRAZY, LIKE "MONDAY: GET KICKED OUT OF NEW SQUAT. TUESDAY: SLEEP IN CLOTHING DROP BOX BY SIDE OF ROAD. WEDNESDAY: MARCH IN PARADE IN DOWNTOWN MIAMI. THURSDAY— BREAK INTO NEW SQUAT. FRIDAY: PLAY SHOW." THE BAND GOT ME THROUGH IT ALL. BEIN' ON STAGE, I'D THINK, "WOW, NO ONE KNOWS THAT I WOKE UP IN AN ABANDONED BUILDING TODAY." IT MADE ME WONDER WHAT LIFE WAS LIKE FOR ALL THE OLD PUNK BANDS THAT I LISTEN TO. WHERE'D ALL THAT HISTORY GO? LIKE, WHAT DID THE CLASH DO EVERYDAY, ~~BUT~~ BESIDES WHEN THEY WERE STANDING AROUND, TRYING TO LOOK COOL? AND WHAT ABOUT THE RAMONES? WERE THEY ALWAYS JUST LEANING AGAINST SOME WALL SOMEWHERE, WITH THEIR LEATHER JACKETS ON? OR WERE THEY OUT WORKIN' SHIT JOBS, OR SELLING DRUGS, OR HAVING DOOMED ROMANCES, OR IN THE FOOD STAMP LINE, OR, WHATEVER, SOMETIMES, TOO?

I REMEMBER PLAYIN' A REAL GOOD SHOW, AND THEN GOIN' TO STAY THE NIGHT AT NICK'S AND TELLING HIM ABOUT IT IN THE DARK, CUZ HIS ELECTRICITY HAD BEEN SHUT OFF, AND WAKING UP TO THE POUNDING ON THE DOOR — WE NEVER ANSWERED IT, CUZ THE ONLY PEOPLE WHO KNOCKED ON NICK'S DOOR WERE THE LANDLORD AND NICK'S MOM AND THEY BOTH ONLY CAME OVER TO YELL AT US... I REMEMBER THAT IF IVY DIDN'T SHOW UP TO TRI-RAILS PRACTICE, YOU'D GET WORRIED THAT SHE'D BEEN CAUGHT, SHOPLIFTING. AND ONE TIME SHE WAS, AND SHE STOLE HER "DADE COUNTY JUVENILE DETENTION ENTER" T-SHIRT AND WORE IT, NOT JUST ON STAGE, BUT ALL THE TIME... I REMEMBER TRYING TO SLEEP IN A METER ROOM THE NIGHT BEFORE THE FIRST CHICKENHEAD SHOW EVER, AND FAILING, BECAUSE OF MOSQUITOS, SO I WENT TO THE PARTY WE WERE SUPPOSED TO PLAY AT, CROWBAR AND ALL, AROUND 12 HOURS TOO EARLY, AT 9:00 A.M., AND WAITED UP ALL DAY TO PLAY... HMMM. MAYBE I DIDN'T WRITE ENOUGH ABOUT THE BAD TIMES. OR JUST THE ORDINARY TIMES. BUT, EITHER WAY, IT WAS ALWAYS FALLING APART, AND MUSIC WAS THE ONLY CONSTANT THING THAT WE HAD.

IT WASN'T ALWAYS NON-STOP VICTORY IN 22. A LOT OF TIMES, ME AND IVY FOUGHT. IT WAS LIKE BEIN' BACKSTAGE WITH THE SUPERHEROS. LIKE WE ALWAYS DID WHAT IT TOOK TO KEEP THE SQUAT GOIN', BUT, WITH ALL THAT HEAT, AND ALL THAT ATTITUDE, IT WAS INEVITABLE. WE FOUGHT. BUT WE DIDN'T FIGHT, THE DAY I BROUGHT HOME THE RADIO.

ITS ALMOST ANOTHER "UP ALL NIGHT" STORY, BECAUSE I'D HAD TO STAY UP ALL NIGHT FOR A FOODSTAMP APPOINTMENT, BECAUSE NO TRUE PUNK COULD GET OUT OF BED EARLY ENOUGH TO GO TO THOSE THINGS. I WENT TO DENNY'S AND THERE WAS IVY, JUST BACK FROM A HITCHIN' TRIP TO GAINESVILLE. AT THE SQUAT, SHE TOLD ME THE WHOLE CRAZY STORY AND I REMEMBER THINKIN' HOW COOL IT WAS THAT SHE WAS GETTIN' ALL RAD AND CRAZY, BUT, HOW MUCH I WISHED SHE'D STAY AROUND, BECAUSE THE SQUAT WASN'T THE SAME ALONE. HE WENT TO SLEEP, AND I STAYED UP, WATCHIN' THROUGH THE CRACK IN THE WINDOW FOR THE FIRST #24 BUS, CUZ, THEN, ACCORDING TO THE BUS SCHEDULE-WALL PAPER, IT WAS 5:13, AND TIME TO HEAD TO MY APPOINTMENT ON SOUTH BEACH. THEN, I WAS GOING TO BUY THE NEW RADIO I'D RECEIPT SCAMMED AND SAVED UP FOR, FOR WEEKS. WHEN I LEFT, I WROTE A NOTE, AND LOOKED AT IVY SLEEPIN' THERE AND JUST FELT REAL GOOD, CUZ I KNEW HOW HAPPY SHE WAS GONNA BE WHEN SHE SAW THE NEW RADIO.

I HAGGLED WITH THE GUY AT THE FLEA MARKET, AND GOT THE RADIO CHEAPER. I HAD 3 BUCKS, SO I BOUGHT A 6 PACK, STOLE A 6, STOLE BATTERIES AND HOPPED THE RAIL HOME AND PUT THE RADIO ON OUR CARD TABLE AND WOKE IVY UP. IT WAS GREAT, LISTENING TO RICHARD HELL AND X AND THE STUN GUNS, IN OUR OWN HOME. IT WAS LIKE THE LAST THING WE NEEDED. I FELL ASLEEP, DRUNK AND SMILIN', AND WHEN I WOKE UP IT WAS DARK, BUT THE RADIO WAS BLASTIN' THE ADVERTS AND IVY WAS WHISTLIN' AND SWEEPIN' AND HAD TOTALLY CLEANED THE SQUAT! IT WAS SUCH A SWEET MOMENT, IT JUST FELT SO HOMEY. THE TERMITES COULD CAVE IN THE FLOOR AND THE BOTTLES WOULD ALL EMPTY AND THE CANDLES ALL WOULD GO OUT AND THE COPS COULD RAID AT ANY TIME, BUT OUT OF THE DARK, OUR MUSIC KEPT PLAYIN'...

A COUPLE OF WEEKS LATER, AT CHURCHILL'S EVERYTHING JUST FELL APART. BEFORE THE SHOW, IVY AND ROBIN ANNOUNCED THAT THEY WERE LEAVING THAT NIGHT ON A ROAD TRIP TO NEW YORK, AND THEN, WE'RE GOING TO CALIFORNIA, AND WEREN'T COMING BACK. THEN, THE CHURCHILL'S OWNER SUDDENLY SAID 'THERE'D BE NO MORE ALL AGES SHOWS AFTER THAT NIGHT. MY BAND WAS IN SAD SHAPE, BUT WE TOOK THE STAGE AS A TWO-PIECE — JUST ME ON GUITAR AND CHUCK SINGIN'. CHUCK SET HIMSELF ON FIRE ON STAGE, AND THE PLACE WENT CRAZY, AND SUDDENLY, CHUCK WAS BEIN' RUSHED OUT TO THE HOSPITAL, EVERYONE HAD TO LEAVE AND IVY AND ROBIN WERE LEAVING TO NEW YORK. IT WAS SUCH AN EXCITING SHOW, BUT THINGS LOOKED BLEAK WITH IVY'S BAND BROKE UP AND MY BAND ON THE ROCKS AND NO PLACE TO PLAY. WE HAD SO MUCH OF OUR PLANS WRAPPED UP IN THE MUSIC.

NOW, 22 WAS OVER, THOUGH I DIDN'T REALIZE IT 'TIL THE COPS CAME AND WOKE ME UP ONE DAY. THIS WAS FUNNY, ACTUALLY, CUZ I SLEPT NUDE. THEY RESPECTED THE WORK WE'D DONE, BUT GAVE ME A COUPLE HOURS TO GET MY STUFF AND LEAVE. MY FRIEND, FLINT, DROVE ME AND MY STUFF TO THE OLD GRAY APARTMENTS. I RIPPED OFF THE LOCK, AND THOUGHT THINGS WOULD BE OK WITH A GOOD BUILDING, AND I COULD LIVE ANYWHERE WITH A RADIO AND A MATTRESS. BUT I WAS ALONE. THE NEIGHBORHOOD HAD CHANGED. I LIVED IN SILENCE. ASTIN' NO SHADOWS AND HEARIN' NO ONE CALL MY NAME. AFTER A COUPLE WEEKS, I WANTED OUT. THEN I CAME HOME AND FOUND THE NEW PLACE RANSACKED. THE RADIO HAD BEEN STOLEN. I KNEW NOW THAT IT WAS TIME TO LEAVE. THE MUSIC WAS GONE...

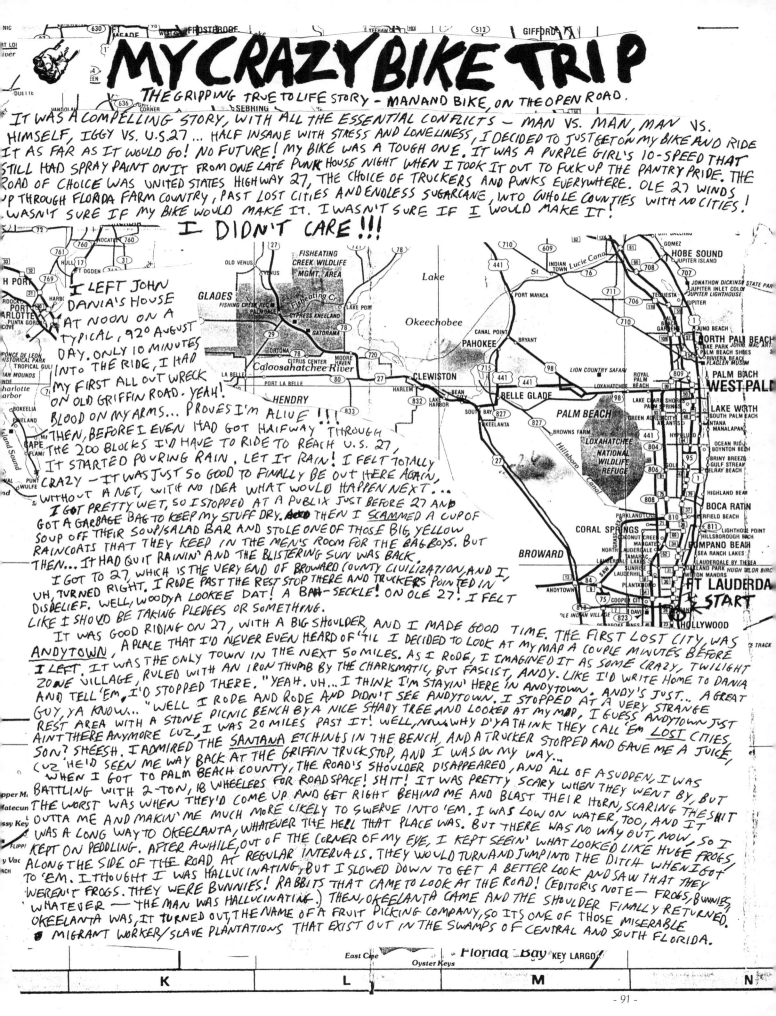

MY CRAZY BIKE TRIP

THE GRIPPING TRUE TO LIFE STORY - MAN AND BIKE, ON THE OPEN ROAD.

IT WAS A COMPELLING STORY, WITH ALL THE ESSENTIAL CONFLICTS — MAN VS. MAN, MAN VS. HIMSELF, IGGY VS. U.S. 27... HALF INSANE WITH STRESS AND LONELINESS, I DECIDED TO JUST GET ON MY BIKE AND RIDE IT AS FAR AS IT WOULD GO! NO FUTURE! MY BIKE WAS A TOUGH ONE. IT WAS A PURPLE GIRL'S 10-SPEED THAT STILL HAD SPRAY PAINT ON IT FROM ONE LATE PUNK HOUSE NIGHT WHEN I TOOK IT OUT TO FUCK UP THE PANTRY PRIDE. THE ROAD OF CHOICE WAS UNITED STATES HIGHWAY 27, THE CHOICE OF TRUCKERS AND PUNKS EVERYWHERE. OLE 27 WINDS UP THROUGH FLORIDA FARM COUNTRY, PAST LOST CITIES AND ENDLESS SUGARCANE, INTO WHOLE COUNTIES WITH NO CITIES! I WASN'T SURE IF MY BIKE WOULD MAKE IT. I WASN'T SURE IF I WOULD MAKE IT!

I DIDN'T CARE!!!

I LEFT JOHN DANIA'S HOUSE AT NOON ON A TYPICAL, 92° AUGUST DAY. ONLY 10 MINUTES INTO THE RIDE, I HAD MY FIRST ALL OUT WRECK ON OLD GRIFFIN ROAD. YEAH! BLOOD ON MY ARMS... PROVES I'M ALIVE!!! THEN, BEFORE I EVEN HAD GOT HALFWAY THROUGH THE 200 BLOCKS I'D HAVE TO RIDE TO REACH U.S. 27, IT STARTED POURING RAIN. LET IT RAIN! I FELT TOTALLY CRAZY — IT WAS JUST SO GOOD TO FINALLY BE OUT HERE AGAIN, WITHOUT A NET, WITH NO IDEA WHAT WOULD HAPPEN NEXT...

I GOT PRETTY WET, SO I STOPPED AT A PUBLIX JUST BEFORE 27 AND GOT A GARBAGE BAG TO KEEP MY STUFF DRY. AND THEN I SCAMMED A CUP OF SOUP OFF THEIR SOUP/SALAD BAR AND STOLE ONE OF THOSE BIG, YELLOW RAINCOATS THAT THEY KEEP IN THE MEN'S ROOM FOR THE BAG BOYS. BUT THEN... IT HAD QUIT RAININ' AND THE BLISTERING SUN WAS BACK.

I GOT TO 27, WHICH IS THE VERY END OF BROWARD COUNTY CIVILIZATION, AND I, UH, TURNED RIGHT. I RODE PAST THE REST STOP THERE AND TRUCKERS POINTED IN DISBELIEF. WELL, WOODYA LOOKEE DAT! A BAH-SECKLE! ON OLE 27! I FELT LIKE I SHOULD BE TAKING PLEDGES OR SOMETHING.

IT WAS GOOD RIDING ON 27, WITH A BIG SHOULDER, AND I MADE GOOD TIME. THE FIRST LOST CITY WAS ANDYTOWN, A PLACE THAT I'D NEVER EVEN HEARD OF 'TIL I DECIDED TO LOOK AT MY MAP A COUPLE MINUTES BEFORE I LEFT. IT WAS THE ONLY TOWN IN THE NEXT 50 MILES. AS I RODE, I IMAGINED IT AS SOME CRAZY, TWILIGHT ZONE VILLAGE, RULED WITH AN IRON THUMB BY THE CHARISMATIC, BUT FASCIST, ANDY. LIKE I'D WRITE HOME TO DANIA AND TELL 'EM, I'D STOPPED THERE. "YEAH. UH... I THINK I'M STAYIN' HERE IN ANDYTOWN. ANDY'S JUST... A GREAT GUY, YA KNOW..." WELL I RODE AND RODE AND DIDN'T SEE ANDYTOWN. I STOPPED AT A VERY STRANGE REST AREA WITH A STONE PICNIC BENCH BY A NICE SHADY TREE AND LOOKED AT MY MAP, I GUESS, ANDYTOWN JUST AIN'T THERE ANYMORE CUZ, I WAS 20 MILES PAST IT! WELL, NOW WHY D'YA THINK THEY CALL 'EM LOST CITIES, SON? SHEESH. I ADMIRED THE SANTANA ETCHINGS IN THE BENCH, AND A TRUCKER STOPPED AND GAVE ME A JUICE, CUZ HE'D SEEN ME WAY BACK AT THE GRIFFIN TRUCK STOP, AND I WAS ON MY WAY...

WHEN I GOT TO PALM BEACH COUNTY, THE ROAD'S SHOULDER DISAPPEARED, AND ALL OF A SUDDEN, I WAS BATTLING WITH 2-TON, 18 WHEELERS FOR ROAD SPACE! SHIT! IT WAS PRETTY SCARY WHEN THEY WENT BY, BUT THE WORST WAS WHEN THEY'D COME UP AND GET RIGHT BEHIND ME AND BLAST THEIR HORN, SCARING THE SHIT OUTTA ME AND MAKIN' ME MUCH MORE LIKELY TO SWERVE INTO 'EM. I WAS LOW ON WATER, TOO, AND IT WAS A LONG WAY TO OKEELANTA, WHATEVER THE HELL THAT PLACE WAS. BUT THERE WAS NO WAY OUT, NOW, SO I KEPT ON PEDDLING. AFTER AWHILE, OUT OF THE CORNER OF MY EYE, I KEPT SEEIN' WHAT LOOKED LIKE HUGE FROGS, ALONG THE SIDE OF THE ROAD AT REGULAR INTERVALS. THEY WOULD TURN AND JUMP INTO THE DITCH WHEN I GOT TO 'EM. I THOUGHT I WAS HALLUCINATING, BUT I SLOWED DOWN TO GET A BETTER LOOK AND SAW THAT THEY WEREN'T FROGS. THEY WERE BUNNIES. RABBITS THAT CAME TO LOOK AT THE ROAD! (EDITOR'S NOTE — FROGS, BUNNIES, WHATEVER — THE MAN WAS HALLUCINATING.) THEN, OKEELANTA CAME AND THE SHOULDER FINALLY RETURNED. OKEELANTA WAS, IT TURNED OUT, THE NAME OF A FRUIT PICKING COMPANY, SO ITS ONE OF THOSE MISERABLE MIGRANT WORKER/SLAVE PLANTATIONS THAT EXIST OUT IN THE SWAMPS OF CENTRAL AND SOUTH FLORIDA.

Memoirs of a SCAM MAN

MORE BIKE TRIPPIN', SCAM LOOSE IN GAINESVILLE, STATE ROAD 60 REVISITED

I DIDN'T STOP, BUT HELD OUT TO SOUTH BAY, A REAL TOWN. IN SOUTH BAY, I TOOK MY FIRST BREAK, DRINKIN' A HALF GALLON OF ORANGE JUICE AND SWIMMING IN A MOTEL'S POOL. IT WAS GETTING DARK AND I WASN'T SURE WHAT TO DO. I HAD BROUGHT JOHN DANIA'S TENT. MY LOOSE PLAN HAD BEEN TO SLEEP IN THE TENT ON ROOFTOPS AND COOK BAKED POTATOES IN CONVENIENCE STORE MICROWAVES FOR MEALS. WELL, I DIDN'T HAVE ANY BAKED POTATOES AND MY GOAL FOR THE FIRST DAY, CLEWISTON, WAS STILL 10, OR SO, MILES UP THE ROAD, A FULL 70 MILES FROM DANIA. SO, I WENT FORWARD TO DEATH ON DARK U.S. 27,

BEAN CITY WAS THE NEXT LOST TOWN, BUT I WAS TOO BUSY BEIN' RUN OFF THE PITCH BLACK, TWO LANE GRAVEL ROAD INTO THE SWAMP AND YELLING, "FUCK!" TO NOTICE IF I PASSED IT OR NOT. YES, THE DECISION TO GO ON TO CLEWISTON WAS NOW, CLEARLY, A BAD IDEA. BUT THEN A PICKUP TRUCK STOPPED, AND THE DRIVER, WHO I'll REFER TO AS "HENRY LEE", SAID HE'D DRIVE ME THE LAST 3 MILES TO CLEWISTON. THERE WERE NO HOUSES OR CITIES AROUND AND THE CENTRAL FLORIDA SKY SPREAD OUT BIG AND BLACK BEFORE HENRY LEE'S RATTLING OLE TRUCK. HENRY LEE SAID HE LIVED IN SOME GUY'S BACK HOUSE WITH NO ELECTRICITY AND SINCE IT WAS GONNA RAIN I SHOULD STAY THERE. WHERE WAS THIS PLACE? "OVER THERE." IN THE SWAMP. THE SKY'D SPLIT OPEN ALL WHITE WITH LIGHTNING AND I'D SEE HENRY'S SCARRED, MEAN FACE AND THINK ABOUT THE SENSELESSNESS OF LIFE OUT IN THE FUCKING SWAMP AND REALIZE JUST HOW FAR FROM ANY LOVE OR JUSTICE I'D ENDED UP... UH, NO THANKS, HENRY LEE, CLEWISTON'S OK WITH ME.

I GOT TO CLEWISTON AND RODE AROUND. IT WASN'T MUCH. 27 WAS MAIN STREET. THE HIGHLIGHT WAS THE "GIT 'N' SPLIT" MARKET WHICH HAD A SIGN OFFERING A BIG DISCOUNT ON SHINERS AND FLATWORMS. SHINERS? FLATWORMS? THESE PEOPLE SURE EAT CRAZY SHIT! I FELT KINDA SILLY WHEN I REALIZED THEY FISHED WITH 'EM... I WENT TO SLEEP ON THE SHORES OF LAKE OKEECHOBEE, BATTLING THE BIGGEST, MOST FEROCIOUS MOSQUITOS I'D EVER ENCOUNTERED TO GET THE TENT UP. IN A COUPLE MINUTES, IT STARTED RAINING. JOHN HAD WARNED ME THAT THE TENT WAS NO GOOD IN A HARD RAIN. SOON, THE TENT WAS FILLING WITH WATER FASTER THAN I COULD BAIL. A SWIMMING BAG! IT MUST OF LOOKED LIKE A HUGE, YELLOW JELLYFISH ALL THRASHIN' AROUND DOWN THERE ON THE SHORE, WITH ME TRYING TO GET OUT OF THE DAMNED THING BEFORE I DROWNED. I WENT TO THE 24 HOUR SHELL STATION TO DRY OFF AND MULL IT OVER. WELL, I'D LEARNED A LESSON ABOUT TENTS. I WOULD HAVE DONE BETTER WITH A GOOD SLEEPING BAG AND A BRIDGE TO GET UNDER.

I WAITED UP ALL NIGHT WHILE IT RAINED AND GOT BACK ON THE BIKE AT FIRST LIGHT. SOON I WAS MILES FROM TOWN, TRULY OUT THERE, WHERE IF YA GOT A FLAT TIRE, THE NEXT THING YOU KNOW, IT'D BE "JOURNAL ENTRY FOR DAY 21: TODAY, I ATE MY OWN FOOT... " IT WAS BEAUTIFUL, YES, WITH THE BIRDS ALL SINGIN' AND A BIG SHOULDER TO RIDE ON AND NO TRAFFIC AND JUST NO FUCKIN' HUMANS! I WAS OFF THE MAP! JUST ME AND MY SPINNIN' WHEELS... AS I GOT FURTHER INTO GLADES COUNTY, THERE WAS DRAMA UNFOLDING, AS I NEARED TWO OF FLORIDA'S STRANGEST TOURIST SIGHTS: CYPRESS KNEELAND AND GATORAMA. EVERY COUPLE MILES, THERE WERE SIGNS FOR CYPRESS KNEELAND, WHICH, AS NEAR AS I COULD TELL, WAS AN EXHIBIT OF THINGS MADE WITH CYPRESS KNEES. THE SIGNS WERE THE REAL INTEREST, AS THEY WERE WOOD LETTERS NAILED ONTO ROADSIDE TREES, WITH SUPPOSEDLY WITTY REMARKS ABOUT THE UPCOMING ATTRACTION, SORT OF A CRAZY, LOW BUDGET SOUTH OF THE BORDER, OUT IN THE SWAMP, MADE OF CYPRESS KNEES. MOST OF THE LETTERS WERE MISSING ON THE SIGNS, SO THEY MADE NO SENSE. AT FIRST, I THOUGHT I'D STUMBLED ONTO SOME WEIRD UNDERGROUND. THEN I REALIZED IT WAS JUST CENTRAL FLORIDA. GATORAMA WAS FIRST, THOUGH. THERE, YOU PAYED REAL CASH TO WALK ON A BRIDGE OVER ALLIGATORS IN A PIT. I RODE BY GATORAMA. IT WAS OPEN. I DIDN'T STOP. SAME WITH CYPRESS KNEELAND. THEIR SIGNS WERE ANNOYING. FUCK THEM... THE NEXT CITY, PALMDALE, WAS ACTUALLY A TRUCKSTOP. GO FIGURE. OK. PEOPLE WORK AT THE TRUCKSTOP. WHERE DO THEY LIVE? ITS ONE OF THOSE GREAT ROADTRIP MYSTERIES, LIKE "DO PEOPLE WHO WORK AT THE RESTAURANTS ON TOLL ROADS HAVE TO PAY THE TOLL ON THE WAY TO WORK EVERYDAY?" WHO KNOWS?

ABOUT 15 MILES UP THE ROAD, A GUY IN AN ORANGE, STATE OF FLORIDA ROAD WORK VAN STOPPED AND ASKED ME IF I NEEDED A RIDE. HE'D SEEN ME LIKE 4 HOURS AND 40 MILES BEFORE, AND THOUGHT I WAS CRAZY, LIKE I WAS SOME AMNESIA VICTIM, LOOSE ON THE LONELY HIGHWAY ON A LAVENDER BIKE. I TOOK THE RIDE, SO I COULD MAKE CHRIS BARROWS' PLACE BY NIGHT. THE GUY TURNED OUT TO BE REAL COOL. HE KNEW ABOUT THE PROPHET!!! HE SAID THE PROPHET HAD GAINED FAME EARLY ON BY PUSHING A CROSS ON WHEELS IN A TRIANGLE FROM BARTOW TO PLANT CITY TO LAKELAND! THEN HE FLIPPED OUT AND GOT A GUN! ONE TIME HE PULLED HIS PIECE OUT FROM UNDER HIS GOWN AND JUST STARTED FIRING INTO THE AIR! THEY PUT HIM IN THE POLK COUNTY MENTAL HEALTH FACILITY, AND SINCE THEN HE'S BEEN IN AND OUT. SAY IT AINT SO, PROPHET! A GUN? MAN. I GOT DROPPED OFF JUST PAST BARTOW. IT WAS HARD TO RIDE NOW, WITH HILLS AND HEAT BEIN' HARSH. I THOUGHT IT COULD BE FROM GOIN' 150 MILES ON ONE CUP OF SOUP AND NO SLEEP, BUT I CHECKED MY BIKE AND MY RIM WAS WAY BENT FROM ALL THE RIDIN' AND X-TRA WEIGHT FROM MY STUFF ON IT. STILL, I RODE ON THROUGH PLANT CITY. ONE TIME, ME AND IVY GOT A RIDE FROM A CHRISTIAN METAL HEAD WHO TOLD US THAT THERE WAS AN "ARMY OF SATAN WORSHIPPERS IN PLANT CITY, TWO THOUSAND STRONG!" BUT BARROWS DIDN'T KNOW ANYTHING ABOUT IT. I GOT KICKED OUT OF A POOL IN THONOTOSASSA, AND, AT LAST, PULLED UP IN FRONT OF CHRIS' TRAILER WHERE I PASSED OUT ON THE LAWN AND WAITED 'TIL HE GOT HOME FROM WORK...

(SORRY — Gainesville's on next page)

I LEFT BARROWS' PLACE, AND HITCHED UP TO GAINESVILLE, TRASHED BIKE AND ALL. IT SEEMS LIKE I
[AL]WAYS INVENT THESE REASONS TO GO ON THESE CRAZY ROAD TRIPS, BUT WHEN I GET WHERE I'M ACTUALLY
[GO]ING, I CAN'T FIGURE OUT WHY I WENT THERE AT ALL, WHAT I REALLY ENJOY IS THE GETTIN' THERE —
[TH]E PUTTIN' OUT THE OLD THUMB AND SEEIN' WHERE I END UP... THIS IS WHAT HAPPENED IN G-VILLE.
[I] GOT THERE, AND DIDN'T EVEN REALLY HAVE A PLACE TO STAY.
SO NOW I WAS HOMELESS IN GAINESVILLE, WHICH MADE ME A LITTLE NERVOUS. G-VILLE IS A
[BI]G SIGHT FOR UNSOLVED STUDENT MURDERS, AND ALSO, AT THE TIME, THERE WAS ALOT OF HYSTERIA
[A]BOUT A MYSTERIOUS WAVE OF CHURCH FIRES ACROSS NORTH AND CENTRAL FLORIDA. THERE WERE
[LI]KE 30 IN 2 YEARS — INCLUDING ONE BURNED TO THE GROUND OFF MAIN STREET G-VILLE.
[I]T WAS, APPARENTLY, A SERIAL CHURCH BURNER — PROBABLY THE FIRST THING OF ITS KIND
[EV]ER, AND RIGHT HERE IN CENTRAL FLORIDA... WELL, THEY ALWAYS LOOK TO BLAME THESE
[TH]INGS ON UNFORTUNATE "DRIFTERS" AND "LONERS", SO I WAS WORRIED ABOUT GOIN'
[SL]EEP ON A BENCH, AND WAKING UP AS "THE GAINESVILLE KILLER". THEN I'D
[H]AVE THREE NAMES, LIKE "IGGY LEE SCAM" AND YOU'D SEE CHUCK FUCKIN' LOOSE
[GO]IN', "WELL, HE SEEMED LIKE SUCH A QUIET KID..." FUCK THAT. LUCKILY,
[ON]E OF THE EASIEST PLACES I KNOW OF TO SURVIVE FOR FREE. THE KRISH-
[NA] CAMPUS, EVERY WEEKDAY, WHICH MEANS YOU DON'T EVEN HAVE TO GO
[TEM]PLE FOR FREE FOOD. I RECOMMEND THE YELLOW STUFF — MUCH SPICIER
[ST]UFF. ALSO, G-VILLE, UNLIKE MIAMI, HAS A PLASMA CENTER INSTEAD
[OF A BL]OOD BANK, SO YOU CAN DONATE TWICE A WEEK. IN FACT, YER
[WI]TH BONUSES, YOU CAN MAKE $30 A WEEK. BUT, I HAD BAD
[TIME] WENT TO THE PLASMA CENTER, BUT I'D GIVEN BLOOD IN
[MIAMI] AGAIN I BEGGED AND PLEADED WITH THE NURSE
[LIK]E IN THE BASTINADO, AND I RAN OUT THE DOOR...
[ON]LY SERVE DURING THE SCHOOL YEAR, WHICH
[AT LE]AST THERE WAS STILL GREAT DUMPSTERS
[KRI]SPY KREME DONUTS, AND LOTS OF
[PRE]TTY FAT...
ITS SO EASY TO LIVE THERE THAT
[T]HERE MORE, WITH THE FREE
[N]O RED, BRICK BUILDINGS. BUT
[O]N THE SURFACE, IT SEEMS
[MU]SIC, AND IS INTO THE
[BE]HIND IT, IT'S ALL
[AN]D KNOWING YOU
[M]USIC WHERE THE
[A]LL EMPTY, LIKE
[N]UTRITION...
[U]NDERSTAND
[LE]THROW
[...] WITH
[...]CE

SUDDENLY
ON TV,
G-VILLE IS
[KRISHNAS] WAS SERVE
TO THEIR CREEPY
THAN THE BROWN
OF A WHOLE-BLOOD
ENCOURAGED TO, AND
TIMING ALL AROUND.
MIAMI TOO RECENTLY TO
'TIL SHE THREATENED TO PUT
THEN, IT TURNS OUT, THE KRISHNAS
STARTED NEXT WEEK. WELL, AT
LIKE HUNGRY HOWIE'S PIZZA AND THE
PLACES TO SCAM CORES, SO I WAS LIVIN'

ITS HARD TO SEE WHY I DON'T LIKE IT
FOOD, AND OLD-STYLE HOMES AND SLEEPY TREES
THERE'S SOMETHING ABOUT COLLEGE TOWNS WHERE
REAL LIBERAL, AND EVERYONE LISTENS TO HALFWAY DECENT
RIGHT CAUSES, BUT THERE DOESN'T SEEM TO BE MUCH
WATERED DOWN AND DEPRESSING LIKE VOTING FOR CLINTON
HATE HIM AND HE HATES YOU OR THAT "PUNK" (ALTERNATIVE)
BANDS MAY WRITE CATCHY SONGS, BUT LISTENING TO 'EM FEELS
BEING FORCE FED A PILE OF BIG-MACS AND STILL DYIN' OF MAL-
UNDERNEATH THE LIBERAL SURFACE, I USUALLY FIND A REAL LACK OF
THING, LIKE WHEN I ASKED A HIP-LOOKING GUY AT THE BAGEL SHOP FOR
ALWAYS, HE WAS TOTALLY PUZZLED. "UH... SURE... WHAT ARE YOU GOING TO
THEM?" "ARE FOR MY ART APPRECIATION CLASS? NO! TO EAT! DUH! OR

I GOT IN A DEBATE WITH THESE BIG CLINTON FANS ABOUT THE NORTH AMERICAN
FREE TRADE AGREEMENT. I SAY ITS TOTALLY WRONG, CUZ ITS A U.S. GRAB FOR
CANADA'S TIMBER AND WATER AND MEXICAN SLAVE LABOR. THEY SAY "NO! THE MEXICANS
WANT TO WORK FOR A DOLLAR AN HOUR! ITS ALL THEY CAN GET..." I GUESS MY
JUDGEMENT OF G-VILLE'S PROBABLY AFFECTED BY BEING HOMELESS THERE. PEOPLE ACTUALLY
WERE REAL NICE TO ME AND I USUALLY FOUND PLACES TO STAY. BILL RADON OFFERED TO PUT
ME UP, THE DAY I WAS LEAVING (MORE BAD TIMING) BUT IVAN GRIPWEED PUT ME UP A BUNCH
FINALLY, THOUGH, I GOT TIRED OF ASKING FOR PLACES TO STAY, SO I HID IN THE TOILET OF
THE UNIVERSITY OF FLORIDA LIBRARY, AND STAYED IN ALL NIGHT! I WAS INSPIRED BY THE CHILD-
HOOD DREAM OF MY FRIEND, KING JAMES, WHO WOULD GO MAKE MAPS OF THE BOCA RATON CITY HALL
WHEN HE WAS 8, AND PLAN TO HIDE OUT AND STAY THE NIGHT AND LIVE OFF THE VENDING MACHINES
IT WAS INCREDIBLE — ME ALONE WITH ALL THOSE ROWS OF BOOKS! THE WHOLE LIBRARY TO MYSELF...
TRULY BEAUTIFUL. I READ ALL NIGHT, HID WHEN IT OPENED AT 9:00 AM, AND LEFT TO SLEEP IN MY
SLEEPY-TALL-GRASS-BY-THE-CREEK-JUST-OFF-13TH-AVENUE-SPOT THAT I ALWAYS VISIT IN G-VILLE.
I ALSO WENT TO CHECK OUT THE SCAM SUMMER HOME, A BEAUTY OF A TWO-STORY
[A]BANDONED HOUSE, WITH GREAT SHADY PORCHES AND BALCONIES, THAT ME AND IVY HAD SPIED ON A
[PRE]VIOUS HITCHIN' TRIP TO GAINESVILLE. THE TOP FLOOR HAD PILES AND PILES OF CLOTHES EVERYWHERE,
[AN]D A MATTRESS. BY THE MATTRESS, ON THE WALL, WERE 6 OR 8 MAGAZINE PHOTOS OF JANET
[JA]CKSON, AND THEY ALL HAD HER FACE SLASHED UP! WAS THIS THE SECRET HOME OF THE
[M]YSTERIOUS CHURCH BURNER, WHO WAS SPURNED BY JANET AND TOOK IT OUT ON ALL THE CHURCHES
[H]E'D NEVER MARRY HER IN? WHO KNOWS? THE BOTTOM FLOOR WAS REAL CLEAN, CUZ THIS NICE,
[O]LD MAN SQUATTED IT AND TOOK GREAT PAINS, HE'D TOLD US, TO MAKE IT A HOME. HE HAD A REAL
[N]ICE PLACE WITH SCRUBBED WINDOWS, AND A MADE BED, AND JUST LOTS OF RESPECT FOR THE PLACE.
[H]E HAD THOUGHT ABOUT FIXING UP THE TOP FLOOR FOR A VACATION SQUAT, AND SPENDING SOME LONG
[SU]MMER DAYS CHATTIN' ON THE PORCH AND SELLING BLOOD UP IN G-VILLE, BUT WE NEVER GOT AROUND
[TO] IT. NOW THAT I NEEDED A PLACE, I DECIDED TO TRY IT OUT, BUT THEN I SAW THAT THE MATTRESS
[W]AS CRAWLIN' WITH LITTLE WHITE BUGS! YIKES! "SCAM PUNKS GETTIN' CRABS" NO WAY!
GAINESVILLE HAS MORE ABANDONED HOUSES WAITING TO BE SQUATTED THAN I'VE SEEN ANYWHERE
[E]LSE, BUT, I SAID, FUK IT. I DECIDED TO JUST GO HOME. PLUS, WHILE I WAS AWAY, HALF OF

UH! CAN'T GO BACK AND F*** IT.

MIAMI WAS DESTROYED BY HURRICANE ANDREW, SO I THOUGHT I'D BETTER GET BACK AND DO SOME RELIEF WORK, AND TRY TO GET IN ON SOME INSURANCE FRAUD SCAMS...

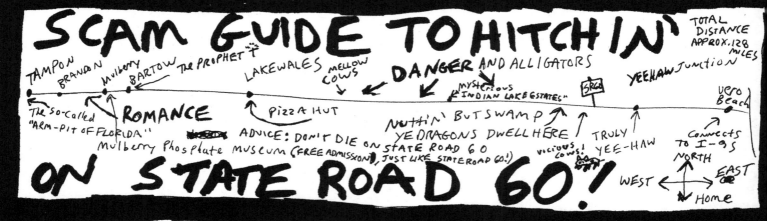

SCAM GUIDE TO HITCHIN'

TOTAL DISTANCE APPROX. 128 MILES

TAMPON BRANDON MULBERRY BARTOW THE PROPHET ✝ LAKE WALES MELLOW COWS   DANGER AND ALLIGATORS   YEEHAW JUNCTION

MYSTERIOUS "INDIAN LAKE ESTATES"   SR60   VERO BEACH

THE SO-CALLED "ARM-PIT OF FLORIDA"   ROMANCE   PIZZA HUT   NOTHIN' BUT SWAMP YE DRAGONS DWELL HERE   TRULY YEE-HAW   CONNECTS TO I-95 NORTH

ADVICE: DON'T DIE ON STATE ROAD 60   VICIOUS COWS!   EAST

MULBERRY PHOSPHATE MUSEUM (FREE ADMISSION) JUST LIKE STATE ROAD 60!)

ON STATE ROAD 60!

WEST ←→ EAST
↓ HOME

THE HITCHIN' NIGHTMARE IS PROBABLY SOMETHING LIKE JOHN DANIA'S STORY ABOUT GETTING A RIDE FROM A COLLEGE PROFESSOR WHO WAS MOVING. WHEN THEY GOT TO THEIR DESTINATION, THE PROFESSOR, WHO, SO FAR, SEEMS LIKE AN OK GUY, SAYS, "YOU CAN SLEEP ON MY COUCH, AND I'LL BUY YOU DINNER IF YOU HELP ME MOVE ALL THIS HEAVY FURNITURE INSIDE." JOHN SAYS, OK. SO HE HELPS OUT, AND THEN HE'S TAKING A SHOWER AT THE GUY'S PLACE, AND HE GETS OUT OF THE SHOWER AND THE "PROFESSOR" IS IN THE BATHROOM, TOO, AND HE'S NAKED! JOHN GETS BACK IN THE SHOWER. THE "PROFESSOR" BEGGED JOHN FOR AWHILE TO HAVE SEX WITH HIM, AND THEN, FINALLY, GAVE UP, SO HE TURNED OUT MORE FUNNY THAN HARMFUL. STILL, THERE'S ALWAYS A LITTLE WORRY ABOUT GETTING PICKED UP BY SOME TOTAL SEX MANIAC PSYCHO KILLER. ON THE OTHER HAND, THERE'S THIS DAYDREAM I ALWAYS HAVE, WHEN I'M STUCK ON THE SIDE OF THE ROAD FOR HOURS, OF MEETING SOME RAD, CRAZY PUNK WOMAN, WHO'LL STOP AND GIVE ME A RIDE AND RESCUE ME, AND THAT'S WHAT HAPPENED WHEN I WAS HITCHIN' HOME FROM BARROWS' PLACE, ON GOOD OLE STATE ROAD 60.

I WAS STUCK IN THE HOT SUN, IN THE HUGE SUBURB, BRANDON, FOR 2 OR 3 HOURS, WHEN SHE PULLED UP, ALL SMILIN', AND I'M THINKING, "OH NO! ITS A GIRL! WHAT DO I DO?" I LOAD MY BIKE IN THE TRUNK AND SEE THE PUNK STICKERS AND THE "FIGHT RACISM" STICKERS ON THE CAR. A PUNK GIRL! THEN, I GET IN THE CAR, ALL STINKY ROADKILL MESS, AND ITS A SEXY, REDHEAD PUNK GIRL! SHE WAS PUNK, TOO, CUZ SHE TOLD ME ABOUT ALL THESE CAVES SHE'D FOUND IN GAINESVILLE THAT I'D NEVER HEARD OF, AND WAS INTO DRINKIN' WINE ON ROOFTOPS AND DIDN'T EVEN NOTICE HOW BAD I SMELLED. SHE DROVE ME 25 MILES PAST HER HOME AND GAVE ME HER NUMBER AND JUMPED ON ME FOR A BIG OLE HUG, AND, MAN, I WAS HOOKED! THE ONLY OTHER TIME A HITCHIN' TRIP HAD EVER HAD SEXUAL TENSION WAS WHEN ME AND IVY GOT A RIDE FROM SOME CREEP IN A VAN, WHO OUTTA NOWHERE, SAID, "YA'LL WANNA HAVE SEX?" (WE DIDN'T). WELL I SUPPOSE YOU WERE EXPECTING SOME STEAMY SEX STORY, HUH? WELL, I'LL SPARE THE READER THE DETAILS OF FURTHER CORRESPONDENCE, VISITING, ROMANCE, AND EVENTUAL ~~blahblah~~, INEVITABLE DUMPING (THAT'S ME BEIN' DUMPED). THIS WAS JUST SUCH A CRAZY WAY TO MEET SOMEONE. IT WAS LIKE A COMMERCIAL FOR HITCH HIKING.

I WAS ALL GOOFY FROM THE ENCOUNTER AND GOT MY NEXT RIDE, AND HUNG OUT THE BACK OF THE TRUCK, HAIR IN FACE, ALL STRAY DOG PANTIN'... DIDN'T EVEN KNOW WHERE I WAS... WELL, I HAD PLENTY OF TIME TO FIGURE IT OUT, CUZ, WHEN I WAS DROPPED OFF ON THE EAST EDGE OF LAKE WALES, NEAR THE COWS, I WAS THERE FOR 12 HOURS! HELLO, COWS... YOU KNOW YOU'RE IN THE SAME PLACE TOO LONG WHEN THE SAME FAMILY DRIVES BY AND YELL "HEY FAGGOT!" 3 TIMES, AND, WHEN YOU START TALKING TO THE COWS. I GAVE AN IMPASSIONED SPEECH TO THE COWS: "COWS! LOVERS OF FREEDOM! TROMP DOWN THAT TINY FENCE AND ENTER THE WORLD OF MEN!" THEY JUST STARED... FINALLY, I GOT A RIDE AT 2:00 AM IN THE BACK OF A PICKUP TRUCK ALL THE WAY HOME. THERE'S NO LIGHTS OUT THERE, SO I JUST LAYED BACK AND WATCHED ALL THOSE STARS IN THE CENTRAL FLORIDA SKY, AND THOUGHT ABOUT THAT GIRL. MAN! THIS ADDED A WHOLE NEW DIMENSION TO THE ROADTRIP, NOT JUST DANGER, BUT ROMANCE AND DANGER! IN BOCA, I BROKE INTO MY FOLKS' PLACE, DRANK A BEER, TOOK A HOT BATH AND READ THE PAPER, ALL DR. THOMPSON-STYLE. THE ROAD TRIP HAD WORKED AND NOW I COULD SAY THAT I'VE SEEN THE PROPHET OF BARTOW, I'VE BEEN TO THE MULBERRY PHOSPHATE MUSEUM, I'VE STAYED THE NIGHT IN THE U. OF F. LIBRARY... AND I FELL IN LOVE ON STATE ROAD 60.

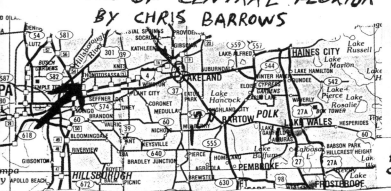

THONOTOSASSA, FLORIDA...
AN EXPOSÉ ON
"THE PRIDE OF CENTRAL FLORIDA"
BY CHRIS BARROWS

A THONOTOSASSA "FAMILY" AS REPRESENTED ON THE SIGN OF THE GROCERY STORE THAT ONLY SELLS BAD MEAT.

In 1975, I was living with my brother and his wife, until his wife threatened to shoot him, ~~n~~ his body, and mix it with the kitty litter. That same day, he found another place to live. ~~i~~s place was called Thonotosassa. We lived in one of two trailers on a lot right off the highway ~~i~~t too long after my brother and I moved out there, he sold the land and the trailers and moved ~~~~ north. So I moved into the other trailer, and rented from the new owners. For the next 17 years ~~p~~aid $130 a month (the rent never went up), and never got bothered about making too much noise ~~~~ anything. It was nice. About a year ago, the landlord told me I'd have to move, because they ~~~~re gonna scrap my trailer and put themselves in a double-wide ("me and the missus gotta think ~~~~ut our future, ya know?") No problem. In short, I live in a house in Tampa now, and I haven't ~~~~n back to Thonotosassa since. What does any of this really mean? I'll tell you.

That little son of a bitch, Iggy, couldn't leave well enough alone. For SCAM #1, he insisted ~~th~~at I write a column about a trailer existence in the rural country. He seemed real fevered to ~~ge~~t a real Hee-haw, hayseed angle to it. So, I naturally wrote about a breastfeeding I witnessed ~~in~~ Ybor City, instead.

For SCAM #2, he enlarged his focus, and wanted a column about the whole town of Thonotosassa- ~~al~~l 12 houses, and 200 trailers, and the fire station, the Circle K, the post office, the grocery ~~st~~ore, the orange groves, the whole shebang. Fuck. So he makes a trip to Thonotosassa, and we ~~we~~nt around. He asked me questions and I would go through the motions of answering him. He captured ~~it~~ all on his tape recorder and that was that. Or was it?

Last month, Iggy wrote from his California office, at SCAM WEST COAST, and said he lost the ~~ta~~pe and needed me to write a story about it. So, I says to Iggy, I says, "Iggy, you write it ~~fr~~om the outsider angle." He writes back with a threatening little letter full of angry noises. He ~~sa~~ys I need to write it. He says I need to tell little country stories with a homespun flair. He ~~sa~~ys I need to tell the things that happened there, like the rape victim that came to our trailer ~~at~~ 2:00 AM, needing a ride home. Or the old lady, covered in blood, carrying a large, dead dog. Or ~~th~~e tree trimmer that got impaled on a tree limb, across the street. Or the launromat with the 3 ~~he~~avily tattooed, 70 year-old women. Or the guy that lived behind us, that dug a 12 foot deep ~~"h~~olding cell", complete with an oxygen tank, to keep his daughter and her friends in, til he got ~~ar~~rested. Or the daily sound of mufflers dragging down the street. Or that Thonotosassa was a ~~du~~mping ground for serial killer's victims (including Bobby Jo Long). Or the 3 8-10 runaway kids ~~wh~~o "turned themselves in" to me at 2 in the morning. Or the time I saw this guy with a shotgun ~~ma~~ke another guy lay face down in the streets while he yelled at him for driving stupid. Or the ~~ga~~ngs of dogs that would make the rounds. Or the gangs of 10 year-old cracker kids on bikes, with ~~th~~eir .22's. Or the Thonotosassa Fire Dept. responding to a trailer fire with an empty water tank. ~~Or~~ the small cafe down the street that sells barbeque gopher and barbeque goat. Or the old lady ~~th~~at had the flashlight tied around her neck at the Circle K, so it would dangle down and ~~il~~luminate the treasures of the trashcans (Iggy saw her—he was very jealous of her wily ingenuity). ~~Or~~ the people that would ride golf carts, riding mowers, and horses to the Circle K to get beer. ~~Or~~ the grocery store that only sells bad meat. Or the female clerks at Circle K that were always ~~ge~~tting abducted. Or the time I got shot at by a state trooper.

But I just can't do it. The people of Thonotosassa are proudly simple, and fiercely inbred. ~~An~~d people just don't talk, if ya know what I mean. There was a rumour that the tree trimmer that ~~th~~ey found impaled across the street was working on an article about Thonotosassa for Maximum Rock ~~an~~d Roll. So I hope you understand, Iggy. The only thing I can say about Thonotosassa is that ~~Fe~~rnando De Soto marched through there a long time ago. I don't know what year, though.

Fidel shot back, "Don't worry. When the revolution triumphs, we will have Marxist books coming out of our ears!"

Who's the Mack?

Police photos of John Dillinger taken in Tucson, A[?] 1/25/34, following the gang's capture. The diamond s[?] pin was worth about $4,000.

SCAM BOOK REVIEWS

THE EARLY FIDEL by LIONEL MARTIN:
"WHAT THE IMPERIALISTS CANNOT PARDON US FOR IS THE DIGNITY, HEROISM REVOLUTIONARY IDEOLOGY, AND SPIRIT OF SACRIFICE OF THE PEOPLE OF CUBA. THEY CANNOT FORGIVE US FOR MAKING A SOCIALIST REVOLUTION IN THE VERY NOSTRILS OF THE UNITED STATES!" — *the young* FIDEL. NOW HERE'S A BOOK THAT DANGEROUS TO READ ON THE #8 BUS ... OR ANYWHERE IN MIAMI, FOR THAT MATTER, BUT RE[?] IF I DID, AND I'VE EVEN BEEN KNOWN TO LEAP UP ONTO A FIRE HYDRANT, ALL CRAZY EYE[?] AND SMELLIN' LIKE CUBAN COFFEE, AND READ QUOTES FROM THE BOOK AT RANDOM TO EL PUEBLO. HERE'S THE TRUE STORY OF A MACKIN' YOUNG MAN, ALL ON FIRE WITH THE LOVE AND POETRY AND HISTORY OF HIS PEOPLE, WHO WAS SICK O[?] THE WAY THINGS WERE GOIN', SO HE TOOK OVER THE ISLAND!!! ONE TIME, T[?] YOUNG FIDEL SMUGGLED THE TEXT OF HIS FAMOUS "HISTORY WILL ABSOLVE ME" PA[?] OUT OF JAIL, ONE PAGE AT A TIME IN FALSE BOTTOMED MATCH BOXES! ALL THOSE OL[?] CUBAN EXILES DOWN ON S.W. 8th STREET WHO SIT AROUND IN THE PARK, PLAYING DOMINOES AND GRIPING ABOUT FIDEL, ALL DAY, ARE JUST [xxx] SORE CUZ THE REVOLUTION DIDN'T GO THEIR WAY. IF THEY'RE SO TOUGH WITH THEIR "KILL CAST[?] FLYERS, WHY DON'T THEY GO DO IT THEN? THE WHOLE WORLD'S WAITIN' NOW FO[?] FIDEL TO DIE, BUT I HOPE HE MAKES IT ANOTHER 25 YEARS! VIVA FIDEL

BLOODLETTERS AND BADMEN by JAY ROBERT NASH: THIS IS THE SHIT. "A NARRATIVE ENCYCLOPEDIA OF AMERICAN CRIMINALS FROM THE PILGRIMS TO THE PRESENT." O[?] SIX HUNDRED PAGES OF CRIME! THE BEST STORY IS ABOUT **JOHN DILLINGER**. DILLINGER WAS TRULY **THE MACK** — A MAN WITH TRUE STYLE, TRAVELLING THE COUNTRYSIDE WIT[?] HIS GANG, ROBBIN' ONE BANK AFTER ANOTHER, DURING THE GREAT DEPRESSION[?] WHEN BANK ROBBERS WERE HEROES AND THE BANKERS WERE THE CRIMINALS. DUR[?] THE EARLY 30'S, AMERICA LOVED DILLINGER, AND NO JAIL COULD HOLD HIM, AND THE **F.B.I.** L[?] LIKE **FOOLS**, TRYIN' TO CATCH HIM. ONE TIME, DILLINGER ESCAPED FROM PRISON USING ONLY A FA[?] GUN CARVED OUT OF WOOD AND PAINTED BLACK WITH SHOE POLISH!!! SHIT. WHENEVER YER DOWN A[?] OUT, REMEMBER THAT ONE, EH... IN JULY, 1934, THE F.B.I. GOT **"THE LADY IN RED"**, CHICAGO MADAM, ANNA SAGE, TO LEAD DILLINGER TO A THEATER WHERE THEY WOULD SHOOT AND KILL HIM, AND THE[?] DID [xx] KILL A MAN THAT NIGHT AND SAY IT WAS DILLINGER, BUT THE BODY HAD DIFFERENT COLORE[?] NONE OF DILLINGER'S SCARS OR GUNSHOT WOUNDS, AND WAS SHORTER AND HEAVIER. IT SEEMS THAT OLE[?] J.D. DISCOVERED THE PLOT AND SENT SOMEONE IN HIS PLACE!!! DILLINGER LIVES!!! IF ALIVE TODAY, DILLINGER WOULD BE 90 YEARS OLD...

The FBI pounded the lodge all night thinking the gangsters were still inside. By morning, their only captives were the gang's girls who had been hiding in the basement.

Dillinger, Hamilton, and Van Meter stole a car and drove out of the trap to St. Paul.

Hoover placed a shoot-to-kill order out on Dillinger and a $10,000 reward. Another $10,000 was offered by five states where Dillinger had robbed banks.

In the next two months half a dozen men who looked like Dillinger were arrested or almost shot. The bandit, however, was nowhere to be found. He appeared briefly at his father's farm for a Sunday chicken dinner in May.

OUTCASTS OF THE SEA
THE STRAIGHT SHIT ON WOMEN PIRATES, SOCIALIST-UTOPIAN PIRATES AND WEIRD PIRATE DRINKS!

Pirates get blamed for a lot of crazy shit. Like this Edward Low guy, who forced one of his prisoners to eat his own lips! What's up with that, huh? But, they weren't all so ruthless. Captain Misson was this crazy, socialist pirate who convinced his men that they shouldn't be bloodthirsty brutes, or, at least, not without a cause. He made a lot of speeches all the time about Liberty and Feedom, and his men were moved to tears. One time, they raided a British ship but, instead of killing everyone, as was the custom, they just took a little food and rum. The Brits were

ANN BONNEY
WHO LOVED AND FOUGHT

so happy that they gave Misson a 21 gun salute! He raided a Dutch ship, gave an impassioned speech, and freed the ships slaves, giving them their master's old clothes. Finally, Misson took his men to a cove in Madagascar and set up a sort of utopian society called Libertatia, that lasted for many years, 'til the natives decideed to destroy them. Said Byron of Misson: "He was the gentlest man who ever scuttled a ship, or slit a throat..."
Blackbeard was a little more G.G. Allin style. He'd set the end of his beard on fire before he jumped into battle, and he drank this crazy home brew called RUMFUSTIAN-- a mixture of beer, gin, sherry, rum and gunpowder! Sounds a little like the Ole Chickenhead wine we made back in the Punk House...
One time, Blackbeard's crew caught Syphilis, so, to get medicine, he docked the ship off Charleston and ravaged the town and took hostages for a month 'til he got the goods. A man of his word, Blackbeard released the hostages unharmed, after robbing them of course, of 15,000 Pounds worth of silver...
The two most famous women pirates were Anne Bonney and Mary Read. Anne was this fiery pirate woman (probably had red hair, too), who married a pretty

TORY ON PAGE 267

BLACKBEARD'S HEAD DANGLING
OVER THE WATER AFTER HIS DEATH

tough pirate, named Calico Jack. For many years they loved, and fought, and raided ships together. Then, Anne fell in love with a particularly brave young man on board---only to find out the man was Mary Read, who had dressed as a man to become a pirate! Finally, their ship got raided and the men chickened out, and only Anne and Mary fought. The ship was captured and Jack was

to be executed, but Anne and Mary lied and said they were pregnant, and lived. Before the execution, Jack was like, o man, o man, my love, I am to die, and Anne said, "If you'd have fought like a man, you wouldn't have to DIE LIKE A DOG!!!"

IT IS COOL TO BE A PIRATE, BUT DON'T GET YOUR HEAD CUT OFF!

WELL I DIDN'T GET TO BACK TO MIAMI RIGHT AWAY, CUZ BUDDHA, CHICKENHEAD DRUMMER AND SCAM CO-FOUNDER, CAME BACK FROM JERSEY, AFTER BEIN' AWAY FOR A WHOLE YEAR. WE DRANK ALOT OF SHLITZ AND PROWLED AROUND BOCA'S EMPTY LOTS AT NIGHT AND IN THE DAY WE'D JAM ALL DAY AT CHUCK'S. ME AND BOOD KNOW THE WHOLE FIRST SCREECHING WEASEL RECORD, YA KNOW, THE ONE THAT THEY'RE ALL EMBARRASSED OF WITH "7-11" AND "SOCIETY MAKES ME WANNA PUKE" ON IT! IF ANYONE WANTS TO PUT OUT CHICKENHEAD DOIN' THE FIRST WEEZEHOLES LP, LET ME KNOW... ONE NIGHT WE ORDERED A PIZZA AND DIDN'T PICK IT UP, AND THEN WENT AND ASKED 'EM IF THEY HAD ANY THROWOUTS, AND THEY GAVE US THE PIZZA WE ORDERED STILL HOT, WHICH WE ATE WITH LEMONADE AND THE RAMONES BLASTIN'... THEN IVY CALLED! SHE HAD BEEN IN NEW YORK CITY AND ATLANTA AND THEN HER AND TIMMY TRI-RAIL HITCHED ALL THE WAY TO OAKLAND, ACROSS COUNTRY. SHE HAD A GREAT SQUAT GOIN', AND TIM AND SCOTTY TRI-RAIL (WHO HAD TAKEN A BUS THERE) AND A BUNCH OF OTHER PEOPLE LIVED THERE. EVERYONE TOLD HER IT COULDN'T BE DONE, THAT A SQUAT WOULDN'T WORK IN THE EAST BAY, BUT SHE DID IT! YO! SHE WAS LIVIN' A REAL LIFE OF CRIME. HER NEW SCAM WAS "RETURNING" HUGE, EXPENSIVE ITEMS FOR STORE CREDIT, WITHOUT A RECEIPT. IF YOU DON'T HAVE A RECEIPT, YOU CAN ONLY EXCHANGE, BUT THAT WAS OK, CUZ SHE "RETURNED" A CAMPING STOVE AND GOT ENOUGH CREDIT TO GET THE TOOLS SHE NEEDED FOR WORK ON THE SQUAT. WELL... I WAS A BIT JEALOUS, SO I KNEW IT WAS TIME TO DUST OFF THE OLE CROWBAR AND HEAD TO MIAMI...

WE WALKED AROUND MIAMI, DIGGIN' DOWNTOWN AND DRINKIN' COLADAS, 'TIL WE FOUND THE SQUAT— A HUGE WAREHOUSE WITH "ZION CORPORATION" WRITTEN ON THE SIDE, ON N.W. 7TH AVENUE AND 17TH. IT'D BE GREAT LIVIN' IN THE ZION CORP. YA KNOW THE CRAZY CONSPIRACY THEORY ABOUT THE ZIONISTS SECRETLY CONTROLLING THE WORLD? WELL, WE COULD MAKE ZION CORPORATION BUSINESS CARDS THAT SAY, "WE SECRETLY CONTROL THE WORLD!" AND SIT AROUND ALL DAY SMOKING CIGARS AND PUTTIN' PINS IN THE MAP! WE COULD PAINT ONE WALL, FROM TOP TO BOTTOM, WITH A PORTAIT OF FIDEL CASTRO'S FACE! WE COULD, AT LEAST, BUILD OUR OWN POOL TABLE... YES, WE HAD HUGE PLANS FOR THIS BIG, EMPTY WAREHOUSE... BUT FIRST WE HAD TO GET IN. WE GOT REAL DRUNK AT A FUNYONS' SHOW AND GOT DROPPED OFF BY THE TARGET. WHAT HAPPENED NEXT IS A DRUNKEN BLUR, BUT WHILE I WAS GOING TO WORK WITH THE CROWBAR, A COP PULLED UP, AND SOON, WE WERE UNDER ARREST! WELL, BEST FRIENDS GOTTA GO TO JAIL TOGETHER, TOO, YA KNOW... IN THE HOLDING CELL, I CARVED "KILL POLICE!" ON THE WALL WITH A SAFETY PIN. YEAH, I GUESS I WAS PRETTY COCKY. I HAD NO WAY OF KNOWING I'D BE THERE FOR THE NEXT 21 DAYS...

CONTACT VISIT REQUEST FORM

COMMISSARY ORDER

NOW I'M DRESSED IN DA COUNTY BLUES...

DA SCAMMAH
IN
DA SLAMMAH

ARTIST CONCEPTION OF IGGY IN JAIL DRAWN BY JANELLE WHILE IN SCHOOL

"Have them arrest us! We'll all have three square meals and a roof!"

— **Tom Wagner of Calvary Chapel, vowing to continue feeding homeless people in Fort Lauderdale's Holiday Park even though city commissioners may outlaw feeding the hungry there.**

I'D BEEN IN JAIL BEFORE, MOST RECENTLY FOR MAKING FUN OF A COUPLE STUPID LOOKING COPS ON SOUTH BEACH, AND USUALLY, ITS NO BIG DEAL. YOU SPEND THE NIGHT AND LEAVE. BUT, NOW, I WAS BEING CHARGED WITH A FELONY — ATTEMPTED BURGLARY ON AN UNOCCUPIED BUILDING — SO IT WASN'T QUITE AS SIMPLE. AFTER BEIN' MOVED AROUND ALOT FOR PROCESSING, ME AND BOOD ENDED UP IN A DORM-STYLE CELL IN THE COUNTY JAIL, WITH ALL THE OTHER NEW FELONY CASES. HERE, WE'D WAIT 'TIL OUR BOND HEARING, TO SEE

IF WE'D GET "PRE-TRIAL RELEASE", A SORT-OF PROBATION THAT LASTS 'TIL YOUR COURTDATE. OTHERWISE WE'D BE STUCK IN JAIL FOR THE WHOLE 21 DAYS. WE WERE PRETTY SURE WE'D GET IT, CUZ WE HAD NO OTHER SERIOUS CRIMES ON OUR RECORDS. BUT WHEN WE FINALLY WENT BEFORE THE JUDGE, THINGS WENT WRONG VERY QUICKLY...

THE BOND HEARING WAS AN UGLY SCENE. THE JUDGE, CRUSTY OLE "MEAN" MURRAY MYERSON, APPEARED BEFORE US ON A LARGE SCREEN TV. ONE AFTER ANOTHER, WE DRAGGED OURSELVES BEFORE HIM, WITH REASONS WHY WE SHOULD BE ALLOWED PRE-TRIAL RELEASE, AND ONE AFTER ANOTHER: "DENIED." HE CALLED MY NAME, AND HE DIDN'T

EVEN LOOK UP FROM HIS PAPERWORK. IT WAS ALL OVER PRETTY FAST. HE SAID THE BOND WAS $3,500. I TRIED TO GET RELEASED TO NICK'S ADDRESS (DENIED), TO MY PARENTS CUSTODY (DENIED), AND TRIED TO GET A LOWER BOND (DENIED). 3 STRIKES, YER OUT. BUDDHA GOT A LOWER BOND, BUT NO RELEASE, WELL, THERE WAS NO WAY OUT, NOW, CUZ I DIDN'T WANT SOMEONE TO COME UP WITH THE MONEY TO GET ME OUT AND THEN HAVE TO FIND A WAY TO PAY 'EM BACK. BETTER JUST DO THE 21 DAYS. THE REASON, IT TURNS OUT, THAT WE DIDN'T GET OUT, IS BECAUSE WE DIDN'T HAVE PERMANENT ADDRESSES. IF I'D HAVE JUST LIED BETTER AND SAID I LIVED AT NICK'S I WOULDN'T HAVE SPENT 21 DAYS IN JAIL... AT LEAST I KNOW NOW.

SCAM LEGAL ADVICE: IF YER HOMELESS OR ON THE ROAD, TRY AND HAVE A GOOD, LOCAL ADDRESS (PREFERRABLY OF SOMEONE YOU KNOW) MEMORIZED. THEY WON'T LET YOU OUT OF JAIL, UNLESS THEY'RE PRETTY SURE YOU HAVE ENOUGH TIES TO THE TOWN TO KEEP YOU FROM SPLITTING BEFORE YOUR COURT DATE. IF YOU TELL 'EM YOU'RE TRAVELLING, THEY'RE GONNA TRY AND FORCE A BIG PILE OF BAIL MONEY OUTTA YA. DON'T BE WORRIED ABOUT LYING, CUZ THEY'RE NOT GONNA CHECK. THE JUDGE MAKES SPLIT SECOND DECISIONS FOR HUNDREDS OF CASES A DAY, SO IF HE ASKS YOU IF YOU'VE EVER BEEN ARRESTED BEFORE DON'T VOLUNTEER ANY INFORMATION TO HIM THAT HE OBVIOUSLY DOESN'T HAVE, IF FOR SOME REASON IT DOESN'T WORK, NOTHING WORSE IS GONNA HAPPEN TO YOU THAN WHAT WAS ALREADY GONNA HAPPEN IF YOU TOLD THE TRUTH...

SO HERE'S IMPORTANT

MORE SCAM LEGAL ADVICE: IF YOU GET BAGGED ON A MISDEMEANOR LIKE SHOPLIFTING, AND YOU HAVE NO ADDRESS, YOU'LL PROBABLY SEE THE JUDGE THE NEXT MORNING. HERE, YOU PLEAD GUILTY AND LEAVE WITH TIME SERVED. DON'T FUCK IT UP. IF YOU START TO SAY ANYTHING BUT "GUILTY" THE JUDGE WILL SAY, "ENTER THE PLEA AS NOT GUILTY AND HOLD UNTIL FURTHER JUDIFICATION" WHICH MEANS YER GONNA BE IN JAIL 'TIL YOU GET A JURY TRIAL WHICH YOU WON'T WIN, TRUST ME, PUNK. IT SUCKS, BUT ITS THE WAY IT WORKS.

JAIL ISN'T THE WORST THING IN THE WORLD, AND ONCE YOU'RE THERE, YER THERE, SO THE BEST THING IS TO NOT PANIC, BUT SIT BACK, STAY OUT OF EVERYONE'S WAY AND MAYBE LEARN SOMETHIN'. THE FIRST YOU'LL BE PUT IN A HOLDING CELL WHICH IS ALOT LIKE A CROWDED BUS AND GO. THERE'S ALOT OF WAITING FOR YOUR NAME TO BE CALLED. PEOPLE MAY FUCK WITH YOU FOR NO REASON, BUT THERE'S ALSO A COMMON BOND, AGAINST THE FUGGIN' PIGS. YOU MAY MEET PEOPLE YOU'D OTHERWISE NEVER MEET.

PEOPLE IN JAIL

THERE'S ALWAYS ONE GUY WHO WON'T STOP YELLING. "IT'S TOO HOT! WHEN DO WE GET FED.?!? WHEN DO I GET MY PHONE CALL?!?" AS IF THE CORRECTIONS OFFICER'S GONNA SAY, "MAN, THAT GUY SURE IS MAKIN' ALOT OF NOISE. WHY DON'T WE JUST LET 'EM GO? DON'T ACT LIKE THIS IN JAIL. I MEAN, I HAVE SOME SELF RESPECT. YA KNOW? I WOULDN'T THINK OF GIVING THE C.O. THE SATISFACTION OF IGNORING ME WHICH IS ALL THEY'LL DO ON WEEKENDS, YOU SEE ALOT OF WELL DRESSED PEOPLE, USUALLY IN FOR D.U.I., WHO PACE AROUND THE CELL AND NERVOUSLY YELL INTO THE PHONE, TRYIN' TO GET BAILED OUT. THEY'LL COMPLAIN TO ANYONE WHO'LL LISTEN THAT THEY DIDN'T DO ANYTHING, THAT THEY DON'T BELONG THERE. WELL FUCK YOU, THEN, TOO GOOD FOR THE JAIL? EH? WHEN THEY COME YER WAY, ROLL OVER AND GO BACK TO SLEEP. SHEESH. THERE'S ALSO THE PEOPLE, THE MAJORITY, WHO ARE IN FOR BEIN' BLACK IN THE WRONG PLACE AT THE WRONG TIME, THERE'S ALWAYS A COUPLE PEOPLE WHO FOR SOME REASON TRY TO SUCK UP TO THE C.O.'S, WHICH IS KINDA LIKE A SHORTCUT THROUGH A PARKING LOT BECOMES "CRIMINAL TRESPASSING" FOR THEM. THERE'S THE PEOPLE, WHO ALWAYS TRY TO TALK TO BUS DRIVERS. WELL, IT DOESN'T GET YOU ANYWHERE, OK? FUCK THE POLICE. FINALLY, THERE IS THE GUY WHO SNORES, SO LOUD THROUGH THE WHOLE THING. THAT YOU WONDER IF MAYBE HE'S CHOKING OR DYING OR SOMETHING. THIS IS THE GUY YOU SHOULD ACT LIKE.

JAIL CONVERSATION

ASKING SOMEONE WHAT THEY DID TO GET IN IS A BAD WAY TO START A CONVERSATION, TOO PERSONAL, A BETTER WAY IS TO ASK SOMEONE WHO HAS BEEN THERE BEFORE (USUALLY NOT THINKING) WHAT THEY THINK WILL HAPPEN TO YOUR CASE. I USUALLY DON'T REALLY TALK TO ANYONE, UNLESS THEY TALK TO ME, OR UNLESS I HAVE SOMETHIN' PARTICULARLY CLEVER TO SAY. DESTROY THE JAIL.

JAIL TERMINOLOGY

WHEN YOU LEAVE THE HOLDING CELL FOR A REAL CELL, IT'LL BE A LITTLE LESS CROWDED AND YOU'LL GET YER OWN BUNK. THIS IS YOUR "HOUSE". YOU MAYBE STANDING BY SOMEONE ELSE'S BUNK IN A DAZE AND BE TOLD "GET YER PUNK ASS AWAY FROM MY HOUSE". PUNK IS FAG. EACH CELL BLOCK HAS AN APPOINTED LEADER, THE HOUSEMAN, THIS POSITION IS WON THROUGH A COMBINATION OF EARNED RESPECT AND BRUTE FORCE, AND COMES WITH ALOT OF PERKS, LIKE ACCESS TO NICE STUFF LIKE CIGARETTES, RADIOS, BOOKS, ETC. IT'S NO USE TO SUCK UP TO THIS MAN, BUT DON'T CROSS HIM EITHER, CUZ HE'S GOT ALOT OF POWER. THE COMMISSARY SELLS STUFF, LIKE JUNK FOOD, STAMPS, BIBLES, NOTHIN' GOOD. YOU CAN ORDER ONCE A WEEK WITH MONEY THAT WAS ON YA WHEN YOU WERE ARRESTED OR THAT IS BROUGHT TO YOU BY FRIENDS OR LOVED ONES, REVOLUTIONARY SUPPORTERS, ETC. THE YARD IS WHERE YOU CAN LIFT WEIGHTS OR WHATEVER. THIS IS WHERE YOU WILL GET BEAT UP BADLY, IF SOMEONE WANTS TO FUCK YOU UP. DON'T GO TO THE YARD. I'M JONES - CLEVER NAME FOR KOOL-AID SERVED WITH CHOW (MEAL).

JAIL HUMOUR

ONE TIME I WAS ARRESTED AND GIVEN A COURT DATE FOR SHOPLIFTING, AMONG OTHER THINGS, A TOOTH-BRUSH. I FORGOT ABOUT MY COURT DATE AND WHEN THAT DAY CAME, INSTEAD OF GOING TO COURT, I WAS GETTING ARRESTED, ETC. A MONTHS LATER I WAS PICKED UP WHILE WALKING AROUND IN BOCA AND TAKEN TO JAIL, WHERE I WAS ISSUED - A TOOTHBRUSH! HA! HA! HA!

(Left margin comic panels with speech, labels:)

SHWOO! GOT A YEETI-PAK!

FUK YOU, YOU UGLY MONKEY! / DA COOM BAK / BONK! / PIG / PIG

DA PIG POORLY DREAMT / PIG!

I DON'T WANT NO... / TI-KEY

INTRODUCING! THE S.I.W.S.!

HAH! / I DONNO... / I KNOW... / KISS / OOOOH / YEAH! / BOMB!

← TO JAIL / KA KA! / BOSARRO AGOVI

WE'RE / HAH / LAH / TI-KEY!

BLACK CROWBARS IN DA HOUR / PIG

SO, ME AND BOOD GOT READY TO TOUGH OUT THE 21 DAYS TOGETHER, CUZ UNLESS WE GOT THE "CAKE FROM MA" (W/THE CROWBAR BAKED IN IT), WE WERE STUCK. BUT WHEN THEY PUT ALL THE NEW CASES IN THE ELEVATOR TO GO TO THEIR NEW CELLS, BUDDHA'S NAME WAS CALLED OUT AT THE 6TH FLOOR. HE GOT OFF THE ELEVATOR, THE DOOR CLOSED, AND THAT WAS IT. I WAS ALONE... I WAS ASSIGNED A CELL ON THE 8TH FLOOR. WHEN I TOLD THIS TO PRISONERS AT THE STOCKADE, A WEEK LATER, THEY WERE SHOCKED. "YOU WERE ON THE 8TH FLOOR?! SHIT! WHAD YOU DO?" APPARENTLY, THE 8TH FLOOR AT THE COUNTY JAIL IS WHERE THE PSYCHOS, MURDERERS, AND PEOPLE-WHO-LIGHT-OTHER-PEOPLE-ON-FIRE END UP.

I SPENT A DEPRESSING WEEKEND THERE ON THE 8TH FLOOR. I FIGURED JAIL WOULD BE EASY IF I COULD GET BOOKS, OR WRITING SUPPLIES, BUT IT TURNED OUT THAT YOU CAN'T GET ANY BOOKS IN THE MAIL, OR FROM VISITORS*. YOU COULD BUY WRITING SUPPLIES FROM THE COMMISSARY BUT I DIDN'T HAVE ANY MONEY OR ANY DESIRE TO HAVE MONEY PUT IN MY ACCOUNT. THERE WERE, HOWEVER, PLENTY OF BIBLES GOIN' AROUND. EVERYONE WAS REALLY INTO GOD, WELL, NOW THAT THEY HAD KILLED SOMEONE, OR WHATEVER, THEY WERE INTO GOD. ESPECIALLY THE HOUSEMAN, THIS 450 POUND, BLACK GUY, WHO ALSO, AS LUCK WOULD HAVE IT, BUNKED UNDERNEATH ME. WHENEVER HE FELT LIKE IT, HE WOULD GIVE ME A LENGTHY SPEECH ABOUT HOW I WAS THROWING MY LIFE AWAY CUZ 1) I DIDN'T BELIEVE IN GOD, AND, 2) I WEAR DIRTY SHORTS. "LOOK AT YOU! ONLY 19 YEARS OLD, WITH THOSE SHORTS!" "I GOT CLEAN UP DUTY, AND THEY'D KEEP GOIN'" "OH, CAN'T YOU DO ANYTHING RIGHT?!? DON'T YOU KNOW HOW TO MOP?" (SO, YOU SEE THAT EVEN IF I GAVE UP MY LIFE 'O CRIME AND "GOT A REAL JOB" IT'D STILL BE THE SAME THING FOR ME - I CAN'T MOP, I DON'T WANNA MOP, FUK YOU) THE WAY YOU MOP, IT'S LIKE YOU DON'T CARE ABOUT GOD, OR NOTHIN'! AND THOSE SHORTS!" EVERYONE SPENT ALL THEIR TIME BARTERING FOR AS MUCH FOOD, OR PHONE TIME (YOU GOT 15 MINUTES A DAY) AS THEY COULD GET, OR WATCHING TV, WHICH WAS ON 24 HOURS A DAY. 24 HOURS OF RAP VIDEOS, JEAN CLAUDE VAN DAMME MOVIES, ANDREW DICE CLAY, FOOTBALL. I JUST SLEPT A LOT, AND THEN EVERYONE WOULD GET ANGRY WHEN I WOULDN'T EAT OR USE MY PHONE TIME. BUT, WITH NO EXERCISE, I HAD NO APPETITE AND, AFTER A COUPLE CALLS EXPLAINING TO CHUCK LOOSE AND MICK WHERE I WAS, I HAD NO DESIRE TO USE THE PHONE. PLUS, IT MADE ME FEEL KINDA TOUGH. I MEAN, THESE WERE THINGS THEY TOOK FROM YOU TO PUNISH YOU AND I DIDN'T WANT THEM TO BEGIN WITH.

ON MONDAY, I WAS MOVED TO THE DADE COUNTY STOCKADE, WHICH WAS LIKE A HIGH SCHOOL GYMNASIUM, FULL OF BUNK BEDS. WHEN I GOT THERE, THEY LINED US UP, 8 AT A TIME, AND GAVE US KWELL DELOUSING SHAMPOO. AND, SO, HERE IT WAS, AT LAST... THE JAIL SHOWER. AH, YES... THEY WANTED ME, WITH MY LONG, BLOND HAIR, IN THAT SHOWER, WITH 7 OTHER BIG, SEX STARVED MEN. I HAD TO LAUGH, BUT I WAS KINDA NERVOUS, AND READY FIGHT AS BEST I COULD, BUT NO ONE EVEN LOOKED AT ME. WHEN I GOT OUT, I SAW THAT BUDDHA WAS HERE, TOO! I WAS PRETTY HAPPY, CUZ HERE, YOU AT LEAST HAD ROOM TO MOVE AROUND, AND, NOW, I WAS BACK WITH BOOD. HE HAD GONE AHEAD AND CALLED HIS MOM TO GET OUT, CUZ HE WAS NERVOUS ABOUT THE 21 DAYS ALONE. WELL, I DON'T BLAME HIM. IF YOU CAN GET OUTTA JAIL, DO IT. I FELT PRETTY BAD FOR LANDIN' HIM HERE IN THE FIRST PLACE, CUZ BOOD'S NOT REALLY A CRIMINAL. AND NOW HIS MOM WAS ALL FREAKED OUT... BUT IT WAS GONNA BE A COUPLE DAYS 'TIL SHE COULD RAISE THE CASH TO GET HIM OUT, SO WE HAD A COUPLE DAYS TO HANG OUT.

IN THE STOCKADE, THERE WERE 90 MEN - ABOUT 75 BLACKS, 10 HISPANICS, 3 "ANGLOS", AND US. THERE WAS, ON THE SURFACE, AT LEAST, A LOT OF RACIAL TENSION, LIKE PEOPLE YELLIN', "GET AWAY FROM MY HOUSE, CRACKER. I HATE FUCKIN' CRACKERS." BUT, MOSTLY, IT SEEMED LIKE IT WAS ATTITUDE, TO FUCK WITH YOU, AND AFTER A WHILE, PEOPLE EITHER WERE COOL TO ME, OR IGNORED ME. THE AVERAGE DAY WENT SOMETHING LIKE THIS: WAKE UP AROUND 1:00 P.M. TRY FOR AN HOUR TO GET BACK TO SLEEP. WAIT IN BED 'TIL "CHOW" AT ABOUT 3:00 (THIS, BELIEVE IT OR NOT, WAS "DINNER TIME"). AFTER "CHOW", EVERYONE HAD TO STAY IN BED DURING "LOCKDOWN", WHILE CLEANUP AND HEAD COUNT WERE DONE, 'TIL ABOUT 5:00. THEN I'D LINGER IN BED. TRY AND BORROW THE CO.'S NEWSPAPER. ME AND BOOD WOULD MAKE A TOUR OF THE WINDOWS, WATCH THE FREIGHT TRAINS GRIND SLOWLY ALONG IN THE RAIN ON NEARBY RAILROAD TRACKS, WONDER ALOUD ABOUT POSSIBILITIES OF GETTING ACID SENT TO YOU, HIDDEN UNDER A POSTAGE STAMP ON A LETTER, AND COUNT THE DAYS. WE PLAYED A LOT OF GIN-RUMMY. EVERYONE ELSE PLAYED SPADES, WHICH IS A REAL COMPLICATED GAME WHERE VICTORY SEEMS TO DEPEND ON HOW HARD YOU SLAM YOUR HAND ON THE TABLE AND HOW MUCH TRASH YOU TALK ON YOUR OPPONENTS WHILE YOU PLAY. I HOPED WE WOULDN'T BE IN LONG ENOUGH TO LEARN THE RULES TO SPADES. AROUND 11:00 P.M. WAS ANOTHER LOCKDOWN FOR HEADCOUNT, AND AT 12:00, IT WAS LIGHTS OUT, BUT YOU COULD STILL WALK AROUND. USUALLY, A SHITTY ACTION MOVIE WAS PLAYED ON TV FOR EVERYONE TO HOWL AT, WHILE I TRIED TO SLEEP, WITH TOILET PAPER BALLS IN MY EARS. I FINALLY SLEEP, 'TIL AROUND 2:40 A.M., WHEN THEY WAKE US UP FOR "CHOW" (THIS ONE IS "BREAKFAST") I FINALLY GET BACK TO SLEEP AROUND 4:00 AM, 'TIL "LUNCH", WHICH IS AT 11:30. PRETTY DULL.

DURING THIS TIME, A WEIRD DRAMA BEGAN UNFOLDING, INVOLVING MY EATING HABITS. SEE, WHEN I GOT TO THE COUNTY, I NOTICED THAT EVERYONE WAS, AT LEAST, 15 OR 20 POUNDS OVERWEIGHT, BECAUSE OF 3 MEALS A DAY AND NOT TOO MUCH EXERCISE. SO, I DECIDED ONLY TO EAT THE FRUITS AND VEGETABLES, AND DO SITUPS AND JUMPING JACKS ON MY OWN. PLUS, THE FOOD SUCKED. IT WAS WRONG! IT WASN'T POORLY PREPARED OR ROTTEN — IT WAS GENETICALLY ALTERED! BUDDHA ATE IT AND FELT SHITTY ALL DAY. WELL, MOST GUYS IN THE STOCKADE WOULD DO WHATEVER THEY COULD TO EAT AS MUCH AS POSSIBLE. THEY'D TRADE AND SAVE MEALS FOR DAYS BEHIND THEIR MATTRESSES. WHEN "CHOW" IS SERVED, THE CRIES GO UP, "I GOT 2 EGGS FOR A MEAT! A BREAD FOR SOMEONE'S PIE! A KIDNEY! I'LL GIVE MY KIDNEY FOR A MEAT!!!" IT WAS PATHETIC. SO I STARTED TRADING MY BREAKFAST TO THIS CRAZY PUERTO RICAN GUY FOR HIS MILKS, FRUITS, AND VEGGIES. WORD GOT OUT THAT THE CRACKER DON'T EAT, AND ALL THESE LEERING, DROOLING STRAYS WOULD DRAG ASS TO MY BUNK EVERY DAY, RIGHT ABOUT CHOW, MAKING THEIR OFFERS, PROMISES, AND, FINALLY, THEIR THREATS. IT GOT KIND OF TENSE, ESPECIALLY CUZ I THINK THEY THOUGHT I DEALT WITH ROBERT CUZ HE WAS WHITE, BUT HE WAS THE FIRST PERSON ME AND BUDDHA MET, BACK AT THE COUNTY, THE DAY OF OUR BOND HEARING. HE WAS JUST THE FIRST PERSON TO ASK ME. PLUS, HE WAS GONNA GET A TABLET, PENS, STAMPS, AND ENVELOPES FROM COMMISSARY FOR ME. SO, EVERYWHERE I WENT, ALL DAY, PEOPLE WOULD TAKE ME ASIDE AND ASK, "MAN, WHY DON'T YOU EAT?" AND I'D HAVE TO EXPLAIN THE WHOLE THING. THIS HAPPENED, SERIOUSLY, LIKE 5 TIMES AN HOUR, EVEN FROM THE SAME PEOPLE. INSANE. I'D GO TO THE BATHROOM AND THE GUY IN THE STALL NEXT TO ME'D SAY, "MAN... I GOT A LUNG FOR YOUR TRAY IN THE MORNING!" SHEESH. NOW, IF ONE GUY WOULD JUST SAY, "I'VE GOT 'JOURNEY TO THE END OF THE NIGHT' BY CELINE..."

*asterisk
"RULES MAY VARY. JAILS ARE DIFFERENT EVERYWHERE, I HEAR, IN BERKELEY, THERE'S EVEN A "PUNK JAIL."

FINALLY, ONE FRIDAY MORNING, AT 4:00 A.M., BUDDHA GOT OUT. HIS MOM WAS GONNA HAVE TO PAY $500, PLUS EGGS AND A MEAT, BUT THEN, SOMEHOW, SHE FOUND OUT ABOUT THE MYSTERIOUS "ALTERNATIVE SERVICES PROGRAM" WHICH ALLOWED HIM TO BE SIGNED OUT TO SOMEONE IN THE COMMUNITY. THIS SOUNDED LIKE MY TICKET OUT, SO I CALLED THE A.S.P. AND GOT NICK TO AGREE TO SIGN ME OUT AND HAD CHUCK LOOSE AND YOUNG FIDEL CALL THE A.S.P. TO BOTHER 'EM ABOUT MY CASE ALOT, CUZ PEOPLE TOLD ME THAT HELPED. THEN, I WENT BACK TO WAITING OUT THE 11 DAYS LEFT. THE WHOLE THING WAS MAINLY JUST FRUSTRATING, CUZ IT WAS SUCH A WASTE OF TIME. I MEAN, I STILL NEEDED A HOME WHEN I GOT OUT. I STILL HAD TO GO OPEN THE ZION CORPORATION. JUST BECAUSE I ENDED UP IN JAIL, DOESN'T MEAN I'M GONNA FREAK OUT AND GET A NORMAL JOB, HOUSE, ETC. I'VE DONE THAT BEFORE, AND I KNOW I DON'T LIKE IT, SO I'VE SET OUT TO FIND A DIFFERENT WAY TO LIVE. I MEAN, JAIL SUCKS, BUT IF YOU'RE GONNA GET MORE SERIOUS' WITH YER LIFE, AND NOT JUST WORK A SHIT JOB, WATCH TV, GET DRUNK, AND COLLECT PUNK RECORDS, THAN THERE'S A GOOD CHANCE YOU COULD END UP THERE (AND EVEN THEN... IT DON'T TAKE TOO MUCH TO LAND IN JAIL IN TODAY'S AMERICA). SO IT FOLLOWS THAT IF YOU CAN'T DO THE THINGS YOU WANT, OR EVEN HAVE A HOUSE AND FOOD, WITHOUT GOING TO JAIL, THEN WE ARE ALWAYS IN JAIL, AND THEY JUST MOVE US INTO SMALLER AND SMALLER CAGES! HOW COULD I BELIEVE SO SERIOUSLY IN SOMETHING AND THEN JUST TURN AWAY AND LIVE LIKE I ALREADY KNOW I HATE IT? LIKE, "OH WELL, I TRIED SQUATTING ONCE. WELL, TIME TO MOVE ON." ~~DOOD PISS~~ I WAS 19 YEARS OLD! THAT'S ANOTHER 60 YEARS OF HAVIN' TO LIVE, KNOWING THAT THAT'S AS FAR AS I GOT! NO AMOUNT OF TRAVELLING, OR BEER DRINKIN', OR ANYTHING COULD HELP ME FORGET THAT...

THINGS WERE PRETTY DULL WITHOUT BOOD. IN A LETTER TO IVY, I WROTE, "I JUST MOVED TO A NEW BUNK, THE BEST ONE YET. ITS WARM, WITH A GOOD VIEW OF THE EXPRESSWAY!" I HAD TO GET MORE RESOURCEFUL TO OCCUPY MYSELF. I WROTE LETTERS ON THE FRONT AND BACK OF COMMISSARY ORDER SLIPS, AND MADE MY OWN ENVELOPES. PEOPLE IN JAIL ARE HIP TO THE ALCOHOL-SOAKING-STAMP TRICK, BUT WITHOUT RUBBING ALCOHOL, THEY USE ROLL ON ANTI-PERSPIRANT TO GET THE CANCELLATIONS OFF! I STUCK MY MILKS UP IN THE AIR CONDITIONING SHAFT TO KEEP 'EM ICE COLD. ONE DAY, THE BUNK NEXT TO ME WAS LEFT VACANT, SO ME AND THESE TWO REAL YOUNG, BLACK KIDS, WHO WERE LIKE 16 AND BEING TRIED AS ADULTS, WE TOTALLY ~~RIPPLE~~ RIPPED APART THE NOW-UNUSED MATTRESS TO GET THE STUFFING OUT TO MAKE PILLOWS (SEE, YOU HAD NO PILLOWS, YOU WERE ISSUED TWO SHEETS, A BLANKET, AND A COUPLE PILLOW CASES). NOW, I SLEPT REAL GOOD ON MY D.I.Y. PILLOW... I ALSO STARTED WORKIN' OUT IN THE LOCKER ROOM-STYLE BATHROOM WITH EVERYONE ELSE. THERE WERE NO WEIGHTS. THEY HAD WATER JUGS TIED TOGETHER WITH ~~CORD~~ RIPPED SHEETS, LIFTED WITH A BROOM HANDLE. YOU MARKED THE NUMBER OF REPS ON THE MIRROR WITH A PIECE OF SOAP...

JAIL SCAMS, JAIL WINE, AND MORE
Pt. III OF 3: IGGY BEHIND BARS

What a fantastic school this prison is! Here, I have forged my vision of the world and have found the meaning of my life. Will it be long or short? I do not know. Fruitful or sterile? But there is something I feel reaffirming itself within me; my passionate desire to sacrifice and struggle.[50] — Fidel

THE COOLEST THING WAS TRYING TO GET AWAY WITH STUFF WITHOUT THE GUARDS KNOWIN', LIKE ONE DAY, ALL THESE GUYS, INCLUDING THE HOUSEMAN, WERE GATHERED AROUND THIS BED, GIGGLING. THEY WERE DRINKIN' THE JAIL CELL WINE! I DECIDED TO MAKE MY OWN, W/ GRAPES FROM "CHOW", SUGAR, AND THE JIM JONES. I MADE IT IN SOMEONE'S OLD COMMISSARY PEANUT BUTTER JAR, AND I HAD TO LOOSEN THE CAP TWICE A DAY. ONE TIME, IN THE BATHROOM, EVERYONE WAS GATHERED AROUND THE EXTENSION CORD TO THE HAIR CLIPPERS. SEE, YOU COULD ALWAYS SHAVE YER HEAD. THE CLIPPERS WERE ALWAYS THERE. BUT, TODAY, EVERYONE ~~WA~~ WAS GATHERED AROUND THE CORD. THEY HAD A CIGARETTE, AND NO WAY TO LIGHT IT, SO WHAT THEY DID WAS PUT PENCIL LEADS IN THE (UNPLUGGED) EXTENSION CORD OUTLET. PLUG IT IN, AND TOUCH A PIECE OF TOILET PAPER TO THE LEADS, WHICH CAUSED A SPARK WHICH CAUGHT THE PAPER ON FIRE, TO LIGHT THE CIGARETTE! THEN THEY ALL SMOKED IN THE TOILET, HIGH SCHOOL STYLE. I'M SURE, BETWEEN 10 GUYS, THERE WASN'T MUCH OF A NICOTINE HIGH, BUT THEY HAD THE GETTING-AWAY-WITH-IT HIGH. I STARTED ~~WRITING~~ FILLING OUT "COUNSELLOUR REQUEST FORMS." THE COUNSELLOUR WAS THIS GUY THAT'S SUPPOSED TO GIVE LEGAL ADVICE AND HELP THE PRISONERS. I WROTE HIM, SUGGESTING WE ORGANIZE A PRODUCTION OF ~~JAILHOUSE ROCK~~ "JAILHOUSE ROCK" TO HELP THE PRISONERS' "SELF-ESTEEM." I WROTE HIM, SUGGESTING HE GET US A MOTIVATIONAL SPEAKER. I SUGGESTED FIDEL CASTRO... FINALLY, I WROTE, "IF I AM NOT LET OUT IN 2 DAYS, I WILL ORDER MY FOLLOWERS TO CALL A NATION WIDE, GENERAL STRIKE, THUS CRIPPLING YOUR ECONOMY AND MAKING THE ENFORCEMENT OF YOUR SO-CALLED LAW IMPOSSIBLE!" I ALMOST GOT IN A LOT OF TROUBLE, BELIEVE IT OR NOT, FOR THAT ONE. A C.O. TOOK ME ASIDE TO MAKE SURE I WOULDN'T "CARRY OUT THIS THREAT." PRETTY FUNNY.

WATCHIN' FOOTBALL GAMES ON TV IN JAIL WAS ALSO KINDA FUN, WITH 90 MEN, ALL CRAZY AND YELLIN' SHIT AT THE PLAYERS AND TALKIN' SHIT TO EACH OTHER, GROANIN', JUMPIN', HIGH FIVIN', AND MAKIN' BETS ON EVERY PLAY. A WHOLE DAY'S CHOW, WON OR LOST, ON EVERY DOWN... I HUNG OUT A LOT WITH THIS BUM, LARRY, I KNEW FROM COCONUT GROVE. WE TALKED ABOUT GROVE SCAMS, LIKE THE GUYS WHO CHARGE MONEY TO PARK YUPPIE CARS BY THE ELEMENTARY SCHOOL, THOUGH ITS FREE TO PARK THERE, AND MAKE A COUPLE HUNDRED BUCKS BEFORE THE COPS CHASE 'EM OFF. LARRY WAS SURPRISED TO FIND THAT I WAS THE PERSON WHO WROTE "KILL POLICE" ON EVERY BUS BENCH IN TOWN... YES, EVEN UP TO THE END, IT SUCKED IN JAIL, BUT I MANAGED TO GET THROUGH IT, AND I'M GLAD THAT ITS NOT A BIG, SCARY MYSTERY TO ME NOW, AND I KNOW WHAT ITS ALL ABOUT. IT FELT GOOD TO KNOW I COULD TAKE IT...

FINALLY, I DECIDED I COULD HAVE ALOT OF FUN, USIN' MY PHONE TIME TO MAKE CRANK CALLS... BUT, THAT NIGHT, THE 20TH, THEY CALLED MY NAME TO LET ME GO! THE CHARGES WERE DROPPED! SEE, I GUESS NO ONE OWNS THESE ABANDONED BUILDINGS TO PRESS CHARGES! EVERYONE GATHERED AROUND ME. "HEY! WHITE BOY'S GOIN' HOME!" WE DRANK THE JAIL CELL WINE I MADE, AND 2 HOURS LATER I WAS FREE. I HAD TOLD EVERYONE THAT I WAS GONNA HOP THE RAIL AND STEAL A 6, BUT THE COOL, OCTOBER AIR AND THE SMELL OF LITTLE HAVANA WAS SO BEAUTIFUL, THAT I JUST WALKED ABOUT 10 MILES TO SIR ROBERT'S PLACE IN THE GROVE. THEN, I STOLE THE 6!

I WAS JUST OUTTA DA **GREYBAR HOTEL** WHEN I HEARD THAT EMIL AND THE **YOUNG FIDEL** WERE DRIVIN' UP TO **D.C.**, TO MEET UP W/ FLINT, SO, SINCE I HAD NOTHING ELSE TO DO AND NOWHERE TO LIVE, I BEGGED UP A SEAT IN THE CAR. AND SCOTTY DECIDED TO COME, TOO, AND WE WERE OFF. EMIL, THE DRIVIN' **MACK**, DROVE THE WHOLE 18 HOURS UP, STRAIGHT, W/ THE YOUNG FIDEL NAVIGATING, AND HOLDING THE TRUSTY SQUEEZE BOTTLE FULL OF SALT WATER, EVER READY TO USE THIS UNLIKELY WEAPON TO **DESTROY** UNSUSPECTING COKE MACHINES ON THE WAY FOR GAS MONEY AND DRINKS. WE ARRIVED IN D.C., **RAIDED** A GIANT SUPERMARKET'S SOUP AND SALAD BAR, AND THEN MY CAR MATES WENT OFF TO SEE SOME TERRIBLE SHOW (CHUMBAWUMBA/FUGAZI) AND I ROAMED DA MEAN STREETS OF THE CAPITOL, SWILLING MY FOOD STAMP BOUGHT **7-11 COFFEE**, CHECKIN' FIRE ESCAPES AND ALLEYS. I GOT ON THE ROOF OF THE D.C. HILTON HOTEL, UP 15 ELEVATOR STORIES, TWO ON THE STAIRS, ONE UP A LADDER, THROUGH A **SECRET FALSE WALL** AND UP A LADDER, THROUGH A HATCH ONTO DA ROOF. YOU COULD SEE EVERYTHING IN TOWN! IT WAS SO BEAUTIFUL! AND... I HAD **SPRAY PAINT!!!** I PRECARIOUSLY LEANED OVER THE EDGE AND SPRAY PAINTED "**U.S. OUT OF HERE!**" ON THE FACE OF THE BUILDING, SO THAT YOU COULD READ IT FOR BLOCKS AND BLOCKS. I MEANT IT! THERE WAS **NO TIME** TO STAND AROUND AND ADMIRE MY WORK, CUZ WE WERE OFF TO **NEW YORK CITY** TO SEE **JAWBREAKER**. WE HAD A DUMPSTERED TV TO GIVE TO **HAUSIPUNGO** TO SMASH ON STAGE BUT WE FORGOT TO GIVE IT TO 'EM. ME AND SCOTTY DRANK **BIG BOTTLES OF BEER** AND GOT **WASTED!** WE STAYED IN JERSEY CITY WHERE I WENT ON A CRAZY SEARCH FOR A **FALLOUT SHELTER** THAT I COULD GET INTO. NO LUCK, SO I SETTLED FOR A F.S. SIGN FROM THE J.C. JUSTICE BUILDING. I CAN ONLY THINK OF TWO FALLOUT SHELTERS IN MIAMI. WHAT WERE THEY GONNA DO? JUST WRITE US OFF? SHEESH. ME AND SCOTT BRAVED A **DUMPSTER FULL OF BEES** TO GET A PILE OF DONUTS AND THEN ME AND J.C. LEGEND, **RAY-RAY** TOOK A WALK BY THE CLOSED DOWN FACTORIES, ABANDONED RAILROAD TRACKS, AND RUNDOWN BUILDINGS, KICKIN' **RAT SKELETONS** IN THE GUTTER, THEN, IT WAS BACK TO **D.C.** WHERE WE WATCHED BRAVE BUMS PLAY CHESS IN DUPONT CIRCLE. AT THE SMITHSONIAN MUSEUM, WHEN YOU'VE CLIMBED THE MILES OF STAIRS UP TO THE ENTRANCE, THERE'S A NET ALONGSIDE THE WALL TO SAVE YOU FROM **FALLING 40 FEET TO YER DEATH**. I JUMPED OFF THE WALL INTO THE NET FOR FUN AND TOURISTS TOOK PICTURES AND TRIED TO MAKE ME KEEP DOING IT BUT IT WAS **TOO PAINFUL**. WE FOUND AN UNUSED SUBWAY SYSTEM BUT COULDN'T EXPLORE IT CUZ WE HAD TO RACE OFF TO **CLEVELAND** WHERE A FRIEND OF FLINT AND YOUNG FIDEL LIVED. THE GUY'S MOM, **A FRIEND OF THE REVOLUTION**, MADE US EAT TONS OF FOOD, AND HE LOANED ME A BIKE. I RODE AROUND AND MET TWO REAL FRIENDLY PUNK GIRLS WITH **BLUE HAIR** IN A DONUT SHOP. WE WALKED TO A PIZZA SHOP WHERE WE ATE PIZZA AND **LEFT WITHOUT PAYING!** THEY WANTED ME TO STICK AROUND, BUT WHEN YOU GOTTA GO, YA GOTTA GO, GO, GO! I RETURNED TO MY TRUE LOVE: **CYCLING** AND RODE AROUND IN SUB **FREEZING TEMPERATURES** IN MY BOXERS, YELLIN' OUT **S.L.F.** LYRICS, AND THEN A GUY NAMED **RINGWORM** LET ME DO 50 ISSUES OF **SCAM** AT HIS WORK. THEN IT WAS OFF TO A FRIEND'S PLACE IN **BALTIMORE**. WE ARRIVED W/ A SACK OF COKES AND SOME SPARE CHANGE. THE RUNDOWN BUILDINGS IN THE RAIN MADE ME FALL IN LOVE W/ THE CITY. I WANTED TO DRINK COFFEE AND WALK IN THE **COLD RAIN** AND DRY OFF IN THE LIBRARY IN A PILE OF BOOKS ON **HOBOS, AND PIRATES AND SPIES**. BUT WE HAD THAT **TRAVEL ITCH**, AND HEADED FOR THE **OPEN ROAD**. BUT FIRST, ANOTHER PAYPHONE ATE MY 5 BUCKS FOR A **CALL TO HELSINKI**. THE OPERATOR SAID THEY'D SEND A CHECK. THIS HAPPENED 8 OR 10 TIMES ON OUR TRIP. THEN WE ENDED UP IN TINY **BOON, NORTH CAROLINA** FOR BEAUTIFUL TREE AND RIPPLIN' CREEK SCENERY. AND **MOUNTAIN CLIMBING IN THE POURING RAIN**. SCOTTY ALMOST GOT LOST OVER THE EDGE. ME AND FLINT TRIED TO GO "**THE IMPOSSIBLE WAY**" AND I SLID 15 FEET DOWN THE FACE OF THE MOUNTAIN! YES, WE LEFT OUR **BLOOD** ON THAT MOUNTAIN, BUT WE CLIMBED IT AND RELAXED TO A BIG MEAL PREPARED BY YOUNG FIDEL. "**TONIGHT WE FEAST, MEN. TOMMORROW WE DRIVE...**" WE HEADED FOR HOME, AND I GOT TO WATCH **GROWN MEN** NEARLY **FIST FIGHT** OVER WHO'S TURN IT WAS TO SIT IN THE FRONT SEAT... AHH. THE ROAD TRIP... I GOT HOME AND MY CHECKS WERE ALREADY WAITIN' FOR ME...

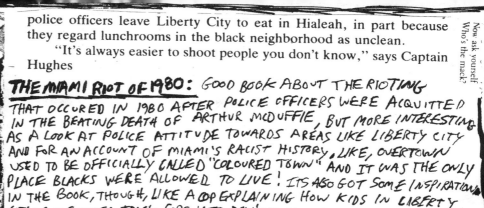

So that's why Ice Cube's dressed up
Because the city is so fuckin' messed up
And everybody's so phoney
Take a little time
To think about your dead homie
Now ask yourself
Who's the mack?

police officers leave Liberty City to eat in Hialeah, in part because they regard lunchrooms in the black neighborhood as unclean.

"It's always easier to shoot people you don't know," says Captain Hughes

THE MIAMI RIOT OF 1980: GOOD BOOK ABOUT THE RIOTING THAT OCCURED IN 1980 AFTER POLICE OFFICERS WERE ACQUITTED IN THE BEATING DEATH OF ARTHUR MCDUFFIE, BUT MORE INTERESTING AS A LOOK AT POLICE ATTITUDE TOWARDS AREAS LIKE LIBERTY CITY AND FOR AN ACCOUNT OF MIAMI'S RACIST HISTORY, LIKE, OVERTOWN USED TO BE OFFICIALLY CALLED "COLOURED TOWN" AND IT WAS THE ONLY PLACE BLACKS WERE ALLOWED TO LIVE! ITS ALSO GOT SOME INSPIRATION IN THE BOOK, THOUGH, LIKE A COP EXPLAINING HOW KIDS IN LIBERTY CITY SOMETIMES TRICK COPS INTO DRIVING INTO AN ALLEY, THEN THEY BLOCK THE CAR IN BY PUSHING A DUMPSTER IN FRONT OF THE EXIT, AND THROW ROCKS AND BOTTLES AT THE CAR! FINALLY, A CURE FOR THE SUMMERTIME BLUES, EH? ONE TIME I WAS WALKIN' UP BY BROWNSVILLE METRORAIL AND I SAW A RAILROAD FLARE ON THE GROUND UNDER THE METRORAIL THAT HAD BEEN PROPPED UP TO FIRE INTO THE TRAIN! YO! **THE COMPLETE BOOK OF RAP LYRICS:** WELL I DON'T REALLY LIKE RAP TOO MUCH BUT THIS BOOK IS VERY HANDY, AND CONTAINS THE ANSWERS TO A LOT OF QUESTIONS, LIKE, O MAN, IGGY WERE SURROUNDED BY THE POLICE, WHAT DO WE DO? HMM... WELL WHAT WOULD **ICE CUBE** DO? PAGE 235 SAYS "ICE CUBE WILL SWARM ON ANY MOTHERFUCKER IN A BLUE UNIFORM!" AH, YES! OF COURSE! SORT OF A

Wanderer, wayfarer, king of the road, he rides the rails a thousand miles from home.

HOBO
Richard Dillof

...BLE FOR CRIMINALS. **MAN IN BLACK** by JOHNNY CASH: ONE TIME ME AND FLINT WERE DRIVIN' ...ROUND LISTENIN' TO JOHNNY CASH, AND SAYIN' MAN, I BET THIS GUY WAS A REAL BAD ASS, ALL ...PPIN' FREIGHTS, AND LANDIN' IN JAIL, FISTFIGHTS, WINE, WOMEN, SONG, ETC. SO, I DECIDED TO CHECK ...T HIS BOOK, WELL, WE WE'RE WRONG! WHAT A POSER! HE DIDN'T EVEN WRITE HALF HIS SONGS! ...E WHOLE BOOK IS A BIG LOVE STORY TO GOD AND AMERICA AND HIS WIFE AND HOW HE TOOK ALL THEM ...TTLE WHITE PILLS AND RUINED HIS MARRIAGE WELL, FUK, THOSE LITTLE WHITE PILLS DID A LOT FOR ...Y BAND, HE DIDN'T HOP TRAINS OR ROB BANKS OR ANYTHING'... HE WAS JUST SOME DUMB HICK LIKE ...VIS, WHO GOT DISCOVERED IN SOME JERKWATER TOWN, SINGIN' LOVE SONGS TO HIS MAMA... ...OUND **FOR GLORY** by WOODY GUTHRIE: THIS IS THE REAL SHIT THAT I WAS LOOKIN' FOR IN THE ...SH BOOK. WOODY TRAVELS AROUND THE COUNTRY, WITH HIS GUITAR, A PICKIN' AND A GRINNIN', AND ...NGIN' SONGS WITH THE PEOPLE. THIS BOOK HAS LOTS OF ACTION — FREIGHT HOPPIN', FIST FIGHTIN', ...RD DRINKIN', ETC., BUT, MORE IMPORTANTLY, FEATURES REAL STRONG WRITING AND GOOD STORIES. ...THRIE USES A LOT OF PHRASES LIKE "HOLLERIN' LIKE 9 CATS IN A BAG.", IF YA KNOW WHAT I MEAN. ...E GREATEST: MY OWN STORY by MUHAAMED ALI: HERE IS THE TRUE STORY OF THAT RAREST ...F INDIVIDUALS, WHO IS BLESSED WITH THAT ELUSIVE COMBINATION OF GREAT POETRY AND ...RD HITTING FISTS! THE TITLE SAYS IT ALL. ALI HAD TRUE STYLE. HE WOULDN'T JUST BEAT HIS ...PPONENT, BUT HE'D ANNOUNCE BEFORE THE FIGHT WHAT ROUND HE'D WIN IN! HERE'S ONE OF ...LI'S POEMS "THIS WILL AMAZE YA/ I'M GONNA RETIRE JOE FRAZIER." THE BOOK FOLLOWS ALI'S RISE ...TTA THE RACIST DEEP SOUTH, THROUGH HIS HEROIC DRAFT DODGING, AND UP TO THE "THRILLA IN ...ANILLA" ITS PRETTY UPLIFTING STUFF, BUT ALSO HAS SOME FUNNY SCENES WHERE HE'S ALWAYS JUST ...ALKIN' AROUND — THIS IS MUHAAMED ALI, RIGHT? — HE'S ALWAYS WALKIN' AND A BUNCH OF KIDS ALWAYS ...OLLOW HIM AROUND, YELLIN' "HEY, CHAMP! YOU GONNA BEAT FRAZIER?" AND STUFF LIKE THAT. ESSENTIAL ...OBO: WELL, I MUST ADMIT I DIDN'T GET ALL THE WAY THROUGH THIS ONE, BUT I KNOW ITS A CLASSIC, ...ECAUSE OF THE COVER, WHICH FEATURES THE HOBO GUY (THAT'S YOU, MAN — THE READER) SITTIN' IN A ...OXCAR WITH A BANJO! I GOT THIS IN A USED BOOKSTORE IN ATLANTA A COUPLE DAYS AFTER HOPPIN' ...Y FIRST TRAIN. SCAM ROAD TRIP ADVICE: BRING A SMILE AND A SONG FOR THE BANJO! **THE DAMNDEST RADICAL: THE BEN REITMAN STORY** — GREAT STORY OF A GUY WHO DID A WHOLE LOT OF ...EVERYTHING: TRAVELLED THE COUNTRY AS A HOBO, WAS EMMA GOLDMAN, THE ANARCHIST'S LOVER, WAS A SKID ...OW CLAP DOCTOR, WROTE THE EXCELLENT "BOXCAR BERTHA" BOOK, ETC... BUT THE BEST STUFF IS ABOUT HIM ...EADING THE HOBO COLLEGE IN CHICAGO. THE HOBO COLLEGES WERE STARTED BY MILLIONAIRE-TURNED-HOBO ...AMES EADS. HOW AS A PLACE WHERE THE MEN OF THE ROAD COULD COME AND SEE PUBLIC SPEAKERS AND ...EBATE EACH OTHER ON THE ISSUES OF THE DAY, ALSO HAS A LOT OF STUFF ON CHICAGO'S "BUGHOUSE ...QUARE" — A PLACE WHERE PEOPLE WOULD GIVE SPEECHES AND ARGUE ...N PUBLIC — SOMETHING I WISH PEOPLE DID MORE NOWADAYS...

an officer can easily get trapped in there," said Captain Hughes. "You ...o in with your car and you can't see around corners once you get into ...hose breezeways, and they push a 'Dempsey Dumpster' into an alley ...ay to block it.

Evans: That guy last night?
Headquarters: Yeah?
Evans: He was hit with Kelites.
Headquarters: He was hit with Kelites?
Evans: Uh-hmm.
Headquarters: Oh, shit.[14]

MORE SCAM BOOK REVIEWS

Never mind your festering pressure cooker cities of handguns, people, and cars. This is the water planet !!

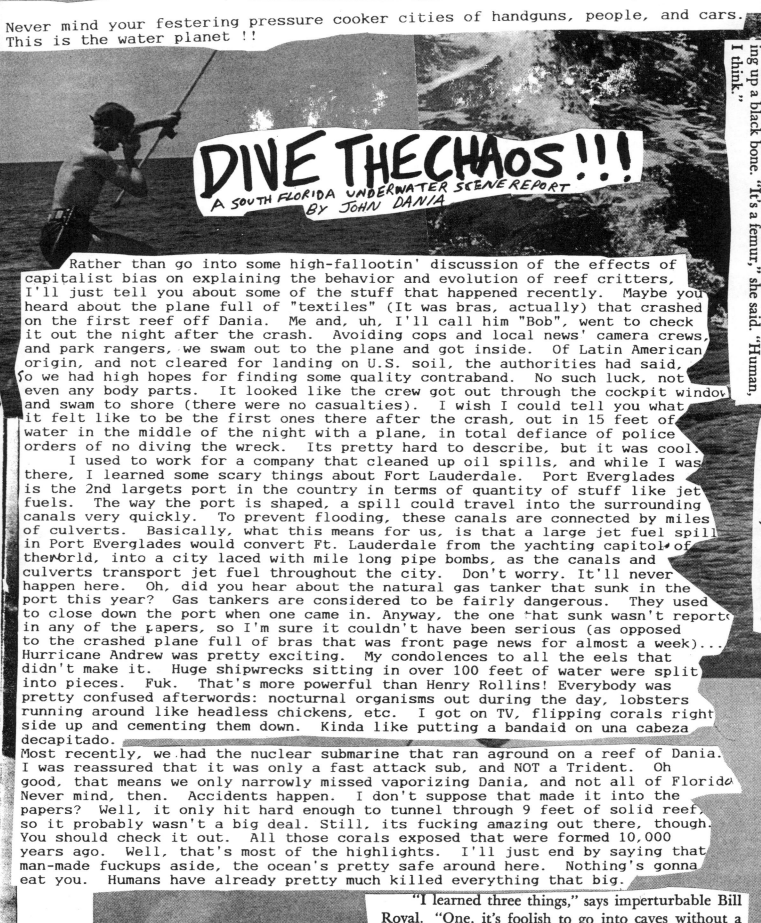

DIVE THE CHAOS!!!
A SOUTH FLORIDA UNDERWATER SCENE REPORT
BY JOHN DANIA

Rather than go into some high-fallootin' discussion of the effects of capitalist bias on explaining the behavior and evolution of reef critters, I'll just tell you about some of the stuff that happened recently. Maybe you heard about the plane full of "textiles" (It was bras, actually) that crashed on the first reef off Dania. Me and, uh, I'll call him "Bob", went to check it out the night after the crash. Avoiding cops and local news' camera crews, and park rangers, we swam out to the plane and got inside. Of Latin American origin, and not cleared for landing on U.S. soil, the authorities had said, so we had high hopes for finding some quality contraband. No such luck, not even any body parts. It looked like the crew got out through the cockpit window and swam to shore (there were no casualties). I wish I could tell you what it felt like to be the first ones there after the crash, out in 15 feet of water in the middle of the night with a plane, in total defiance of police orders of no diving the wreck. Its pretty hard to describe, but it was cool.

I used to work for a company that cleaned up oil spills, and while I was there, I learned some scary things about Fort Lauderdale. Port Everglades is the 2nd largets port in the country in terms of quantity of stuff like jet fuels. The way the port is shaped, a spill could travel into the surrounding canals very quickly. To prevent flooding, these canals are connected by miles of culverts. Basically, what this means for us, is that a large jet fuel spill in Port Everglades would convert Ft. Lauderdale from the yachting capitol of theworld, into a city laced with mile long pipe bombs, as the canals and culverts transport jet fuel throughout the city. Don't worry. It'll never happen here. Oh, did you hear about the natural gas tanker that sunk in the port this year? Gas tankers are considered to be fairly dangerous. They used to close down the port when one came in. Anyway, the one that sunk wasn't reporte in any of the papers, so I'm sure it couldn't have been serious (as opposed to the crashed plane full of bras that was front page news for almost a week)... Hurricane Andrew was pretty exciting. My condolences to all the eels that didn't make it. Huge shipwrecks sitting in over 100 feet of water were split into pieces. Fuk. That's more powerful than Henry Rollins! Everybody was pretty confused afterwords: nocturnal organisms out during the day, lobsters running around like headless chickens, etc. I got on TV, flipping corals right side up and cementing them down. Kinda like putting a bandaid on una cabeza decapitado.

Most recently, we had the nuclear submarine that ran aground on a reef of Dania. I was reassured that it was only a fast attack sub, and NOT a Trident. Oh good, that means we only narrowly missed vaporizing Dania, and not all of Florida Never mind, then. Accidents happen. I don't suppose that made it into the papers? Well, it only hit hard enough to tunnel through 9 feet of solid reef, so it probably wasn't a big deal. Still, its fucking amazing out there, though. You should check it out. All those corals exposed that were formed 10,000 years ago. Well, that's most of the highlights. I'll just end by saying that man-made fuckups aside, the ocean's pretty safe around here. Nothing's gonna eat you. Humans have already pretty much killed everything that big.

"I learned three things," says imperturbable Bill Royal. "One, it's foolish to go into caves without a safety line tied to yourself. Two, you shouldn't dive alone. Three, there's no treasure chest in Ponce de Leon Springs."

There's a vast amount of gold and silver in wrecks lying on the ocean floor. Hundreds of millions of dollars worth. Almost every ocean and coast can claim a

ing up a black bone. "It's a femur," she said. "Human, I think."

BOCA RATON EMPTY LOTS AND SHIT

BOCA SUCKS. ITS BEEN SAID A MILLION TIMES. I EVEN GOT DETENTIONS IN HIGH SCHOOL FOR WEARING A SHIRT THAT SAID IT. BIG DEAL. I LIVED THERE FOR AWHILE, AT MY MOM'S PLACE, LAST OCTOBER, BETWEEN ROAD TRIPS AND MY BAND'S TOUR, AND MANAGED TO FIND ALL KINDS OF CRAZY STUFF IN THE EMPTY LOTS AND WOODS UP IN NORTH BOCA. I'D GET ALL TANKED ON ICED TEA, AND EVERYDAY WHEN MY MOM CAME HOME FROM WORK, I'D HEAD UP TO THE RAILROAD TRACKS, NORTH OF YAMATO, TO HANG OUT IN THE ABANDONED BUS BEHIND HI-SEA MUSIC, AND WRITE LETTERS, SING S.L.F. SONGS TO MYSELF AND THINK ABOUT THIS GIRL I LIKED. AH YES... IT WAS OCTOBER AND I WAS IN LOVE, AND OCTOBER WAS TOTALLY MY FAVORITE MONTH CUZ THE WEATHER GOT BREEZY AND COOL AND THE DAYS GOT SHORT; ALL BITTERSWEET, WINDIN' DOWN, STIFF BREEZE INTO THE END OF THE YEAR... I'D **CLIMB** AROUND ON THE WHISPERING PINE TREES AND SIT ON THE ABANDONED FREIGHT CARS THERE AND THINK ABOUT OCTOBERS PAST, LIKE WHEN I WAS 14 AND I HAD JUST STARTED HIGH SCHOOL, MY BEST FRIEND AND I HAD KIND OF A BET ABOUT WHICH ONE OF US WOULD GET LAID FIRST (PRETTY LAME, I GUESS, BUT, HEY, WE WAS KIDS). ONE DAY, SCHOOL WAS CANCELLED CUZ OF A TROPICAL DEPRESSION THAT FLOODED ALL THE ROADS. MY FRIEND CALLED ME UP AROUND 3:30 THAT DAY AND SAID, WELL, UM... I WON THE BET, AND IT WAS LIKE WE'RE HERE NOW, AND EVERYTHING'S GONNA BE REAL DIFFERENT FROM NOW ON. HALLOWEEN CAME, W/OUR FIRST REAL PARTY AND BEER AND BANDS AND WE STAYED OUT ALL NIGHT W/ THESE CRAZY CHICKS (AND SLEPT IN ONE GIRL'S YARD, CUZ NO BOYS ALLOWED INSIDE) AND NEVER CALLED HOME. WE DIDN'T CARE! YO! BUT, YEAH, THE BUS, THE FREIGHT CARS, THE TREES... IT WAS A GREAT SPOT THAT BROUGHT BACK THAT INTENSE, INSPIRED FEELING LIKE I WAS TOTALLY ON THE THRESHHOLD OF SOME OF SOME REALLY AMAZING DISCOVERY. LIKE WHAT? LIFE? YEAH! I'D EVEN GO THERE AT NIGHT AND WRITE ON THE CRUMBLY CONCRETE NEXT TO THE TRACKS, BY CANDLELIGHT, AND THE FLORIDA EAST COAST HOTSHOT FROM MIAMI TO J-VILLE WOULD ROLL BY, BLOWIN' OUT MY CANDLES AND TAKIN' MY THOUGHTS W/ IT, AND I'D THINK, "SOMEDAY I'M GONNA HOP ONE OF DEM DAMN TRAINS..." I HAD THIS FANTASY OF SOMEHOW LIVING IN ONE OF THE ABANDONED FREIGHT CARS, AND ALL A SUDDEN, WAKING UP ONE DAY IN RICHMOND, OR SOMETHING, WHEN THE TRAIN HAD BEEN UN-ABANDONED. ME AND BUDDHA ALSO THOUGHT OF LIVIN' IN THE BUS. WE HAD THIS WEIRD IDEA WHERE WE'D BE PIRATES, ONLY INSTEAD OF A SHIP WE'D HAVE A BUS. INSTEAD, WE WENT TO MIAMI, GOT CAUGHT OPENING A SQUAT, AND WOUND UP IN JAIL... ACTUALLY, THIS GUY WHO, I GUESS, WORKED FOR F.E.C. LIVED IN A TRAIN CAR THERE W/ A SIGN ON IT THAT SAID "CAMP CAR" AND ONE NIGHT I KNOCKED ON HIS DOOR TO ASK HIM ABOUT IT, LIKE "WOW! YOU LIVE IN A TRAIN CAR W/ ELECTRICITY AND EVERYTHING! WHAT'S IT LIKE?" BUT HE WAS REAL GRUMPY, GET LOST, AND THEN, ONE DAY, HIS CAR WAS GONE... PROWLING AROUND IN WOODS NEAR THERE I'D FIND CRASHED SHACKS, HIDDEN SWINGS, AND LOTS OF ROTTED COUCHES, MATTRESSES, AND SIGNS OF ENCAMPMENTS BY LONG DEAD CIVILIZATIONS. SURROUNDED BY LOGS (APPARENTLY USED AS CHAIRS) IN A CIRCULAR CLEARING, WAS A TRASHED, TOTALLY STRIPPED VOLKSWAGON. HOW'D IT GET THERE? DID ALIENS BRING IT THERE? DID THE NATIVES WORSHIP IT AS A SYMBOL OF RUNNIN' DOWN CULTURE? I PHONED MY LONG TIME FRIEND, LEONARD NIMOY, OF TV'S IN SEARCH OF, TO ASK HIM WHAT HE THOUGHT, BUT HE HAD NO IDEA. I KNEW I WAS ONTO SOMETHING, AND SOON, SURE ENOUGH, I CAME THROUGH A CLEARING, RIGHT INTO THE LIVING ROOM, OF THE PEOPLE WHO LIVE IN THE WOODS. THE PEOPLE WHO LIVE IN

BOCA RATON MEANS "MOUTH OF THE RAT" IN SPANISH. BIG DEAL.

1993

SUN	MON	TUE	WED	THU	FRI	SAT
LQ 8	NM 15	FG 22	FM 30		1	2
3	4	5	6	7	8	9
10	11	12				

1993

RAT MOUTH EMPTY LOTS AND OCTOBER SAP SHITZ CONT.

THE WOODS 1) SMELL BAD 2) DRINK BUSCH BEER 3) DON'T CARE. IT WAS PRETTY AMAZING TO FIND PEOPLE LIVING IN THE WOODS, SURROUNDED BY UNSTOPPABLE "PROGRESS" AND DEVELOPMENT IN SOUTH FLORIDA. SO SINCE I "DISCOVERED" THE I TOOK THEIR BEER AND MADE THEM CARRY STUFF AROUND FOR ME... UM.. ANYWAYS, I EXPLORED OUT OF THE WOODS, TOO, EVE FINDING A PERFECTLY GOOD BIKE UNDER A PILE OF CEILING DEBRIS IN A BURNED OUT BUILDING ON U.S. 1. SOMETIMES, I'L RIDE UP TO BOYNTON, WHICH IS A CRAZY PLACE, EVERYTHING CLOSED FOR THE SEASON. I'D LOOK FOR TH ABANDONED MINIATURE GOLF COURSE THAT I THOUGHT I SAW FROM THE HIGHWAY, OR RIDE NORTH TO FIND OUT WHAT THE HELL HYPOLUXO WAS ALL ABOUT... BUT THIS IS ABOUT BOCA... BESIDES EMPTY L BOCA ALSO HAD THE WORLD'S GREATEST DUMPSTERS, LIKE I'D GO TO WINN-DIXIE, HOPING FOR ONE APP AND FIND 23 BAGS OF SUPERBRAND POTATO CHIPS, OR SOME SHIT LIKE THAT. ONE TIME, I FOUND 48 HEINEKEN BEERS (2 CASES). FUK! ONE NIGHT, WHEN I WAS FEELIN' PRETTY BRAVE, I CHECKED OUT THE BOCA POLICE STATION DUMPSTER AND FOUND A HUGE, 30 PAGE REPORT, STAMPED "CONFIDENTIAL" ALL ABOUT AN UPCOMING KLAN RALLY IN BOCA, AND HOW COPS PLANNED ON CONTROLLING THE CROWD, VIDEOTAPING PRO AND ANTI K.K.K. DEMONSTRATORS, AND INFILTRATING THE CROWD W/UNDERCOVERS WHO WOULD ALL BE WEARING LIME GREEN WRISTBANDS...! IT EVE HAD PHOTOS AND REPORTS ON PEOPLE WHO WERE EXPECTED TO ATTEND THE RALLY... PRETTY CREEPY, I WENT BACK W/ A CAR ONE TIME AND GRABBED 4 OR 5 BAGS OF THEIR TRASH, WHICH WE WENT THROUGH ON CHUCK'S PORCH, BUT DIDN'T FIND ANYTHING REAL COOL. YEAH BOCA SUCKS. THE COPS ARE HARSH AS HELL AND IT'S GOT THESE UGLY PINK BUILDINGS AND ITS A DULL, ALL WHITE SUBURB, BUT I'M GLAD I DID GO BACK, AFTER I HAD THOUGHT I HAD LEFT HOME FOREVER. MAY I HAD A BETTER ATTITUDE THE 2ND TIME AROUND. ITS FUNNY, CUZ WHEN I WAS A KID, BEFOR BOCA WAS REALLY CLEANED UP, ME AND MY MOM WOULD DRIVE BY THESE VACANT LOTS AND YOU COULD SOMETIMES SEE GUYS SITTING IN THE CLEARING, DRINKING. I'D SAY, "MOM, WHY ARE THO MEN THERE", AND SHE'D SAY, "DON'T EVER GO NEAR THOSE MEN! THEY'RE BUMS!!!" AND NOW, I'M ONE OF THE FREAKY MEN, HANGIN' OUT IN THE WOODS, DRINKIN' BEER, AN WORSHIPPING TRASHED CARS AND GREY, WINDY OCTOBER, AND SMASHED HUTS, AND STILL SEARCHIN' FOR SOMETHING TO FILL THE EMPTY LOT IN A MAN'S SOUL...

SWORDFIGHTING IS PUNK!!!

"THEY SAY, 'THE PEN IS MIGHTIER THAN THE SWORD', BUT I SAY, 'FUCK THE PEN... CAUSE YOU CAN DIE BY THE SWORD'!"
—SLAYER

CLINK!
CLINK!

DA SHLITZ
SCAM
DA CROWBAR

I WAS THINKING THAT ITS ABOUT TIME THAT SWORDFIGHTING CAME BACK INTO STYLE. LIKE ON THE STREETS, IN BARS, PEOPLE CHALLENGING EACH OTHER TO DUELS... IT'D BE GREAT IF ALL THE STREET GANGS GOT INTO THE SWASH BUCKLING THING INSTEAD OF DRIVE-BY'S. THAT WAY LESS INNOCENT BYSTANDERS GET HURT AND YOU COULD BE WALKING DOWN THE STRE AND SEE A GANG OF GUYS IN RED BANDANAS YELL, "ON GAURD, CRIPS!" AND JUMP OUT OF A TRUCK AND LIKE JUST DASH A ROLL AND HOP AND PARRY AND THRUST RIGHT OUT ON THE STREETS. WHAT A SHOW! I'D ALSO LIKE TO SEE MORE PEOPLE WITH SWORDS SWINGING FROM CHANDELIERS AND BIG CURTAINS AND STUFF. THANKS. THAT'S ALL I WANTED TO SAY.

THE SATANIC & OTHER MYSTERIOUS RELIGIOUS [AN IVY STORY] HAPPENINGS TOUR OF MIAMI

FIRST OFF I'D LIKE TO SAY THAT THESE ARE REAL EXPERIENCES I'VE HAD OVER THE PAST YEARS WITH THE <u>UNDERLORD ALMIGHTY</u>...

FERNISAL PARK / N.W. 22 AVE BACK IN MY HEAVY METAL THRASHIN' YEARS ME & SOME OTHER METTLERS USED TO GO HANG OUT IN THIS <u>SATANIC TREE HOUSE</u>.. THE TREE ITSELF WAS CLAD IN LADIES UNDERWEAR AND VARIOUS BONES OF ANIMALS.. WHEN YOU GOT UP TO THE INSIDE OF THE TREEHOUSE YOU'D READ PRAISES TO <u>SATAN</u> SCRAWLED ON THE WALLS WITH FLOURESCENT PAINT & SPRAY PAINT....

SIMPSON PARK / MIAMI AVE / BRICKELL THERE'S BRICKELL'S NOTORIOUS SIMPSON PARK, A PLACE WHERE JUNKIES, <u>MADMEN, OZZY</u>, METALHEADS, AND MEMBERS OF THE OCCULT NAMELY <u>SANTERIA WORSHIPPERS</u> WOULD ROAM COME NIGHTTIME, A PLACE WHERE ONCE YOU WALKED IN YOU COULD BE LOST FOR HOURS IN THE WRANGLING FOREST. IT WAS BASICALLY A PIECE OF LAND SURROUNDED BY A CORAL WALL, NOT REALLY A PARK TO STROLL IN JUST THERE TO PRESERVE A PIECE OF FLORIDA'S NATURAL HABITAT... MY FRIEND CAROL ONE NIGHT WAS DRINKIN' AND WALKIN' AROUND IN THE PARK & SUDDENLY STUMBLED UPON A <u>SACRIFICIAL GROUND</u> WHERE THERE WAS A <u>DECAPITATED GOAT</u> LYING IN A CIRCLE OF STONES. SHE TOOK A PICTURE OF IT AND OTHER BIZARRE THINGS SURROUNDING IT...

LITTLE HAVANA / S.W. 8 ST. A NEIGHBORHOOD MADE UP OF SEMI-RUN DOWN APTS, & AND OLD COTTAGES DATING BACK TO THE 20's AS IS THIS IS THE OLDEST NEIGHBORHOOD IN MIAMI. I LIVED IN BRICKELL, HOME OF DELINQUENTS WHO WERE ALWAYS OUT LOOKING FOR TROUBLE, THEY <u>(BOYS ON BRICKELL (B.O.B.)</u> USED TO HANG OUT AT THE METRORAIL (BRICKELL) STATION RIGHT ACROSS THE STREET FROM MY HOUSE. YOU WILL ALSO FIND A GREAT MANY OF THE RESIDENTS ARE INVOLVED WITH <u>SANTERIA</u>, A SPANISH RELIGION... ONE NIGHT I WOKE UP TO SIRENS SCREAMING ACROSS THE WAY TO FIND OUT A <u>MAN</u> HAD BEEN TIED TO A <u>TREE</u>, <u>BURNT ALIVE</u> IN A <u>SANTERIA RITUAL</u>. HE HAD COINS AND CORN GRAINS PLACED AT HIS FEET, TOKENS OF THE <u>SANTERIA</u> RELIGION, HE DIED TWO DAYS LATER IN JACKSON MEMORIAL HOSPITAL... WAS IT ALL FOR OZZY? WE'LL FIND OUT NEXT TIME...

ALPHA + OMEGA CHURCH / S.W. 32 AVE / MIAMI A GIRL WE'LL CALL TATIANA WHOM I'D KNOWN FROM SCHOOL HAD ASKED ME TO ATTEND <u>ALPHA & OMEGA</u> WITH HER AND I DIDN'T HAVE ANY OBJECTION TO DOING THIS. SO I WENT ON A WEDNESDAY NIGHT AND IT TURNS OUT IT'S A SPANISH SPEAKING CHURCH. SO I WATCHED ON & AFTER A WHILE I STARTED SEEING PEOPLE WALK UP TO THE PASTOR (CHRISTIAN SPANISH ROCK BAND IN THE BACKGROUND) AND HE PUTS HIS HANDS ON THEIR FOREHEADS AND STARTS SCREAMING STUFF & THOSE PEOPLE START HAVING CONVULSIONS AND PASS OUT ON THE GROUND... THIS IS PRETTY ENTERTAINING NOW... THEN TATIANA ASKS (URGES) ME TO GO UP AND TAKE PART. SO I JUST WANTED TO SEE THE LOOK

ON HIS FACE WHEN **PENTAGRAMS** BURNED THEIR WAY INTO HIS SKIN... SO I WENT UP AND HE PUT HIS HANDS ON MY HEAD AND STARTED SCREAMING AND I WAS JUST STANDING THERE... I COULD TELL HE WAS GETTING NERVOUS BUT I STILL DIDN'T HAVE ANY CONVULSIONS AND EVERYONE LOOKED AT ME AS IF I HAD THE **DEVIL** IN ME... LITTLE DID THEY REALIZE THAT IT WAS THE POWER OF **OZZY** AMEN!

CORAL WAY (S.W. 22 ST.) & 12 AVE. A WEEKEND FILLED WITH **EVICTIONS, ROBBERIES, HOSPITALIZATION**... ME & IGGY WERE SHOPPING CARTING OUR STUFF TO NOWHERE REALLY AND FOUND 2 OPENED SALVATION ARMY CLOTHES DROP BOXES AND DECIDED TO STAY IN ONE FOR THE NIGHT... SO WE PUT OUR SHOPPING CART IN ONE AND SLEPT IN THE OTHER, WHEN I WOKE UP I WENT OUT TO GET SOMETHING AND FIND MYSELF STANDING IN FRONT OF A **BARKING DOG** AND HEAR A **HISSING SOUND** COMING OUT OF THE OTHER BOX. I GET PAST THE **DOG** TO FIND THIS **BUM** WITH MY MARILYN MONROE BOOK & MY UNDERWEAR IN HIS LAP AND HE WAS SPRAY PAINTING SWASTIKAS, **PENTAGRAMS**, & CROSSES ALL OVER THE INSIDE WALLS... WITHOUT A WORD HE RAN AWAY AND HIS DOG RAN AFTER HIM...

SATANIC ZOO / CRANDON BEACH / KEY BISCAYNE AS FAR AS I CAN REMEMBER THE **SATANIC ZOO** USED TO BE AN ACTUAL ZOO THAT CLOSED DOWN IN THE EARLY 80'S AND SINCE WAS INFESTED WITH **SATAN ⊗ WORSHIPPERS**, DRUGGIES, & THE KEY RATS A LOCAL GANG OF JR. HIGH KIDS... WALTER WHO WAS A KEY RAT REMEMBERED SEEING MANY OF THE GUTTED OUT CAGES & BUILDINGS TURNED INTO SHRINES FOR **SATAN** AND MANY TIMES SAW DOMESTIC ANIMALS SLAUGHTERED TO **SATAN**, THERE WAS ALSO A MOTEL ON THE BEACH THAT WAS ABANDONED RIGHT NEAR THE ZOO WHICH ALSO HAD TRACES OF **SATAN ⊗ WORSHIPPING** WALTER SAID IT WAS TRULY A SIGHT TO SEE AS IF LIKE AN ANIMAL ZOO BUT INSTEAD A **SATANIC ZOO.**

BLACK SABBATH REUNION / NEWPORT BEACH OK, SO I HEAR **SABBATH** WAS HAVING A REUNION SHOW IN SO. CALIFORNIA... MY HEART & I JUMPED 10 FT. HIGH... I WAS PRETTY EXCITED SO OFF I GO TO FIND 20⁰⁰ & A RIDE THERE. I GET BOTH FROM MY FRIEND JAMES. SO THE NIGHT BEFORE THE SHOW WE DRIVE DOWN AND GET THERE AT 10 AM. WE DECIDED TO GO TO THE BEACH WHERE WE GOT SURROUNDED BY POLICE AND 2 OF OUR FRIENDS GOT ARRESTED!! SO WE HAD TO DEAL WITH **EL HOMBRE** AND MAKE SOME DEALS WITH THE **DEVIL**... ALL I COULD THINK OF WAS **OZZY**, YOU KNOW? WE HAD TO RAISE A LOT OF BAIL BUT FINALLY GOT IRA OUT TO SEE HIS DYING WISH... WE MADE IT TO THE SHOW MIDWAY THROUGH **OZZY'S** SOLO ACT, MISSING SEPULTURA & **SABBATH** WITH **ROB HALFORD** FROM JUDAS PRIEST SINGING... SO THIS **METAL CHICK** TELLS ME THAT SABBATH HAS ALREADY PLAYED... AND SHE OFFERS ME HER **BINOCULARS** SINCE SHE FELT BAD FOR ME... I'M FEELING PRETTY DOWN, BUT WAIT SOME GUY GETS ON THE MIKE AND SAYS "ALRIGHT YOU WANNA HEAR SOME FUCKIN' HISTORY ??!!! "YEEAAHH!!! OZZY COMES OUT WITH A WHITE TASSLE SHIRT AND HIS KIDS AND THANKS EVERYBODY FOR A GREAT LIFE... **BLACK SABBATH** STARTS WITH BLACK SABBATH, ALSO PLAYED MY FAVE **PARANOID** AND OTHER CLASSIC METAL HITS I WON'T NAME OFF CUZ I DON'T WANNA... WELL 4 PITS BROKE OUT CUZ **OZZY** SAYS THE CRAZIEST MOTHERFUCKER'S GONNA PARTY WITH HIM BACKSTAGE... ALL HELL BROKE LOOSE... I SAW DOZENS OF SECURITY GUARDS RUSHING TO EXTINGUISH FIRES THAT HAD BEEN SET ALL OVER THE AMPHITHEATER... BUT LITTLE DID THEY REALIZE THAT THE **DEVIL & OZZY** WILL NEVER BE EXTINGUISHED. **HAIL SATAN.** THE END. ⊗

HAIL SATAN ALMIGHTY...   666   666   666   666   KING OF THE DAMNED...   666

666

"Let's" "Steal" "Electricity"

WITH CHUCK LOUSE

STEALING FROM LIGHT POLES

SERVICE PLATE (TAKE IT OFF)

TIGHTEN THIS-A-WAY ← WIRE NUT

ENDS SPLICED TO REVEAL WIRE INSIDE

OLD EXTENSION CORD

SCREW IT FIRMLY OVER THE WIRES

① FIRMLY GRASP THE TWO GREEN WIRES THAT ARE WIRE NUTTED TOGETHER ② UNSCREW THE NUT, BEING CAREFUL NOT TO TOUCH THE WIRE ③ PUT THE GREEN WIRE FROM YOUR EXTENSION CORD ALONG SIDE THE OTHER TWO GREENS ④ PUT THE WIRE NUT BACK ON, SCREWING IT ONTO ALL THREE WIRES. ⑤ REPEAT PROCESS FOR DA' WHITE WIRE ⑥ ONCE AGAIN FOR DA' BLACK ⑦ PLUG INTO THE "FEMALE" END OF THE EXTENSION. ⑧ GO, MAN, GO!

• SOME STUFF TO REMEMBER •

★ AVOID TOUCHING EXPOSED WIRES THAT ARE PART OF AN ELECTRIC CIRCUIT. ALSO, AVOID TOUCHING ANYTHING METAL THAT'S TOUCHING A WIRE ★ ALWAYS USE A SCREWDRIVER OR A PAIR OF WIRE CUTTERS THAT HAVE A RUBBERIZED HANDLE. ★ WHEN WORKING WITH LIVE WIRES, STAND ON A WOODEN BOARD, OR SIMILAR NON-CONDUCTIVE SURFACE, SO, YOU... UH... "FLOAT", OR ARE NOT PART OF AN ACTIVE CIRCUIT.

STEALING FROM GROUND MOUNTED-TYPE FLOODLIGHTS

① HEY, SAME THING AS ABOVE, ALSO WORKS FOR OVERHEAD MOUNTED-TYPE SPOTLIGHTS.

STEALING FROM LIGHT POLES THAT LOOK LIKE THIS

SERVICE PLATE

① HEY, THIS IS KNOWN AS A "220 CIRCUIT". GO GREEN TO GREEN, BLACK FROM THE EXTENSION TO EITHER OF THE 2 REDS OR BLACKS, AND WRAP THE WHITE AROUND A NAIL AND HAMMER IT INTO THE GROUND.

NAIL

4 BLACK OR 4 RED WIRES

"JUMPING OUT" A METER BOX

① THIS IS THE STEPS FOR JUMPING A METER DEVICE OUT OF A CIRCUIT TO ALLOW POWER INTO A SYSTEM (HOUSE OR OTHER BUILDING) ② GET 2-1' LENGTHS OF 10 AWG WIRE (AVAILABLE AT ANY HARDWARE STORE). USING AN INSULATED SCREW DRIVER, CONNECT THE 2 WIRE LENGTHS AS INDICATED. THIS SHOULD PROVIDE A PATH FOR ELECTRICITY AROUND THE FUSE OR CIRCUIT BREAKER, AND INTO THE BUILDING.

FUSE

CONNECT HERE. AND HERE.

10 AWG WIRE

SERVICE PANEL

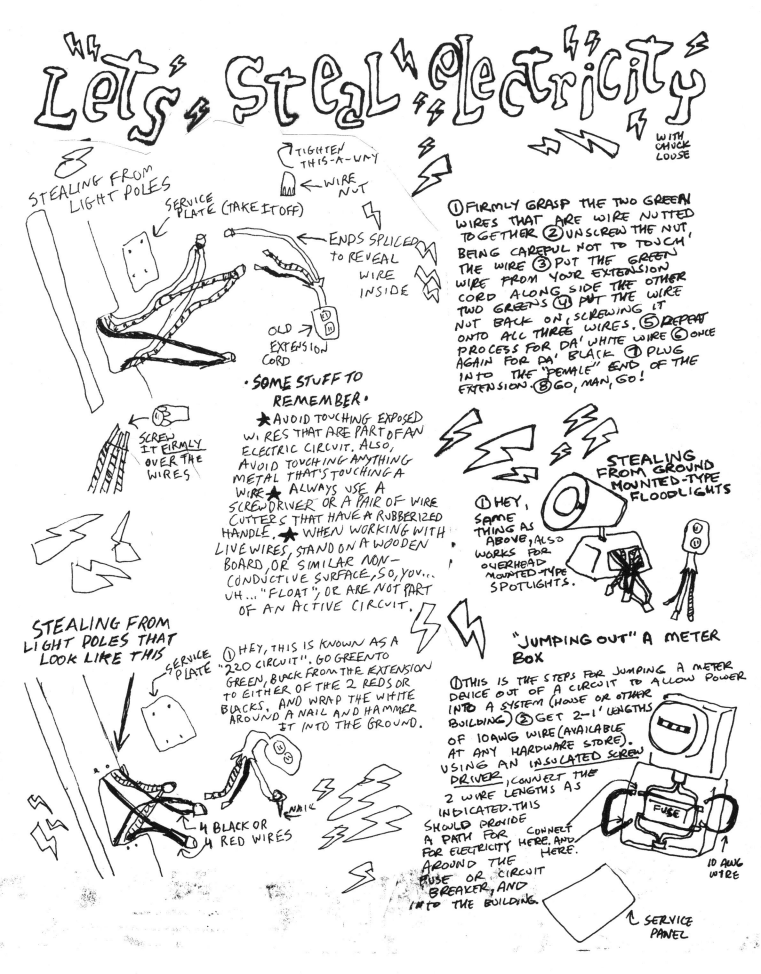

More Let's Steal Electricity

STILL WITH CHUCK LOOSE

MORE ABOUT "JUMPING OUT" A METER BOX

A LOT OF TIMES, ELECTRICITY TO A BUILDING WILL BE DISCONNECTED AT THE POWER LINE, AT A POINT BEFORE IT DROPS DOWN TO THE METER. IN THAT CASE "JUMPING OUT" IS USELESS AND THE POWER COMPANY HAS TO TURN POWER ON TO THAT CIRCUIT, FUCKERS. SOMETIMES, THE FUSE BOX OR CIRCUIT BREAKER WILL BE EQUIPPED WITH A SIMPLE ON/OFF SWITCH WHICH MAY BE ALL THAT IS NEEDED TO BE ENERGIZED TO ALLOW POWER INTO THE BUILDING. OH YEAH, THE WIRING IN SOME BUILDINGS MAY BE SO AGED AND DECREPIT THAT, IF ELECTRICITY IS ALLOWED TO FLOW THROUGH IT, THE HEAT CAUSED BY THE ELECTRON FLOW CAN MELT THE PLASTIC INSULATING THE WIRING AND EVEN CAUSE A FIRE. YOW! A WAY TO AVOID THIS IS TO BYPASS THE OUTLETS INSIDE THE BUILDING BY SPLICING AN OLD EXTENSION CORD INTO THE WIRING. IT'S PRETTY MUCH THE SAME DEAL AS SPLICING INTO A LIGHT POLE. ① MAKE SURE ALL THE BREAKERS ARE "OFF" EXCEPT FOR THE ONE YOU'RE GONNA TAP INTO ② UNHOOK THE WIRE TO THE CIRCUIT BREAKER ON THE SIDE COMING FROM THE OUTSIDE. SPLICE THAT WIRE WITH A WIRE NUT (AVAILABLE AT ANY HARDWARE STORE) TO THE "HOT" WIRE (BLACK) ON THE EXTENSION. HOOK THE GREEN AND WHITE WIRES AROUND A NAIL AND HAMMER THAT SUCKER INTO THE WALL, OR FLOOR, NEAR THE BOX. OH YEAH, BE CAREFUL, HAVE FUN

AND DON'T GET ELECTROCUTED!

POWER LINE

METER

INTERIOR BUILDING OUTLETS

FUSE OR CIRCUIT BREAKER (WHERE YOU "JUMP IT OUT")

GOES TO OUTSIDE (FUSE OR CIRCUIT BREAKER AND METER)

FUSE BOX INSIDE BUILDING

WIRE GOES FROM OUTSIDE, THROUGH CIRCUIT BREAKER AND TO INSIDE OUTLETS.

ON/OFF CIRCUIT SWITCHES

HOOK TOGETHER W/ WIRE NUT

HAMMER TO WALL OR FLOOR

THE Enjoy Coke ® © INC etc
scam...

HA HA HA... HAD TO DO IT.

OR MONEY FOR NOTHIN'
AND YOUR COKES FOR FREE!

Ⓐ MORON, OR ANY OTHER TYPE 'O' SALT.

↳ CASH CARD CODE.

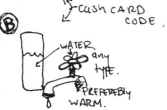

Ⓑ WATER any type. PREFERABLY WARM.

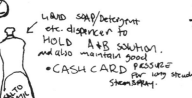

Ⓒ LIQUID SOAP/DETERGENT etc. dispencer to HOLD A+B solution. and also maintain good
• CASH CARD PRESSURE for long steady steam SPRAY.

Ⓓ ELECTRONIC DOLLAR INTAKE!
* MUY IMPORTANTE!

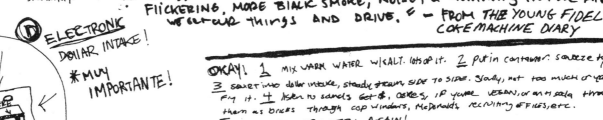

BLOW UP CLOSE VIEW OF DOLLAR INTAKE

DWARFS HUMAN BEINGS IN SIZE AND POWER!

Ⓔ • CANCER DISPENSER, OPERATIVE OF THE MAN
• SOCIAL CONTROL IMPLEMENT OF CORPORATES.
• BAD!
• SORT OF MONEY MACHINE
• PIGGY BANK

...ELECTRO SMOKE, BUZZING AND HUMMING, 50 d and an ICETEA. OVER FRIED IT. QUICK AND PAINLESS. Got to REMEMBER NOT TO USE SO MUCH. "HUNT THE MACHINE. STALK IT. (- FROM THE TAO of ELECTRO SABITAGE) UN-SUSPICIOUSLY AND GRACEFUL JUST AS WE BELONG THERE IN THAT TIME AND SPACE IN THAT PATCH OF CEMENT IN FRONT OF THE SODA DISPENSER calling to US, CRYING to be LIBERATED, DESTROYED. EYES LEFT EYES RIGHT, BEHIND, AH CLEAR, ON THE TARGET. OUT COMES THE SALINE SOLUTION, TAP WATER AND SALT, DESTROYERS of MACHINES (I HEAR it could be USED ON ANYTHING, LOCKS, CARS, ATM MACHINES, ETC... I'VE EVEN HEARD of RUMORS OF PUNKS BREAKING INTO U.S. MAXIMUM TOP SECURITY UNDERGROUND MILITARY INSTALATIONS WITH NOTHING BUT SALTWATER AND CROWBARS). THE STEADY STREAM IS SPRAYED SIDE TO SIDE, ONE TO TWO PASSES UNTIL THE DOLLAR INTAKE SOUND is made SHORTENING THE $ INTAKE (SALT thins out the WATER wich short circuits THE ELECTRONIC INTAKE) SO EASILY DOES it SURRENDER ITS BANK, "the LOOT" CHANGE IS SPIT OUT, TOO FAST TO COLLECT, I get ON MY KNEES AND BOW BEFORE THE CHANGE RETURN HANDS cupped in SERVICE, collecting the donated COINS to the CAUSE. "THE CAUSE." COMES UP AND JOINS ME AS I begin THE SECOND STREAM TO SHOOT THE CANCEROUS DISPENSERS. INTERNAL HEMORAGING AND SLUGGISH NOISE, ORGANS RUPTURING, BONES BREAKING, it VOMITS CANS AFTER CANS, UNTIL The dispenser can't HOLD ANY MORE. WE LAUGH FEVERISHLY REMEMBERIN' THE SCENE IN THE CLASSIC I (EMPIRE STRIKES BACK) WHERE THE SNARED AT AT@ FALLS, VICTORY IS OURS, THE DISEASE DISPENSER DESTROYED, POCKETS FILLED, ELECTRONIC FLICKERING, MORE BLACK SMOKE, NOISE, a humming in the AIR, we gather our things AND DRIVE. 〜 - FROM THE YOUNG FIDEL COKE MACHINE DIARY

OKAY! 1 MIX WARM WATER W/SALT. lots of it. 2 put in container. squeeze type! 3 squirt into dollar intake, steady stream, SIDE TO SIDE. Slowly, not too much or you'll FRY it. 4 listen to sounds get $, COKES, if you're VEGAN, or anti soda throw them as bricks through cop windows, McDonalds recruiting OFFICES, etc. 5 IF you FAIL TRY & TRY AGAIN!

MOST SODA, COKE & PEPSI ARE ROCK + ROLL, SOCIAL sedatives, CULTURE THEFT, home and abroad. PART OF THE "COOL SCHOOL" sponsorers of "THE MAN" THE companys That FED OF your pARents Blood, "disease for your support" DESTROY COKE. HAVE FUN. ENJOY LIFE.

13.

Ⓕ DUH.

CHANGE RETURN

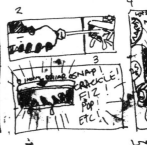

1 2 3 SNAP! CRACKLE! FIZ! POP! ETC! 4 LOTS OF MONEY 5 CA$HING (lots o drinks) CANCER! KERPLUNK!

↙ VERY IMPORTANT ✳

GETTING AWAY WITH IT
TRUE CRIME STORIES

ONE TIME, BACK IN THE FT. LAUDERDALE PUNK HOUSE, ME AND MIKE CRACK WERE UP ALL NIGHT ON LOTSA BEER AND ACID, WHEN WE DECIDED TO GO ON A ROAD TRIP TO ORLANDO. THE DETAILS NOW ARE HAZY BUT THE PLAN INVOLVED 1) RESCUING (KIDNAPPING?) THIS GIRL WHO LOVED MIKE BUT WHOSE FAMILY KEPT THEM APART AND 2) SNEAKING INTO DISNEYWORLD AND 3) MORE DRUGS. FIRST, WE NEEDED A DRIVER TO DRIVE MIKE'S CAR. MILO AGREED TO DRIVE WHEN HE GOT OFF WORK, LATER THAT AFTERNOON. WE NEEDED A BACK UP DRIVER SO MIKE DECIDED TO TEACH ME TO DRIVE. WE TOOK CHUCK LOOSE TO WORK AND THEN IT WAS MY FIRST TIME BEHIND THE WHEEL. OK, MIKE SAYS, THIS ONE IS FORWARD, THIS IS STOP, SO GO. I FLATTEN A STOP SIGN. YOWL! THIS IS FUN! NO, NO, IGGY, SAYS MIKE, DON'T HIT THE SIGNS. OK. SOON I'VE REALLY GOT THE HANG OF IT, SO I TAKE HER OUT ON I-95 AND TURN UP THE RADIO REAL LOUD. DRIVIN'S COOL. NO PROBLEM. NOW WE NEED MORE DRUGS. WE GO BACK TO THE PUNK HOUSE AND MIKE, CLAIMING TO BE THE HEAD OF AN ART GALLERY ON LAS OLAS, PHONES A LOCAL ART SUPPLY STORE AND ARRANGES FOR A CAN OF A VERY RARE AND POWERFUL INHALENT, THAT NO SOLD, BUT NOT JUST TO ANYONE, NORMALLY FOR USE IN AIRBRUSHING, TO BE MADE AVAILABLE TO US. "I'LL SEND MY BOY DOWN TO GET IT AT 2:00" SAYS MIKE. NOW, ITS OFF TO WESTSIDE MARKET FOR MORE BEER. THE BEER IS NO PROBLEM. THEY KNOW US AT WESTSIDE. IN THE MONTHS WE'VE LIVED IN THAT NEIGHBORHOOD, THEY'VE COME TO UNDERSTAND OUR UNIQUE PROBLEMS AND TO LEARN OUR STRANGE HABITS. THE MAN SAYS "SEE YA, DUDE" AND WE LEAVE WITH THE BEER. IT IS SHAPING UP TO BE A BEAUTIFUL DAY. THE SUN IS FULLY UP, THE BIRDS ARE SINGING, MIKE STOPS TO ADMIRE A GARDEN FULL OF BLUE FLOWERS ON THE WAY HOME. EVERYONE KNOWS, SAYS MIKE, THAT MORNING GLORIES ARE HALLUCINOGENIC BUT FEW KNOW THAT ALL BLUE FLOWERS HAVE SOME HALLUCINOGENIC PROPERTIES. WE DROP THE BEER AND DIVE INTO THE GARDEN, STUFFING THE FLOWERS IN OUR MOUTHS! BUT AFTER A MINUTE OR SO I SAY, SHIT, WE BETTER GET OUT OF HERE. WHAT IF THE OLD WOMAN WHO LIVES HERE WAKES UP TO LOOK OUT THE WINDOW AND SEES A COUPLE CRAZY-EYED, BEER MAD ANIMALS EATING HER FRONT YARD? BAD CRAZINESS. NOW, WE NEED NEW TIRES FOR THE CAR, SO ITS OFF TO A GAS STATION ON U.S. 1 TO HAVE 'EM PUT ON. WE HAVE NO MONEY. THE MECHANIC GOES TO WORK ON THE TIRES AND WE PROTECT OUR IDENTITY BY PRETENDING TO BE HOMESICK SWEDES WHO DON'T SPEAK MUCH ENGLISH. WE NOD AND SAY "YAW! YAW!" ALOT. EVENTUALLY THE CAR'S READY AND WE DRIVE AWAY AND GET LOST IN TRAFFIC WITH THE NEW TIRES (80 BUCKS A TIRE, I THINK). NO PROBLEM, WE PICK UP THE INHALENT, AND GO GET MILO AND BUDDHA AND ARE ON OUR WAY. SLOWLY, THE TRIP DEGENERATED INTO FIGHTING AND GENERAL DRUNKEN CURSING. MILO IS INSANE. NO ONE CAN STAND HIM. MIKE DIES AFTER DOING TOO MUCH INHALENT. HE JUST SLOUCHES OVER, SMILE ON HIS FACE. MIKE! MIKE! WE SCREAM AND SLAP HIM. FINALLY HE COMES TO, AND IS PISSED CUZ I THREW HIS INHALENTS OUT THE WINDOW. THE LAST GASP OF THE TRIP COMES WHEN WE DINE AND DASH A PERKINS' FAMILY RESTAURANT IN CENTRAL FLORIDA SOMEWHERE AND GET CHASED BUT, OF COURSE, GET AWAY. AFTER THAT, WE'RE ALL PRETTY MEAN AND SICK. MAYBE ITS THE INSECTICIDE ON THE BLUE FLOWERS? WE END UP JUST DRIVIN' HOME, BUT, IN A ROUNDABOUT WAY, THIS IS THE STORY OF HOW WE STOLE 4 BRAND NEW TIRES.

A LOCAL TRUE CRIME LEGEND IS YOUNG FIDEL'S FRIEND, ALAN, WHO IS FAMOUS FOR DOING THINGS LIKE STEALING A WALKMAN WHILE IN RADIO SHACK WITH HIS MOM! THEY LEAVE, HE PULLS IT OUT OF HIS PANTS AND SHE'S YELLIN' "I'M SHOCKED, ALAN, TAKE IT BACK!" AND HE'S LIKE, "YEAH, RIGHT." ALAN BOUGHT A HAND HELD NINTENDO GAME ONCE, PUT SOME KINDA TRASH IN THE BOX, RESEALED THE SHRINK WRAP SOMEHOW, SO EXPERTLY THAT YOU COULDN'T TELL IT HAD BEEN OPENED, AND RETURNED THE BOX FOR HIS MONEY BACK. ONE TIME, WHEN ALAN WANTED A FAX MACHINE, HE WENT TO OFFICE DEPOT AND BOUGHT ONE, RAN TO THE CAR, DUMPED OUT THE FAX AND PUT IN BLOCKS OF WOOD AND WENT BACK TO THE LADY WHO SOLD IT TO HIM, AND SAID HIS MOM WANTED HIM TO TAKE IT BACK. SHE WAS ABOUT TO GIVE HIM THE MONEY WHEN SHE GOT CALLED AWAY AND THE MANAGER CAME OVER AND STARTED TO OPEN THE BOX! QUICK ALAN, THINK! ALAN SAID WAIT, IF I FIND A BETTER DEAL ON THIS SOMEWHERE ELSE YOU GUYS WILL PAY THE DIFFERENCE, RIGHT? THE MANAGER SAYS YES AND ALAN TAKES THE BOX TO LOOK FOR A BETTER DEAL... WELL, IT ALMOST WORKED.

I WAS A TEENAGE RUNAWAY...

story by BEN WEASEL

SUBURBO MILK 100%

HAVE YOU SEEN ME?

MISSING

A FACT STORY

I was 14 years old the first time I ran away from home. I was hanging out in the smoking area, which we called THE PIT, at Homo High with my friend Phil. Phil was the same age as me but he was a pretty big guy muscle-wise, a big Greek with the same feelings of hatred that I had toward being forced to attend an all-boy's Catholic highschool.

It was one of those boring, cold days when the sun is shining but it's still only about 35 or 40 degrees outside. We had nothing to smoke but cigarettes and we both somehow decided that going back to class after lunch was a dumb idea.

"Let's run away," I said brightly.

"Yeah!" said Phil, probably more out of a need to show he wasn't afraid than anything else.

My next door neighbor Tom had recently moved down to Nashville. He was in his twenties, but a cool guy. I'd talked about running away a zillion times before and he'd always told me not to come to his house but I figured he'd change his mind once he saw us at his doorstep.

I was all for leaving right then, but Phil had to stop by his house.

"My leg's all fucked up," he said. "I gotta get my antibiotics from home."

Phil lived about a mile or so from our school, right behind the public highschool, Hersey. We went to his house and got his antibiotics. Then he said he wanted to stop by Hersey.

I was starting to get impatient. It was already around 2:00.

"I gotta see my sister and tell her I'm going," he said. "She'll be all pissed off if I leave and don't tell her."

Jesus, this was getting ridiculous. I tried to act all stern.

"Don't let her talk you out of it."

"I won't."

"We're going, y'know. Your sister's gonna try to talk you out of it, but we're going."

"I know, I know."

We hung out near the main entrance of the school until the last class was out. Phil walked around trying to find his sister. He finally saw one of her friends and got her to go get the elusive sister.

When sis showed up, she didn't really try to talk him out of it too much. I could tell she sorta thought it was cool. He said his goodbyes and we left. Once we were outside the school, he pulled three twenties from his pocket.

"Where'd you get that?"

"My sister gave it to me. I guess it wasn't such a dumb idea to stop here, was it?"

Having $1.25 to my name, I was in no position to argue.

We walked and walked and walked. We had our thumbs out there in the cold for three hours but nobody picked us up. We were headed in what we thought was the general direction of a highway, but we couldn't be sure. Around 5:00 we stopped in a gas station and got a map. We were right by I-294, which, according to the map, led down to highway 80. From there it was just a quick jaunt to I-65 south, which went right into Nashville. We walked up the on-ramp, sat on a guardrail and stuck out our thumbs. Within a couple of minutes, we were picked up and got a ride down to some unfamiliar exit. We got off and tried thumbing again. No luck. We started walking down Ogden Avenue and soon saw a sign informing us we were in Downers Grove. I consulted my map but I couldn't find the town. We kept walking. We walked for hours, stopping only to eat a couple of 25 cent hamburgers at McDonald's - they had a special going for Valentine Day weekend.

As it got colder and darker, I suggested that we look for a motel. We stopped at five of them. The first four refused to give us a room 'cause we had no I.D. to prove we were 18. The last motel was next to an I-HOP. The old guy behind the counter didn't wanna give us a room, but we laid the pity stuff on him pretty hard and he relented. In a couple of minutes we were in the room watching TV.

The next morning, we were out of the room and eating breakfast in the I-HOP by 8:00. After we finished, Phil got a box of Marlboros for each of us. We sat smoking and drinking water, sorta hanging around avoiding the inevitable.

"Do you wanna go home?" he asked.

"No," I said. And I didn't. But this was gonna suck, standing out on the highway all day. We hadn't been too lucky with rides last night, so I didn't think we had much chance to make it to Nashville by night. I thought about it for a while and then gave him as much of a pep talk as I could muster. We headed back out on Ogden toward the highway.

This time, we'd been on the ramp for only a few minutes when we got a ride. The guy was a real prick though, telling us to watch the upholstery and whatnot, being a real pain in the butt. He finally let us out on an off ramp just off of I-65. As I was getting out of the car, the door handle came off in my hand. I don't even know how, I mean, I didn't do anything but open the fucking door. The guy got all pissed off but we just laughed at him; he was backing up traffic and had no way to go but forward.

Pretty soon, a big old Cadillac pulled up and we climbed in. The back seat was huge and the machine was being skippered by a forty-ish guy wearing an expensive looking suit and reeking of Old Spice and arrogance. I gave him the standard speech about how we were running away 'cause our parents were fucked and all, making sure to say that Phil's parents beat him regularly (which wasn't really true, but what the hell).

He started talking about drugs, wanting to know if we had any Rush or Locker Room. He was really into poppers, kept talking and talking about them, all the time cranking out his Beethoven or whatever the hell classical shit he was listening to. Phil asked him to turn the station once (and I elbowed him in the ribs good for THAT one) but he just said, "This is wonderful music, you can really appreciate it when you're speeding." I made up some bullshit about me being a big-time speed dealer in Chicago and having to get out of it 'cause of the law. The idiot bought it. He woulda bought anything. He was the kinda guy who would buy an ounce of pure oregeno from you, then call you up the next week and thank you for the great dope.

He drove us pretty far, all the way down to the bottom of Indiana, but I think he finally dumped us 'cause he was getting annoyed; we were fucking around in the back seat and making fun of him behind his back. I knew it wasn't a bright move, but the guy was so flaky and flamboyant and silly, I couldn't help it. And Phil had no concept of tact at any time.

We walked down the highway for about a half hour and were finally picked up by some burnout looking guys in a black Camaro. They asked us if we had any weed and we told them we didn't. Two miles later we were back pounding the pavement.

"Fucking assholes anyway," I said.

"Yeah, we shoulda told 'em we had pot."

Phil was starting to irritate me. "If we told 'em we had pot, they'd want some. Then what?"

"Then nothing. We'd kick the shit out of them."

I didn't bother mentioning that these guys woulda slaughtered us. Phil always got a little pissy when his own stupidity was pointed out to him.

We were outside a town called Shephardsville, in Kentucky. We wandered down the street off the highway until we found a McDonald's. We were almost broke. We had gone through a drive-thru with the Cadillac guy and spent way too much money. We bought a pack of cigarettes and had enough dough left for two 25 cent hamburgers.

I went up and ordered and the girl behind the counter asked where we were from.

"Chicago," I said, tired of answering the same old questions. "We ran away from home." She was really nice to us and all, and when she handed our bag to us, it was crammed full of burgers and fries. We practically salammed her, then slinked off to a corner to wolf down the food. We hung around the McDonald's until it was getting to be ridiculous, then headed out into the cold again. For some reason, I thought that it would get warmer after we crossed the state line into Kentucky. After all, this was the South.

We got back on the highway at around 7:30 P.M. and started walking, and we kept walking. We walked for miles, every so often having to cross a bridge, and of course every time we did, a few trucks would barrel past leaving us shaking on the bridge, feeling like we were about to be knocked to our death.

RAN AWAY FROM HOME AT AGE 15

DEBBIE HAS BEEN ON DRUGS SINCE SHE WAS 14

FATHER AN EXECUTIVE AND AN ALCOHOLIC

MOTHER DIED 1 YEAR AGO— WITHOUT CHRIST

HER PARENTS DIVORCED WHEN SHE WAS 7

It was really cold now, and totally dark but for the occasional set of headlights. We had been walking for what seemed like hours; neither of us had a watch, but I'd occasionally count up to a minute and start over in a lame attempt to keep track of time. Things looked bad. We had no money for a room and cars were whipping by as if they didn't see us. Phil kept lagging behind, complaining about the pain in his leg. I kept walking faster, trying to keep warm.

We were getting desperate. The trucks seemed to be coming closer and no one gave any signs of pulling over. My thumb was almost frozen from hanging there in the cold. I prayed, literally. I didn't even really believe in God, but I was so fucking low I prayed for a car to pick us up. And about twenty seconds after I finished my little prayer, a car pulled over.

It was a green Charger, a real studmobile. We ran up to the car, pulled open the door and dove into the back seat: "THANKYOUTHANKYOUTHANKYOU." The guy driving the car was black. His name was LeRoy and he was from Kankakee, driving down to Atlanta to see his brother or something.

"Got any weed?" he asked.

"No, sorry," I said, every muscle in my body clenched up in a one-man attempt to access his brain with my fervent "DON'T KICK US OUT DON'T KICK US OUT DON'T KICK US OUT" mental chant. He didn't kick us out.

Instead, he chatted amiably with us about general crapola. I looked at the clock on the dash. It was 10:30. Three hours out in the freezing cold, waiting for a ride. At some point, LeRoy pulled over to get gas. When he came back from the cashier's, he had big foot long hot dogs and a six pack of Schlitz Malt Liqour 16-ouncers. We were in hog heaven. We ate and drank heartily, our spirits only dampened by the fact that we had no cigarettes left. LeRoy was more than happy to bum us a few. When we hit Nashville, he dumped us at a Denny's and gave us a pack of his Salems. What a prince.

I swaggered into the Denny's, still slightly drunk from my two beers, and whipped open the phone book in the lobby. Tom's name was nowhere in the book. I called Information. No luck. He had just moved down, maybe he didn't have a phone yet.

Our moment of glory, shattered. We were fucked and we knew it. It was just about then that Phil noticed the sticker on the side of the phone booth.

"Let's call," he said.

"The RUNAWAY HOTLINE???" I almost screamed. "They'll turn us in! We'll spend the night in jail!"

"Well, we're not sleeping here," he said, which was obvious. The Denny's employees were already shooting us nasty looks.

I called. A man answered and I told him we were runaways and needed a place to stay.

"Where are you?" he asked.

I looked out the window at the street sign. "Murfreesboro Road" I answered.

"Okay," he said, "There's a Mission on Murfreesboro, just go left and walk down until you see it."

"How far?" I asked.

"I don't know," he said, "I've never been to Nashville."

We started the long walk. The place was nowhere in sight. We were starting to get into a kinda lousy area too. We walked by a club that was closing down. A well-dressed older guy was getting into his car. I asked if he knew where the Mission was and he offered to give us a ride. We were there in a few minutes.

We walked in and were showed to our sleeping quarters. We both had top bunks in a six man room. The walls were painted puke green. Everyone was asleep. The guy below me was snoring like a sow. The guy under Phil had no legs. Cockroaches scampered merrily on the walls.

"Should we get outta here?" I asked.

"I'm too tired," said Phil. "I gotta sleep."

We fell asleep after about an hour of whispering back and forth about the creepiness of the place. We were woken up what seemed like a minute later. It was 6:00 A.M. and some old guy with a deformed face was telling us to eat this slop in a green bowl. It appeared to be stale mucus. We declined and got outta there despite his protests, the security guard guy making a half assed attempt to keep us from leaving.

It was Sunday morning, so maybe everyone was at church. The only things on Murfreesboro Road were smashed booze bottles and puddles of blood and vomit. We headed back the way we came from. Phil saw a Greyhound station and suggested we go in for a nap.

We went into Greyhound and laid down on two benches. Just as I was drifting off to sleep, I heard a voice.

"You guys run away from home?"

It was a friendly, clean cut looking fellow, mid-thirties maybe, neatly trimmed mustache, short black hair.

Phil, of course, was involved in a conversation with him already. I pulled him aside.

"He says we can go to his house and crash," he said.

I figured the guy was okay, he was all friendly and whatnot, just waiting at the bus station for his friend whose bus hadn't showed up.

"Okay, let's go," I said.

As soon as we got into the guy's car, I smelled a rat. His junky old shitmobile was covered with fast food wrappers and dirty snotrags. He started telling us about his knife that he had got in the war or some shit.

"Cool," I said absentmindedly.

"You don't believe me?" he said, and he pulled out a big switchblade.

Phil thought it was cool. I thought we'd best not piss this creep off.

We got to his house and on the way to the door, he explained that he really lived in the basement but his doctor friend owned the house and didn't mind him hanging out upstairs. Always thinking ahead, I told him that we had to make a phone call to Chicago soon 'cause we had a lead on a place to stay.

When we walked in, the first thing we saw was a huge Doberman sitting inside a cage in the middle of the floor.

"I'd better not let him out," The Creep said as the animal growled at us angrily. "You guys like MTV?"

Sure, we liked MTV - it was still fairly new back then and pretty cool to a couple of fourteen year old delinquents.

Phil and I sat down on a love seat in front of the TV and watched lame-ass Duran Duran.

"You want something to drink?" asked The Creep.

"A glass of water would be good," I said.

"Oh c'mon, how about something a little stronger? Rum and Coke?"

It was 6:30 in the morning fer chrissakes. Phil jumped at the chance for alcohol. The Creep came over with two huge glasses of rum and coke, mostly rum. I hated hard liquor and this stuff tasted like shit. Phil was gulping his down. The Creep had been offering us a shower on the way over. Now he was telling us what we really needed was a warm bath.

"I don't take baths," I said, "I could really use a shower though."

"The shower's broken."

"Oh well, I'll pass...."

Phil was oblivious. The Creep left for a minute and came back carrying a pair of satin shorts in each hand.

"Y'all be more comfortable in these," he said.

Sirens, bells, flashing lights. My heart was pounding from fear now.

"I don't think so," I said.

"Yeah, we're fine," said Phil, a funny little quizzical look on his face. I was sitting on the left side of the couch, Phil on the right. The Creep had been sitting on the edge of the couch by Phil. Now he squeezed in next to him. Pat Benatar was on MTV asking us to hit her with our best shot.

"Man, she's hot," said Phil.

"Oh yeah, " said The Creep. "There's nothing like a big, wet tongue around your dick."

Sirens went off in my head once again. I vowed to play it cool. No sudden moves.

"Yep," he continued, "Nothing like a nice piece of ass."

"Or a nice, warm pussy," I offered.

He wasn't impressed. "Sure you don't want to put these on?" he said, waving the shorts. "I can run a warm bath for you."

Phil was finally beginning to catch the drift, the fucking dolt. He put down his glass and shot me a look. The Creep went to the kitchen for a minute and Phil leaned over to me.

"He's weird," he said.

"No shit," I answered. "He's a fuckin' homo. He wants our ass."

"Lemme do the talking," I said. "Whatever I say, you agree. We gotta get outta here." My only hope was that if the guy got rough, Phil would clock him good. He was only 14, but he was a pretty tough guy.

The Creep came back and continued urging us to take baths and get into his queer little shorts. I'd occasionally comment about the fact that it was almost time for us to make our call. I kept watching the digital clock on top of the TV, waiting for it to hit 6:55. I had decided that's when we were leaving.

The Creep kept making vague references to his knife and his dog. Finally the time came.

"We gotta make that call," I said. "Is there a pay phone around here?"

"Well there's one right down at the corner," he answered. "But you can call from here."

FUCK!!! I thought fast. "Well, it's a long distance call."

"That's alright," he said. "Just keep it short."

I had him now. "Well, the thing is, I gotta get directions from this girl and it's gonna take a long time." That sounded good. Now to add a little fuel to the fire. "Plus my girlfriend is over there and she's gonna wanna talk to me."

He looked reluctant, but I could tell he didn't want us making a long call to Chicago. He gave us long, drawn out directions to the phone booth on the corner. We were almost at the door when he did a little hop and wound up in front of us.

"Y'all comin' back, right?" he asked. The dog was barking now, sounding like it wouldn't mind chowing on our nuts.

"Oh yeah," said Phil. "We're just gonna make this phone call and then we'll come right back."

The Creep looked suspicious, but he unlocked the door and let us go. We walked down the steps and onto the street. As soon as we were past the house, we ran.

About a block later, we were still running, but cracking up.

"This is gonna make a great story," said Phil. "Only when we tell it, let's say you kicked the guy in the balls and I punched him in the face."

I agreed and we kept running until we were back on Murfreesboro. We were even farther away from civilization than before. At least there were cop cars whizzing by every ten seconds. We were on the middle of a bridge when I looked back and saw The Creep behind us in his car. He saw me spot him and yelled, "Hey, where ya goin'?"

We both gave him the finger and yelled "Fuck you, homo," and such at him. He looked kinda pissed, and we started running. By the time we were off the bridge and halfway through a vacant lot, we realized he had turned around.

We kept walking and walking, but now Phil was really whining about his leg. At one point, I turned around to see him two blocks behind me. We kept stopping so he could rest but it was getting ridiculous.

After what seemed like 20 miles, we reached the Denny's where we had been dumped the night before.

"I'm going home," said Phil. "I'm gonna call my dad and have him pick me up. You can go too."

"You PUSSY!" I shouted. "What the fuck is wrong with you? We made it, we're here!"

"We're never gonna find Tom," he said. "He's not even in the phonebook." He was probably right, but I spent about twenty minutes trying to talk him out of it anyway. It was no good. He gave me half a pack of Salems and two dollars he had swiped from The Creep's house. I turned my back and kept walking.

After a while I stopped at a 7-11 type joint called the Hot Spot and bought a soda. I hung around for a while until the guy behind the counter got suspicious.

I spilled my guts to him and told him if I could just use his phone to call Chicago, I'd be outta there.

He let me into the back room and I called Tom's mother's house, hoping to reach his sister. Of course, I got his mother instead. She told me she didn't have the number but that she'd call me back. I gave her the number at the Hot Spot and went back out to browse around magazines and stuff. When she called back, she said she had spoken to my parents and that if I wanted to come home, I had to call Judy somebody, some friend of my parents from their Toughlove group.

"Sorry," I said. "I'm not coming home." I thought maybe I could get a job at the Hot Spot and sleep in the storeroom for a while. The guy behind the counter was the manager and he seemed to like me.

We got to talking and he told me after his shift I could come to his house for dinner. He lived with his wife, her sister and her brother-in-law. I was a bit skeptical, but having no other choice, I agreed.

He bought me a hot dog, and when his shift ended we got into his car and headed for his house. I was pretty happy, I mean, he'd bought me a pack of cigarettes (but he got Salems, 'cause that's what I had been smoking) and he seemed okay.

We got to his house, a nice little ranch type thing in the suburbs. Walking in was like the fuckin' Waltons at Christmastime. The manager was a born again Christian and so was everyone who lived there. Well, at least they made a big spaghetti dinner. I sat down and dug in.

"Ummm... we say grace before we eat, Ben." It was the guy's wife. I felt myself turning red.

The brother-in-law spoke up. "Do YOU want to say grace?"

"Uh, I don't really know any prayers," I said. All I knew was GODISGREATGODISGOOD and something told me that wouldn't cut it with these Jesus jumpers. Somebody said a big long prayer and then we ate. Well, sort of. I mean, it was the worst spaghetti I'd ever had, like out of a can. I forced as much into myself as possible before giving up.

"Not hungry?" asked the manager.

"No, I don't eat much," I said, which was only a half lie anyway.

After dinner I went out for a smoke. When I came back inside, they let me shower and gave me a pair of pajamas that were way too big. I hated pajamas but I put them on to please them. They also convinced me to call those friends of my parents. I did and it was worked out that I'd fly back the next day, Valentine's Day, and get picked up by these mysterious friends.

Then they gave me some comic books and pulled out the couchbed for me. As soon as they went to bed, I ditched the crummy jammies and fell asleep.

The next day I was up bright and early to make the 10:00 A.M. flight to Chicago. The manager and his family waited for me at the airport until I boarded. Then they gave me a hug and their names and phone number on a card and told me to call them collect after I'd gotten back and settled in. It was really weird, I mean these people really acted like they LIKED me.

It was only a 45 minute flight. I was met at O'Hare by a pudgy lady and her sheepish looking husband. I got in their car and they took off in the wrong direction.

"Where are we going?" I asked.

"You'll know when we get there," was the only answer I got to that oft-repeated question.

They were Toughlove parents, and they explained that their daughter was the problem child in their family. Right, I'd have to look her up. We pulled up in front of a Marine Recruiting Center in Palatine. They brought me inside and left. A big jocko marine took me into a small back room with an empty desk and two chairs. Immediately the guy started screaming at me. The usual crap, about how I was an ungrateful little asshole, I was killing my parents, etc. He was right up in my face, little pieces of his spit hitting me in the nose. I just sat there and took it. Then he ordered me to empty my pockets.

I did as he said. He told me to take the pin off my jacket. I layed it down on the table. He pulled out a manila envelope, wrote "PERSONAL EFFECTS" on it in big block letters and started doing an inventory on a sheet of paper.

"One comb, black," he said in his professional military voice. I smirked at him and he squinted his beady little eyes at me.

"I could kick the living shit out of you right now and there's not a goddamn thing you can do about it," he said quietly.

I didn't believe him. "I dare you," I said.

More in-my-face roaring from the prick.

"I'm not going into the army, " I said.

This enraged him more than anything else. "YOU'RE TALKING TO A GODDAMN MARINE!!!" he screamed. "YOU ADDRESS ME AS SIR!"

"Yessir," I mumbled.

He sat back down and continued his inventory.

"37 cents, change. One Zippo lighter." He opened it up and pulled out the fluid filter, finding nothing of course. He put it back together and dropped it in the envelope.

"One wallet, brown. One mairjawanna leaf pin, gold." This he dropped into the wastebasket.

"Hey," I said. "Whattya think you're doing?"

"You don't want your father to see that, do you?"

"Fuck that," I said. "Give it back." He put it into the envelope reluctantly, giving me the squint again.

After he finished, he left the room and I sat there for five hours until my old man showed up. He put me in the car, handing me my personal effects envelope minus my pin, lighter and cigarettes. He drove me to my uncle's house in Highland Park, where I spent the next three days sitting on the couch doing nothing, occasionally getting my aunt to turn her back so I could cop a few drags from her cigarette.

Finally I was picked up by the old man and brought home. I got a three hour long lecture about how things were gonna change and all that bullshit. After it was over, I said, "No way," walked outside and started off down the street. Hell, it was my first night back in town. I had to have a little fun.

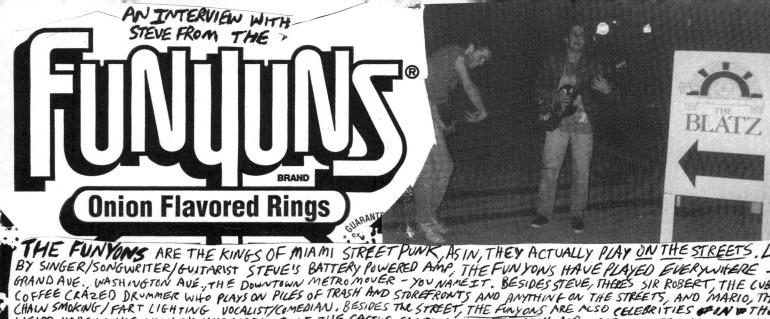

FUNYUNS®

BRAND

Onion Flavored Rings

THE FUNYONS ARE THE KINGS OF MIAMI STREET PUNK, AS IN, THEY ACTUALLY PLAY ON THE STREETS. L[ED] BY SINGER/SONGWRITER/GUITARIST STEVE'S BATTERY POWERED AMP, THE FUNYONS HAVE PLAYED EVERYWHERE - GRAND AVE., WASHINGTON AVE., THE DOWNTOWN METRO MOVER - YOU NAME IT. BESIDES STEVE, THERE'S SIR ROBERT, THE CUB[AN] COFFEE CRAZED DRUMMER WHO PLAYS ON PILES OF TRASH AND STOREFRONTS AND ANYTHING ON THE STREETS, AND MARIO, TH[E] CHAIN SMOKING/FART LIGHTING VOCALIST/COMEDIAN. BESIDES THE STREET, THE FUNYONS ARE ALSO CELEBRITIES ON THE WEIRD "OPEN MIKE NIGHT" UNDERGROUND AT THE CACTUS CANTINA ON THE BEACH, AND WERE WRITTEN ABOUT IN TH[E] NEWTIMES AS OPEN MIKE STARS. STEVE'S SONGS ARE USUALLY REAL CATCHY, FUNNY POP PUNK. HITS INCLUDE "I'M [IN]TO IT," "THE QUANTUM PHYSICS SONG", "BIGGER CAGES, LONGER CHAINS" AND "MOVIN' TO SEATTLE", WHICH T[O THE] TUNE OF "GOIN' TO THE CHAPEL" GOES "MOVIN' TO SEATTLE, GONNA GET A BRAND NEW FLANNEL, MOVIN' TO SEATTLE, GONNA BE THE NEXT NIRVANA, MOVING TO SEATTLE, GONNA FEED COURTNEY LOVE BANANAS..." OK, I LOVE THESE GUYS. WHAT MORE CAN I SAY? I INTERVIEWED STEVE, CUZ I WAS ALWAYS KIND OF INSPIRED BY THE FACT THAT HE'S A DENNY'S WAITER, A TEACHER, AND A BIT OLDER, BUT HE'S STILL OUT THERE DOIN[G] STUFF, AND THAT'S PRETTY PUNK, EH?

i: So yer a waiter at Denny's...

S: all right. Maybe 50 bucks.

i: How'd you do on tips last night?

S: all right. Maybe 50 bucks. This one group of people were taking a real long time to examine their menu, while they drank their coffee, and it is true that the menu has a new layout, but i couldn't figure out why they were taking so long. I went over and said, "Look, i just want to make sure you aren't going to memorize the menu and go start a 'Lenny's', or a 'Kenny's', or something, and they laughed uproariously. They still gave a lousy tip! There are no funny denny's stories.

I: And you've got this teaching job...

S: i teach physics lab to freshman physics students at F.I.U. I work in a lab where were studying the surface properties of metal.

I: like Judas Priest?

S: Fuck off.

I: How long have you been doing THE FUNYONS? Did you try to do a real band... S: Hey, wait a minute!!!

I: Soory, eh... I mean a normal, four piece band and couldn't, so you just did it alone?

S: No, I was friends with THE METHADONE ACTORS and I wrote a song for them that I thought they could use, but their singer, Mario, thought it wouldn't be good with them, so me and him and their drummer, Betty, started THE FUNYONS. This was bout a year and a half ago.

I: When did you start playing in the streets

S: Right away. That's what I always wanted to do, cuz.. well, in a club, you end up preaching to the converted, or, uh, the unconvertible. When you play in the streets, you play to anyone who walks by.

I: Where was the first place you played?

S: I think it was 9th Street, between Washington and Collins, on Miami Beach. Betty was pretty shy about playin in public so we had to get her real stoned and tell her we were just gonna practice in a spot where no one would ever walk by. But after a while, she got into it and we did it alot. But now, Robert's the drummer, and he wants everyone to see what a freak he is.

I: Do you run into people at Denny's who've seen you play?

S: No. Well, I'm sure I've told some people that I work with about it, but its so far removed from their everyday life, that they don't really see me going out on the streets, playing obnoxious music.

I: How'd you get into the open mike scene?

S: we just kind of walked by the Cactus Cantina one night when it was open mike night, and decided to play it. (KREAMY 'LECTRIC SANTA drummer, Tim, walks by and says "Tell 'em how you rode to the top on K.L.S.'s coat tails") S: and after that, it has just been a ride to the top on K.L.S.'s coat tails... We ARE open mike stars.

I: What about the other regulars at open mike? the real hopeless ones...

S: Well, they're not hopeless, but, uh, I guess they should be. I can't imagine why anyone would want to do a Dylan cover... Well, there's alot of sad, whiny folk songs about how we should all hold hands and the world would be a better place. That girl, Noodles, did a song about butterflies, then she got to the top on K.L.S.'s coat tails. There's Phil T. Rich. He's this bald guy that does kinda simple, crude, offensive songs that aren't really clever in any way, like this song he does about how much he likes to have sex with pygmies. The barmaid that hates us, cuz we try and sneak in all the underage kids, she really likes that pygmy song. She requests it every time.

I: What about yer FUNYONS tour of Chicago last year?

S: Well, that wasn't THE FUNYONS, really. It was a Steve tour of Chicago. But, I took the battery powered amp to Chicago and played everywhere. I played Wrigley Field. I stormed up the Pablo Picasso statue, with my amp mounted on my backpack, and played up there. I played at the Hard Rock Cafe in downtown Chicago. These rugrats from the burbs were heckling me, and yelling at me to play RUSH.

I: So you hit em with the guitar!

S: Right. I hit em with the guitar and jumped up and down on their legs until I heard them break. The guys on the corner selling the stolen gold jewelry came over and told me that if I had any problems with ANYBODY, that they'd care of it, so we were getting protection from the local hoods in da hood. The weird thing is that there were alot of street musicians in Chicago, but they all had permits. They were music for THE MAN! I: what usually happens when the cops run you out...

THE BOTTOM OF THE BAG: FUNYONS INT-VW PT II

down here? S: Well, Downtown, they say, "Go to Miami Beach." In Miami Beach, they say," Go to Coconut Grove." In the Grove, they say, "Go to New York." (pauses dramatically) But, I guess if you went everywhere that people told you to go... you'd be nowhere, man. I: Don't worry. I'll edit that out. S: Thanks. Sorry. I: So what are some of the cooler places you've played? S: Well, we played outside of a Rave in downtown Miami. The Rave was selling those "Smart drinks", so we sold this shitty, warm, unsweetened Kool-Aid, and called it "Stupid Drinks" People'd buy it and think they were getting dosed, but they'd just get stupid. We made 15 bucks playing outside of Lollapalooza, and I think we were the real alternative that day. We were playing out front of Uncle Sam's one night, and these promoters from Def American came by and heard us and wanted us to play at Club One, the disco on South Beach, at this promo party for a new C.D. for a band called "Digital Orgasm". They were gonna play the C.D. all night, then stop the music at midnight and and we'd play and go crazy for a couple minutes then they'd play the C.D. again. They said we'd get paid, get drinks, blah, blah, blah, etc. I: What happened? S: We got blah, blah, blah, etc. Not only did we get no money or drinks, but I had to give the bathroom attendant a buck. All we got was a shitty "Digital Orgasm" C.d. But it was this cavernous disco, and we play with no amplification, except for my battery powered amp, and they have this huge video screen of us, behind us, with all these TV's. People couldn't hear us at all. Robert just ran around banging on stuff, and everyone just kinda left the dance floor. I: What's the song, "I'm Used to It" about? S; Well, everyone says its a love song, but its not. Its about alienation. I wrote it when I was 19, and I barely knew the chords to it. Its about my walk to school, and I guess, being a lonely, young man, I'd try to look people in the eye, or say hello, or make acquaintances with people on the way, and I noticed that no matter where you go, if you look people in the eye, they just look away. I'd walk to school every morning and see the same people walking their dog or whatever and they'd just pretend they didn't know me. Its about how lonely you can be even walking down the street with a crowd of people.

← PHOTO: Steve ALONE IN A crowd of people

LETTER FROM STEVE: TO HIS FANS

IGGY: HERE ARE THE CHICAGO PICTURES AND THE LYRICS YOU ASKED FOR. MY FAVORITE PICTURE IS THE ONE IN FRONT OF WRIGLEY FIELD. VERY CHICAGO. FUNYONS PLAYED ALL OVER AS USUAL LAST WEEK. JUST ME AND MARIO WENT OUT, AND WE MADE 25 BUCKS, PLUS A SMALL BAG OF COCAINE!!! WHAT IS THIS?!? 1979?!? NO, JUST WASHINGTON AVENUE AS USUAL. WE PLAYED A STUNNING SET AT THE PHOTO-STUDIO FOYER NEXT TO WASHINGTON SQUARE WITH DOZENS OF ONLOOKERS AND EVEN DOC (vicious idiot Boomer) AND THE REST OF THE DWARVES THERE. THEY DIDN'T TRY AND BEAT US UP. I THOUGHT THIS WOULD BE A GOOD PLACE TO STAGE A REAL ALTERNATIVE TO THE SQUARE. ONE SHOW, AT THE CACTUS, WE WERE ALL SICK, BUT WE WERE WELL RECEIVED...

I'M NOT SURE WHICH LYRICS YOU WANT, SO HERE'S A BUNCH OF 'EM THAT I'M PARTICULARLY HAPPY WITH.

"...YOU STANDING IN THE SUPERMARKET AISLE, YOU LOOK AWAY IF I THREATEN TO SMILE I'M USED TO IT..." — "I'M USED TO IT"

"HEY, MAN, LET'S PRETEND ITS 1968 AGAIN YOU DIG LIFE AND I'LL DIG LOVE WE'LL SIT AROUND AND DO A LOT OF DRUGS DID WE TURN INTO OUR PARENTS YET?" — "STEVE HATES HIPPIES"

"ONCE UPON A TIME, I WAS FALLING IN LOVE, NOW I'M ONLY FALLING APART. NOTHING I CAN ♥ SAY..." — TOTAL ECLIPSE OF THE HEART

"CALL IT THE 'MAGIC OF IMAGINATION', JUST ANOTHER ARYAN VACATION, AND EVERYONE MUST SALUTE THE 'UBERMOUSE" — "FASCIST FUN FACTORY"

write to Steve Funyons, bother him to ord Funyons songs: FUNYONS 3244 WEST TRADE #4 COCONUT GROVE FL 33133

Coconut Grove is in The house, yo!

- 117 -

THE PUNK ROCK PICNIC!

PUNK ROCK PICNIC! Sunday May 30th

THERE WAS REALLY NOWHERE FOR PUNK BANDS TO HAVE GOOD SHOWS IN SOUTH FLORIDA, ESPECIALLY AFTER CHURCHILL'S QUIT LETTING KIDS IN, SO THE PUNKS WERE DRIVEN UNDERGROUND AND THUS THIS WAS BORN

WE WOULD JUST GET A GENERATOR, AND FOOD, AND BEER AND BANDS AND HAVE A SHOW IN THE MIDDLE OF NOWHERE! FUCK THE CLUBS! THESE SHOWS COULD BE AS GOOD AS YOU WANTED 'EM TO BE. WE STARTED HAVIN' 'EM IN AN EMPTY LOT WAY OUT PAST S.W. 157TH IN KENDALL, BUT THE BEST ONE I SAW WAS AT THIS CRUMBLY, ABANDONED WAREHOUSE IN KENDALL THAT HAD BEEN FUCKED UP BY THE HURRICANE. AUDACITY FROM GEORGIA PLAYED, BUT THE BEST PART WAS ALL THE OTHER STUFF. ME AND FLINT STOLE A BUNCH OF SHOPPING CARTS FOR SHOPPING-CART SMASH 'N' RIDE RINK, AND BOWLING BALLS FOR THE PUNK ROCK BOWLING ALLEY. EMIL BROUGHT 6 CASES OF DUMPSTERED "GREEN SLIME" PUDDING THAT GOT ALL OVER EVERYONE. THERE WAS SCHLITZ AND STOLEN WINE AND A "PIN THE SYRINGE ON SID" GAME, AND, OF COURSE, THE HUGE BONFIRE. AUDACITY PLAYED GREAT RAMONESISH PUNK AND I AIR-GUITARED AND PUSHED MY CART AROUND THE FIRE ALL NIGHT, AND WOKE UP HUNGOVER, CRUSTY, GREEN AND SMILIN' THE NEXT DAY! THE KENDALL EMPTY LOT IS NOW UNDER SUBURBAN HOUSES, AND THE WAREHOUSE IS A FUNCTIONING BUSINESS. ONLY WE, THE PUNKS, KNOW THAT THOSE WERE THE SIGHTS OF SOME OF THE BEST PUNK SHOWS EVER IN MIAMI!

PUNK ROCK SHOW

THIS IS A FREE PICNIC!
BUT, YOU ARE ENCOURAGED TO BRING A CAN OF FOOD FOR FOOD NOT BOMBS. SO, BRING BEER, INHALANTS, JUNK FOOD, OR WHATEVER, AND GO!

HEY! YOU THERE!
LOOKEE...IT'S THE RETURN OF...
PUNK & PICNIC
SUNDAY, NOV. 22 — CAVITY (FORMERLY CRAWL)
PLUS
SUNDAY, NOV. 29 — AUDACITY FROM GEORGIA

PUNK ROCK SHOW! CHICKENHEAD

KILLER KANE

AUDACITY

CITY OF MIAMI

PUNK PICNIC — THEME NOON

CAVITY — MIAMI'S OWN SLOW, LOUD, AND PAINFUL

STUN GUN — POP-ISH PUNK ALL THE WAY FROM MISSOURI

Che Canadiens — THE ONLY BAND WHO STILL BELIEVE IN CHELSEA

KILLER KANE

CHICKENHEAD/AUDACITY I PUNK THEME PARK

PICTURED ABOVE: JOEY JACKAL, IQ AFTER CUTTIN' HIS HEAD WITH A RAZOR AT THE KENDALL D-ROCK PICNIC SPOT...

- 118 -

THE ROCK 'N' ROLL LIFESTYLE:

TAKIN' A BAND LIKE CHICKENHEAD ON TOUR SEEMS TO KIND OF MAKE A MOCKERY OF THE WHOLE BAND TOUR EXPERIENCE, WHICH IS GOOD, I THINK, CAUSE BANDS ARE REALLY SERIOUS ABOUT EVERYTHING THESE DAYS. THEY WRITE LENGTHY TOUR DIARIES FOR LOCAL ZINES ABOUT WHAT AN ORDEAL TOURING IS, AND WORSE, THEY WRITE STOOPIT SONGS ABOUT TOURING, LIKE THAT JAWBREAKER SONG WHERE THE LINE IS "20 MINUTES IN I BROKE ANOTHER FUCKIN' STRING." ANOTHER STRING? OMAN, HOW DO YOU, YA KNOW, MANAGE TO COPE WITH IT? SHEESH! THERE ARE NO GOOD SONGS ABOUT TOURING! ITS FUN. DON'T LET ANYONE TELL YA DIFFERENT. I MEAN, YOU LEARN A COUPLE CHORDS AND THEN GET TO TRAVEL THE COUNTRY WITH YOUR BEST FRIENDS. ITS LIKE THE BIGGEST SCAM OF ALL.

WE DRIVE STRAIGHT UP TO RICHMOND FOR THE FIRST SHOW, AND ME AND CHUCK LOOSE IMMEDIATELY GO TO WORK, CASHING OUR TRAVELLER'S CHECKS, FOR THE DOUBLE-YER-MONEY-TRAVELLER'S-CHECK-SCAM, WHICH IS WHERE YOU GET CHECKS, BUY CHEAP ITEMS WITH EACH ONE TO GET THE CHANGE IN REAL MONEY (WITHOUT SHOWING YOUR I.D. MOST STORES WON'T CHECK) AND REPORT THE CHECKS LOST OR STOLEN FOR A "REFUND", THUS DOUBLING YOUR CASH. AFTER WE DID THAT, IT WAS OFF TO THE FIRST SHOW.

AT THE SHOW, CHUCKY DRINKS A HALF A BOTTLE OF VODKA AND STARTS PUKING ALL OVER THE CLUB, ABOUT 2 HOURS BEFORE WE'RE SUPPOSED TO PLAY. A LOT OF PEOPLE POINT AND LAUGH. MANY RUN TO GET OUT OF THE WAY. IT WAS A LOT LIKE ONE OF OUR SHOWS. I FIGURED CHUCK WAS "GOING SOLO." CHUCK PASSES OUT IN A PUDDLE OF PUKE AND THESE NICE RIOT GRRLS WHO BOOKED THE SHOW HELPED ME CLEAN HIM OFF A LITTLE. WE'RE NOT WORRIED, CUZ HE'S TOTALLY PASSED OUT, BUT, STILL, YA KNOW, FLAMMABLE. THE SHOW WILL GO ON. BUT, THEN, BUDDHA GETS KICKED OUT OF THE CLUB FOR DRINKING A BEER THAT WE HAD SMUGGLED INTO THE CLUB. I TRY VERY DIPLOMATICALLY (UNUSUAL FOR ME) TO EXPLAIN TO THE CLUB OWNER THAT THIS IS ALL A BIG MISUNDER- STANDING, CUZ IN MIAMI, UNDERAGE KIDS ARE JUST ALLOWED TO BRING THEIR OWN BEER INTO CLUBS... OK, WE HAVE TO PLAY WITHOUT BOOD, AND DECIDE TO ENACT THE CHICKENHEAD "SCORCHED EARTH POLICY" TOWARDS THE EVIL CLUB. BUT THEN THE OWNER SAYS WE CAN'T PLAY AT ALL, SO WE PACK UP. I DISCREETLY URINATE ON THEIR DANCE FLOOR, AND ON THE WAY TO THE VAN, DECIDE TO SPRAY PRINT SOMETHING CLEVER ON THE SIDE OF THE CLUB. ABOUT 25 GUYS SURROUND THE VAN SO WE CAN'T LEAVE. THEY WANT TO KICK MY ASS. THE COPS COME AND I WRITE ALL THE PERTINENT PHONE #'S ON MY ARM, CUZ I'M SURE I'M HEADIN' TO JAIL. BUT, SINCE I HAVE ALL THAT TRAVELLER CHECK MONEY, I OFFER 20 BUCKS TO THE OWNER FOR HIS WALL, AND THAT WORKS, AND WE GET THE HELL OUT OF TOWN...

NEXT UP WAS A BASEMENT SHOW IN ANNAPOLIS. IT WAS DARK DOWN THERE. I DON'T REMEMBER MUCH. THEN IT WAS UP TO JERSEY FOR A SHOW ON W.F.M.U. EVERY BAND THAT GETS A CHANCE SHOULD PLAY HERE. IT WAS A LOT OF FUN, AND WE EVEN MANAGED TO FINISH THE LYRICS TO SOME OF THE SONGS BEFORE WE WENT ON THE AIR. THE NEXT DAY WAS THE WORST STORM FOR THE TIME OF YEAR, IN OVER 50 YEARS, AND ME AND SCOTTY GOT TO SEE SNOW FOR THE FIRST TIME EVER, YES, WE WERE A FLORIDA BAND TOURING IN THE DEAD OF WINTER. I ALMOST LOST MY TAN. THAT DAY, DESPITE THE WEATHER, THIS GUY, JOHN, GETS US A SHOW AND AN AUDIENCE AT THE LAST MINUTE IN HIS BASEMENT. PRETTY COOL. JERSEY WAS FUN. WE RAIDED THE WALDBAUM'S SUPERMARKET IN JERSEY CITY EVERY NIGHT. AND BY NOW, BUDDHA HAD PUT TOOTHPASTE IN HIS HAIR, I HAD THE LOGO OF THE BAND, CRIME, PAINTED ON MY CHEST, AND WE'D ALL DECIDED THAT WE SHOULD TALK LIKE CANADIANS. SO, WE SAID "SOORY ABOOT THAT, EH?" AND "WHY ARE YOU TALKING ABOOT, EH?"

THE NEXT NIGHT AT ABC NO RIO, THINGS WERE GOIN' REAL WELL. THIS GUY OFFERED TO DO 100 ISSUES OF SCAM AT HIS WORK AND MAIL 'EM TO ME. I FOUND SOMETHING CLOSE TO CUBAN COFFEE AT A RESTAURANT UP THE STREET. I MET THIS REALLY COOL FOREIGN GIRL, WHO WAS JUST... UM... REALLY NEAT AND BEAUTIFUL AND FROM ANOTHER COUNTRY AND SHIT... SO, WE GO TO PLAY (AND THE GIRL'S RIGHT UP IN FRONT WINKIN' AT ME... GOSH) AND AFTER 2 MINUTES, CHUCK'S ALL BLOODY AND COVERED WITH MARMALADE (AND WE'D PUSHED OUR AMPS TO THE EDGE OF THE STAGE, SO WE PLAYED IN THE CROWD). THE GUY WHO WE'RE STAYING WITH, WHO LOANED ME HIS GUITAR, COMES RUNNING UP AND TAKES THE GUITAR OFF ME! WHAT A STATEMENT. THE END OF THE SHOW! EVERYWHERE WE GO, THEY SAY, "DAMN." CHICKENHEAD IS FUCKIN' UP THE PROGRAM. I WAS PRETTY PISSED OFF. OH YEAH, THE GIRL DISAPPEARED. TALK ABOUT BORN TO LOSE. SHEESH.

THE SHOW IN BALTIMORE THE NEXT DAY TOTALLY MADE UP FOR IT. WE BROUGHT PINATAS THAT WERE COP'S HEADS THAT THE GIRL WE WERE STAYIN' WITH, FAITH, MADE. THE SHOW RULED. 30 TOTALLY PULL ON PAINT-INKED KIDS JAMMED TOGETHER IN A BASEMENT. WE SCREENED OFF A BUNCH OF SHIRTS. THEY'LL BE TALKIN' ABOUT THE PIT THAT DAY FOR YEARS. UM... THE LAST SHOW WAS IN PHILADELPHIA. IT WAS A WEIRD ENDING TO THE TOUR. WE MET THESE 2 SQUATTER GUYS WALKIN' AROUND ON SOUTH STREET, AND TOOK 'EM TO THE SHOW, AND SAID THEY WERE IN THE BAND SO THEY'D GET FREE BEER. AT THE END OF OUR SHOW, THE 2 GUYS AND HIS 16 YEAR OLD, RUNAWAY GIRL (ALL TRASHED), WHO ARE 3/5 OF OUR AUDIENCE, DECIDE THEY WANT TO GO HOME WITH US! SO ME AND BOOD FORCE THE OTHERS TO LET US BRING 'EM TO MIAMI, CUZ WE WANT TO BE A BAND THAT MAKES A DIFFERENCE IN PEOPLE'S LIVES - YA KNOW, BY GETTING 'EM WASTED AND DRAGGING 'EM A THOUSAND MILES FROM HOME. SO, ALL 8 OF US PILE IN THE VAN AND DRIVE HOME. AT HOME, I TRY TO CALL JOHN DANIA AND TELL 'EM HOW THE TOUR WENT BUT ALL I CAN SAY IS "EH" AND "ALLROOT" AND JOHN HANGS UP ON ME. SAYS TO CALL HIM WHEN I'M NORMAL.

CHICKENHEAD GOES ON TOUR!

ACTUALLY "TOUR SPIEL" BY THE MINUTEMEN IS A GOOD SONG. AND "TRAVELLIN' BAND" WHERE THEY SAY "AT THE LAST SHOW, SOMEONE GOT EXCITED, THEY HAD TO CALL THE STATE MILITIA"

RETURN TO MIAMI • FLINT, GOLIATH, AND THE U.F.O.'S • RUNNIN' FROM COPS. LOVE LETTERS • CHRISTMAS BLUES. RESCUED BY PIRATES • MUTINY!

IT WAS GREAT TO BE BACK IN MIAMI AFTER THE TOUR, SEEIN' FLINT AND YOUNG FIDEL'S NEW "KIDS VS. COPS" GRAFFITI PAINTINGS ALL OVER TOWN, AND RIDIN' THE METRORAIL IN AND SEEIN' THAT THE PEOPLE WHO LIVE IN THE BOXCARS HAD RIPPED BACK THE FENCE AND WERE BACK IN THEIR RIGHTFUL HOMES, AND MEETIN' ALL KINDS OF CRAZY FUCKS DOWNTOWN, LIKE THE WOMAN WHO WAS PASSING OUT HOMEMADE "CHRISTMAS CARDS" ORDERING EVERYONE TO KILL THEMSELVES NOW, SO THAT THE U.F.O.'S COME RETURN BY NEW YEAR'S TO DO GOD'S WORK... AH YES, EVERYTHING SEEMED POSSIBLE DOWN THERE.

I WENT TO SEE FLINT, AND HE HAD JUST RETURNED FROM A PROFITABLE HITCH HIKING/GREYHOUND/ WALKING TOUR. IT SEEMS THAT GREYHOUND KEPT LOSING HIS LUGGAGE, POOR GUY LOST LIKE 4 BAGS. BUT, IT WAS OK, CUZ GREYHOUND PAY $150 BUCKS FOR EACH "LOST BAG." HE WAS HOPING TO GO ON ANOTHER TRIP SOON, AND LOSE SOME MORE BAGS.

FLINT SAYS TO ME, "YA KNOW, IGGY, I'M REALLY INTO THIS DAVID AND GOLIATH MYTH FROM THE BIBLE." UH, I'M NOT SURE WHAT YOU MEAN. "WELL, THE GOVERNMENT IS THIS BIG, GIGANTIC GOLIATH THAT THINKS ITS INDESTRUCTABLE, AND WE'RE DAVID, ALL SCRAPIN', USIN' WHATEVER TOOLS WE CAN, TO FIND THE WEAK SPOT AND TOPPLE THE WHOLE THING!" HMM... OK... "SO WHAT I DID WAS, I GOT THIS SLINGSHOT AND I'VE BEEN SHOOTIN' OUT THE WINDOWS OF COP CARS WITH MARBLES..." YO! FLINT! TIMMY TRI-RAIL WAS BACK FROM CALIFORNIA, TOO, AND HIM AND SCOTTY WERE GOING OUT TO PLAY GUITARS IN THE STREETS ALOT. I SAW YOUNG FIDEL AND HE SAID HE COULDN'T EVEN TELL ME WHAT HE WAS WORKIN' ON, SINCE HE'D HITCHED BACK FROM COLORADO! HE JUST SAID, "CHECK THE HEADLINES — YOU'LL KNOW..." IT SEEMED LIKE ALOT MORE WAS GOIN' ON IN MIAMI, EVERYONE GETTIN' ALL CRAZY AND RAD ALL OF A SUDDEN. AFTER WATCHING SO MANY FRIENDS SETTLE DOWN, IT SEEMED LIKE ALOT OF MY FRIENDS SEEMED TO REALLY KNOW WHAT THEY WANTED TO DO, AND WE'RE GETTIN' REAL HARDCORE ABOUT IT. IT WAS SO EXCITING, LIKE IT WAS ALL OUT THERE, A WHOLE CITY, A WHOLE WORLD O ROMANCE AND DANGER AND I WAS ALL SWEATIN' 19 YEARS READY TO EXPLODE ALL OVER IT.

BUT, FIRST, I STILL HAD THE KIDS FROM PHILADELPHIA TO WORRY ABOUT, AND THEY WEREN'T QUITE AS EXCITED WITH MIAMI, AFTER THEY SOBERED UP. THEY DECIDED TO HOP TRAINS HOME, FLINT AND I DROVE 'EM OVER TO THE F.E.C. TRAIN YARD IN HIALEAH, AND WE'RE HANGIN' OUT, WAITIN' TO FIND OUT WHERE THEIR TRAIN WAS GONNA BE, WHEN THE TRAIN COP CAME. HE RAN OUR (FAKE) NAMES THROUGH THE COMPUTER AND THE KIDS SAID, UH RELAX, HE'LL JUST THROW US OFF THE YARD, BUT IT WAS TAKING WAY TOO LONG AND I KNEW WHAT WAS UP AND SURE ENOUGH, HALF A MILE DOWN THE ONLY ROAD INTO THE YARD, I SAW THE METRO-DADE POLICE CAR TURN IN. SO I TOOK OFF RUNNIN', HOPPIN' OVER TRAIN AFTER TRAIN, TO THE BARBWIRE FENCE, THEN OVER THAT, AND OVER THE CANAL ON A PIPE THAT CROSSED IT, AND OVER ANOTHER FENCE OUT ONTO MILAM DAIRY RD. WHERE I HID BEHIND A DUMPSTER FOR TWO HOURS. I NEVER SAW THE PHILLY KIDS AGAIN...

I WALKED AROUND THE CITY THAT NIGHT, FOR A LONG TIME, FINALLY FEELIN' FREE. I WALKED ABOUT 10 MILES, AND WENT BY 22, OLE 22, AND SAW THAT LOCAL GRAFITTI ARTIST LEGEND, LUCIANO JAMES HAD DIGNIFIED THE FACE OF MY OLD HOME WITH ONE OF HIS PAINTINGS! THEN I PAID MY RESPECTS TO THE CORAL WAY CHRIST WITH MY OWN GRAFITTI, AND WENT TO DENNY'S TO WRITE A LOVE LETTER TO THE RAD, CRAZY REDHEAD. THE HEAD COOK CAME OVER AND SAID, "MAN, YOU'VE BEEN WRITIN' UP A STORM, THERE! YOU MUST BE WRITIN' A LOVE LETTER! WELL, IF YOU NEED ANY ADVICE, COME TO ME, CUZ I'M THE MAN." I SAID, "SURE THING", BUT IT DIDN'T REALLY MATTER WHAT I WROTE. IT WAS CLEAR THAT SHE DIDN'T LOVE ME, BUT I DIDN'T CARE. I LIKED THE IMAGE.

True or False Questions

THE SO-CALLED "GATEWAY TO OPA-LOCKA", THE MOST, ANYONE KNOW WHO "ABOMB" IS? THE ABOMB" GUY FOT

AFTER A WEEK OF JUST DIGGIN' MIAMI, IT WAS CHRISTMAS, AND I HAD TO GO UP TO BOCA FOR
AND PRACTICE, BUT FIRST I WANTED TO OPEN THE ZION CORPORATION, ONCE AND FOR ALL. I STORMED
PTO IT, READY TO KICK DOWN THE FRONT DOOR, BUT WHEN I STOOD THERE IN FRONT OF THE PLACE FOR
HE FIRST TIME SINCE I WAS ARRESTED THERE, I SAW THAT IT WAS ALREADY OPEN! INSIDE, THE
LACE WAS FULL OF THE USUAL: THE RUSTY, BROKEN LIGHTERS, THE BLACK SPOONS, AND THE RIPPED
T PHOTOS OF NAKED WOMEN. GREAT. MY FUTURE SQUAT WAS A CRACKHOUSE. BRIGHT SIDE? NO
UMAN FECES. YEA. MY RIDE THEN TOLD ME THEY WEREN'T GOING TO BOCA AT ALL. I TRIED TO GET ON
HE 77 BUS NORTH. THE BUS DRIVER WOULDN'T LET ME ON THE BUS! I'M STILL NOT SURE WHY.
WATCHED THE BUS PULLED AWAY, NOW LAUGHING CRAZILY. AH YES... SOME GREATER FORCE WAS
PPARENTLY WORKING AGAINST ME. BEST TO RIDE IT OUT. I INNOCENTLY STROLLED THROUGH A
OLIDAY GUN BATTLE A COUPLE BLOCKS NORTH, THEN WALKED 2 MILES ONTO THE WRONG HIGHWAY, ONLY
O HAVE TO WALK BACK TO HITCH. THIS, I THOUGHT, IS WHERE IT GETS REAL GOOD. IT'LL BE A GREAT
TORY — YOU HAD THE SHIT DAY, BUT THEN YOU GET A RIDE FROM A GANG OF CRAZY PUNKS AND YOU GO
OB A BANK OR SOMETHING, OR YOU GET THE RIDE FROM "THE GIRL OF YOUR DREAMS." I FINALLY GOT
RIDE FROM AN OFF DUTY WACKENHUT COP WHO HATES "NIGGERS AND FAGS." OH WELL. HE DROPPED
E 8 MILES FROM BOCA, AND I SAID, NO MORE RIDES, SANTA, I'LL JUST WALK...

BUT HERE IS THE COOL PART ABOUT PIRATES

BUT THEN IVY CALLED ME A COUPLE DAYS LATER AND SAID SHE WAS AT BECKY FUNN'S HOUSE IN
ELRAY! SHE WAS BACK FROM CALIFORNIA FOR A WEEK WITH A CARLOAD OF DIRTY, SMELLY FREAKS,
ROM BERKELEY, AND THEY WERE COMIN' TO GET ME TO GO TO MIAMI! GREAT. BUT WHERE, I ASK,
RE WE GONNA STAY? IVY JUST SAYS, "WHO CARES? WE'LL JUST FIND A BUILDING AND BREAK IT
PEN AND STAY IN IT! IT'LL BE EASY!" IT SOUNDED GREAT. YEAH! WHO CARES?!? WE'LL BE
IRATES! WHAT WE WANT, WE'LL TAKE! LET'S GO!

SO THEY COME TO GET ME IN THE BRAVE PIRATE SHIP. IVY AND BECKY AND DRIVER, JAMES, AND
EFF AND STEVE ALL PILED IN THIS TINY BLUE CAR, AND I'M ONE MORE, AND THERE'S AN
BNOXIOUS GRATING SOUND FROM ONE OF THE WHEELS RUBBIN' FROM TOO MUCH WEIGHT, BUT THE
AR'S MADE IT ALL THE WAY FROM CALIFORNIA, YES, AND NOT A VALID DRIVER'S LICENSE OR TITLE
R REGISTRATION AMONG US, SO IT IS A PIRATE SHIP. WE SET SAIL FOR MIAMI, AND OUR FIRST
ARGET, THE X-TRA SUPERMARKET, WHERE IVY FILLS A SHOPPING CART W/ GROCERIES AND JUST
USHES IT OUT THE DOOR! NOW WE'RE SET FOR THE WEEK, WITH RICE, BEANS, BREAD, FRUIT,
EGETABLES, COFFEE GROUNDS AND, OF COURSE, BEER! WE BRIEFLY CONTEMPLATE TAKING ALL OF
HE EMPLOYEES HOSTAGE AND PUTTING 'EM IN THE GAOL BUT, WE JUST PILE INTO THE TOUGH,
LUE CAR AND LEAVE INSTEAD.

THEN IT WAS OFF TO MIAMI LAKES FOR 7-11 COFFEE, WARM BEER AND GUITARS, AND TO MEET UP
ITH SCOTT, TIMMY, ANDY, AND BUDDHA. THEY DECIDED THAT THEY SHOULD GO PLAY GUITARS AND MAKE SOME
ONEY ON THE STREETS OF THE GROVE. YO! SINGIN' PIRATES! WHATEVER IT TAKES!

Walking back to Grand and taking a turn toward
the Bay one can't help but notice Sailboat Bay. This
is the home of The Mutiny, a private club. Food,
spirits and live entertainment are the attractions. The
place is cozy and has a large following.

WHILE THEY PUT THE HAT OUT ON GRAND AVE.
BY COCOWALK, ME AND JAMES WANDERED AROUND
COCONUT GROVE, SCOUTIN' UP TROUBLE.
I POINTED OUT THIS HUGE OLE ABANDONED
BUILDING ON THE CORNER OF McFARLANE AND
SOUTH BAYSHORE. IT WAS A HOTEL, CALLED
THE MUTINY, BUT NOW IT RIDES THE SKYLINE,
LIKE A GHOSTSHIP, ALL CREEPY AND
DARK, 12 STORIES HIGH...

THE DISCOVERY OF THE MUTINY!

UTINY!
IRCA
1973

continued
on next
page, yes

IT'S ALL WRAPPED UP MASTER— SOON WE WILL HAVE OUR ONE WORLD GOVERNMENT, THANKS TO OUR PEOPLE IN KEY POSITIONS!

A DREAMIN' AND A SEARCHIN' AND FINDIN' A NEW HOME (CONTINUED)

I SAID I'D ALWAYS WANTED TO GO IN THAT PLACE AND SEE WHAT ITS LIKE, BUT I NEVER SEEM TO BE NEAR IT IN THE DAYTIME. I DON'T THINK IT'D BE TOO GOOD AN IDEA TO GO IN IT AT NIGHT. WE CROSS THE EMPTY LOT ACROSS FROM THE COCONUT GROVE CHAMBER OF COMMERCE AND PEACOCK PARK TO GET A BETTER LOOK, AND SEE THAT PART OF THE FENCE IS DOWN AND ALL OUTSTRETCHED, JUST LIKE ROLLIN' OUT THE RED CARPET. "YEAH" SAYS JAMES, AS WE START HIGH STEPPIN' OVER THE BARBWIRE SAYS AND THE FENCE, "IT'S PROBABLY A BAD IDEA TO GO IN AT NIGHT." WE LOOK AROUND THE BOTTOM FLOOR, ALL BOARDED UP, BUT JAMES SAYS "THAT'S HOW YOU WOULD GET IN" POINTING AT A SERIES OF PIPES AND LEDGES RUNNIN' UP TO THE 2nd FLOOR BALCONY AND OPEN WINDOW, ALL PERFECT LIKE STEPS. "YEAH, BUT ITS PROBABLY DUMB TO GO IN WITHOUT A FLASHLIGHT" HE SAYS, WHILE WE'RE CLIMBING UP. SOON, WE'RE INSIDE. "YEAH, YOU'D BE A FOOL TO GO IN A PLACE LIKE THIS AT NIGHT." YEP, YEP. THE INSIDE WAS AMAZING. THE FLOOR WAS TOTALLY STRIPPED, SO IT WAS JUST A LONG, CONCRETE ROOM, LIKE A HUGE STUDIO APARTMENT, RUNNING THE LENGTH OF THE BUILDING. WE DECIDED NOT TO CLIMB ALL THE WAY UP THE STAIRS, 'TIL WE GOT THE REST OF THE CREW. BUT, NOW, WE HAD A COOL PLACE TO STAY. THE OLD MUTINY SIGN EVEN HAD A LITTLE PIRATE ON IT.

BACK AT THE GAP, THE MONEY WAS ROLLIN' RIGHT IN. IT WAS REAL FUNNY WATCHIN' DRUNK GROVE YUPPIES GIVE WHOLE DOLLARS TO HEAR ACOUSTIC VERSIONS OF "SKINHEADS SMOKE DOPE" AND "WE'RE GONNA FIGHT." JEFF, TIM, ANDY, AND SCOTT TOOK TURNS PLAYIN', AND WHOEVER WASN'T PLAYIN', WOULD STALK AROUND THE GROVE, TABLE DIVIN' FROM ALL THE OUTDOOR RESAURANTS. "HEY MAN, YOU GONNA FINISH THAT SALAD, OR JUST LOOK AT IT ALL NIGHT.?" EVERY SO OFTEN, YOU'D FIND A HALF DRUNK BEER TO COME BACK AND ENJOY WHILE LISTENING TO 🍴 FIFTEEN SONGS DONE LIVE AND IN PERSON. IT WAS A LOT OF FUN, AND AFTER A COUPLE HOURS, THEY HAD 35 BUCKS. GOOD, NOW WE COULD GET MORE 7-11 COFFEE AND GAS FOR THE PIRATE SHIP (SAME THING). AND BEER!

IT WAS TIME TO TAKE THE LOOT AND OUR BIG BOTTLES OF BEER TO OUR NEW HIDEOUT, THE MUTINY, BUT WE STOPPED ON THE WAY SO IVY COULD SPRAY PAINT PENTAGRAMS ALL OVER THE NEW WAVE DISCO, "CLUB ANARCHY." THEN WE ALL CLIMBED IN THE MUTINY, JUST AS IT STARTED TO POUR RAIN AND THUNDER AND LIGHTNING, AND SET OUT TO EXPLORE THE PLACE, WITH RAIN SPLASHIN' IN THE ELEVATOR SHAFT AND BROKEN GLASS CRUNCHIN' UNDERFOOT AND AN OCCASIONAL RAT RUNNIN' THROUGH THE FLASHLIGHT BEAM, THE RAT ALL SCARED AND EXCITED AS US PROB'LY... IT TURNED OUT ALL 12 FLOORS WERE LIKE THE 2nd — IT WAS JUST A BIG CONCRETE SKELETON, WITH HOLES IN THE FLOORS WHERE PIPES USED TO BE, AND SOME WINDOWS IN, SOME SMASHED OUT. 12 STORIES OF PIRATE PLAYGROUND! AND WAY UP TOP WAS SORT OF A FLOOR 13, A TINY ROOM ON THE ROOF WHERE THE ELEVATOR MACHINERY USED TO BE. THIS WAS THE PLACE TO BE, WE FIGURED, PIRATES ON FLOOR 13 OF THE REAL CLUB ANARCHY.

BUT THERE WAS ALREADY SOMEONE IN THERE! THIS POOR GUY, WILL, IS TRYIN' TO SLEEP UP THERE ALL COZY IN THE BEST ROOM IN THE HOUSE, AND ALL A SUDDEN 10 DRUNK AND ROWDY KIDS COME BARGING IN WITH BEER AND GUITARS, BUT ITS ALLRIGHT, HE SAYS. HE'S ABOUT OUR AGE AND PRETTY EXCITED TO HANG OUT AND DRINK AND HEAR US GO ON ABOUT OUR ADVENTURES, AND, PLUS, HE'S KIND OF A JUNKY, IT SEEMS, SO HE WASN'T SLEEPIN' TOO WELL ANYWAYS. WILL SAYS A HANDFUL OF BUMS ARE PROBABLY LURKIN' THERE IN THE BUILDING, PRETTY HARMLESS, AND THAT, IN THE MORNING THERE'S A SECURITY GUARD THAT WATCHES THE OUTSIDE PROPERTY, BUT HE'S EASY TO AVOID, AND DOESN'T CARE ANYWAYS, AND ONCE, EVERY 3 MONTHS OR SO, THE COPS'LL RAID THE PLACE AND BOOT ALL THE BUMS OUT, BUT DON'T SWEAT IT, NOW, CUZ THERE'S NO WAY THEY'RE GONNA COME ALL THE WAY UP HERE IN THE DARK. THEY'RE TOO SCARED!!!

SO THERE WE WERE IN THE CATBIRD SEAT 13 FLOORS UP WITH THE MOST AMAZING VIEW OF RAINY, SLEEPY MIAMI ALL SPREAD OUT BEFORE US FOR MILES AND MILES. WHERE DO WE STRIKE NEXT?!? AH YES, IT WAS TRULY BEAUTIFUL. I CAN'T BELIEVE HOW GREAT THINGS ARE SOMETIMES - NO MONEY, NO JOB, AND LIVIN' LIKE A KING WITH A PENTHOUSE SUITE ON BEAUTIFUL BISCAYNE BAY. I GOT ALL DRUNK AND DREAMY, SPYIN' ON THE CITY, AND ALL A SUDDEN IT HIT ME: I SHOULD LIVE HERE! IT WAS PERFECT — YOU HAD TO CLIMB ALL TREEHOUSE STYLE TO GET IN, YOU HAD THIS AWESOME VIEW, AND IT WAS CALLED

MUTINY!!! NOT JUST A PLACE TO LIVE BUT A CALL TO ACTION!!!

THE NEXT MORNING, WHEN WE WENT TO LEAVE, WE SAW THE SECURITY GAURD (←I HAVE NOW BEEN AWAKE TOO LONG! -ED) FOR THE FIRST TIME. HE WAS A LARGE, BLACK GUY, SITTIN' IN A BIG, BLUE STATION WAGON. WE WERE A LITTLE WORRIED 'ABOUT LEAVIN', UNTIL I SAW THAT HE WAS HOLDIN' UP, AND INTENTLY ADMIRING, A PORNO CENTERFOLD! SO WE SNUK OUT THE WINDOW BEHIND HIM, ALL SMIRKIN', BUT SILENT, AND HE NEVER SAW US. WE HAD LEFT THE MUTINY! JUST IN TIME TO SEE THE OWNER OF CLUB ANARCHY SHOW UP IN FRONT OF THE CLUB AND SEE IVY'S GRAFFITTI FOR THE FIRST TIME, IT WAS PRETTY FUNNY. HE STARTED YELLIN' ALL KINDS OF CUSSWORDS AT THE GUY WHO WAS WITH HIM, WHILE WE WATCHED, SAFELY ACROSS THE STREET.

THE REST OF THE WEEK BROUGHT MORE CRAZINESS. ONE NIGHT, DENNY'S ON CORAL WAY WAS GIVING US THE USUAL NO-REFILL BULLSHIT, EVEN THOUGH WE HAD BOUGHT ALOT OF FOOD (WITH GUITAR-EARNED CASH). SO, AFTER A DRAMATIC SHOUTING MATCH WITH THE PINHEAD MANAGER, WE LEFT AND JAMES SNUK AROUND BACK AND CUT SOME WIRES AND TURNED OFF THEIR ELECTRICITY! THEN, I WENT DOWN TO VARADARO'S AND RECEIPT SCAMMED 14 BUCKS 'O BEER CASH, AND DROVE THE BLUE BOMBER BY DENNY'S AND SAW THE EMPLOYEES ALL MILLIN' ABOUT IN FRONT – ANGRY AND IN THE DARK! ITS 'BOUT TIME WE GOT THOSE FUCKERS BACK! DOWN IN THE GROVE, THERE WAS PLENTY OF TROUBLE TO GET INTO. COCONUT GROVE USED TO BE THE HIPPIE SECTION OF TOWN, BUT, NOW, ITS MORE YUPPIE-STYLE AND TOTALLY PACKED WITH THE OLDER, THIRTYSOMETHINGS AND THE POORER KIDS WHO CAN'T MAKE IT IN SOUTH BEACH. WITH THE NEW YEAR'S HOLIDAYS, IT WAS MORE PACKED DOWN THERE THAN EVER. THERE WAS ALOT MORE GUITAR PLAYIN' IN THE STREETS, ALOT OF TABLE DIVIN', AND GOOD DRUNKPUNK SPORTS, LIKE CHASIN' AFTER RILKSHAW DRIVERS AND BUSSES TO STICK "FUCK SHIT UP!" STICKERS ON 'EM. JEFF WENT SWIMMING AT THE OLE 22 POOL, ON TOP OF THE MAYFAIR HOTEL, ONE NIGHT. A HOTEL EMPLOYEE CAME AND TOLD JEFF THAT SINCE HE WASN'T STAYIN' AT THE HOTEL, HE'D HAVE TO GET OUT OF THE POOL. JEFF WAS ALL TOO HAPPY TO. HE SWIMS NAKED! THE EMPLOYEE STARTED FLIPPIN' OUT – "GET BACK IN! NO, GET OUT! NO – AARGH!" AND, MOST NIGHTS, WE STAYED UP IN THE MUTINY!

SOMEWHERE IN ALL THIS, I FOUND TIME TO PLAY A SHOW WITH MY BAND, IN THE OLE KENDALL ABANDONED WAREHOUSE, WITH THE DARK HARDCORE, MEREL FROM JERSEY. AFTER THE BANDS WE'RE DONE, IVY, JEFF, TIM, AND SCOTT WENT UP AND PLAYED A BUNCH OF GREAT SONGS THAT THEY HAD WRITTEN IN THEIR SQUAT BACK IN OAKLAND. THEY WERE GREAT! NO SHIT! I WAS ALMOST MOVED TO DRUNKEN TEARS BY IVY'S SINGIN'. WHO KNEW SHE COULD SING THAT WELL?

SUDDENLY, THOUGH, THE WEEK WAS OVER, AND I WAS PRETTY DOWN. EVERYONE WAS GONNA LEAVE, AND I WAS GONNA BE TRYIN' TO SQUAT, ALL ALONE AGAIN, IN MIAMI. WELL, POOR ME, RIGHT? BUT EVERYTHING SEEMED CRAZIER THAN EVER, REALLY SPIRALLING OUTTA CONTROL. I DIDN'T KNOW WHAT TO DO. SHOULD I BRAVE THE ROUGH ZION CORPORATION NEIGHBORHOOD, AND TRY AND PLANT FLOWERS IN OVERTOWN, OR SHOULD I TRY THE RICH, UPSCALE, BUM HATING, SECURITY GUARDED COCONUT GROVE? MY BAND WAS THINKING OF TOURING, BUT THEN, BOOD AND SCOTT AND TIM WERE THINKIN' OF MOVIN' TO CALIFORNIA TO DO A BAND WITH IVY, WHICH WOULD END MY BAND. SOMETIMES IT SEEMS HARD TO COMMIT TO SOMETHING WHEN EVERYTHING AROUND YOU SEEMS TO BE FALLING APART AND GOIN' CRAZY. I DECIDED TO DO THE ONLY SANE THING – GO CRAZY, TOO. I DECIDED TO TRY TO SQUAT THE MUTINY!

I REMEMBER, WHEN I MOVED OUTTA FT. LAUDERDALE, WHEN I DID MY FIRST ZINE, I THOUGHT I KNEW ALL THE ANSWERS. NOW, I COULD SEE THAT I HARDLY KNEW ANYTHING. THAT'S GOOD. ITS MORE EXCITING THAT WAY...

WRITING ABOOT DA MUTINY, EH – FROM "MIAMI-CITY OF THE FUTURE" by T.D. AHMAN

He wasn't scared by the car bomb, but the managing editor of *El Herald* sure was scared a few nights later when we visited the Mutiny Club in Coconut Grove. At the Mutiny, which, according to Drug Enforcement Agency officials, was at that time the favorite watering hole of the more established cocaine cowboys, the patrons arrived in magenta Cadillac convertibles and the parking "valets" wore uniforms out of *The Merry Widow*. The membership cards were gold, and even the baked potatoes came wrapped in gold foil, which matched the gold medallions on the young men at the bar. The waitresses, over black net stockings, wore skirts that ended in the vicinity of the *mons veneris*. At that time there was a soufflé chef at the Mutiny who called himself Pierre but who was really named Mohammed. He was Iranian, and when I asked him one time how an Iranian soufflé chef had managed to get a job in a place where the staff was predominantly Cuban, Mohammed replied, "Compassion for a fellow refugee. I explained Khomeini was just like Castro,

a revolution betrayed."

At the Mutiny the tables didn't have chairs. They had leather-covered, swiveling, executive armchairs, and when the guy who ran the discotheque got going, the laser beams bouncing off your baked potato reminded you of that car bomb exploding, but that wasn't why you went to the Mutiny. You went to the Mutiny to look at the killers.

Not, I'm sure, that our fellow revelers saw themselves as criminals. In their eyes they were bulwarks against anarchy—law enforcement officers, if you will, taking a night off at the Mutiny, because these were men who believed deeply in law and order. The only problem was that, in their particular profession, there wouldn't be any law and order if they weren't there to enforce it.

Pt. 4 — MUTINY IN MIAMI!

WITH CROWBARS... WITH SLINGSHOTS... WITH GUITARS...

WHATEVER IT TAKES!!!

AUGUST 28

"Will The Real Grove Businessmen Please Stand Up"

MRS. BETTNER
CITY MANAGER REESE

MIAMI HERALD, if I were a little old lady in tennis-pumps and rolled down elastic socks, I would shake my straw shopping bag at you and declare, "You really fucked it up this time...pause you can't fool me!"

Now, while you suck your teeth back into your collective mouths, I just want to tell you that I am a member of the 25 and under set, and although I use soap and water every night on my body it just doesn't cut it when 12 hours pass and there is no deodorant in the house. Occassionally I pass for one of Coconut Groves more odiferous "Hippies", and I fall into that category without remorse.

On Friday, July 25, 1969, the MIAMI HERALD ran an article entitled, CLEAR OUT GROVE HIPPIES, REESE TOLD. This was later ammended to read, SET HIPPIES STRAIGHT, REESE TOLD. In either case, the article stated that..."City Manager Melvin Reese's staff interviewed 32 adult business people, responsible employees and residents in the central Coconut Grove area" and that the investigation "showed that businessmen were concerned that they were losing customers because of the hippie image becoming attached to the Grove." The article further stated that Mrs. Elizabeth Bettner, who, incidently has aspirations for the legislature, said that "hippies were dangerous" that they "...robbed people and burglarized Grove stores." A lot of other things were said, also ... and they will be dealt with by the rest of the staff ...

Feeling sufficiently outraged, Mike Wells and I set out to interview most of the business establishments in the central Grove area to find out what all of the uproar was about. Each establishment was asked four basic questions:

1. Have you been interviewed by the City Commission?
2. Has your establishment been vandalized or burglarized by "Hippies"?
3. Do you feel that "Hippies" keep business away from the Grove?
4. Do you have any additional comments about the "Hippies"?

The following represents the results of that survey:

Westinghouse X-ray Division:
No interview by Commission. "I don't have any complaints. They don't hurt our business. I think if they were left alone there wouldn't be any trouble."

Grove Bar and Grill:
No interview by Commission. No stealing. No vandalism. No complaints. "Why don't they (the police) leave them alone?"

Carl Miller TV Service:
No interview by Commission. No complaints about business.

Interior Designers:
No interview with Commission. No robbery. No vandalism. No effect on business.

Pan American Photo Shop:
No interview with Commission. No stealing. No vandalizing. A customer in the shop complained, "I don't think I can take my girl down to the Park anymore. The last time I was there I heard too many nasty words."

Bicycle Shop:
No interview by Commission. "Yes they've stolen from me ... a lot of other people have stolen from me too ... not just "Hippies"."

Steel's Barber Shop:
No interview by Commission. No stealing. No vandalism. "I don't get any business from them because they don't get their hair cut ... but they don't keep any of my regular customers away."

Grove Beauty Shop:
No interview by Commission. No stealing. No vandalism. "They don't give us any business ... I'd cut their hair for free if I thought it would do any good."

Burt's Village Shops:
No interview by Commission. Some shoplifting. No vandalism. "Our customers come from the higher, middle income bracket. Some of them call me and say they are afraid to come to the Grove because of the 'Hippies'. I think that they create an unpleasant atmosphere, they are grubby and dirty and they linger on the sidewalks ... therefore they do drive my business away.

Grove Village Inc.:
A jewelry store not interviewed by the Commission. No complaints at all. "I wish there were more of them. Who has been interviewed by the Commission? I sure would like to know!"

Twice Around Shop:
No interview by Commission. No stealing. No vandalism. "We don't like some of the littering ... and the type who are dirty are not pleasant to have around ... but even they are nice when they come in here. What is a 'Hippie' anyway? I think that most of them are just kids with no place to go. I've often wondered why they haven't put a pool in the park ... and more ping-pong tables ... and open up the building for them at night ... that would get them off the street and sidewalk, don't you think?"

Kirsten Travel Agency:
Have been interviewed by Commission. Was not available for comment.

Vanity Box:
No interview with Commission. No vandalizing. No stealing. Some customers complain about being afraid to come to the Grove.

Little Jack Horner Shop:
No interview by Commission. No vandalizing. No stealing. "We don't encourage them to come in here."

Maiji Originals:
No interview by Commission. "My shop has been robbed twice. Once by two people with motocycle hats on. Are they 'Hippies'? My husband and I used to walk down (McFarlane) there at night but not any more. They block the sidewalk and some of them are dangerous with those bicycles ... nearly ran me down."

Rexall Drugs:
No interview by Commission. No complaints at all.

Adam's Apple:
Were interviewed by Commission. Hippies steal from them. Hippies keep business out of the Grove. Hippies shouted obscenities at a couple customers one day when they came into the store.

Grove Furriers:
Were not interviewed by Commission. No stealing. No vandalism. No complaints.

Grove Cleaners:
No interview with Commission. No complaints.

Minna Lee Dress Shop:
No interview by Commission. No complaints.

Art Fugate:
No interview by Commission. No stealing. No complaints. "If it weren't 'Hippies' it would be somebody else. I'd like to know who the Commission interviewed."

Thomas and Cook Inns:
No interview by Commission. No stealing. No vandalism. No complaints. "If I were to give you any complaint it would be purely a personal viewpoint and would have absolutely nothing to do with business."

Foremost Liquours:
No interview with Commission. No stealing. No vandalism. "We dig you."

Campbell's Fine Antiques:
No interview with Commission. No stealing. No vandalism. No complaints about business. "I'd like to find out who the 32 people were that the Commission interviewed."

Maison de Marie:
No interview with Commission. "I don't want to discuss it".

Burt's Grocery:
No interview by Commission. No robbery. No vandalism. Some objections to those people who are dirty or smell bad. Some pilfering ... but mostly by a little group of real young colored kids who hit nearly every store in the Grove. "Do you think maybe they (the Hippies) will riot ... or damage the stores in the Grove because of this?"

Smart Shop:
No interview with Commission. No stealing. No vandalism. "I think they mind their own business." They don't keep customers away.

Poodle Parlour:
Was not interviewed by Commission. "The so-called "Hippies" have not harmed my business... in fact my business has increased in the last 4-5 months."

Bachelor Of Arts:
Was not interviewed by Commission. "I have no objection to people because of the way they look. I don't care to be around anyone who physically stinks and I don't care for them littering up the sidewalk in front of my store. But the people who do that are not just "Hippies". They don't keep my customers away there

There is one aspect of the latest Kennedy tragedy that has not been discussed. That is the moral implication of Kennedy's tragedy to the Country's concept of what morality really is.

It's strange how we condemn death at first hand and condone it at a distance. There are few of us that cannot at least roll over and go to sleep when it comes to the death of millions in Biafria and India - or Indonesia (how many have heard of the 300,000 deaths there - even wide awake liberals), yet quiver behind locked doors for a week after a robbery been committed in the neighborhood.

We march or write letters and hold up signs when DOW, UNION CARBIDE, or DUPONT make the chemicals and bombs for antisepticly far removed genocide and the destructions of war is general, but point a morally righteous finger at a man when a pretty girl happens to be sitting beside him when his car goes off the bridge.

The whole country knows that Old Joe Kennedy built his family fortune rum running. We, on the other hand, do not like to discuss that this fortune so illgotten accomplished two things; one it contributed to the, ever growing number of alcoholics and broken homes that we have in this country and two, financed John's ascendency to the presidency. A strange paradox indeed.

The contention is that if it is good for business, it's all right for some deaths, however regretable, to occur. If it is personal, on the other hand, it must be as pure as the proverbial driven snow. We condone all kinds of immorality in the business

(cont. on page 21)

CIRCLE BARBER

the Mainline

WHILE THE CITY SLEEPS...

PIONEER LIFE IN COCONUT GROVE

On a more bizarre note, the 12-story **Mutiny Hotel** (2951 South Bayshore Drive, Coconut Grove; 305-442-2400) offers 100 individually styled theme rooms. An Amazon room has bamboo wallpaper and mirrored ceilings, while an African suite sports animal skin bedspreads and draped fishing nets. The decor throughout the hotel, though, has begun to show signs of wear and tear. Deluxe.

EVERYBODY IN COCONUT GROVE KNOWS ABOUT THE OLE MUTINY HOTEL. TO THE YUPPIES AND TOURISTS WHO POUR INTO THE GROVE ON THE WEEKENDS, ITS A CURIOUS BLACK HOLE IN THE SKYLINE, ALL DARK AND DISTANT IN THE MIDDLE OF ALL THIS CITY LIGHT. TO DEVELOPERS, ITS A FRUSTRATING EYESORE, ROTTING ON EXTREMELY VALUABLE BAYSHORE LAND, TOO CLOSE TO ITS SURROUNDINGS TO DEMOLISH AND TOO COSTLY TO BRING UP TO CODE. THE COPS WHO HANG OUT ACROSS THE STREET FROM THE MUTINY, AT THE COCONUT GROVE CHAMBER OF COMMERCE, KNOW THAT US BUMS SLEEP IN THERE SOMETIMES, SO THEY KEEP AN EYE ON THE PLACE. BUT, TO ME, THE MUTINY WASN'T JUST AN ABANDONED BUILDING. IT WAS A PLACE WHERE DREAMS COULD COME TRUE. ALL I'D HAVE TO DO WOULD BE LOCK UP THE TOP FLOOR WITH A GOOD, DEADBOLT AND I'D BE SET UP WITH A HUGE, CRAZY PIRATE MANSION BY THE SEA! WITH ALL THAT SPACE, I COULD DO JUST ABOUT ANYTHING I WANTED. PLUS, THE PLACE HAD THE COOL PIRATE IMAGE. I ENVISIONED A PIRATE RADIO TRANSMITTER ON THE ROOF AND LIVE BROADCASTS FROM THE SQUAT! I COULD SPRAY PAINT "MUTINY!" ALL OVER TOWN, WITH A STENCIL OF A COP WALKIN' DA PLANK! ANYTHING! IT WAS EXCITING, HOW YOU COULD TAKE THIS BIG, INTIMIDATING, SCARY THING AND WORK ON IT, AND, SLOWLY, MAKE IT ALL YOUR OWN. KINDA LIKE YER LIFE.

BUDDHA AND TIM HAD SAID THEY MIGHT MOVE IN WITH ME, BUT IT WAS UP TO ME TO SETTLE THE PLACE. SO, BATTLING A FEVER AND A BAD COUGH, ME AND MY SLEEPING BAG HEADED TO THE MUTINY TO CONQUER OUR NEW HOME. BUT, WHEN I GOT TO THE SUPER-SECRET-SPY-STYLE ENTRANCE, THE PIPES YOU HAD TO CLIMB UP TO GET IN HAD BEEN REMOVED FROM THE WALLS! SHIT! MUTINY AT THE MUTINY! I GO TO LOOK FOR A NEW WAY IN, AND COME UPON SOME OLD 2ND FLOOR BUMS, BUMMIN'. THEY SAY, YEAH, A MAINTENANCE GUY CAME AND CUT IT ALL DOWN, WE SAW THE WHOLE THING, FUK. I MANAGE TO CLIMB INSIDE, AND SEE THAT, EVEN WORSE, THE STAIRWELL IS BOARDED UP! WHAT THE FUCK?!! EVERYTHING'S ALWAYS HARD. WHAT CAN I SAY? DID I TELL YA I WAS SICK? ANYWAY, NOW, I'VE GOT TO RUSH AND FIND A PLACE OPEN TO GET A NEW CROWBAR. THE FIRST TWO HARDWARE STORES WERE CLOSED, SO I WENT TO THE CORAL WAY SEAR'S. I THOUGHT I MIGHT HAVE TO BREAK INTO MY NEW RADIO FUND (BUCKS), BUT ONCE INSIDE THE STORE, I INSTINCTIVELY GRAB A 30 DOLLAR WRENCH SET AND A CROWBAR AND "RETURN" THE WRENCHES WITHOUT A RECEIPT. THE GUY AT THE REGISTER, A TOTALLY CLEAN LOOKIN', LATIN KID IN A PAISLEY VEST — I SWEAR I AM NOT MAKING THIS UP— HE SAYS, "HEY, I KNOW YOU! YOU'RE IGGY CHICKENHEAD!" INSTINCTIVELY, MY GRIP TIGHTENED AROUND THE CROWBAR. PEOPLE OFTEN RECOGNIZE ME THESE DAYS, SOMETIMES THEY JUST WANT AN AUTOGRAPH, BUT SOMETIMES THEY WANT TO FIGHT.. BUT ITS OK. I GUESS HE JUST SAW US PLAY ONE TIME, AND HE TALKS ABOUT IT <u>FOREVER</u>, WHILE I SWEAT IT OUT, MAKING SURE HE DOESN'T MAKE ANY STRANGE MOVES FOR THE PHONE TO CALL SECURITY. FINALLY, HE GIVES ME THE NEW CROWBAR AND THE 21 BUCKS DIFFERENCE, AND I GET THE HELL OUT OF THERE. GOOD THING HE DIDN'T KNOW ME AS "IGGY SCAM"...

BACK AT THE MUTINY, I HAPPILY RIP THE BOARD OFF THE STAIRWELL DOOR, STORM UP THE 12 FLIGHTS OF STAIRS AND WAVE MY CROWBAR TRIUMPHANTLY AT THE SLEEPIN' CITY. WELL, I WAS IN. I HAD NO IDEA HOW SERIOUS THE PERSON WHO BOARDED UP THE STAIRWELL WAS TAKING THIS, SO, I FIGURED, I'D JUST IGNORE IT, AND GO AHEAD WITH MAKING MY HOME.

FOR A WEEK, OR SO, IT WAS JUST ME, UP THERE IN MY SLEEPING BAG, ALONE AT THE TOP OF 12 STORIES OF DARK EMPTY BUILDING. IT WAS WINDY AND COLD, IN JANUARY, BUT THAT SOMEHOW MADE THE PLACE MORE HOMEY, CUZ I'D SNUGGLE UP IN MY SLEEPING BAG AND BE SO WARM THAT WHEN I GOT UP IN THE MORNING, I DIDN'T WANT TO GET OUT A BED. I'D JUST LAY THERE, SMILIN' AND WATCHIN' THE PIGEONS BUILD NESTS IN MY ROOF. THE PIGEONS WERE QUATTIN' MY SQUAT! I INSTALLED A DEAD BOLT AND SPENT THE DAYS SWEEPIN' THE PLACE OUT. THE PLACE BECAME MORE COMFORTABLE WHEN JOHN DANIA DONATED A MATTRESS AND NICK GAVE ME A RADIO. I FOUND THAT I COULD MAKE TEA BY LEAVIN' TEA BAGS IN A JUG OF WATER OVERNIGHT. I ALSO FOUND THAT THE COCONUT GROVE LIBRARY, RIGHT NEXT DOOR TO THE MUTINY, THREW AWAY BOOKS— GOOD BOOKS LIKE STEINBECK, TWAIN, CONRAD'S "HEART OF DARKNESS". SO, I'D DUMPSTER BOOKS AND SIP MY TEA IN THE SUN ON THE BALCONY. AND ENJOY THE VIEW.

FROM THE 12TH FLOOR, I COULD SEE CITY HALL 24 HOURS A DAY, BUT THEY COULDN'T SEE ME! AND THE SUNRISES OVER THE BAY WERE INCREDIBLE. I'D STAY UP & WALKIN' AROUND ALL NIGHT, AND COME HOME FOR THE SUNRISE. FROM THE OTHER BALCONY, I COULD SEE THE WHOLE CITY ASLEEP IN GREY, AND I'D FEEL ALL TENSE AND TINGLY AND CRAZY IN LOVE, LIKE DREAMIN' AWAKE, MISTY MORNING RUSHIN' THROUGH EMPTY STREETS, ALLEYS, CRACKS, TREETOPS, EARLY MORNING BIRDS NESTS, AT THE SPEED OF SUNRISE LIGHT... ITS KINDA HARD TO EXPLAIN. ITS JUST THAT EVERYTHING SEEMED POSSIBLE, YA KNOW?

HOME, SWEET HOME

COMIN' HOME, YOU COULD ALWAYS SEE THE MUTINY FROM THE METRORAIL. WHEN YOU GOT THERE, THERE WERE TWO ENTRANCES. IF THE GUARD WAS IN FRONT, YOU WENT ACROSS THE EMPTY LOT, IN BACK, OVER THE TRAMPLED FENCE, UP ONE STUMP, ONTO A BRANCH, ONTO THE BALCONY, AND INCHED ACROSS TO THE OPEN WINDOW. IF THE GUARD WAS IN BACK, YOU LOOKED BOTH WAYS, DUCKED IN THE HOLE IN THE FRONT FENCE, WENT UP THE WOOD STEPS TO THE OLD, OUTDOOR BAR BY THE OLD MUTINY POOL AND JACUZZI, AND CLIMBED UP THE METAL MONKEY-BAR-STYLE BEAMS AND INTO THE SMASHED IN WINDOW THERE. YOU COULD HEAR TIM AND BUDDHA, OR TIM AND SCOTT PLAYIN' GUITARS BY ABOUT THE 10TH FLOOR. AT THE 12TH FLOOR, THERE WAS NO SECRET KNOCK. I MEAN, WE ALL HAD KEYS. EXCEPT TIMMY ALWAYS LOST HIS, SO I'D BE IN THE MUTINY, WRITING, AND ALLA SUDDEN THESE LEGS WOULD COME DANGLIN' IN THE HOLE IN THE ROOF, AND THEN, PLOP! THERE WAS TIM...

I WAS NO LONGER ALONE IN THE MUTINY. TIM HAD FINALLY BEEN KICKED OUT OF HIS FOLKS' HOUSE FOR GOOD, SO HIM AND HIS ACOUSTIC BASS HAD MOVED IN. IT WAS A PRETTY EXCITING OCCASION, AND WE CELEBRATED TIM'S DESCENT INTO POVERTY BY WAITING IN LINE FOR THE FREE SHOES - "THE BOBOS" - AT A CHURCH IN DOWNTOWN MIAMI, AND BY APPLYING FOR FOODSTAMPS TOGETHER. THE FOOD STAMPS WERE EASILY CONVERTED INTO REAL CASH, AND THE 7-11 IN COCONUT GROVE SOLD CHEAP WINE TO KIDS. THINGS WERE GOOD.

BUT, ALMOST IMMEDIATELY, THERE WERE SEVERAL PROBLEMS THREATENING TO RUIN MY LIFE, WHEN I HAD THE WORST SCAMMIN' WEEK IN MY LIFE. FIRST, I WAS ARRESTED FOR TRYING TO WALK OUT OF MERVYN'S WITH A NEW PAIR OF CONVERSE ON. IT WAS BAD FORM. I HADN'T REALLY NEEDED THE SHOES, SO I WAS ABUSING THE SCAM. I KNEW THE RISKS... THEN, SOMEONE BROKE IN THE SQUAT AND STOLE OUR RADIO. I HAD THOUGHT THE BACK STAIRWELL WAS PERMANENTLY LOCKED, BUT, I GUESS, I WAS WRONG. THEN, I GOT CAUGHT STEALIN' A NEW DEADBOLT AT SEAR'S. AN UGLY SCENE... THAT NIGHT, ME AND NICK GOT REAL DRUNK ON THE STREETS, AND NEEDED MORE BEER, BUT 7-11 WAS CLOSED, SO WE HAD TO GO TO THE POOR SIDE OF THE GROVE FOR MORE. THE GROVE IS RIGIDLY SEGREGATED, AND THE DIVIDING LINE BETWEEN THE YUPPIE SIDE AND ONE OF THE HARSHEST HOODS IN MIAMI IS 32ND AVENUE. IT CAN BE ROUGH OVER THERE, BUT I FIGURE I SHOULD JUST WALK WHEREVER I WANT, YA KNOW? PLUS, USUALLY I LOOK TOO SCUMMY TO BE MUGGED, AND NEVER HAVE ANY MONEY. WELL, NICK HAD MONEY, AND THIS GUY WITH A KNIFE MADE NICK GIVE HIM HIS 12 BUCKS. WHILE NICK WAS BEIN' ROBBED, IT DRUNKENLY OCCURRED TO ME TO SAVE THE DAY. I GOT OUT MY SLINGSHOT THAT I ALWAYS CARRIED WITH ME, AND STARTED HUNTIN' ON THE GROUND FOR ROCKS. THE MUGGER GUY WENT, "HEY, WHAT THE HELL ARE YOU DOIN'? CUT IT OUT!" AND KINDA DISTRACTEDLY PUNCHED ME, LIKE SWATTIN' A FLY, AND IT BROKE MY NOSE! THERE WAS BLOOD EVERYWHERE! MYSTERIOUSLY, MY BLOOD FORMED ON THE GROUND IN THE SHAPE OF CHRIST ON THE CROSS AND, NOW, CHRISTIANS FROM ALL OVER THE WORLD MAKE A YEARLY PILGRIMAGE TO THE CORNER OF 34TH AND GRAND TO SEE IT. TRULY AMAZING. MORALE WAS LOW. WE NEEDED A QUICK, WINNABLE GROUND WAR AGAINST AN UNQUESTIONABLY EVIL ENEMY TO RESTORE OUR FAITH IN THE SCAM. SO WAS LAUNCHED...

SUBS

Please take a moment to complete this card. Your input is valu[able] and important to help monitor the quality of product and servic[e]

Day: ___

Ag[e] ___

Are ___

WE WILL BEAT YOU, MIAMI SUBS!

THE WAR ON MIAMI SUBS!!!

#109
COCONUT GROVE

☐ Local Resident - over 20 minutes driv[e]
☐ Traveler/Tourist - from where? ___

		Excellent	Good	Fair
Condition of outside store, parking lot, landscaping, etc. TRASH CANS HAVE PUNK GRAFFITTI	✓	Excellent	Good	
Windows, dining room, tables, floor, music, condiment stand, etc. GOOD EXCEPT CONDIMENT STAND SHOULD HAVE CRACK	✓	Excellent	Good	
Clean and properly stocked TOILET PAPER EASY TO STEAL	✓	Excellent	Good	
Well groomed, clean uniforms, name tags, etc.		Excellent	Good	

MIAMI SUBS, ON THE CORNER OF GRAND AND MC FARLANE, A BLOCK AWAY FROM THE MUTINY, WAS ME AND TIM AND BUDDHA'S MAIN HANG OUT SPOT. YOU COULD SCAM COKES INSIDE AND SIT AT THE OUTDOOR TABLES, AND SEE WHAT WAS GOIN' ON IN THE NEIGHBORHOOD. AT FIRST, THE MANAGER, CHRIS, STARTED TRYING TO STOP US FROM STEALIN' THE COKES. THEN, HE WENT SO FAR AS TO ASK US NOT TO SIT AT THE TABLES ANYMORE. CHRIS (HE HAD A NAME TAG) WAS WEIRD. LIKE, HE'D BE IN THERE EVERY DAY FROM SAY NOON TO 3:00 AM. HE'D RUN OUT FROM BEHIND THE COUNTER AND TRY AND TAKE MY COKE, AND I'D SAY, "CHRIS, YOU'RE

WORKIN' TOO HARD. COME SIT OUT AT THE TABLES AND RELAX..." HE HATED ME. WE FINALLY JUST STOLE ALL OUR SQUAT FURNITURE FROM MIAMI SUBS. WE'D GO AT 3:00 AM, STEAL TABLES AND HAUL 'EM UP THE 12 FLIGHTS OF STAIRS. WE GOT A BUNCH OF CHAIRS, TOO. I WENT IN WITH TOOLS AND GOT THEIR HUGE, TOILET PAPER ROLLS, AND, AS AN AFTERTHOUGHT, RIPPED OFF ONE OF THEIR CHEAP TOILET SEATS FOR THE MUTINY PISS BUCKET Ø. WE BEAT 'EM LIKE A GONG, AND LEFT OUR MARK OUTSIDE, THE PLACE ON THE USA TODAY MACHINE. IT SAID "MUTINY! USA TODAY — TOMMORROW THE WORLD!"

INSPIRED BY OUR SUCCESS AT MIAMI SUBS, ME AND TIM RAIDED THE SHERATON HOTEL IN BRICKELL FOR PILLOWS, TOWELS, SHEETS, AND SOAP. THE SQUAT WAS REALLY LOOKIN' GREAT, WITH FURNITURE AND FLYERS ON THE WALLS. TIM BROUGHT UP A COUCH THAT FOLDED OUT INTO A BED, AND A NEW RADIO, AND I GOT KEROSENE LAMPS AND BOB'S BARRICADE LIGHTS (NON BLINKING). THE FINAL TOUCH WAS TIM AND SCOTT LAYING DOWN CARPET IN ONE AREA. CARPET = HOME.

BUDDHA MOVED IN, SCOTT AND BECKY HUNG OUT ALL THE TIME, WE HAD A COUCH, AND SHELVES, AND A DR. HUNTER S. THOMPSON ACTION FIGURE, AND THE COMPLETE BOOK OF RAP LYRICS. WE WERE SET. SOMEHOW, THE BIG, SCARY BUILDING HAD BECOME PRETTY LIVABLE. WHEN YOU'D COME HOME, AFTER CREEPIN' THROUGH THE CRAZY COCONUT GROVE CROWDS, AND SNEAKIN' IN, AND CLIMBIN' UP THE 12 FLIGHTS OF DARK STAIRS, COMIN' IN THE 12TH FLOOR SEEMED LIKE ENTERING ANOTHER WORLD. IT WAS SO SECRET AND HIDDEN. SOMEDAYS I WOULDN'T EVEN WANT TO LEAVE. I'D JUST DRINK TEA, BLAST THE BUZZCOCKS, PRACTICE SHOOTIN' BOTTLES WITH MY SLINGSHOT, READ, WRITE, DIG THE VIEW, WHATEVER. JUST DO IT ALL IN A MAD FRENZY TO ARRIVE AT THAT ELUSIVE COMBINATION OF CAFFEINE AND LOUD PUNK AND THE SOUND OF SMASHING GLASS THAT I NEED TO WRITE SOMETIMES. TIM AND BOOD ONLY REALLY STAYED IN THE MUTINY HALF THE TIME, BUT FOR ME, IT WAS DEFINATELY THE GREATEST HOME I'D EVER HAD. HEY! BLACKFLAG PAID MONEY TO LIVE IN THAT CHURCH, BUT WE WERE LIVIN' FREE! VIVA LA SCAM!

THE MUTINY WILDLIFE

IN THE MUTINY, WE HAD PETS. KIND OF. WELL, WE HAD THIS RAT. MAYBE RATS, BUT WHEN YOU'VE GOT RATS, YOU TEND TO THINK ITS JUST ONE — MAKES IT SEEM MORE LIKE A PERSONAL WAR WITH THIS ONE RAT. THE RAT WAS OK WITH ME, AS LONG AS HE DIDN'T EAT OUR FOOD. IN FACT, WE WERE DOING A MUTINY SQUATTER KIDS' MOVIE, BASED ON LASSIE, ONLY WITH LASSIE AS A CLEVER, PUNK RAT THAT WARNS THE PUNKS WHEN THE PIGS ARE COMIN'. I'VE ALWAYS WANTED TO DIRECT. WE HAD TONS OF 'EM. WE TRAINED 'EM TO CARRY MESSAGES AND SENT 'EM TO THE POLICE STATION WITH NOTES SAYING, "YOOZE GUYS ALL SUCK!" THE SOMEWHAT MORE PLENTIFUL WAS THE PIGEON POPULATION. WE HAD TONS OF 'EM. PIGEONS' MOANING AND PURRING IN THE ELEVATOR SHAFT SOUNDED HOLY AND SAD, LIKE GHOSTS. FINALLY, I STARTED SEEING THIS RACCOON HANGIN' OUT BY THE BACK ENTRANCE ALOT, SO WE HAD THE COOL ANIMAL CRIMINAL TYPES THERE, TOO. PRETTY COOL. HE OFFERED ME A JOINT, BUT I DON'T SMOKE.

FAMOUS PEOPLE IN COCONUT GROVE

EVERY NEIGHBORHOOD HAS FAMOUS PEOPLE — YOU KNOW, THE PEOPLE THAT ARE ALWAYS IN ONE PLACE, NO MATTER WHAT, OR ARE ARE KNOWN FOR TRULY DRAMATIC BEHAVIOUR IN PUBLIC. THEY ALL HAVE THAT CELEBRITY MYSTIQUE — LIKE YOU CAN'T IMAGINE SEEING THEM ANYWHERE BUT IN THEIR ONE PLACE, AND YOU ALWAYS WONDER "WHAT THEY'RE REALLY LIKE." I'M REALLY INTO THE NEIGHBORHOOD CELEBRITIES. IT SEEMS LIKE THEY'VE MADE IT BIG ON A LEVEL WHERE IT REALLY MATTERS — ON THE STREETS OF WHERE THEY LIVE. IN COCONUT GROVE, IT NEVER FAILED TO BRIGHTEN MY DAY TO SEE THE MATHILDA MAN. I'D ALWAYS WALK IN AND OUT OF THE GROVE ON MATHILDA STREET, INSTEAD OF 32ND AVE, CUZ THERE WERE TREES, NO TRAFFIC, AND, SOMETIMES, GOOD TRASHPILES. BUT, THE BEST THING WAS THIS OLD MAN WHO JUST SAT OUT IN HIS YARD, EVERYDAY, FOR MOST OF THE AFTERNOON, JUST WAVING AT AND TALKING TO EVERYONE WHO WALKED BY. ONE TIME, I WAS WALKIN' BY AND HE SAW MY THERMOS AND BOOK AND SAID, "ALLRIGHT — YOU GOT YOURSELF SOMETHING TO DRINK, SOMETHIN' TO READ — NOW YOU JUST NEED A SHADY TREE AND YOUR ALL SET!" I DON'T KNOW. I JUST REALLY LIKED THIS GUY. HE WAS KIND OF A THROWBACK TO ANOTHER TIME. WHEN I WAS A KID, MY MOM WOULD SEND ME TO BORROW A CUP OF SUGAR OR MILK FROM THE NEXT DOOR NEIGHBOR, BUT, THESE DAYS, MY MOM WOULDN'T THINK OF BORROWING MILK OR ANYTHING FROM ANYBODY, EVEN THOUGH THE SAME PEOPLE LIVE NEXT DOOR. ALL THE NEIGHBORHOOD WATCH STUFF HAS EVERYONE HOLED UP TO THEMSELVES, SCARED AND SUSPICIOUS OF PEOPLE ON THEIR OWN BLOCK, SO, I WAS ALWAYS GOOD TO SEE THIS ONE MAN, AFTER ROWS OF FENCES, BARKING DOGS, AND "THIS HOME PROTECTED BY..." SIGNS, WHO HAD THE COURAGE TO DO WITHOUT ALL THAT AND JUST SIT OUT IN HIS YARD AND BE NICE TO PEOPLE. ONE GUY WHO TRULY DIDN'T GIVE A SHIT WAS THE LAUGHING GUY. HE WAS THE DIRTIEST, GRUBBIEST GUY YOU EVER SAW, AND HE'D COME LURKIN' UP THE STREET, ALL DARK AND MYSTERIOUS, AND STAND IN THE MIDDLE OF HUGE, FRIDAY NIGHT CROWD, AND JUST START LAUGHIN' THIS LOUD, CRAZY LAUGH, AND YELLIN' MOSTLY UNINTELLIGIBLE INSULTS AT PEOPLE. HE PICKED HIS SPOTS WELL, LIKE A COP WOULD BE TELLING THE FUNYONS THEY COULDN'T PLAY IN THE STREETS, AND HE'D COME UP AND START LAUGHIN'. THE BEST PART, THOUGH, WAS THE LAUGH ITSELF. IT WAS A TRUE MASTERPIECE — A DRAMA IN 3 PARTS. IT STARTED WITH HIS EYES ALL BUGGIN' AND A BIG, RASPY ROAR OF "HRHAAAHAH — " AND IT ROSE AND SPUTTERED, THEN HE LURCHED FORWARD AND SPIT OUT ONE AT A TIME, "HLAACH.. HLAACH... HLAACH..." THEN HE DREW BACK AND SUCKED IN AIR, ALL WHEEZY, WHISTLIN', LIKE HE WAS GONNA SUCK IN ALL THE AIR, EVERYWHERE, "HREEHEHE HEEHSH" THEN, STARTED OVER. YOU COULD HEAR IT FROM JUST ABOUT ANYWHERE IN A 5 BLOCK RADIUS! HE MADE EVERYONE REAL NERVOUS, BUT HE WAS MY HERO. IT WAS SO PURE, YA KNOW? LIKE, YOU CAN'T LAUGH IN THE STREET FOR SPARE CHANGE. HE WAS THE FREE-EST MAN I EVER SAW. EVERY ONCE IN A WHILE, SOME NEIGHBORHOOD CELEBRITY WOULD LET DOWN THEIR GUARD AND REVEAL TO YOU, AND YOU ALONE, SOME DARK SECRET. THIS HAPPENED TO SCOTTY ONE NIGHT WITH THE DOOBIE BROTHERS GUY. THE DOOBIE BROTHERS GUY WAS THIS BLACK GUY IN HIS LATE 20'S, WHO FUCKED UP PARKING METERS FOR A LIVING ON MCFARLANE BY THE CHAMBER OF COMMERCE. WHEN TIM AND SCOTT AND BUDDHA HAD THEIR ACOUSTIC GUITARS WITH THEM, HE'D STOP 'EM, SOMETIMES 3 TIMES A NIGHT, AND MAKE ONE OF THEM PLAY THE BASSLINE TO THIS SHITTY DOOBIE BROS. SONG, WHILE HE PLAYED THE GUITAR PART AND SANG. HE'D SHOW YA BOTH PARTS OF THE SONG, AND WHEN THE CHANGE CAME, HE'D QUIT SINGIN' AND YELL, "CHANGE!" I PLAYED WITH HIM SOMETIMES. WHEN THE OTHER GUYS WERE SICK OF DOING IT, AND HE JUST NEVER GOT SICK OF IT. HE'D SEE YA AND SAY, "HEY, LET'S PLAY THAT SONG!" IT WAS CRAZY. I MEAN, IMAGINE THIS GUY GOING THROUGH HIS WHOLE

LIFE KNOWIN' THIS ONE SONG, AND WITH NO GUITAR TO PLAY IT ON, AND THEN WE COME ALONG... WELL, ONE NIGHT, SCOTT GOT CAUGHT ALONE WITH D.B. AND D.B. TOOK THE GUITAR AND PLAYED A COUPLE ENTIRELY DIFFERENT SONGS — SONGS THAT SCOTT HAD NEVER HEARD BEFORE, THAT D.B. MUST HAVE WRITTEN HIMSELF. ANYONE WHO HAS EVER PARKED A CAR IN COCONUT GROVE ON A WEEKEND KNOWS OLE D.B., AND HERE HE WAS, DEBUTING HIS SONGS, HIS ART, HIS HEART AND SOUL, FOR SCOTT! IT WAS RIGHT UP THERE WITH THE TIME ANDY POWELL WAS AT FIREHOSE'S SHOW, AND A DRUNKEN MIKE WATT PUT HIS ARM AROUND ANDY AND TOLD HIM HOW MUCH HE MISSED D. BOON, OR THE TIME IN 5TH GRADE WHEN MY BEST FRIEND WON BACKSTAGE PASSES TO VAN HALEN AND GOT SNEERED AT BY DAVID LEE ROTH! D.B. HASN'T PLAYED THOSE SONGS FOR ANYONE SINCE...

A WEIRD KIND OF FAME WAS ENJOYED BY TRACEY YOUNG. HE WAS THIS BLACK GUY IN HIS EARLY 20'S WHO WAS THE THE ALL-NIGHT, HEAD MANAGER OF THE 24-HOUR, COCONUT GROVE WOOLEY'S SUPERMARKET (NOT TO BE CONFUSED WITH THE BRICKELL WOOLEY'S). IT WAS THE ONLY 24-HOUR SUPERMARKET IN THE GROVE, SO, AROUND 2:00 AM, EVERYONE IN THE GROVE — ALL THE DRUNK CLUB GOERS, AND RESTAURANT WORKERS, AND YUPPIES, AND HOMELESS PEOPLE, AND STARVING ARTIST TYPES, AND HIPPIES — WOULD END UP BUYING STUFF FROM HIM. THERE WAS A BIG SIGN WITH HIS NAME ON IT, AND HE HAD A NAMETAG, SO EVERYONE KNEW HIS FULL NAME — TRACEY YOUNG. IT WAS WEIRD TO WATCH HOW PEOPLE WOULD TRY TO GET CLOSE TO HIM, LIKE THEY'D SAY, "ROUGH NIGHT, HUH, MR. YOUNG?", OR, "SEE YA, TRACEY." JUST CAUSE YOU SAW HIM EVERY NIGHT, YOU'D GET USED TO THE STABILITY OF IT, AND YOU'D THINK, SUBCONSCIOUSLY, "HE'S A GOOD GUY." WHEN YOU HAD NO IDEA WHAT HE WAS REALLY LIKE AT ALL. I MEAN, I COULDN'T IMAGINE THE GUY GOING HOME OR ANYTHING. I KINDA THOUGHT THEY KEPT HIM ON ICE IN THE BACK. BUT, MAYBE THE STRANGEST THING ABOUT THE WHOLE NEIGHBORHOOD FAME THING, IS HOW THE FAMOUS PEOPLE LOOK AT YOU. TRACEY YOUNG KNEW ME AS THE APPARENTLY HOMELESS GUY WHO WOULD COME IN THE STORE EVERY NIGHT AROUND 3:00, SOMEHOW SPEND A HALFHOUR IN THE STORE (I WAS IN THE BACK BY THE BATHROOM, EATING), AND THEN ONLY BUY A QUART OF WHOLE MILK. HE NEVER SAW ME IN A DIFFERENT SHIRT ALL THE MONTHS I WENT THERE. ON MOST NIGHTS, HE SOLD BEER TO MY FRIEND, SIR ROBERT, COCONUT GROVE'S CRAZED PUNK ROCK GENIUS, AND HIS ROOMMATE, SASHA, THE HARD DRINKING, RUSSIAN PHOTOGRAPHER. TRACEY YOUNG PROBABLY THOUGHT ROBERT WAS A FREAK, CAUSE OF HIS MEMORABLE APPEARANCE — LONG, BLACK HAIR IN FACE OVER BIG GLASSES, ARMY JACKET, WEIRD ANIMAL PRINT PANTS, HUNCHED OVER, REAL THIN, CLUTCHING DA SHLITZ... PLUS, ROBERT AND SASHA WENT IN ONE NIGHT WITH SASHA, IN THE BIG SOVIET, IN A GORILLA OUTFIT. THEY BOUGHT A BANANA... SO THEN, TRACEY WOULD FLIP OUT WHEN HE SAW ME AND ROBERT COME IN TOGETHER. HE COULDN'T FIGURE OUT OUR CONNECTION TO EACH OTHER, AND HE WAS USUALLY SO STUNNED THAT SIR ROBERT COULD BUY A 6, AND I COULD JUST KINDA FOLLOW HIM OUT THE DOOR WITH MINE, AND TRACEY WOULDN'T NOTICE AND RING IT UP. MAYBE THE FAMOUS PEOPLE THINK WE'RE FAMOUS..

WENDY'S HEAPIN' PLATE 'O FREE SALAD

DA SHLITZ DA CROWBAR

SCAM SAYS! THANKS, WENDY'S!

SCAM PUNKS AT WENDY'S

WENDY'S ON U.S. 1 AND RED ROAD: TWO YEARS' FREE FOOD, AND RUNNING...

STEP 1: STEP 2: STEP 3: STEP 4: TAKE SPARE CHANGE STEP 5: CUP O SOUP

THE 8-BALL 6-PACK   THE BEER CAN TAB   Put tab in meter

SECRETS OF THE GROVE REVEALED!!!

THE BEST SHOW IN TOWN is still FREE. GO TO SCAM PUNKS' DRINKIN' SPOT #12 (THE FIRE ESCAPE OF COCONUT GROVE ELEMENTARY SCHOOL, ON THE GRAND AVENUE SIDE) AND DRINK SOME BEER, ALL HIDDEN UP THERE BY TREES. DOWN TO THE LEFT, WATCH THE PARKING LOT GUYS 1) CHARGE PEOPLE TO PARK IN THE EMPTY LOT THERE, AND 2) RUN AWAY WHEN THE COPS SHOW UP. ALWAYS EXCITING. MEANWHILE, DOWN ON MCFARLANE, THE PARKING METER GUYS HAVE MADE IT BIG, WITH AN ARTICLE ABOUT 'EM IN THE NEW TIMES, BUT THEY STILL CAN NOT BE STOPPED. THEIR SECRET? TECHNOLOGY! THEY PUT TIME ON PARKING METERS WITH THEIR BEER CAN PULL TABS, THEN ASK YOU FOR THE CHANGE YOU WOULD HAVE PUT IN THE METER! THE BEER OF CHOICE? SAYS THE DOOBIE BROTHERS GUY, "IT'S THE 8-BALL..." YOU READ IT HERE FIRST... EVER WONDER WHERE YOUR SPARE CHANGE ENDS UP? WELL, SOME OF IT DOES GO TO FOOD, AND THE GROVE BUMS ALL EAT THE 99¢ "CUP OF SOUP" THING THAT THEY SELL AT 7-11 AND YOU HAVE TO MICROWAVE. WHEN ITS COOKED, THEY EAT A LITTLE OFF THE TOP, THEN FILL IT UP WITH THE FREE MEAT SAUCE (AS FEATURED IN SCAM #1)! OVERHEARD AT 7-11: A COP TOLD ANOTHER OF MIAMI FINEST THIS JOKE: "HOW CAN YOU TELL WHEN YOUR WIFE NEEDS TO GO ON A DIET? WHEN SHE SITS ON YOUR FACE, YOU CAN'T BREATHE." HMM... MAYBE, I'M TELLING IT WRONG... FREE BEER CAN SOMETIMES BE HAD AT THE OBNOXIOUS NEW BUDWEISER STORE, WHERE THEY SELL BUD SHIRTS, HATS, ETC. THEY HAVE A KEG OF "FREE SAMPLES" THAT THEY VERY SELECTIVELY ISSUE. ME AND SCOTT, BOTH UNDERAGE, GOT FREE BEER, BUT THE BUD STORE REPORTEDLY TOLD JEFF OTT, "YOU NEED SHOES TO COME IN HERE, MAN..." THE GROVE FORGETS ITS HIPPY ROOTS AGAIN...

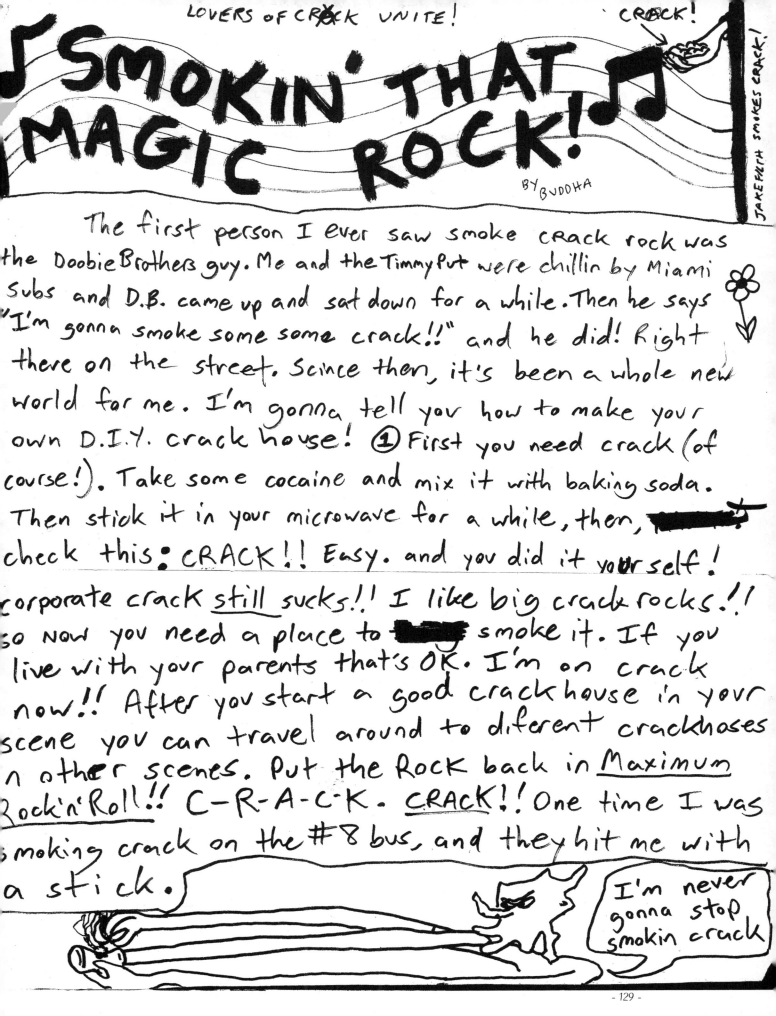

they work their way right into the heart of major cities. There they hole up under buildings and in bushes and trees and eat anything from garbage to crayfish.

¡BASURERA AQUI!

STORIES ABOUT TRASH!

EAT IT! USE IT! LIVE IT!

THAT'S RIGHT, MICHELLE! BARRY FOUND A BABY IN A DUMPSTER!

ISN'T THAT WILD?

THERE'S THIS **WEIRD PORNO UNDERGROUND**. PEACHES' RECORDS IN BOCA HAS HAD A DUMPSTER FULL OF PORNOS, AT LEAST 3 TIMES, INCLUDING A HUGE PILE OF DIRTY PAPERBACKS. IT'S FUNNY TO LEAVE 'EM IN FREE NEWSPAPER BOXES. ONE TIME, TIM FOUND A WHOLE BOX OF DILDOS, WIGS, AND VIDEOS IN A DUMPSTER ON MAIN STREET IN MIAMI LAKES, OVER BY COACH DON SHULA'S PLACE. HE BROUGHT 'EM UP TO CHUCK'S PLACE AND A BUNCH OF PEOPLE TOOK TURNS TRYING ON THE WIGS AND DILDOS. WEIRD. SPEAKING OF WEIRD UNDERGROUNDS, THE **MASONIC** **LODGE** TRASH SCENE IS STILL PRETTY MYSTERIOUS. JOHN DANIA GOT CHASED AWAY FROM THE HOLLYWOOD MASONIC LODGE TRASH AT 3:00 AM BY A SCREAMING WOMAN IN A WHITE ROBE! I'VE CHECKED THE HUGE SCOTTISH RITE TEMPLE AND YORK RITE TEMPLE, ON THE RIVER, A LITTLE NORTH OF DOWNTOWN MIAMI, ONLY TO FIND BAGS OF PUBLIX DELI CHICKEN BOXES. THESE PEOPLE SECRETLY CONTROL THE WORLD?!? SHEESH. IN MIAMI SPRINGS, ON ROYAL POINCIANA DRIVE, THE MIAMI SPRINGS LODGE HAD A PILE OF SHREDDED XEROXES OF IN SPANISH. YOU'D THINK IT WOULD AT LEAST BE IN ESPERANTO. IT WAS JUST THE AGENDA FOR A PUBLIC MEETING. OH WELL... **THE COCONUT GROVE CHAMBER OF COMMERCE**, ON McFARLANE, ACROSS FROM **THE MUTINY** HAS LOTS OF OFFICIAL CITY LETTERHEADS FOR MAKING OFFICIAL LOOKING FLYERS, OR WHATEVER. I USED TO ALWAYS CHECK THEIR TRASH TO SEE IF THERE WAS ANY STUFF IN THERE ABOUT US... THE VELVET CREME ON U.S. 1 BY U. OF M. IS A SURE THING FOR DONUTS AND GOOD MUFFINS (I RECOMMEND THE CHOCOLATE CHIP MUFFIN). PLUS ALL THESE CORAL GABLES AND SOUTH MIAMI COPS HANG THERE. ONE TIME, I HAD SO MANY MUFFINS THAT I STUFFED A WHOLE BUNCH UP A COP CAR'S TAIL PIPE! OH, I ALSO FOUND PORNOS THERE ONCE, TOO. I GAVE 'EM TO EMIL, IN EXCHANGE FOR A RIDE TO GET MY BOLT CUTTERS TO CUT THE LOCK AT THE CORAL GABLES PUBLIX, OFF U.S. 1. THEY JUST GOT NEW LOCKS, SO I GAVE UP, BUT EVERY PUBLIX LEAVES BREAD, MUFFINS, AND DONUTS (PUBLIX BRAND) OUT ALL NIGHT, USUALLY IN FRONT OF THE STORE!!! SO I STILL GOT THEIR FOOD THE FUCKERS. IN SOUTH MIAMI, I DUMPSTERED ALL THIS MAKE UP ONCE, AND DIDN'T KNOW WHAT TO DO WITH IT, 'TIL I SAW A COP CAR BY BAKERY CENTER! I WROTE "FUCK THE" OVER SOUTH MIAMI POLICE W/ MAGENTA LIPSTICK! AT THE KARATE SCHOOL ON DIXIE IN DANIA I FOUND A PERFECTLY GOOD NINJA IN THEIR TRASH... AFTER I GOT MUGGED IN THE ROUGH SIDE OF THE GROVE, I WALKED THROUGH THERE AT 3:00 AM, ON A PEACE MISSION, HANDIN' OUT VELVET CREME MUFFINS. PEOPLE THOUGHT I WAS CRAZY, BUT A COUPLE PEOPLE WERE PRETTY STOKED. DIDN'T HAVE MUCH TROUBLE AFTER THAT. CHRIS START DUMPSTERS SNARE DRUM HEADS. CHUCK LOOSE DUMPSTERS T.V.'S AND V.C.R.'S IN BOCA. CLEVELAND'S LEGENDARY, **DAVEY**, DUMPSTERS BIKE PARTS. ONE TIME, ME AND NICK WERE WALKING ON MARY STREET, IN THE GROVE, AND WE SAW A PUNCHING BAG ON A TRASH PILE!!! WE HAD IT ALL PLANNED OUT — WE'D PUT OUT WEIRD PAMPHLETS DECLARING NICK TO BE THE NEXT **LEADER OF CUBA**, AND IT'D HAVE A PICTURE OF NICK, W/ A BIG CIGAR IN HIS MOUTH, HITTIN' THE PUNCHING BAG! IT WAS A SURE THING. BUT, OF COURSE, WHEN I CAME BACK W/ THE SHOPPING CART, THE BAG WAS GONE... ONE MAN'S TRASH IS ANOTHER MAN'S ASCENDENCY TO POWER! I CHECKED THE TRASH CAN BEHIND OPEN **BOOKS AND RECORDS**. THERE WERE A COUPLE K.F.C. BISCUITS IN THERE. TASTED PRETTY GOOD.

Sesión Pública

JOSE MARTI PEREZ LODGE No. 371
F.& A.M.

Maestro de Ceremonia: V.H. Rafael Bermeosolo P.M.

y saludo a los asistentes, por el Venerable Maestro

A.

less creatures in their mouths. In Seattle I spotted one out in front of a movie theater, waiting in the shadow of the curb for the crowd to go in so it could move back to its den in the sewer.

These masked bandits are prolific in almost every city across the country, with the exception of hot, arid places. They are as sly as weasels and feed quietly on the castoffs of civilization. People usually think o

HERE WAS ALWAYS A BIG CROWD OF PEOPLE ON THE STREETS OF COCONUT GROVE, AND IT WAS A LOT OF FUN JUST TO HANG OUT ON THE STREET WITH NOTHING TO DO. IT WAS KINDA LIKE LIVING A RAMONES SONG, OR SOMETHING...

THE AREA AROUND THE MUTINY WAS THE CENTER OF IT ALL — CRUISIN' CARS ON THE STRIP, BLASTIN' BASS, ROLLERBLADERS, RICKSHAW DRIVERS, CARALARMS GOING OFF, THE HIPPIE KIDS BEATIN' ON BONGOS IN PEACOCK PARK, THE GUYS WHO SOLD THE HIPPIE KIDS HANDFULS OF SHRUBBERY AS POT, THE PARKING METER GUYS, THE COOL, MIAMI-STYLE BUMS, THE YUPPIES AT THE OUTDOOR CAFES WHO IGNORED 'EM (UNTIL AT THE END OF THE NIGHT, WHEN THEY FOUND THEIR CAR WINDOW SMASHED IN AND STEREO GONE...), THE JOHNNY ROCKETS HAMBURGER PLACE BLASTIN' '50'S MUSIC... IT WAS A HUGE, STUPID YUPPIE CARNIVAL, ALMOST EVERY NIGHT, BUT IT WAS FUNNY, CAUSE IN THE SHADOWS OF ALL THIS CRAZINESS WAS US, ALL SILENT AND STEALTHY, TAKIN' CROWBARS TO BOARDED UP BUILDINGS AND TABLE DIVIN' DINNERS, AND SNEAKIN' INTO MIAMI SUBS TO SCAM COKES...

WHEN I FIRST MOVED TO THE GROVE, THIS CROWD OF PEOPLE COULD BE PRETTY INTIMIDATING, LIKE — HERE'S EVERYONE IN THE WORLD, SEEMINGLY HAVING A GOOD TIME, AND HERE'S ME SLINKING ON UP TO MY BIG, DARK, EMPTY BUILDING. BUT, SOON, I WAS HAVING SUCH A GOOD TIME IN THE MUTINY, THAT I REMEMBERED IT WAS MY NEIGHBORHOOD, NOT THEIRS. I COULD DO ANYTHING I WANTED WITH IT. WE HAD NO MONEY, SO THE STREETS WERE OUR PLAYGROUND, AND THE CROWD WAS A HUGE, BUILT-IN, AUDIENCE. PLUS, THE COPS ARE ALWAYS IN UNIFORM, AND SNARLIN' AND MAKIN' NO SECRET OF HOW HATEFUL THEY ARE, AND THE SUITS ARE ALWAYS IN UNIFORM, AND STRESSED AND HAVIN' NO FUN. I FELT A RESPONSIBILITY AS A PROUD AND NEARLY-FAMOUS, COCONUT GROVE BUM TO SHOW 'EM HOW MUCH FUN I WAS HAVING.

THE COCONUT GROVE ARTS FESTIVALS TURNED OUT TO BE SOME OF THE MOST FUN I'D HAD IN A WHILE. THERE'S ALWAYS THESE BIG, WEEKEND-LONG FESTIVALS IN THE GROVE, AND THEY BLOCK OFF SOME STREETS TO CARS, AND MORE YUPPIE SAPS THAN EVER, FROM ALL OVER SOUTH FLORIDA, POUR INTO THE GROVE TO BUY USELESS SHIT AND EAT OVERPRICED FOOD. THE STREETS THAT THEY BLOCK OFF ARE SOUTH BAYSHORE AND McFARLANE — THE STREETS RIGHT IN FRONT OF THE MUTINY! SO I CAME HOME FROM EMIL'S HOUSE TO FIND A THOUSAND PEOPLE IN FRONT OF MY HOUSE! SHIT! I HADN'T THOUGHT OF THAT. I COULDN'T GO HOME, SO I TRACKED DOWN TIM AND BUDDHA AT SCOTT'S, AND FOUND THEY'D HAD THE SAME PROBLEM. BUT, THEY CAME DOWN TO THE GROVE ANYWAYS, TO PLAY GUITARS IN THE STREETS. OR, SCOTT AND TIM PLAYED GUITARS FOR CASH, WHILE ME AND BOOD FOUND CARDBOARD BOXES ON THE GROUND, PUT 'EM OVER OUR HEADS, AND RAN HEADLONG INTO THE CROWDS, SCREAMING, "AAARGH! WE HAVE BOXES ON OUR HEADS!" IT WAS FUCKIN' FUN! WE MOVED TO THE CORNER OF GRAND AND McFARLANE, BY THE GAP, WHERE THEY PLAYED ALL NIGHT, AND DRUNK PEOPLE ON THE BALCONY OF SAN MARINO'S RESTAURANT, ABOVE THEM, KEPT DROPPING WHOLE DOLLAR BILLS, TRYING TO MAKE A BASKET IN THEIR CHANGE CUP, SO IT REALLY WAS RAININ' MONEY! SINCE IT WAS THE ART FESTIVAL, I CARRIED A SIGN FOR A WHILE THAT SAID, "YO! RAPPIN' IS ART!" AND WE MADE A SIGN THAT SAID "FREE ART." WITH AN ARROW POINTING AT TIM AND SCOTT. THEN, THIS WEIRD, DRUNK COUPLE CAME UP AND STARTED FULL-ON MAKING OUT, GROPING, REMOVING CLOTHES NEXT TO US, SO WE WROTE "FREE LOVE!" ON THE SIGN, WITH AN ARROW POINTING TO THEM! I FINALLY GOT TO PLAY GUITAR, TOO, SEIZIN' THE ACOUSTIC, AND DOING LOUD, SPRAWLIN', JUMPIN' ON FIRE DRUNK, ROLLIN' ON THE SIDEWALK VERSIONS OF "NERVOUS BREAKDOWN" AND "I LIKE DRUGS." PEOPLE THREW ASH AT ME, BUT I WOULD NOT STOP! I ALSO JUMPED ON THE BACK PORCH OF A DELIVERY TRUCK, AND HUNG ON FOR A RIDE ALL AROUND THE GROVE, WITHOUT THE DRIVER KNOWING. IT WAS JUST A GREAT NIGHT, FINALLY TOPPED OFF AFTER THE FESTIVAL WAS LONG OVER, WHEN THE GROVE WAS EMPTY, BY FINDING A VENDOR'S CART THAT WAS STOCKED WITH FRUIT AND JUICE. I STOLE A PILE OF BANANAS, THAT I GAVE OUT TO BUMS, AND FRUIT AND ORANGE JUICE FOR THE SQUAT. YO! SCAMMIN' IS ART!

BY NOW, TIM, BUDDHA, AND SCOTT WERE A BAND CALLED THE CANADIANS, WITH TIM ON BASS, BOOD ON GUITAR, SCOTT ON DRUMS (AND IVY WOULD SING IF SHE CAME BACK FROM CALIFORNIA). THEY WEREN'T "CIRCLE A ..." THEY WERE "CIRCLE, EH..." THEY PLAYED OUT BY THE GAP A LOT WITH SCOTT AND BUDDHA TRADING OFF ON GUITAR. THEY WERE REALLY THE FIRST COCONUT GROVE STREET MUSICIANS, BUT THERE WERE ALREADY A LOT OF WEIRD STREET PERFORMERS, LIKE THE CRUSTY, OLE MASSAGE GUY, WHO WAS SORT OF A LIVING LEGEND, HAVING GIVEN MASSAGES ON MAIN HIGHWAY FOR ALMOST 20 YEARS, SHEESH! WHO THE HELL EVER HEARD OF A STREET MASSEUSE?!? ON "COCONUT GROVE"! ON GRAND AVENUE, THE CANADIANS HAD TO BATTLE FOR STREET SPACE AND SPARE CHANGE WITH THE DREADED SNAKE GUY. HE WAS THIS SWEATY, LITTLE GUY WHO HAD A BIG SNAKE THAT HE WOULD PUT ON PEOPLE, AND MAKE THEM PAY TO BE PHOTOGRAPHED WITH. IT COST 10 BUCKS TO HOLD THAT STOOPIT SNAKE! THE CANADIANS WOULD BE TRYING TO PLAY A SONG TO SOMEONE, AND HERE WOULD COME THE FUCKIN' SNAKE GUY, "OH NO! ITS SKIN JUST LOOKS SLIMY. IT'S ACTUALLY VERY DRY. HERE — TOUCH IT. IT EATS WHOLE RATS ALIVE!"

THE SNAKE GUY WAS AN ASSHOLE. STILL, THEY MADE A LITTLE MONEY EVERY NIGHT, BECAUSE THEY WERE REALLY GOOD - REAL CATCHY, SHORT SONGS, KINDA LIKE EARLY <u>DESCENDENTS</u>, OR <u>S.L.F.</u> PEOPLE (BESIDES THE DOOBIE BROTHERS GUY) STARTED STOPPING 'EM IN THE DAY, ASKING, "ARE YOU GONNA PLAY TONIGHT?" THEIR MUSIC, IN THE DARK, ON THE 12TH FLOOR, COULD REALLY MAKE THE MUTINY FEEL HOMEY, BUT IT WAS MORE FUN TO SEE 'EM PLAY OUT IN THE STREETS. PLUS, IF THEY MADE ANY MONEY, THEY'D USUALLY BUY ME A BEER. THANKS, GUYS.

THE CANADIANS WERE GAINING NOTORIETY IN OTHER WAYS THAN THEIR MUSIC IN THE STREETS. TIM GOT CAUGHT STEALING AT WOOLEY'S, AND THE DAY MANAGER, EDDIE RIVERA, WOULD NOW SCREAM AT HIM AND FOLLOW HIM ALL AROUND THE STORE WHENEVER HE CAME IN. THESE MANAGER GUYS ARE ALWAYS SO HIGH-STRUNG! SHEESH! THEN THERE WAS THE BAKED POTATO THING. WE COULD TABLE DIVE AND GET GROVE RESTAURANTS TO GIVE US FOOD, BUT STILL HAD NO WAY TO COOK OUR OWN FOOD. THEN, ONE NIGHT, I DUMPSTERED A BAG OF POTATOES AT PUBLIX AND IT HIT ME — THINGS WOULD BE DIFFERENT FROM NOW ON, BECAUSE WE'D COOK BAKED POTATOES IN THE MICROWAVE OVEN AT 7-11! I DIDN'T KNOW WHY I HADN'T THOUGHT OF IT BEFORE. SO, WE BUMMED BUTTER OFF OF CAFÉ SCI SCI, AND STORMED INTO 7-11 WITH OUR POTATOES AND WENT TO WORK. THINGS TURNED UGLY, FAST. ONE WORKER TRIED TO TAKE OUR POTATOES, WHILE THE OTHER SCREAMED REPEATEDLY, "THERE IS NO FREE HERE! THERE IS NO FREE HERE!" LOOKING BACK, WHAT'S SO FUNNY IS NOT THAT WE COOKED THE POTATOES, BUT HOW MUCH A DIFFERENCE I THOUGHT IT WAS GOING TO MAKE IN OUR LIVES. OH WELL. WE ESCAPED WITH OUR DINNER, JUST AS THE WHOLE 7-11 WAS ON THE BRINK OF ANARCHY, AND MADE OUR WAY, WITH STEAMIN' POTATOES ON PAPER PLATES, THROUGH THE CROWDS, TO THE MIAMI SUBS TABLES TO EAT. CHRIS CAME OUT TO GIVE US YET ANOTHER HALF-HEARTED SPEECH ABOUT SITTING AT THE TABLES. I REALLY LIKED CHRIS, AND I WOULD REALLY MISS HIM WHEN HE WAS FIRED A COUPLE WEEKS LATER, BUT, HERE, HE WAS, CLEARLY, OUT OF LINE. AT THIS POINT, WE SHOULD HAVE BEEN DEMANDING PROTECTION MONEY FROM HIM FOR HIS SHITTY MIAMI SUBS! HE WAS LUCKY. FINALLY, HE WENT AWAY EXASPERATED, AND WE GOT TO EAT OUR HOT, BUTTERED POTATOES. THEY WERE GOOD!

IT'S NOT REALLY GOOD, OF COURSE, TO HANG OUT ON THE STREETS ALL THE TIME. IT CAN BE PRETTY TIRING, NOT HAVING A PLACE TO RELAX, HAVING TO KEEP YOUR GUARD UP ALL THE TIME IN THE FACE OF THOSE HUGE CROWDS. AND BEING SNEERED AT AND SPIT ON AND HARRASSED BY THE POWERS THAT BE CAN STING A LITTLE MORE THAN I MAY LET ON. OR JUST NOT BEING ABLE TO BE SURE WHO YOU COULD TRUST, AND GETTING RIPPED OFF. LIKE, TIM AND BOOD GOT RIPPED OFF ON POT DEALS BY THIS GUY, FRED, ALL THE TIME. WHENEVER I SAW 'EM, THEY WERE "LOOKING FOR FRED..." BUT, I MEAN, THAT IT'S GOOD TO BE OUT IN THE STREETS WHERE PEOPLE WALK AND LIVE, OUT IN THE WORLD. AND IF YOU CAN TREAT AN ABANDONED BUILDING LIKE A BIG BLANK SLATE YOU CAN DO ANYTHING WITH, THEN YOU CAN HAVE THE SAME ATTITUDE ABOUT YOUR NEIGHBORHOOD, TOO. STILL, I WAS GLAD I WASN'T OUT THERE ALL THE TIME. LUCKILY, I LIVED ON THE 12TH FLOOR, SAFELY ABOVE ALL THE ANTS, AWAY FROM THE SHOUTING, WHERE YOU COULD LOOK DOWN ON IT ALL, AND HEAR THAT ONE DISTINCT GROVE SOUND... THE LAUGHING GUY'S

LAUGH ↑

PUNK SHOW!

WITH THE BAD BOYS OF THE FOLK/PUNK SET... Anarchist "W"

THE FUNYONS
(ONE GUY W/ GREAT SONGS, ANOTHER GUY WHO LIGHTS HIS FARTS AND A GUY WHO DRINKS ALOT O' CUBAN COFFEE AND BEATS ON TRASH CANS. NO FUTURE.)

with the debut of

THE CANADIANS, eh.
← Hoser-core. Ex-IntenseMassacre, KillerKane, ChickenHead, SALT n' PEPA, eh.
[THE CANADIAN INVASION IS HERE. THEY'VE COME FROM A BOAT FROM CANADA FOR YOUR WELFARE, JOBS, CHEAP BEER, AND SPARE CHANGE. NO SLEEP 'TIL TORONTO!]

THIS IS BASICALLY AN ACOUSTIC SHOW
BUT AT LEAST IT'S NOT IN SOME SHITTY CLUB, AND IT'S FREE, AND ILLEGAL (VERY PUNK)

FRIDAY FEB. 19TH AT ABOOT 10, EH? (THAT'S CANADIAN TIME, EH)

AT THE GAP CLOTHING STORE IN COCO WALK IN COCONUT GROVE. TAKE U.S. 2 TO S.W. 32nd. GO SOUTH TO GRAND AVE. TAKE LEFT. IT'S A FEW BLOCKS UP. YER ENCOURAGED TO BRING BEER, FOOD, DRUGS, WHATEVER IT TAKES

Hey pal, you R trespassing and loitering. Got any I.D.?

I gonna have to TAKE YOU IN!

♪ Oh la la, I love to play guitar ♪

?!?!?

FUCK YOU, YOU UGLY MONKEY!

BOOM!

A VICTORY, FOR THE COMMON MAN.

THE REVOLUTION WILL NOT BE AMPLIFIED!!!

REVIEW OF THE FUNYONS/CANADIANS STREET SHOW

THE <u>FUNYONS</u> AND <u>CANADIANS</u> PLAY SO MUCH ON THE STREET CORNER IN FRONT OF <u>THE GAP</u> AT COCOWALK THAT WE DECIDED TO SEE WHAT WOULD HAPPEN IF WE MADE A FLYER FOR A "REAL" SHOW ON THAT CORNER. BEFORE THE SHOW, STEVE FUNYONS SAID HE WASN'T AFRAID TO GO TO JAIL — THAT IF THE COPS TRIED TO STOP THE SHOW, HE'D KEEP PLAYING AND LEAD THE CROWD ON A MARCH THROUGH THE GROVE. YO, STEVE! WELL, IT TURNED OUT TO BE MUCH LESS DRAMATIC. ABOUT 20 KIDS CAME CUZ OF THE FLYER AND SAT IN A BIG CIRCLE AROUND THE FUNYONS, COMPLETELY BLOCKIN' THE SIDEWALK. ABOUT 20 OTHER PEOPLE STOPPED TO WATCH, TOO, SO THE FUNYONS PLAYED TO A HUGE, APPRECIATIVE CROWD OF ABOUT 40 OR SO. ONCE AGAIN THEY SHOWED THAT THEY WERE THE MASTERS OF STREET PUNK, WITH ROBERT LEAPIN' AND FLAILIN' ALL OVER HIS TRASH DRUMS, STEVE BELTIN' OUT THE HITS FOR HOURS, AND MARIO, OF COURSE, SHOWIN' UP LATE, BUT MAKIN' UP FOR IT WITH A COUPLE QUICK JOKES. THE CANADIANS, WITHOUT THE FUNYONS' AMP, COULDN'T REALLY BE HEARD AND THE CROWD LOOKED CONFUSED, BUT NOT AS CONFUSED AS THE CANADIANS WHO HAD GUZZLED A TON OF ROBO TO LOOSEN UP... THE FUNYONS WERE BROUGHT BACK BY POPULAR DEMAND, AND EVERYONE GOT

DRUNK ON THE STREETS, WATCHIN' 'EM. PUNK ROCK GARY STARTED A PIT! THE COPS JUST WALKED BY AND SNEERED. THE MAN CAN'T BUST OUR MUSIC! AFTER THE SHOW, SCOTTY BECAME THE FIRST PERSON TO PUKE IN THE MUTINY, AND I GOT TO WATCH IT FALL AND SPLAT 12 FLOORS DOWN. TAKE THAT, COCONUT GROVE!

THE BEST SWINGSET IN ALL OF MIAMI HAS TO BE

IN PEACOCK PARK IN COCONUT GROVE. I'M NOT TRYING TO START ANY NEIGHBORHOOD RIVALRIES. FACTS ARE FACTS. THE PEACOCK PARK SWINGSET IS WELL-OILED, IN THE DARK AT NIGHT, AND A SHORT WALK FROM FREE COKES, A DUMPSTER FULL O GOOD BOOKS, AND BEAUTIFUL, BISCAYNE BAY. ONE TIME, AROUND NOON, BUDDHA AND I SPIED AN OPEN, UNATTENDED FRIDGE FULL O BEER BEHIND THE BAR AT GROVE CALLOWAY'S, SO WE HELPED OURSELVES TO A COUPLE FREE BEERS (CANADIAN BEERS, OF COURSE, EH), WHICH WE DRANK ON THIS SWINGSET. WE WERE SWINGIN' REAL HIGH, WHEN BOOD SHOUTS, "HEY! LET'S JUMP OFF WHEN WE GET AS HIGH AS WE CAN GO!" SO WE JUMP, AND BUDDHA JUST KINDA THUDS, BUT I MUSTA FLEW FIFTEEN FEET, AND LANDED, LAUGHIN', ALL WIND KNOCKED OUT, ON MY BACK, FACING THE SWINGS! IT WAS INCREDIBLE!!! IS THIS A GREAT SWINGSET, OR WHAT? **MORE FREE LONG DISTANCE CALLING** CAN BE HAD, BESIDES THE OLE 22 PHONE AT THE MAYFAIR. THE GRAND BAY HOTEL, ACROSS FROM CITY HALL, ON SOUTH BAYSHORE HAS A PHONE BY THE POOL. ASK THE OPERATOR FOR AN OUTSIDE LINE. THEY HAVE MY FAVORITE JACUZZI IN TOWN, TOO... **SECRET OF THE GROVE UNREVEALED:** WHEN WE MOVED INTO THE MUTINY, ON THE INSIDE OF THE 12TH FLOOR DOOR, SOMEONE HAD DRAWN A STICK FIGURE IN A CIRCLE WITH THE WORDS, "GONE FISHIN" THEN, I SAW THE SAME FIGURE, CIRCLE, AND "GONE FISHIN" ETCHED IN THE CEMENT BY THE PAYPHONES AT PEACOCK PARK ACROSS THE STREET FROM THE MUTINY. NO ONE I ASKED KNEW ANYTHING ABOUT WHO COULD HAVE DONE IT. IMAGINE HOW FREAKED OUT I WAS WHEN I WAS WALKING ACROSS THE PEACOCK PARK BASEBALL FIELD AT 4:00 AM, ONE NIGHT, AND SAW THE STICK FIGURE, CIRCLE, AND "GONE FISHIN" DRAWN IN THE DIRT OF THE ENTIRE INFIELD!!! IT MADE ME FEEL REAL WEIRD AND ALONE, LIKE I WAS THE ONLY PERSON WHO SURVIVED A NUCLEAR WAR, OR SOMETHING...

RECIPES FOR SUCCESS®

Recipes for preparing delicious, nutritious meals the whole family will enjoy.

Make Every Meal A Success Story.

THE BEST THING ABOUT LIVING WITH A BUNCH OF OTHER PUNKS, SOMETIMES, IS JUST COOKING TOGETHER. YA KNOW — MAKING HUGE, CRAZY, COMMUNAL FEASTS WITH FOOD THAT YOU MANAGED TO ALL SCRAPE TOGETHER, SOMEHOW. FEASTS THAT TAKE ALL DAY TO COOK AND LIKE 5 MINUTES TO EAT. SO FAR, THE MUTINY, OR EVEN THE 22 HOUSE HAD BEEN REALLY LACKING THAT, WITH NO COOKING AT ALL. BUT, FINALLY, WE FIGURED WE COULD COOK WITH CHARCOAL FIRES ON THE MUTINY'S CEMENT FLOORS. IT WAS GREAT! IT WAS LIKE THE LAST THING WE NEEDED TO HAVE A REAL HOME. I MEAN, I HAD THOUGHT WE WERE PRETTY SET WHEN WE GOT THE COMPLETE BOOK OF RAP LYRICS, BUT MAN CAN NOT LIVE BY DOPE RHYMES ALONE. HE NEEDS SOUP, TOO. WORD.

TASTY! SOPA DE MUTINY (CON PAN) OR, THE MUTINY SOUP WITH BREAD YOU WILL NOT PUKE!

HERE'S WHAT YOU DO. FIRST, DUMPSTER THE POTATOES AND ONIONS AT WOOLEY'S. MAKE SURE THE PSYCHO MANAGER DOESN'T SEE TIM AND START YELLING AT HIM. GO INSIDE, PUT SOME GARLIC IN YOUR POCKET, AND STEAL THE CHARCOAL WITH THE OLE "LEFT HAND SCAM" (HOLD CHARCOAL IN OTHER HAND WHILE PAYING FOR 2 RAMEN PACKS. THEY ASSUME THE CHARCOAL IS YOURS, OR DON'T NOTICE IT.) THE RAMEN (+ CHARCOAL) IS 32¢. PAY WITH A FOODSTAMP. TAKE THE CHANGE AND BUY A BOTTLE OF VODKA! GO BACK INSIDE, AND LEFT-HAND A POT AND SKILLET, WHILE BUYING A BAG O CARROTS AND SOME CORN BREAD MIX. THAT'S $1.52. PAY WITH FOODSTAMPS. THAT'S ALL THE FOOD YER GONNA NEED, SO YOU CAN TRADE ALL THE REST OF YOUR STAMPS IN NOW, FOR CRACK! GO UP TO DA MUTINY AND SIT IN THE SEMI-DARK-LIGHT OF THE BOB'S BARRICADES LIGHT AND CUT VEGETABLES WITH YOUR BEST FRIEND, BUDDHA AND LISTEN TO THE NIP DRIVERS AND THE CIRCLE JERKS AND TALK ABOUT HOW HUNGRY YOU ARE, AND DIG THE COOL WIND AND MOON ON THE BAY. SOAK THE CARROTS/TATERS/ONIONS/GARLIC FOR A COUPLE HOURS, THEN START THE FIRE AND PUT THE SOUP ON AND START MAKIN' THESE THICK, KINDA CHEWY CORN CAKE SLABS ON THE SKILLET, AND HUDDLE 'ROUND THE FIRE TO KEEP WARM, AND GRAB THE CAKES AS THEY'RE BARELY DONE, CUZ YOU'VE BEEN WAITIN' ON THIS ALL AFTERNOON. IF THE FIRE STARTS TO DIE CUZ OF HUMIDITY, SOAK THE FUCKER WITH KEROSENE! YOW! LET THE SOUP BOIL FOR A LONG TIME, SO THE VEGGIES GET GOOD AND SOFT AND THE FLAVOR COMES OUT. LEAVE THE LID ON, YOU FUCK! WHEN ITS BOILING UP GOOD, ADD THE TWO RAMEN PACKS AND THE MYSTERIOUS "FLAVOR PACKS". STIR, STIR, SIT, WAIT A FEW, THEN SERVE IT UP! 3 QUART POT STUFFS 3 HUNGRY PUNKS! EAT, LAUGH, TALK, SMOKE, WHATEVER — THEN LISTEN TO THE CANADIANS JAM A FEW TOONS, LIVE AND IN PERSON. WASH OUT THE POT, AND PUT ON SOME TEA WHILE THE COALS ARE STILL A GLOWIN'. YO, PUT YER FEET UP! A SOUP SCAM IS GOOD FOOD!

THERE'S THIS PROBLEM I HAVE SOMETIMES, WHERE MY DREAMS ARE SO BIG AND CRAZY THAT, WHEN THE REALITY JUST TURNS OUT REAL GOOD, AND NOT TOTALLY, NON-STOP AWESOME, I GET A LITTLE DOWN. THIS HAPPENED WITH THE MUTINY. TIM AND BOOD JUST DIDN'T LIKE IT AS MUCH AS ME, AND SPENT LESS AND LESS TIME THERE. THIS FRUSTRATED ME A LOT, AND THEN A SHOW WE WERE SUPPOSED TO PLAY TURNED OUT SHITTY AND I GOT REAL STRESSED. LUCKILY, I HAD AN ESCAPE. IVY HAD A LUNG INFECTION AND WAS COMING BACK TO MIAMI TO USE HER MOM'S MEDICAID AND TO SING FOR THE CANADIANS. I NEEDED A ROAD TRIP TO QUIT WORRYING ABOUT OTHER PEOPLE, TO GET IN TOUCH WITH MYSELF. SO I WENT TO MEET HER ON THE WAY.

25¢

Adventure

APR.

PT. 5: SCAM PUNKS HOPPIN' TRAINS

Adventure
(Registered U. S. Patent Office)

Vol. 116, No. 2   for   Best of New Stories

December, 1946

MY FIRST TRAIN TRIP

When a man gets the blues, he catches a freight train and rides.

I HAD ALWAYS WANTED TO HOP TRAINS, but I guess I was waiting for Ivy or Greta, or someone else who's done it before to come to Florida and show me how. But then, Ivy called and said she was finally leaving for Miami, from Oakland, by trains, and I knew that Screeching Weasel and The Pink Lincolns were playin' in Atlanta at the end of the month, and I wanted to see 'em, so Ivy says, "I'll meet ya there," and the challenge was issued. Freight hoppin' it was gonna be. But, just takin' the bus out to the train yard in Hiahleah, and tryin' to hop didn't sound too exciting. It wasn't dramatic enough. Like, if I didn't make it, then what? Just take the bus home? No. I decided to hitch up to Tampa, and, once and for all, sweep that Rad, Crazy, Redhead off her feet. Or, at least, throw myself at her feet. It was probably hopeless, but, at least it had style.

The ride up to see her was great. State Road 60, 1-2-3. I got there in 4 hours, with 3 rides, and got dropped by the le Burger King by the I-75 overpass. I called her up and she was all excited to see me, so she said she'd come and get me right away! Yo! SCAM medicine: Hit the road! Never fails--- the magic thumb! Things were lookin' great. I went into BK and the same manager was there from the last time I'd come to see her. Last time, he'd said, "Shit. You white boys are crazy. There's no girl worth hitch hiking from Fort Lauderdale for." When I came in, now, he said, "Hey, Ft. Lauderdale! You still here for that girl? You crazy! CRAZY!" Yeah, yeah, crazy. He gave me a free coke and one of those Burger King crowns to present to my queen. I went outside, all whacked on free caffeine, and free travel, and sappy, snuggly thoughts, and waited for her to come.

Well, she never came... Hours later, the cop who almost busted me for vagrancy, told me where her house was, 5 miles away. I walked there, knocked, and was greeted by her roommate who looked at me with pity, and said, "She'll be down in a minute. She came down the stairs in a bathrobe. She was, it turns out, with ANOTHER MAN! She said something had come up, but I could still stay there. Ugh. I wanted to leave, but the cop had followed me to her house. I sat in the corner all night with my crown on, in a daze. When morning came, some guy came down the stairs with a suitcase and grunted at me on his way out the door. He was from out of town, too?! ? Where does she get all these men? O travellers, beware when passing random on State Road 60. Look straight ahead, and plug your ears with wax, cuz you'll hear the most beautiful singin' in the world, and you'll think your in love, but she really has claws and wants to wreck your ship on the rocks, so she can eat you alive!

I left and stole Peanut Butter and a plastic spoon from

Publix, and went out to thumb to the train yard on ole State Road 60, the road that got in this mess in the first place...

I WAS HEADING FOR BARTOW, to get on U.S. 17, north to Lakeland, to hop my first train. It turns out that I'd misread the train info that my friend, Greta, had sent me, and thought that (SBD) by Tampa, meant that only southbound trains left from there, when it actually meant that the Seaboard Railway Yard was there. So I went to Lakeland cuz that was the nearest place that I thought I could catch a train from. Lakeland is a creepy little town, midway between Orlando and Tampa. All I knew about it was that I had been stuck there in the dark, in the rain, while hitch hiking more times than anywhere else in Florida. Also, one time I was near there and decided to call this girl, who had ordered SCAM, and written me a bunch of times. She had turned out to be a diehard racist! She said "I don't like blacks... they don't work and leech off welfare" Don't work and leech off welfare? Did you even READ my zine?! Fuck off, ya subnormal Central Florida Scum! I figured that Lakeland ought to have three K's in it: LAKKKELAND.

The hitching to LaKKKeland went well. I now had an instant bond with people who gave me rides. "So are you just hitchin' around for the hell of it, or..?" Oh, I hitched up to see this girl. "Oh yeah?" Yeah, but, check this: I get to her house, and she's with another guy! "No!" Yep. "Man, that's harsh! Have a beer." Don't mind if I do...

I got dropped off at the deserted LaKKKeland Amtrak station in the pouring rain, and sat there, against a wall, slowly eating peanut butter and realizing, with the cold rain, and empty train station, that, finally, this was it. I was totally alone. There was nothing to do but catch the train. It was real exciting, but, I was also a little nervous. It was kind of like the feeling you get while youre in Ki nko's, making $300 worth of copies, with $1.50 in your pocket. I went to look for the train yard, singin' out loud, gettin' anxious about the lonely drama that was unfolding out here on the flipside of town, under the silent, Central Florida sky, between me and the train I'd soon have to get on. After an hour or so, I still hadn't found the yard, when, from behind me, I heard, comin' slow and sure, a train. My train. It went grindin' on past me, indifferent, and I watched it, all in a trance, and then, alla sudden, here was the last car goin' by, and I was up and chasin' it, all flailin' and laughin', and then I grabbed the grain car's ladder, and swung up on, all proud Hobo-style, and waved goodbye to my imaginary audience. I did it! I was finally on a train! Now, I just had to find out where it was going...

I figured it'd be just my luck to end up on a train going completely the wrong way, or, with the way things were goin' I'd end up on one that was supposed to run off a cliff, or something, but, it was just headed into the LaKKKeland yard.

THE SWINDLER TALKED TOO MUCH AND THEN...

IN A DINGY BOHEMIAN RESTAURANT, A TOUGH-LOOKING WAITER EAVESDROPS WHILE HELEN DEMARE, ASPIRING YOUNG WRITER, HEARS BAD NEWS FROM HER "LITERARY AGENT"....

YOU MEAN ALL MY MONEY IS GONE, MR. ROWE, AND YOU'RE NOT PUBLISHING MY STORY?

NOW, NOW, SISTER. I'LL LEND YOU TRAIN FARE HOME

Actually, though, I had so much adrenalin from catchin' the train, that I wouldn't have been too upset if I was goin' the wrong way. At least I knew I could do it, now. In the yard, I found a brakeman who told me that the next train north wouldn't be 'til 6 or 8, the next morning, so I just walked to Circle K (they should have Circle KKK) and stole my nightly quart of milk and some insect repellent, and laid down to sleep in my ole New Kids On The Block sleeping bag, behind the D.M.V. building. At this point, you might be thinking, "Well, he's sleeping on cold, damp concrete, by a major highway, with it raining all around, and there's mosquitos all over, and he got his heart broke by Tampa, and there's no way out, and he's surviving entirely on orange juice and peanut butter... " But, listen, it was awesome, OK? I wouldn't shit ya. I mean, this was turning pro hobo, ya know? Like, Pass-the-gritty-coffee, ya fuck! I knew when and where a train was gonna be ready to go, and all I had to do was get there and get on it.

I WOKE UP, JUST AFTER SUN UP, AND raced over to Circle K to get more juice, for the train, and to SCAM a wake-up thermos 'o coffee. Over at the yard, my train was exactly where it was supposed to be, but I found a brakeman to ask to make sure, and then, found a spot on the porch of a grain car, put my sleeping bag down as a cushion, and waited. I wasn't really sure if I was doing everything involved with this train hopping thing correctly, but, now that I was out there doin' it, I was glad that I was doing it alone, and hadn't waited any longer for anyone to show me how. I guess I was ignoring my own advice. People are always saying things like, "I want to go on a big road trip, but I need to save up more money first," or, "As soon as I move away from this town, things'll be better"--- always ignoring the present, putting off their dreams for some future Promised Land, a future that gets further and further away. Or things are never good enough, now. "There's nowhere to have shows," or "We can't find a bass player." I'm usually the one who says just start now, anyways, and see what happens. Now, Chickenhead and The Canadians share one guitar, a shitty duct-taped drum set, and two members, and we have shows in empty lots, ride dumpstered bikes, go on tour without a record (or without really knowing songs), etc., etc. I don't know why I'd waited this long to take the trains. It was fun!

After what seemed like forever, suddenly, and with little fanfare, my train Ca-chunked into motion, and we were off! I grabbed some coffee and raised a salute to Fidel and MUD FLAP, And Chickenhead, cuz those are the stickers on my thermos, and held on for the ride. After a while, I realized I was safe and could relax, cuz it wasn't scary at all. It was like riding in the back of a pick-up truck, all breezy, and sunny, and sleepy. The scenery was real nice, and showed what 99% of Florida's really like--- rural, sparsely populated, and wide open, and green. Still, we didn't go through any tunnels, or over any huge bridges, or by any waterfalls, or anything. The train did go through some real North Central Florida hotspots--- Lochloosa, Bushnell, Lawtey, and even Hawthorne, where it went real slow through the center of town, and I stood out on the porch, wavin' to the masses all Truman '48-style. The Iggy Scam Whistle Stop Tour! In a lot of places, the railroad tracks were right through backyards, and people had chairs set up to watch it go by. I saw dads with kids on their shoulders, pointin' at the train, and kids on bikes throwin' rocks at the train, and teenage girls, who came out to the tracks to just stand and smoke in the twilight and watch the train race off, away from the setting sun, to SOMEWHERE ELSE. Man! Finally after 12 hours, my train came to a stop in Baldwin...

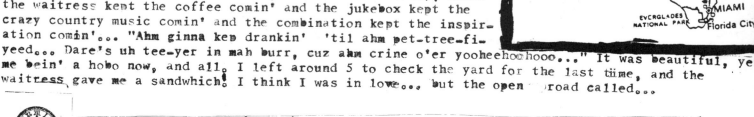

IN BALDWIN, I CELEBRATED MY BIG RIDE, with a little peanut butter on the porch 'o my car and waited, but as it became finally dark, I realized that this train was, unfortunately, not going any further. A brakeman told me that there wouldn't be any trains headin' up Waycross way 'til at least midnight. At midnight, they told me to try back at 3 or 4. Well, I wasn't gettin' anywhere, but I wasn't stressin' it, cuz now that I'd hopped a train, I felt real confidant. I'd get a ride on a helicopter if I had to! I wasn't worried. Besides-- Baldwin had a Waffle House...

I went to Waffle House and flew the sign "Atlanta or Waycross" to maybe scare up a ride, and wrote furiously, while the waitress kept the coffee comin' and the jukebox kept the crazy country music comin' and the combination kept the inspiration comin'... "Ahm ginna kep drankin' 'til ahm pet-tree-fi-yeed... Dare's uh tee-yer in mah burr, cuz ahm crine o'er yooheehoohooo..." It was beautiful, ye me bein' a hobo now, and all. I left around 5 to check the yard for the last tiime, and the waitress gave me a sandwhich! I think I was in love... but the open road called...

AT THE YARD, a cool, old guy brakeman said, "To be honest, there ain't but one train u Waycross a day, and it could be anytime from now 'til sundown." Well, it still wasn't sun UP, and I was 12 hours from missin' my date with Ivy, so I was runnin' 'outta time. I decided to dust off the ole thumb. It was total dark, no traffic, but, hey, at least I had total, one-on-one contact with every car, right? I needed to get just past Lake City on I-10, to catch I-75 north to Atlanta, and it only took two rides. When I got dropped at the big intersection on 10 and 75, the sky fullon opened up with buckets of rain, so I ran for the overpass, where I watched all that poundin' rain and wind whippin' trees and thunder 'n lightni kind of in awe, not hatin' it too much, since I was all dry and warmand such in my sleepin' bag. I found a pile of peppermint patties in my pocket that I had grabbed back at the Waffle House. Mint chocolate ?!? Iggy Scam, you ARE prepared! With 5 hours of road and most of a day to get there, I smiled and went to sleep.

When I woke up, I saw that this was a pretty popular bridge to get stuck under in the rai cuz there was traveller graffiti there, datin' back to the early '70s. There was a wide variety from the typical "Randolph Lee Portlack of 1851 Held Lane, Redwood Valley, California was here on April 17, 1975. Wish good luck to travellers. I made it here in 12 days." to the truly amazing, like "I, Norge Dietrich Himmler, bestow the following curse upon Jim Horton, Apopka city police officer: That all the pain, trouble, and toils, and frustrations that I suffer shall be a dozen times over put on him, that his marriage to Betty Lanzilli, Apopka city police dispatcher, and mother of Kelly Wose, my best friend, will fail within 2 years, and, finally, that he shall suffer a permanent disability within these 2 years, leaving him paralyzed, but fully conscious, for the rest of his life, which will be long indeed. Read this, travellers, and carry the word to him. I can not, for to see him again is my death"--Norge Dietrich Himmler

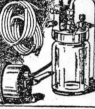

o, Norge, I know how it is, man! My favorite, though, was from the road poet, Harold Rife (exclusively published in SCAM), who, way back on 1-11-80 wrote "Some of us must forever follow the lonely roads of life without a companion. And there are those who follow the roads of life with their loved one. Then there are those who are happy with just staying at home with their loved ones. I am neither, FOR I AM THE "REBEL".AAh... the man bled those words-- the angst, the proud defiant "rebel", laughing in the face of convention, sleeping under bridges, etc... Classic. I dug a marker out of my bag and wrote my own huge essay there under the bridge, all about my trip so far, and then wrote, "I'm leaving the marker here for you to write yer own story here." and wedged the marker up into the corner. A bridge between travellers past and travellers of the future...

My dry place in the world was rapidly shrinking there under the bridge, so I left my toasty bag and once again went out to the road to hitch. It was still raining, but not as much, and I didn't mind, cuz beautiful fog had the road ahead all shrouded in mystery, and I was feelin' smart for bringing garbage bags to keep my stuff dry. It was a long wait there in the rain, about 2 hours, but I finally got a ride, and he was going all the way! Atlanta. Now I could relax. Or, so I thought. Outside of Macon, 120 miles from Atlanta, the driver starts fallin' asleep at the wheel! He goes to a gas station and drinks 2 large coffees, but then, 60 miles outta A-town, he says, "Man, I'm sorry. I'm gonna have to stop and sleep, and yer gonna have to get another ride." Just then I remembered the pills that Chuck Looseslipped me when he dropped me off at I-95 to start my trip, and said, "Relax. I have drugs. You'll make it if you take these," and handed him 5 white crosses. The driver ate the pills, and we made it to Atlanta in record time. Whatever it takes!

We finally came into Atlanta, and there was the skyline, shootin' up all pro big city style outta the Deep South, and I felt pretty excited. A couple daysbefore I had left Miami, some old guy at a show gave me a big, dumb speech about how I was gonna get real tired soon of livin' how I do. Hmmm... I wonder what I'll get tired of first-- thesunrises over the bay in The Mutiny, or the rendezvous with rad, crazy women in faraway places... I called Ivy at Andy Powell's (cuz he was livin' there in 'Lanta at his dad's) and hopped the MARTA train to meet em.

WHEN I GOT OFF THE MARTA, IVY WAS THERE, WITH HER NEW TRUCKER HAT ON, and Andy's right behind her, and we're together again. We stalk off in the rain to a Subway where Andy's friend, Jay, worked to get free food all night. It was one of those great reunitin' times, when yer with yer good friend, racin' down the streets of some city you don't know, tryin' to take it all in, and havin' no idea where you are, and yer both all bustin' out, tryin' to tell the whole story at once, and you just want to have it all frozen there for a minute, yes, ya feel so good... We end up takin' over Subway, with stiff socks and big bags all in a pile, and us all wet and stinky, sippin' cokes and swappin' stories, just like back in ole Miami.

Ivy's story was a little more dramatic than mine. She'd left Oakland, against doctor's orders, and had a crazy, two week adventure. She'd caught out of Oakland, alone, with a bottle of Southern Comfort, been kicked off the train in Davis (the bull gave her 5 bucks, though), broke into an abandoned building to stay the night in Sacramento, hitched to Roseville. People kept giving her money. She made 80 bucks! She caught an eastbound, out of Roseville, with Paco, the tramp, this crafty ole veteran hobo who knew how to tell where a train was headed, just by the number of engines it had, or where it was in the yard, or the numbers and letters on the engine. Her and Paco split up in Pueblo, where she fell off a movin' train, when she tried to get on, and it was going too fast. She cursed the train, and it stopped at the light, so she got it all the way to Ft. Worth. She ended up in Little Rock, where she stayed in an abandoned cottage for 2 days with this crazy, old hobo guy and a guy who called himself, "The proffessional hitch hiker". Two Christians gave her 20

BUCKS, AND THEN, RUNNING OUT OF TIME TO MEET ME, SHE JUST HITCHED
ONE RIDE, FROM LITTLE ROCK TO ATLANTA, ~~ALONG~~ WITH A TRUCKER.
THAT'S WHERE SHE GOT THE TRUCKER HAT. SHE ALSO HAD ALL KINDS
OF RAILROAD STUFF LIKE UNION PACIFIC FIRST AID KITS AND SOUTHERN
PACIFIC RAILROAD FLARES. SHE WAS TOTALLY PREPARED, AND HERE
I WAS WITH NOTHIN' PACKED TO SAVE MY LIFE BUT AN OLD
BLACK FLAG |||, TAPE... HER STORIES WERE SO EXCITING AND
CRAZY, THAT I TOTALLY WANTED TO JUST JUMP ON ANOTHER TRAIN,
TO ANYWHERE, AND JUST KEEP GOING. BUT, FIRST, WE WOULD
HANG OUT IN ATLANTA.

THE P.LINCOLNS/WEEZEHOLES SHOW WAS OK. IVY AND ME
PASSED OUT A BUNCH OF BLOWN UP BALLOONS, AND EVERYONE
JUST KIND OF STARED AT US, DRILY. THE REST OF THE WEEK, WE
JUST WALKED, AND TALKED, AND CAUGHT UP. IT WAS GOOD TO BE
TOGETHER, BUT ATLANTA WASN'T TURNING OUT TO BE THAT GREAT,
CUZ WE WERE STAYING WAY OUT ON THE EDGE OF TOWN WITH JAY,
AND HIS ROOMIES WERE JUNKIES WITH PSYCHOTIC, SPLIT-PERSON'
ALITIES. ONE GUY, WHEN HE WAS ON, AND FEELING GOOD, TOLD US,
"THIS IS MY DREAM... I JUST WANT TO WALLOW IN IT..." SHEESH!
WHAT A TIRED OLD MOVIE TO RELIVE. BUT THAT'S KINDA HOW THE
WHOLE TOWN FELT — EVERYONE ACTIN' OUT SOME BAD PART.
JUNKIES BEIN' JUNKIES, ASSHOLES AT THE SHOW BEIN' ASSHOLES AT THE SHOW, HICKS BEIN' HICKS, AND
COPS BEIN' COPS. IT WAS TIME FOR US TO LEAVE.

WE WENT TO THE CSX YARD TO TRY AND CATCH A TRAIN DOWN TO JACKSONVILLE, WHERE WE'D ONLY
NEED ONE FLORIDA EAST COAST TRAIN TO GET HOME TO MIAMI. I LIKE TRAIN YARDS. THEY'RE LIKE WHOLE
UNDERGROUND WORLDS, AT THE END OF OBSCURE BUS LINES, OUT ON THE EDGE OF TOWN, AND OFF THE CITY
MAPS. THEY'RE SURROUNDED BY BIG TREES AND FENCES, OR MOATS, AND WHEN YA SNEAK ON 'EM, THEY'RE ALL
EERY AND SILENT, WITH JUST THE FAR OFF SOUNDS OF RUMBLIN' MACHINES AND COLLIDIN' METAL AND
ENGINES GRINDIN' BACK AND FORTH. THEY EVEN HAVE THEIR OWN COP WHO USUALLY DRESSES REAL NICE,
DRIVES A WHITE TRUCK, OR BLAZER, AND HAS A STUPID MUSTACHE. ITS KINDA NEAT TO THINK ABOUT ALL
THIS SECRET ACTIVITY GOIN' ON, 24 HOURS A DAY, KNOWN TO FEW, BUT ITS EVEN COOLER TO THINK THAT
THE TRAIN THAT COMES BARRELIN' THROUGH THE OUTSKIRTS AND CROSSROADS OF YER TOWN, RIPPIN' THROUGH
THE MIDDLE 'O THE NIGHT, MAY BE CARRYIN' A BOXCAR FULL OF CRAZY SCAM PUNKS! YO!

IVY HAD SCOUTED THE YARD THE NIGHT BEFORE, AND WAS TOLD THAT ALL THE SOUTHBOUNDS STOP
BEFORE THIS ONE TUNNEL, AND WE'D JUST HAVE TO MAKE SURE IT WAS HEADED TO J-VILLE BEFORE WE
GOT ON. THE BRAKEMAN SHE HAD TALKED TO ALSO SAID THERE WAS A CREW CABIN THERE THAT WOULD
BE SAFE TO WAIT IN AND STAY WARM AND OUTTA SIGHT OF THE TRAIN PIG. I WAS SO ANXIOUS TO
LEAVE TOWN, AND COULDN'T WAIT TO SEE OUR TRAIN STOPPIN' AT THE TUNNEL. BUT, WE DIDN'T SEE OUR
TRAIN THAT DAY. THE ONLY THING THAT STOPPED BY OUR SHACK WAS THE CLEAN, WHITE BLAZER OF THE
CSX TRAIN POLICE...

IT WAS SPECIAL AGENT R.L. JOHNSON, A THIN, BLACK MAN OF ABOUT 50, WHO HAD A STRONG,
DEEP SOUTH ACCENT, WAS WELL DRESSED, AND HAD A STUPID MUSTACHE. WE HOPED HE'D JUST BOOT US OFF
THE YARD, AS IS THE CUSTOM, BUT, INSTEAD, HE PUT ALL OUR STUFF IN HIS BLAZER AND DROVE US TO HIS
OFFICE. HE STARTED RUNNIN' OUR NAMES THROUGH THE COMPUTER, AT THE OFFICE, AND SAID, "YOU CAN
GO AHEAD AND FINISH EATIN' IF YA WANT (WE WERE EATIN' PEANUT BUTTER WHEN BUSTED). NOW, I WAS
WORRIED, CUZ, USUALLY, ITS THE "NICE" ONES WHO ARE GONNA FUCK YOU UP. IF A COP, OR
SECURITY GUARD BELLOWS IN YOUR FACE ABOUT HOW HE SHOULD JUST KICK YOUR ASS, AND YOU'LL BE
LUCKY IF YA GET 3 YEARS, AND HOW THEY'LL TEAR A KID LIKE YOU TO PIECES IN PRISON, ETC. ETC.
THEN YOU'LL PROBABLY BE OK, IF YOU JUST DO YER PART AND ACT REAL SCARED AND STICK TO YOUR
STORY. HE'LL PROBABLY LET YA GO. WHEN THE COP OFFERS YOU SMOKES AND SAYS, "YOU WANT SOME
M AND M'S?" GET SET FOR JAIL. THIS COP IS "JUST DOING HIS JOB" AND IS TRYING TO REACH SOME
INTERNAL PEACE WITH THE FACT THAT HIS JOB PUTS PEOPLE IN THE BOX. HE'S A GOOD GUY, RIGHT? BUT RULES
ARE RULES...

AFTER A TENSE 20 MINUTES, OR SO, R.L. ANNOUNCES, "IVY, YOU HAVE A WARRANT OUT FOR
YER ARREST IN PALM BEACH COUNTY, FLORIDA." (HE STARTS OFFERING HER CIGARETTES). "I'M
GONNA HAVE TO CALL THE POLICE, TO TAKE YOU TO JAIL..."

THE FOLLOWING IS AN EXCERPT FROM MY JOURNAL, WRITTEN JUST HOURS AFTER IVY WAS TAKEN TO JAIL

I CAN'T BELIEVE I'M STILL IN SHITLANTA!
FUCK THIS PLACE! THEY NEVER SHOULD HAVE
REBUILT THIS FILTHY, DOOMED CITY! THE NORTH WON!
THIS PLACE SHOULDN'T EXIST! AAAAARRGH!!!

Be prepared to defend oneself.

SO, I WAS STUCK IN ATLANTA, AND, NOW, WITHOUT IVY. THE COP WHO CAME TO TAKE HER TO JAIL GAVE ME A RIDE TO THE JUNKIES' HOUSE. AMAZING. BACK IN THE DAYS, THEY'D SIT IN THE HOBO JUNGLE, DRINK GRITTY COFFEE. IGGY SCAM GETS A UNIFORMED COP TO DRIVE HIM TO A HOUSE FULL OF DRUGS. IT WAS FUCKING COLD, AND I WAS PRETTY ALONE, YES, AND I COULD HEAR, "I CAN SEE CLEARLY..." BY SCREECHING WEASEL BLASTIN' OUTTA THE HOUSE AND PEOPLE LAUGHIN' AND YELLIN'. SHIT. I DIDN'T KNOW WHAT I WANTED TO DO, BUT I KNEW I DIDN'T WANT TO GO IN THERE AT ALL. I WAS SICK OF THE TIRED, OLD MOVIES. I PICKED UP OUR 3 PACKS AND 2 SLEEPING BAGS AND WALKED AWAY, UP THE HILL. IT FELT GREAT. SOMETHINGS JUST HAVE TO BE DONE ALONE. UP THE STREET A LITTLE WAS AN ABANDONED HOUSE THAT ME AND ANDY HAD GONE IN BEFORE. I WENT INSIDE, LIT A CANDLE FOR IVY, WROTE AWHILE, AND WENT TO SLEEP.

THE NEXT MORNING, I HID OUR STUFF AND WALKED DOWN TO THE JAIL TO CHECK ON IVY'S CASE. THE COP HAD SAID THAT PALM BEACH COUNTY WOULD NEVER PAY TO EXTRADITE HER THERE FOR A 2-YEAR OLD SHOPLIFTING CHARGE, AND, SINCE NO CHARGES WERE BROUGHT AGAINST HER BY CSX, SHE'D BE OUT AS SOON AS THE PAPER WORK ON THAT CLEARED. MAYBE EVEN THE NEXT MORNING... WELL, THAT DIDN'T TAKE INTO ACCOUNT THE COMBINED NEGATIVE ENERGY OF BOTH PALM BEACH AND SHITLANTA — AN INTANGIBLE, PSYCHIC BLACK HOLE WITH IMMEASURABLE EFFECTS. AT THE JAIL, SURE ENOUGH, THEY COULDN'T EVEN FIND HER NAME IN THE COMPUTER... OUTSIDE, I CONSIDERED THE ATLANTA DOWNTOWN SKYLINE. AH YES... ATLANTA. SO BIG. SO MODERN. SO... SO... <u>FLAMMABLE</u>!! WOULD WE EVER GET HOME?!?

THINGS TO DO WHILE YOUR FRIEND'S IN JAIL

I RAN INTO ANDY POWELL AT THE BUS STOP BY MY ABANDONED HOUSE, AND HE SAID HIS FOLKS WERE LEAVING TOWN, AND I COULD STAY AT HIS PLACE, SO I MOVED THE <u>SCAM</u> OFFICES OUT TO DECATUR, AND CALLED ALL OVER, EVERYDAY, TRYING TO GET IVY OUTTA JAIL. I WAS PRETTY BUMMED OUT, BUT, SOON, I REALIZED THAT FEELING LIKE I WAS "STUCK" ONLY MADE IT WORSE. SOMETIMES GETTING 'STUCK SOMEWHERE CAN BE GOOD, CUZ IT FORCES YA INTO NEW SITUATIONS. SO, I GAVE EXPLORING ATLANTA ANOTHER CHANCE, AND, I FEEL A LITTLE GUILTY, BUT I MUST ADMIT, I ENDED UP HAVING FUN WHILE IVY WAS IN JAIL...

I LOVE WALKING AROUND BIG CITIES ALONE. THERE'S SO MUCH TROUBLE TO GET INTO! THERE'S PLENTY OF WALLS TO TAG, AND ROOFS TO GET ON, AND POOLS TO HOP, AND HOTELS TO GET CHASED OUT OF, TRASH TO PLAY WITH, AND PEOPLE TO WATCH. ON MY FIRST DAY EXPLORIN' ATLANTA, I HIT THE PEACHTREE CENTER HOTEL — 76 STORIES OF FUN! IT WAS LIKE ONE OF THOSE CHOOSE-YER-OWN-ADVENTURE-BOOKS FROM WHEN YOU WERE A KID: "IF YOU GO RIGHT, YOU GET THE FULL PLATES 'O LEFTOVERS FROM ROOM SERVICE, AND HALF A BOTTLE

OF WINE. IF YOU GO LEFT, YOU GET THE PINCH FROM DA GUY-WITH-NO-NECK." I DIDN'T MAKE IT ON THE ROOF, OR GET WINE, BUT I DID SWIM, TAKE A HOT SHOWER, EAT TONS OF GREAT STILL-WARM PASTA AND PASTRIES, AND BURP IN THE FACE OF THE-GUY-WITH-NO-NECK ON MY WAY OUT THE DOOR. ACTUALLY, IT REMINDS ME OF SOMETHING I DIDN'T GET AROUND TO DOING THIS ISSUE—THE SCAM BOARD GAME. THERE'S TWO GAME PIECES—YOU CAN EITHER BE THE SCAM "UNK GUY, OR THE WILL SHATTER PIECE FROM THE FLIPPER GONE FISHIN' RECORD. IT'D BE STUFF LIKE, "YOU LOOK PATHETIC AND STRANGERS GIVE YOU 4 BUCKS. MOVE AHEAD 2 SPACES." OR "THE SANDWICHES THAT YOU ATE IN THE DARK BY THE DUMPSTER WERE REALLY DIAPERS. GO BACK 6 SPACES AND PUKE!" MAYBE NEXT TIME...

THE NEXT DAY, ANDY GAVE ME HIS DAD'S MONTHLY MARTA TRAIN PASS TO EXPLORE THE CITY WITH, BUT IT WAS SUCH A GREAT DAY FOR WALKIN' AND SINGIN', ALL DARK 'N' DRIZZLY, THAT, INSTEAD OF TURNING LEFT TO MARTA, I TURNED RIGHT AND WALKED ABOUT 6 MILES TO DOWNTOWN. ON THE WAY, I FOUND SOME SPRAY PAINT ON A TRASHPILE, AND THEN, A GREAT UNDER-THE-BRIDGE SPOT, WITH RIPPLIN' CREEK, DRIPPIN' TREE SCENERY. I DID SOME GRAFFITTI 'TIL MY PAINT RAN OUT. THEN, I FOUND A DECENT USED BOOKSTORE THAT PASSED THE SCAM USED BOOKSTORE TEST, MEANING THAT THEY DON'T REALLY EXPECT YOU TO PAY THEIR OUTRAGOUS PRICE, ARE EASILY TALKED DOWN, AND GLADLY GIVE A DISCOUNT TO US YOUNG AND ENTHUSIASTIC, BUT SMELLY AND POOR, BOOK LOVER TYPES. AT A SUPERMARKET I STOLE ROLLS AND DID A RECEIPT SCAM. WHEN THE BUM OUTSIDE ASKED FOR 40¢, I GAVE HIM A WHOLE BUCK AND TOLD HIM HOW I GOT IT, AND HE WAS LIKE, "YO! THAT'S A GOOD SCAM, MAN!" PEOPLE ARE ALWAYS GLAD TO HEAR ABOUT PEOPLE GETTIN' AWAY WITH STUFF LIKE THAT. I TOOK A WALK UP LUCKIE STREET WHICH IS KINDA CRUELLY NAMED, CUZ THAT'S WHERE ALL THE PROJECTS ARE—ON LUCKIE STREET UP TOWARDS THE GEORGIA TECH LIBRARY. BUT, BEFORE I GOT TO THE LIBRARY, I SAW THIS FIERY OLD BLACK WOMAN STREET PREACHER, ALL LOUD AND SKINNY, WALKIN' AROUND WITH A SANDWICH BOARD, THAT SAID, "REPENT!", YELLING, "REPENT! REPENT FOR THE LORD!" SHE SEES ME AND YELLS, "LOOK AT YOU BOY! YOU BETTER REPENT! YOU'RE A REBEL, AND YOU'RE GOING STRAIGHT TO HELL!" I LEAPED UP, ALL FIST PUMPIN', "AMEN!" AND FELT REALLY GOOD FOR THE FIRST TIME ALL WEEK...

I RODE THE MARTA AROUND AND HEADED BACK TO ANDY'S, LATE. AT THE DECATUR MARTA, I MET A HOMELESS WOMAN WHO I GAVE MY LAST ROLL TO. SHE SAYS, "YA KNOW, I'M ALWAYS FINDING STUFF, SEE?" AND SHE SHOWS ME A FREE DRINK TICKET TO SOME BAR. I SAY, "I FIND STUFF, TOO" AND SHOW HER MY RED, TOY GUN THAT SHOOTS SPARKS. SHE YELLS, "GET THAT AWAY FROM ME!" SHE EXPLAINS, "IF YOU EVER PULL A GUN ON ME, IT WILL TURN AROUND AND SHOOT YOU, AND YOU'LL SPEND THE REST OF YOUR LIFE TRYING TO MAKE UP FOR IT THROUGH MY ESTABLISHED, RELIGIOUS ORDER!" I SAY, WHOOPS, I, UH, MEANT NO HARM. SHE SAYS, ITS O.K., GET LOST... FINALLY, TO END MY GREAT DAY, I DRANK A THERMOS 'O SCAMMED COFFEE ON THE CREAKIN' SOFTLY PORCH SWING OF AN ABANDONED HOUSE AND WATCHED THE RAIN AND MY CLOUDY BREATH. THE FIREBREATHIN' IGGY SCAM! YO! I'M FROM FLORIDA. THAT CLOUDY BREATH THING IS STILL KINDA A NOVELTY TO ME, I GUESS.

I WAS GLAD I GAVE ATLANTA ANOTHER SHOT. ONE NEAT THING ABOUT IT IS THAT PEOPLE SEEMED REAL FRIENDLY THERE. A COUPLE PEOPLE JUST CAME UP TO ME AND TALKED TO ME ON THE STREET LIKE, "YER NOT FROM AROUND HERE, ARE YOU?" AND I'D TELL 'EM ABOUT IVY IN JAIL AND WE'D TALK ABOUT COPS AND POVERTY. MAYBE CUZ ITS SUCH A POOR CITY, AND MOSTLY BLACK, PEOPLE FEEL MORE TIGHT KNIT. PEOPLE WERE ALWAYS TALKIN' TO EACH OTHER ON THE BUS, OR TRAIN. NOT LIKE THE TOTAL ISOLATION IN MIAMI. I SAW THESE TWO GUYS WHO HAD MET ON THE TRAIN, TALKIN'. WHEN THE ONE GUY SAID, "WELL, HERE'S MY STOP..." INSTEAD OF "SEE YA", OR "GOOD NIGHT..." THE OTHER GUY SAYS, "BE STRONG." THAT WAS GREAT, LIKE THERE WAS SOME UNDERSTANDING OF LIFE AND STRUGGLE THERE. I REALLY DUG THAT. BE STRONG, BE STRONG. SHIT.

WHAT WOULD FIDEL DO IN THIS SITUATION?

FINALLY, AFTER 5 DAYS, PALM BEACH COUNTY TOLD FULTON COUNTY NOT TO HOLD IVY FOR EXTRADITION ANYMORE, AND SHE WAS OUTTA JAIL. NOW, WE HAD TO GET HOME, WITH IVY'S WARRANT STILL IN EFFECT AND HER LUNG INFECTION GETTING WORSE AND WORSE, IT SEEMED LIKE THE SENSIBLE THING TO DO WOULD BE TO JUST HITCH HOME. IT SOUNDED TERRIBLE. WE NEEDED A BETTER ENDING TO OUR STORY THAN 3 DAYS ON THE SIDE OF THE ROAD BEGGING FOR RIDES. WE NEEDED STYLE, LIKE JOHN DILLINGER. WHEN DILLINGER WAS WANTED ALL ACROSS THE COUNTRY, WITH HIS PICTURE EVERYWHERE, HE'D ROLL INTO A TOWN, CALL THE CHEIF OF POLICE AND SAY, "HI. THIS IS JOHN DILLINGER. I'M IN TOWN TO KILL YOU"! YEAH! SO, WE DECIDED TO SNEAK BACK INTO THE YARD THAT IVY HAD BEEN ARRESTED IN, UNDER COVER OF THE NIGHT, RISKING CERTAIN JAIL, TO CATCH OUR TRAIN HOME.

ONE THING WAS FOR SURE: ATLANTA OWED US A TRAIN, AND WE DID CATCH ONE, BUT IT WAS A BATTLE RIGHT UP TO THE END. AT THE YARD, NO TRAIN CAME BY SUNUP, SO WE MADE OUR WAY OVER THE MOAT, THROUGH THORN BUSHES TO MAKE A WELL-HIDDEN HUT TO CRASH OUT IN. WE USED BRANCHES AND LEAVES AND OUR UMBRELLA AND TOWELS AND A STOLEN AMERICAN FLAG TO MAKE A GOOD, TOUGH ROOF, AND WE CRAWLED IN AND BUNDLED UP AND LAUGHED AND TOLD STORIES AND ATE PEANUT BUTTER AND NODDED OFF TO SLEEP. AND THEN THE RAIN CAME TO PUT OUR BRAVE, D.I.Y. HUT TO THE TEST. UM... IT FAILED PRETTY BADLY. AH, YES... DOLOR DE VIDA. I JUST KINDA SAT THERE, SHIVERING AND GIGGLING A LITTLE EVERY TIME A NEW LEAK SPAT A STREAM OF WATER IN MY EYE. IT WAS PRETTY FUNNY, ACTUALLY, AND I HAD ALREADY DECIDED, "I WON'T DIE IN ATLANTA!", LIKE, I WON'T GIVE 'EM THE HONOR, YA KNOW? SO IT WAS OK. WE LEFT THE HUT, AND WALKED SEVERAL MILES, IN THE RAIN, IN THE

"FLORIDA BOUND BLUES"

by Leroy Carr

[The Famous Migration Blues]

WRONG DIRECTION, LOOKING FOR A REPAIR YARD THAT DIDN'T EXIST, AND ENDED UP OFF THE YARD, BY THE FULTON COUNTY DOG POUND. WE SAT IN THE MUD AND ATE PEANUT BUTTER IN NUMB DESPAIR. THERE'S ALWAYS A POINT WHERE THINGS ARE SO BAD, THAT IT BECOMES HILARIOUS, AND, LUCKILY WE REACHED THAT POINT WHEN OUR PLASTIC SPORK BROKE IN THE PEANUT BUTTER. WE JUST STARED AT IT AND STARTED LAUGHIN' FOR LIKE 5 MINUTES. THEN, WE WENT INTO THE POUND AND IVY VISITED EVERY DOG AND FELT BETTER AND WHEN WE CAME OUT, THE SUN WAS OUT...

IT WAS ABOUT FUCKING TIME, YA KNOW. I STORMED INTO THE YARD, WET AND CRAZY, AND ASKED A CONDUCTOR, WHO WAS SITTIN' IN AN ENGINE, ABOUT TRAINS TO J-VILLE. HE SAID, "THIS TRAIN'S GOING THERE IN 20 MINUTES." I RAN AND GOT IVY AND OUR STUFF AND WE SCURRIED ACROSS THE YARD, IN BROAD DAYLIGHT, AND CROSSED OVER TRACKS, AND TRAINS, AND CREPT UP ON OUR TRAIN, REAL SLOW, THE BRAKEMAN TURNED HIS HEAD AND, GO! WE'RE ON! ME AND IVY AND OUR COLLECTIVE BODY ODOR JAM INTO THE BACK ENGINE'S TOILET, AND HIDEOUT, ALL STOWAWAY STYLE, HEARTS BEATIN' HEAVY WHEN MEN COME INTO OUR ENGINE... FINALLY, OUR TRAIN GIVES A POWERFUL LURCH FORWARD, AND, I THINK I CAN, I THINK I CAN, I KNOW I CAN... YO. WE'RE OUT OF ATLANTA!

JACKSONVILLE: THE PUNK ROCK BOWLING ALLEY, JIMMY THE TRAMP, BEANS AND MORE...

WE HITCH HIKED ACROSS JACKSONVILLE, FROM THE WAY NORTH WEST SIDE, WHERE OUR CSX TRAIN DROVE US OFF, TO THE WAY SOUTHEAST SIDE, WHERE THE FLORIDA EAST COAST YARD AND THE TRAINS HEADIN' HOME WERE. WE GOT A RIDE FROM A NICE OLD GUY WHO JUST HAPPENED TO BE GOIN' ABOUT A BLOCK FROM THE YARD. HE POINTED OUT THE BRIDGE THAT WENT OVER IT, AND DROPPED US OFF BY A SUPERMARKET UP THE STREET AND WE WERE TOTALLY HAPPY TO BE WHERE WE NEEDED TO BE. WE GOT FOOD AND STOLE JUICE AND GOT A SHOPPING CART TO HAUL OUR STUFF AROUND IN. AS SOON AS WE STARTED PUSHIN' THE OLE CART, A GUY STOPPED HIS TRUCK AND GAVE US 5 BUCKS, SO I GUESS WE LOOKED ESPECIALLY DESPARATE, OR MAYBE ESPECIALLY BRAVE. WE USED THE CASH TO LIVE IT UP WITH LIME-AID AND COKES AT THE MR. BURGER AND FRIES. IT WAS A MELLOW SATURDAY AFTERNOON THERE AT THE MR. B. AND F. JUST SHOOTIN' THE SHIT AND LISTENING TO THE TWO OLD, ORIENTAL GUYS WHO RAN THE PLACE TALK ABOUT THE MOVIE "COMA" AND DRINK BEER, BEHIND THE COUNTER, WITH THIS OLD, BLACK GUY, IN A MAILMAN UNIFORM.

THEN, WE WENT DOWN TO THE BRIDGE OVER THE YARD, HID OUR STUFF, AND HOPPED A WALL INTO THE YARD TO SEE HOW TO GET OUR TRAIN HOME. WE HAD ONLY WALKED ABOUT A HALF MILE, WHEN WE CAME UPON SOME CONDUCTORS IN AN ENGINE WHO TOLD US THAT WE WERE, BASICALLY, RIGHT AT THE SPOT, THAT A TRAIN TO MIAMI WOULD LEAVE FROM IN 4 OR 5 HOURS. EVERYTHING WAS FALLING INTO PLACE.

WE WENT BACK UNDER THE BRIDGE, WHERE THERE WAS A GREAT COUCH/HOME SET-UP, IN A SHADY AREA, SOME 50 YARDS LONG. THERE WAS ALSO AWESOME GRAFFITTI (THAT WE ADDED TO, OF COURSE) AND MORE 99¢ QUART BEER BOTTLES THAN I'D EVER SEEN IN ONE PLACE IN MY ENTIRE LIFE. THE BEST GRAFFITTI THERE WAS A SMALL STRIP OF PICTURES IN A ROW, STARTING WITH A GUN SHOOTING BULLETS, THEN A GUY RUNNING, A GUY SWINGING ON A VINE, THEN A PICTURE OF A HEROIC LOOKIN' GUY'S FACE, THEN A GUY WITH A JETPACK ON HIS BACK FLYIN' AND SHOOTIN' A RAYGUN, THEN ANOTHER GUN, A STERN, EVIL KRUSCHEV-LOOKIN' GUY, THEN A SUBMARINE, THEN A GUY SWIMMING! IT WAS THIS WHOLE CRAZY MINI-ADVENTURE COMIC WITH NO WORDS! WE SET UP 10 BOTTLES AT A TIME, IN A LINE, AND HAD THE PUNK ROCK BOWLING ALLEY, ROLLING QUARTS AT 'EM, AT HIGH SPEEDS, FOR THE MIGHTY SOUND OF EXPLODING GLASS!!! YO! WE QUIT, THOUGH, WHEN THE GUY WHO LIVED UNDER THE BRIDGE CAME HOME. HIS NAME WAS JIMMY AND HE'D HOPPED TRAINS FROM TEXAS AND ENDED UP IN

J-VILLE. WE GAVE HIM 3 FOODSTAMPS AND TRAIN INFO. AND HE GAVE US 2 WARM BEERS (WHICH WE'D SAVE FOR THE TRIP HOME) AND A BOTTLE OF DUMPSTERED VITAMINS, WHICH, HE CLAIMS, HE HAS MANAGED TO LIVE ~~OFF~~ EXCLUSIVELY OFF OF, FOR WEEKS, WITH NO FOOD. OK, JIMMY... WHATEVER...

AT 8:00, ME AND IVY WENT TO SCAM MORE COKES FOR THE ROAD, BUT THIS GIRL OUTSIDE OF BURGER KING GAVE IVY 5 MORE BUCKS, SO WE WENT TO SHONEY'S, WHERE IVY LIVED IT UP WITH FRIED OKRA, AND I GOT A TON OF COFFEE. WE BROUGHT JIMMY BACK A BOX OF LEFTOVERS AND HEADED FOR THE YARD, FULL-ON READY TO GO, WHICH IS GOOD, CUZ IT TURNS OUT WE HAD REAL DRAMA AHEAD OF US...

OUR TRAIN WAS NOT PUT TOGETHER YET, SO WE WALKED ON THE FAR SIDE OF THE YARD, ON A LITTLE DIRT PATH BY THE DITCH AND FENCE, FOR A WAYS, THEN CROUCHED IN THE SHADOWS OF A FLATBED TRAIN ON THE FAR TRACK, TOTALLY OUT OF SIGHT, STEALTHY SHIT. THE YARD WAS WELL LIT BUT, IF THE FLAT BED STAYED PUT, WE'D HAVE COVER TO WALK SAFELY, AND THEN, CROSS OVER THAT TRAIN, WHEN WE GOT TO OUR ENGINE. OUR PATH WAS OVERGROWN, WEEDY, AND LOOKED UNUSED BY CARS, SO WE FELT SAFE. OUR TRAIN STARTED LINING UP, AND WE REALIZED WE WERE TOO FAR NORTH IN THE YARD, SO WE SNUK OFF SOUTH, DUCKIN', CROUCHIN' WHEN ENGINES WENT BY, OR WHEN CARS WENT BY ON THE MAINROAD. WE WERE TAKIN' NO CHANCES WITH IVY'S WARRANT STILL IN EFFECT, NEEDIN' TO GET HOME DESPARATELY, CUZ IVY'S REAL SICK, NOW, HACKIN' UP PHLEGM WITH BLOOD IN IT. THEN, WE SEE A CAR WITH ITS LIGHTS OFF, WAY BEHIND US, ON OUR PATH! WE DIVE INTO THE DITCH AND SIT, WHILE THE MOSQUITOS EAT US UP, AND THE ANTS CRAWL ALL OVER US. AND OUR TRAIN IS STILL BEIN' PUT TOGETHER. FINALLY, WE HAVE NO CHOICE, BUT TO GET UP AND RUN FOR IT... BUT THE CAR'S GONE! SO, WE START WALKING REAL FAST TO THE HEAD OF A BIG, ANXIOUS MOFO TRAIN, CHUGGIN' WITH 3 BIG ENGINES, CARRYIN' A MILE OF AUTO CARS ALL THE WAY DOWN TO MIAMI. WE'RE WALKING AND CROUCHIN' IN THE SHADOW OF THE FLATS, WHEN THE FLAT TRAIN STARTS MOVIN', AND WE'RE SOON TOTALLY EXPOSED IN THE CENTER OF THE YARD! FASTER, FASTER WE WALK, CARRYIN' TONS 'O BAGS, IVY COUGHIN', WHEEZIN', SPIT SHIT. THE TRAIN COP KEEPS DRIVIN' BY OUR TRAIN, SHINING A SPOTLIGHT, AND CRASH! WE HIT THE ROCKS AND WAIT, AND HE GOES BY AND WE GET UP, LOSIN' MORE TIME, GOIN' EVEN FASTER, HALF-RUNNIN', 'TIL WE'RE AT THE HEAD OF THE YARD. THE FENCE NOW GROWS FROM 5 FEET TO 15 FEET TALL, BARBWIRED, AND I SWEAR I HEAR STRAY DOGS IN THE SWAMP BEYOND, BARKIN', NO SHIT, AND WE'RE TOTALLY RAMBO-STYLE NOW, WITH NO WAY OUT! THEN, OUR TRAIN CA-CHUNKS INTO MOTION, AND WE'RE NOWHERE NEAR THE FRONT. WE BREAK INTO A FULL RUN, ONLY TO HIT THE ROCKS AGAIN WHEN THE TRAIN COP GOES BY, AND THEN WE'RE UP, JUMP, RUN, JUMP AND RUN, WITH UNRIDABLE AUTOMOBILE CARRIERS THE ONLY CARS ON THE TRAIN, WE HAVE TO MAKE THE ENGINE TO RIDE AT ALL, AND THE TRAIN COP STOPS AHEAD, WITH HIS HEADLIGHTS SHININ' ON THE FRONT OF THE TRAIN, SO IF WE DON'T GET ON AND OUT, WE STAND THERE, IN THE SPOTLIGHT, WAITING TO BE ARRESTED. YO! HOME OR 21 DAYS! WE'RE FULL ON RUNNIN', STUMBLIN', WHEEZIN', BLOOD SPITTIN', BAGS BREAKIN' AND I FEEL WATER ON MY LEG AND SMELL THAT IT'S THE BEERS SPLITTIN' OPEN IN MY BAG. FINALLY, WE COME RIGHT UP TO THE ENGINE, BUT THERE'S A BRAKEMAN STANDIN' RIGHT THERE! WE WAIT, BEFORE HE SEES US, PANTIN', HEART BREAKIN', FUK, SHIT, HE WON'T MOVE, SO... HERE GOES! IVY CLAMBERS ON UP PAST HIM AND I FOLLOW, AND WE'RE HITTIN' THE WALL, ITS ALL BREAKIN' UP INTO THIS ONE MOMENT, HOME, OR, JAIL, AND OUR STUFF'S UP AND, YO! WE'RE ON THE TRAIN! IT FELT SO HARDCORE! BUT, IT WAS A SHORT RIDE...

AS SOON AS WE GET IN THE ENGINE, WE HEAR ON THE RADIO, "YEAH. WE GOT A COUPLE HOBOS ON THERE... LET'S PICK 'EM OFF..."

SCAM PUNKS GOIN' HOME!

SO THERE WE WERE, NOWHERE TO RUN, AND I WAS ADDIN' UP 21 DAYS IN MY HEAD TO SEE IF I'D BE IN JAIL ON MY BIRTHDAY. BUT TO MAKE A LONG STORY A LITTLE SHORTER, THE TRAIN COP JUST LET US GO, SAYIN' HE FELT SORRY FOR US AND WISHES WE HAD BEEN ON THE TRAIN. WE WISHED HE WAS UNDER IT. WE JUST HITCHED HOME ON I-95. I WAS BUMMED CUZ I WANTED TO SEE MY OLD HOME TOWNS OF FT. LAUDERDALE AND BOCA BY TRAIN, BUT WE HAD TO GET HOME.

IT WAS 2:00 A.M. AND THE ONLY CARS OUT IN J-VILLE WERE COPS, SO WE WENT TO WAFFLE HOUSE TO FLY THE "MIAMI" SIGN. BUT, WHEN WE SIT DOWN, WE REALIZE WE NEITHER WANT NOR CAN AFFORD COFFEE. SO, IN A RARE MOMENT OF CRUELTY, WE USED OUR LAST ~~25~~ QUARTER TO PLAY THE WAFFLE HOUSE SONG ON THE JUKEBOX! WE ESCAPED OUT THE DOOR JUST AS THE "WE THANK YOU!"'S STARTED FULL-ON AND THE HELPLESS PATRONS REALIZED IN HORROR WHAT WAS HAPPENING TO THEM. WE GOT A RIDE TO DAYTONA BY SUNUP, AND WERE STUCK THERE SO LONG THAT WE MADE A SIGN WITH A BIG MASONS LOGO ON IT, TO HOLD UP. NOW, LET'S SEE WHO SECRETLY CONTROLS THE WORLD! WELL, IT DIDN'T SEEM TO HELP, BUT FINALLY WE GOT HOME. ALL 4 RIDES WERE WITH RAILROAD WORKERS. IVY SAID THEY OWED US...

AFTER THE TRIP, I FELT SO TOUGH. THE TRAIN PART WAS SO EXCITING AND ALL THE BAD STUFF HAD HELPED ME PROVE A LOT OF STUFF TO MYSELF. AT A CERTAIN POINT, I'D MADE THE DECISION TO LIVE THE WAY I DO, AND I ALWAYS KNEW THAT THE HOMELESSNESS, AND JAIL, AND ALL THAT WAS OUT THERE WAITING FOR ME. IT WAS A GREAT RELIEF TO DEAL WITH THESE THINGS AND SEE THEY WEREN'T SO BAD... IN DELRAY BEACH, WE CALLED BECKY FUNN TO COME GET US, AND STOLE ICE CREAM AND SAT IN THE SHADE TELLING OUR LONG, CRAZY STORIES. ICE CREAM, GOOD FRIENDS, GOOD STORIES... I WAS HOME! AND, FINALLY, MORE AT HOME WITH MYSELF...

DAILY PLANET
AND THE MIAMI FREE PRESS   25¢

A ROZZER OF DROPSY

CHURCH NEWS

PARK RESURRECTION

SOCIAL CONDEMNING VALUE

IN SNIDE

Vol. II No. II Sept. 11 — Sept. 26   *All the news unfit to print*   Outside Florida **35¢**

UPS LNS   *application for 2nd class mailing permit pending Miami, Fla.*   Smut

PARK IS LIBERATED

FROM FOOLS ON THE HILL

COCONUT GROVE PARK WAS LIBERATED FROM THE POLICE LAST SUNDAY, BUT ONLY DUE TO THE PRESENCE OF THE MASS MEDIA.

AN ESTIMATED 600 PEOPLE ATTENDED THE FIRST MUSICAL LOVE-IN SINCE CITY MANAGER MELVIN REESE ORDERED A POLICE CRACKDOWN ON "HIPPIES" IN THE PARK.

"I GUESS THIS SHOWS ELIZABETH BETTNER WHERE IT'S AT," SAID PRESS/PLANET PUBLISHER JERRY POWERS OVER THE MIKE SUNDAY. THE ENTIRE CROWD CHEERED. MRS. BETTNER, (LIZZIE) WAS THE WOMAN WHO BROUGHT CHARGES OF INDECENT CONDUCT AGAINST THE PEOPLE USING THE PARK ON WEEKENDS. SHE FORCED REESE AND THE POLICE TO START THEIR "CLEAN UP" CAMPAIGN. Continued on page 2

Pt. 6: RETURN TO THE MUTINY!

BOXING IN THE STREETS · CHEAP RED WINE · BLACKENED VOODOO.
BIKE WRECKS · BAGELS NOT BOMBS · RATS · ROLLER SKATES
WATERMELONS · SCAM AT SEA · CASTRO · LENNY

BACK TO THE BAY

THIS PHOTO IS THE VIEW OF THE MARINA FROM THE MUTINY BALCONY AT NIGHT TIME ↑

"THE BAY FED AND HOUSED AND CLOTHED ITS PEOPLE. IT CAST UP VIA THE WRECKS OFF THE REEF FLORIDA REEF EVERYTHING FROM A GRAND PIANO TO SILK SHAWLS AND A FANCY CARRIAGE. NOBODY WAS EVER SURPRISED, ONLY PLEASED, AT WHAT THE SEA WASHED IN. INTO THE SUN-SPLASHED ISOLATION ONE DAY FLOATED A RAILROAD FREIGHT CAR. THE PEOPLE OF CUTLER, SOUTH OF THE GROVE, EYED IT SPECULATIVELY, THEN TURNED IT INTO A POST OFFICE... HURRICANE WEATHER WAS A PURE LARK. A GOOD HURRICANE WOULD WASH IN PLENTY OF WRECKAGE: CHEESE AND CANDLES, SOAP AND BAGS OF FLOUR, FINE OLD WINES AND WHISKEY. YOU NEVER KNEW WHEN YOU GOT UP IN THE MORNING, WHAT THE BAY WOULD WASH IN BEFORE SUNDOWN..."
— HELEN MUIR, WRITING IN "MIAMI, U.S.A." ABOUT THE EARLY COCONUT GROVE SETTLERS.

IT WAS GOOD TO BE BACK IN THE MUTINY, BACK TO THE BAY. THAT GREAT MUTINY VIEW HADN'T CHANGED, BUT EVERYTHING ELSE IN THE MUTINY WAS DIFFERENT. WHILE I WAS GONE, TIM AND BUDDHA HAD MOVED OUT AND HAD GONE BACK TO THEIR PARENT'S HOUSES. LEFT UNATTENDED, THE SQUAT HAD BEEN BROKEN INTO AND EVERYTHING WAS STOLEN — THE RADIO, MY TAPES (WHY DO THEY ALWAYS TAKE ALL THE TAPES? ARE THE SQUAT THIEVES INTO THE DICKIES AND SOCIAL DISTORTION, TOO? SHEESH.), MY SLINGSHOT, MY JAMES BOND SCAM PHONE, MY CAMERA, MY SCISSORS, AND EVEN MY BASKETBALL THAT I'D TRADED A COUPLE SHITTY STOOGES TAPES TO BOOD FOR BACK IN '88. NO MORE LATENIGHT, BAREFOOT B-BALL AT THE COURTS UNDER THE METRO-RAIL AT DOUGLAS ROAD... MY LAYOUT AND ZINE STUFF WAS DUMPED OUT AND HAD ALL LONG SINCE BLOWN AWAY AND WAS GONE FOREVER. ROTTEN FOOD WAS EVERYWHERE, AND THE RATS HAD TAKEN OVER.... IT WAS REALLY SAD TO SEE MY HOME DISRESPECTED LIKE THAT, BUT IT WAS ALSO GOOD, MAYBE, TO MAKE A NEW START. AFTER THE LONG, CRAZY TRIP HOME FROM ATLANTA, IT FELT LIKE WE WERE WEARY WAGON TRAIN SETTLERS, WHO'D TRAVELED THOUSANDS OF MILES, TO THIS GOOD PLACE BY THE WATER TO REST AND MAKE OUR HOME.

WE WENT TO WORK, MAKING THE MUTINY A HOME AGAIN, WITH KIND OF A NEW ATTITUDE. WE DIDN'T GO OUT OF OUR WAY TO REPLACE THE STUFF THAT WAS THERE BEFORE, OR GO STEAL A LOT OF NEW STUFF FOR THE PLACE. IT SEEMED KINDA EMPTY FEELIN', LIKE STUFF IS JUST STUFF, WHETHER YOU BUY IT OR STEAL IT. WE DIDN'T WANT TO ALWAYS FEEL A NEED FOR SOMETHING MORE, OR TO MAKE LIFE TOO COMPLICATED. OF COURSE, I THINK ITS BETTER TO STEAL STUFF THAN BUY IT, IF YOU CAN, BUT ITS ALSO GOOD TO WONDER WHY YOU NEED IT AT ALL. ALSO, IVY WAS SICK AND NEEDED TO RELAX MORE, SO THAT SET THE TONE. I WANTED TO SLOW DOWN A LITTLE AND APPRECIATE WHAT WAS THERE — THE SUMMER, THE CITY, MY FRIENDS — AND TO TAKE MY TIME AND SIT BACK IN THE MUTINY AND WATCH THE BAY AND SEE WHAT WASHED UP.

IVY'S MOM GAVE US A HEADSTART BY DONATING AN OLD TAPE PLAYER AND A SMALL STERNO STOVE, AND THEN WE STARTED TO KINDA JUST FIND STUFF, AND WHATEVER WE FOUND, WE USED. I FOUND A TOUGH, OLD WOOD TABLE AND BROUGHT IT UP TO THE MUTINY, FOR THE NEW SCAM OFFICE. I "FOUND" A COUPLE OF THOSE BIG, 3-GALLON, CONSTRUCTION SIGHT WATER COOLERS ON THE BACK OF A COUPLE SOUTHERN BELL TRUCKS, AND BROUGHT 'EM UP TO THE SQUAT TO STORE WATER IN. AND, ONE DAY, IVY AND I WERE WALKIN' BY

THIS BAR, AND THE SIDE DOOR WAS OPEN, AND A BARB-B-QUE GRILL WAS ON THE SIDEWALK, THERE. IVY SAYS, "HEY, LET'S TAKE IT." SO WE LOOKED BOTH WAYS, AND, UH... CROSSED THE STREET WITH IT... I'M STILL NOT SURE WHETHER IT WAS TRASH, OR IF WE STOLE IT. THEN, THROUGH SOME MAGIC COMBINATION OF DUCT TAPE, ROPE, AND PUNK ROCK DETERMINATION, WE MANAGED TO GET THE HUGE, SOOTY OLE THING UP ONTO THE 2ND FLOOR BALCONY, AND THEN CARRIED IT UP THE 12 FLIGHTS OF STAIRS TO COOK ON. HAVING TO DRAG EVERYTHING UP THE 12 FLIGHTS OF STAIRS WAS KIND OF COOL. IT MADE YOU FEEL PRETTY TOUGH...

I MADE MY OFFICE THERE ON THE 12TH FLOOR, AWAY FROM THE BAY, ON THE FAR SIDE OF THE MUTINY. I PUT THE BIG, WOOD TABLE BY THE WINDOW, WHERE I COULD LOOK DOWN ON THE CHAMBER OF COMMERCE AND THE COPS, THOSE HELPLESS ANTS, AT ALL TIMES, AND PLOT THE OVERTHROW OF THE EXISTING CITY GOVERNMENT. THERE WERE NAILS IN THE WALL WHERE I COULD HANG MY COOL, OLD GUY HAT AND MY UMBRELLA. AT NIGHT, I'D FIRE UP THE KEROSENE LAMP, ALL OILY AND SMOKY, AND DRINK GOOD, STRONG TEA AND LISTEN TO THE RAIN SPLASH IN FROM THE HOLE IN THE ROOF, AND READ, AND WRITE AND WATCH THE STREETS. PEOPLE HEADING TOWARDS BARS WAS 2:00 A.M. SMALL GROUPS OF PEOPLE YELLING, CLAPPING, OR FISTFIGHTING WAS 3:00 A.M. AND, FINALLY, THE EMPTY STREETS WAS 4:00 A.M., AND TIME TO LEAVE AND RIDE MY BIKE 'TIL THE SUNRISE...

THE OFFICE WAS GREAT, BUT THE BEST THING ABOUT THE NEW MUTINY WAS WHEN WE WE HAD OUR FIRST BIG FEAST. IVY AND I WOKE UP IN THE AFTERNOON, ONE DAY, AND DECIDED TO MAKE A BIG SOUP. THE PROCESS TOOK ALL DAY. WE SPLIT UP AND WENT UP AND DUMPSTERED A LITTLE OF THIS, AND STOLE A LITTLE OF THAT, AND BEGGED UP SOME KEY INGREDIANTS AT THE BACK DOORS OF SOME GROVE RESTAURANTS, AND THEN MET BACK UP AT THE SQUAT TO PUT IT ALL TOGETHER AND SEE WHAT WE'D GOT. IT TURNED OUT THAT WE WERE HAVING CARROT AND POTATO AND MUSHROOM NOODLE SOUP, WITH FRIED PLANTANOS, CORN BREAD CAKES, AND ½ A BOTTLE OF RED WINE! IT WAS TOTAL HUNTER AND GATHERER STYLE. WE DIDN'T DO IT EVERYDAY, BUT I REALLY DID LIKE THAT REAL BASIC APPROACH TO LIFE, LIKE SPENDING A LOT OF TIME FINDING AND PREPARING AND MAKING FOOD — FOOD FOR SURVIVAL. IT MADE YOU REALLY APPRECIATE THE FOOD AND THE LIFE IT PROVIDED, AND THE COLD WATER SWIRLIN' INTO YOUR CUP, OUT OF THE COOLER, WAS VALUABLE, CUZ THERE WAS SO LITTLE OF IT... AT THE LAST MINUTE, WE'D REALIZED WE'D FORGOTTEN TO GET BUTTER, SO I WENT BACK OUT, TO TRY AND BUM SOME OFF CAFE SCI SCI, AND SAW BY THE LIBRARY DUMPSTER, TWO UNOPENED BEERS! ONE FOR ME, AND ONE FOR IVY! WHEN I CAME BACK WITH THE BUTTER AND BEER, IT WAS AFTER DARK, AND IVY WAS WEARIN' HER TRUCKER HAT AND HER BEST, BLUE DRESS, AND SINGIN' ALONG TO HER BLUES TAPES AND DANCIN' AROUND, LIGHTIN' CANDLES. THE FOOD WAS ALMOST DONE. SHALL WE EAT OUT ON THE BALCONY TONIGHT? WHY NOT? I PUT ON MY COOL, OLD GUY HAT AND WE ATE AND ATE AND SIPPED OUR WINE ON THE BALCONY, IN THE COOL BREEZE AND CANDLELIGHT... THE MUTINY WAS HOME AGAIN. AND IT WAS FRIDAY NIGHT IN COCONUT GROVE AND WE WERE OVERLOOKING HUNDREDS OF PEOPLE BELOW US. IT WAS CRAZY HOW ALL THESE PEOPLE SEE THIS BIG, DARK BUILDING AND WOULD NEVER GUESS WHAT WAS REALLY GOIN' ON UP HERE — PEOPLE LIVIN', LAUGHIN', LOVIN', ETC... WE WERE THE TRUE UNDERGROUND!

IVY AND I WERE STILL THE ONLY ONES WHO LIVED FULLTIME IN THE MUTINY, BUT TIM AND SCOTT HUNG OUT A LOT, WRITING SONGS WITH IVY AND FILLIN' THE 12TH FLOOR WITH MUSIC. BECKY FUNN, THE MUTINY HEAD CHEF, HUNG OUT FOR DAYS AT A TIME. SHE WENT TO COOKING SCHOOL SO SHE ADVANCED THE BIG FEASTS TO MORE AMBITIOUS PROJECTS, LIKE CREAMY GARLIC SAUCE OVER POTATOES AND SPINACH, PASTA, TOMATO SAUCE AND MOZZARELLA. RAFAEL, KENDALL'S OWN GUITAR HERO, CAME OVER SOMETIMES TO BUY BEER WITH MONEY HE'D FOUND IN CLOTHES AT THE DRY CLEANERS HE WORKED AT, AND TO LISTEN TO THE RAMONES. IVY'S MOM EVEN STAYED THE NIGHT, ONE NIGHT, WHEN SHE GOT IN A FIGHT WITH HER BOYFRIEND. SHE HELPED IVY SWEEP AND CLEAN, LISTENED TO MUSIC, AND WENT WITH IVY IN THE MORNING TO ST. HUGHES CHURCH FOR THE FREE FOOD BOX...

IT WAS GOOD TO HAVE SUCH A CRAZY HOME, AND STILL BE ABLE TO HAVE ALL OUR FRIENDS OVER, BUT THERE WERE UNINVITED GUESTS, TOO — THE RATS! THEY WERE INSANE! IVY WANTED TO KILL 'EM, BUT I HAD A LOT OF RESPECT FOR THEM, CUZ THEY COULD CLIMB WALLS AND CHEW THROUGH JUST ABOUT ANYTHING. THEY WERE LIKE THE PUNKS AND WE WERE THE YUPPIES AND THEY WANTED OUR FOOD! ONE TIME, WE HEARD A KNOCK AT THE DOOR, AND I OPENED IT TO SEE THIS BIG, WOODEN RAT. IVY GOES, "OH, HOW SWEET! THEY MADE US A BIG RAT!" AND STARTED TO WHEEL IT IN, BUT I YELLED, "IVY! NO!"

WO CLOSED THE DOOR. IT WAS A TROJAN RAT! STILL, THE RATS WERE USEFUL, TOO. I MAILED RAT TURDS TO FOOD COMPANIES, TELLING 'EM THAT THE TURD WAS IN MY FOOD, AND GOT FREE STUFF. AND, ONCE, I FOUND A DEAD RAT AND LEFT IT INSIDE THE JOHNNY ROCKET'S HAMBURGER PLACE. THEIR MANAGER HAD BEEN A LITTLE UPPITY, YELLING AT IVY FOR TABLE DIVING. IT WAS TIME TO SHOW 'EM THAT THE MUTINY PUNKS WERE BACK!

MY TOUGH FUCKIN' BIKE !!!

THERE'S NOWHERE TO GO. GETTIN' THERE IS THE FUN. GETTIN' THERE IN A CAR USUALLY SUCKS, SO I'M REALLY INTO BIKES, AND I ALWAYS SEEM TO HAVE A GOOD ONE. MY PURPLE GIRLS' BIKE GOT STOLEN FROM DADELAND SOUTH METRO-RAIL. SOMEONE ACTUALLY CUT MY LOCK! WELL THEY CAN HAVE THE BIKE, BUT I BET THEY CAN'T RIDE IT MOST OF THE WAY TO TAMPA! THERE IS A SPECIAL ROOM IN HELL FOR BIKE THIEVES, YES.

I WAS BUMMIN' WITHOUT A BIKE, BUT THEN I SAW THAT THE BIKE I'D FOUND IN AN ABANDONED BUILDING, UNDER A PILE OF RUBBLE, IN BOCA, WAS JUST SITTIN' UP AT CHUCK LOOSE'S PLACE, ALL LONELY AND PROUD AND READY TO SING — POETRY UNWRITTEN — SO I BROUGHT IT TO THE MUTINY. SINCE I DIDN'T HAVE A LOCK AT FIRST, I CARRIED IT UP 12 FLIGHTS OF STAIRS TO RIDE AROUND THE SQUAT! I EVEN LEARNED A COOL STUNT, WHERE I'D RIDE REAL FAST, THEN GRAB ONTO ONE OF THE PIPES HANGIN' FROM THE CEILING, AND THE BIKE WOULD KEEP GOIN' WITHOUT ME, FOR 10 FEET, OR SO, THEN WRECK. DIDN'T I TELL YA IT WAS TOUGH?

I GOT A LOCK, AND WAS ALMOST READY TO TAKE MY NEW, TOUGH BIKE OUT ON THE MEAN STREETS 'O MIAMI, BUT FIRST I CUT UP AN OLD INNER-TUBE AND STRUNG IT ACROSS THE HANDLEBARS FOR A D.I.Y. SLINGSHOT! THERE'S NO BIKE LANES IN MIAMI, AND TONS OF TRAFFIC, SO YOU HAVE TO BE PREPARED TO DEFEND YOURSELF. ONE TIME, SOME STOOPIT CAR CUT ME OFF AND MADE ME WRECK AND I ALMOST THREW MY BIKE THROUGH THEIR WINDSHIELD! FUCKERS!

NOW, I WAS READY. I'D RIDE MY TOUGH BIKE ALL NIGHT, THROUGH 4:00 A.M. STREETS, THROUGH DESERTED DOWNTOWN, SHOOTIN' BETWEEN SKYSCRAPERS, AND UP TO THE PRODUCE DISTRICT, AND PAST THE JUNKYARDS, ALONG THE MIAMI RIVER, AND INTO THE TOUGH NEIGHBORHOODS WHERE THE STRAY DOGS ON THE CORNER, WOULD CHASE ME OFF THEIR BLOCK. MY TOUGH BIKE ALWAYS GOT AWAY! IT WAS FUNNY, THOUGH. IT WAS LIKE THE STRAY DOGS WORKED THE GRAVEYARD SHIFT ON THE CORNER, WHILE THE LOCAL HOODS SLEPT. THEN, I'D HEAD DOWN TO RICH CORAL GABLES' DUMPSTERS AND GOLF COURSES. ON A GOLF COURSE, YOU CAN'T REALLY SEE THE GROUND AT NIGHT, SO ITS LIKE RIDING YOUR BIKE IN SPACE! YOU GO UP AND DOWN ALL THOSE LITTLE HILLS, ALL ROLLERCOASTERIN' AND YELLIN' OUT, AND THEN, YOUR AIRBORN, ALLASUDDEN, AND WRECKIN' IN THE SANDTRAP! YOU CAN ALSO WRITE HUGE MESSAGES, 15 FEET ACROSS, IN THE SAND, LIKE, "SO YOU DON'T HAVE ANY SPARE CHANGE, HUH?" THEN, I'D RIDE HOME TO THE GROVE, AS FAST AS I COULD, DOWN ACROSS THE PEACOCK PARK BASEBALL FIELD, AND STRAIGHT TO THE WATER OF BISCAYNE BAY, ACROSS THE STREET FROM THE MUTINY...

ONE DAY, IVY GOT A TOUGH BIKE, TOO. TIM, FROM FAROUT RECORDS, FOUND IT IN A DUMPSTER IN KEY WEST! IT HAD A BASKET AND A BELL WITH A 3-D PICTURE OF A TYRANOSAURUS REX ON IT! GRR! STOMP! YO! IVY STOLE THE NEW TIRES IT NEEDED, AND NOW WE WAS A GANG TEARIN' UP THE STREETS OF THE GROVE. ONE DAY, WHEN WE WERE BIKIN' AROUND, WE FOUND A CRATE OF BANANAS IN A PUBLIX DUMPSTER. WE WERE ABOUT TO LEAVE WITH THE CRATE BALANCED ON MY HANDLEBARS, WHEN I DECIDED TO, FIRST, TRY AND JUMP THIS MAKESHIFT RAMP BEHIND THE STORE. I MADE IT! SOMEHOW, LAUGHIN', ALMOST DYIN', ETC, I MADE IT. BUT THAT WASN'T GOOD ENOUGH! I NEEDED MORE SPEED, MORE DISTANCE TO ACHIEVE TRUE FLIGHT AND THE EFFORTLESS GRACE THAT WE NORMALLY FIND ONLY IN ANIMALS... ANYWAY, IT DIDN'T HURT TOO BAD, THE CRASH. I TOLD IVY TO BEND OVER TO HEAR MY LAST WORDS, BUT SHE KICKED ME AND MADE ME GET UP AND GO TO THE HOSPITAL, CUZ I WAS BLEEDIN' A TINY BIT FROM THE HEAD. I GAVE THE HOSPITAL A FAKE NAME AND MADE 'EM RUN ALL SORTS OF X-RAYS, AND I WAS O.K. SO GOES MY CAREER AS A COCONUT GROVE EVEL KNIEVEL...

AFTER I LEFT THE HOSPITAL, I WENT TO SCAM A COKE AT MCDONALD'S AND WHEN I CAME OUT, NOT 3 MINUTES LATER, MY BIKE WAS GONE. SHE LEFT ME! NOT EVEN A NOTE! I GUESS I SHOULD NEVER HAVE MISTREATED HER ON GRAND AVENUE FOR 8 BUCKS! OH WELL... BUT THEN, TIMMY SAID I COULD HAVE HIS BIKE, THAT VERY SAME NIGHT! IT WAS A TOUGH ONE, TOO, BUT I GUESS THEY ALL ARE. IT WAS AN ALL-STRIPPED DOWN, BASIC BLACK BEAUTY, AND I RODE IT ALL THE WAY FROM P.S.N. TO LITTLE HAVANA (18 MILES) IN ONE HOUR! YO! I PUT THOSE BANANAS ON THE HANDLEBARS, AT SCOTTY'S HOUSE, AND ME AND IVY AND THE TYRANNOSAURUS REX AND MY NEW, TOUGH BIKE RODE HOME...

15 CANS OF SIMILAC! ∧ FABLE...

WHEN WRITING ABOUT ALL THE STUFF THAT ME AND IVY HAVE STOLEN, OR WHATEVER, I DON'T WANT TO GIVE PEOPLE THE IMPRESSION THAT WE NEVER GET CAUGHT, THAT WE'RE SUPERHEROS OR SOMETHING. SOMETIMES WE DO GET CAUGHT, AND SOMETIMES, IT'S EVEN WORSE...

ONE DAY, I NEEDED A LITTLE SPENDING MONEY, SO I WENT TO DO THE RECEIPT SCAM AT THE WINN-DIXIE ON N.W. 7TH AND DOUGLAS ROAD. INNOCENTLY, I PICKED A RECEIPT UP OFF THE GROUND THAT LOOKED LIKE A GOLD MINE. IT HAD 15 CANS OF SIMILAC, THE BABY FORMULA ON IT! AT $2.15 A CAN, I'D MAKE WELL OVER 30 BUCKS! I WENT IN THE STORE AND SCOOPED PRACTICALLY A WHOLE SHELF OF SIMILAC INTO A WINN-DIXIE BAG, AND WENT TO "RETURN" IT. I WAS JUST ABOUT TO BE HANDED THE LOOT, WHEN THE CASHIER STOPPED AND SAID, "OH, WAIT. SORRY, SIR. YOU CAN'T GET A REFUND IN CASH FOR THIS, CUZ IT WAS PAID FOR WITH A W.I.C. (GOVERNMENT WELFARE FOR POOR MOTHERS TO BUY BABY FOOD WITH) CHECK. YOU CAN ONLY EXCHANGE IT FOR A DIFFERENT KIND OF SIMILAC..."

OUTSIDE THE STORE, I STOPPED AND CONSIDERED MY NEW BAG FOR A GOOD LONG WHILE. WHAT HAD GONE WRONG? I WAS NOW THE OWNER OF ALL THIS SIMILAC. FIFTEEN CANS, APPARENTLY WORTHLESS... BUT, I COULDN'T JUST LEAVE IT BEHIND, COULD I?

I MUST HAVE DRAGGED THAT DOOMED SACK OF SIMILAC ON MY BIKE TO TEN DIFFERENT STORES, ALL OVER MIAMI SWEATING BUCKETS AND MUMBLING CRAZILY IN THE SOUTH FLORIDA HEAT AND ANGRILY SHAKING MY FISTS AT THE SUN, THE BLANK SKY, THE CRUEL GODS... AT EACH STORE IT WAS THE SAME THING "YOU CAN ONLY EXCHANGE THESE, SIR..." MY LIFE HAD SUDDENLY GONE WRONG. MY HEART WAS HEAVY AND I SANG THE BLUES:

"I'SE GOT TROUBLE BY DA TRUCKLOAD AND A BAD LUCK BY DA SACK.
I SAYS I GOTS TROUBLE BY DA TRUCKLOAD AND A BAD LUCK BY DA SACK.
THINGS JESS AIN'T BEEN RIGHT, SINCE I GOT ALL DAT SIMILAC..."

FINALLY, A BROKEN MAN, I MADE MY WAY TO SKID ROW, TO THE POOR SIDE OF THE GROVE, TO GIVE AWAY MY SIMILAC. I PEDALED SLOWLY UP AND DOWN THE STREETS, LIKE A FALLEN ICE CREAM MAN, UNTIL I FOUND SOME KIDS. IT MUST'VE BEEN PRETTY WEIRD — THIS SWEATY MANIAC WITH A BIG BAG OF BABY FOOD, ALL FOR FREE, BUT THEY SAID THEIR MOM WOULD USE IT AND TOOK IT, AND, AT LAST, I WAS FREE...

BARNEY VS. THE U.S.S. HELLSPAWN!

THE MUTINY WAS REAL COMFORTABLE. I COULD FORGET IT WAS A SQUAT, PRETTY EASY, WHEN I WOKE UP IN THE MORNING. I'D ALWAYS YAWN, PISS, STRETCH, PUT ON SOME CUBAN COFFEE (WE'D STOLEN A STOVE TOP (WBAND MAKER) AND IT'D BE KINDA LIKE THE ROUTINE "NORMAL" PEOPLE GO THROUGH, I GUESS, BUT THEN A PIGEON WOULD COME FLAPPIN' BY ME, AND I'D REALIZE THAT I BETTER GO CHECK ON IVY, MAKE SURE THE RATS HADN'T CARRIED HER OFF IN THE NIGHT... STILL, WE GOT JUST ABOUT EVERYTHING FOR FREE, WE HAD THAT BALCONY VIEW, AND I SPENT SO MUCH TIME JUST LAYIN' OUT BY THE POOL, THAT IT FELT LIKE WE WERE FILTHY RICH. AND, IN A WAY, I GUESS WE WERE. WE HAD EVERYTHING. WE HAD NOTHING. IT WAS ALL THE SAME. THERE WAS NOTHING TO DO BUT PUT ON SOME TEA, AND SEE WHAT BREWED UP.

ONE DAY, WE HAD JUST WOKE UP — ME, IVY, BECKY, AND TIMMY, AND WE'RE MAKIN' SOME TEA, AND HANGIN' OUT. ANOTHER ONE OF THOSE TERRIBLE COCONUT GROVE FESTIVALS WAS GOIN' ON ACROSS THE STREET, IN PEACOCK PARK, AND THERE WAS SOME REALLY AWFUL JAZZ BAND ON A STAGE BLASTING BAD MUSIC INTO OUR SQUAT. BUT, THEN IT GOT WORSE. BARNEY, THE PURPLE DINOSAUR, TOOK THE STAGE! HIS VOICE WAS BOOMING OVER THE P.A. INTO OUR HOME! "I LOVE YOU, KIDS!" AAARGH! WE HAD TO STOP HIM! IVY ESPECIALLY HATES BARNEY, AND SHE QUICKLY SCRAWLED ANTI-BARNEY MESSAGES ON ANY PAPER AVAILABLE AND MADE US ALL LEAVE THE MUTINY AND RUN OUT INTO THE STREETS TO PROTEST BARNEY. SO, HERE I AM, 15 MINUTES OUT OF BED, STORMING THROUGH A HUGE CROWD OF PARENTS, HOLDING A PAPER PLATE THAT SAID, "BARNEY IS A TOOL OF THE DEVIL!", WHILE IVY LED THE WAY, YELLIN' "STOP HIM! STOP BARNEY! HE'S RUINING OUR KIDS!" SHE WAS HEADING RIGHT TOWARDS THE STAGE. "GOOD GOD," I MUTTERED TO MYSELF, "SHE'S GOING TO ASSASSINATE BARNEY!" BUT, BEFORE WE COULD WEED OUR WAY THROUGH TO THE STAGE, BARNEY WAS FINISHED, AND HIS HANDLERS WHISKED HIM AWAY. WE COULDN'T FIND HIM ANYWHERE. IVY WENT UP TO A COP AND DEMANDED, "WHERE'S BARNEY?" THE COP KIND OF CHUCKLED, "OH, HE WENT HOME. BARNEY'S GONE." IVY SAID, "BARNEY'S EVIL. HE'S TEARING APART FAMILIES." THE COP LOOKED REAL UPSET. "WHAT'S WRONG WITH YOU? EVERYBODY LIKES BARNEY..." OBVIOUSLY, THE COP WAS ANOTHER HELPLESS DUPE WHO HAD BEEN WON OVER BY BARNEY'S FRIENDLY, PURPLE BRAND OF FASCISM, WE HAD TO LOOK ELSEWHERE.

BEHIND THE STAGE, THERE WAS NO BARNEY, BUT WE DID SEE THE D.J. FROM LOVE 94 WHO WAS EMCEE-ING THE FESTIVAL. I ASKED HIM FOR SPARE CHANGE. HE WENT AWAY REAL QUICK. WELL, THE SEARCH FOR BARNEY WAS HOPELESS, AND THE D.J. WAS PROBABLY GONNA GET A COP TO BOOT US FROM THE FESTIVAL... THEN, WE FOUND OUR ESCAPE. THE OUTDOOR STAGE WAS RIGHT UP AGAINST THE SHORE OF THE BAY. ON THE ROCKS, ALL WASHED UP AND SAD, WAS A BOAT! WE ALL RAN TO THE ROWBOAT AND STARTED CLEANING IT OUT. THE OARS WERE ON THE ROCKS A FEW FEET AWAY. WE COULDN'T BELIEVE IT. IVY AND I HAD WANTED A BOAT FOR YEARS. WE EVEN WROTE IT ON OUR "THINGS TO DO" LISTS: "MAKE FLYER, DUMP PISS BUCKET, FIND BOAT..." AND NOW, HERE WAS ONE JUST WASHED UP FOR US!

WE DIDN'T SINK AND DIE. THE REST IS GRAVY. WE ROWED OUT TO THE FIRST LITTLE ISLAND IN THE BAY. IT WAS PRETTY CLOSE TO THE SHORE, BUT SEEMED SO DISTANT, AND FAR AWAY AND PEACEFUL WHEN WE GOT TO IT. IT WAS DESERTED — JUST TREES AND PARTS OF WRECKED BOATS. IF WE'D HAVE HAD TREASURE, WE WOULD HAVE BURIED IT. IT WAS A REAL HOT DAY

AND WE WERE CRASHIN' THROUGH THE TREES ALL JUNGLE EXPLORER STYLE, LOOKIN' FOR THE BEST FUTURE PICNIC SPOT, THE BEST FUTURE BURYIN' TREASURE SPOT, THE BEST FUTURE MAKIN' OUT SPOT, THE BEST FUTURE FISHIN' SPOT, THE BEST FUTURE CAMPFIRE SPOT, ETC., JUST MAKIN' ALL SORTS OF CRAZY PLANS THAT WE'D PROBABLY NEVER GET AROUND TO CARRYIN' OUT, NOT THAT IT REALLY MATTERED. WE RESTED ON A WRECK IN THE SHADE AND LOOKED OUT AT THE HORIZON FOR AWHILE. AH... THE SEA. WE WERE YOUNG. WE HAD BOATS. WHAT ELSE MATTERED? WELL, WE WERE HUNGRY, SO WE DECIDED TO ROW BACK TO LAND, GO RAID THE WENDY'S SALAD BAR, AND COME BACK TO THE ISLAND LATER. WE ROWED TO THE COCONUT GROVE MARINA, TIED UP THE BOAT, WITH THE LITTLE ROPE THAT WAS ALREADY TIED TO IT, AND SPRAY PAINTED "USS HELLSPAWN" ON IT. IT WAS A TOUGH LOOKIN' OLE BOAT, AND I COULDN'T WAIT TO GO OUT AND PUT THE MUTINY FLAG ON THE ISLAND (OR... TO MAKE A MUTINY FLAG, FOR THAT MATTER)

BUT WHEN WE CAME BACK, WE COULDN'T FIND THE BOAT ANYWHERE. THE TIDE HAD GONE OUT. I THOUGHT MAYBE IT HAD JUST WASHED AWAY. BUT, IT HADN'T, BECAUSE WE FINALLY FOUND IT TIED TO THIS MOTORBOAT THAT BELONGED TO THIS WEIRD, INBRED MARINA FAMILY. THEY WERE TRYING TO STEAL OUR BOAT! WE TALKED TO THEM ABOUT IT, BUT THEY CLAIMED IT WAS THEIRS AND THEY HAD JUST BOUGHT IT THAT MORNING. CONVENIENTLY ENOUGH, THEY RAN AROUND THE MARINA TRYING TO PRODUCE WITNESSES, LIKE "HEY, THESE KIDS ARE TRYING TO TAKE THE BOAT I JUST BOUGHT THIS MORNING (WINK WINK) YOU KNOW — THE BLUE ONE..." IT DEGENERATED INTO A SHOUTING MATCH AND I REALIZED, WAIT, WHO NEEDS THE BOAT, IF ITS JUST ONE MORE THING WE'LL HAVE TO WORRY ABOUT, TO HAVE TO PUT A LOCK ON? SO THEY TOOK THE BOAT. I GUESS YA CAN'T REALLY OWN A BOAT, ANYWAYS. YOU JUST BORROW 'EM FOR AWHILE.

OUT IN THE BAY, OUR ISLAND WAS NOW UNREACHABLE AND MYSTERIOUS AGAIN. IT WAS ALL RIGHT, THOUGH. WE'D BEEN THERE ONCE. WE'D GAINED AND LOST IT ALL IN ONE DAY. THE BEST FUTURE PICNIC SPOT REMAINED OFF THE MAP...

THE "BAGELS, NOT BOMBS" MOVEMENT

I OPENED A 2nd OFFICE, OUT OF THE MUTINY, AND OUT IN THE WORLD. IT WAS IN A HUGE, VACANT LOT FULL OF BIG, SHADE TREES RIGHT ON GRAND AVENUE AND ABOUT 35TH, ON THE POOR SIDE OF THE GROVE. A BIG, WHITE OVERTURNED REFRIGERATOR (LEFT BY THE PREVIOUS OFFICE HOLDERS, NO DOUBT) SERVED AS A DESK, AND I HAD SEVERAL MILK CRATE CHAIRS SCATTERED ABOUT FOR IMPORTANT VISITORS TO SIT IN. AND... I HAD A PHONE! THERE WAS A PAYPHONE AT THE SIDEWALK IN FRONT OF THE LOT! MY NUMBER WAS 305-567-1581. THE LOCAL DRUG DEALERS GOT A LOT MORE CALLS THAN ME, THOUGH. I GOT ONE CALL. THE PHONE RANG AND I PICKED IT UP. THE VOICE SAID, "DO YOU SPEAK SPANISH?" NO. "DO YOU WANT TO HAVE SEX?" NO! I HUNG UP. ONE TIME, THOUGH, GRETA CALLED AND TALKED TO SOME LITTLE GIRL, WHO ANSWERED THE PHONE, FOR AWHILE, BUT I WASN'T THERE. OH WELL.

AT THIS OFFICE, I'D SIT SOME AFTERNOONS AND GIVE AWAY FREE FRUIT, COOKIES, BAGELS, AND GOOD, STRONG ICED TEA. IT WAS LIKE A SOCIALIZED LEMONADE STAND — THE REFRESHMENTS, NOT BOMBS! I WAS NEVER ABLE TO GET A FOOD NOT BOMBS! GOING IN MIAMI. I COULDN'T FIND A DRIVER OR PEOPLE WHO WERE ABLE TO HELP, SO I FINALLY FIGURED I'D JUST START SMALL AND DO WHAT I COULD, AND MAYBE, THROUGH THAT SMALL EFFORT, MEET SOME PEOPLE IN THE NEIGHBORHOOD WHO'D OFFER UP A CAR, OR A KITCHEN, OR A PLACE TO STORE FOOD. BUT EITHER WAY, I COULD RELAX IN THE SHADE ON HOT, HEAVY DAYS AND DRINK GREAT ICED TEA, AND READ, AND WRITE, AND TALK TO PEOPLE WHO STOPPED BY TO EAT AND DRINK AND SIT.

HOW I GOT THE FOOD: I STOLE TEA BAGS AND ICE AND BREWED TEA AT SIR ROBERT'S PLACE AND PUT IT IN A 3-GALLON COOLER. I GOT THE MANAGER OF THE BAGEL EMPORIUM ON U.S. 1, BY THE UNIVERSITY, TO GIVE ME THE THROWAWAYS. THE MANAGER OF THE TINY COMMODORO MARKET ON S.W. 27 AND U.S. 1 GAVE ME A BOX A WEEK OF WHATEVER HE HAD. ONE TIME, IT WAS A BOX OF KEEBLER'S COOKIES' PACKAGES. ONE TIME, IT WAS A CRATE OF THE MYSTERIOUS, HAIRY ROOT, MALANGA... THE MAJOR LABEL STORES WOULDN'T COOPERATE, BUT I LEARNED THAT THE PUBLIX ON S.W. 27 and CORAL WAY THREW EVERYTHING OUT AT NOON, SO I GOT GRAPES, WATERMELONS, PEARS, APPLES STILL COLD FROM THE STORE. I'D PUT ALL THE STUFF IN A CRATE AND PEDAL WITH IT ON MY TOUGH BIKE'S HANDLEBARS TO THE OFFICE. THIS WORK TOOK A LITTLE OF THE ALIENATING EDGE OFF OF HOMELESSNESS AND POVERTY. LIKE, I ENJOYED GOING INTO THE SUPERMARKETS (USUALLY WITH IVY) TO MEET THE MANAGERS, TELL THEM OUR POSITION AND WHAT WE WERE ATTEMPTING TO DO. YOU'D FIND OUT WHAT THE PEOPLE IN THE STORES WERE LIKE. THE SMALL, FAMILY-OWNED STORES WERE USUALLY KIND, BUT DIDN'T REALLY HAVE THE WEALTH TO THROW MUCH STUFF OUT. THEY'D GIVE WHAT THEY COULD. THE BIG STORES LIKE PUBLIX, WOOLEY'S, AND VARADARO'S, OF COURSE, THREW OUT TONS OF STUFF, BUT WOULDN'T KICK DOWN. IT MADE YOU FEEL EVEN BETTER ABOUT RIPPING 'EM OFF FOR SO LONG...

I'M REALLY INTO THE IDEA OF WORKING FOR CHANGE ON A NEIGHBORHOOD LEVEL. LIKE, THE BLACK PANTHERS GOT STARTED WHEN LOTS OF KIDS WERE GETTING KILLED CROSSING THIS ONE INTERSECTION IN THE GHETTO, BUT THE CITY OF OAKLAND WOULDN'T PUT UP A STOPLIGHT. SO, HUEY

NEWTON WENT AND PUT UP HIS OWN STOP SIGN, AND STOOD BY IT WITH A GUN! THE CITY PUT UP THE LIGHT... I USED TO READ THE NEWSPAPERS REAL CLOSELY AND GET REAL UPSET OVER EACH NEW TERRIBLE THING THAT WAS HAPPENING IN THE WORLD, BUT I REALIZED THAT BEING AWARE OF ALL THESE PROBLEMS DIDN'T DO ANYTHING. IN FACT, IT MADE ME FEEL OVERWHELMED BY THE SHEER AMOUNT OF PROBLEMS IN THE WORLD. BUT, STARTING FROM THE BOTTOM UP, INSTEAD, IT WAS EASY TO FIND WAYS ALL AROUND ME TO PRACTICALLY APPLY MY BELIEFS. LIKE, I THINK HOUSING AND FOOD ARE THE TWO MOST IMPORTANT ISSUES. PEOPLE NEED FOOD, SO YOU FEED THEM. PEOPLE NEED HOUSING, SO YOU TAKE IT. MIAMI'S A TOWN THAT'S DESPARATELY LACKING ALOT OF SENSE OF COMMUNITY, BECAUSE EVERYTHING'S BUILT FOR TOURISTS, THE CITY'S REAL POOR, AND OVER HALF THE PEOPLE WHO LIVE THERE HAVE MOVED FROM SOMEWHERE ELSE. I JUST FELT LIKE I WANTED TO TRY AND MAKE MY CITY, MY NEIGHBORHOOD A LITTLE MORE LIKE THE KIND OF PLACE I WANTED TO LIVE IN...

AND I THINK IT WORKED A LITTLE, TOO. PEOPLE WILL RESPOND IF YOU MAKE A LITTLE EFFORT. I GOT TO MEET ALOT OF PEOPLE WHO STOPPED THERE AT THE SHADY, SCAM OFFICES, AND ALOT OF OTHER PEOPLE IN THE GROVE KNEW US, TOO. PEOPLE WERE VERY FRIENDLY TO US. LIKE, THE GUYS AT THE SPOKES ON THE GROVE BIKE SHOP LET US LOCK UP OUR BIKES THERE ALL NIGHT, AND EVEN DID SOME FREE, MINOR REPAIRS FOR US. RESTAURANTS GAVE US FREE BREAD, BUTTER, OR GARLIC, OR WHATEVER LITTLE ITEMS WE NEEDED FOR COOKING — OR SOMETIMES, HUGE MEALS. AND ALL THE BUMS KNEW WE WERE SQUATTIN' THE MUTINY. THEY'D SAY, "YOU GUYS STILL UP THERE?" AND LOOK UP ALL FOGGY AND DREAMY AT THE MUTINY, CUZ THE PLACE REALLY DID KINDA CAPTURE THE IMAGINATION. THE NEIGHBORHOOD WAS STARTING TO FEEL A LITTLE MORE TIGHT KNIT. ONE NIGHT, THE DOOBIE BROTHERS GUY EVEN BOUGHT IVY DINNER. HE SAID, "HEY, YOU GUYS! LET'S GO EAT!" AND TOOK US TO 7-11, WHERE HE BOUGHT IVY THE 99¢ CUP OF SOUP! HE COOKED HIS AND IVY'S SOUP IN THE MICROWAVE, THEN TOOK HIS AND LEANED OVER ALL CONFIDENTIALLY, "WATCH THIS!" AND STARTED FILLING IT WITH THE FREE MEAT SAUCE! IT WAS LIKE THE COCONUT GROVE BUM SECRET HANDSHAKE! WE WERE IN...

BUT THE BIGGEST HONOR WAS WHEN JOE COOL WANTED TO MOVE INTO THE MUTINY. EVERYBODY IN THE GROVE KNEW JOE COOL. HE WAS THIS THIN, BLACK HOMELESS GUY IN HIS LATE 30'S, WHO ALWAYS WORE SHORTS, PULLED-UP, WHITE SOX, TENNIS SHOES, SHORT SLEEVED SHIRTS, AND A "NEWPORT" CIGARETTES HAT. HE WAS THE TOTAL RELAXED, MIAMI-LOOKIN' GUY, AND HE ALWAYS HAD THIS BIG SMILE. YOU'D BE SMILIN', TOO, IF YOU WERE JOE COOL, CUZ HE HAD BEEN AROUND SO LONG THAT EVERYTHING WAS FREE. RESTAURANTS FED HIM, & EVERYONE ALWAYS SEEMED TO OWE HIM A BEER, OR A SMOKE, AND THE COPS WOULD SEE HIM DRINKIN' IN PUBLIC AND JUST SAY, "HI, JOE!" HE WAS ABOVE THE LAW. I THINK HE WAS ALSO REAL HAPPY CUZ HE WAS USUALLY DRUNK. BUT IVY HAD KNOWN HIM SINCE SHE WAS A CRAZY, 12-YEAR OLD, COCONUT GROVE STREET KID AND HE WAS A REAL GOOD GUY. HE WAS THE UNOFFICIAL KING OF COCONUT GROVE, AND HE WANTED TO LIVE WITH US!

WE WENT AND STOLE A LOCK FOR JOE AND HE MOVED IN ON THE 9TH FLOOR. THEN, THIS KID, GRASSHOPPER, WHO WAS KIND OF A SMART ASS COCONUT GROVE STREET VETERAN, ABOUT MY AGE, WANTED TO MOVE IN ON THE 10TH FLOOR. IVY SAID IT WAS COOL, CUZ SHE'D KNOWN HIM FOR YEARS, TOO. HE WAS PRETTY FUNNY, ALWAYS GOIN' ON ABOUT THIS EXPENSIVE CAR HE HAD SOMEWHERE, OR HIS RICH GIRLFRIEND WHO, HE SAID, LIVED IN THE EXCLUSIVE CONDOS ON GROVE ISLE. SO, UH, GRASSHOPPER... WHY ARE YOU LIVIN' ON THE 10TH FLOOR OF AN ABANDONED BUILDING THEN? IT WAS COOL HAVING OTHER PEOPLE LIVE THERE, THAT WAY WE FELT MORE SECURE, MORE IN CONTROL OF ALL THAT BIG, DARK BUILDING, AND WE KNEW WHO WAS THERE — COOL PEOPLE, AND NOT CREEPS. THIS WAY THERE WERE MORE PEOPLE LOOKIN' OUT FOR EACH OTHER. AND, NOW, WE HAD NEIGHBORS TO BORROW CUPS OF SUGAR FROM. IT WAS KINDA FUNNY. THERE WAS A BIG CONDO NEXT DOOR TO THE MUTINY. WE WERE LIKE THE ANTI-CONDO. THEY WERE ALL LIT UP, WE WERE ALL DARK AND CREEPY. THEY HAD SECURITY GUARDS TO KEEP CRIME AWAY FROM THEIR HOME. WE HAD SECURITY GUARDS THAT KEPT US AWAY FROM OUR HOME...

THERE WERE SOME NEW FIXTURES IN THE HOOD, TOO. THERE WAS TONY THE BUM, AND KEVIN THE HOMELESS HIPPIE, WHO ALWAYS SAID, "FEED YER HEAD, NOT THE FEDS, DUDE!" AND THE VULGAR PARKING ATTENDANT. THE V.P.A. WAS THIS CHEERFUL, YET OBSCENE LATIN GUY WHO PARKED CARS LEGALLY IN A LEGITIMATE GARAGE. HE WAS ALWAYS HUNGOVER AND SWEATY, BUT KINDA FUN. HE CUSSED ALOT IN HIS THICK, SPANISH ACCENT, AND WHEN WOMEN WALKED BY, HE'D GROWL, "I VANT YAR BAW-DEE!" AND HIS EYES WOULD BULGE OUT. THEN THERE WAS JOKER, THE LAST TRUE PUNK ROCKER. HE WAS THE LEADER OF THE GROVE RATS, A CUTE LITTLE GANG OF 14 YEAR OLD, SCHOOL SKIPPIN', DRUG TAKIN' FUCKUPS. HE HAD "THE LAST TRUE PUNK ROCKER" TATTOOED ON HIS ARM. HE LIVED IN A BUSH IN PEACOCK PARK. I GUESS HE HAD A GOOD THING GOING, FEEDING ACID TO ALL THESE KIDS AND GETTING THEM TO DO STUFF FOR HIM — KIND OF A MINOR LEAGUE MANSON — BUT HE WAS KIND OF A DICK. STILL, HE DID TELL ME, "IF YOU EVER GET KICKED OUT OF YER PLACE, YOU CAN LIVE IN MY BUSH, MAN. IT'S A REAL GOOD BUSH. I MADE A DOOR ON IT!" WHAT A PRINCE, THAT GUY.

I THOUGHT WE KNEW EVERYBODY NOW. THEN, ONE DAY, IVY, AND BECKY, AND ME WERE MAKIN' SPAGHETTI LUNCH, WHEN THERE WAS ALOT OF BANGIN' ON OUR DOOR. IT WAS PRETTY SCARY. WHO COULD IT BE? IT WAS THE MUTINY SECURITY GUARD! HE WAS ON A ROUTINE SEARCH OF THE PLACE, WHEN HE FOUND US. SHIT! HE WANTED IN, SO I DECIDED TO BE REAL NICE AND GIVE HIM A TOUR. HE WAS TOTALLY BLOWN AWAY, AND, FINALLY, AGREED NOT TO TELL ANYONE WE WERE THERE. I WAS STILL WORRIED, THOUGH. THEN, THE NEXT DAY HE KNOCKED AGAIN. HE WAS LONELY AND WANTED TO TALK! WE TALKED FOR 45 MINUTES ABOUT HOW BORING HIS JOB WAS, AND WHEN HE LEFT, HE SAID, "YOU DRINK BEER?" OF COURSE! HE SAID, "I'LL BRING SOME UP SOMETIME!"

WINE VALLEY DAYS

ONE DAY IVY AND I WERE WALKIN' UP McFARLANE TOWARDS MIAMI SUBS, WHEN WE SAW THAT THE BAR, GROVE CALLOWAY'S WAS CLOSED FOR GOOD. IT HAD BEEN THIS OBNOXIOUS, YUPPIE EYESORE, SPILLIN' DRUNK JOCKS INTO THE STREETS 'TIL WAY LATE, EVERY NIGHT, BUT THEY HAD GONE OUT OF BUSINESS NOW. SCORE ONE FOR THE PUNKS! WE WENT UP TO THEIR OUTDOOR BAR AREA AND PROWLED AROUND AND SAW THAT THEY HAD LEFT ALL KINDS OF GREAT STUFF THERE: TWO OLD-STYLE KEROSENE LAMPS, ALL KINDS OF PAINTS, CHALK, BOXING GLOVES, ROLLER SKATES AND A BIG, 3-LITER BOTTLE OF CHEAP, RED WINE, CALLED WINE VALLEY! WE TOOK ALL THE STUFF UP TO THE SQUAT, AND GAVE JOE COOL SOME LAMPS AND BECKY AND IVY PAINTED ALL OVER THE WALLS. BUDDHA WAS BACK IN TOWN, LIVIN' AT THE MUTINY, TOO. THINGS WERE STILL REAL GOOD.

A COUPLE DAYS LATER, I WAS ROLLER SKATIN' AROUND THE SQUAT WHEN DAVIS, THE LONELY SECURITY GUARD CAME BACK UP. I TRIED TO SHOW 'EM MY NEW SKATES, BUT HE CUT ME OFF, AND TOLD ME THAT "THEY" WERE THINKING OF PUTTING IN SECURITY LIGHTS IN ON THE 12TH FLOOR — OUR FLOOR! AND, "THEY" HAD BOARDED UP THE BACK ENTRANCE AND WOULD FIX THE FENCE SOON. THIS WAS BAD. WHO KNEW WHO "THEY" WERE, OR WHAT "THEY" WERE CAPABLE OF? THAT'S ONE THING ABOUT SQUATTING — SOMETIMES THERE'S ALOT OF PROBLEMS WITH "THEM." SO, DAVIS LEAVES, AND IVY, OUR BRAVE COMRADE IVY, WHO SO COURAGEOUSLY LED THE ASSAULT ON X-TRA AND SQUATTED IN OAKLAND WHEN IT "COULDN'T BE DONE", SHE HAD TO GO TO A DOCTOR'S APPOINTMENT. SO ME AND BUDDHA WATCHED THE MEN FIXING THE FENCE, FROM THE BALCONY, AND TRIED TO THINK OF WHAT TO DO. I MEAN, HERE WAS DRAMA: WE WERE ON TOP, WITH ONE EXIT BOARDED UP AND A GUARD BY THE OTHER ONE. WHAT IF WE COULD NEVER GET OUT? WE LOOKED AROUND AND TOOK STOCK OF THE SITUATION — WE HAD ROLLER SKATES, BOXING GLOVES, THE COMPLETE BOOK OF RAP LYRICS, BUCKETS OF PAINT, CUBAN COFFEE, AND THE 3-LITER BOTTLE OF WINE. JUST THE VERY EXISTENCE OF THE WINE VALLEY WAS AN INSPIRATION — LIKE SOMEWHERE, MEN GUZZLE RED WINE OUT OF BIG MOUTH BOTTLES, BY THE LITER! ITS ALWAYS A GOOD YEAR FOR WINE LIKE THAT! THINGS LOOKED GOOD. IF WE NEVER GOT OUT, THEY'D FIND US COVERED IN PAINT, BELCHING BAD RAPS AT EACH OTHER, BETWEEN DRUNKEN BOXING MATCHES...

WE MADE CUBANO, LISTENED TO BLACK FLAG, ANSWERED CHICKENHEAD MAIL, AND KEPT ROLLER SKATING AROUND. JOE COOL CAME OVER AND WE GOT OUT THE WINE VALLEY FOR OUR DISTINGUISHED VISITOR. JOE CAME OVER ALOT AND TOLD GOOD STORIES, HE WAS LIKE THE EYES AND EARS OF THE 'HOOD. HE TOLD US ABOUT THE OLD MUTINY, AND THE DRUG RING THAT MADE ITS HOME THERE. WHEN THEY GOT BUSTED THE HOTEL WAS SEIZED BY THE GOVERNMENT AND CLOSED FOR A FULL YEAR, THE ROOMS WERE IN TACT, WITH RUNNING WATER, AND BUMS LIVED IN IT IN SPLENDOR THAT MADE US LOOK PRETTY POOR. JOE ALSO TOLD US ABOUT FINDING WALLETS FULL OF CASH ON THE SHORE WHERE WE FOUND THE BOAT. RICH PEOPLE WHO LIVED ON BOATS DROPPED THEIR WALLETS OVERBOARD, AND THEY

HAD TO WASH UP SOMETIME, HE SAID. YOU COULD TELL THAT JOE HAD ALOT OF FAITH IN THE BAY. IT'D ALREADY BROUGHT HIM TWO WALLETS, FILLED WITH A COUPLE HUNDRED BUCKS EACH! "BUT DON'T GO DOWN THERE AT NIGHT," HE WARNED. "THEY'VE FOUND 3 BODIES DOWN THERE THIS YEAR... "THAT'S THE WAY IT WAS WITH THE BAY," HE SAID. SOMETIMES YOU GOT RICH, SOMETIMES YOU GOT BODIES... AS FAR AS THE MUTINY WENT, JOE SAID NOT TO SWEAT IT. NO ONE WOULD EVER DO ANYTHING WITH THE BUILDING, CUZ THEY'D HAVE TO SINK MILLIONS INTO IT JUST TO BRING IT UP TO CODE.

IT HAD TURNED OUT TO BE A REAL GOOD DAY. JOE WENT HOME AND BUDDHA AND I MADE SPINACH, MOZZARELLA, PASTA AND TOMATO SAUCE, WITH PLENTY MORE PAPER CUPS OF WINE VALLEY. BUT WASN'T THE SQUAT ABOUT TO BE BUSTED? WELL, I'D USE MY CROWBAR TO TAKE OFF THE BACKBOARD AND MY PLIERS TO TAKE APART THEIR CHEAP, LITTLE FENCE. AND THEN WHAT? WELL, I'D WAIT AND SEE... I WAS A LITTLE WORRIED, BUT ALSO CONFIDENT, TOO. WE WERE DRUNK AND WE HAD TOOLS! WHATEVER IT TAKES! ITS THE SURVIVAL THING— WE HAD THE ENERGY GENERATED BY MEN PUSHING SHOPPING CARTS, AND THE WARMTH OF THE TRASH CAN FIRE OF THE PEOPLE WHO LIVE IN THE BOX CARS, AND THE MECHANICAL, CALM CERTAINTY OF THE METER GUYS, SLIPPIN' THE BEER TAB IN TO FUCK UP THE PARKING METER FOR THE MILLIONTH TIME... AND WE HAD ENOUGH WINE VALLEY LEFT FOR ~~one~~ TONIGHT. WE POURED OURSELVES THE LAST OF THE BOTTLE AND RAISED OUR PAPER CUPS IN A TOAST, AND DOWN IT WENT, WARM AND RED, LIFE'S BLOOD, TO THE MUTINY.

THE LAST OF THE GREAT ROMANCES

It was summertime and I was in love. It was one of the Last Great Romances, between me, my brave bike, The City of Miami, and the-Girlfriend-that-I-didn"t-have I went everywhere on that bike, exploring everywhere I could in Miami, in love, but with no girl. I guess it was meant to be. The bike was only built for one.

My bike took me to the weekend flea market in the parking lot of Bobby Maduro Statdium, which is quite a cultural event, in a quiet part of town: families, food, and rows and rows of tables, piled high with apparently useless junk. Me and the-girl-I didn,t have, we could have got tiny Puerto Rican flags and shoelaces and matching rings, that were actually obscure car parts. Still, alone it wasn't so bad. I bought a ½ half used can of spray snow for 27¢ and wrote "Chickenhead" on a wall by I-95, and then toured the produce district, which is also a weekend time-sharing resort for bums. Here's what you get: Big couches on the loading decks, plenty of booze, and a good seat at the trashcan fire! Then I saw clever graffitti on the public housing over by N.W. 20th Street and 24th ave. It said: "Boys in the H.U.D."

We would have been quite a pair, me and my girl in Little Havana, like dominoes in Maximo Gomex park, a smouldering flame in the Alleged Fast Luck district. We could have walked mano a mano from one end of 8th street to the other, drinking cubano, singin' and yellin'.

Ah yes... but I was alone, and the only singin' was from a lonely rooster somewhere off the main street, a song for the sun, lost in city life. It was allright, though, bein' alone. There was mystery in every market, and botanica, and rincon cafeteria, and I went in every one just to look around and ask questions. One store must have been the Little Havana Supply Store, cuz they only sold like 5 things: white undershirts, cigars, dominoes, cool old guy hats, and Saint Lazarus candles. I asked the guy who ran the place what the secret was behind the orange water coolers, with the free water that are in the counter windows of all the restaurants there. Is it an old Cuban tradition? Is this how it is in Havana? He looked alarmed. "Senor, the weather, it is hot. The people LIKE the free ice water."

The summer raged on and my bike brought me to the greatest spots. The trailer park pool on 79th street, by Northside Metrorail was an enormous pool, all splashin' out with summer, with a huge stone lion's head on one end and a bunch of crazy kids jumping off it into the water. It would have been good, me and a girl, with nothing better to do than lay in the school's out sun and wait for the ice cream man. Well, I didn't have any money for ice cream anyways. But dreamin's free. I took a walk and ended up exploring the train yard. A brakeman yelled, "Hey keep yer head up, kid! These trains sneak up on ya!" Yo! Don't sweat it, man! I won't die just yet.

My bike even took me out to breakfast, at the Publix dumpster on LeJeune road in Coral Gables. I found a huge crate of bananas, boxes of fresh strawberries, cold, cold watermelons, just thrown out. I had no girl to share my breakfast with, but, here, I wasn't alone. The manager of Publix came out to yell at me. "Hey you! Get away from that trash!" Uh, sorry, can't hear ya. Got a banana in my ear. Yuk yuk. I started to pedal away with my food. "I never want to see you here again. ARE YOU LISTENING TO ME ?!?"

Ya think I'm A SAP? TELL it to my crowbar!

NO!!!

I pedaled away laughing. It was another great day, the kind of day where I expected to come around a corner, and finally, there SHE'd be. She'd be in front of Publix, sparechangin' for money for tampons, all punk and crazy and some fat yuppie would just walk by her and pretend not to hear her and she'd scream, "OH FINE ... I'll **JUST FUCKING BLEED TO DEATH THEN** !!!" and I'd ride up all cool, like "Relax. Care to join me for some strawberries in the shade ?" and she'd get on my tough bike's handlebars, and we'd ride off into the sunset, or Miami Springs, or whatever...

But, it never happened. And I can't say I mind too much. I'd wake up in The Mutiny and look across the city from my balcony, and know it was all out there. It was all mine. I was 20 years old with nothing for sale and nothing better to do than to chase romance up rooftops and shout at the sunrise. And, alone, or not, it was always good to dumpster those cold watermelons on those impossibly hot, dizzy days, when the summer seemed to split wide open, red and raw and wet with adventure. Watermelon days. And we dove in headfirst, me, my bike, and the girl-friend-I-didn't-have, in the last of The Great Romances.

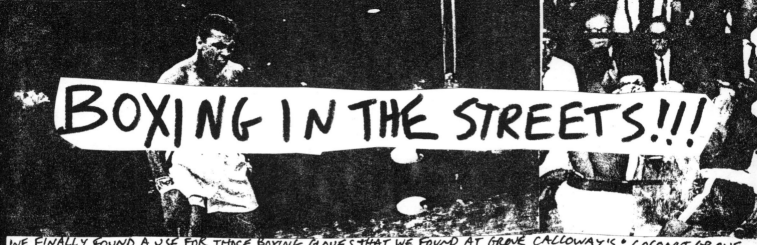

BOXING IN THE STREETS!!!

WE FINALLY FOUND A USE FOR THOSE BOXING GLOVES THAT WE FOUND AT GROVE CALLOWAY'S: COCONUT GROVE STREET BOXING! ONE DAY, BUDDHA, IVY, AND I MADE A SIGN THAT SAID, "FIGHT THE CHAMPION!" AND WENT IN THE STREETS TO TRY AND GET STRANGERS TO PAY 9 BUCKS TO FIGHT IVY!

WE WENT DOWN TO GRAND AVENUE TO FIGHT. IVY HAD ON THE GLOVES AND A DRESS WITH LITTLE PUNK HEARTS ALL OVER IT. SHE PULLED UP HER SOCKS, STUCK AN UNLIT CIGARETTE IN HER MOUTH, AND WAS READY TO BOX! BUDDHA HELD THE SIGN, WHILE I SHOUTED INSULTS AT PASSERS BY: "C'MON AND FIGHT THE CHAMPION! C'MON — YOU SIR! PUT YOUR MANHOOD ON THE LINE AND FIGHT THE CHAMPION! WHAT? ARE YOU A WIMP?!? GO BACK TO KENDAL YA SAP! SHE'LL KICK YOUR ASS! ONLY 9 BUCKS!" NO ONE WANTED TO FIGHT HER. SHE LOOKED PRETTY TOUGH.

SO, UNCHALLENGED, IVY REMAINED THE CHAMPION AND WE STARTED TO LEAVE. BUT, JUST THEN, THESE KIDS CAME UP, AND ONE SAYS, "HERE'S OUR CHAMPION!" AND PUSHES FORWARD HIS RELUCTANT LOOKIN', 14 YEAR-OLD BROTHER. HE SAYS, "HOW MUCH? 9 BUCKS?" AND HE TURNS TO HIS FRIENDS AND THEY DIG IN THEIR POCKETS, AND, SOO, THEY HAVE THE 9 BUCKS, AND WE HAD A FIGHT! I GUESS WE HADN'T EXPECTED THIS...

I SAY, WELL, IVY, IT'S YER CALL ... AND SHE SAYS, "ALLRIGHT! LET'S GO!" AND THE KID GETS REAL EXCITED AND BARELY GETS THE GLOVES ON. SHE GOES BAREFISTED. WE'RE OVER BY THE GAP, AND THE RESTAURANT CROWD ON THE 2ND LEVEL OF COCOWALK IS LOOKIN' DOWN, GAINING INTEREST, AND THE PEOPLE ON THE SIDEWALK CLEAR OUT A CIRCLE AND EGG IT ON, AND THE NEXT THING YOU KNOW, THE KID LEAPS AT IVY AND POPS HIS PADS, KA-POW! ON HER HEAD, AND SHE'S DUCKIN', FLAILIN' AT HIM, AND THE FIGHT'S ON, SERIOUS! ME AND BUDDHA LOOK AT EACH OTHER IN DISBELIEF, LIKE "WHAT HAVE WE BECOME A PART OF HERE?" WAS THIS GOOD, OR BAD?

THE KID LANDS A COUPLE GOOD ONES. HE'S GOT ALOT MORE REACH THAN IVY, BUT SHE'S SLIPPERY, DUCKIN' LOW THEN LUNGIN' IN, AND HE'S CUSSIN', SPITTIN', THEY'RE BOTH GRUNTIN', FUK, KAPOW!, SHIT, SPIT, HIT IT WAS CRAZY. WE'D CLEARLY TURNED OVER A NEW LEAF HERE. THE HIPPIES WANTED FREE LOVE, BUT WE WERE OUT HERE BOXING THE MASSES!

THEY KEEP FIGHTIN', TO THE DELIGHT OF A HUGE, SUNDAY AFTERNOON GRAND AVENUE CROWD. FINALLY, IVY GRABS THE KID'S LEG AND PUSHES HIM BACK A FULL 3-FEET, AND, IN THE EXCITEMENT, I YELL, "THE POLE, IVY! GRIND THE FUCKER INTO THE TELEPHONE POLE!" BUT THEN... IT'S OVER. SHE SAYS, "I WIN. I GOT YOUR LEG." THE KID GOES, "I LOST?" SHE SAYS, "YEP!" HE DIDN'T EVEN CONTEST IT, SO I GUESS HE KNEW DEEP DOWN, THAT IT WAS TRUE. I PUT OUT MY PALM AND HIS BRO SMACKS THE 9 BUCKS INTO MY HAND. I HAND IT TO IVY AND RAISE HER ARM AND CALL TO THE BALCONY, "LADIES AND GENTLEMEN — THE CHAMPION!" TO MIGHTY APPLAUSE, AND WE WALK AWAY. IVY HAD A BLACK EYE!

WELL, I GUESS THERE'S NO REASON WHY A PERSON CAN'T MAKE AN HONEST LIVING WITH THEIR FISTS. AND JUST SO YA KNOW — I GOT NONE OF IVY'S 9 BUCKS. I'M NOT A PIMP. MAYBE, INSTEAD OF BUMS PARKING CARS, NOW YOU'D SEE BUMS FIGHTING DRUNKS IN THE STREETS FOR SPARE CHANGE, AFTER THE BARS CLOSE. EITHER WAY, NOW THE WHOLE GROVE KNEW THAT IVY WAS THE CHAMPION.

HAPPY BIRTHDAY, SCAM!!!

TURNIN' 20, LENNY THE SUPERHERO, HOMEMADE BOATS, MORE...

OH...ANOTHER CROWBAR... UH...THANKS!

HERE'S YER PRESENT! HAPPY BIRTHDAY!

MY 20TH BIRTHDAY CAME, AND I DIDN'T GO TO DENNY'S FOR THE FREE MEAL. FOR SOME REASON, I WANTED TO GO A WHOLE BIRTHDAY WITHOUT ANYONE SAYING "HAPPY BIRTHDAY TO ME". SO, I DECIDED TO GO TO THE COCONUT GROVE MARINA

THE MARINA'S A PRETTY CRAZY PLACE AT NIGHT, AND A PRETTY EASY PLACE TO FIND PEOPLE TO TALK TO. FOR INSTANCE, I WAS ONLY THERE A COUPLE MINUTES BEFORE SOME WIDE-EYED BOAT DWELLER, WITH PUKE IN HIS BEARD, CAME UP TO ME AND SAID, "I'M GONNA FUCKIN' KILL MY OLD LADY!" HE GAVE ME A BEER. IT WAS THE ONLY PRESENT I GOT ALL DAY.

WHEN ALL THE PEOPLE WHO LIVE ON THE BOATS AREN'T OUT SHRIMPING, OR FISHING, OR SALVAGING, OR RUNNIN' DRUGS — WHICH IS MOST OF THE TIME — THEY LIKE TO JUST SIT AND DRINK ON THEIR BOATS. I THINK PEOPLE WHO LIVE ON BOATS SEEM LIKE THEY WANT TO BE LEFT ALONE, YA KNOW? THAT'S DEFINATELY TRUE HERE, CUZ THERE'S NO LAW AT THE MARINA, EXCEPT THAT KINDA UNWRITTEN "YOU JUST DON'T DO THAT, MAN. YA JUST DON'T..." WHITE-TRASH KINDA LAW. THAT'S

BECAUSE THE MARINA IS UNDER COAST GUARD, NOT POLICE, JURISDICTION, AND THE COAST GUARD'S NEVER AROUND. SO THINGS GET DRUNKER AND CRAZIER AS THE NIGHT GOES ON, THE LEVEL RISING LIKE THE TIDES. PEOPLE SHOUTING TURNS INTO PEOPLE PUNCHING TURNS INTO GUYS WRAPPED UP IN NETS, PASSED OUT IN ROW BOATS, FALLING IN THE WATER. EVERYONE ALWAYS MAKES UP AT THE END OF THE NIGHT. IT'S REALLY SWEET... THE MARINA'S LIKE THE RETIREMENT HOME FOR ALL THE EARLY 80'S COCAINE DAYS' HEROS, ALL THE "SMUGGLER'S BLUES," AND "MARGUERITAVILLE" CROWD. THEY MADE IT BIG ON THEIR BOATS AND GOT BUSTED. IT'S A UNIQUELY MIAMI KIND OF WHITE TRASH, I THINK.

I WENT TO THE MARINA TO BORROW LENNY'S ROWBOAT. LENNY, YOU MAY REMEMBER, IS THE BIG CRAZY, ROARIN', REDHEAD, 3-TOOTHED, DRUNK/NUDIST/INVENTOR, WHO RAISED IVY, WAY BACK IN PT. 1 OF THIS TOME. THESE DAYS, HE'S A SHRIMPER WHO LIVES ON A BOAT IN THE MARINA. HE HAS A ROWBOAT THAT HE SAID WE COULD USE WHENEVER WE WANTED. LENNY HAD BUILT IT HIMSELF, ONLY HE BUILT IT WRONG, SO THAT IT ALWAYS TIPPED OVER. BUT, SO FAR, I HAD HAD GOOD LUCK WITH IT. WE NEVER REALLY TOOK IT OUT, CUZ HAVING A BOAT WASN'T THE SAME AS FINDING A BOAT, AND WE NEVER WENT BACK TO THE ISLAND. BUT, TIM, IVY, AND I DID TAKE IT ONCE, 5 OR 6 MILES DOWN THE SHORE TO FIND THIS BEAUTIFUL, SECLUDED BEACH SPOT THAT IVY HAD BEEN TO ONCE. WE NEVER REALLY FOUND IT, BUT PARKED THE BOAT, AND TRUDGED AROUND THIS MANGROVE FOREST, LOOKIN' FOR BODIES, AND ATE WATERMELON, AND THEN ROWED BACK IN THE DARK, ALL KA-CHUNK! KA-CHUNK! ON BIG WAVES POUNDIN', WATER SPLASHIN' IN, CURRENT PUSHIN' US AT ROCKS, WATER FULL 'O SHARKS, PIRATES, SEA MONSTERS, ETC. IT WAS FUN. WHEN WE TOLD LENNY WHERE WE WENT, HE SAID THAT WAS THE SECLUDED BEACH PARADISE FROM IVY'S CHILDHOOD — BUT THE HURRICANE HAD LEVELED IT. SO SOMETIMES YOU REALLY CAN'T GO BACK.

LENNY WAS A SUPERHERO. WHY? BECAUSE HE DIED 3 TIMES, AND INVENTED A MACHINE THAT COULD SAVE THE WORLD! YOU COULDN'T JUST USE THE ROWBOAT. FIRST YOU HAD TO GO ON HIS BOAT SO HE COULD SHOW YOU HIS INVENTION AGAIN. "IT'S THEM!" LENNY WOULD GROWL FROM OUTTA A PILE OF OLD MILWAUKEE CANS AND SWARMIN' FLIES. "THEY DON'T WANT MY MACHINE TO BE MADE, BECAUSE THEN, THEIR EMPIRE WOULD BE RUINED!" THE MACHINE USED MAGNETS. HE HAD TWO TOY CARS ON A TRACK, WITH MAGNETS GLUED TO THEIR BACKS, AND HE'D LINE THE CARS UP SO THAT THE REPULSION OF THE SAME MAGNETIC POLES WOULD MAKE THE CARS ROLL AWAY FROM EACH OTHER. "DO YOU SEE THAT?!?" HE'D ROAR. "HERE! COME DO IT YOUR ELF!" I'D GO AND LINE UP THE CARS, DO THE MAGNET THING, AND THEY'D ROLL AWAY FROM EACH OTHER. "WHEN MAGNETS CIRCLE A COPPER COIL, IT CAUSES ELECTRONS TO COME LOOSE AND RUN THROUGH THE COIL. DO YOU KNOW WHAT THAT IS?" YEAH. IT'S ELECTRICITY. "EXACTLY!" LONG PAUSE. "SEE... WHAT THEY DON'T WANT YOU TO KNOW IS THAT WE DON'T NEED THESE BIG FUEL COMPANIES, THIS GAS POLLUTION, NUCLEAR WASTE. WE NEED MAGNETS! " ALL OF LENNY'S MACHINES USED MAGNETS. "NO ONE WILL HAVE TO PAY ELECTRIC BILLS! THE MAGNETS KEEP RUNNING BY THEMSELVES!" HE WANTED TO HAVE A MACHINE WHERE MAGNETS PROPELLED THEMSELVES AROUND THE COPPER COIL — A PERPETUAL MOTION MACHINE. AND HE HAD DEVELOPED IT RIGHT HERE ON A BOAT IN THE COCONUT GROVE MARINA! "I'M TOO OLD," LENNY WOULD SAY. "THIS MACHINE WON'T HELP ME. I WON'T BE AROUND." SAID LENNY, "I'M DOIN' IT FOR THE KIDS!"

FINALLY, I GOT TO TAKE THE BOAT OUT. LENNY SAID, "WHERE ARE YA GONNA GO?" I DON'T KNOW. THE ISLAND, MAYBE. "WHY THE HELL YA WANNA GO OUT THERE?!! THERE'S RATS AS BIG AS DOGS! TELL HIM ABOUT THE ISLAND!" AND THE DRUNKS ON THE BOAT NEXT DOOR NODDED, "BIG AS DOGS, YEP." I DIDN'T REALLY WANT TO GO TO THE ISLAND, AT ALL, I JUST WANTED TO BE ALONE, TRY AND GET A HANDLE ON THIS TURNIN' 20 YEARS-OLD THING. I PUSHED OFF AND LENNY CALLED OUT, "AT LEAST TAKE A STICK! THOSE RATS ARE CRAZY!" LENNY JUST WANTED ME TO STICK AROUND. HE WAS A SUPERHERO, BUT HE WAS AS LONELY AS THE REST OF US.

I ROWED OUT PAST THE BOATS, PAST THE ISLANDS, EVEN PAST THE MARINA HOUSEBOATS, AND THEN I QUIT ROWIN' AND JUST SAT THERE. THE MOON WAS FULL, THE AIR WAS CLEAR, THE BOAT DIDN'T TIP OVER—

IT WAS A GOOD NIGHT FOR REMINISCIN'... I WAS THINKIN' ABOUT HOW FAR I HAD COME SINCE I FIRST MOVED TO MIAMI. I MOVED THERE RIGHT WHEN I TURNED 18. TURNIN' 18 WAS EXCITING, BECAUSE, MY JUVENILE ARREST RECORD WOULD BE CLEARED AND I'D FINALLY BE ELIGIBLE FOR FOOD STAMPS. MIAMI HAD BEEN SO INTIMIDATING AT FIRST, BUT I'D BUMBLED MY WAY THROUGH THE TOUGH TIMES, SOMEHOW. I REMEMBER, WHEN I TURNED 19, I DID A PHONE INTERVIEW ON MY BIRTHDAY, FROM A PAYPHONE IN DOWNTOWN MIAMI, WITH A STOLEN CALLING CARD #. I WAS IN BETWEEN PLACES, A LITTLE UNSURE ABOUT EVERYTHING, AND THOUGHT, "WHY DOES THIS KID WANT TO INTERVIEW ME ABOUT SCAMS WHEN MY SCAMS ARE GONNA GET ME KILLED HERE ON THE STREETS OF MIAMI?" THE VERY NEXT DAY, I MOVED INTO THE 22 HOUSE AND SAW THAT IT COULD BE DONE, THIS SQUATTING THING. AND NOW, HERE I WAS AT 20, WITH THE BEST SQUAT YET. I GUESS, NOW THAT WE KNEW WHAT WE WERE DOING, I WAS FEELING NOSTALGIA FOR THE BUMBLING DAYS. THE OLD INNOCENT, BUMBLING DAYS, LIKE WHEN ME AND BUDDHA WOULD FORCE TOURING BANDS TO EAT DUMPSTER PIZZA, BACK IN THE PUNK HOUSE, OR THE TIME WHEN I GOT MY FIRST PAIR OF BOLT CUTTERS. I GOT THE BIG ONES, CUZ THEY'D CUT MORE. THEY WERE VERY BIG. AS BIG AS A MAN! YOU COULDN'T TAKE THEM ANYWHERE IN PUBLIC WITHOUT RISKING CERTAIN ARREST. THEY WERE SO BIG THAT THEY WERE TOTALLY USELESS. ONE TIME, I TRIED TO TAKE 'EM OUT IN A SHOPPING CART, HIDDEN UNDER OTHER STUFF, BUT GOT DISGUSTED, AND RATTLED THE CART HOME... LIVING IN THE MUTINY HAD REMINDED ME OF THOSE DAYS, CUZ OF THE WAY WE JUST FOUND EVERYTHING WE NEEDED. I LIKED THAT. SCARCITY MADE THINGS SIMPLE AND PURE, MORE SPECIAL. AND THINGS WERE MORE SPONTANEOUS - LIKE IN THE BUMBLIN' DAYS.

I THOUGHT ABOUT IT A LOT WHEN THESE GIRLS FROM THE GROVE RATS ASKED ME, ONE NIGHT, TO BUY THEM BEER, CUZ THEY WEREN'T OLD ENOUGH. WELL, I WASN'T OLD ENOUGH, BUT THE 7-11 SELLS TO ME. I HADN'T BOUGHT BEER IN A LONG TIME BECAUSE I'D DECIDED ONLY TO DRINK BEER THAT I FOUND. AND I FOUND UNOPENED BEERS ON THE STREETS ALL THE TIME! OR, SOMETIMES, THERE'D BE HALF A PITCHER AT AN OUTDOOR BAR'S TABLE. JUST ENOUGH TO GET A BUZZ, AND RIDE AROUND ON MY BIKE. I EVEN FOUND 48 BEERS ONE NIGHT, BEFORE CANADIANS' PRACTICE, IN A DUMPSTER! IT REMINDED ME OF WHEN BEER WAS MORE SPECIAL, LIKE FIRST YOU'D HAVE TO LIE TO YOUR MOM TO GET CASH. THEN, YOU'D STAND IN FRONT OF 7-11, AND FIND SOME CREEP TO BUY FOR YOU. YOU GAVE THEM A TEN. THEY CAME OUT WITH A 6-PACK, AND TOOK ONE. THEY KEPT THE CHANGE. YOU TOOK YER 5 BEERS THROUGH THE FOREST, ACROSS THE SWAMP, INTO A CAVE, AND SAID "NO COPS WILL BOTHER US HERE!", JUST BEFORE THE COPS CAME AND YOU HAD TO HIDE THE BEER AND HOPE THEY DIDN'T SMELL IT ON YOUR BREATH. ONE OF YOUR FRIENDS WOULD EAT A HANDFUL OF PINE NEEDLES - "THIS GETS THE SMELL OFF MY BREATH SO MY MOM WON'T KNOW." THEN HE PUKES ALL OVER AND YOU CARRY HIM HOME. YOU HAD TO DO ALL THIS BEFORE 10:00 PM, OR YOU'D GET GROUNDED. NOW, THAT'S DRAMA!

THE GROVE RATS WERE GREAT. THEY WERE RUNAWAY KIDS. RUNNING AWAY FROM HOME WAS ALWAYS SO MUCH FUN! THAT WAS PUNK, MAN - DEFIANT, PROUD, "FUK YOU ALL, I'LL DIE IN THE STREETS BEFORE I EVER COMPROMISE TO YOUR SHIT" - I GOT EVERYTHING FROM RUNNIN' AWAY: SELF RELIANCE, LOVE OF NOWHERE IS HOME, LIFE WITHOUT A NET, SCAMS, AND THE ABILITY TO LAUGH IN THE FACE OF ALL THAT LONELY. FRIENDS WOULD HELP ME OUT, CUZ I WAS DOING "IT" AND WE WERE ALL DEFIANT AND BRAVE AND SPECIAL TOGETHER, WITH PEOPLE SNEAKING ME INTO THEIR ROOMS WITHOUT THEIR PARENTS KNOWING, GIVING ME RIDES, FOOD, SUPPORT TO SEE HOW LONG IT COULD LAST, WITH COPS LOOKIN' FOR ME, AND OPTIONS RUNNING DOWN, I'D STEAL A 12-PACK AND DRINK AND WALK ON THE RAILROAD TRACKS AND SING LOUD AND GO UP TO THIS GIRL'S WINDOW AND KNOCK AND WAKE HER UP TO SEE IF SHE COULD SNEAK ME IN. WE'D WHISPER AND LAUGH THROUGH THE SCREEN AND IT WAS SERIOUS AND DRAMATIC, YES, VERY DRAMATIC, BECAUSE I HAD A CRUSH ON HER (AND SHE DIDN'T KNOW, NO WAY). I'D SNEAK HER BEERS THROUGH THE HOLE IN HER SCREEN AND SAY GOODBYE, AND SHE'D SAY GOOD LUCK. WHEN I SAW HER THE NEXT DAY IN SCHOOL, SHE'D FLASH A NAUGHTY SMILE AND SAY SHE HAD DRANK THE BEERS AFTER 1st HOUR AND HAD A BUZZ AND THAT WAS THE SHIT, CUZ EVEN BEER MEANT SOMETHING SPECIAL THEN! NOW IT'S THERE WHENEVER I WANT. IN THE TWO YEARS I'D BEEN IN MIAMI, ME AND IVY HAD LOST A LOT OF THAT INNOCENCE. BUT IT HAD TO GO. IT WAS GOOD, TURNIN' 20, AND SEEING THAT. WE HADN'T SO MUCH LOST IT, AS TRADED IT FOR EXPERIENCE, AND NOW WE KNEW HOW TO DO STUFF. WE COULD KEEP GOING, INSTEAD OF TRYING TO HOPELESSLY BRING IT BACK, DRINKING ALL THE TIME, SAYING, "SEE, I'M STILL YOUNG AND PUNK..." IN MIAMI, I'D LEARNED TO LET STUFF GO, JUST APPRECIATE THE SMALL THINGS, CUZ THE SMALL THINGS, THE HIDDEN THINGS ARE MIAMI. WHEN I WAS WORRIED EARLY ON ABOUT NOT GETTING THINGS DONE, OR THE SCENE BEING TOO SMALL I'D MISSED OUT ON THE REAL CITY — THE COLD POOLS AND WATERMELONS ON THE HOT DAYS, THE SMELL OF DINNERTIME IN LITTLE HAVANA, THE GUYS WHO HAD IT ALL IN LOST IT IN THE MARINA, THE GUYS WHO HAD IT ALL, LOST IT, AND WANTED CASTRO TO DIE SO THEY COULD GET IT BACK IN MAXIMO GOMEZ PARK, THE GREAT PUNK PICNICS THAT ERUPTED ON VACANT LOTS, NOW COVERED BY YUPPIE HOUSES. MIAMI DREAMS BIG AND CRAZY AND TRIES TO BUILD PARADISE IN THE PATH OF HURRICANES. THE MUTINY WAS OUR PARADISE. IT COULD GO ANY MINUTE. IN MIAMI, I LEARNED TO LET IT.

OUT THERE IN THE BOAT, I GOT CARRIED AWAY DREAMIN' AND REMEMBERIN'. THE FULL MOON ON THE BLACK WATER WAS SO BEAUTIFUL. IT'S HARD TO DESCRIBE WHAT IT FELT LIKE OUT THERE, TO BE THERE ON MY BIRTHDAY, SURROUNDED BY WATER, IN A TINY HOMEMADE DINGY - JUST ME AND THE MOON AND THE BLACK SEA, TURNIN' TWENTY, TURNIN' A HUNDRED, TURNIN' A THOUSAND, WHATEVER, JUST TOTALLY OUT OF TIME, FLOATIN' ACROSS CENTURIES, JUST THIS WATER, MOON AND ME. IT WAS DEFINATELY A SPECIAL TIME. BACK AT THE MARINA, SOME GUY WAS YELLING, "GIVE ME THE FUCKING MONEY, PETER!" AND LENNY WAS SITTING UP, ASLEEP, SMILING AND SOAKING WET. I GUESS HE'D FALLEN IN THE WATER AGAIN. I'D MADE IT. A WHOLE BIRTHDAY WITH NO "HAPPY BIRTHDAYS." IT MADE IT MEAN THAT MUCH MORE! 12 DAYS LATER, WHEN IVY AND BUDDHA AND BECKY AND TIM AND ANDY FINALLY REMEMBERED AND SURPRISED ME WITH A CAKE...

TIME TO LEAVE

ONE OF THE COOLEST THINGS ABOUT LIVIN' IN THE MUTINY, REALLY WAS JUST THE LONG AFTERNOONS, HANGIN' OUT AND TALKIN' WITH IVY. OR DRINKIN' TEA AND SWEEPIN' THE PLACE, AND LISTENIN' TO MUSIC. JUST BEIN' INSIDE IT WAS FUN. THE AIR WAS HEAVY AND SALTY, THE BREEZE WAS COOL OFF THE BAY, AND THAT GREAT VIEW JUST WENT ON AND ON — BLUE AND BLUE AND BLUE AND BLUE. DREAMY, SLEEPY AND BLUE. EXCITING STUFF STILL HAPPENED, SURE, LIKE WHEN THE CANADIANS PLAYED THEIR FIRST SHOWS AS A FULL BAND, OR WHEN I HAD TO MISS THE COCONUT GROVE BED RACES, AGAIN, SO MY BAND COULD RECORD OUR 7" THAT DAY. AND — I HAD STARTED PLAYIN' DRUMS IN A BAND, WITH BECKY FUNN ON BASS AND ANDY POWELL ON GUITAR/SINGIN'. ANDY WAS BACK FROM ATLANTA, AND HE WAS LIVIN' IN A METER ROOM IN MIAMI LAKES, SO WE WORKED ON A SONG CALLED, "I LIVE IN A METER ROOM." WE HAD NO PLACE TO PRACTICE, SO BECKY FOUND A MEDICAL CENTER BY HER HOUSE IN DELRAY, WITH AN OUTDOOR PLUG, SO WE SET UP AND PRACTICED AT NIGHT THERE, AFTER OFFICE HOURS. STILL, THE BEST STUFF WAS JUST THE DAY TO DAY MUTINY LIFE. JOE COOL CAME OVER TO HANG OUT. I ROLLER SKATED AROUND THE SQUAT, IVY AND BUDDHA WROTE A GREAT SONG, ON ACOUSTIC GUITAR, IN 5 MINUTES, RIGHT BEFORE MY EYES, ONE MORNING. WE SAT ON THE BALCONY AND WATCHED THE CRAZY, NEW NIGHT TIME SECURITY GUARD TALK TO HIMSELF AND YELL AT THE TREES ALL NIGHT. AND ONE TIME, IVY SAVED A RAT FROM DROWNING, AFTER IT HAD FALLEN INTO THE MUTINY PISS BUCKET!

ONE DAY, I WENT OUT EARLY TO TRY AND SURPRISE IVY WITH BREAKFAST BEFORE SHE GOT UP. I DUMPSTERED THE GRAPES, STOLE THE CHEESE AND ORANGE JUICE, AND GOT THE HEALTH FOOD STORE TO GIVE ME THEIR BREAD. ON THE WAY HOME, FOR STYLE, I STOPPED BY THE STILL-ABANDONED GROVE CALLOWAY'S TO FIND A PICNIC BASKET TO CARRY THE STUFF AND A PITCHER TO PUT THE JUICE IN AND AN ICE BUCKET TO KEEP THE FRUIT AND CHEESE COOL. THE GROVE CALLOWAY'S WAS LIKE THE TRASH STORE. WE COULD JUST GO IN, WHENEVER, AND GET WHAT WE NEEDED!

IT WAS A GREAT BREAKFAST AND A GREAT DAY. IT STARTED FULL ON, POURIN' RAIN, AND WE DRANK TEA AND WATCHED IT, STUCK INSIDE, BUT TRAVELLIN' LIGHT YEARS ON CAFFEINE AND GOOD CONVERSATION. WE BOTH HAD KIND OF A TRAVEL ITCH, AND WE SPENT ALL DAY TALKIN' ABOUT OTHER PLACES, IVY TOLD ME CRAZY STORIES ABOUT GETTIN' CHASED BY COPS IN NEW YORK CITY AND SQUATTIN' IN OAKLAND, AND HOW SHE COULDN'T WAIT TO HOP TRAINS AGAIN. I TOLD HER HOW I WANTED TO JUST RIDE MY BIKE ALL UP THE COAST OF CALIFORNIA SOME DAY, AND HOW I WANTED TO GO TO ST. LOUIS AND WALK BY THE MISSISSIPPI. LUCKILY, WE WERE LEAVIN' PRETTY SOON. MY BAND WAS GOIN' ON TOUR AGAIN, AND, THEN, IVY AND TIM WERE GONNA TAKE TRAINS TO CALIFORNIA, WHERE OUR TOUR ENDED, AND BUDDHA, AND SCOTT WERE GONNA STAY THERE AND DO THE CANADIANS THERE. THEN, I PLANNED TO TRAVEL AROUND FOR AWHILE. IT LOOKED LIKE MY BAND WOULD BE OVER, BUT THAT WAS COOL. A LOT OF BANDS ARE REAL SERIOUS ABOUT IT, DOING A RECORD, THEN A TOUR, THEN A TOUR OF EUROPE EVERY YEAR, NOTHING TO SNEER AT, I GUESS. SOME WOULD EVEN CALL IT A PUNK ROCK SUCCESS STORY. BUT IT SOUNDED KINDA DULL TO ME IT WAS TIME FOR ME TO GO OUT ALONE AND PUT THE SCAM ON THE LINE AGAIN. IVY PUT ON HER ROBERT JOHNSON RECORD AND GOT OUT HER TRAIN MAP AND RAN HER FINGER ALONG THE ROUTE TO CALIFORNIA, THROUGH NEBRASKA, OKLAHOMA, NEVADA — ALL THOSE BIG, CRAZY PLACES, AND SANG ALONG "DOWN AT THE CROSSROADS" AND I KNEW IT WAS TIME TO LEAVE...

PEOPLE ALWAYS SAY TO ME ABOUT SQUATTING — "WELL, YOU NEVER KNOW WHEN YER PLACE WILL GET BUSTED..." I ALWAYS THINK, "YEAH, BUT YOU COULD KEEP WORKIN' AT THAT SHITTY JOB FOREVER... HELL, YOU MIGHT EVEN GET A PROMOTION." I'M GLAD THAT IT DOESN'T HAVE TO LAST FOREVER, THAT I CAN KEEP MOVING ON BEFORE THINGS GET TO STALE. THE MUTINY WAS SUCH A SPECIAL PLACE, BUT THERE WASN'T MUCH LEFT WE COULD DO, BUT TURN IT INTO

SOME KIND OF BIG EMPIRE. IT SOUNDED TOO COMPLICATED. IT WAS NEAT TO THINK THAT WE'D JUST GET TO LEAVE THE PLACE INTACT— LIKE THE SCAM MUSEUM, YA KNOW, PUT UP A PLAQUE ON THE WALL WITH THE STORY OF THE MUTINY, LOCK IT AND LEAVE. IT SEEMED LIKE THE BEST WAY TO APPRECIATE THE PLACE...

THAT NIGHT, I WAS IN GROVE CALLOWAY'S, WHEN I SAW THAT THE FORMERLY PADLOCKED REFRIDGERATOR WAS OPEN AND FULL OF BEER AND WINE! HUNDREDS AND HUNDREDS OF REALLY EXPENSIVE BEERS AND WINE! TIM AND I FILLED A COUPLE BASKETS AND WENT UP TO THE SQUAT. AFTER WE GOT DRUNK, TIM SAID HE'D DECIDED TO MOVE BACK IN TO THE MUTINY. IT WAS PRETTY EXCITING, ME, TIM, AND BOOD, TOGETHER AGAIN...

THE NEXT DAY, WE DECIDED TO CELEBRATE WITH LUNCH. BUDDHA WENT TO GET BREAD, TIM PUT ON THE ROLLER SKATES AND WE TIED A ROPE TO MY BIKE AND I GAVE HIM A TOW UP TO WOOLEY'S WHERE HE'D GET JUICE. I RODE UP TO VARADARO AND STOLE THE FELAFEL MIX. I MET TIM BACK AT WOOLEY'S, AND GAVE HIM A TOW BACK. HE TOTALLY WIPED OUT ON DAY AVE., BUT WE MADE IT. STYLE COUNTS IN THE GROVE, YA KNOW. WE MET WITH BUD AT GROVE CALLOWAY'S, AND GOT MORE BEER, AND WENT UP TO THE 12TH FLOOR.

IVY HAD GONE TO A DOCTOR'S APPOINTMENT, SO IT JUST US 3 FOR LUNCH. THE FELAFEL WAS GREAT. THEN BOOD SAID, "LET'S DRINK!" TIM HAD TO LEAVE TO GET ALL HIS STUFF, BUT ME AND BOOD DRANK ALL DAY ON THE BALCONY. WE DRANK THIS CRAZY BEER CALLED BLACKENED VOODOO THAT TASTED GREAT. JOE CAME OVER AND SAW THE TWO UNOPENED WINE BOTTLES, AND SAID "WHAT THE HELL ARE YOU WAITIN' FOR? LET'S OPEN THOSE UP!" THE THREE OF US HATCHED THIS CRAZY PLAN TO GO BACK AND GET THESE GOLF CLUBS THAT I'D SEEN AT THE GROVE CALLOWAY'S AND MAKE A MINIATURE GOLF COURSE ON THE 6TH FLOOR. JOE LEFT AND SAID HE'D COME BACK LATER, AND ME AND BOOD JUST KEPT DRINKIN'. WHEN WE RAN OUT, WE JUST WENT DOWN AND GOT MORE! IT WAS TOO MUCH, ALL THAT BEER AND ALL FOR FREE.

IT WAS SUCH A GREAT, LONG DAY, WITH BEER AND THE BALCONY AND THE BAY SPLASHIN' IN AND OUT. WE GOT FALLING OUT OF CHAIRS DRUNK, AND RAISED TOASTS TO EVERYONE WE KNEW. "AH... THIS ONE'S FOR IVY, WHO BOXED MEN IN THE STREETS FOR CASH!", "THIS ONE'S FOR JOHN DANIA, WHEREVER THE HELL HE IS!", OR "THIS ONE'S FOR SIR ROBERT AND PRIYA — THE NICEST PEOPLE IN COCONUT GROVE!" AFTER A WHILE, WE WERE DOWN TO "THIS ONE'S FOR THE GUY WHO PLAYED DRUMS ON THE FIRST CIRCLE JERKS RECORD! WHAT DRUMMING!" WE DRANK A LOT OF BEER BEERS THAT NIGHT, BUT WE KNEW A LOT OF PEOPLE, YOU KNOW. WE WATCHED THE CRAZY SECURITY GUARD JUMPIN' AROUND IN THE PARKING LOT, YELLING AT THE FENCE. JOE CAME BACK AND SAID, "LET'S GO GET THOSE CLUBS! C'MON!" BUT WE JUST STAYED TO LOOK AT THE BAY. AH... THE BAY. "SOMETIMES YA GOT RICH, SOMETIMES YA GOT BODIES." THAT NIGHT, WE GOT RICH. TOMORROW? WHO KNOWS?

THE END

SCAM PUNKS!

DA CROWBAR

1994

3:36 AM the 28TH JANUAR KINKO' South S.F. CA. on CHRIS GAMBL Birthd

ORDER SCAM #2
FOR ONE DOLLAR
2629 - 19th STREET
SAN FRANCISCO, CA
94110

THE SHOES: 2/6/93 - 1/28/94. THANKS, JOHN!

SCAM PUNKS MAIL
4787 S.W. 154 AVE.
MIAMI, FL 33185

SEND TO:

LAST MINUTE NOTE: DUE TO A MISUNDERSTANDING
BLACKLIST IS SELLIN' MY ZINE FOR TOO MUCH. YOU
CAN ORDER FROM THEM IF YOU WANT IT REAL FAST, OR
FROM 2629 - 19th STREET, S.F., CA 94110 FOR ONE BUCK
IF YOU CAN STOMACH A SMALL WAIT.

"BISCAYNE BOULEVARD"
BY IGGY SCAM

53 Sun-up Over Bay Biscayne, Miami, Florida

Gone, gone, gone -- the orange groves, the swamp; gone is the old
Bay shore. The Tequesta who traded at the mouth of the river should have
sent for another deck when they saw the boats on the horizon, the ships
of the men who sailed the seas to bring the sweet smell of orange blossoms
back to the King's table. Somebody should have watched the back door. And
now they're all gone, too, like the shills who subdivided the swamp and
poured the concrete. Gone with all the money, and all that they left behind
was maps of underwater plots of land and 6 lanes of cracked pavement.
Biscayne Boulevard.

Gone, all gone, but still they come, down, down. From Tifton, from
Waycross. From Jersey from Philly -- a timeless southbound procession. Down
to the bottom. To Biscayne Boulevard.

Where the faces of the men on the sidewalks look like the faces in
Greyhound stations everywhere. Where the sun shines all the time.

Like the flourescent lights in the 13th Avenue holding cells, downtown.

"You remember with your body, kid, not with your brain," warns
a Biscayne oldtimer. He was talking about the war, but could have been
talking just as well about springtime or a girl. Or that 4:00 AM breeze of
Biscayne Bay. The breeze that haunts the open window, that haunts an empty
bed -- a ghost of a scent of orange blossoms, warm and sweet, that still
haunts the cracks in the pavement. Six lanes of traffic, where men drive all
night. With windows open. Under the towering palms, under an empty handed
moon, where men once ripped apart the jungle searching for 7 cities of
Gold, for the fountain of youth.

And where they are still searching for them to this day. And finding
them in neon pink and blue, the names of cheap motels.

Still searching on Biscayne Boulevard, with the shill's map, in neon
pink and blue. Where they should have sent for a different deck, where they
should have watched the back door, but now its all gone, with the money.
Under the towering palms, under the empty-handed moon. Where there's a
ghost of a scent, warm and sweet. Where a 4:00 AM breeze remembers springtime. Where the sun always shines.

But its all gone.

SCAM #3

ONE BUCK SUMMER '97

"FOR TODAY'S ACTION PUNKS"

Greetings from...

miami!

SLEDGEHAMMERS TO THE STREETS!

THIS ISSUE:
FREE TRIP TO
EUROPE, INSTANT
BEER PLEASURE,
CRIME WEEK, SHLITZ
CRACK ART, TURD
ATTACKS, DESCENDENTS,
MAPS, BACKROADS,
THE DALAI LAMA,
TRUCKERS, BIKES ON
TRAINS, RADIO,
SCAM TREASURE HUNT,
ALEX TREBEK, AND SPRAY
PAINT...

MIAMI
TORTURING BY
MIND CONTROL

SCAM EMPLOYEE OF THE MONTH! —

(FOR A RECORD 38TH YEAR STRAIGHT)
pictured on LEFT: Actual
CEMENT ETCHING in
Downtown MIAMI!

yo! its...

SCAM #3

WELL, HERE IT IS, THE "SUMMER '97" ISSUE OF THE SCAM, AND I CAN HARDLY BELIEVE THAT IT CAME OUT, WITH THINGS BEING SO HECTIC HERE LATELY. IN THE LAST COUPLE OF WEEKS, I BROKE MY COLLARBONE IN A FREAK BICYCLE ACCIDENT, BUT STILL HAD TO PLAY GUITAR AND SING WITH MY BAND FOR 3 SHOWS IN 4 DAYS, STEAL BLANK TAPES FOR A TAPE COMP. I PUT OUT, HELP OUT AT FOOD NOT BOMBS FEEDINGS IN COCONUT GROVE, SET UP A F.N.B. BENEFIT SHOW, AND PUT TOGETHER THIS "VANDALISM ART" SHOW AT THIS PLACE IN MIAMI, WITH PHOTOS OF VARIOUS SPRAYPAINTINGS, CRIMES, AND ALTERED BILLBOARDS I WAS RESPONSIBLE FOR... NOW, I'M ABOUT TO MOVE OUT OF MY HOUSE AND FIND A RIDE OUT OF MIAMI, SO THIS IS JUST GOING TO HAVE TO BE THE FINISHED ZINE. ITS MY BIRTHDAY PRESENT TO MYSELF THIS YEAR!

OLDTIMERS WHO STILL REMEMBER THE LAST ISSUE, WHICH CAME OUT SOMETIME BACK WHEN DINOSAURS FREELY ROAMED THE EARTH, WILL NOTE THAT THIS ISSUE IS WAY SMALLER. THIS IS BECAUSE 1) I WANT TO DO A SHORTER, MORE EASILY XEROXED ZINE THAT COMES OUT MORE OFTEN, AND 2) ITS SUMMERTIME AND MY HEAD IS SPINNING AND I WANT TO BE OUT RIDING TRAINS AND EXPLORING NEW CITIES AND PLAYING MUSIC AND POOL HOPPING AND STEALING BEER, AND NOT SITTING AROUND WRITING A FANZINE! THIS SHOULD BE THE FIRST OF SEVERAL ZINES FROM ME THIS YEAR, AS I'VE GOT PARTS OF THE NEXT COUPLE DONE ALREADY, AND, THOUGH IT WAS NICE TO HAVE A NEAT TIDY ENDING TO THE LAST ENORMOUS ZINE, I THINK THE SHORTER-AND-MORE-FREQUENTLY-APPEARING APPROACH WILL BE MORE FUN, URGENT, AND CHAOTIC — YA KNOW, LIKE LIFE.

BY THE WAY, WITH THIS BIRTHDAY, I JUST TURNED 24, AND I'M PRETTY HAPPY ABOUT IT. THIS COULD BE THE THING I WANT TO SAY MOST IN THIS ISSUE, BECAUSE I'VE NOTICED ALOT OF PEOPLE MY AGE FONDLY REMINISCING ABOUT "THE OLD DAYS" WHEN "JUST HAVING FUN AND BEING A KID WAS WHAT BEING A PUNK WAS ALL ABOUT..." AND I CAN'T HELP BUT THINK, "HEY! GET OVER IT, ALREADY! YOU'RE NOT A KID!" BESIDES, BEING A KID WASN'T REALLY FUN ANYWAYS. MY PARENTS, TEACHERS, AND THE COPS TRIED TO STOP ME FROM DOING EVERYTHING I WANTED TO DO. I HAD NO RIGHTS, AND EVEN THE OLD PUNKS WERE SNOTTY AND CONDESCENDING. FUCK THAT! I'LL TAKE 24, WHEN I CAN DO WHATEVER I WANT!

TERSE REMINDER

THOUGH I FEEL THAT THE ERA OF CORPORATE INTEREST IN THE PUNKS IS NEARING AN END, I STILL WANT TO SAY THAT IF YOU ARE WRITING AN ARTICLE ABOUT "THE ZINE REVOLUTION", OR ANY SUCH SHIT, PLEASE LEAVE ME OUT OF IT, OR AT LEAST CHECK WITH ME FIRST! AS A PUNK AND A CRIMINAL, I HAVE NO INTEREST IN THIS ATTENTION.

This book will tell you:
★ "Reversal of Fortune" - the author's story
★ Special Senior Citizens' Section: tips, stories and s
★ 3 new factors why we get involved in scams   ★ 70+ descriptions of the most current scams

Hey Iggy: Thanks for that zine you left us. We're gonna have toilet paper for a fuckin' year!
Lee, Memphis, TN

LETTERS
WWW//SUK.MY.ASS.

IGGY: Hey, thanks for the zine! I kind of like it when a zine shows up really late and you'd forgotten all about it, cause then this mysterious envelope shows up at your door, and you get all excited and curious.
Sue, Baltimore, MD

AS USUAL, SCAM HAS A NEW MAILING ADDRESS. PLEASE NOTE THAT YOU ORDER THE ZINE FROM RECESS RECORDS AND NOT DIRECTLY FROM ME! IF YOU SEND ME CASH, I SWEAR, I'M GOING TO USE IT ON BEER, OR THE BUS, OR SOMETHING. THIS TIME, I'M INTERESTED IN HEARING ABOUT TRIPS TO CUBA, OR PRACTICAL ADVICE ON STARTING A PIRATE RADIO STATION. OH YEAH, AS USUAL, ANYONE WHO CAN HELP WITH FREE XEROXING, LET ME KNOW!

ORDER SCAM #3:
2 BUCKS TO
RECESS RECORDS
P.O. BOX 1112
TORRANCE, CA 90505

ALL PROCEEDS GO TO SEND THE EDITOR TO CUBA!!!

WRITE ME:
IGGY
P.O. BOX 1224
MIAMI, FL 33133
ATTENTION! NO BACK ISSUES, NO FUTURE ISSUES, ANCIENT CHICKENHEAD 7" IS NOW ON CALIFORNIA'S RECESS RECORDS!!!

Dear Mr. (IGGY SCAM): The claim you submitted pertaining to your lost luggage has been reviewed, and we have arrived at the settlement value in the amount of $250.00, as indicated on the attached check.
Greyhound is committed to providing quality service and regrets the inconvenience you experienced. We hope you will give us another opportunity to provide your future transportation needs.
Sincerely, Angenetta Overstreet, claims examiner. Greyhound Lines, Inc. Dallas, TX

Dear MR. (IGGY SCAM): The claim you submitted pertaining to your lost luggage has been reviewed and we have arrived at the settlement value in the amount of $1250.00, as indicated on the attached check. In addition, we have enclosed a flight coupon in the value of $400.00 to be used towards your next flight.
Continental Airlines is committed to providing quality service and regrets the inconvenien inconvenience you experienced. We hope you will give us another opportunity to provide your future transportation needs.
Sincerely, Continental Airlines, Inc.

ED. --- WELL, WHAT CAN I SAY? I JUST LOSE SHIT.

HEY IGGY! DIG THIS CINEMA SCAM! GET FILMS FROM FRIENDS, PUT PROJECTOR IN EMPTY LOT, STEAL ELECTRICITY FROM NEARBY BILLBOARD, BRING COOLER FULL OF BEER, HOT DOGS ON PORTA-GRILL, LAWN CHAIRS! ALL FILM, NO VIDEO, NO COPS, ALL FUN!
BILL DANIEL, WAXAHACHIE, TX

"BROKE..."

So, did I ever tell you about the time when I was broke? I mean, COMPLETELY broke? I didn't even have foodstamps, I was so broke. I had spent them all in one week, by getting up every morning, buying an orange, and using the change to buy a bottle of vodka! Like I said, we're talking BROKE!

I had mapped out a daily Walk-Of-Poverty that took me past the table scraps of some of the city's finest restaurants, the dumpsters of upscale markets, and the backyard fruit trees of the rich and famous. But, before I could go on my daily search for food, I'd always have to break out the duct tape. My shoes had become so full of holes, that I had been keeping them together with duct tape. Then, when they completely fell apart, I threw them away, and started wrapping the tape around my FEET! It was a long walk.

Finally, the long awaited morning of my food stamp appointment arrived. Everyone knows that no true punk rocker can get up at 7:00 AM to go to these things, so I had to try to walk around and stay awake all night. First, I went into Denny's, but, since I was broke, I could only order hot water, and the waiter started cussing at me in Spanish, so I had to leave, and start walking, just to stay awake. It was a good night: I was only chased by three stray dogs, and only stopped, for no reason, by cops, twice. I will say this for the cops around here: they may act like assholes, but they've never beat me up (this is an example of the so-called twenty-something generation's "diminished expectations", I'm sure). Anyways, it wasn't a bad night. I found eight whole garbage bags of bagels in a dumpster! I can't believe they just throw them away!

I got to the food stamp office with time to spare, and spent it reminiscing about the good, old days of welfare, like my first breathless and excited application, only days after my 18th birthday. When it comes to food stamps, I'm totally "old school". When I started getting them, you only got $106 a month, but now, after six years, with "Cost-of-Living" increases, we're all the way up to $120!

Lately, though, the food stam office has been more of a downer. I blame welfare reaform. So, wait--- with this new Welfare Reform Law, and all --- does this mean that I won't be able to get food stamps in several different states at the sam time anymore? It is, of course, too early to tell, and I haven't read the fine pint of the law, but that just may be the case!

I know from experience that there are any number of sweet, old ladies, compassionate Haitian women, and big-hearted, black ladies who call you "baby", that work as food stamp case workers, here in town, and always approve your case, no questions asked. But it seems like years now that I've been getting tough, old Valdez. Valdez is a severe-looking, Cuban guy in his 40's, who looks at you, with a permanen scowl, framed by a bristly, black goatee. Valdez' hard eyes stare back, black and cold, like coal on Christmas morning. Of course, no one really knows what goes on inside the head of an inscrutable man like Valdez, but I'm starting to think that Valdez may actually HATE poor people!

I think back on all the well-crafted, hard luck stories that I've used in food stamp offices across the country, over the years. In Arkansas, I said I'd come to ton to join an up-and-coming country music band, but got kicked out and had to pawn my guitar. Down in Biloxi, I was fired from a shrimp boat, because I was a better picker than the captain's son. Out West, in Eureka,, when my case worker asked, "Are you homeless?", I gave her my most innocent, heartbreaking look, and replied, "No, Ma'am. I live in a bush on 'T' Street. All the stories are the sae; all roads lead to the food stamp office. As Valdez starts his usual interrogation, I consider that this ridiculous, fictional past is not too unlikely as a real future.

If Valdez was a cartoon, you'd always draw him with steam coming out of his ears. He hammers away, "If you're homeless, where do you take showers?!? Where do you cook food ?!?" He, apparently, hasn't considerred that homeless people may not, in fact, get to take showers. Valdez gets more and more frustrated as we navigate this confusing world between my lies, and his total lack of understanding. But, since he doesn't believe anything I say, it doesn't really matter what I tell him. When he finally snorts, "Well, why haven't you been looking for a job?!?" I just grin. "My girlfriend left me. And I've been drinking ever since."

Reluctantly, Valdez finally approves my case, and within an hour, I had my stamps and had expertly made several $1.05 purchases to get enough change to buy some tall, ice-cold cans of malt liquour. As I recall, malt liquour tasted good that year. But, I had to try and drink the cold beer on the left side of my mouth, because the teeth on the right side were killing me. Maybe my wisdom teeth were coming in. Maybe my teeth were just on the verge of total collapse. Who knows these things? I often wonder exactly where the line between young, excited punk rocker living in abandoned buildings, and crazy, toothless wino living in the street lies. I've given it lots of thought, and have decided that if all my teeth fell out, and I had to get false teeth, I'd just have to laugh it off somehow, like my friend did when he accidently cut off his finger at work.

I decided to go see if the Free Clinic could help me with my teeth. First, I had to hop the subway. I felt bad that I had no change for the Guy-with-no-legs at the foot of the stairs by the main train station. See, even that shows how tough times are. There used to be a blind guy at that spot, possibly the best panhandling spot in town. Then there was a guy with one hand. Now, its a guy with no legs, and the one-handed guy can't get a spot within 10 blocks of the station! Soon, it'll just be a little nub, with a cup, and folks'll still be walking by, saying they don't have any money!

When I got to the clinic, I got right in to see the doc, a real, kindly, gentle, old Nazi, with stiff, gray sideburns, a set of big, white teeth, and a look on his face that said he'd be happier setting fire to oil wells in Iraq. He punched my nose a couple times, strangled me a bit, and said I was fine, but that he'd go ahead and give me an appointment for May 10, 2003, at 6:00 AM, anyways. I promised to be there. At the subway, I ignored the new signs that said "FARE EVASION IS A SIN", and hopped the rail home.

When I got home, though, I couldn't believe my good luck! In the mailbox, was 25 bucks in cash from my distributor for old magazines I'd sold them!

Twenty-five dollars, in those days, was alot of money to a young, starving writer. I used the money to purchase a loaf of fresh-baked bread, an onion, and four of the finest quality pens for my writing. My writing is very important to me. I ate the bread and onion, in my tiny room, while watching two men fist

fight in the streets below my window. Then, I ate the pens. I am very hungry these days. You can see that being a young, starving writer, while certainly glamorous, has its drawbacks. Like, for one thing, I can't get a date. I consider a personal ad:" Y.S.W seeks S.F...", but I have to save my cash to get my glue stick out of the pawn shop.

But it was a great night there in my room. For weeks, I had been saving the half-full cans of beer that frat boys threw at me from passing cars, and, now, I finally had enough to get drunk with, while I listened to music. It was true that I only owned one record, but, I loved to listen to it, on both the 33 RPM, and 45 RPM speeds, all night!

OK, I'LL ADMIT THERE'S A BIT OF A HOLLYWOOD TOUCH TO ALL THIS GLAMORIZATION OF POVERTY YOU SEE HERE AND IN OTHER ZINES, SOMETIMES, IT SEEMS LIKE WE'RE LOOKING BACK, NOSTALGIACALLY, LAUGH TRACK AND ALL, AND SAYING," THIS IS HOW WE LIVED BEFORE..." I WONDER, SOMETIMES, BEFORE WHAT? THE "REVOLUTION"? OUR "BIG BREAK"? THE "DOOMSDAY COMET"? WHO KNOWS?.
ALL I'M SAYING IS, MAN, WAS I BROKE...

ANIMAL SACRIFICE, BEER SPITTING, DANCING TAMPONS AND OTHER LOCAL SHITZ !!!

FIRST OF ALL, I'M NOT INTO TALKING ABOUT "THE OLD DAYS" TOO MUCH, BUT I COULDN'T HELP BUT NOTICE, LATELY, HOW MUCH BETTER EVERYTHING SEEMS IN MIAMI NOW, THEN WHEN I GOT INTO PUNK. SHOWS ARE MORE FUN, LOCAL BANDS ARE BETTER, THERE'S MORE PLACES TO PLAY, AND YOU'RE A MILLION TIMES LESS LIKELY TO GET BEAT UP AT A SHOW. SOME OLDTIMERS MAY LIKE TO TRY AND GLAMORIZE THE OLD "DANGEROUS" DAYS, BUT I, PERSONALLY, NEVER FELT THAT THE THREAT OF GETTING JUMPED BY 10 SKINHEADS IN A SOUTH BEACH ALLEY, BY THE CAMEO, MADE A SHOW ANY MORE EXCITING, ESPECIALLY WHEN THE SHOW IN QUESTION WAS SOME FAKE-ASS SHIT LIKE A SPEED METAL BAND AND A STRAIGHT EDGE BAND OPENING UP FOR THE FUCKING CIRCLE JERKS FOR 15 BUCKS! DUH!

1997: YEAR OF "THE REGION"?

FOR THOSE WHO DON'T KNOW, "THE REGION" IS A LOOSELY DEFINED GEOGRAPHICAL TRIANGLE WITH POINTS IN MIAMI, CHATTANOOGA, TENNESSEE, AND EXTENDING WEST POSSIBLY FAR AS LITTLE ROCK, ARKANSAS, WHERE A WHOLE ARMY OF BAD-AS-HELL BANDS ARE KNOWN, NOT FOR RIPPING OFF SOME COOL, RETRO-STYLE, BUT FOR HOW MUCH ENERGY, AND SPIT, AND SWEAT THEY BRING TO THE STAGE - BASICALLY, JUST HOW HARD THEY ROCK! YO! AFTER A COUPLE YEARS OF GOING BACK AND FORTH, PLAYING EACH OTHER'S TOWNS, THE REGION ROCKERS ARE ALL GOING ON TOUR. LOS CANADIANS WENT THIS SPRING, AND THIS SUMMER, LOOK FOR MIAMI'S DARVIS BROWN AND THE SMOKE ASSES WITH CHATSWORTH, GA'S THE MORONS, CHATTANOOGA'S DRILLER KILLERS AND THE SPAWN SACS, MIAMI'S KREAMY 'LECTRIC SANTA, AND MAYBE LITTLE ROCK'S CHAOS L.R. HUNTSVILLE, AL'S JOEY TAMPON AND THE TOXIC SHOCKS, AND CHATTANOOGA'S JACKPALANCE BAND, AND MIAMI'S THE STUN GUNS.

GETTING THE ROCK ON IN MIAMI

MY NEW FAVORITE PLACE TO HAVE SHOWS IS THE BACKSTAGE UPON N.W. 7TH AVE. AND 122nd STREET IN THE "FAILING RESTAURANT AND DISCOUNT AUTO PARTS" DISTRICT. IT'S PRETTY SMALL WITH NO STAGE, SO YOU SEEM TO FEEL MORE CROWD/BAND ENERGY, AND THERE'S TOTAL PUNK CONTROL! ANYONE CAN PLAY, YOU CAN WORK THE DOOR IF YOU FEEL LIKE IT, AND YOU'RE FREE TO CHARGE WHATEVER YOU WANT, BECAUSE THE OWNER DOESN'T TAKE A CUT. INSTEAD, HE MAKES HIS CASH BY SELLING COLD CANS OF CHEAP BEER, RIGHT OUT OF THE 12-PAK BOX! AFTER A COUPLE YEARS OF THE PRO-STYLE SHOWS AT CHEERS, WHERE WELL-SCRUBBED YOUNGSTERS DUTIFULLY RECREATE ENTIRE QUEERS AND NOFX RECORDS WITHOUT EVEN SEEMING TO ENJOY IT, IT WAS EXCITING TO GO TO THE BACKSTAGE AND SEE UFC, THE POSSESSORS OF SOUTH FLORIDA'S LARGEST MOHAWKS STOMP AROUND THE DANCE FLOOR, SPITTING BEER ON EACH OTHER, WHILE STOPPING AFTER EVERY SONG, SO THE BASSIST COULD TEACH THE GUITARIST THE NEXT SONG! AT THE BACKSTAGE IT FEELS LIKE PUNK NEVER GOT FAMOUS.

CONTINUED ON NEXT PAGE ➔

INSTANT REDNECK ATTACK

IF YOU'RE EVER IN CHATTANOOGA, CHECK OUT THE PLEASANTLY NAMED "INSTANT BEER PLEASURE" LOUNGE, CUZ THAT'S WHERE SOME GREAT SHOWS HAPPEN, AS WELL AS INSPIRATIONAL PUNK VICTORIES OVER LOCAL REDNECKS. THE 'NECKS GOT ROWDY AT THE LOS CANADIANS SHOW AND ASKED AUDIENCE MEMBER, CANDY, IF SHE WAS A BOY, OR A GIRL. THERE WERE SOME BACK AND FORTH INSULTS, 'TIL SPAWN SACS DRUMMER, QUANNAH, TOLD THE REDNECKS, IN TRUE QUANNAH-INCOMPREHENSIBLE STYLE "YOUR MOTHER'S A TOMATO!" NOT WANTING TO ADMIT THEY DIDN'T KNOW WHAT THAT MEANT, THE REDNECKS TRIED TO FISTFIGHT THE PUNKS, BUT THE WHOLE CROWD GANGED UP ON THE 3 'NECKS AND TOLD 'EM WHAT WAS UP! AFTER THE 'NECKS WERE GONE, THE SHAFFERS PLAYED PROVING, ONCE AGAIN, THAT THE ROCK IS UNSTOPPABLE!!!

I THINK MY FAVORITE BACKSTAGE SHOW, SO FAR, WAS A COUPLE WEEKS AGO WHEN REGION ROCKERS, JOEY TAMPON AND THE TOXIC SHOCKS CAME TO TOWN. FIRST, THE 'BONEHEADS, LED BY THEIR MADMAN DRUMMER, TORE THROUGH A TIGHT, STRAIGHT AHEAD ATTACK, AND EVEN BROKE OUT A DILKS COVER. THEN, MY BAND, THE ~~BLUE~~ HIDDEN RESENTMENTS SWEATED OUT A WHOLE 12-PAK, BROKEN COLLARBONE AND ALL. BUT, THEN THE TOXIC SHOCKS BURNED THE SHIT TO THE GROUND WITH DRUMMER, GREG, FULLY RISING OFF THE DRUM STOOL TO HIT THE CRASH, EVERY TIME, AND BASSIST, NEIL, BREAKING HIS STRAP, BUT FINISHING THE SET, WITH IT WRAPPED, NOOSE-LIKE AROUND HIS CHOKING NECK! YO! WHEN BIG HECTOR, OF DARVIS BROWN, PUT ON THE TAMPON SUIT AND STARTED MOSHING EVERYBODY DOWN, THE PLACE WENT NUTS — WALL TO WALL DANCING, WITH NO HINT OF VIOLENCE; JUST JUMPING, YELLING, BEER SPITTING FUN WITH THIS BIG, HAPPY TAMPON IN THE MIDDLE OF IT!

BUT THE SHOW OF THE YEAR MAY HAVE BEEN THE NEW BOMB TURKS SHOW DOWN AT CHEERS. I WAS SORT-OF SKEPTICAL OF THE TURKS, CUZ I THOUGHT THEY MIGHT JUST BE SOME RETRO-BANDWAGONEERS ON A BIG LABEL, BUT I FIGURED I'D STEAL A BOTTLE OF WINE AND GO TRY AND SNEAK INTO THE SHOW. WELL, THEY TOTALLY BLEW ME AWAY BY SPLITTIN' THE SKULLS OF THE AUDIENCE FOR WELL OVER AN HOUR WITH PURE BAD ASS ROCK! THE CROWD DANCED LIKE HELL FOR THE WHOLE SHOW, AND I THOUGHT WE WERE GONNA CAVE THE FLOOR IN, EVEN THOUGH, I KNOW ITS, TECHNICALLY, NOT POSSIBLE. RECLUSIVE, OLDER PUNK ROCKERS DRAINED THEIR BEERS AND EXECUTED THEIR FIRST STAGE DIVES IN YEARS! IT WAS GREAT, AND I WAS TOTALLY CONVINCED BY THE STRENGTH OF THE TURK ROCK TO GO STEAL THEIR NEW CD FROM SPEC'S! IT WAS JUST ONE OF THOSE RARE SHOWS WHERE A BAND CAN MAKE A HUGE ROOM FULL OF PEOPLE FEEL LIKE THEY'RE ALL PART OF THE SAME THING. AFTERWARDS, I TABLE DIVED PIZZA SLAPS AT CASOLA'S ACROSS THE STREET WITH ALL THESE PUNKS WHO I'D NEVER MET BEFORE, AND FELT LIKE I KNEW ALL THESE RAD, NEW PEOPLE...

BANNED FOR LIFE?

AS OF THIS WRITING, THE WORD IS THAT CHEERS IS CLOSING. THIS NEWS COMES ABOUT A MONTH AFTER I WAS PERSONALLY "BANNED FOR LIFE" FOR TRYING TO SNEAK INTO THE DARVIS BROWN/ MORONS SHOW WITH A POORLY FAKED STAMP. FOR LIFE, HUH?

SPEAKING OF "BANNED FOR LIFE", JUST ABOUT ANYONE WHO IS ANYONE HAS BEEN BANNED FOR LIFE FROM CHURCHILL'S, BUT, USUALLY, OWNER, DAVE DANIELS, THE SLEAZY, DRUNKEN, BRIT, IS TOO TRASHED TO REMEMBER THAT HE KICKED YOU OUT. FOR INSTANCE, CAVITY, WAS GIVEN THE BOOT WAY BACK IN 1992 WHEN THEY WERE CALLED CRAWL BECAUSE THEIR DIRGE, FEEDBACK ATTACK CLEARED OUT THE WHOLE BAR. THESE DAYS, THEY PROBABLY BRING THE PAINFUL CAVITY ROCK TO CHURCHILL'S ONCE A MONTH!

JUST ABOUT EVERY SHOW THAT CHANGED MY LIFE, THAT EVER MATTERED TO ME, THAT CAUSED ME TO STILL BE WIDE AWAKE WHEN THE SUN CAME UP, HAPPENED AT CHURCHILL'S, AND ITS STILL A GREAT PLACE TO SEE SHOWS. BUT I THINK ITS STATUS AS A LOCAL "INSTITUTION" HAS TAKEN SOME ENERGY OUT OF IT. MAYBE DAVE'S RECENT PUBLIC THREATS TO SELL THE PLACE WILL LIGHT A FIRE UNDER THE CROWD, AND MAKE IT SEEM MORE SPECIAL, OR MAYBE THE SHOWS WILL JUST KEEP GETTING A LITTLE MORE DULL AND PEOPLE WILL KEEP DRINKING MORE TO TRY AND COVER IT UP. WHO KNOWS?

THE CLOSING OF CLUBS MAKES ME THINK OF THIS SKID ROW DOUGHNUT SHOP I USED TO HANG OUT IN IN SAN FRANCISCO. THE COUNTER GUY WOULD ALWAYS BAN PEOPLE FOR LIFE FOR BEING TOO DRUNK, OR SLEEPING ON THE TABLES, OR TRYING TO FENCE STOLEN PROPERTY. BUT, AFTER A COUPLE WEEKS OF WORKING THERE, THE COUNTER GUY WOULD, INVARIABLY, LOSE HIS MIND AND QUIT. THEN THERE'D BE A NEW COUNTER-GUY AND ALL THE DUDES WHO GOT BANNED WOULD SLOWLY COME BACK. THE COUNTER GUYS, AND CLUBS COME AND GO, BUT WE, THE PUNKS, WILL STILL BE HERE!

FREE FOOD, FREE COFFEE, FREE PRACTICE, TWO DOLLAR SHOWS

MIAMI FOOD NOT BOMBS IS NOW SERVING FREE, VEGETARIAN FOOD ON SUNDAYS AT 2:00 PM (OR, UH, CLOSE TO IT) AT THE EMPTY LOT ON GRAND AVENUE AT MARGARET STREET IN COCONUT GROVE, NEXT TO THE FINA GAS STATION, 2 BLOCKS WEST OF THE POST OFFICE. BELIEVE IT, OR NOT, LAKE WORTH HAD A FOOD NOT BOMBS FOR MONTHS THAT NO ONE DOWN HERE KNEW ABOUT. THEY SERVE THURSDAY AFTERNOONS AT JOHN PRINCE PARK ON LAKE WORTH BOULEVARD, WEST OF I-95 A BIT, ON THE LEFT.

THE NEW YESTERDAY AND TODAY RECORDS IS NOW OPEN IN LOVELY, DOWNTOWN SOUTH MIAMI, AND IS NOW FULLY UNDER PUNK CONTROL, AS STARCRUNCH RECORD LABEL GUY, CHRIS (WHO PUT OUT

REPRINTED WITH NO PERMISSION FROM 1979 FANZINE "MOUTH OF THE RAT", ISSUE #11 FROM BOCA RATON, FL!

I GUESS YOU CAN CALL IT "THE END OF AN ERA". THE TUESDAY AND WEDNESDAY NITE FORAYS INTO PUNK ROCK ARE A THING OF THE PAST, TIGHT SPACE IS MOVING TO GREENER PASTURES. I NEVER THOUGHT I'D MISS A PLACE THAT ~~████~~ CHARGED $1.50 FOR BEER, ABUSED MY FRIENDS, UNDER PAID IT'S OPENING BANDS AND THREW ME OUT FOR DANCING BUT I ACTUALLY GOT A LUMP ■ IN MY THROAT ■ DURING THE CICHLIDS LAST SET THERE. LIKE ROBT. SAID WELL IT'LL HAPPEN SOMEWHERE ELSE BUT IT JUST WON'T BE THE SAME... YEAH, FUCK IT I WILL MISS THE PLACE..... SO NOW IT'S SAT. NITE AND I CAN'T HELP BUT WONDER WHERE THAT PLACE WILL BE.....THERE ARE A FEW PEOPLE AND PLACES PLOTTING AND PLANNING AND IT WILL BE INTERESTING

TO SEE WHAT WE'LL HAVE TO PUT UP WITH AND GO THROUGH IN THE INTERIM...OF COURSE, WE'LL SEE THE EAT, THE GIRLS AND THE CICHLIDS AROUND BUT IT WILL BE GREAT WHEN WE FIND A CLUB WE CAN "ALL" CALL HOME...IT'S OUT THERE SOME-WHERE... SOME PEOPLE ARE TALKING WARE-HOUSE AND THAT COULD BE OUR BEST BET, SURELY SOMEWHERE BETWEEN MIAMI AND WEST PALM BEACH THERE IS A WAREHOUSE... IN THE MEANTIME IT LOOKS LIKE IT'S EVERY MAN FOR HIMSELF.......

(CONTINUED FROM)

THE STUNGUNS, LOS CANADIANS, KREAMY 'LECTRIC SANTA, THE DRUG CZARS...) IS SLOWLY BUYING IT FROM THE OLD OWNER. THE NEW STORE ALSO FEATURES VIDEO RENTAL AND MAY POSSIBLY HAVE SHOWS! IT IS CONVENIENTLY LOCATED, BY THE WAY, NEAR TWO WEIRD, OFTEN OVERLOOKED SOURCES OF FREE COFFEE ——— THE WINN-DIXIE GROCERY STORE, AND... THE WAITING ROOM AT TIRE KINGDOM ON U.S. 1! NO SHIT! SOUTH MIAMI — "EPICENTER OF FREE COFFEE"!

SPACE CADET STUDIOS REMAINS A GOOD EXAMPLE OF PEOPLE WORKING LIKE HELL TO DO STUFF, INSTEAD OF JUST SITTING AROUND TALKING ABOUT IT. THEY'VE BEEN DOING DIFFERENT TYPES OF SHOWS, USUALLY ONLY FOR TWO BUCKS, WHERE THEY HAVE AN "ART OPENING" IN THE FRONT ROOM AND THEN A COUPLE BANDS PLAYING IN THE BACK ROOM. THEIR INCREDIBLE FREE REHEARSAL SPACE FOR BANDS IS NO LONGER AVAILABLE, BECAUSE SOME PEOPLE DELIBERATELY TRASHED THEIR EQUIPMENT, BUT THEY'RE SUPPOSED TO BE OPENING A NEW SPACE FOR REHEARSAL THAT WILL HAVE ONE ROOM STILL AVAILABLE FREE OF CHARGE! EVEN COOLER, THOUGH, IS HOW, THROUGH BIG BROTHERS/BIG SISTERS ASSOCIATION, THEY'VE ALLOWED THEIR SPACE AND MUSICAL INSTRUMENTS TO BE USED BY GROUPS OF INNER CITY KIDS, WHO WOULDN'T ORDINARILY HAVE THE EXPOSURE TO EXPENSIVE EQUIPMENT!

WHEN THESE ANTI-CRIME STICKERS (FIG. A) SUDDENLY APPEARED ALL OVER DOWNTOWN AND LITTLE HAVANA, WE, THE CRIMINALS, HAD TO STRIKE BACK! SO ME AND IVY MADE THESE FLYERS (FIG. B), WITH THE HELP OF CHUCK LOOSE'S EXTENSIVE LIBRARY OF GAY COP PORNOGRAPHY, AND I USED TRUSTY OLE 3M SPRAY GLOO TO PUT 'EM UP NEXT TO THE OTHER STICKERS, EVERYWHERE! JASON HUDSON TOOK ONE AND FAXED IT TO LOCAL AM RADIO CELEBRITY, NEIL ROGERS, WHILE HE WAS ON THE AIR, AND, ACCORDING TO JASON, ROGERS BROKE OUT LAUGHING AND SPENT THE REST OF THE SHOW JOKING ABOUT IT...

FIG. A↗ FIG. B↗

FEDEX SCAMMED

WHILE WORKING ON THIS ISSUE ON MANY LATE NIGHTS AT THE BRICKELL KINKO'S, I COULDN'T HELP NOTICE THAT OFTEN, ESPECIALLY ON SUNDAYS WHEN THERE'S NO FEDEX PICKUP, THE FEDEX PICKUP BOX WOULD BE FULL, SO PEOPLE WOULD JUST LEAVE THEIR PACKAGES OUTSIDE THE BOX TO BE PICKED UP. THIS MEANS THE AIR BILL, THAT CONTAINS THE FEDEX ACCOUNT NUMBER (MAIL EQUIVALENT OF CALLING CARD #) AND ALL OTHER PERTINENT INFO. THAT YOU NEED TO SEND A PACKAGE, IS IN FULL VIEW FOR ANYONE TO COPY DOWN AND USE! TRY IT WITH SOMETHING UNIMPORTANT FIRST TO SEE IF THE # WORKS, AND DON'T USE YOUR REAL NAME...

SCAM AND PUNK SHIT IN THE LIBRARY

IN AN EFFORT TO REACH MORE OF OUR TARGET AUDIENCE — YOU KNOW, BUMS — SCAM IS NOW AVAILABLE IN THE SAN FRANCISCO MAIN PUBLIC LIBRARY AND THE UNIVERSITY OF MONTANA LIBRARY AT MISSOULA. IT WAS PRETTY EXCITING TO GET IN THE RAD OLD SF LIBRARY BEFORE THEY SWITCHED BUILDINGS. IF YOU'RE DOWN THERE, CHECK IT OUT, CUZ THEY'VE GOT EVERY ISSUE OF MUDFLAP! I'M SORT OF WORRIED ABOUT THIS MONTANA THING, THOUGH. I'M AFRAID THE WHITE SEPARATIST MILITIA GUYS ARE GOING TO USE THE RECEIPT SCAM TO BUY AK-47'S! FUK!

MEANWHILE, MY BIG MIAMI-PUNK-IN-THE-LIBRARY PROJECT HAS SORT OF STALLED FOR NOW. THE HEAD OF THE FLORIDA ROOM WAS VERY ENTHUSIASTIC ABOUT MY DONATING A "LOCAL MUSIC COLLECTION" WHICH WAS, OF COURSE, ALL PUNK. I DONATED A SMALL PILE OF STUFF LIKE SCAM, SUBURBAN RELAPSE ZINE, CHICKENHEAD, LOS CANADIANS, THE EAT, MORBID OPERA, K.L.S. "WE CAN'T HELP IT IF WE'RE FROM FLORIDA" COMP., ETC... AND, NOW, A YEAR LATER, ITS ALL STILL IN SOME MYSTERIOUS VAULT AWAITING "CLASSIFICATION." MAYBE IF YOU, THE SCAM READER BUG 'EM ABOUT IT...

BY THE WAY, DID ANYBODY BESIDES ME AND IVY SEE THE EXHIBIT OF "COURTROOM SKETCHES OF MIAMI" IN THE MAIN LIBRARY? IT WAS TOTALLY HILARIOUS; A "WHO'S WHO?" OF MIAMI IGNOMINIOUS DEFEAT, WITH ALL THE GREATS AND NEAR GREATS LIKE INDICTED COMISSIONER DAWKINS, INDICTED CITY MANAGER ODIO, INDICTED MIAMI BEACH MAYOR, ALEX DAOUD, INDICTED HIALEAH MAYOR, RAUL MARTINEZ, AS WELL AS TED BUNDY, THE YAHWEH-BEN-YAHWEH, SHERIFF NICK NAVARRO, THE MIAMI RIVER COPS, AND, OF COURSE, GENERAL NORIEGA! NOW THAT'S AN ART EXHIBIT!

I READ IT IN THE HERALD!

THE DRUG, SPEED, LONG UNAVAILABLE IN SOUTH FLORIDA, IS SOON TO HIT THE MARKET HERE, REPLACING HEROIN, ACCORDING TO THE DEA, AND I CAN'T WAIT. SINCE I MOVED AWAY FROM THE WEST COAST, WHERE SPEED IS THE DRUG OF CHOICE, I'VE MISSED THE MYSTERIOUS 4:00 AM GARDENERS AND MECHANICS — THE LURKING HENCHMEN AND MAD INVENTORS OF THE FAILED SUBURB. ASK NOT WHO THE TOOTHLESS, MUSTACHIOD HESHER STANDS IN HIS YARD FOR AT DAWN — HE STANDS FOR YOU!

FREE PUNK SHOWS IN THE SWAMP!

WITH SUMMER COMING UP, HOPEFULLY THE PROUD, MIAMI TRADITION OF JUST TAKING A GENERATOR TO THE MIDDLE OF NOWHERE, AND HAVING A PUNK SHOW, WILL CONTINUE. OVER THE LAST COUPLE YEARS, THERE'S BEEN A BUNCH OF GOOD SHOWS AT A MYSTERIOUS EVERGLADES BOAT LAUNCH OFF KROME AVENUE, WITH TONS OF BEER, SPRAYPAINTED SHIRTS AND FOOD SOLD TO PAY THE BANDS, AND BANDS FROM THE REGION, LIKE LES TURDZ VANBUILDERASS, AND CRACKROCK, AND LOCAL ROCKERS, AGAINST ALL AUTHORITY, PIN KAI, AND THE CRUMBS. WE NEVER HAD ANY TROUBLE FROM COPS, BUT, ONE TIME WE DID HAVE TO MOVE A BUNCH OF CARS WHEN A STUNNED FISHERMAN SHOWED UP TO ACTUALLY LAUNCH A BOAT...

THE "ANDRE AGASSI SCAM"?

AGASSI

PUT

MILLIONS CHEER FOR ANDRE AGASSI, THE TEMPER-MENTAL, SHAVEN-HEADED TENNIS STAR AND HUSBAND OF BROOKE SHIELDS AS HE WINS TOURNAMENT AFTER TOURNAMENT. DOZENS SHOUT, "HELL, YEAH!" AS TIMMY PUT, THE LOVABLE, LITTLE, BALD BASSIST OF LOS CANADIANS SENDS HEARTS SKYWARD WITH HIS SOARING, MELODY BASS LINES. NOW, ONE TELEVISION COMMERCIAL HAS BROUGHT THEM TOGETHER IN MIAMI LEGEND, FOREVER...

TIMMY GOT HIS "BIG BREAK" WHILE WORKING HIS DAY JOB AS DELIVERY GUY FOR A COCONUT GROVE HEALTH FOOD STORE. WHEN HE DELIVERED FOOD TO THE SET OF A COMMERCIAL FOR THE UPCOMING LIPTON TENNIS TOURNAMENT AT KEY BISCAYNE, THE AD EXECS WERE IN THE PROCESS OF TRYING TO FIND SOMEONE TO PLAY AGASSI, AS A JOKE, IN A COMMERCIAL FOR THE TOURNAMENT. ONE EXEC SAID, "HOW ABOUT THE DELIVERY GUY?" HE WAS HIRED RIGHT AWAY.

IN THE COMMERCIAL THAT AIRED FOR A MONTH ON LOCAL TV, TIMMY, HOLDING A TENNIS RACKET AND KEEPING HIS TATTOOS WELL OUT OF SIGHT, WAS QUESTIONED AS AGASSI BY VETERAN ESPN TENNIS ANALYST, CLIFF DRYSDALE. WITH HIS TRADEMARK, CLIPPED, BRITISH ACCENT, DRYSDALE ASKED TIMMY, "ANDRE, WILL YOU MAKE #1 AGAIN?" TIMMY'S RAMBLING AD-LIB RESPONSES WERE ABOUT HIS LOVE OF HIS AND BROOKE'S NEW, SOFT PUPPY, AND ABOUT THE INDESCRIBABLE BEAUTY OF THE ACTUAL SHADE OF A TENNIS RACKET. WHILE HE ANSWERED, CLIPS WERE SHOWN OF TIMMY STUMBLING AROUND A TENNIS COURT, AND FLAILING AT TENNIS BALLS, AS WELL AS CLIPS OF DRYSDALE, DEEPLY INTERESTED, NODDING STUDIOUSLY.

TIM GOT PAID AND HIS NEIGHBORHOOD CELEBRITY INCREASED, ALONG WITH HIS TIPS, BUT THAT SEEMED TO BE THE END OF IT.

BUT, THEN, WORD GOT BACK TO TIMMY THAT ANDRE HIMSELF HAD SEEN THE COMMERCIALS AND HAD LOVED THEM. TIMMY WAS ASKED TO APPEAR ON COMEDIAN AND FAILED TALK SHOW HOST, DENNIS MILLER'S HBO SPECIAL THAT WAS COVERING THE LIPTON TOURNAMENT! HE WAS GIVEN A FULL TENNIS OUTFIT AND WAS TOLD THAT HE WOULD BE PRESENTING AN AWARD TO ANDRE, AS ANDRE. PRETTY DRY STUFF, TO BE SURE, BUT WHO SAID TENNIS WAS FUNNY?

BEFORE THE SHOW, TIM GATHERED TOGETHER LOS CANADIANS T-SHIRTS AND RECORDS FOR ANDRE AND BROOKE. THE CANADIANS WERE PLANNING A TOUR AND, BEFORE HE LEFT FOR THE

WISH YOU WERE HERE!

SINCE MIAMI'S "OFFICIAL" IMAGE IS BASED ON POSTCARD SCENES — YA KNOW, BIKINIS AND HOTELS — I THOUGHT IT'D BE FUN TO FUCK WITH. SO I MADE THE ABOVE POSTCARDS, ON REAL POSTCARD STOCK, OF BIKINI GIRLS WITH HUGE PENISES AND THE MIAMI CRACK HOUSE, AND TOOK 'EM OUT AND STUCK 'EM IN POSTCARD RACKS IN GIFT SHOPS ALL OVER TOWN, NEXT TO THE NORMAL ONES! CHUCK SCAMMED THE CARDSTOCK COPIES AT HIS WORK...

TAPING, TIMMY ANNOUNCED THAT HE INTENDED TO ASK ANDRE FOR $10,000 TO FINANCE THE TOUR. "ANDRE WILL GIVE IT TO ME. I KNOW HE WILL," SAID TIM.

BUT, AT THE TAPING, ANDRE NEVER SHOWED AND TIMMY WAS TOLD THAT HIS PRESENTATION WOULDN'T BE TAPED. TIM'S NEW JOB WAS TO MINGLE IN THE CROWD AS ANDRE. INSTEAD, HE SAT AROUND THE SET ALL DAY, GUZZLING COMP. BEERS IN A DULL RAGE.

WHEN IT CAME TIME TO ANNOUNCE THE AWARD, TIMMY AND SOME TENNIS PRO WERE ANNOUNCED BY DENNIS MILLER. TIMMY WAS TOO DRUNK TO READ THE TELEPROMPTER, SO HE TRIED TO AD-LIB A PRESENTATION, BUT THE TENNIS PRO REFUSED TO PLAY ALONG. THE CROWD WAS STUNNED. MILLER, THE SMUG BASTARD, APOLOGIZED SMIRKINGLY TO THE CROWD, CALLING TIMMY, "A MONKEY VENTRILOQUIST." IT WAS AN UGLY SCENE. TIMMY'S STAR HAD CRUELLY FALLEN JUST BEFORE HIS RISE TO CABLE TV STARDOM, DINNER WITH ANDRE AND BROOKE, THE WORLD OF THE $10,000 HANDSHAKE... BACKSTAGE, TIMMY DRUNKENLY YELLED AT EVEN MORE WASHED UP COMEDIAN, PAULY SHORE (A FELLOW PRESENTER) AND, FINALLY CORNERED A CHANNEL 10 SPORTS REPORTER, DEMANDING A HUNDRED BUCKS! "I'M ANDRE, DAMN IT!" HE BELLOWED.

TIMMY NEVER DID MEET ANDRE. A COUPLE DAYS LATER AGASSI LOST IN A SURPRISE, FIRST-ROUND UPSET TO AN UNRANKED ARGENTINIAN. BUT UNRANKED DELIVERYGUY, TIM, HAS MOVED ONTO A NEW PRINT AD FOR LOCAL RECORD STORE SPEC'S!

SANTERIA VS. THE COPS!

TO KEEP THE POLICE AWAY

Grind sage leaves into a powder and blow on your door.

TO ESCAPE THE LAW

Rub your head with two quail hens. Bite their heads off and let the blood drip on your head. Spread their feathers up and down the street.

VOODOO IS PUNK!

CRUDE, BUT EFFECTIVE...

JUST AFTER CHRISTMAS, MY OLD RUSTY BIKE THAT HAD SERVED ME FOR ALMOST 2 YEARS (AN ALL-TIME RECORD) GOT STOLEN OUTSIDE OF A LITTLE HAVANA BAKERY. I WAS GOING TO DIE WITHOUT ONE, SO, AFTER A COUPLE WEEKS OF THINKING ABOUT IT, I FINALLY WENT TO A LOCAL DEPARTMENT STORE, GRABBED A FLOOR MODEL MOUNTAIN BIKE, AND... UH... HEADED FOR THE DOOR! IT WAS SO EXCITING! AS I HEADED FOR THE DOOR, I THOUGHT, "I CAN'T BELIEVE ITS REALLY HAPPENING!" I GUESS NO ONE SAW ME, BUT I RODE LIKE HELL, ANYWAYS, TO A FRIEND'S HOUSE WHERE I SCRATCHED OFF THE SERIAL #S. WITHIN AN HOUR IT WAS SPRAY PAINTED BLUE AND ALL MINE. NOT EXACTLY A SCAM, BUT...

ANIMAL SACRIFICE IN THE NEWS

IT CAN BE REALLY HARD TO WRITE ABOUT AND LIVE IN MIAMI AT THE SAME TIME, SOMETIMES, AS EVERY DAY, THE NEWS BRINGS SOME INCREDIBLY RIDICULOUS STORY. CHECK THIS MIAMI HERALD STORY: "A MIAMI HUSBAND AND WIFE CLAIMING TO OFFER A MANATEE SKULL, A FROZEN BALD EAGLE, A HUMAN FETUS, AND OTHER HUMAN BODY PARTS FOR SALE TO SANTERIA PRIESTS HAVE BEEN ARRESTED FOR ALLEGED VIOLATIONS OF FEDERAL WILDLIFE LAWS." HOW MUCH OF THIS SHIT CAN YOU TAKE EVERY DAY? "THE COUPLE WERE ARRESTED AFTER A METRO-DADE COP, POSING AS A SANTERIA PRIEST, PAID $1600 FOR TWO FROZEN OWLS, A HAWK, TWO ELEPHANT TUSKS, AND A RABBIT FETUS..." SHEESH!

NEXT TIME THE GUYS ON GRAND AVENUE ASK, "ARE YOU STRAIGHT, MAN?" I'M GOING TO SEE IF THEY CAN SCORE ME SOME RABBIT FETUS!

PUNCH LINE TO THIS LONG JOKE: "HEY! THIS ISN'T RABBIT FETUS!!! ITS A BAG OF OREGANO!"

A voodoo curse caused a scuffle between two neighbors. The fight began about 10:41 a.m. Thursday when one neighbor accused the other of placing a voodoo object on her doorstep in the 6400 block on Indian Creek Drive. Both women suffered minor scratches to their arms. Police warned them to stay away from each other.

TO OBTAIN A PRISONER'S RELEASE (MIAMI STYLE!)

A rooster   Cemetery dust

Cotton thread in red, black, white, yellow, blue, green, and brown

Sacrifice the rooster to Elegua. Toast the rooster's feathers and grind them to a powder. Mix the powder with the dust.

Tear out the rooster's tongue and wind it tightly in the different colored threads. It is to be given to the prisoner to unwind in his or her cell.

Sprinkle a light, but steady, stream of powder from the Orisha's house to the jail and back again.

THE ROAD TO TALLAHASSEE IS PAVED WITH GROSS AND UNNATURAL ACTS!!!

THE TRUE, SHOCKING STORY!

THERE'S THIS KIND OF UNWRITTEN LAW OF HITCH HIKING WHERE IF YOU'RE WALKING UP TO THE ON-RAMP, AND SOMEONE'S ALREADY THERE, YOU'RE SUPPOSED TO WALK PAST THEM TO A WORSE SPOT, THAT, IF POSSIBLE, IS OUT OF SIGHT OF THE FIRST HITCHER. A BUNCH OF PEOPLE IN ONE SPOT HAVE LESS CHANCE OF GETTING RIDES, AND SINCE THE FIRST HITCHER WAS ALREADY WAITING, POSSIBLY FOR DAYS, YOU GIVE 'EM THE GOOD SPOT. THE SOONER THEY GET OUT OF THERE, THE SOONER YOU WILL, TOO.

SOMETIMES THIS CAN BE KIND OF A DRAG, LIKE, I REMEMBER, IN CALIFORNIA, SOMETIMES THERE'D BE SO MANY HITCHERS, THAT IT'D SEEM LIKE THEY WERE BEING DROPPED OUT OF HELICOPTERS, JUST IN FRONT OF ME, THE WHOLE WAY UP THE COAST. OR I'D BE WALKING UP TO SOME DESOLATE ROAD, IN THE MIDDLE OF NOWHERE, READY TO DROP MY PACK AND PUT OUT THE THUMB, WHEN SOME CRUSTY, OLD HIPPY AND HIS DOG CRAWL OUT OF THE ROADSIDE SHRUBS AND GET THERE FIRST. I'D WEARILY ASK HIM THE USUAL QUESTIONS: "WHERE YA HEADED?" HE'D SAY, "GARBERVILLE." I'D SAY, "HOW LONG YA BEEN HERE?" HE'D REPLY, "SINCE 1973." HE'D ASK IF I'D BEEN AT "THE SHOW", MEANING THE GRATEFUL DEAD SHOW. HIS DOG WOULD ASK ME IF I HAD ANY POT, ETCETERA, ETCETERA. THEN, I'D WALK ON UP THE ROAD...

BUT, IN FLORIDA, THERE'S LESS COMPETITION FOR RIDES, SO THAT'S WHY I WAS SURPRISED WHEN I HIT THE I-10 RAMP, HEADED WEST TO TALLAHASSEE, ONLY TO SEE THIS OTHER GUY WITH 3 HUGE BAGS AND A RADIO. HE WAS RIGHT AT THE PERFECT SPOT, TOO, JUST WHERE THERE WAS ENOUGH SHOULDER TO PULL OVER AND THE CARS WERE STILL GOING SLOW ENOUGH TO STOP. HE SAID HE WAS GOING TO ST. LOUIS; PRETTY FAR. HE'D HAVE TO TAKE I-10 TO NEW ORLEANS, AND THEN GET ON I-55 NORTH, OR "NARTH" AS THEY'D SAY IN ST. LOUIS. I WAS ONLY GOING ABOUT 100 MORE MILES AND I HAD ALL DAY SO I WASN'T TOO WORRIED ABOUT GETTING THE SHITTY SPOT, UP AHEAD, ACTUALLY ON THE FREEWAY. I WISHED THE GUY LUCK AND HEADED UP THE ROAD.

WELL, NO CARS STOPPED FOR AGES. IT SUCKED, BUT I KNEW I MUST BE AT THE RIGHT SPOT, BECAUSE OF ALL THE COBWEB-COVERED SKELETONS, HOLDING SIGNS THAT SAID, "TALLAHASSEE", ON THE SIDE OF THE ROAD. HA HA! THAT'S A JOKE, KIDS. HITCH HIKING HUMOUR IS VERY IMPORTANT TO ME IN THOSE LONG GAPS BETWEEN RIDES. I USED TO FEEL BAD WHEN I WAS STUCK FOR HOURS AND NO ONE WOULD STOP... THEN I MET A MAN WITH NO THUMB! BUH DUM BUMP! WELL, I STILL HAD ALMOST A WHOLE DAY AHEAD OF ME... THEN, FINALLY, A RED TRUCK DRIVEN BY AN OLD, WHITE HAIRED GUY PULLED UP AND STOPPED. I HAD A RIDE!

BUT, INSIDE THE TRUCK, MY SPIRITS QUICKLY SANK. RIGHT AWAY, I KNEW SOMETHING WAS WRONG. I HAD SAID, "I'M GOING TO TALLAHASSEE, WHERE ARE YOU HEADED?" HE SHRUGS AND NONCHALANTLY SAYS, "OH, I DON'T KNOW... 8, 10, 12 MILES UP THE ROAD? SOMETHING LIKE THAT..." HERE'S AN IMPORTANT CLUE FOR FIRST-TIME HITCHERS: IF YOUR RIDE DOESN'T KNOW WHERE THEY'RE GOING, THEY ARE PROBABLY GOING TO ASK YOU TO FUCK THEM! ITS TRUE. SURE ENOUGH, THE GUY TURNS OUT TO BE A CREEP. I'M SITTING, SOMEWHAT STIFFLY, STARING STRAIGHT AHEAD, THINKING, "WELL, LET'S GET THIS OVER

OVER WITH - GO AHEAD AND MAKE YOUR MOVE..." HE STARTS ASKING QUESTIONS LIKE, "WHERE ARE YOU FROM?" AND "DO YOU GO TO SCHOOL IN TALLAHASSEE?" — JUST THE USUAL SMALL TALK, BUT, THEN, I HEAR A VERY AUDIBLE "ZIP!" AS HE SLOWLY UNZIPS HIS PANTS! I'M NOT REALLY AFRAID OF THIS PATHETIC OLD MAN. INSTEAD, I HAVE A MORBID FASCINATION. IS HE REALLY GOING TO, YA KNOW TAKE IT OUT?!? HE KEEPS TALKING, NOW WORKING HIS HAND INTO HIS PANTS. "DO YOU WORK IN MIAMI? DO YOU HAVE A GIRLFRIEND?" FINALLY, THE SUSPENSE IS TOO GREAT, AND I HAVE TO LOOK. SURE ENOUGH; THERE IT IS: THE MEAT! HE'S NOT ONLY GOT IT OUT, BUT HE'S FULLY MASTURBATING! NOW, I'D HAD ENOUGH. "AH GOD, WOULD YA JUST PULL OVER RIGHT HERE?!? LET ME OUT!" I YELL, IN DISGUST. ACTUALLY, IN HUNDREDS OF RIDES, IN THE U.S, CANADA, MEXICO, GERMANY, POLAND, ETC, I HAVE ONLY BEEN PROPOSITIONED LIKE THIS 5 or 6 TIMES, AND NEVER THREATENED, BUT THIS GUY WAS THE MOST PATHETIC AND CRUDE OF ALL. HEY, KEEP YOUR STUPID, OLD PENIS TO YOURSELF, JERK! SHEESH! HE PULLS OVER, MEEKLY, AND I START WALKING.

LUCKILY, HE HAD PULLED OVER AT AN EXIT. MAYBE I SHOULD'VE STAYED WITH THE RIDE. IT PROBABLY WOULD'VE TAKEN THE OLD GEEZER ALL THE WAY TO TALLAHASSEE TO GET OFF, ANYWAYS, AND THEN I'D BE WHERE I NEEDED TO GO. OH WELL... I WALKED UP THE ON-RAMP TOWARDS THE "BEST SPOT", AND, IN AN EXACT REPLAY OF EARLIER THIS MORNING, THERE'S OLE "ST. LOUIS" WITH HIS 3 HUGE BAGS AND RADIO, AGAIN! SHIT. IT LOOKS LIKE THIS GUY'S GONNA DOG MY TRAIL THE WHOLE WAY. BUT, ITS NOT HIS FAULT, AND I WAVE AND SMILE AS I WALK UP. "AH, IT'S YOU AGAIN..." HE LAUGHS AND SAYS, "WHAT ARE YOU TRYIN' TO DO, MAN? WALK TO TALLAHASSEE?" THAT WAS PRETTY FUNNY. WE MIGHT AS WELL LAUGH; IT LOOKED LIKE WE WERE BOTH HAVING SOME PRETTY LOUSY LUCK, AFTER HITCHING ALL DAY TO END UP IN THE MIDDLE OF NOWHERE, A MIGHTY 8 MILES FROM WHERE WE BOTH STARTED. I SAID, "NO, I'M NOT WALKING. IT JUST SEEMS LIKE IT. SOME CREEP PICKED ME UP IN BALDWIN AND STARTED JERKIN' OFF, SO I MADE HIM LET ME OUT HERE."

ST. LOUIS' EYES GET WIDE AND HE STARTS LAUGHING LIKE CRAZY. FINALLY, HE SAYS, "WAS IT AN OLD WHITE HAIRED GUY? IN A RED TRUCK?!?"

Scams in Cuba are more brazen, more common than ever

(SCAM EDITORS REPLY: "WE TAKE FULL CREDIT!")

ALEX TREBEK AND THE INTERNATIONAL HOBO UNDERGROUND
A SCAM EXCLUSIVE!!!

TREBEK: MILD MANNERED GAME SHOW HOST... OR RUTHLESS HOBO SMUGGLER?!?

THIS STORY COMES TO ME FROM SCAM TRAVEL EDITOR, BRAD. LAST SUMMER, BRAD AND IVY WERE ON A TRAILER TRAIN TO PHILADELPHIA WHEN THE TRAIN COP SAW 'EM, AS THEY ENTERED PHILLY'S TRAIN YARD. THEY DOVE OFF THE MOVING TRAIN AND RAN LIKE HELL, BUT STILL GOT CAUGHT. THE TRAIN COP WAS A REAL FUCKER, OF COURSE, WITH A MUSTACHE, AND INSTEAD OF JUST BOOTING 'EM OFF THE YARD, HE DROVE THEM BACK TO HIS OFFICE TO INTERROGATE THEM AND THREATEN THEM FOR AN HOUR! THE COP GAVE 'EM THE USUAL SCARE SPEECHES: 1) "I'M GONNA GIVE YOU 30 DAYS IN JAIL!" 2) "THE YARD IS IN A BAD NEIGHBORHOOD WHERE THEY'LL KILL YOUR WHITE ASS, NO QUESTIONS ASKED IN A SECOND" AND, OF COURSE, 3) "JUST LAST WEEK THEY FOUND SOME GUY ON THE TRACKS, OBLITERATED BY A TRAIN, BLOOD EVERYWHERE, THEY HAD TO SCRAPE 'EM OFF THE TRACKS, ETC." WHEN YOU HOP TRAINS, AFTER AWHILE, EVERYONE

"ALEX TREBEK" CONT.

TELLS YOU ABOUT HOW THEY KNOW SOMEONE WHO LOST A LEG IN A TRAIN ACCIDENT. EVENTUALLY, YOU JUST SHRUG AND THINK, "OH WELL... ANOTHER LEG ON THE PILE"... ANYWAYS, I'M SURE BRAD HAD KINDA TUNED HIM OUT, 'TIL THE PIG ASKED BRAD IF HE WAS IN THE F.T.R.A. THE FREIGHT TRAIN RIDERS OF AMERICA. YOU SEE F.T.R.A. GRAFFITI ALL OVER THE PACIFIC NORTHWEST TRAIN YARDS. DEPENDING ON WHO YOU ASK, THE F.T.R.A. IS EITHER A VERY DANGEROUS TRAIN RIDING GANG WHO THROW PEOPLE OFF MOVING TRAINS, IF THEY DON'T BELONG TO THE F.T.R.A., OR A HARMLESS AND PATHETIC GROUP OF BEARDED OLD MEN WHO LIVE OUTSIDE THE FOODSTAMP OFFICE IN PASCO, WASHINGTON. BRAD TOLD THE COP HE'D NEVER HEARD OF THE F.T.R.A. THE COP SAID HE FOUND THAT HARD TO BELIEVE SINCE "THE FTRA ARE A NATIONWIDE DRUG SMUGGLING RING, WITH TIES TO COLOMBIA, WHO HAVE MEMBERS IN EVERY MAJOR AMERICAN CITY WITH A RAILYARD!" BRAD SHRUGGED. COPS WILL SAY ANYTHING. THE COP WENT ON "LOTS OF GUYS - RICH GUYS, LIKE LAWYERS AND BUSINESSMEN — THEY DRESS UP LIKE HOBOS AND SMUGGLE COCAINE AROUND THE COUNTRY ON FREIGHT TRAINS.... IT'S ALL OUT OF L.A.! ACTORS, ALEX TREBEK... ALL THOSE GUYS..." "WAIT A MINUTE! ALEX TREBEK?!? THE WITTY, URBANE, WELL-DRESSED HOST OF TELEVISION'S 'JEOPARDY'..." "?!? THE COP SAYS, "YEAH... THE GUY FROM JEOPARDY!" HE'S A BIG GUY IN THE F.T.R.A. THOSE RICH GUYS LOVE TO PLAY HOBO. A COUPLE MONTHS OUT OF THE YEAR... GET ALL GRUBBY-LOOKIN'. HOP A TRAIN... SMUGGLE DRUGS..." WELL, FINALLY, THE COP LET BRAD AND IVY GO, BUT THIS TREBEK-THING STILL HAUNTS VS. ALEX TREBEK IS A TRAIN HOPPING DRUG SMUGGLER "A COUPLE MONTHS OUT OF THE YEAR"? AS THEY SAY ON "JEOPARDY!" — "WHAT IS 'RIDICULOUS'?"

BUT WHAT IF ITS TRUE... ESQUIRE MAGAZINE JUST RAN A BIG STORY ON BORED YUPPIES WHO HOP TRAINS. FROM HOPPING TRAINS TO SMUGGLING DRUGS IS JUST A SHORT LEAP FOR A BORED YUPPIE.. NOW, IN TRAIN YARDS I STILL HAVE NIGHTMARE VISIONS OF GETTING ON THE WRONG BOXCAR. JUST AS THE TRAIN STARTS MOVING REAL FAST, I NOTICE A FIGURE LURKING IN THE DARK CORNER OF THE CAR. ITS TREBEK... HE LEANS CLOSE AND SAYS, "A RUTHLESS GANG OF DRUG SMUGGLING HOBOS BASED ON THE WEST COAST, OF WHICH I AM THE LEADER..." I SAY, "UH... THE FTRA? WAIT..." IT'S TOO LATE. TREBEK LEAPS OUT OF THE DARK AND HURLS ME OFF THE MOVING TRAIN! DAYS LATER, THEY WILL HAVE TO SCRAPE ME OFF THE TRACKS... THE LAST WORDS I HEAR: "ANSWER IN THE FORM OF A QUESTION!" AND TREBEK'S SINISTER LAUGH FADING OUT IN THE ROAR OF THE TRAIN... HE SMILES

IN THE DARK, WITH A BRIEFCASE OF HEROIN AND, NOW.... MY FOOD STAMP CARD.
WELL, IT'S BECOME A MID THING FOR BORED YUPPIES AND BORED PUNKS TO HOP TRAINS. SCAM'S EDITORIAL POSITION ON THIS IS THAT FREIGHT HOPPING IS NOT ONLY ILLEGAL, BUT VERY DANGEROUS. IF YOU MUST HOP TRAINS, FOR GOD'S SAKE, WATCH OUT FOR TREBEK! HE'S OUT THERE, AND HE RIDES AT NIGHT...

DA BANNERS

SCAM TREASURE HUNT!

DA SLOPPY LAYOUT

WHILE ON AN EPIC FREIGHT HOPPING TRIP, A COUPLE SUMMERS BACK, I FOUND MYSELF WAITING ON AN EASTBOUND TO KANSAS, IN PUEBLO, COLORADO. I HAD PRETTY MUCH DONE ALL I COULD DO THAT MORNING IN PUEBLO: I HAD FILLED MY WATER JUG SHAVED IN THE SAFEWAY GROCERY STORE TOILET, GOT A YUPPIE CAFE TO GIVE ME FREE FOOD, EXPLORED THE OLD TOWN, TOOK PICTURES OF AN OLD HOTEL, DID SOME GRAFFITI, AND MADE AN EXTENSIVE STUDY OF PUEBLO'S CREEPY, WHITE POWER GRAFFITI, OF WHICH THERE IS PLENTY. FINALLY, BORED AND LONELY, I GOT A COUPLE BEERS AT 7-11... ONE FOR ME, AND ONE FOR IVY, WHO HAD TOLD ME SHE MIGHT BE TAKING TRAINS OUT OF CALIFORNIA THAT SUMMER. SHE WOULD PROBABLY END UP GOING THROUGH PUEBLO, TOO. SO I FOUND AN EXCELLENT HIDING SPOT FOR THE BEER AND MAILED HER A MAP OF HOW TO FIND IT. SHE NEVER MADE IT TO PUEBLO THOUGH, SO IF ANYONE WANTS A QUART OF SKLITZ MALT LIQUOR WHEN THEY'RE STUCK IN PUEBLO, HERE'S WHAT YOU DO: THE 4TH STREET BRIDGE, IN OLD TOWN, GOES OVER THE EAST END OF THE TRAIN YARD, UNDER THE BRIDGE AGAINST 15-20 PILES IS WHAT LOOKS LIKE AN OUTHOUSE, A LITTLE WOODEN SHED THAT IS UNLOCKED. INSIDE BACK TO THE BOX, STRAIGHT AHEAD 15-20 PACES IS WHAT LOOKS LIKE AN ELECTRIC POWER BOX, WITH YOUR UNLESS SOMEONE FOUND IT, IS IVY'S BEER. SHE SAID SHE DOESN'T MIND IF YOU DRINK IT...

SHLITZ KRIEG BOP!!!

A DRUNKEN INSIDE ACCOUNT OF THE FIRST ANNUAL COCONUT GROVE EASTER SHLITZ HUNT!

THINK OF IT AS A VICTORY FOR BEER

ARE YOU READY, PUKES, FOR THE

1st ANNUAL COCONUT GROVE EASTER SHLITZ HUNT?!

FIRST PRIZE: 12-PAK OF SHLITZ. 2ND PRIZE: THERE IS NO 2ND PRIZE! ALL PARTICIPANTS GET TO KEEP THE BEER THEY FIND!

MAP OF HUNT

MIAMI POLICE
DA
LOOSELY DRAWN COP WITH A BEER HIDDEN ON HIS HEAD

OAK
COCO PUNKS
GRAND AVE
MAIN
PEACOCK PARK
S. BAYSHORE
THE WATER

THE HUNT GOES FROM OAK AVE. SOUTH TO THE WATER NO FURTHER WEST THAN 32nd OR EAST THAN 27th, AND NOT PAST THE COCONUT GROVE PLAYHOUSE ON MAIN. THERE WILL BE NO BEER HIDDEN IN THE MARINA SO THE SALTY GUYS DON'T GET IT ALL

THE HUNT STARTS AROUND NOON AT THE CLOCK IN FRONT OF COCOWALK AND ENDS AT 2:00 SO TOM CAN GO TO WORK

PICTURED ABOVE: 7-11 CELEBRITY, SNARLY, HANDS ANDY THE VICTORY 12-PAK, MOMENTS BEFORE WE STOLE IT!!!

IT WAS THE SCAM PUNKS' DREAM COME TRUE — FULL, UNOPENED CANS OF GOOD OLE SHLITZ IN THE STREETS, THE ALLEYS, ON THE ROOFTOPS, ON THE STAIRWELLS, IN THE FOUNTAINS, EVEN IN THE TREES OF COCONUT GROVE! I'VE ALWAYS WANTED TO HAVE SOME BIG, CITY WIDE EASTER EGG HUNT, SO, FINALLY, THIS EASTER THE FIRST ANNUAL COCONUT GROVE EASTER SHLITZ HUNT WAS BORN. BEFORE SUNRISE ON EASTER SUNDAY, ME, IVY AND CARRIE HID 70 CANS OF SHLITZ, ALL ORNATELY DECORATED IN THE RED AND WHITE SHLITZ LABEL, IN THE GROVE BETWEEN 27th AND 32nd AVE, FROM OAK AVE. TO THE WATER. EXCEPT WE DIDN'T PUT ANY IN THE MARINA CUZ THOSE SHRIMPER DUDES CAN SNIFF OUT AN UNOPENED SHLITZ A MILE AWAY. ITS GENETIC, OR SOMETHING.

HIDING THE BEER IN ALL THE WEIRD SPOTS LIKE THE MAYFAIR FOUNTAINS AND PEACOCK PARK BASKETBALL NETS WAS FUN, BUT IT WAS HARD TO BREAK WITH A FULL LIFETIME OF DRINKING EXPERIENCE AND JUST PUT A FULL BEER DOWN AND WALK AWAY. IT WAS OK THOUGH, CUZ ME AND IVY STOLE ALL THE BEER FROM X-TRA SUPERMARKET.

AROUND NOON WE WOKE UP OUR SHLITZ HUNTERS—THE GRIZZLED HUNGOVER SHLITZ LOVING RESIDENTS OF THE GROVE DRUNK HOUSE. WE MET AT THE BIG CLOCK IN FRONT OF COCO-WALK AND EXPLAINED THE RULES: YOU GET TO KEEP ALL THE BEER YOU FIND AND WHOEVER FOUND THE MOST IN 2 HOURS WON AN ADDITIONAL NEW 12-PAK! THE HUNT WAS ON! YO!

WATCHING THEIR HOPELESS, SWEATING, HUNGOVER SEARCH FOR THE BEERS WAS MORE FUN THAN HIDING THE SHLITZ. ONE BEER WAS DUCT-TAPED ON TOP OF THIS HUGE, STONE ANCHOR BY THE SAILING CLUB. SHLITZ HUNTER, CINQUE, ACTUALLY SAT ON THE ANCHOR WONDERING WHERE TO LOOK NEXT! DUH! FINALLY, AFTER 2 HOURS, WE MET BACK AT TCBY WHERE BUDDHA WAS WORKING AND COUNTED THE BEERS. ANDY POWELL WAS THE FIRST SHLITZ HUNT WINNER WITH A MEASLY TOTAL OF 7 SHLITZ! ABOUT 45 BEERS WERENT FOUND SO WE WENT AROUND DRINKING AND GATHERING BEER AND WENT TO 7-11 TO AWARD ANDY HIS GRAND PRIZE — 12 COLD SHLITZ!

ANDY WAS GIVEN THE 12-PAK IN A CEREMONY IN THE 7-11 BEER AISLE. VETERAN BRICKELL 7-11 WORKER, SNARLY, WHO HAD JUST TRANSFERRED TO THE GROVE, WAS PHOTOGRAPHED HANDING ANDY HIS VICTORY SHLITZ, WHILE ALL THE PEOPLE IN THE STORE APPLAUDED. IVY MADE HIM TAKE A PLAQUE MADE OF CUT UP SHLITZ BOXES AND EVERYONE RUSHED TO CONGRATULATE HIM. IN ALL THE CHAOS, I TOOK THE VICTORY TWELVE AND WALKED OUT — WITHOUT PAYING! IT WAS THE SHLITZ HUNT BEER HEIST!!! EVERYONE GOT DRUNK AND ANDY TOOK HIS WINNING HAUL TO THE STUDIO TO RECORD WITH THE STUN GUNS. STILL NOT ALL THE BEER WAS FOUND AND I KNOW FOR SURE THAT TO THIS DAY THEY STILL FIND SHLITZ IN THE ALLEYS OF COCONUT GROVE.

FIG. 1

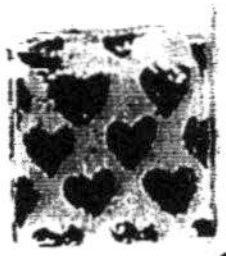

"HEARTS"

CrackArt

...AND OTHER DRUGS   BY IVY

FIG. 2

"LIL DEVILS"

FIG. 3

"STARS"

FIG. 4

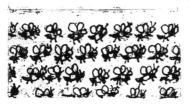
"CRACK 'O THE IRISH"

   LAST SUMMER, I took a vacation to New York City to visit my pal, Little Mike. Brad and I jumped trains to get there from Miami. We were in a hurry to make a deadline, because we wanted to get there in time for THE DICKIES show. We made it and it was such a great show! While I was in New York, I stayed at Mike's, but he had to work alot. He had a job as a dogwalker. One of the dogs he walked was Phil Donahue's. Mike said it ate its own shit!

   Anyway, while Mike was at work, I walked all over the city, or hopped the subway, everyday. I only had to pay for the subway like once, or twice, the whole time I was there! In different parts of town I started collecting drug baggies that I found on the ground. I got really into it and I even convinced Mike to start finding and saving them for me to, when he was out walking Phil's dog. There was a bunch of different decorations on them. It got so that when I was hanging out with Brad and Mike, I'd be paying more attention to looking down and searching the streets! I was addicted the drug baggies!!! One night, we ran into Iggy Pop eating dinner with his girlfriend at some outdoor cafe! But, I was still more interested in my baggies...

   Well, I found baggies of all different patterns and colors. They were beautiful! They were really found everywhere, all over town, but there were more, it seemed, around Central Park.

   I never did find the "gun print" baggie I heard about, or the one with the "kissing lips" on it that Mike told me about, and, soon, it was time to leave New York, but I'm still collecting them, and, hopefully, I'll find them one day. In Miami, that shouldn't be TOO hard!

FIG. 5

FIG. 6

FIG. 7

FIG. 8

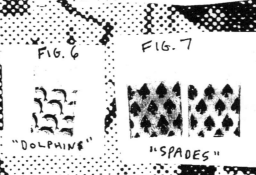
"BUMBLEBEES"   "DOLPHINS"   "SPADES"

"HERSHY'S KISSES"

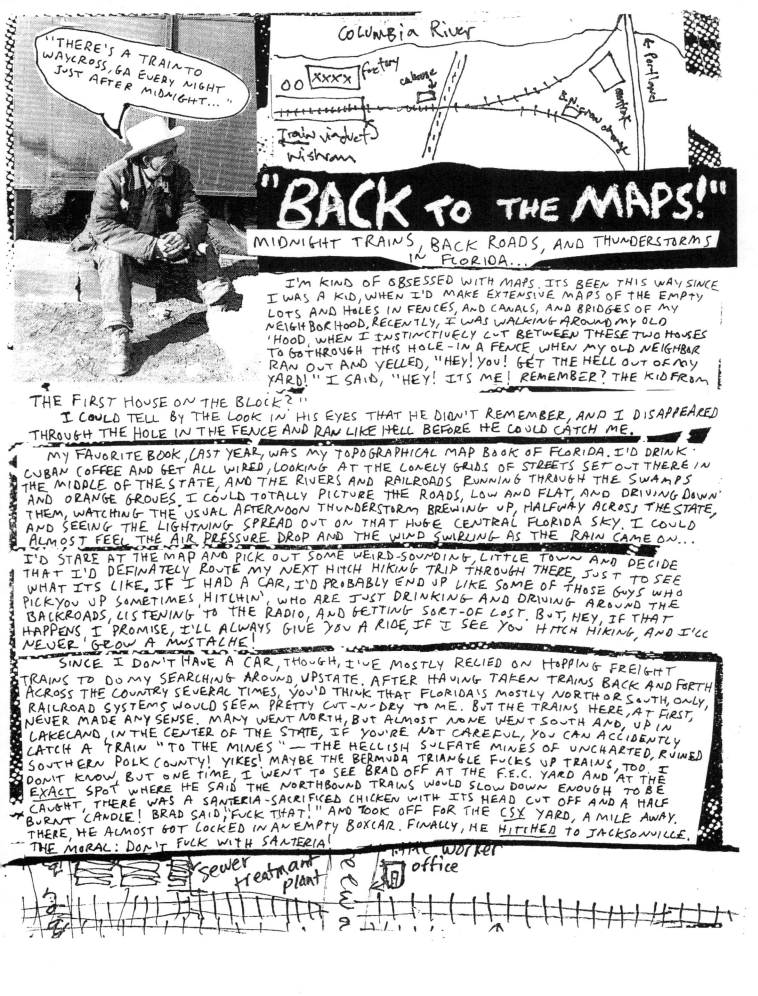

"THERE'S A TRAIN TO WAYCROSS, GA EVERY NIGHT JUST AFTER MIDNIGHT..."

Columbia River

factory
caboose
to Portland
S.N. flow change
Train viaduct
Wishram

"BACK TO THE MAPS!"

MIDNIGHT TRAINS, BACK ROADS, AND THUNDERSTORMS IN FLORIDA...

I'M KIND OF OBSESSED WITH MAPS. ITS BEEN THIS WAY SINCE I WAS A KID, WHEN I'D MAKE EXTENSIVE MAPS OF THE EMPTY LOTS AND HOLES IN FENCES, AND CANALS, AND BRIDGES OF MY NEIGHBORHOOD. RECENTLY, I WAS WALKING AROUND MY OLD 'HOOD, WHEN I INSTINCTIVELY CUT BETWEEN THESE TWO HOUSES TO GO THROUGH THIS HOLE-IN A FENCE WHEN MY OLD NEIGHBOR RAN OUT AND YELLED, "HEY! YOU! GET THE HELL OUT OF MY YARD!" I SAID, "HEY! ITS ME! REMEMBER? THE KID FROM THE FIRST HOUSE ON THE BLOCK?"

I COULD TELL BY THE LOOK IN HIS EYES THAT HE DIDN'T REMEMBER, AND I DISAPPEARED THROUGH THE HOLE IN THE FENCE AND RAN LIKE HELL BEFORE HE COULD CATCH ME.

MY FAVORITE BOOK, LAST YEAR, WAS MY TOPOGRAPHICAL MAP BOOK OF FLORIDA. I'D DRINK CUBAN COFFEE AND GET ALL WIRED, LOOKING AT THE LONELY GRIDS OF STREETS SET OUT THERE IN THE MIDDLE OF THE STATE, AND THE RIVERS AND RAILROADS RUNNING THROUGH THE SWAMPS AND ORANGE GROVES. I COULD TOTALLY PICTURE THE ROADS, LOW AND FLAT, AND DRIVING DOWN THEM, WATCHING THE USUAL AFTERNOON THUNDERSTORM BREWING UP, HALFWAY ACROSS THE STATE, AND SEEING THE LIGHTNING SPREAD OUT ON THAT HUGE CENTRAL FLORIDA SKY. I COULD ALMOST FEEL THE AIR PRESSURE DROP AND THE WIND SWIRLING AS THE RAIN CAME ON...

I'D STARE AT THE MAP AND PICK OUT SOME WEIRD-SOUNDING, LITTLE TOWN AND DECIDE THAT I'D DEFINATELY ROUTE MY NEXT HITCH HIKING TRIP THROUGH THERE, JUST TO SEE WHAT ITS LIKE. IF I HAD A CAR, I'D PROBABLY END UP LIKE SOME OF THOSE GUYS WHO PICK YOU UP SOMETIMES, HITCHIN', WHO ARE JUST DRINKING AND DRIVING AROUND THE BACKROADS, LISTENING TO THE RADIO, AND GETTING SORT-OF LOST. BUT, HEY, IF THAT HAPPENS, I PROMISE, I'LL ALWAYS GIVE YOU A RIDE, IF I SEE YOU HITCH HIKING, AND I'LL NEVER GROW A MUSTACHE!

SINCE I DON'T HAVE A CAR, THOUGH, I'VE MOSTLY RELIED ON HOPPING FREIGHT TRAINS TO DO MY SEARCHING AROUND, UPSTATE. AFTER HAVING TAKEN TRAINS BACK AND FORTH ACROSS THE COUNTRY SEVERAL TIMES, YOU'D THINK THAT FLORIDA'S MOSTLY NORTH OR SOUTH, ONLY, RAILROAD SYSTEMS WOULD SEEM PRETTY CUT-N-DRY TO ME. BUT THE TRAINS HERE, AT FIRST, NEVER MADE ANY SENSE. MANY WENT NORTH, BUT ALMOST NONE WENT SOUTH AND, UP IN LAKELAND, IN THE CENTER OF THE STATE, IF YOU'RE NOT CAREFUL, YOU CAN ACCIDENTLY CATCH A TRAIN "TO THE MINES" — THE HELLISH SULFATE MINES OF UNCHARTED, RUINED SOUTHERN POLK COUNTY! YIKES! MAYBE THE BERMUDA TRIANGLE FUCKS UP TRAINS, TOO. I DON'T KNOW, BUT ONE TIME, I WENT TO SEE BRAD OFF AT THE F.E.C. YARD AND AT THE EXACT SPOT WHERE HE SAID THE NORTHBOUND TRAINS WOULD SLOW DOWN ENOUGH TO BE CAUGHT, THERE WAS A SANTERIA-SACRIFICED CHICKEN WITH ITS HEAD CUT OFF AND A HALF BURNT CANDLE! BRAD SAID, "FUCK THAT!" AND TOOK OFF FOR THE CSX YARD, A MILE AWAY. THERE, HE ALMOST GOT LOCKED IN AN EMPTY BOXCAR. FINALLY, HE HITCHED TO JACKSONVILLE. THE MORAL: DON'T FUCK WITH SANTERIA!

sewer treatment plant
worker office

ONE TRAIN, IN PARTICULAR THAT I ALWAYS WONDERED ABOUT WAS THE FAMOUS "ORANGE JUICE TRAIN" THAT SUPPOSEDLY RAN FROM SOMEWHERE IN FLORIDA, ALL THE WAY TO NEW JERSEY! I'D HEARD TALK OF IT AND HAD EVEN FOUND IT MENTIONED IN THE HUGE PILE OF TRAIN MAPS AND INFO. I'VE ACQUIRED. IT SHOWS UP IN MY INFO. ON ROCKY MOUNT, NC: "A GOOD PLACE TO CATCH A FAST RIDE ON THE ORANGE JUICE TRAIN" AND THAT WAS IT. NO TRAIN WORKERS I TALKED TO KNEW ANYTHING ABOUT IT UNTIL ONE TIME, IN RICHMOND, VA, A WORKER TOLD ME HOW TO CATCH OUT SOUTH. AS HE WAS WALKING AWAY, I YELLED "WHAT ABOUT THE ORANGE JUICE TRAIN?" THE TRAIN WORKER YELLED BACK, OVER HIS SHOULDER, "YEAH, HE COME THROUGH HE-YAH'..." AND WAS GONE BEHIND A ROW OF TRAINS.

WALKING BACK, TOWARDS TOWN, ON THE TRACKS, I WAS EXCITED THAT SOMEBODY HAD FINALLY HEARD OF IT. THEN, BEHIND ME, A TRAIN WAS COMING AROUND THE CORNER AND I GOT OFF THE TRACKS TO WATCH IT GO BY. I COULDN'T BELIEVE IT: ONE CAR, AFTER ANOTHER —THE WHOLE TRAIN— WAS BRIGHT, ORANGE FREIGHT CARS THAT SAID, "TROPICANA" ON THE SIDE! THERE IT WAS, TAKING ITS TIME, CHUGGING NORTH RIGHT PAST ME — THE GODDAMN OJ TRAIN!

I NEVER FOUND OUT HOW TO CATCH THE OJ TRAIN, BUT I DID FIGURE OUT THE HIALEAH YARD TO GET OUT OF MIAMI, REAL EASY. EVERY NIGHT, EXCEPT SUNDAY, A NORTHBOUND TRAIN LEAVES THE YARD, HEADED ALL THE WAY TO WAYCROSS, GEORGIA! ITS NICE TO KNOW THAT MIDNIGHT TRAIN'S ALWAYS THERE FOR YOU. I DEVELOPED A PERFECT SYSTEM: ABOUT ONCE A MONTH, WHEN I GOT RESTLESS IN MIAMI, I'D TAKE OFF ON A 3, OR 4 DAY TRIP. I'D RIDE THE MIDNIGHT TRAIN UP TO THE YARD IN BALDWIN, FL, OUTSIDE JACKSONVILLE, HITCH HIKE TO SOME LITTLE TOWNS, AND TRY TO READ ALL THE BOOKS I BROUGHT AND DRINK PLENTY OF BEER AND COFFEE ALONG THE WAY. IT NEVER FAILED TO CLEAR MY HEAD.

I THINK MY FAVORITE LITTLE TRIP WAS THE ONE WHERE I ENDED UP IN TALLAHASSEE FOR THE FIRST TIME. I BROUGHT BEER UP TO THE YARD, AND WHEN MY TRAIN FINALLY GOT THE GREEN LIGHT AND TOOK THAT SUDDEN LURCH FORWARD, I CRACKED OPEN MY COLD BEERS, FELT THE BREEZE COMING IN, AND LOOKED OUT THE BOXCAR DOOR AT THE CLOSED STORES AND EMPTY STREETS GOING PAST AS I LEFT TOWN. I FELL ASLEEP, AS USUAL, WHEN THE TRAIN STARTED GOING REAL FAST THROUGH THE DARK IN WESTERN PALM BEACH COUNTY. WHEN I WOKE UP THE SUN WAS COMING UP OVER AN ORANGE GROVE. ROWS AND ROWS OF TREES IN THE FLATTEST PART OF THE WORLD!

I GOT TO BALDWIN THAT AFTERNOON, AND, AS USUAL, HEADED STRAIGHT FOR THE WAFFLE HOUSE, ACROSS THE STREET FROM THE TRAIN YARD. I'M MORE A REGULAR AT THIS WAFFLE HOUSE IN BALDWIN THAN I AM AT MOST PLACES IN MIAMI. ITS ALWAYS SO GOOD TO GET THAT FIRST CUP OF COFFEE AFTER 16 HOURS ON A TRAIN.

AT WAFFLE HOUSE, I DRANK CUP AFTER CUP, LOOKING OUT THE WINDOW AT TRAINS MOVING BACK AND FORTH IN THE YARD, WITH MY MAPS SPREAD OUT AROUND ME. THIS IS WHERE I DECIDED TO HITCH HIKE WEST, TO TALLAHASSEE, AND STAY THE NIGHT IN THE F.S.U. LIBRARY.

THE STAYING-THE-NIGHT-IN-THE-LIBRARY-THING IS PRETTY FUN, AND I'VE DONE IT 4, OR 5 TIMES NOW. YOU JUST HIDE REAL GOOD WHEN THE LIBRARY'S CLOSING, WAIT AWHILE FOR EMPLOYEES AND CLEANING CREWS TO LEAVE, AND THEN COME OUT AND HAVE THE WHOLE DARK, QUIET LIBRARY TO YOURSELF! I DID GET CAUGHT BY THE CLEANING LADY AT TULANE IN NEW ORLEANS, ONCE, BUT SHE WAS SO PUZZLED THAT SHE JUST LET ME OUT. "YOU SURE LIKE TO STUDY!" SHE

"PUTTING THIS DREAM TOGETHER"

"Ministering to America's Truckers"
John 14:27

THE TRUCKER'S CHAPEL OF BALDWIN, FL

ONE OF BALDWIN'S PROUD LANDMARKS IS ITS "TRUCKER'S CHAPEL", WHICH SITS ON THE LOT OF THE UNION 76 TRUCKSTOP. ITS A WHOLE, FUNCTIONING CHURCH, COMPLETE WITH PEWS AND ORGAN, INSIDE AN 18-WHEELER! YOU GOT TO ADMIT, CHRISTIANS SURE ARE DILLIGENT, IF THE PUNKS WORKED THIS HARD, WE'D CONTROL THE WORLD! ANYWAYS, THEIR FREE PAMPHLET, "PUTTING THIS DREAM TOGETHER" RELATES THE INSPIRING STORY OF THE "HOLY ROLLER", REV. JOE HUNTER. HUNTER WAS LOST TO THE EVILS OF BOOZE AND LITTLE WHITE PILLS 'TIL ONE FATEFUL NIGHT IN 1971 ON A ROUTINE RUN TO GREENVILLE, S.C. HE LOST CONTROL OF HIS RIG AND ALMOST DIED! HE ACCEPTED CHRIST, SAVED HIS MARRIAGE, AND SOON BEGAN MINISTERING IN AMERICA'S TRUCKSTOPS! TODAY THE TRUCKER CHAPEL EMPIRE HAS 33 IN 14 STATES AND 4 RIGHT HERE IN FLORIDA! I'VE NEVER SEEN A SERVICE IN THE ONE IN BALDWIN, THOUGH, AND ON A 30° NIGHT, ONCE, I WENT TO SEEK WARMTH IN IT, ONLY TO FIND IT LOCKED!

MARVELED. BUT IN A COLLEGE LIBRARY, ITS ALWAYS SEEMED PRETTY LOW-RISK.

I HITCHED WEST AND MADE IT TO OUR STATE CAPITOL IN GOOD TIME. SO THIS WAS TALLAHASSEE? WHAT A DRAG. MIAMI SHOULD SECEDE, I SWEAR. I GUESS I EXPECTED MORE CHARMING, OLD SOUTHERN HOUSES, AND LESS ENDLESS BOULEVARDS TO NOWHERE, LINED WITH STRIP MALLS AND FAST FOOD PLACES. I DID ADMIRE TALLAHASSEE'S TRULY DESPERATE, LITTLE GHETTO. NOW HERE WAS A PLACE WHERE A MAN COULD GET KILLED FOR NO REASON. I EVEN FOUND A CRACK BAGGIE WITH A "HERSHEY'S KISS" PRINT THAT I'VE KEPT TO THIS DAY! I FOUND A COUPLE CHICKEN HEADS ON THE TRACKS, TOO; PROBABLY LEFT BY HOMESICK COLLEGE KIDS FROM MIAMI. AFTER I GOT REFUSED AT THE BLOOD BANK, THOUGH, FOR LACK OF LOCAL I.D., I BAILED TO THE LIBRARY.

THE F.S.U. LIBRARY TOTALLY MADE UP FOR EVERYTHING. I FOUND ALL THESE BOOKS I'D BEEN LOOKING FOR, PLUS OTHERS ABOUT FLORIDA RUMRUNNING AND THE SECRET GRAFFITI UNDERGROUND OF DENVER. THEN I WENT TO WORK, CHECKING OUT THE LAYOUT OF THE PLACE. I COULDN'T FIND ANY UNLOCKED CLOSETS OR FORGOTTEN STUDY ROOMS TO HIDE OUT IN, BUT THE STAIRS WENT UP ONE FLOOR PAST THE ACTUAL LIBRARY, WHERE THEY ENDED AT A LOCKED DOOR. I TOOK MY BOOKS UP TO THE TOP OF THE STAIRS AND WAITED THERE FOR THE LIBRARY TO CLOSE. IT SEEMED PRETTY UNLIKELY THAT ANYONE WOULD COME UP THERE FOR ANY REASON, AND I'D BE SAFELY IN ALL NIGHT.

WELL, NO ONE WENT UP THERE, BUT I GUESS I WAS SO TIRED FROM TRAVELLING THAT I FELL ASLEEP UP THERE. I SLEPT HARD AND WHEN I WOKE UP, THE FLOURESCENT LIGHTS WERE STILL ON AND I HAD NO IDEA WHAT TIME IT WAS. I CREPT SLOWLY DOWN THE STAIRS, EXPECTING TO FIND THE LIBRARY ALL TO MYSELF, BUT IT WAS FULL OF STUDENTS. IT WAS THE NEXT MORNING! I'D SLEPT THROUGH THE WHOLE NIGHT AND MISSED ALL OF THE FUN OF HAVING THE WHOLE LIBRARY TO MYSELF!

SINCE I WAS JUST USING THE LIBRARY AS A HOME BASE AND AN INDOOR PLACE TO SLEEP, IT OCCURRED TO ME THAT I WAS, IN EFFECT, SQUATTING AN EXISTING, NON-ABANDONED BUILDING! THIS IS CLEARLY AN ADVANCEMENT OF SORTS. MY NEXT INNOVATION IN SQUATTING WILL INVOLVE TELLING PEOPLE "GOODBYE" AND PRETENDING TO LEAVE THEIR HOUSE, BUT, INSTEAD, HIDING UNDER THE SINK, WHERE I WILL SECRETLY LIVE AND EAT THEIR FOOD! MAYBE I'M ALREADY LIVING IN YOUR HOUSE. HAVE YOU THOUGHT OF THAT?!?

AFTER I WAS DONE WITH MY RESEARCH, I VOLUNTARILY GAVE UP MY LIBRARY HOME TO GO HANG OUT AND GET DRUNK WITH THE BAND, LES TURDZ WHO LIVED IN T-HASSEE THEN. TWO DAYS AND COUNTLESS SHLITZ LATER, BRIAN TURD OFFERED TO DRIVE ME TO CHATTAHOOCHIE, A SCARY, LITTLE TOWN, 30 MILES WEST OF TALLAHASSEE, WHERE TRAINS DID CREW CHANGES BETWEEN NEW ORLEANS AND BALDWIN.

I STUDIED MY MAPS AND DECIDED ON A COUPLE OF OPTIONS: 1) I COULD TAKE A TRAIN WEST AND GO TO GULF BREEZE, FL TO TRY AND FIND THE UFO WATCHERS. ABOUT 20 YEARS AGO THERE WERE SEVERAL FAMOUS UFO SIGHTINGS THERE, AND I READ THAT TO THIS DAY, THE PARKS OF GULF BREEZE ARE FILLED, NIGHTLY, WITH FOLKS WITH BINOCULARS AND TELESCOPES, WHO ARE TRYING TO GET A GLIMPSE OF ONE! 2) I COULD RIDE THE TINY APPALACHICOLA NORTHERN RAILROAD, SOUTH TO THE GULF OF MEXICO. THE AN IS ONE OF THE LAST OF THE LITTLE, SHORT LINE, INDEPENDENT RAILROADS IN THE U.S. AND IT ONLY HAS ABOUT 80 MILES OF TRACK, DOWN FROM CHATTAHOOCHIE, THROUGH THE APPALACHICOLA NATIONAL FOREST TO PORT ST. JOE! OR, 3) I COULD GO ALL THE WAY TO NEW ORLEANS. OR 4) I COULD GO HOME.

TRUCKER'S NEWS

PEOPLE ALWAYS ASK ME, "SO, IGGY, WHAT ZINES DO YOU READ?" AND I NEVER HESITATE TO TELL 'EM MUDFLAP, TALES OF BLARG!, AND, OF COURSE, THE TRUCKER'S NEWS! EVERY ISSUE FEATURES THE LATEST TRUCKER GEAR, TRUCKSTOP NEWS, AND TRUCKERS SPEAKING OUT ABOUT THEIR PROBLEMS WITH THE COMPANIES AND THE I.C.C. BUT THE BEST PART IS THE STORIES ABOUT TRUCKERS WITNESSING CAR WRECKS ON THE INTERSTATE, AND THEN PULLING OVER TO PULL CHILDREN OUT OF THE BURNING WRECKAGE! WHEN ASKED TO STICK AROUND TO ACCEPT A REWARD, THE TRUCKER ALWAYS POLITELY DECLINES, AND SAYS, "NAW... I GOT TO GET THIS LOAD TO YUMA BY TONIGHT..." FACE IT. TRUCKERS ARE RAD! LAST ISSUE HAD AN ARTICLE ON A TRUCKSTOP THAT HAD A CHRISTMAS "TOYS FOR TOTS" DRIVE. ALL THE TRUCKERS GOT ON THE CB RADIO AND TALKED IT UP AND THE TRUCKSTOP RAISED AN ALL-TIME HIGH IN CHRISTMAS TOYS! THE TRUCKERS WERE HIGHBALLIN' FOR THE KIDS!

AT CHATTAHOOCHIE, ME AND BRIAN DECIDED TO DRINK SOME MORE SHLITZ WHILE WE WAITED FOR MY TRAIN. WE GOT A 6-PAK AND WALKED DOWN THE TRACKS, PAST THE CREW CHANGE SPOT. A LITTLE WAYS DOWN, WE FOUND AN ABANDONED HOUSE THAT WAS OPEN AND HAD A NICE, SHADY PORCH. INSIDE, THERE WAS A LOT OF OLD CLOTHES, AND OUT FRONT WAS REMAINS OF A FIRE PIT, SO YOU COULD TELL IT WAS A 4-STAR HOTEL ON THE FLORIDA HOBO CIRCUIT. WE DRANK BEER ALL AFTERNOON, AND JUST WATCHED TRAINS GO BY. IT WAS JUST SUCH A RELAXED SPOT THAT WE DIDN'T WANT TO LEAVE.

TRAINS CAME AND WENT AND I STILL HADN'T DECIDED WHAT I WANTED TO DO. SO WE GOT MORE BEER AND WALKED BACK TO OUR PORCH. WHAT CAN I SAY? WE LOVE OUR SHLITZ! BRIAN EVEN TOLD ME THAT ONE TIME, HE HAD WANTED TO MOVE AWAY FROM MOBILE, SO HE DECIDED TO MOVE TO MILWAUKEE, WHERE HE'D NEVER BEEN, AND KNEW NO ONE, JUST BECAUSE THAT'S WHERE SHLITZ COMES FROM! EVERY TIME WE FINISHED A SIX, THERE'D BE THIS LONG, AWKWARD MOMENT WHERE WE WERE SUPPOSED TO SAY "GOODBYE", BUT, FINALLY, BRIAN WOULD GO, "UH... LET'S GET SOME MORE..."

SUDDENLY, IT WAS LATE AT NIGHT, AND WE WERE DRUNK AS HELL. BRIAN STUMBLED OFF TO DRIVE HOME AND I SAID, "WHAT THE HELL? I'LL RIDE THAT A.N. DOWN TO THE OCEAN!" A WORKER AT THE CREW SHACK TOLD ME THAT A.N.'S YARD WAS "ABOUT A MILE DOWN THE TRACKS" SO I STARTED STUMBLING THAT WAY, SLOWLY. IT WAS PITCH BLACK OUT THERE, AND I COULDN'T SEE ANYTHING. CHATTAHOOCHIE'S SORT-OF... UH... "RURAL" I COULD SMELL TRASH FIRES AND HEAR HOWLING DOGS, BUT COULDN'T SEE THE DOGS. THEN I FELL AND TWISTED MY ANKLE REAL BAD AND LAID THERE ON THE TRACKS. THIS MUST BE HOW PEOPLE "FALL ASLEEP ON THE TRACKS" I'VE ALWAYS WONDERED ABOUT THAT, LIKE, WHO JUST LAYS DOWN TO GO TO SLEEP ON THE TRACKS?!?

FINALLY, I DECIDED, "FUCK A.N.!" AND WENT BACK TO THE CSX YARD, WHERE I SPRAY PAINTED MESSAGES ON TRAIN CARS FOR MY FRIENDS IN OTHER CITIES AND MY GIRLFRIEND BACK HOME. IN LESS THAN AN HOUR, THE EASTBOUND ROLLED IN, AND I WAS ON MY WAY BACK TO BALDWIN.

THAT MORNING, IN THE WAFFLE HOUSE, OVER COFFEE AND THE SUNDAY PAPER, I DECIDED TO GO THROUGH JACKSONVILLE, SOUTH TO ST. AUGUSTINE, WHERE I'D NEVER BEEN BEFORE. I PUT MY THUMB OUT AND MANAGED TO GET DOWN THERE PRETTY FAST, STEALING A QUART OF BEER IN DOWNTOWN JAX ON THE WAY. ST. AUGUSTINE IS KNOWN WIDELY AS "THE OLDEST CITY IN AMERICA" BECAUSE IT WAS FOUNDED BY SPAIN LONG BEFORE THE PILGRIMS, AND THOSE OTHER TRENDIES SHOWED UP ON THE SCENE, UP NORTH. THERE'S A HUGE, RAD OLD SPANISH CASTLE OVERLOOKING A BAY AND LOTS OF OTHER BUILDINGS THAT ARE "THE HISTORIC..." THIS, OR "THE OLDEST..." THAT. I WAS AFRAID IT MIGHT BE A LOUSY, FLORIDA TOURIST TRAP, BUT ACTUALLY, I REALLY LIKED THE HUGE, OLD TREES AND NARROW STREETS. I STOLE MORE BEER FROM THE (HISTORIC) WINN-DIXIE GROCERY STORE AND WALKED AROUND IN A PLEASANT, LIGHT DRIZZLE.

GOING TO ST. AUGUSTINE REALLY TURNED OUT TO BE A GREAT IDEA. I DRANK MORE BEER AND HUNG OUT BY THE GLOOMY CASTLE IN THE FOG. I DUMPSTERED A PIZZA FOR DINNER AT THE (OLDEST) PIZZA HUT, AND FOUND THIS RAD, SEEDY MARINER AREA WITH PEOPLE LIVING ON OLD, FUNKY, WOOD BOATS IN A CHANNEL, AND PLENTY OF SCUMMY, SHRIMPER DUDES WALKING AROUND IN RUBBER BOOTS. WHEN I WAS READY TO SLEEP, I FOUND THIS PRETTY AMAZING ABANDONED HOME ON THE MAIN DRAG! IT LOOKED PRETTY VACATED, SO I BROKE IN AND DOVE IN THE WINDOW TO FIND IT FULLY FURNISHED!

I SLEPT ON THE BED THERE, AND IN THE MORNING LIGHT, NOW SOBER, I SAW THAT NOT ONLY WAS IT FURNISHED, BUT THERE WAS OTHER STUFF IN IT, LIKE A BIKE WITH 2 FLATS, RECORDS, AND A WEIGHT SET! I GUESS I COULD HAVE FIXED THE BIKE AND STAYED THERE AWHILE. THE "FOUNTAIN OF YOUTH", A TOURIST SPOT, WAS DOWN THE STREET, SO THEORETICALLY, I COULD LIVE THERE FOREVER! BUT WHEN I HEARD VOICES OUTSIDE, I STARTED THINKING MAYBE MY PLACE WASN'T SO ABANDONED! WELL, I LIKED IT A LOT, BUT LIVING THERE FOREVER SURE WOULD SUCK, ANYWAYS.

I SNUCK OUT A BACK WINDOW AND WENT TO GET COFFEE, SOMEWHERE. IT WAS TIME TO TAKE ANOTHER LOOK AT MY MAPS...

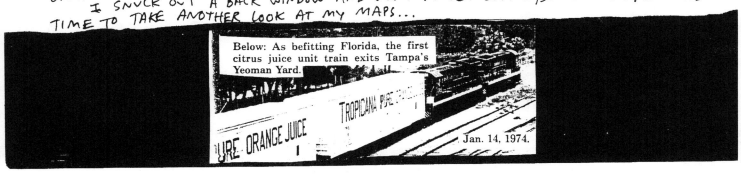

Below: As befitting Florida, the first citrus juice unit train exits Tampa's Yeoman Yard.

PURE ORANGE JUICE   TROPICANA PUR...   Jan. 14, 1974.

STASH LIKE ME or IGGY MADE ME GROW A MOUSTACHE AND WALK AROUND WITH IT STUCK ON MY FACE! or THE PUBLIC EMBARASSMENT OF CHUCK LOOSE

So, I moved to Ft. looderdale many moons ago because, like, as everybody knows, FT. LAUDERDALE IS PARTY TOWN U.S.A.! WHOO! HOOOOO! BOOOBS!! For those of youse who doubt it and insist that "yourtown, U.S.A." is **THE** place to party it down, I believe I need only reference the 1962 film "Where the boys are" and it's numerous offspring; just about every low budget film that came out in the early to mid eighties which bore the moniker "spring break" somewhere in it's title. 'Nuff said, jack. Anyhoo, besides being the (unfortunately for <u>this</u> party animal, former) spring break capi-

tal of the world, and boasting the most tiki-styled bars per capita in entire dammned United States, Ft. Lauderdool bears another claim to fame! A LOT OF MUSTACHES! Although I'm not sure how we rate "per capita" against a city where mustaches are REALLY king, like, lessee, San Francisco, fer example, Ft. Lauderdale's got a peck of 'em...the main differ-ence betweenst the "Ft. Lauderdale Moustache" and

Fig.A Me before; peppy, sassy, new wave, antisocial, but happy.

Fig.B Me after; Surly, Figity, Not afraid to use the word "muff" in normal conversation anywhere else though,is it's connotation.. to have a "lip buddy" in Ft. Lauderdale means one of three things: 1."I really like the guy from QUEEN who kicked it and am trying to carry on his memory.Bo Rhap Forever!" 2."I'm underage and trying to fool the 7-11 clerk into selling me a six pack of red dog" or 3."I am a Fort Lauderdale guy...I came here on spring break 20 years ago, and never left. I like Jimmy Buffet and can tell the difference between a Snook and a Marlin. I drink miller high life exclusively and can tell you the location of every clandestine after-hours cocaine bar in the pompano area". Since I've already grown a moustache for reasons 1 and 2, Mr. Iggy Scam convinced me that it would be "a good thing" to grow a moustache and go undercover the infiltrate the world of #3: The Ft. Lauderdale Guy. It is never a "good thing" to grow a moustache, kids. Ask any cop. And anyhoo, I really don't think that Ft. Lauderdale, or even it's surrounding county of Broward has any more mustaches than does Iggy's HQ of Dade county...but then again, truth or factual accounting don't make for good 'zine writing...hum.."creative embellishment" does. Ho ho! So, all in the name of "A funny article for SCAM" I got on down to business...I had my roommates hide my razors from me with the agreement that they would not give them back until I resembled Tom Selleck or a reasonable facsimile thereof. To begin, I started growing the "Generation x-style goatee" thingee around my mouth, so I would at least be able to go to the punk rock show and not be mistaken for a narc. Once my face was heavy with the fruit of my hyperactive teststosrone-producing glands, I trimmed and tapered until...wahla..the pride of all leathermen and cops...the lip worm! Ech! Ok, so now i gots a moustache, I gets an "I eat it raw at the Half Shell Raw Bar" tshirt, I listened to "maragitaville" ten times in a row, and I even went on down to a construction sight to get the ambiance goin' and my mojo workin'. Wahoo! bring on the hot tubs and hawaiian shirts! I am Mister Fort Lauderdale! Hell yeah! Ok, so the first place I decided to go to show off my new facial disgrace was...where else, einstein? A1A-BEACHFRONT AVENUE! And home of the world famous parrothead lounge! For those of you not in "the know", The "world famous Parrothead Lounge" is "a little out of the way place" on "the world famous Ft. Lauderdale strip" (as the sign above the door reads) featuring "Ft. Lauderdale's most atomic 10 cent chicken wings". Egad! What could be more a home away from home for a "Ft. Lauderdale guy" like me? I Bellied my newly moustachio'd self up to the bar, sure that the bartender would immediately take a liking to the clever tshirt I had chosen to wear(see fig. B), the color of which really accented the auburn highlights in my new facial hair. Hot Dawg! I ordered a Hot Dawg! Sorry, I just put that in there 'cause it rhymed...actually I summoned the barkeep thusly "My good man!" I exclaimed "I will have one of your finest top shelf Strawberry Margaritas whilst you spin me tales of baiting crab traps and all-night booze fueled fishing jaunts at the Pompano Pier." Hmmmm... I didn't expect this. Absolute silence....the barguy stared right through me...was it disbelief? disgust? was he jealous of my moustache? And then it hit me! The bottle thrown at my head from the other side of the bar! No, I'm just kidding. Actually what hit my was the realization that the barguy had a nose ring and was wearing a Jane's Addiction T-shirt. Land Sakes! This guy was 100% Gen-X! He weren't a "Parrothead at all!" What gives? Dejected, and actually pretty embarrassed that I had actually let Iggy talk me into growing this stupid thing, I sat in the corner of the bar, sucked down my weak and watery margarita and left post haste. "Where are the real parrotheads?" I asked myself as I walked down the beachfront...indeed! where was the "Moustache Nation" I'd heard so much about? With my Moustache-sense pushing me at 110%, I continued onward, searching for a fellow fur face. The only other people I saw bearing the 'stash were a couple of cops hangin' out at the Waffle House, and some short waffle-eyed woman who nearly bore down on me, astride her runaway 3-wheeled beach cruiser. Then...whatzit?!?...like an Oasis in the desert..like a candy cane to a hypoglycemic..like..like...um...like a bottle of any kind of alcoholic beverage to my roomates..there it was...yes! waaah! the "WORLD FAMOUS ELBO ROOM as featured in 'Where The Boys Are'". Surely this would be the Moustache homeland. A REAL Ft. Lauderdale Guy bar! As I sauntered in, I immediately noticed the "Moustache friendly" atmosphere. There was a "moustaches only" water fountain. Bathrooms labeled "Men", "Woman", and "Moustache"...yep...uh huh...well, actually, there was some crappy cover band hammering out a pretty rotton cover of "Smells like teen spirit" whilst a room fulla 20-something year old's danced in iridescent shirts.Yep, the whole moustache idea was pretty much a flop...and in the HEART of Ft. Lauderdale, no less. Sheesh. So I went home, dejected, to shave and listen to Motorhead. Fini.

" Ruining It For the Rest of us ... "

by GRETA S.

Have you ever said that phrase to any one? The first time I noticed someone saying that, it was gay scenesters saying it to gay punks. My roommate Tom used to complain about how he, though very gay with his pink triangle pins and public display of boyfriend, would get hissed at and sneered at in the Castro, because he was too punk. He told me, too, that there was a well-defined schism between the "straight-acting, straight-looking" people and the drag queens and queer punks, to where there would be opining in the written organs of the scene, and accusations back and forth. The straight-actings would use the above phrase, and the more flamboyant would reply "Sellout!" or "Go back to your closet!"

Tom's not my roommate anymore, he moved to L.A. and builds cool little machines out of outdated nuclear technology. In SF there evolved this sort of punk-oriented bike scene, people making bike actions and bike games and riding and drinking and carousing, and even doing political-type, anti-corporate environmental activities. As time has gone by, though, I noticed an increase in the usage of the above phrase. Once in the Mission, I was juggling a beer and tooling around at 22nd and Bryant when a sour-looking cyclist road up to me and said, "Get on the right side of the street! It's people like you who are RUINING IT FOR THE REST OF US!"

- 182 -

I think, now wait a minute, the oil companies are sponsoring political murders in Nigeria, and environmental terrorism and brainwashing all over the globe, and some goody two shoes cyclist thinks a drunk punk aimlessly trolling a near-empty intersection in the Mission is RUIN-ING IT? That little incident, repeated hundreds of times, signalled splintering and infighting amongst those who have the energy for that kind of thing, and the rest of us have just gone about our business. This phrase is a symptom, like hives or night sweats, of an insecure, defensive and self-abnegating mentality. Whenever it's used, it's used to put down people who have TOO MUCH IN COMMON. It specifies that

the RUINER is also one of US.

I'm sure you've noticed it in the punk scene. You may even have said it to someone. Someone said it to me, for graffiti. A punk telling another punk YOU"RE RUINING IT over graffiti? I have always consid-ered graffitti to be one of the Articles of Confederation of punkdom. If we can't do graffitti, at least, are we really punks anymore? You know, there comes a time for many people when they DO want to quit being a punk. There's no shame in that, I guess. But you can't have it both ways. You can't quit being a punk, then go around in punk's clothing telling other people they're wrecking the scene.

When punks have to attack their friends to protect their scene, then its TOO LATE! The enemy is already within.

Fuck THE REST OF THEM!

SOME SCAM REVIEWS

THE DESCENDENTS SHOW 3/97: I USUALLY HATE REUNIONS, BUT THE DENTS HAVE BEEN A BAND, WITH A DIFFERENT SINGER, THAT'S BEEN TOURING NON-STOP FOR 10 YEARS... AND THEY MADE A NEW RECORD THAT IS WAY BETTER THAN MOST OF THEIR OLD ONES AND BLOWS AWAY MODERN FAKE-ASS POP LIKE THE QUEERS. BASICALLY THE DENTS ALL-OUT, FURIOUS, URGENT APPROACH TO THE ROCK HAS INSPIRED ME FOR YEARS, AND IF YOU CAN'T PLAY LIKE THAT, YOU MIGHT AS WELL QUIT PLAYING!

MILO PROVED HE WAS A BAD ASS BY GETTING IVY AND BUDDHA INTO THE SHOW FOR FREE! I COULDN'T FIND A WAY IN, BUT LISA FROM MORBID OPERA PAID MY WAY! I THINK THE 80'S -STYLE OF THE SHOW HAD PUT HER IN AN EXALTED STATE. THANKS, AGAIN, LISA!

SO, EVERYONE DANCED LIKE HELL ALL NIGHT. IT WAS VERY FUN, BUT ALSO WEIRD CUZ I HAVEN'T BEEN TO A HUGE, 3000 PERSON, PUNK ROCK SPECTACLE LIKE THAT SINCE YE OLDE DAYS. YOU KNOW — COPS ATTACKING STRAGGLERS OUTSIDE, BOUNCERS ON THE ATTACK, YOU DANCE ALL NIGHT WITH A GIRL YOU WILL REMEMBER FOR YEARS AND WILL NEVER SEE AGAIN, UNDERLYING SKINHEAD MENACE, SOME KID PUKING BY YOUR CAR... THE WHOLE WORKS. THE GIRL WHO SHARED HER SCHLITZ AND KISSED ME AT THE LAST SHOW WAS THERE WITH HER BOYFRIEND... THE COPS WERE STOPPING PEOPLE FROM PASSING OUT FLYERS AND WE'RE RANDOMLY TAKING I.D.'S... IT WAS A HEAVY SCENE.

OH YEAH, THE SHOW WAS IN HALLANDALE, A TOWN THAT ACTUALLY HAS AN "ANTI-MOSHING" ORDINANCE ON THE BOOKS! NO SHIT! AS FAR AS I KNOW, THOUGH, THERE WERE NO ARRESTS FOR MOSHING AT THE SHOW...

I GOT IN JUST IN TIME FOR THE START OF THE SHOW. WHAT CAN I SAY? I WAS EXCITED. THEY PLAYED LIKE HELL FOR AN HOUR AND A HALF. EVERYONE I KNOW WAS THERE. THEY'D ALL COME BOBBING UP ON THE DANCE FLOOR FOR A SECOND AT A TIME. THE BOUNCER MAULED SOME DUDE, SO I SPIT ON THE BOUNCER AND HELD MY MIDDLE FINGER UP AT HIM, YELLING "FUCK YOU!" HE MOTIONED LIKE "C'MON UP HERE AND SAY IT!" HE WAS AS BIG AS A CAR. NEEDLESS TO SAY, I MANAGED TO STAY ON THE OTHER SIDE OF THE PIT ALL NIGHT, AND MADE SURE NO ONE PICKED ME UP AND CARRIED ME OVER TO HIM!

SUDDENLY IT WAS ALL OVER, AND WE ALL WENT OUTSIDE, SWEATY AND OVERJOYED, ONLY TO SEE A COP, MUSTACHE AND ALL, PUMMELING A CRYING, 15-YEAR OLD, RAVER GIRL. THE COPS PUSHED THE CROWD BACK. WE ALL YELLED INSULTS. I BEANED THE LADY COP IN THE HEAD WITH MY FLYERS, AND GOT THE HELL OUT OF THERE, BUT I HAD TO GO BACK FOR BUDDHA WHO SEEMED TOO DRUNK TO KNOW THAT HE SHOULDN'T JUST STAND THERE, YELLING IN THE COPS' FACE.

WITHIN MINUTES, THE CROWD WAS TOTALLY DISPERSED. CARS SCREECHED AWAY. I SAW THE BASS PLAYER, JUST STANDING AROUND, SO I WENT UP TO HIM. WE TALKED ABOUT WHAT A BAD ASS THE DRUMMER IS, FOR A MINUTE; THAT'S ALL. THEN MY RIDE DROVE UP. THAT WAS IT. IT WAS TOTAL CHAOS! I COULDN'T SLEEP AND SPENT THE WHOLE NIGHT RIDING MY BIKE AROUND, DRINKING BEER, AND SINGING "BIKEAGE" REAL LOUD...

I mean, A SCAM REVIEW ↗

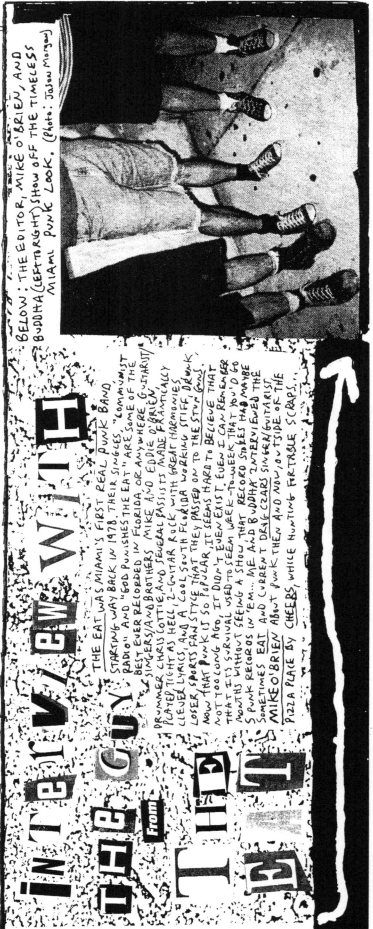

BELOW: THE EDITOR, MIKE O'BRIEN, AND BUDDHA (LEFT & RIGHT) SHOW OFF THE TIMELESS MIAMI PUNK LOOK. (Photo: Jason Morgan)

INTERVIEW WITH THE GUY from THE EAT

THE EAT WAS MIAMI'S FIRST REAL PUNK BAND, STARTING WAY BACK IN 1978. THEIR SINGLES, "COMMUNIST RADIO" AND "GOD PUNISHES THE EAT" ARE SOME OF THE BEST EVER RECORDED IN FLORIDA, OR ANYWHERE. GUITARIST/SINGERS/AND BROTHERS, MIKE AND EDDIE O'BRIEN, DRUMMER CHRIS COTTIE, AND SEVERAL BASSISTS MADE FRANTICALLY CLEVER LYRICS, AND A COOL SOUTH FLORIDA WORKING STIFF, DRUNK LOSER, SPORTS FAN STYLE THAT THEY PASSED ON TO THE STUD GUNS. PLAYED TIGHT AS HELL, 2-GUITAR ROCK WITH GREAT HARMONIES NOW THAT PUNK IS SO POPULAR, IT SEEMS HARD TO BELIEVE THAT NOT TOO LONG AGO, IT DIDN'T EVEN EXIST. EVEN I CAN REMEMBER THAT IT'S SURVIVAL USED TO SEEM WEEK-TO-WEEK. THAT YOU'D GO MONTHS WITHOUT SEEING A SHOW, THAT RECORD STORES HAD MAYBE 5 PUNK RECORDS IN 'EM... ME AND BUDDHA INTERVIEWED THE SOMETIMES EAT AND CURRENT DRUG CZARS SINGER/GUITARIST MIKE O'BRIEN ABOUT PUNK THEN AND NOW, OUTSIDE OF THE PIZZA PLACE BY CHEERS, WHILE HUNTING FERTRASLE SCRAPS...

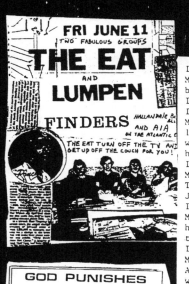

THE EAT VS. THE '70'S!

IGGY: So you guys started playing in 1980?
MIKE: No, it was 1978. My brother had this basement---it was like the only one in Florida, up by the Broward/Dade line...
I: Why'd you guys staat
I: Why'd you guys start playing? Were you guys punk rockwers?
M: No. There were no punk rockers. My brother and Cottie were in country cover bands. Back in 1972. They all met when Eddie and Cottie both answered the same ad in the music paper. It was with this guy who was a roadie for the Jefferson Airplane. He wrote rock operas, and thought he was real brilliant.
I: You mean, he did alot of drugs.
M: Yeah. He did codeine and wrote rock operas. I was only 15, so I was their little roadie. Their first gig was in the cripple ward at Jackson Memorial Hospital! They did BYRDS covers, Jefferson Airplane... a couple of the guy's little rock operas. This was in 1973.
I: uh... That's when we were born.
M: So they're playing and its all these cripples in bed---burn victims and shit. They played horrible. Horrible! But the doctor came up and told them that this was really the best kind of therapy for these people.
I: Would you say your audiences today arte similarly crippled?
M: well,.. We've seen some pretty strange shit looking off that stage over the years...
Anyways, they kept playing through the 70's as a cover band. Eventually, Cottie went on tour with David Alan Coe...
I: The cocaine snorting, fighting freak?
M: Yeah, he did coke with George Jones... Anyways, I took over on drums. We played THE WHO, CHEAP TRICK, ROXY MUSIC.... We were called The Fire Ants for awhile, but one day we were sitti: around practice talking, and I was saying "Well, We eat. It Eats. Everything eats. So, We became The Eat...
I: uh... that's pretty heavy, man. "Everything eats"... And what kind of drugs were you on?
M: Mostly just marijauna with a few other chemicals...
So Cottie got kicked off the David Alan Coe tour when he broke his foot, so he came back to Miami. Our guitarist quit, so I went to guitar, and Cottie joined up. That's when we decided to play originals. We wrote "Dr. TV", "Catholic Love"...

THE EAT "GO PUNK"!

I: Did you guys listen to punk?
M: Yeah, by then we listened to Ramones, New York Dolls.... It was a natural   progression from the glitter shit. We made a conscious decision: "Let's go punk."
I: So you didn't have red hair, or a mohawk, or anything?
M: No. There was no punk. I was 21 years old when I just "went punk."
The whole punk scene was THE CICHLIDS who were like power pop with a few covers. THE POLICE played in 1978. That was where alot of the people who became punks later met. Suddenly, it all just exploded in 1979, but it was dangerous, because people were real threatened by it. There was always people who came to shows just to fuck with you---rednecks, and shit.

THE EAT VS. DISCO AND THE SOUND GUY!

I: Wait, this is getting dull. Did you guys ever kill anybody, or what ?!?
M: Well, we did drop a cinder block on this guys head once while we were playing. He was a re asshole. He was very surprised, because most people don't expect musicians to drop cinder blocks on them.
I: Was he a nazi, or something?
M: We could have been the nazis... We were a mean ass group.
B: But weren't there more mean people around?
M: Yeah, everyone was pissed off cuz they thought we were trying to destroy music   as they knew it... We'd get this sneering criticism in The Miami Herald. We got in the Herald for playing a "Punk meets Disco" party in the Grove somewhere. The disco people unplugged us in the first song, "Jimmy B. Goode", which we always opened with! So, the guy from Mouth of the Rat fanzine, David Parsons, took a picture off the wall and smashed it and the glass frame got all over and cut all these disco people. They were bleeding all over. The cops came but somehow we got away. It was like 5 punks, and 200 disco fuckers...
I: and the disco people were on cocaine...

M: You bet... So it was in the paper. They said we were ruining everything... Eventually, as we put out records and stuff, they went as far as "Well, this is OK, ya know, if you like this sort of thing..." Also, we had some trouble at our second show, up in Boca, at FAU.
I: FAU? That's where me and Beod are from! You could, like hit a baseball from our houses to FAU Campus...
M: Wow. Our 2nd show was there with THE CICHLIDS in '79. We were OK. But when THE CICHLIDS started playing, they were kicking the monitors and stuff, so the sound guy wanted to fight them. Sound guys always hated punk bands.
I: Yeah, I've almost been beat up by the sound guy a bunch of times. What's up with that shit
B: Yeah, like the rednecks don't come to shows to fight you anymore, but there's still the fucking sound guy!

MYSTERY LYRICS OF "COMMUNIST RADIO" REVEALED!

B: You guys sing about Miami alot...
M: Well, its sort of a perverse thing, getting to be from here, so why not? "Money for the Police"-- that's a song about the River Cops (For out of towneres:The cops in the 80's used to seize coke shipments so they could sell it themselves! Isn't that rad? That led to the fame River Cop case)
"Hiahleah"-- that's about the racetrack...
I: But wait... What are the actual lyrics to "Communist Radio"? No one knows.
M: Ya know, those are just bullshit lyrics. We were filming this video thing and the song didn' have lyrics, so I just made 'em up on the spot. I always expected to go back and change 'em but I never got around to it. I'm pretty sure its "I walked out on the Indian Ocean. I wore boots but they didn't show. I got caught up in the commotion. Communist Radio"...

BORINGTON
JOURNAL #2

"I MAY NOT AGREE WITH WHAT YOU SAY, SO IF YOU SAY IT AGAIN I'LL KICK YOUR FUCKIN FACE IN" - STIV BATORS

STEAL THIS RAG

GUNS AND DRUGS: THE EAT'S 1980 TOUR!

I: So you guys actually went on tour?
M: Yeah in 1980. We did 2 shows in New York City, 2 shows in North Carolina, a couple in Florida, one in Atlanta... It was good. We brought guns and alot of speed.
I: GUNS ?!? What For? Rad Miami style?
M: Our manager was a gun collector nut. When we left on tour, he presented us all with our ow gun. Things were going good on tour, but on the way back -- we'd been doing tons of speed all week-- we'd start arguing and then threatening each other with the guns. It was a bad id
I: What about The Eat Coke Mirror that Chris Cottie has?
M: Our manager made that, too. He'd make us shirts, silkscreen stickers...
I: make coke mirrors...
M: Yeah, why not? It was fun, we just gave all the stuff away.
B: How were the shows on tour?
M: The New York City ones were weird. We played with some weird Scottish band in kilts, and a Bruce Springsteen cover band. The Carolina shows went great. We were the nasty punk band from Miami, and they didn't have punk there, so they loved us...
M: Have you seen the video where we're playing at the old Open Book and Records? That was right after that tour.
B: Its in the same plaza in Ft. Lauderdale where the tracks are, where the Mudhouse and Far Out Records were later (92-95).
I: No shit! Is that the one that features shots of the young Paul Enema and the young Aesop Hickey moshing together in the crowd?
B: No, that's a Gay Cowboys in Bondage show... (Ed. note: Hickey is really from Florida, though they are now ashamed of their roots and deny it...)
I: Didn't you guys just give away your records, too?
M: Well, we gave away alot of 'em. We first got our 7" on New Year's Eve '79/80. It was the "New Wave New Year's" with THE CONTORTIONS at the Sunrise Musical Theater. 2000 people came' threw a ton of records out into the crowd... they were getting stepped on, broken.
I: and now its worth a ton of money...
M: Yeah, I'm waiting for the price to go up so I can sell the ones I got left...

I: What are the differences in shows between then and now?
M: Well, the crowd sizes are about the same. The kids look the same... The only thing is now its OK to have long hair.
I: well,I told this guy at The Pink Lincolns show to stop punching everybody and he yelled, "Fuck you, Longhair!" It was pretty old school, I thought. SO me and Dood knocked him

out by dropping a cinder block on his head, and then we took a bunch of pictures of him with a long blonde wig on while he was passed out...
M: Another difference is The Eat didn't stand around tuning, or wasting time. WE'd play 23, songs for an hour and when you'd come offstage you'd be totally soaked and fucked up. With Eat I'd always cut my right finger open, just playing so hard, and blood would splatter all over my guitar. For some reason, I never got cut when I played with MORBID OPERA, or now with THE DRUG CZARS... just THE Eat. Also then, bands hated other bands. They all thought the were gonna be famous, so they'd try to step on you and keep you down.

EAT ON TOUR

PLUS: MO-DETTES, STRAIT JACKETS, Milk Me

THE EAT

PREMIER CLUB

715 S. 21 ave. Hollywood
FRI. & SAT., MAY 9 + 10

Plus Special Guests CHARLIE PICKETT & THE EGGS

A Lonely Surprise for All Our Little Friends

SH.EGM.

PEACE
LOVE

THIS IS NOT, NOR IS IT INTENDED TO REPRESENT, A SOLICITATION TO PERFORM SEX FOR COMPENSATION.

BIENVENIDO LOS PUNKS CUBANOS SE HA ESPANOL

THE EAT VS. "FATHER TIME"!

I: Where are the people now who came to your shows in 1980?
M: Who knows? Alot came out of the woodwork for our last reunion.. I'm glad I'm still doing it. I'll be doing it til I'm dead...
I: Did you ever think you'd still be playing in 1997?
M: No way. I thought in 1997, it'd be a police state, which it sort of is.
I: That's cuz you live in Broward. Down here, you can just give the cops a few bucks and its good!
M: I'm surprised that punk turned into this whole lifestyle thing... We were just working shitty jobs and trying to make it through the week. WE were like normal guys who played in th band...
I: Are The Eat playing ever again?
M: Yeah, Ivy says we have to play in June, so I guess we'll do whatever she says. Somehow The Eat won't die. We're still trying to kill it.
I: How about "Kill The Eat! Night"...? You could bring a knife and get in free...
M: Well, the thing is, we could just die, anyways. You see Cottie; he's a walking heart attack... He could have died at our last show. Me, too. We're old...

JUST ABOUT THEN IS WHERE WE CALLED IT QUITS SO WE COULD GO WATCH THE NEW BOMB TURKS' SET. THE OLD EAT 7"'S ARE STILL INCREDIBLY RARE, BUT LOOK FOR THE COMPLETE WORKS OF THE EAT ON ONE CD, SOON, FROM LOCALS STARCRUNCH RECORDS. MEANWHILE, CHECK OUT MIKE'S GREAT NEW BAND WITH THE EAT'S CHRIS COTTIE, BUDDHA, AND A TRUE BAD ASS OF LOCAL ROCK, ROACH MOTEL AND MORBID OPERA'S JEFF HODAP ON LEAD GUITAR THEY'RE CALLED THE DRUG CZARS AND HAVE A 7" ON STARCRUNCH...

THE 5 MINUTES THAT CHANGED PUNK?

PLAY FASTER!

CLICK GULP

EXCLUSIVE INSIDE ACCOUNT OF RICHMOND, VA'S FIRST "REALLY SHORT SHOW" BY IGGY SCAM

WHEN I WAS 11 YEARS OLD, RONALD REAGAN SAID "THIS IS THE GENERATION THAT MAY FACE ARMAGEDDON" AND "THE DAY AFTER", THE MOVIE ABOUT THE AFTERMATH OF A NUCLEAR WAR BETWEEN THE U.S. AND THE FORMER U.S.S.R. SHOWED ON TV. MAYBE THIS IS WHY I CAN'T WRITE A SONG THAT'S LONGER THAN 90 SECONDS, OR SIT THROUGH TODAY'S 5 BAND, 6 HOUR SHOWS WHERE BANDS PLAY 45 MINUTE SETS. FUK! SAM AND I DECIDED SHOWS ARE GETTING WAY TOO LONG, SO WE INVENTED "THE REALLY SHORT SHOW." THE IDEA WAS TO GET A BUNCH OF BANDS TO JUST PLAY ONE SONG, BUT THEN WE REALIZED SOME WISE-ASSES WOULD PROBABLY PLAY A 10-MINUTE SONG. SO THE RULES WERE THAT EVERY BAND PLAYS EXACTLY ONE MINUTE, OR LESS, AND IF A MINUTE COMES UP AND THEY DON'T STOP PLAYING, WE KICK THEIR ASSES! NO EXCEPTIONS! ON A COUPLE DAYS NOTICE, WE GOT THIS BAR TO LET US DO THE SHOW, GOT A HANDFUL OF BANDS TO AGREE TO PLAY, AND GOT FLYERS OUT. THE REST IS HISTORY. ABOUT 100 PEOPLE SHOWED UP TO SEE THE FIRST "REALLY SHORT SHOW" BUT, LIKE WOODSTOCK, THAT FIGURE WOULD BALLOON IN THE WEEKS FOLLOWING THE SHOW TO OVER 100,000 PEOPLE WHO CLAIMED TO HAVE BEEN THERE FOR "THE 5-MINUTES THAT CHANGED PUNK FOREVER..."

FIRST, SAM EXPLAINED THE RULES TO THE BANDS AND CROWD, AND THEN, JUST PAST MIDNIGHT, THE SURF-ROCK-INSTRUMENTAL TRIO, THE FRESH-O-MATICS STARTED OFF THE SHOW. THEY PLAYED AS TIGHT AND ENERGETIC A SURF TUNE AS YOU COULD EXPECT FROM THREE KIDS WHO'D NEVER SEEN A WAVE. BUT TROUBLE BREWED WHEN THEY DELIBERATELY IGNORED THE SIGNAL TO QUIT AT THE ONE-MINUTE MARK! THE CROWD LOOKED ANGRY AND CONFUSED, SENSING THAT THEY WERE BEING BETRAYED. BUT, I LEPT UP AND PULLED THE GUITARIST TOWARDS THE EDGE OF THE STAGE, AND HE QUIT PLAYING AND THEN THE DRUMMER SAW THAT I MEANT BUSINESS AND SPLIT! YOU CAN'T FUCK WITH THE "REALLY SHORT SHOW" LIKE THAT AND GET AWAY WITH IT!

FOR SOME REASON, PROBABLY BECAUSE THERE WAS ONLY 4 "REAL" BANDS, I WAS SUPPOSED TO PLAY A SONG NEXT. SO I ELECTED TO DO A NUMBER CALLED "SOMEBODY BUY ME A BEER" WHERE I JAMMED THE MICROPHONE IN MY MOUTH AND GURGLED AND HOWLED WHILE I PLAYED DRUMS BUT THE MIKE KEPT FALLING OUT OF MY MOUTH, AND MY TIME WAS RUNNING OUT, SO I FINALLY JUST DOVE OFF THE BASS DRUM INTO THE CROWD. IT WAS PRETTY WEIRD, I GUESS, BUT A LOT OF PEOPLE DUG IT, WHICH MADE ME WISH I HAD SHIRTS AND CD'S TO SELL, CUZ EVERYONE KNOWS THAT "MERCH" IS HOW YOU MAKE IT ON TOUR.

NEXT UP WAS THE (YOUNG) PIONEERS WHO PLAYED A REAL GOOD SONG THAT WAS ABOUT 45 SECONDS LONG. THEY WERE FOLLOWED IMMEDIATELY BY ACTION PATROL. A.P. APPARENTLY TOOK THE "REALLY SHORT SHOW" VERY SERIOUSLY AS EVIDENCED BY THE FACT THAT THE BAND MEMBERS ALL WORE PLASTIC BAGS OVER THEIR HEADS, THUS CUTTING OFF THEIR OXYGEN AND NOT GIVING THEM MUCH MORE THAN A MINUTE TO LIVE! THE SINGER, A LARGE, HEAVY KID WITH GLASSES INHALED HELIUM TO MAKE HIS VOICE REAL HIGH AND THEN JUMPED AROUND LIKE A MANIAC THROUGH THE WHOLE SONG. THE MUSIC WAS FAST AND SLOPPY AND THE MINUTE ENDED WITH THE ASPHYXIATING GUITARIST AND THE BIG VIRGINIAN ON THE FLOOR IN THE PIT! YO! THE COMBINATION OF THE (YOUNG) PIONEERS TIGHT, DANCY, MINUTEMEN-ISH RUMBLE AND ACTION PATROL'S SPASTIC, CHOKING SPRAWL MADE FOR THE BEST 2 MINUTES OF PUNK I'VE SEEN IN YEARS! THIS WAS "THE REALLY SHORT SHOW" AT ITS FINEST...

MEN'S RECOVERY PROJECT BROUGHT THE EVENING TO A CLOSE AT ABOUT 12:08. THEY SPENT NEARLY THEIR WHOLE MINUTE SETTING UP AN ELABORATE SLIDE SHOW AND PUTTING ON RAINCOATS, ONLY TO SUDDENLY BREAK INTO A FURIOUS, GUITAR DRIVEN, 5-SECOND ATTACK. AND THAT WAS IT. THE STUNNED CROWD FILED OUT OF THE BAR, SPENT AND SPEECHLESS FROM RELEASED TENSION.

THE FUTURE OF PUNK, "THE REALLY SHORT SHOW", HAS ARRIVED! AS FAR AS I'M CONCERNED, IF A BAND CAN'T ROCK FOR ONE MINUTE, WHO WANTS TO HEAR THEIR LAME, FAKE-ASS SHIT FOR A HALF HOUR?!?

WELL, WHAT CAN I SAY? ITS JUST THE RECORD THAT CHANGED MY WHOLE LIFE COMPLETELY, AND IRREVERSIBLY...

(E.G. 1A: THE FLYER)

IVY, KRISTIANA, ERIC, KERRIE, AND OF COURSE, PUNCH, FOLLOWED ME AND THE BOOD WITH THE CART WHILE HENRY'S TORTURED SCREAMS AND GREG'S SNARLING, SAVAGE GUITAR ATTACK SCARED THE SHIT OUT OF UNSUSPECTING DOWNTOWN PEDESTRIANS! BUT THE BEST PART WAS WHEN WE WENT INSIDE THE RESTAURANT AT THE GOVERNMENT CENTER METRO-RAIL AT THE END OF THE RECORD WHEN ITS HENRY AND THE DRUMS AND WE PUSH THE CART REAL SLOW, WHILE PEOPLE STARE IN HORROR, AND HENRY SCREAMS "NOBODY COMES IN! NOBODY COMES IN! STAY OUT!" FUCK YEAH! THEN BOBBY LOAD SHOWED UP WITH BEER AND WE ALL WENT AND DRANK AT THE RIVER!

DAMAGED IN DOWNTOWN!
MONDAY FEBRUARY 5TH
AT 4:00 PM

IGGY AND BUDDHA WILL BE PLAYING BLACK FLAGS 'DAMAGED' LP ON A HUGE RADIO DOWNTOWN. WE WILL BE PUSHING THE RADIO IN A SHOPPING CART FROM THE OLD...

DA CEARIST BUILDING

PATCHING EAR!

RAW BUTTOCKS!

X-TRA

COURTHOUSE ON FLAGLER UP AVENUE TO MICARY'S THEN RIGHT MIAMI AVENUE TO MM BRICKELL BRIDGE, RIGHT ON FLAGLER ... BACK TO MIAMI AVE BRIDGE THEN OUR ROUTE TO GET DRUNK IN SUZMARTI PARK!

FIGHT BACK WITH FECES!!!

TRUE LIFE STORY OF A CRUDE AND SHOCKING ATTACK...

OK, I'LL ADMIT THAT ITS POSSIBLE THAT THE COCONUT GROVE ARTS FESTIVAL STARTED OUT SORT-OF RAD, LIKE ALOT OF 60'S HIPPIE NEIGHBORHOOD STUFF IN THIS COUNTRY, BUT THESE DAYS ITS CLEARLY NOTHING MORE THAN A DRUNKEN/YUPPIE MESS. AN EXPENSIVE BLOCK PARTY WITH PEOPLE SELLING ALOT OF FAKE-ASS CRAFTS AND KNICK-KNACKS AND JEWELRY AND PAINTINGS OF SUNSETS— BASICALLY, ITS PRETTY FUN TO FUCK WITH.

SO, I WAS WONDERING HOW A YOUNG ARTIST LIKE ME COULD, YA KNOW, GET MY "BIG BREAK" AND SHOW MY STUFF AT THE FESTIVAL, FINALLY, I DECIDED I'D JUST HAVE TO TAKE IT OUT THERE AND TAKE A CHANCE AND SHOW IT

I WENT IN A PORTO-LET AND TOOK A SHIT ON A PAPER PLATE, AND THEN TOOK IT IN A BAG TO THE MAIN DRAG OF THE FESTIVAL, WHERE I DISCREETLY UNVEILED IT WITH A SIGN THAT SAID "LOCALLY PRODUCED ORGANIC ART" AND A PRICE TAG: "$4,000." AND LEFT IT OUT THERE WITH ALL THE OTHER OVERPRICED SHIT. I WAS NERVOUS, 'CUZ IT WAS MY FIRST SHOWING AND ALL, BUT IT WENT PRETTY WELL. I TOOK OFF, AND IVY STOOD BY IT FOR AWHILE, YELLING "OH GROSS! LOOK AT THAT! SOMEONE SHIT ON A PLATE!" TO MAKE SURE PEOPLE SAW IT. SHE'S SO SWEET THAT WAY, ALWAYS SO SUPPORTIVE OF MY ART....

(FIG.2A)
PICTURED ABOVE: QUANNAH, DRUMMER FOR CHATTANOOGA, TN'S THE SPAWN SACS PROUDLY MODELS HIS NEW TATTOO OF A BIG TURD STEAMING IN THE SUN, WITH BEAUTIFUL BISCAYNE BAY BEHIND HIM...

← DON'T FUCK WITH THE SCAM!

FAKE ASS MAINSTREAM SHIT IMITATES LIFE

OK, SEEING RANCID FILM A VIDEO AT THE TRAIN YARD IN WEST OAKLAND, WHILE I WAS THERE TO HOP A TRAIN WAS BAD ENOUGH. HAVING MTV'S REALWORLD SHOW UP TO BOTH MY BAND AND IVY'S BAND'S SHOWS LAST YEAR WAS WORSE. BUT, NOW, IN A NEW U2 VIDEO FILMED IN MIAMI, THEY SPEND LIKE ½ THE VIDEO STANDING IN FRONT OF THE MURAL ON 8TH STREET THAT WAS ON THE COVER OF SCAM #2! SHEESH! WHAT'S NEXT? FUCKING ALANIS MORRISHIT, DUMPSTER DIVING WITH PUNCH?

IVY AND I, DISGUSTED ON OUR DAILY WALK THROUGH THE GROVE AT SEEING YET ANOTHER UNBELIEVABLY UGLY PINK AND BLUE YUPPIE CONDO IN THE LOT WHERE A NICE, OLD HOUSE AND TREES USED TO BE, CAME UP WITH WHAT WE THOUGHT WAS A PRETTY FUNNY IDEA TO FIGHT IT. INSTEAD OF VANDALIZING IT, PER SE, YOU COULD JUST GET A BUNCH OF CONCERNED CITIZENS TO GO IN THE MIDDLE OF THE NIGHT AND REPAINT IT A LESS OFFENSIVE COLOR! YOU KNOW, LIKE A LIGHT GREEN... THIS IS OBVIOUSLY RIDICULOUS AND IMPRACTICAL, BUT, FOR THE "VANDALISM ART SHOW" I DECIDED TO GO PAINT BIG, BLUE POLKA DOTS ON A PASTEL, YELLOW CONDOS OUTER WALL. OK, SURE, THIS IS SORT-OF FASCISM, BUT NO MORE THAN REAL ESTATE FASCISM THAT NEVER ASKED THE PEOPLE WHO ACTUALLY LIVE HERE HOW WE WANT OUR NEIGHBORHOOD TO LOOK! SO, USING A STENCIL, I PUT UP THE DOTS AND IT LOOKED SO COOL! I EVEN THOUGHT THAT THEY'D AGREE WITH ME AND LEAVE IT UP. MAYBE POLKA-DOTTED BUILDINGS WOULD BECOME A GROVE CRAZE AND I'D BE PAID TO DO MY ART ON SEVERAL BUILDINGS!

BUT, AT 9:00AM, I RODE BY TO GET THE PICTURE, AND THEY WERE ALREADY COVERING IT! THE WORLD WILL NEVER ← KNOW... BUT THEN I SAW THIS RAD CLIPPING OF SOMEONE IN A FT. LAUDERDALE, GAY NEIGHBORHOOD WITH THE SAME IDEA!

WILL THE CITY OF MIAMI SURVIVE? THAT'S THE BURNING QUESTION IN TOWN THESE DAYS (THE ANSWER IS USUALLY "WHAT DO YOU MEAN BY SURVIVE?"). BY NOW READERS IN OTHER TOWNS HAVE UNDOUBTEDLY HEARD ABOUT THE CITY MANAGER RESIGNING, AS THEY SAY, IN DISGRACE AND IT TURNING OUT THAT HE NOT ONLY TOOK BRIBES, BUT HID THE CITY'S $68.2 DEBT. NOW, WE'RE SUPPOSEDLY GOING TO GO BANKRUPT ANY DAY. OUR SUDDEN BANKRUPT STATUS IS M SHOCK TO ANYONE WHO HAS EVER BEEN STUCK WITHOUT TOILET PAPER IN THE LIBRARY TOILET. BUT I BELIEVE "THE MAGIC CITY" WILL SURVIVE. THE OTHER DAY, I GOT STUCK WITHOUT T.P. IN THE LIBRARY CRAPPER, AND WAS AT A LOSS, 'TIL A FRIENDLY, FELLOW-MIAMIAN'S HAND APPEARED UNDER THE STALL WITH A ROLL OF TOILET PAPER! THAT'S THE SPIRIT,

JUST BEFORE X-MAS '95, 2 APARTMENT COMPLEXES IN E. LITTLE HAVANA

BRICKELL VILLAGE

publix

THESE EDITION IS A PLEASURE

OPENING MAY '96

DEVELOPER: CORAL WAY VENTURE. L.P.

WERE KNOCKED DOWN TO BUILD THIS

MIAMI! WE CAN DO IT! NEXT YOU'LL SEE OVERTOWN RESIDENTS OFFERING TO TEAR DOWN THEIR OWN HOMES TO MAKE WAY FOR THE MAYOR'S NEW BASKETBALL ARENA!

BY THE WAY, TO RAISE CASH, LETS CHARGE THE SUBURBS PROTECTION MONEY! CORAL GABLES PAYS UP, OR WE SEND THE FIVE-THREE KILLAS TO PARTY ON THE MIRACLE MILE! THIS COULD WORK ON BROWARD COUNTY TO THE NORTH, AS WELL. BROWARD, WHERE ALL THE OLD BURT REYNOLDS-STYLE CRACKERS MOVED "WHEN THE CUBANS TOOK OVER" IS NO MATCH FOR OUR SUPERIOR GUNPOWER! LET'S PLANT THE CUBAN FLAG IN DOWNTOWN FT. LAUDERDALE AND MAKE PATOIS THE OFFICIAL LANGUAGE!

PUBLIX SUPERMARKET... ONE BLOCK FROM AN EXISTING HYDE PARK SUPERMARKET! E. LITTLE HAVANA IS SUDDENLY... "BRICKELL VILLAGE!"

"NOSTALGIA FOR AN AGE YET TO COME"
THE CIA IN MIAMI HISTORY

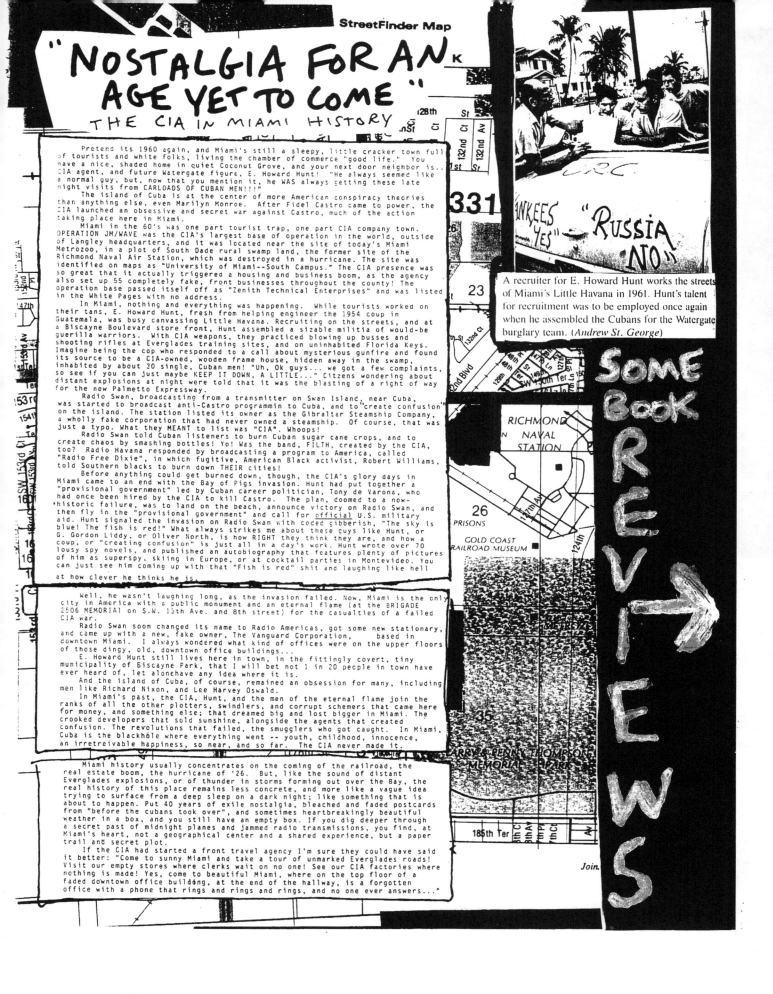

Pretend its 1960 again, and Miami's still a sleepy, little cracker town full of tourists and white folks, living the chamber of commerce "good life." You have a nice, shaded home in quiet Coconut Grove, and your next door neighbor is... CIA agent, and future Watergate figure, E. Howard Hunt! "He always seemed like a normal guy, but, now that you mention it, he WAS always getting these late night visits from CARLOADS OF CUBAN MEN!!!"

The island of Cuba is at the center of more American conspiracy theories than anything else, even Marilyn Monroe. After Fidel Castro came to power, the CIA launched an obsessive and secret war against Castro, much of the action taking place here in Miami.

Miami in the 60's was one part tourist trap, one part CIA company town. OPERATION JM/WAVE was the CIA's largest base of operation in the world, outside of Langley headquarters, and it was located near the site of today's Miami Metrozoo, in a plot of South Dade rural swamp land, the former site of the Richmond Naval Air Station, which was destroyed in a hurricane. The site was identified on maps as "University of Miami--South Campus." The CIA presence was so great that it actually triggered a housing and business boom, as the agency also set up 55 completely fake, front businesses throughout the county! The operation base passed itself off as "Zenith Technical Enterprises" and was listed in the White Pages with no address.

In Miami, nothing and everything was happening. While tourists worked on their tans, E. Howard Hunt, fresh from helping engineer the 1954 coup in Guatemala, was busy canvassing Little Havana. Recruiting on the streets, and at a Biscayne Boulevard store front, Hunt assembled a sizable militia of would-be guerilla warriors. With CIA weapons, they practiced blowing up busses and shooting rifles at Everglades training sites, and on uninhabited Florida Keys. Imagine being the cop who responded to a call about mysterious gunfire and found its source to be a CIA-owned, wooden frame house, hidden away in the swamp, inhabited by about 30 single, Cuban men! "Uh, Ok guys... we got a few complaints, so see if you can just maybe KEEP IT DOWN, A LITTLE..." Citizens wondering about distant explosions at night were told that it was the blasting of a right of way for the new Palmetto Expressway.

Radio Swan, broadcasting from a transmitter on Swan Island, near Cuba, was started to broadcast anti-Castro programmin to Cuba, and to "create confusion" on the island. The station listed its owner as the Gibralter Steamship Company, a wholly fake corporation that had never owned a steamship. Of course, that was just a typo. What they MEANT to list was "CIA". Whoops!

Radio Swan told Cuban listeners to burn Cuban sugar cane crops, and to create chaos by smashing bottles! Yo! Was the band, FILTH, created by the CIA, too? Radio Havana responded by broadcasting a program to America, called "Radio Free Dixie", in which fugitive, American Black activist, Robert Williams, told Southern blacks to burn down THEIR cities!

Before anything could get burned down, though, the CIA's glory days in Miami came to an end with the Bay of Pigs invasion. Hunt had put together a "provisional government" led by Cuban career politician, Tony de Varona, who had once been hired by the CIA to kill Castro. The plan, doomed to a now-historic failure, was to land on the beach, announce victory on Radio Swan, and then fly in the "provisional government" and call for official U.S. military aid. Hunt signaled the invasion on Radio Swan with coded gibberish, "The sky is blue! The fish is red!" What always strikes me about these guys like Hunt, or G. Gordon Liddy, or Oliver North, is how RIGHT they think they are, and how a coup, or "creating confusion" is just all in a day's work. Hunt wrote over 70 lousy spy novels, and published an autobiography that features plenty of pictures of him as superspy, skiing in Europe, or at cocktail parties in Montevideo. You can just see him coming up with that "Fish is red" shit and laughing like hell at how clever he thinks he is.

Well, he wasn't laughing long, as the invasion failed. Now, Miami is the only city in America with a public monument and an eternal flame (at the BRIGADE 2506 MEMORIAl on S.W. 13th Ave. and 8th street) for the casualties of a failed CIA war.

Radio Swan soon changed its name to Radio Americas, got some new stationary, and came up with a new, fake owner, The Vanguard Corporation, based in downtown Miami. I always wondered what kind of offices were on the upper floors of those dingy, old, downtown office buildings...

E. Howard Hunt still lives here in town, in the fittingly covert, tiny municipality of Biscayne Park, that I will bet not 1 in 20 people in town have ever heard of, let alonehave any idea where it is.

And the island of Cuba, of course, remained an obsession for many, including men like Richard Nixon, and Lee Harvey Oswald.

In Miami's past, the CIA, Hunt, and the men of the eternal flame join the ranks of all the other plotters, swindlers, and corrupt schemers that came here for money, and something else; that dreamed big and lost bigger in Miami. The crooked developers that sold sunshine, alongside the agents that created confusion. The revolutions that failed, the smugglers who got caught. In Miami, Cuba is the blackhole where everything went -- youth, childhood, innocence, an irretrievable happiness, so near, and so far. The CIA never made it.

Miami history usually concentrates on the coming of the railroad, the real estate boom, the hurricane of '26. But, like the sound of distant Everglades explosions, or of thunder in storms forming out over the Bay, the real history of this place remains less concrete, and more like a vague idea trying to surface from a deep sleep on a dark night; like something that is about to happen. Put 40 years of exile nostalgia, bleached and faded postcards from "before the cubans took over", and sometimes heartbreakingly beautiful weather in a box, and you still have an empty box. If you dig deeper through a secret past of midnight planes and jammed radio transmissions, you find, at Miami's heart, not a geographical center and a shared experience, but a paper trail and secret plot.

If the CIA had started a front travel agency I'm sure they could have said it better: "Come to sunny Miami and take a tour of unmarked Everglades roads! Visit our empty stores where clerks wait on no one! See our CIA factories where nothing is made! Yes, come to beautiful Miami, where on the top floor of a faded downtown office building, at the end of the hallway, is a forgotten office with a phone that rings and rings and rings, and no one ever answers..."

A recruiter for E. Howard Hunt works the streets of Miami's Little Havana in 1961. Hunt's talent for recruitment was to be employed once again when he assembled the Cubans for the Watergate burglary team. (*Andrew St. George*)

SOME BOOK REVIEWS

A LONG-DISTANCE BUS LEAVES THE HIGHWAY

TO MAKE ANOTHER STOP ON THE MAIN STREET OF ANOTHER STUNTED CITY.

WHAT IS THIS? WHERE ARE WE?

MONGRELT

THE OFFICIAL SCAM PUNKS GUIDE TO THE MIAMI METRORAIL !!

If you miss your stop, simply get off at the next station and take the train going in the opposite direction.

I LOVE THE METRO-RAIL. TO ME ITS MUCH MORE THAN SOMETHING TO THROW BIG BEER BOTTLES AT AS IT RACES PAST THE PUNK SHOW AT CHEERS; ITS ANOTHER CHARMING EXAMPLE OF HOPELESSLY INEPT CITY PLANNING. EVERY TIME IT RUMBLES PAST, EMPTY AND SAD, ON ITS SLOW, INEVITABLE JOURNEY TO THE GARMENT SWEATSHOPS, FLOODED ROADS, AND SANTERIA REMAINS OF HIALEAH, OR THE VAST WASTELAND OF KENDALL'S MALLS AND EXPRESSWAYS, I GET ALL WISTFUL. TO LOVE THE METRORAIL IS TO LOVE MIAMI, IN ALL ITS FADING GLORY. NAY-SAYERS SAY THE METRORAIL DOESN'T GO A LOT OF PLACES, BUT WHERE DOES IT GO? OUR STATION BY STATION TOUR STARTS DOWN AT THE SOUTH END AT **DADELAND SOUTH** — SIGHTS: OBSERVE THE 11th ANNIVERSARY, THIS YEAR OF THE FAMED "DADELAND MASSACRE" WHERE RIVAL DRUG SMUGGLERS SHOT IT OUT WITH MACHINE GUNS IN MAYHUE'S LIQUOUR IN 1980, IN FULL DAYLIGHT, IN THE MIDDLE OF A CROWDED MALL! A COUPLE SMUGGLERS BIT IT AND THE MESSAGE WAS SENT TO THE REST OF THE WORLD THAT MIAMI WAS BASICALLY A LAWLESS DODGE CITY RULED BY COLOMBIANS WITH UZIS — A PERCEPTION THAT HAPPILY SURVIVES TO THIS DAY! SCAMS: BORDER'S BOOKS ACROSS U.S. 1 FROM STATION HAS ALL THE FREE BOOKS AND COFFEE YOU COULD ASK FOR... HOPPABILITY: THE STATION HAS TWO ENTRANCES SO YOUR CHANCES OF CATCHING ONE UNGUARDED ARE DECENT. **DADELAND NORTH:** THE RAIL DOES **NOT** GO TO THE AIRPORT, OR ANY MAJOR STADIUM, BUT HAS **TWO** STOPS FOR THIS ANCIENT MALL. I DREAM THAT ONE DAY DADELAND MALL WILL BE LIKE MALLS UP IN BROWARD COUNTY — ABANDONED AND COVERED ON THE INSIDE WITH TEENAGE GANG GRAFFITI, A REFUGE TO SKATERS AND UNDERAGE DRINKERS. UNTIL THAT DAY, YOU SHOULD SKIP THIS DULL STOP. **SOUTH MIAMI** — A TRIP TO "SOMI" MEANS A TRIP TO THE "FREE" WENDY'S SALAD BAR AT RED ROAD. STATION IS SMALL, NEARLY UNHOPPABLE, AND ONE TIME THE GUARD TRIED TO PUNCH MY FRIEND, BRAD, FOR NO REASON. PROCEED WITH CAUTION! **UNIVERSITY:** THERE'S LOTS OF FREE SHIT AT THE UNIVERSITY, LIKE THE LIBRARY AND THE PIANOS AND DRUMS IN THE MUSIC BUILDING. THERE'S A "CIRCLE K" AND A DOMINO'S PIZZA NEXT TO EACH OTHER ON PONCE DE LEON, WHERE ONE TIME I DUMPSTERED PIZZA, HEATED IT IN THE "CIRCLE K" MICROWAVE, BOUGHT BEER, AND JUST SAT OUTSIDE THE STATION, DRINKING BEER AND PIZZA ALL DAY! IT WAS SO FUN! I THOUGHT I'D END UP DOING IT ALL THE TIME BUT SOMEHOW, I'VE NEVER GOT AROUND TO DOING IT AGAIN... **DOUGLAS ROAD:** THIS IS PROBABLY THE EASIEST STATION OF ALL TO HOP BECAUSE OF A CRUCIAL ARCHITECTURAL FLAW IN THE STATION'S DESIGN THAT HAS THE TURNSTILES AT ONE ENTRANCE BLOCKED FROM THE VIEW OF THE GUARD STATION BY THE ELEVATOR! HOP AWAY! SIGHTS: A HUGE COMMUNITY HAS SPRUNG UP IN HOMEMADE SHACKS UNDER THE RAIL, SERVING AS AN EXCELLENT STUDY IN URBAN PLANNING. JUST LIKE PITTSBURGH, FOR EXAMPLE, RISING AT THE INTERSECTION OF THREE RIVERS, THIS "CITY" HAS SPRUNG UP IN CLOSE PROXIMITY TO A NATURAL SOURCE OF WEALTH (3-WAY INTERSECTION OF U.S. 1, BIRD, AND DOUGLAS IS GREAT FOR "WORKING THE SIGN") AND A TRADING POST (MOBILE GAS STATION SELLS 50¢ TALL CANS OF MALT LIQUOUR!) **COCONUT GROVE:** THE STATION NAME IS THE LAST LINK TO ANYTHING RESEMBLING "THE GROVE" AS ALL THE FLOPPY, OLD, WOOD HOUSES UNDER HUGE SHADE TREES ARE BULLDOZED TO MAKE WAY FOR THE UGLY, PINK/BLUE PASTEL TOWNHOMES WITH HUGE GATES AROUND THEM. RECOMMENDED ACTIVITY: STEAL CD'S FROM **SPEC'S**. CHASE RICKSHAW DRIVERS. GO TO THE SUNDAY DRUM CIRCLE IN PEACOCK PARK AND GET LECTURED BY A MYSTIC BUM. BUY FAKE DRUGS FROM A CRAFTY OLD STREET GUY. GET RUN OVER BY ROLLERBLADERS, ETC. **VIZCAYA** — THIS STATION HAS A VERY NICE STONE FOUNTAIN IN FRONT OF IT, AND, IF YOU'RE LUCKY YOU MAY ARRIVE AT THE STATION ON THE ONE DAY A YEAR THAT THE CITY HAS MONEY TO RUN WATER IN IT. THIS IS THE NEAREST METRORAIL STATION TO MADONNA'S HOUSE. **BRICKELL** — THIS IS STILL MY FAVORITE STATION. FROM THE PLATFORM, YOU CAN SEE TONS OF HUGE TREES, TALL BUILDINGS, AND THROUGH A CRACK IN THE SKYLINE, BISCAYNE BAY. THIS STOP IS A 5-MINUTE WALK FROM AN EASY-TO-STEAL-FROM **HYDE PARK MARKET** AND EXCELLENT DRINKING SPOTS ON THE RIVER, THE BAY, AND IN SEVERAL PARKS, AS WELL AS KINKO'S AND DOWNTOWN ITSELF, AND THE BREAD DUMPSTER AT BRICKELL EMPORIUM! OH YEAH, THE 2-DOLLARS-FOR-HUGE-PLATE-OF-BEANS-AND-RICE-PLACE IS RIGHT THERE, TOO, ON 8th STREET. **GOVERNMENT CENTER** — EASY AS HELL TO HOP, RIGHT IN DOWNTOWN, NEXT TO THE MAIN LIBRARY, AND YOUR TRANSFER SPOT TO THE REAL FUN OF THE MINI-DOWNTOWN ONLY- RAIL, THE METROMOVER. STEVE AND I USED TO DO FUNYONS SHOWS ON THE MOVER. WITH HIS BATTERY-POWERED GUITAR AMP AND A SNARE DRUM, STUNNING COMMUTERS. ONE TIME, ABOUT 8 OF US WENT AND GOT DRUNK AS HELL ON THE MOVER, JUST RIDING IT

AROUND THE LOOP ALL NIGHT. THE MOVER'S ALL RICKETY, LIKE A SMALL-TOWN ROLLER COASTER AND THERE'S ALL THESE SCARY TURNS WHERE IT LOOKS LIKE YOU'RE GOING TO FALL OFF THE TRACK TO YOUR DEATH, SEVERAL STORIES DOWN, AND, OF COURSE, SINCE ITS IN MIAMI, THERE'S NO REASON TO BELIEVE THAT IT WON'T FALL, YA KNOW? IT WAS PRETTY FUN. **OVERTOWN/ARENA:** SIGHTS: THE SOON-TO-BE-ABANDONED MIAMI ARENA. THE HEAT AND THE PANTHERS ARE MOVING OUT LEAVING ANOTHER SPORTS ARENA PROJECT THAT DID NOTHING BUT HELP FUCK UP AN ALREADY FUCKED UP NEIGHBORHOOD. MY DREAM IS THAT THE DOWNTOWN HOMELESS WILL STORM THE ARENA WITH CROWBARS, AND TAKE IT OVER, BUT THE REAL ARENA FUTURE IS PROBABLY MORE BLEAK. BEST CASE: IT BECOMES "WORLD'S #1 INDOOR FLEA MARKET." WORST CASE: IT IS TURNED INTO A NEW JAIL. RECOMMENDED ACTIVITY: DRINK MALT LIQUOR IN "CRACK ALLEY" AND MARVEL AT THE SHEER HOPELESSNESS OF IT ALL. **CULMER:** QUITE FRANKLY, A ROUGH AREA. SIGHTS: CRACKHOUSES AND THE WOMEN'S DETENTION CENTER. HOPPABILITY: I DOUBT IT. YOU MAY HAVE NOTICED THAT THE JOGGING PATH UNDER THE RAIL ENDED AT BRICKELL AND WAS NOT RESUMED NORTH OF THE RIVER. THIS IS BECAUSE PEOPLE SOUTH OF THE RIVER JOG AND FOLKS UP NORTH OF THE RIVER RUN! **CIVIC CENTER:** THIS MAY LOOK LIKE ANOTHER EXCITING DOWNTOWN AREA, BUT DON'T GET OFF THE RAIL HERE CUZ ITS A TRAP! THERE'S NOTHING HERE EXCEPT THE JAIL, THE COURTHOUSE, AND THE HOSPITAL — THE INTERSECTION OF BUREAUCRACY AND HUMAN MISERY! YIKES! ITS ACTUALLY PRETTY HOPPABLE, EVEN AFTER A NIGHT IN JAIL, BUT, I SAY, ITS BETTER TO SKIP THE CIVIC CENTER EXPERIENCE ALTOGETHER! **SANTA CLARA** — THIS OFTEN OVERLOOKED STATION IS A GREAT STOP IF YOU WANT TO DRINK BEER ON THE LOADING DOCKS OF MIAMI'S PRODUCE DISTRICT, GO TO THE HUGE, WEEKEND FLEA MARKET IN THE PARKING LOT OF BOBBY MADURO STADIUM, OR IF YOU HAPPEN TO BE AN EMPLOYEE OF THE CITY OF MIAMI WASTE PAPER FACILITY. SIGHTS: IN THE TRADITION OF MIAMI'S DOOMED NEW "ATTRACTION", "RIVERWALK" ALONG THE FILTHY RIVER, DOWNTOWN, I SUGGEST "TRACKWALK." GO NORTH FROM THE STATION ON 12TH AVE. TO THE TRACKS AND TURN LEFT FOR 10 BLOCKS OF PURE HUMAN WASTE! HERE'S WHAT YOU GET: COUNTLESS BAGS OF ROTTING SACRIFICED ANIMALS FROM SANTERIA RITUALS, ROTTING FRUIT, SINISTER GRAFFITI, HUMAN FECES IN THE SUN, BROKEN LIGHTERS, PORNO MAGS, AND ZOMBIES ON CRACK! ON A HOT DAY, THE TRUE PAIN OF LIFE IS FELT. ● THE CITY COULD ALSO SAVE MONEY WITH AN ATTRACTION LIKE THIS — INSTEAD OF HAVING A SHUTTLEBUS, THEY COULD JUST HAVE A GUY CHASE YOU BACK TO THE METRORAIL! **ALLAPATTAH:** SIGHTS — CONTINENTAL BLOOD BANK, ONE BLOCK WEST ON 36TH STREET! **EARLINGTON HEIGHTS:** THIS STATION IS A SHORT WALK FROM THE ABANDONED GRAVEYARD WITH WEEDED OVER HEADSTONES, THE EVERPRESENT STENCH OF DEATH, AND LOTS OF SEVERE LOOKING, HALF-ZOMBIE DUDES LURKING BACK THERE IN THE TREES! EVEN IN BROAD DAYLIGHT ITS SCARY AS HELL, AND THEY DIDN'T NEED A FENCE TO KEEP ME OUT! **BROWNSVILLE:** NOT BAD FOR A PLEASANT AFTERNOON TRIP TO THE BIG THRIFT STORE AND A LUNCH OF CISCO AND 25¢ HONEY BUNS, AVAILABLE AT ANY CORNER STORE. PROBABLY, HOWEVER, A BAD PLACE TO STAND AROUND, LATE AT NIGHT, WITH AN OPEN MAP, ASKING RANDOM PASSERSBY HOW TO GET TO THE BEACH. **DR. MARTIN LUTHER KING, JR. PLAZA** — SIGHTS: HEARTBREAKING VIEW OF NEIGHBORHOOD HOUSING PROJECTS FROM PLATFORM SHOWS HOW THE CITY CUTS ALL THE LIMBS OFF THE TREES, LEAVING THESE MUTILATED STUMPS. SUPPOSEDLY, THEY DO THIS SO COPS CAN SEE INTO THE PROJECTS, AND SO "CRIMINALS" (READ: ALL RESIDENTS) HAVE "NOWHERE TO HIDE." **NORTHSIDE** — SERVICES 79TH STREET, THE HOME OF HIP-HOP PIRATE RADIO, INDOOR FLEA MARKETS, AND THE URBAN TRAILER PARK. THERE'S A GREAT POOL IN ONE TRAILER PARK, WEST OF STATION ON 79TH, AND THE BIGGEST BOLT CUTTERS THE LAW ALLOWS ARE ON SALE IN THE FLEA MARKET. CHECK OUT THE ABANDONED INDUSTRIAL PARK THAT DOUBLES AS THE "NORTHSIDE ART GALLERY" — A HUGE 2-STORY BUILDING FULL OF FULL WALL MURALS OF LOCAL GRAFFITI. ITS ALL COOL AND DARK AND PEACEFUL INSIDE, LIKE A MUSEUM, AND THERE'S JUST ROW AFTER ROW OF PIECES! **TRI-RAIL** — UP THE TRACKS IS CSX TRAIN YARD FOR BEER DRINKING, SPRAY PAINTING, AND FREIGHT HOPPING. EAST HIALEAH IS FUN AND ABANDONED ON SUNDAYS, BUT IS ALSO THE "EPICENTER OF STRAY, RABID DOGS", SO BE CAREFUL! **HIALEAH** — THE RAIL BARELY ENTERS THE SEPARATE PLANET OF THE CITY OF HIALEAH, AS IF IT IS AFRAID, OR SOMETHING. FROM THE PLATFORM YOU CAN JUST FEEL THE SANTERIA AT WORK! THIS IS YOUR STOP FOR THE BEAUTIFUL, OLD RACE TRACK. **OKEECHOBEE** — NOT ALL THE WAY TO LAKE OKEECHOBEE, BUT FEELS LIKE IT. THE UNLUCKY HORSESHOE-SHAPED CYCLE OF THE RAIL COMES TO AN END HERE, ON U.S. 27, AMID TRUCKSTOPS AND STRIP CLUBS, OFFERING "THE FREE FRICTION LAP DANCE." THIS IS ALSO A COUPLE BLOCKS FROM THE LANDFILLS AND BODY DUMPING SPOTS OF THE QUAINT TOWN, MEDLEY. IF YOU JUST WANT TO SAY YOU'VE BEEN THERE... SO THE RAIL BASICALLY STARTS AND ENDS... NOWHERE! YOU MIGHT WANT TO PICK UP A 6-PAK HERE. ITS A LONG RIDE BACK TO DADELAND...

TO KILL THE TIME, A YOUNG CIVIL ENGINEER SHOWS MR. KNIPL HIS GRANDIOSE PLANS FOR BRIDGES WHICH WILL NEVER BE BUILT.

"79TH STREET RADIO"

⑨

Fig. 2 — The basement makes a good station location if it is dry.

MY FRIEND, CINQUE, WAS THE ONE WHO FIRST FOUND THE NORTHSIDE BLACK POWER PIRATE RADIO STATION, WAY DOWN ON THE LEFT OF THE FM DIAL. YOU COULD ONLY TUNE IT IN, UP ON THE NORTHSIDE, SO WE'D LISTEN TO IT WHILE WE DROVE DOWN 79TH STREET, WHENEVER I WENT TO HIS HOUSE. YOU COULD TELL IT WAS PIRATE RADIO, BECAUSE OF THE # OF TIMES THE DJ'S WOULD SAY "MOTHERFUCKER" IN EVERY SENTENCE AND BECAUSE OF THE RAD, CRAZY SHIT THEY PLAYED. THEY'D PLAY ALL THIS POORLY RECORDED LOCAL RAP, LIKE THIS ONE SONG, "TOO MANY SUCKAS, NOT ENOUGH STRETCHAS" WHERE THE GUY RAPS, "LIVIN' IN THE 'M', THE 'I', THE 'A,M,I/ SOMETIMES I GOTTA ASK MYSELF 'WHY?'" OR THEY'D PLAY 2PAC, AND THEN, EVERY COUPLE OF BEATS, THE DJ'S WOULD CUT IN OVER IT AND JUST SCREAM, HOWL, OR GO "UH!" AND THE MUSIC WOULD CUT OUT COMPLETELY!

MOST OF THE TIME, THERE'D BE 4, or 5 DJ'S ALL IN THE ROOM WITH THE MIKE, ALL TALKING AND YELLING AND TELLING JOKES OVER THE MUSIC. IT WAS JUST TOTALLY LOUD, CHAOTIC, AND FUN. THEY EVEN TOOK PHONE CALLS, SOMEHOW. THEY'D PLAY A BEAT AND PEOPLE WOULD CALL UP TO RAP OVER IT, OVER THE PHONE! YO! TALK ABOUT D.I.Y.!

ACTUALLY, THEY WERE NEVER REALLY POLITICAL AT ALL. WE CALLED IT THE "BLACK POWER" STATION BECAUSE OF ONE TIME WHEN THEY WERE TAKING CALLS, AND THIS DUDE CALLED UP AND SAID, "SOUTHERN BELL VAN'S BEEN PARKED OUT IN FRONT OF MY HOUSE FOR 3 DAYS... THERE AIN'T NOTHIN' WRONG WITH THE GODDAMN PHONE!! ITS THE WHITE MAN SPYING ON US AND TRYING TO KEEP US DOWN!" LIKE I SAID, IT WAS A GREAT STATION.

BESIDES BEING REALLY GREAT RADIO, "THE STATION", AS WE CALLED IT, WAS EXCITING. WHO WERE THESE GUYS? WHERE DID THEY BROADCAST FROM? AND HOW DID EVERYONE KNOW THEIR # TO CALL IN, WHEN THEY NEVER GAVE IT OUT OVER THE AIR? WHEN THE DJ'S TALKED, I'D LISTEN TO SEE IF THERE WAS EVEN SOME DISCERNABLE CODE THAT THEY USED, BUT COULDN'T CATCH ONE. I NEVER FOUND OUT ANYTHING, REALLY, AND EVENTUALLY I MOVED AWAY FROM MIAMI.

BUT, AFTER ALL MY PLANS FELL APART, ONE BY ONE, LAST YEAR, I FOUND MYSELF BACK IN MIAMI, TRYING TO SORT IT ALL OUT. I ENDED UP LIVING UP ON THE NORTHSIDE, OFF 79TH STREET. GOOD OLE 79TH STREET — HOME TO THE "WELCOME TO MIAMI" WATERTOWER, AND THE I.N.S. BUILDING. SIX LANES OF ROAD, FROM BEACH TO SWAMP, FULL OF RUSTY, OLD AMERICAN CARS BLASTIN' BASS. THE URBAN TRAILER PARK, AND THE INDOOR FLEA MARKET. THE 99¢ QUART OF MALT LIQUOR...

I ALWAYS THOUGHT 79TH STREET, AND NOT THE BEACHES, OR HOTELS, WAS THE TRUE HEART OF MIAMI. YOU LOOK AT EVERYTHING AND THINK "THIS WAS ALL ONCE SOMEBODY'S IDEA OF A GOOD IDEA." IT WAS GOOD TO COME HOME TO. THERE'S ALWAYS ROOM FOR ONE MORE BAD IDEA ON 79TH STREET. BAD CREDIT? NO CREDIT? NO PROBLEM!

RIGHT AWAY, I STARTED TRYING TO TUNE IN THE STATION, BUT I COULDN'T SEEM TO FIND IT. I DIDN'T KNOW IF MY RADIO HAD BAD RECEPTION, OR IF THEY'D JUST GONE OFF THE AIR. I WASN'T EVEN SURE OF THE EXACT FREQUENCY. I BECAME SORT-OF OBSESSED WITH FINDING OUT WHAT HAPPENED TO 'EM, BUT THERE WAS NO WAY TO FIND OUT.

¡ATENCIÓN!

"79th STREET RADIO" cont.

Es prohibido tener Gallos in la Ciudad. Si Ud. es el Dueño del Gallo, sea notificado que está quebrando la Ley. El Department of Animal Control y el Departamento de Policía han sido notificado de este...

MEANWHILE, I KEPT BUSY TAKING LONG BIKE RIDES TO EXPLORE THE NORTHSIDE, AN ALMOST TOUCHING DAILY TOUR OF THE VERY ARCHITECTURE OF DEFEAT. THERE WAS SAD, OLD BOBBY MADURO STADIUM, NAMED FOR A CUBAN BASEBALL STAR WHO NEVER MADE THE MAJORS. ORIGINALLY, IT WAS BUILT IN THE 50'S BY A CUBAN FINANCIER TO LURE MAJOR LEAGUE BASEBALL TO MIAMI. BUT, EVEN THEN, IT WAS BUILT TOO SMALL. THE FINANCIER LOST ALL HIS MONEY, BACKING CASTRO, AND THEN, LATER, BACKING ANTI-CASTRO REVOLUTIONARIES. BY THE 80'S THE STATION WAS A SHELTER AND PROCESSING CENTER FOR NICARAGUAN REFUGEES. NOW, ITS HOST TO A WEEKEND FLEA MARKET IN ITS PARKING LOT.

A LITTLE EAST AND NORTH IS THE SO-CALLED "MIAMI DESIGN DISTRICT", WITH ITS EMPTY, EMBARRASSED STREETS AND 1980'S PASTEL MURALS. THE IDEA, AS OLDTIMERS TELL IT, WAS TO BRING ARTISTS AND CLOTHING DESIGNERS TOGETHER IN A THRIVING, NEARLY HISTORIC, CENTRAL CITY AREA. IT DIDN'T WORK, AND TODAY YOU'D BE LUCKY TO BRING TOGETHER ONE LOST TOURIST AND ONE AGGRESSIVE PANHANDLER DOWN THERE. IF THE "MIAMI DESIGN DISTRICT" WAS A BOOK, IT'D COST 25¢ AT A THRIFT STORE, AND BE ON THE SHELF NEXT TO "THE GREAT STOCK MARKET CRASH OF 1988" AND "EAT TO WIN."

AH, PLANS, PLANS, PLANS. DOOM, DOOM, DOOM. I WASN'T SURE HOW IT WAS GOING TO WORK OUT, BUT MY CURRENT PLAN WAS TO PAY MY VERY CHEAP RENT BY COMMITTING VARIOUS MANAGABLE CRIMES, LIKE STEALING CD'S AND SELLING THEM. SO FAR, SO GOOD. I NOTICED, AND EVEN ENJOYED THE ABSURDITY OF CRIME AS A RENT-PAYING JOB. LIKE, MOST PEOPLE COMMUTE DAILY FROM THE SUBURBS TO THE CITY, ALL DRESSED UP, FOR WORK. I GET CLEANED UP A LITTLE AND HEAD OUT THE OTHER WAY, TO LURK AROUND THE 'BURBS HITTING VARIOUS, SOFT STORES. TO SUPPLEMENT MY INCOME AS A CAREER CRIMINAL, WHEN TIMES GOT ROUGH, I'D SOMETIMES PICK UP A LITTLE CASH, WRITING RECORD REVIEWS FOR THE LOCAL FREE WEEKLY. IT JUST ISN'T EASY BEING A YOUNG, STARVING CRIMINAL.

JUST WHEN I'D PRETTY MUCH FALLEN IN LOVE WITH THE NORTHSIDE, FOR ITS OWN SAKE, AND HAD GIVEN UP THE SEARCH FOR THE STATION, I FOUND WHAT COULD HAVE BEEN A STRANGE CLUE. I WAS RIDING AROUND THIS NAMELESS AREA THAT I'D STARTED CALLING THE "D.C.C." MOST CITIES, I FIGURED, HAD THE "CENTRAL BUSINESS DISTRICT" — THE "C.B.D." BUT MIAMI HAD THE "DEVESTATED CITY CENTER" — THE "D.C.C." ITS ALL UNUSED WAREHOUSES, HUGE FENCED-OFF LOTS OF WEEDS AND RUBBLE, BOARDED-UP PROJECTS, AND TRACKS WITH NO TRAINS. THERE'S EVEN A LITTLE GRAFFITTI AND IT ALWAYS MAKES ME THINK, "IF YOU TAG IN THE MIDDLE OF THE FOREST AND NO ONE'S THERE TO SEE IT..." BUT, THIS TIME, I WAS THERE, AT THE END OF A DEAD END STREET TO SEE WHERE SOMEONE HAD SPRAY PAINTED,

"TAPE RADIO 61.5 W-E-E-D."

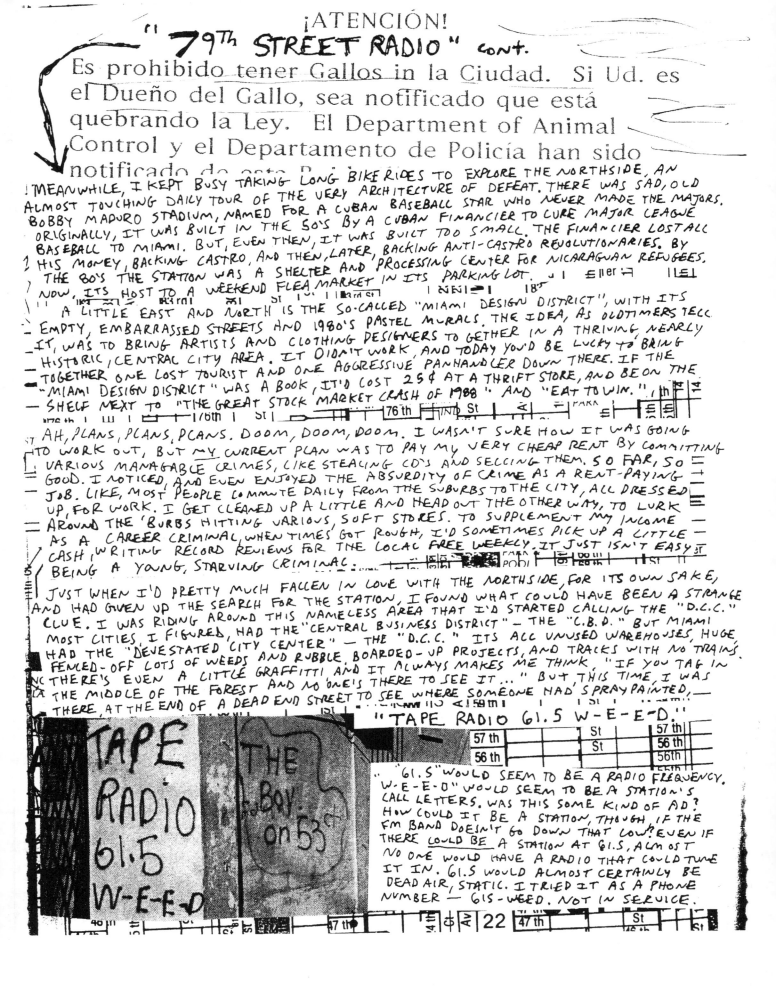

"61.5" WOULD SEEM TO BE A RADIO FREQUENCY. "W-E-E-D" WOULD SEEM TO BE A STATION'S CALL LETTERS. WAS THIS SOME KIND OF AD? HOW COULD IT BE A STATION, THOUGH, IF THE FM BAND DOESN'T GO DOWN THAT LOW? EVEN IF THERE COULD BE A STATION AT 61.5, ALMOST NO ONE WOULD HAVE A RADIO THAT COULD TUNE IT IN. 61.5 WOULD ALMOST CERTAINLY BE DEAD AIR, STATIC. I TRIED IT AS A PHONE NUMBER — 615-WEED. NOT IN SERVICE.

- 194 -

"Code violation is rampant

Mervyn Adirim, a Westchester resident since 1959, says his neighborhood has gone from being spotless to resembling "a Third World country."

these days," Adirim, 64, said. "I have neighbors who have chickens."

I FIGURED THAT SINCE THERE'S REALLY NEVER ANY PEOPLE DOWN IN THE D.C.C., IF 61.5 WAS SOMEHOW A STATION, THEY WERE PROBABLY BROADCASTING FROM A WAREHOUSE ON THAT STREET, AND THAT THE BROADCASTERS, THEMSELVES, HAD PROBABLY PAINTED IT. BUT, LATER THAT SAME DAY, I FOUND THE EXACT SAME SPRAYPAINTED MESSAGE, IN THE SAME WRITING AND BLACK PAINT, 30 BLOCKS NORTH IN LITTLE HAITI.

WELL, I NEVER DID FIND OUT WHAT IT MEANT, BUT THAT NIGHT, IT WAS HOT AS HELL OUTSIDE, SO I WAS JUST LAYING AROUND, FEELING SWEATY AND MISERABLE, WHEN I CHECKED THE RADIO FOR THE FIRST TIME IN WEEKS AND, I COULDN'T BELIEVE IT! THE STATION WAS BACK ON THE AIR! DJ FUNKY-ONE WAS ON, PLAYING MUSIC AND TAKING CALLS. HE'D PLAY A LITTLE INSTRUMENTAL BEAT PART, AND THEN SUDDENLY CUT IN, COMPLETELY OVER THE MUSIC, PUT THE CALLER ON THE AIR AND YELL, "WASSUP?!?"

"I WANT TO SAY TWO TIMES FOR LITTLE HAITI", A GIRL CALLER WOULD SAY. DJ FUNKY-ONE WOULD SAY, "ALLRIGHT, BABY, LITTLE HAITI'S IN THE HOUSE... WASSUP?!?" THE NEXT CALLER WANTED TO SAY ONE TIME FOR THE LARCHMONT CLICK. "ARRIGHT! WASSUP?!?" ONE TIME FOR ARENA TOWERS, ONE TIME FOR THE SIX-EIGHT, ONE TIME FOR EDISON, TWO TIMES FOR THE SEVEN-FOUR BOYZ, AND A SHOUT OUT TO SHADOW MAN. IT WENT ON ALL NIGHT, MUSIC AND CALLS. OUTSIDE MY WINDOW, THE STATION SIGNAL WAS FLYING STRONG OVER THE DARK ROWS OF STREETS AND AVENUES, PAST THE OPEN WINDOWS AND OPEN APARTMENT DOORS AND FRONT PORCHES; THE WHOLE SAD, CITY OUT THERE SWEATING IN THE NIGHT. I DRANK SOME TALL CANS FROM THE 79TH AND BISCAYNE BEER SPECIAL, AND LISTENED, AND IT FELT LIKE EVERY RADIO IN THE NORTHSIDE MUST BE TUNED IN.

I FINALLY, AFTER A WHILE, HEARD THE PHONE NUMBER GIVEN OUT, SO, ONE AFTERNOON, WHEN ONLY MUSIC WAS ON AND THEY WEREN'T TAKING CALLS, I CALLED ANYWAY, I COULDN'T BELIEVE IT WHEN DJ. FUNKY-ONE ACTUALLY ANSWERED. I SAID, "UH, WHAT ARE YOU GUYS CALLED?"

HE SAID, "WE'RE THE SPACE STATION!"

"WHERE DO YOU BROADCAST FROM?"

"CAROL CITY."

"DO YOU, UH, HAVE A LICENSE, OR ANYTHING?"

DJ FUNKY-ONE STARTED LAUGHING. "YEAH, YEAH, WE GOT ALL THAT SHIT!" AND HUNG UP.

CAROL CITY WAS AT THE VERY NORTH END OF THE COUNTY. IT HAD ORIGINALLY BEEN A WHITE, SUBURBAN SUBDIVISION, BUT, EVENTUALLY, ALONG WITH OPA-LOCKA, WAS WHERE CITY PLANNERS TRIED TO GET THE RISING BLACK POPULATION OF THE 60'S TO MOVE TO, WHEN THE CITY NEEDED NEW SLUM LAND AS FAR AWAY FROM DOWNTOWN AS POSSIBLE. THESE DAYS, ITS A SEEDY, MENACING RESIDENTIAL SPRAWL OF LITTLE HOMES AND GANG GRAFFITTI, KNOWN WIDELY AS A PLACE WHERE KIDS FROM WHITE, SUBURBAN SUBDIVISIONS GO TO BUY DRUGS

I RODE UP THERE, BUT FOUND NO MORE GRAFFITTI CLUES TO THE STATION'S WHEREABOUTS. LATER, WITH A CAR RADIO, I FOUND THAT YOU COULDN'T EVEN GET THE STATION THAT WELL, NORTH OF 125TH STREET, ABOUT 60 BLOCKS SOUTH OF CAROL CITY, SO I THINK DJ FUNKY-ONE WAS PROBABLY LYING ABOUT CAROL CITY.

SO, I STARTED KEEPING MY EYES OPEN FOR ANY NEW CLUES ON MY RIDE HOME FROM THE MORE WEALTHY SOUTHERN PARTS OF TOWN, WHERE I WAS "WORKING." IT WAS A LONG RIDE HOME, BUT ALWAYS INTERESTING. WHEN YOU LEFT DOWNTOWN FOR THE NORTHSIDE, IT WAS LIKE CROSSING OVER ONTO THE FLIPSIDE OF THE POSTCARD. YOU RODE OUT OF THE PINK AND BLUE, NEON GLARE OF AIRCONDITIONED MALLS, CHAIN STORES, GATED CONDOS, HOTELS AND SKYSCRAPERS, INTO

A DARK, NARROW MAZE OF FUNKY, OLD, WOOD HOUSES, HAND PAINTED SIGNS, AND CORNER STORES. THE SUBURBS HAVE THE POLICE PROTECTION; THE NORTH SIDE HAS VOODOO. MIAMI BEACH HAS FASHION MODELS FROM EUROPE AND SOUTH AMERICA; 79th STREET HAS A COUPLE 6'5" BLACK DUDES IN WIGS AND MINISKIRTS. WITHOUT MONEY, YOU'VE GOT TO IMPROVISE...

IT MADE ME THINK OF THE BOOK, 1984, AND HOW, IN IT, THERE WAS ABOUT 10% OF THE POPULATION THAT WAS FULLY INDOCTRINATED INTO THE PARTY, WAS CONSTANTLY UNDER SURVEILLANCE BY AND RECEIVING PROPAGANDA FROM THE TELESCREEN, AND HAD THE GOVERNMENT JOBS AND RELATIVE SECURITY. THEN THERE WAS THE REST OF THE PEOPLE, "THE PROLES" LIVING IN VAST, UNPOLICED OUTER REGIONS OF GHETTO, SURVIVING ON THE BLACK MARKET AND LIVING UNDER CONSTANT THREAT OF FALLING ROCKET SHELLS. THE PARTY MEMBERS WEREN'T SUPPOSED TO GO TO THE NEIGHBORHOODS OF THE PROLE'S, BUT WINSTON WOULD ALWAYS SNEAK OUT THERE TO GO BROWSE AT OLD JUNK SHOPS AND MEET HIS GIRL IN THE STREET. WHEN I'D RIDE INTO OVERTOWN, IT ALWAYS FELT LIKE THAT, LIKE I WASN'T ALLOWED TO BE THERE.

ONE OF THE NORTHSIDE'S BIGGEST MIDDLE FINGERS TO THE WHOLE MIAMI SUN AND FUN FANTASY WORLD IS IMPENETRABLE LITTLE HAITI WITH ITS VOODOO AND BACKROOM GAMBLING AND POLITICAL GRAFFITI. I'D SIT AT MY FAVORITE SPOT, IN THE SHADE, BY THE ABANDONED RAILROAD TRACKS AND WATCH HUGE, STRONG, HAITIAN WOMEN WALK BY WITH BASKETS ON THEIR HEADS AND ROOSTERS RUNNING IN THE WEEDS AT THEIR FEET. THE OLD MILE MARKER ON THE TRACKS SAID "362" WHICH WOULD BE THE MILAGE TO JACKSONVILLE, BUT NO TRAIN RUNS ANYMORE, THAT WAY, AND I WONDER HOW MANY MILES IT IS TO PORT-AU-PRINCE. THERE'S FREIGHT CONTAINERS ALL OVER LITTLE HAITI, INCLUDING TWO IN THE CHURCHILL'S PARKING LOT. THEY'RE HARDLY NOTICABLE BUT I'VE SEEN PEOPLE DRIVE UP TO 'EM, AT ALL HOURS OF THE DAY, AND QUICKLY LOAD, LIKE, 10 REFRIDGERATORS INTO THEM! THE FREIGHT GOES BACK TO HAITI, VIA BOATS ON THE MIAMI RIVER. ITS NO SECRET, TOO, THAT ALMOST ALL STOLEN BIKES END UP ON THESE BOATS, TOO! YOU CAN SEE 'EM GOING OFF TO SEA WITH HUNDREDS OF BIKES ON THE ROOFS! NOW, ANYONE WHO KNOWINGLY BUYS A STOLEN BIKE, FOR WHATEVER REASON, IS SCUM IN MY BOOK. STILL, THE THOUGHT OF MY LAST BIKE WITH THE CAVITY AND MISTER T EXPERIENCE STICKERS STARTING ITS NEW LIFE IN HAITI DEFINATELY CAPTURES MY IMAGINATION. GOOD LUCK, OL' RUSTY!

LITTLE HAITI ALSO REPRESENTS ONE IN A LONG SERIES OF MIAMI'S CHEERFUL IRONIES. STARTED OUT AS AN ANTI-SEMITIC, WHITES ONLY PARADISE, MIAMI BEACH WAS SAVED FROM FINANCIAL RUIN... BY VACATIONING NEW YORK JEWISH MILLIONAIRES. MIAMI, ENVISIONED THE SAME WAY, NOW HAS 2 CUBAN MAYORS AND IS MAJORITY HISPANIC. AND THE NEIGHBORHOOD WHERE LITTLE HAITI IS WAS ONCE KEPT WHITES-ONLY BY THREAT OF LYNCHING! IF THEY'D LIVED TO SEE HOW THEIR PLANS TURNED OUT!

WELL, FINALLY ONE DAY I GOT A HUGE CLUE WHEN THE STATION WAS APPARENTLY HAVING AN ON AIR LIVE PROMO PARTY! DJ FUNKY-ONE SAID, "C'MON DOWN! WE GOT ALL THIS GREAT FOOD DOWN HERE AT MAMA'S KITCHEN! WE GOT THE FRIED CHICKEN PLATE FOR 5 BUCKS AND MAMA'S CONCH DINNER FOR 7 BUCKS!" COULD IT BE?!? DJ FUNKY-ONE AND A PIRATE RADIO TRANSMITTER, LIVE IN A RESTAURANT?!!
THE ADDRESS THEY GAVE OUT WAS ONLY A COUPLE BLOCKS AWAY IN THE HEART OF LITTLE HAITI, BUT WHEN I GOT THERE THERE WAS NO RESTAURANT AT ALL — JUST 2 BLACK DUDES ON A COUCH IN FRONT OF THIS TINY HOUSE CUT UP INTO FOUR EFFICIENCIES. I SAID, "UH... ARE YOU GUYS WITH THE RADIO STATION?"
THEY LOOKED AT ME LIKE I WAS CRAZY AND NODDED. I MAY HAVE BEEN CRAZY. BIG DEAL.
"THIS IS MAMA'S KITCHEN?" I COULD SMELL CHICKEN. THEY SAID IT WAS.
I SAID, "BUT WHERE'S DJ FUNKY-ONE? WHERE'S THE STATION?"
THEY BROKE UP LAUGHING AND ONE GUY SAID, "EVERYONE WANT TO KNOW THAT!"

SO, "MAMA'S KITCHEN" WAS REALLY JUST SOME GUY'S MOM'S KITCHEN. I ENDED UP BUYING A FROZEN CUP OF CHERRY KOOL-AID FOR A QUARTER, AND SITTING AT MY FAVORITE SPOT, SUCKING ON IT IN THE SUMMER HEAT AND LAUGHING. NOW THAT I'D MET 2 PEOPLE FROM THE STATION THE WHOLE THING WAS EVEN MORE MYSTERIOUS!
WELL, I GUESS I DON'T MIND NOT KNOWING, AND NOW I'LL PROBABLY NEVER FIND OUT MORE ABOUT THE STATION, BECAUSE IT WAS TIME TO MOVE AWAY FROM THE NORTHSIDE. MY PLAN HADN'T FAILED. IT HAD WORKED TOO WELL. THE STORE THAT I WAS STEALING ALL MY CD'S FROM WAS GOING OUT OF BUSINESS.
BUT I HAD ONE LAST SATURDAY NIGHT WITH THE STATION. ONE LAST NIGHT OF THE STATION SENDING OUT THE MIAMI-STYLE BASS TO BE PACKAGED AND DELIVERED TO THE SUBURBS VIA 79th STREET IN A GREAT RUSTING 1971 OLDSMOBILE. ONE LAST RIDE THROUGH THE RUINS AND FAILING STREETS AND THE BAD IDEAS THAT TALKED TO YOU LATE AT NIGHT. LIKE RADIO.

JOHN SAYS: FAKE KIDNAPPINGS REALLY WORK!!!

A column by JOHN DANIA w/ guest appearance by THE DALAI LAMA →

PICTURED: DALAI LAMA (CENTER) WITH WELL WISHERS, INCLUDING RX-CHICKENHEAD BASS HOLDER, DANIA, RIGHT OF D.L.

I Went to a Barbecue with the Dalai Lama's Ninja Bodyguard

This summer, Students for a Free Tibet got passes to Lollapalooza. Passing up the heavy temptation to scalp the tickets, I started planning our attack. It was pretty funny trying to get people together - I'd call up these people from Columbia and NYU and go "hey, I got free tickets to Lollapallooza! Wanna go?" College students are easy prey... No one really believed we would go through with it, so they all quickly agreed to help out with my plan for guerilla theater. It wasn't 'til about the day before the concert when they started getting nervous: "uh, what do mean I have to dress like a Tibetan nun?"

The bands sucked, the crowd was bored. Lollapallooza was ripe for takeover. We had a couple people dress up as "peaceful Tibetan demonstrators", who marched up to the bleachers and began shouting slogans, waving a Tibetan flag, and holding a "China out of Tibet" sign. As you can imagine, this was a bit out of place at Lollapallooza, and people wondered what was going on. Enter the Chinese Occupation Force, who charge the demonstrators, knocking them down and kicking and clubbing them senseless. This really got everyone's attention - now hundreds of people are squinting down at us wondering "who are those guys, and why are they beating up those other guys?" Next (this was the hard part) we went up into the stands and actually talked to people and passed out flyers. Some people quickly snapped back into drone-mode and were impossible to reach, but lots of them were still curious enough to want to talk to us. Some of the response was pretty depressing, like the pack of skin heads who wanted to know if we needed any help beating them up, but mostly it went pretty well.

This was a HUGE improvement over the year before, when we just sat at a booth and wondered why no one would talk to us except for an occasional confused drunk. (Several people came up and pointed to our banner and said "Uh, like, how do I get a 'free tibbet'?) Guerrilla theater works! Short of grabbing people by the throat and yelling at them, it's the shurest way to get people to pay attention to you. When my friend Christy's squat was facing eviction in Amsterdam, they built a raft and staged this whole series of dramas up and down the canals, covering all of downtown. They tore down the building anyway, but at least they went out with style.

A few of us went down to Florida a while ago, to mess with a place called Splendid China. It's a theme park, in the shadow of Disney World, completely owned by the Chinese government. I'm not making this up! When it opened, the Miami Herald wrote a piece calling it the "torturer's theme park". You should check it out (after hours) some time - it's got to be one of the weirdest exhibits of propaganda anywhere. They've got a miniature Great Wall, replicas of palaces they destroyed, and little prostrating figurines all over the place. It's a trip.

Anyway, we blocked the entrance by locking ourselves together with this hardcore Greenpeace-inspired gear, and shut the place down for most of the day. A busload of Taiwanese showed up to help us out, burning flags and chanting slogans (you know, like "off the pigs" and stuff). It was pretty funny - one person (I'll call her Sarah, cuz that's who it was) acted as the police liaison, so all communication with the cops went through her. The Captain in charge of the arrest - standing right next to us - would be like "Sarah, could you please inform the demonstrators that if they do not cooperate when we attempt to put them in the van that they will be charged with resisting arrest?"

We weren't really all that slick though, and we couldn't quite get the hang of our Greenpeace gear. Once the cops figured out that we weren't chained together as permanently as we said we were, they just pulled us apart. "Hey, man, that hurts!" I said. "It's gonna hurt - it's called a pain pry", replied the cop, smiling for the first time. Oh. Still, they had to call the fire department with the Jaws of Life or whatever in case they needed to cut the stuff off of us, and the chaos lasted for several hours. We watched station wagons full of little kids with their faces pressed to the glass start to drive in, and then turn around in a near panic when they saw the scene we created. Hi kids! Free Tibet - torture isn't splendid!

A few months ago, eight Tibetans went on a hunger strike in front of the United Nations - pledging to go until death if necessary. You would laugh if you heard how little they were willing to die for, but it's still much more than the UN offered. If it wasn't for the intervention of the Dalai Lama to end the strike on the 13th day, I have little doubt that there would've been dozens of deaths by now. There was a whole list of Tibetans who were ready to take the place of anyone who died, to make sure the hunger strike could continue.

As you can imagine, working with people who are that committed to freedom is pretty humbling. I feel sort of uncomfortable talking about what I've done, or tried to do, to help them out. One time this monk came to the US. He had just escaped from Tibet, having spent around 27 years in prison. They had tortured him pretty badly, but his mind was in good shape. Anyway, when someone introduced me to him, he got really emotional - he kept thanking me over and over for my help. He wouldn't let go of my hand. The whole thing freaked me out pretty bad - what do you say to somebody whose whole life was nothing but sacrifice, standing there and thanking YOU for helping out?

Since China invaded Tibet in 1949, over a million Tibetans have died at the hands of one of the most brutally oppressive regimes in the history of mankind. People are being tortured to death in secret cells for no greater crime than daring to speak out in public. There's a lot more to say, but if you're interested you can find out for yourself easily enough. Reading is FUNdamental.

I'm 27 now, and like most of you I've seen a lot of shit go down in this country - enough to make me want to punch someone in the face when they start talking about how this is a free country, or spouting some fucking bullshit about their "rights" or the constitution. I've been beaten up by cops, I've seen women clubbed senseless for exercising their "right" to peaceful protest, and I've gotten frantic calls in the middle of the night from friends in jail.

Et fucking cetera. You can get all the evidence you could ever want that the land of the free ISN'T just from the front page and the 6:00 news. No shit, right? So there are plenty of reasons to be pissed off in this country, and there's a lot to fight for. All of this is what makes it difficult for some people to understand why I have dedicated so much of my time to helping Tibet. Some people think the situation in Tibet is hopeless, some say Tibet will be free within two or three years. All I know is, if no one fights back, it's over - whether it's in Tibet, Burma, or Florida.

Turkey Hammock

60

FLORIDA AND SMUGGLERS
"♫ THEY MOVE IT THROUGH MIAMI, THEY SELL IT IN L.A.! ♫"

Florida's always been the kind of place where anyone with a boat, or a plane, can find someone to meet them in a mall parking lot with a suitcase full of cash! With 8,400 miles of coastline, countless acres of unpopulated swamp and farmland to land planes on, and a convenient proximity to fully corrupt, 3rd world island nations, Florida's always been a smuggler's paradise. And, since the rumrunners of Prohibition, smuggling has been a part of South Florida life. Sometimes, in subtle ways, like the occasional story in the Herald about a bale of pot -- the so-called "square grouper" -- washing up on the beach, or stories you hear about people buying brand, new Mercedes with paper bags full of $100 bills. Then, there's less subtle ways, like the time in 1981 when a bail of pot dropped out of a plane that was being tailed by the Feds, AND crashed through the roof of this senior citizen's trailer, west of Ft. Lauderdale! Said the old codger, "Its just one of the hazards of living here."

Big Bill McCoy, probably the most famous rumrunner of all time, was just a poor cracker, building boats in Florida, 'til he said, "Fuck that weak shit!" and split for the big cash, up north, where he established "Rum Row" off the coast of New York. He sat out in International Water, with a boat full of brew. and anyone who wanted could come out and buy it off him. He was known for having the best quality stuff, which is where the phrase "The Real McCoy" came from!

Here in town, Miami managed to survive the lean real estate bust years, after the Hurricane of '26, and the years of the Depression, by providing a steady flow of liquour to tourists, from the dryer North, at fancy, Miami Beach hotels. The violation of Prohibition was well known and out in the open. When the coast guard shot it out with smugglers at the mouth of the Miami River, in full view of tourists dining at a fancy hotel, the public and the Miami Herald were outraged... at the Coast Guard!

Cuba was where the good rum came from, and was a fairly safe haven for smugglers. But, under cruel dictator, Gerardo Machado, who was known as "El Gallo' (The cock), because of his policy of torturing student activists with castration, smugglers who tried to make money on the return trip, by bringing guns to revolutionaries in Cuba, were shot on the spot, if caught.

By the 1970's, smuggling was back, and very much in the open, as Florida was a major entry point for pot coming into the U.S. Even as an elementary school kid, I knew what the guy who lived across the street from me, who had the wild, all-night parties, meant when he said he was working in "Imports and Exports". In a December, 1981 issue of Miami magazine, a Ft. Myers sailor is quoted as saying, "Anywhere you sail in the Bahamas, you're going to see little strobe lights flashing in the water at night, and then high-powered boats going out to make the pick-ups. The lights are attached to bales of drugs." Tourism was down, and the local economy was in decline, but, mysteriously, new high rises and developments were going up all over town, often as a way to launder drug money. Its not clear just how much of Miami's skyline was built with drug cash, but a Miami real estate economist testified in Senate subcommitte

FROM "TRAFFICKING: INSIDE THE AIR AMERICA RING" BY BERKELEY RICE

Finding suitable planes was never a problem for drug smugglers. There were thousands of planes sitting around Florida's airports that one could buy, lease, borrow, or steal for a quick run to Colombia. ''Back in the early eighties,'' one airport manager told me, ''most of the dopers used cheap throwaway planes. You could find them anywhere, and get them fixed up enough to make a run or two.''

hearings in 1981, that between 100 and 150 million dollars in Miami were "directly attributed to the affluence generated by the narcotics traffic."

In the early days of pot smuggling, the smugglers had a good image as good, old boys with boats, or planes, who were just out having fun, and trying to make a good living, by beating the cops and bringing in something that everyone wanted anyways. On the Labor Day, 1977, Jerry Lewis Muscular Dystrophy Telthon, even, two mysterious, bearded guys appeared, on live TV, donating $10,000 in cash "for the kids, from the Blockade Runners."! Later, when the risk of smuggling increased, with greater coast guard presence, many smugglers switched to the more valuable Cocaine. Much more money could be made with the same size shipment of cocaine. This led to the gun battles in mall parking lots, and other drug violence that Miamians have come to know so well. What's with the mall parking lot thing anyway? I wonder if they all started meeting in mall parking lots, before, or AFTER, MIAMI VICE ?

Drug planes landed everywhere. Smugglers would pay farmers, upstate, to let them land on their farm, and pay a local sheriff $50,000 to just stand there and make sure nothing went wrong. Before the stretch of I-95, between Ft. Pierce and Cocoa was completed, planes would use the paved part as a night time runway.

Boats could make it in, anywhere, too. One Ft. Lauderdale operation bought up expensive houses on Ft. Lauderdale's canals, and would bring boats right up to the back door! Then, they'd hire elderly couples in winnebagos to drive the stuff north, out of Florida, and they'd hire Krishnas to watch the stuff, because they knew the Krishnas wouldn't take anY!

With all this cash around, the Miami Police decided they wanted a cut, too. In the early '80's, the force was ordered to comply with new affirmative action laws, and to have all officers live within the city limits of Miami. Since the cops were overwhelmingly white, and lived in the 'burbs, there was a frantic svcramble to find new cops, and almost anyone was hired, whether they passed all the tests, or not. For a couple years, the city was plagued by these new cops, who would take bribes, steal evidence, and even do stuff like pick up prostitutes and use their badge to get a free hotel room! Then, the "Miami River Cops", came along. They would work together to stake out and catch drug dealers, so that they could seize the drug shipments and sell them themselves! Yo! They got caught, and got their name on the same night, when they raided a freighter on the Miami River to get all the cocaine, and a couple of the dealers drowned after trying to jump off and swim away.

It wasn't always just drugs and rum, ya know. Sometimes they smuggled REAL LIVE PEOPLE! Chinamen paid smugglers to take them into the U.S. from Cuba in Prohibition days, and Cubans paid during the Mariel Boatlift. Just last year the Herald ran a story about a Haitian freighter coming into the Miami River. As it docked, 20 or 30 dudes jumped ship, swam to land, and started running like hell, through downtown, in all different directions! Many of them hailed cabs and got away, but most were caught--- with a twenty dollar bill and a piece of paper with a Little Haiti address!

But, what about the case of Everglades City? In 1983, federal agaents blockaded the two roads into the tiny town on the west coast of Florida, and raide it, arresting 193 of the town's 600 residents for drug trafficking charges! The papers across the country called it the "Town gone bad", but everyone in town said they were just trying to find a new living with their knowledge of boats and the Florida coast, after the government announced a ban on commercial fishing in the Everglades. Fishing, and the already-banned alligator poaching were the town's livlyhood. The just-trying-to-make-a-living argument is the same one that one-armed smuggler, Harry Morgan, made, as the main character of Hemingway's Key West smuggling novel, TO HAVE AND HAVE NOT.

The good, old boy smugglers have given way to Cartel-controlled, multi-national operations. Corporate smuggling still sucks! But, Florida's frontier-style attitude and contempt for Federal law proudly remain. As one of the agents who raided Everglades City said, "They ask why I'm down there bothering them. They act like the laws don't even apply to them --- like they don't even belong to the United States!" Or as one of the captured smugglers put it, better I think: "One thing I won't do is bait hooks for some Yankee fisherman!"

The transfer of the cocaine to the Colombians followed a similarly antiseptic routine designed to avoid unnecessary contact. According to Cooper, "The Colombians would drive up from Miami the day before and check into the Holiday Inn out on Route 27. They'd leave their cars in the parking lot with a spare set of keys for each one. The ground crew would pick up the cars that evening and drive out to a place near the field. After the coke arrived they would load the duffel bags into the cars' trunks and drive them back to the motel. Then they'd call the Colombians from a nearby restaurant to say the shipment had arrived. The following morning the Colombians would get in their cars and take off with the coke. The two groups never met."

UNITED STATES OF AMERICA

Type/Caté- · Code of issuing / code du pays · PASSPORT NO /NO. DU PASSEPORT
gorie · State · USA émetteur
P · 044545880
Surname / Nom

"SPRECHENZE SCAM?"
OR... HOW I GOT A FREE TRIP TO EUROPE!!!

IT ALL STARTED WITH A BROKEN COPY MACHINE IN A MEMPHIS KINKO'S. I WAS OUT HOPPING TRAINS AROUND THE COUNTRY AND SELLING THE LAST ISSUE OF THE SCAM. I WAS SORT-OF LOW ON FUNDS, BUT THEN THIS GUY OUTSIDE OF THE SHOW TRADED ME A $100 KINKO COPY CARD FOR ONE ZINE! WHAT A GUY! I WAS SO STOKED, CUZ I COULD COPY 15 OF THE HUGE ZINES FOR $100.

BUT, AT KINKO'S, THINGS TURNED OUT EVEN BETTER. THE MACHINE IN THE FAR CORNER OF THE STORE, NEARLY OUT OF SIGHT OF THE EMPLOYEES AT THE COUNTER, WAS BROKEN SO THAT IT WORKED WITHOUT THE CARD AND COST NOTHING!

I SHOWED THE COUNTER GUY MY 100 BUCK CARD AND ASKED HOW MANY 2-SIDED, 8½ by 11 COPIES I COULD MAKE ON IT, SO THAT HE'D KNOW THAT I HAD IT AND WOULDN'T GET ALARMED WHEN I MADE A TON OF COPIES. THEN, I RAN OFF MY 15 ZINES ON THE BROKEN MACHINE. IF ANYONE QUESTIONED ME ABOUT IT, I COULD JUST TURN OVER THE CARD, AND I'D STILL BE AHEAD.

BUT, NO ONE QUESTIONED ME. I WENT BACK, 3 DAYS IN A ROW, ON SEVERAL DIFFERENT SHIFTS, MAKING HUGE PILES OF ZINES! I WOULD PUT THEM IN BOXES AND USE THE FEDEX SCAM TO SEND THEM AHEAD TO FRIENDS IN TOWNS I PLANNED TO STOP IN. FINALLY, THE STORE WORKERS STARTED LOOKING AT ME FUNNY, SO I SENT OUT ONE LAST BATCH, AND CAUGHT THE AFTERNOON FREIGHT TO ARKANSAS. WITHIN A WEEK, I WAS ON A TRAIN TO PORTLAND, FROM FARGO, AFTER FLOODING THE MIDWEST WITH SCAMS AND MAKING TONS OF CASH.

MY CASH KEPT ME 'TIL I MADE IT BACK AROUND THE COUNTRY AGAIN TO BOSTON, WHERE I RAN OUT OF MONEY ON THE SAME DAY THAT THE FIRST SNOW OF THE YEAR FELL. WHOOPS! THIS WAS NO PLACE FOR A FLORIDA BOY IN SHORTS. EVEN WORSE, THOUGH — I WAS ALREADY SICK AS HELL AND IT WAS THANKSGIVING SO THE FREIGHT YARDS WERE DEAD! HELP!

THE NEXT DAY, I FOUND AN ANCIENT COPY CARD IN MY BAG THAT HAD 35 BUCKS ON IT. THAT WOULD ONLY MAKE LIKE 4½ ZINES, BUT I HAD AN IDEA. I WENT TO KINKO'S AND, SOMEHOW, CONVINCED SOME SNOTTY, "HOT-LESS" BOSTON BASTARD IN A SWEATER THAT MY FOLKS HAD BOUGHT IT FOR ME, THAT I COULDN'T USE IT, AND THAT I HAD TO HAVE CASH BACK. HE FINALLY GAVE IT TO ME! TALK ABOUT THANKSGIVING! I'VE NEVER, BEFORE, OR SINCE, BEEN ABLE TO EVEN GET TWO BUCKS BACK FROM A CARD!

THE CASH WAS EXACTLY ENOUGH TO CATCH A GREYHOUND DOWN TO D.C., WHERE, HOPEFULLY, IT'D BE WARMER. WHEN I BOARDED MY 2nd BUS, FROM NEW YORK CITY TO D.C., I CHECKED MY BAG AND THE LUGGAGE GUY ACCIDENTLY HANDED ME TWO CLAIM STUBS FOR MY ONE BAG. I COULDN'T BELIEVE IT! SOMETIMES THEY MAKE IT SO EASY ON YOU! IT WAS A GREAT RIDE.

IN D.C., OF COURSE, MY 2nd BAG, THE ONE THAT NEVER EXISTED, COULD NOT BE FOUND. I WENT TO THE COUNTER AND REPORTED IT LOST, AND WITHIN A COUPLE MONTHS, AFTER A LITTLE PAPERWORK AND A COUPLE PHONE CALLS, GREYHOUND SENT ME $250 FOR MY MISSING BAG! IT MADE ME SORT OF KICK MYSELF FOR NOT RIDING THOSE THINGS BEFORE!

I HOPPED SOME FAST TRAINS AND HITCHED SOME RIDES AND MADE IT DOWN TO FLORIDA TO PICK UP SOME ZINES THAT CHULK LOOSE HAD COPIED FOR ME AT HIS WORK, AND THEN SPLIT TOWN THE NEXT DAY WITH F.Y.P. AND THE CRUMBS. I RODE WITH THEM TO BERKELEY. BY THEN, I HAD ENOUGH CASH TO RENT THE CLOSET AT LEFTY AND MR. STARCHY'S PLACE.

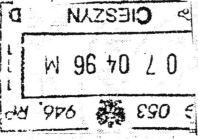

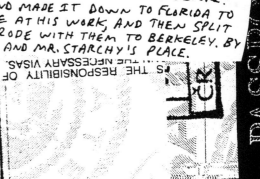

I TOOK LONG WALKS IN THE HILLS. I DRANK STRONG COFFEE. I WAITED. BUT, THE GREYHOUND CHECK STILL, AT THAT TIME HADN'T COME. SO, I WENT OVER TO SAN FRANCISCO AND GOT A WELFARE CHECK. ALL THIS TIME, IT'D BEEN RAINING LIKE HELL IN THE BAY AREA. IT HAD RAINED FOR FIVE WEEKS. RIVERS WERE FLOODED ALL OVER THE STATE. I WANTED TO SEE THE SUN, AND GO SWIMMING, SO INSTEAD OF PAYING MORE RENT, I GOT A CHEAP AIRPLANE TICKET TO FT. LAUDERDALE WITH THE WELFARE CASH.

AT THE FT. LAUDERDALE AIRPORT, SCAM RAILROAD EDITOR, CHANDLER, MET MY PLANE AND "STOLE" MY LUGGAGE FOR ME. I REPORTED IT "LOST", AND DID THE WHOLE, ONE MAN, GOOD COP/BAD COP ACT WITH THE AGENT AT THE LOST AND FOUND DESK: "WHERE THE HELL IS MY LUGGAGE, DAMN IT?!? I JUST GOT OFF A CROSS COUNTRY FLIGHT! I'M SORRY, I MEAN, I KNOW ITS NOT YOUR FAULT, BUT..." THEY ASSURED ME THAT NIGHT, ON THE PHONE, THAT THE LUGGAGE WOULD ARRIVE ON THE NEXT FLIGHT FROM SAN FRANCISCO, AND I THOUGHT, YEAH RIGHT, I'M SITTING HERE LOOKING AT IT.

AFTER ALL THE PAPERWORK, I GOT $1250 IN A CHECK, AND, TO MY SURPRISE, A $400 COUPON TOWARDS MY NEXT FLIGHT! AFTER PAYING OFF CHANDLER, I STILL HAD PLENTY OF BEER MONEY.

AFTER A COUPLE MONTHS, THOUGH, ALL THAT SUN AND FUN GOT TO ME. I FIGURED I COULD HOP TRAINS TO GO ANYWHERE IN THE U.S., SO I SHOULD USE THE COUPON TO GO OVERSEAS. I SHOPPED AROUND AND FOUND IT WAS THE LAST DAY OF A SPECIAL ON FLIGHTS TO FRANKFURT, GERMANY. SO I RODE TO THE AIRPORT ON MY BIKE AND USED THE COUPON. THE TICKET CAME OUT TO $406.

SO, OK, I LIED. THE TRIP TO EUROPE COST 6 BUCKS.

THE ABANDONED MALLS OF BROWARD COUNTY

FAILED SUBURBS ARE MORE FUN THAN FAILED INNER CITIES. ANYONE WHO HAS EVER RIDDEN THE BUS IN BROWARD COUNTY KNOWS THAT ALL THE ROUTES ARE DESIGNED SO THAT THE BUS STOPS FOR TEN WHOLE MINUTES AT ANY ONE OF THE VARIOUS RUINED, ANCIENT, NEARLY UNINHABITED MALLS AROUND BROWARD. THE POMPANO FASHION SQUARE... CORAL SKY... THERE'S PROBABLY ONE IN MARGATE, TOO, WHEREVER THE HELL THAT IS... THE BUS DRIVER USUALLY PARKS, TAKES A SMOKE BREAK, AND GETS ALL WISTFUL, TUGGING AT HIS MUSTACHE WHILE STARING AT THE EMPTY PARKING LOT. NO ONE GETS ON, OR OFF THE BUS. FINALLY, YOU LEAVE.

WHENEVER I'M BACK HOME IN THE 'BURBS, RIDING BROWARD BUSSES, I THINK OF HOW WRECKED EVERYONE'S PARENTS WERE WHEN WE ALL BECAME TEENAGERS AND STARTED DOING DRUGS AND SKIPPING SCHOOL. WE WERE TURNING THE WHOLE PERFECT SUBURBAN PLAN TO SHIT BEFORE THEIR EYES. NOW, TEN YEARS LATER, I SEE EVEN THE LITTLE BROTHERS AND SISTERS OF MY OLD FRIENDS HAVE GONE THE SAME ROUTE. AND THERE'S THE PARENTS STILL STUCK IN THEIR NEAT, LITTLE ROWS OF HOUSES, WITH PERFECT LAWNS, AND 320 DAYS OF SUN A YEAR, OR WHATEVER. I FEEL BAD FOR THEM, BUT STILL CAN'T HELP BUT THINK, "WELL, WHAT DID YOU EXPECT, ANYWAYS?"

SO, WHEN I'M OUT SPENDING MY TIME, NOT GOING TO COLLEGE, NOT BECOMING A DOCTOR OR A LAWYER, NOT GETTING MARRIED, I LIKE TO MAKE AN OCCASIONAL PILGRIMAGE TO THE SPIRITUAL HEART OF SOUTH FLORIDA — THE ABANDONED MALL, AND THE WINDSWEPT PARKING LOT. THE OLD HOLLYWOOD FASHION SQUARE IS COMPLETELY BOARDED UP THESE DAYS, BUT THE BUS STILL STOPS THERE. THE FIRST TIME I WENT THERE, I FOUND LOTS OF GANG GRAFFITTI AND EMPTY BEER BOTTLES ON THE ROOF, WHERE THE PARKING USED TO BE. THROUGH A CRASHED IN SKYLIGHT I COULD SEE AN INDOOR FOUNTAIN FULL OF TRASH AND A RED PENTAGRAM SPRAY PAINTED ON THE FLOOR! YO, OZZY! I MANAGED TO PEEL BACK SOME BARBWIRE AND A BOARD AND BREAK INTO THE FORMER JORDAN MARSH DEPARTMENT STORE, BUT INSIDE, IT WAS PITCH BLACK, AND I DIDN'T HAVE A FLASHLIGHT, SO I LEFT.

I WENT BACK AND DRANK BEER ONE TIME WITH QUANNAH AND SOME KIDS FROM CHATTANOOGA. ITS A GREAT DRINKING SPOT OR SKATING SPOT. I'D LOVE TO HAVE A SHOW THERE. I GUESS IT WASN'T MUCH OF A PLACE FOR A PERFECT CITY, BUT, REALLY, LIKE I SAID, "WHAT DID YOU EXPECT?"

DRAMA! INTRIGUE! BUTTCRACKS! BRIBERY! (BUT, NO PUKE...) ITS THE STORY OF...
CALLE PUNK-O !!!

In honor of Little Havana's yearly street festival, CALLE OCHO (on 8th street), CALLE PUNK-O (literally "Punk Street") was born. 100 punks, 5 bands, countless boxes of cold beer, and one generator were brought together in East Little Havana's Jose Marti Park, under the huge I-95 overpass, on the banks of the deadly Miami River, for a truly Miami-style punk show. And, unlike all the other punk picnics out in the Everglades, this time we had permission to be there! Norberto Rivas, the elusive and mysterious Park Director had told me, weeks before the show that we didn't even need a permit, if we weren't charging admission and didn't expect more than 500 people. So, to pay the out-of-town bands, the punks' deep cover team at Kinko's, John and Faith, made tons of CALLE PUNK-O stickers, and a bunch of shirts featuring Jose Marti, "The Father of Cuban Independence", with a green mohawk, and we sold 'em all.! For me, having set up the show, the most fun part, of course, was getting a hundred people to say the words "CALLE PUNK-O" with a straight face.

As it turned out, it was Jose Marti's birthday! So, as the punks filled one side of the park, scores of Cuban demonstrators rallied around the Marti statue on the other side of the park! Now, the main challenge would be making sure they didn't see the shirts and kill us! the

As tugboats pulled huge ships, bound for South America, down the river, and downtown's skyscrapers loomed just across the river, Daiton, GA's, THE SPADES kicked off the after-noon's drunken Rock. Singer/bassist, Forest sang the hell out of a handful of 3-chord, Misfits style rockers, and drummer, Matt, kept his smoke lit in his mouth through the whole set! HEY SHMECKY, the band formerly known as Los Canadians, tore through the next 10 or 15 minutes in true Canadian style. Next up was Dalton's legendary THE SHAFFERS. But, then, the generator mysteriously quit working, and the crowd was treated, instead, to the now-familiar punk picnic sight of Chuck Loose's Buttcrack, as he bent over his often faulty generator, trying to get it working.

This seemed like a good time to bring out Ralph, The Puking Guy. Ralph had earned himself actual billing on the flyer by promising that he would be able to PUKE ON STAGE for money to pay the bands! Before the show, he had told me, excitedly, that he had been gearing up to the puke all morning with a breakfast of doughnuts, pie, chocolate bars, and 3 entire coladas of Cuban coffee! Yuck! With the stench rising off the river, he was a walking time bomb of puke! Ralph walked through the crowd with a cup, securing cash donations, while from the "stage", I yelled at everyone not to

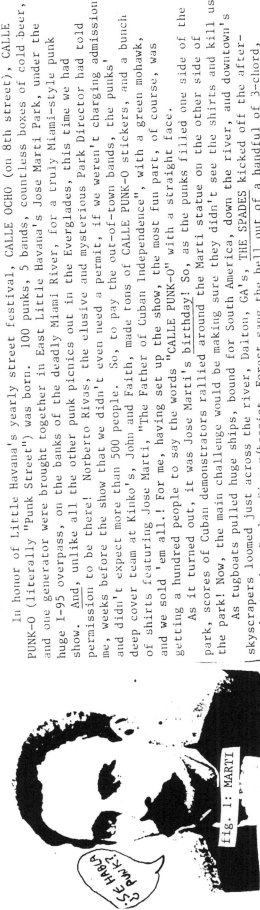

¿SE HABLA PUNK?

fig. 1: MARTI

CONTINUED ON NEXT PAGE, FUCKER...

WHO NEEDS THE FUCKIN' TRI-RAIL?!?

THE TRI-RAIL KEEPS RAISING THEIR FARES, AND, AS ME AND BRAIN FOUND OUT, YOU CAN'T EVEN DRINK BEER ON IT! NOT EVEN A LITTLE. WHAT'S UP WITH THAT SHIT?!? BUT, IF YOU'RE GOING NORTH FROM MIAMI TO FT. LAUDERDALE YOU CAN RIDE A FREIGHT TRAIN! THE MIGHTY NORTHBOUND TRAIN LEAVES THE CSX YARD IN HIALEAH AROUND MIDNIGHT, OR A LITTLE LATER, AND IT ALWAYS STOPS AT STATE ROAD 84 IN FT. LAUDERDALE! THIS IS YOUR FREE RIDE, PUNKS! YOU CAN TAKE BEER, AND, YOUR BIKE. (CATCH OUT UNDER THE 103rd STREET BRIDGE!

← 103rd street →

S ← → N

Fig. 1: Metro Rail

leave, because soon we would be treated, one and all, to a real, live, gross puking man!

People gathered around Ralph. Tension mounted. Could he really do it ?!? Like, without using his fingers ?!?

Well, to make a long, painful story short, Ralph just didn't have it that day. He couldn't do it. I felt real bad for him; I mean, here was a truly tortured artist at work. But what consolation could you really offer the guy ? "I'm sure you'll puke again, someday"? This was getting too absurd! The show was falling apart. The generator wasn't fixed. Chuck Loose's buttcrack mocked a drunk and impatient crowd.

We looked for an outdoor outlet at the park, but couldn't find any. Then, we were approached by a mysterious, old, white-haired, Cuban guy, who spoke little English, but merely took our extension cord, walked into the park office, and plugged us in! We were saved! The SHAFFERS started playing again, and the crowd danced like hell. Dust rose, and beer spilled, and spit flew. The show was going great, but when THE CRUMBS were about to play, a young guy in a park department shirt came running up, frantically, saying we had to stop! He said the old, white-haired guy didn't actually work for the park, and that he just hung out there! We didn't have a permit, so we could use the park, but not the power...

Thinking quick, Tom from Ft. Lauderdale, who had somehow managed to attend the show, while being on house arrest, stepped forward and peeled a crisp, new 20 dollar bill out of his wallet. "Are you sure we can't just use it a little ?" he asked.

The park kid smiled and took the 20! "Like, I said, you can only use the power for two more hours, 'til I get off..." he corrected himself. He was a corrupt, park department worker! Of course, as a MIami citizen, I am shocked and outraged at this corruption at all levels of city government, but, the show must go on!

THE CRUMBS played, and then, before AGAINST ALL AUTHORITY could play, the cops showed up. Technically, we were all legal, but would the actual law stop the man from trying to bust our music? The cops talked to the park kid, and... he stayed bought! He told them we were fully allowed to be there, with permission from Rivas, and the cops split in 5 minutes! Yo! A.A.A, of course, wrote an anti-cop song about it right there on the spot. Just kidding.

With the corrupt park guy, the weird, but kindly, old Cuban dude, the cops, and Jose Marti out of the way, there was only one last miami-style problem we could encounter (barring Voodoo or Santeria attack): surly, gang members from the neighborhood. A bunch of young gang kids were watching the show. They were there with Ivy's sisters, who were in the gang, too. One of the kids got moshed too hard during AAA's set, and he took it personally, so he started throwing rocks at the band and crowd. It almost got really tense but at this crucial moment, Ivy's sister rushed to the stage, grabbed the mike, and, apparently making fun of the punk rock style, she screamed,

"¡TE AMO! ¡Y SI NO ME AMAS, MATO A SU PERRO!"

which loosely translates as " I love you. If you don't love me, I'll kill your dog!" And the gang kids started laughing at us instead. The rest of the show went fine, everyone got drunk as hell in downtown, and CALLE PUNK-O would go down in Miami history as a true punk victory over the man!

HYDE PARK MARKET (32nd Ave + US 1): BECAME THE FIRST LOCAL GROCERY STORE WITH CARPET AND A SUSHI BAR, AND SPENT ALOT OF CASH ON NEW CAMERAS, BUT ITS STILL JUST AS EASY TO RIPOFF AS IT ALWAYS WAS, AS SOME AISLES DON'T HAVE CAMERAS! D.H. TARGET: WHEN YOU DEVELOP FILM AT TARGET, THEY PUT IT OUT IN A BIN WHEN ITS DONE, SO YOU CAN GO GET IT AND RIP IT OFF WITHOUT HAVING TO EVER LET AN EMPLOYEE SEE YOU! WINN-DIXIE SUPERMARKET (32 + Coral Way): THIS IS THE NEW STORE ON THE SIGHT OF THE SADLY MISSED X-TRA STORE. I GUESS X-TRA WAS SO EASY TO STEAL FROM THAT WE PUT 'EM OUT OF BUSINESS. I SWEAR, I EVEN WENT TO X-TRA ON DATES, AND YOU COULD ALWAYS DRINK

→ A SCENE REPORT FOR CRIMINALS

BEER AND MAKE OUT IN THE BEER AISLE AT 3:00 AM! W.D. HAS PULLED OUT ALL THE STOPS, WITH BULK FOOD, FREE COFFEE, LOTS OF FREE SAMPLES, AND EVEN A GUY IN A PLANTAIN SUIT AT THE GRAND OPENING! BUT IT CAN'T WIN MY HEART, AS NEW CAMERAS AND IN-STORE WACKENHUT HAVE MADE FILLING A BACKPACK WITH BEER HARD. ☺ TEXAS TACO — NOTORIOUS LOCAL LEGENDARY DUMPSTER DIVER AND METER-ROOM DWELLER, PUNCH, TIPPED ME TO THIS PLACE'S FREE COKE REFILLS. ANYTIME A NEW RESTAURANT LIKE THIS OPENS, YOU HAVE TO GO TRY OUT THE EMPLOYEES AND SEE IF THEY'RE THE KIND OF PEOPLE WHO ARE GONNA TRY AND FIST FIGHT YOU OVER A COKE. I GOT THE COKE CUP AND WENT UP IN FULL VIEW OF THE KID AT THE COUNTER, STARED HIM IN THE EYE, AND FILLED IT UP. HE DIDN'T DO ANYTHING! HE'S SOFT. THE PUNKS'LL OWN HIM. THE PLACE HAD PRETTY GOOD TABLE DIVING, TOO, I MIGHT ADD, BUT THE BLARING TV'S SORT OF TURNED ME OFF. I SAY STICK TO TACO BELL.

"HIGHWAY 301 REVISITED..."

SPAWN SACS

DA THUMB

IT WAS A WEEK OF DEJA-VU, OR SOMETHING LIKE IT. SURELY, I'D BEEN HERE BEFORE, WHERE NOTHING I TRIED TO DO SEEMED TO WORK AT ALL. IT STARTED WITH LITTLE STUFF, LIKE MY FAVORITE PRODUCE DUMPSTER WHERE I ALWAYS GOT FRUIT, WAS SUDDENLY PADLOCKED. I COULDN'T EVEN FIND A USED CUP TO SLAM COKES AT TACO BELL. THEN I GOT CAUGHT STEALING BECAUSE OF A FREAK ACCIDENT INVOLVING A KID WITH DOWNS SYNDROME. I WAS TRYING TO "LEFT-HAND" A 12-PAK OF BEER, BY HOLDING THE BEER BELOW THE COUNTER WITH MY LEFT HAND AND BUYING A 12¢ BANANA WITH MY RIGHT HAND. BELIEVE IT, OR NOT, THIS ALMOST ALWAYS WORKS. THE CASHIER HANDED ME MY CHANGE AND HADN'T NOTICED THE BEER, BUT THE DOWNS SYNDROME KID, IN LINE BEHIND ME WITH HIS DAD, FOR SOME REASON, STARTED POINTING AND YELLING, "BEER! BEER! THAT MAN HAS BEER, DAD!" THE DAD SAID, YES, SON, THAT MAN HAS BEER. THE CASHIER SAID, "HEY, MAN! YOU HAVE BEER! WANT TO TRY PAYING FOR THAT?!?" WITH A QUICK LOOK AROUND THE STORE, I COULD SEE IT WOULD BE IMPOSSIBLE TO KILL THE CASHIER, AND GET AWAY. WHAT THE HELL, I BOUGHT THE BEER, AS I HAD NO CHOICE, LOSING MY LAST SIX BUCKS.

THEN I GOT PERMANENTLY BOOTED FROM THE APARTMENT COMPLEX POOL THAT I'D BEEN SWIMMING IN EVERY DAY FOR NEARLY A YEAR. THE APARTMENT MANAGER, A GUY ABOUT MY AGE WITH A TAN-SURFER LOOK, SAID IN A FRIENDLY, CONFIDENTIAL TONE, "REALLY SORRY, DUDE. YOU KNOW, I DON'T CARE IF YOU SWIM HERE, BUT YOU KNOW ITS NOT UP TO ME..." WE LOOKED AT EACH OTHER FOR A LONG, UNCOMFORTABLE MOMENT WHILE HE TRIED TO SHRUG, SYMPATHETICALLY, AND I WONDERED WHAT HE MEANT. WHO WAS IT 'UP TO'? WHAT WERE WE UP AGAINST?!?

THEN, MY GIRLFRIEND CAME BACK TO TOWN, BUT ONLY SO WE COULD BREAK UP, IN PERSON. SHE SAID, "BEING ALONE'S BEEN GREAT. I'VE JUST BEEN READING LOTS OF BOOKS!"

I SAID, "READING BOOKS? NO, NO, NO. I WRITE, SO I CAN TELL YOU FROM EXPERIENCE: BOOKS ARE TOTALLY OVERRATED."

SHE LEFT, ANYWAY, BUT I THOUGHT IT WAS A GOOD LINE.

WELL, SURE, I'D ANTICIPATED THIS BREAK UP, POSSIBLY SINCE OUR FIRST KISS, BUT I DECIDED TO ACT LIKE IT WAS A REAL, BIG DEAL, ANYWAY, BY ATTEMPTING A NIGHT OF RASH AND IRREVERSIBLE BEHAVIOR TO PAY TRIBUTE TO MY EX. I TOOK OFF ON MY BIKE WITH A HUGE BAG OF BEER AND SPRAY PAINT. I ENDED UP IN THE TRAIN YARD, BUT THERE WAS NOTHING GOING OUT. REALLY, OF THIS PERIOD OF MY LIFE, I REMEMBER VERY LITTLE, BUT I THINK I WRECKED AND BROKE MY CHAIN AND ENDED UP PUSHING THE BIKE HOME 6 MILES IN A SHOPPING CART, COVERED IN BEER, BLOOD, GREASE, AND PAINT. SOME TRIBUTE.

I COULD SEE WHAT SCIENTISTS CALL A "TREND", CLEARLY DEVELOPING HERE. I WAS DOOMED. FINALLY, I WENT BACK TO THE YARD, THE NEXT DAY, AND CAUGHT OUT FOR BALDWIN. A VACATION WOULD DO ME GOOD, THOUGH, REALLY, I HAVEN'T HAD A JOB IN 6 YEARS...

IN BALDWIN, AT WAFFLE HOUSE, I WAS A REGULAR ALL RIGHT. THE SAME WAITRESS WHO WOULD ONLY GIVE ME ONE FREE REFILL OF COFFEE, MY LAST TWO TIMES IN TOWN, WAS THERE AGAIN! SHE STILL WOULDN'T KICK DOWN, AND I LEFT TO HITCH HIKE TO GAINESVILLE, A DULL AND SMUG, LITTLE COLLEGE TOWN IN THE CENTER OF THE STATE, WHERE I WOULD BE SURE TO FEEL BETTER ABOUT MYSELF. AT LEAST THE COLLEGE LIBRARY'S REAL GOOD.

I HOPE THIS STORY DOESN'T SOUND TOO PESSIMISTIC. I WAS JUST HAVING A LITTLE RUN OF BAD LUCK. SOMETIMES YOU JUST CAN'T GET ANYTHING RIGHT. BUT I WAS STILL GLAD TO BE OUT HITCH HIKING ON A NICE DAY, AND I STILL CAN'T BELIEVE HOW EXCITING, AND CRAZY AND UNPREDICTABLE LIFE CAN BE.

THAT'S WHY, WHEN MY FIRST RIDE PULLED OVER THERE AT THE INTERSECTION OF HWY. 301 AND I-10, I WENT AHEAD AND GOT IN, EVEN THOUGH I WAS TOTALLY STUNNED, AND DIDN'T KNOW WHETHER TO LAUGH, OR CRY.

THE RIDE WAS THE OLD, WHITE HAIRED GUY. IN THE RED TRUCK.

IT WAS COLD AS HELL, BELOW 30°, AND YOU COULD SEE EVERYONE'S BREATH AS THEY WALKED UP. THERE WAS STILL ALOT OF PEOPLE THERE, THOUGH. I WAS SURPRISED TO REALIZE THAT I'D NEVER REALLY BEEN TO ONE OF THESE THINGS BEFORE. I HAD SHOWN UP IN LITTLE ROCK THAT MORNING ONLY TO FIND OUT THAT ALL MY FRIENDS WERE GOING DOWNTOWN FOR THE BIG MARCH TO PROTEST LITTLE ROCK POLICE BRUTALITY, WHICH THERE IS A CONSIDERABLE AMOUNT OF. YOU KNOW, "THE LONG SHADOW OF LITTLE ROCK" AND ALL... I WAS PRETTY TIRED FROM A LONG, COLD WEEK ON TRAINS, MY OWN PERSONAL MARCH AGAINST THE HIGH COST OF AIRPLANE TICKETS, BUT, IT SOUNDED PRETTY RAD, SO I WENT DOWN TO CHECK IT OUT, WITH CINDY, WHO ALSO HAPPENED TO BE PASSING THROUGH. WE WERE THE "OUTSIDE AGITATORS"!

THE MARCH WAS SUPPOSED TO START AT THIS CHURCH. THE ONLY PEOPLE WHO SHOWED UP WERE VERY WELL-DRESSED, BLACK PEOPLE FROM THE SURROUNDING POOR NEIGHBORHOOD, AND THE CHEERFULLY, SCUMMY GREEN-HAIRED, DREADLOCKED, AND PIERCED PUNKS OF L.R... BLACKS AND PUNKS? IT OCCURRED TO ME THAT THE AVERAGE LITTLE ROCK CITIZEN MAY ACTUALLY WANT AND EXPECT THE COPS TO BEAT US UP, LIKE "WELL, THAT'S WHAT WE PAY 'EM FOR..."

NO ONE REALLY KNEW WHAT TO DO. EVERYONE MILLED ABOUT NERVOUSLY FOR AWHILE, BUT THEN, A COUPLE SPEAKERS CAME UP TO TALK, AND EVENTUALLY, THE DIFFERENT PEOPLE IN THE CROWD STARTED OPENING UP AND TALKING TO EACH OTHER ABOUT POLICE ATTACKS THEY'D SUFFERED. IT

"THE MARCH"

WAS EXCITING TO SEE DIFFERENT NEIGHBORHOODS COME TOGETHER AND TO SEE HOW MUCH IT MEANT TO EVERYONE TO TELL THEIR STORY AND NOT TO FEEL ALONE. IT SEEMED TO ME THAT THIS GESTURE OF BEING HERE TO SPEAK AND LISTEN AND MARCH IN THE FACE OF SUCH A HOSTILE TOWN WAS THE ONLY THING THAT REALLY MATTERS, THIS SIMPLE FAITH IN PEOPLE AND THE WORLD WHICH MAKES EVERYTHING ELSE POSSIBLE.

THE ACTUAL MARCH ITSELF, THROUGH L.R.'S FADING DOWNTOWN TO THE POLICE STATION WAS FUN AS HELL. ACTUALLY BEING "THE NEWS", MAKING SOMETHING HAPPEN IN A QUIET TOWN WAS EXCITING. AND I LIKED THE LOOK ON THIS ONE MUSTACHE-WEARIN' COP'S FACE AS HE HAD TO STAND THEIR AND LISTEN TO OUR VARIOUS ATTACK STORIES. HE DIDN'T LIKE IT.

WHEN I GOT BACK TO MIAMI, ME AND IVY STARTED TALKING ABOUT TRYING TO DO A FOOD NOT BOMBS HERE, AGAIN. WE'D TRIED TO START ONE UP, FOUR YEARS AGO, WHEN WE LIVED IN A SQUAT IN COCONUT GROVE TOGETHER, BUT WE COULDN'T REALLY FIND ANY PEOPLE WHO WERE INTERESTED IN HELPING. I DID HAVE A BAGEL AND PRODUCE CONNECTION AND I'D GO OUT, SOMETIMES AND GIVE IT ALL AWAY AT THIS EMPTY LOT ON GRAND AVENUE, BUT, EVEN THEN, I WAS HAULING THE BOXES AROUND ON MY BIKE HANDLEBARS AND IT JUST WASN'T SOMETHING I COULD REALLY DO EVERYDAY.

SINCE THEN, WE'D BEEN IN AND OUT OF MIAMI AND HAD ALWAYS FELT WE DIDN'T WANT TO TRY TO START SOMETHING IF WE WERE JUST GOING TO LEAVE TOWN SOON, ANYWAYS. THIS YEAR, I KNEW I WAS GOING AWAY FOR THE SUMMER FOR SURE, AND SHE WAS THINKING ABOUT IT. BUT WE'D HEARD OTHER PEOPLE TALKING ABOUT WORKING ON STARTING ONE, SO WE FIGURED, WE MIGHT AS WELL TRY IT AND SEE HOW IT TURNS OUT.

ITS FUNNY THAT, SINCE WE'D LIVED IN THE GROVE FOR YEARS AND KNOW LOTS OF PEOPLE THERE, AND CARE ABOUT THE NEIGHBORHOOD, I THINK WE WOULD HAVE GONE AHEAD AND DONE ANY KIND OF FOOD GIVEAWAY, EVEN WITHOUT CALLING IT "FOOD NOT BOMBS." WHAT I MEAN IS, WHY DO YOU HAVE TO DO SOMETHING A CERTAIN WAY, JUST BECAUSE THAT IS THE WAY ITS DONE IN OTHER CITIES? HOWEVER, I HAVE ALWAYS AGREED COMPLETELY WITH THE BASIC FOOD NOT BOMBS IDEA OF TRYING TO CREATE A NEIGHBORHOOD, PUBLIC SPACE TO BRING PEOPLE TOGETHER THROUGH FOOD SHARING. ITS REAL SIMPLE AND PRACTICAL, LIKE SQUATTING, WHERE, IF YOU NEED A HOUSE, YOU GET A CROWBAR AND GO GET ONE.

MAYBE ITS THE ACTUAL "FOOD NOT BOMBS" NAME THAT HAS A NEGATIVE CONNOTATION, THOUGH. MAYBE ITS SORT-OF HOKEY, LIKE GRETA SAYS: "I THINK THEY COULD AT LEAST USE A COMMA." OR MAYBE THE NAME HAS, UNFORTUNATELY, COME TO

REMIND ME OF A HANDFUL OF FLAKES AND IDIOTS I'VE RUN INTO, ACROSS THE COUNTRY, WHO ARE CONNECTED WITH IT. LIKE THE SNOTTY, LITTLE DO-GOODERS AND HOLIER-THAN-THOU FINGER POINTERS WHO SPEND ALL THEIR TIME PATTING THEMSELVES ON THE BACK AND TELLING EVERYONE ELSE HOW THEY'RE NOT DOING ANYTHING, OR THE TEENAGE REVOLUTIONARY WHO GETS FRUSTRATED AND QUITS WHEN "THE REVOLUTION" DOESN'T START AFTER 2 WEEKS OF JOYLESS, AWKWARD FEEDINGS IN A DECREPIT, INNER CITY PARK. THE WHITE KIDS WHO CALL BUMS "THOSE PEOPLE" AND THE ONE F.N.B. GROUP THAT REFUSED TO SERVE, AND, INSTEAD, THREW AWAY A CASE OF DONATED POTATO CHIPS BECAUSE THEY WEREN'T VEGAN. AND, OH YEAH, WHAT ABOUT THE INEVITABLE POT SMOKING, CONSPIRACY THEORIST WHO WANTS TO START EVERY MEETING BY SAYING, "WILL ALL THE FEDERAL AGENTS IN THE ROOM PLEASE IDENTIFY THEMSELVES," BECAUSE THEY READ IN A BOOK, OR SOMETHING, THAT A FEDERAL AGENT IS REQUIRED TO DO THAT, IF ASKED. WHO WANTS TO EAT LUNCH WITH THOSE PEOPLE?!?

OK, SO ITS EASY TO JUST PUT STUFF DOWN, AND NOT SO EASY TO DO IT. BUT, REALLY, ISN'T THIS THE KIND OF SHIT THAT KEEPS ALOT OF BASICALLY GOOD AND GENEROUS PEOPLE FROM WANTING TO GET INVOLVED?

WE ENDED UP DECIDING TO GO AHEAD AND CALL IT "FOOD NOT BOMBS" THOUGH, BECAUSE WE DO AGREE SO STRONGLY WITH THE BASIC IDEAS. WELL, EXCEPT FOR THE PART ABOUT "CONSENSUS." WE DON'T GIVE A SHIT ABOUT "CONSENSUS."

SO, WE MADE A TON OF FLYERS FOR A FIRST MEETING AND WERE PRETTY SURPRISED WHEN ABOUT 15 PEOPLE ACTUALLY SHOWED UP. SOME WE KNEW, SOME WE DIDN'T. MOST OF THEM HAD BEEN SITTING AROUND, LIKE US, WONDERING IF THERE WAS ANYBODY ELSE OUT THERE WHO WAS INTERESTED IN DOING ANYTHING LIKE THIS. THE MEETING WAS SORT OF AWKWARD AND EXCITING, LIKE THE MARCH IN L.R., IN HOW IT FELT LIKE SOMETHING WAS HAPPENING THAT HADN'T HAPPENED HERE BEFORE. WHEN IN DOUBT, MAKE A FLYER.

WE DECIDED TO COOK AT IVY'S HOUSE IN THE GROVE, AND SERVE A COUPLE BLOCKS AWAY AT THIS EMPTY LOT ON GRAND AVENUE. THE SITUATION IN THE GROVE IS PRETTY HEAVY THESE DAYS. THE GROVE IS VERY RIGIDLY, RACIALLY SEGREGATED BY S.W. 32nd AVENUE, WITH THE MALL, COCOWALK, THE TOURIST SHOPS, AND ONE OF THE WEALTHIEST, WHITE AREAS IN THE CITY LIMITS TO THE EAST, AND ABANDONED STORE FRONTS, CRACKHOUSES, SHOTGUN SHACKS, AND ONE OF THE POOREST BLACK GHETTOS TO THE WEST. 32nd MAY BE THE MOST DRAMATIC DIVISION BY ONE STREET THAT I'VE EVER SEEN IN THE WHOLE COUNTRY, BETWEEN "HAVES" AND "HAVE NOTS." BUT, LATELY, THE OLD GROVE WOOD HOUSES HAVE BEEN DISAPPEARING ON THE WHITE SIDE, AS THEY'RE TORN DOWN TO MAKE ROOM FOR FORTRESS-LIKE, GATED CONDOS. NOW, THE DENSITY'S GREATER, AND THERE'S MORE "HAVES" THAN EVER WHO ARE PARANOID ABOUT CRIME. POLICE HAVE BEEN MAKING THE WEST SIDE PAY WITH A NEW POLICY OF FACE-DOWN-ON-THE-SIDEWALK SEARCH-AND-FRISKS OF BLACK YOUTH ON THE STREETS. OFTEN, WHEN COPS STOP PEOPLE ON THE WEST SIDE, A CONFRONTATION DEVELOPS WHERE BLACK PASSERSBY START THROWING BOTTLES AND YELLING INSULTS AT THE COPS. IT WOULD SEEM THAT THE BUNKER MENTALITY OF THE WHITE SIDE AND THE SEARCH AND DESTROY MISSION OF THE POLICE, MIXED IN WITH A HOT SUMMER COULD BRING ABOUT SOME TERRIBLE RIOT. AND 32nd AVENUE AND GRAND, WHERE THE TWO SIDES MEET, IS ALREADY THE EPICENTER OF MUGGINGS, DRUG DEALS, PURSE SNATCHINGS, CAR BURGLARY, ETC, IN THE WHOLE GROVE.

THE EMPTY LOT WE CHOSE TO SERVE AT IS, MORE OR LESS, ON THAT LINE, AT GRAND AND MARGARET, A COUPLE BLOCKS WEST OF 32nd AVE., ACROSS FROM THE FINA GAS STATION WHERE EVERYONE IN THE GROVE, INCLUDING MANY OF MY FRIENDS, BUY THEIR HEROIN AND CRACK. I LIKED THE IDEA OF PUTTING A LITTLE LIGHT DOWN THERE, IN THE HEART OF THE SHIT, AND I LIKED USING AN EMPTY LOT, AND TAKING IT AWAY FROM DRUG DEALERS. AND, AT THAT SPOT, WE COULD BE CONVENIENTLY LOCATED BETWEEN THE POOR FAMILIES OF THE WEST SIDE, AND THE HOMELESS OF THE EAST. IT WAS STILL A LITTLE TOO FAR FOR THE SHRIMPER GUYS DOWN AT THE MARINA, THOUGH. THOSE GUYS HATE LAND.

FIRST, OBVIOUSLY, WE WERE GOING TO NEED FOOD. WE FIGURED OUR BEST BET WAS TO HIT UP THE PRODUCE DISTRICT WAREHOUSES, UP BY CIVIC CENTER, FOR THE HUGE BOXES OF VEGETABLES AND FRUIT THAT THEY OFTEN HAVE TO THROW OUT AT THE END OF THE DAY. IVY, WENDY, AND ME WENT UP THERE TO CHECK IT OUT. I ALWAYS LIKE GOING UP TO THE PRODUCE DISTRICT, ANYWAY, BECAUSE ITS TOTALLY CRAZY, WITH PEOPLE EVERYWHERE, AND ROTTING FRUIT AND TIRES AND TRASH IN THE STREETS, AND HOMELESS PEOPLE TRYING TO SELL YOU BOXES OF DUMPSTERED STUFF. BUT, I LIKE THIS PART OF FOOD NOT BOMBS, ALOT, THE SORT-OF DETECTIVE WORK OF GOING OUT TO WEIRD PARTS OF TOWN TO MEET THE PEOPLE THERE AND TELL THEM ABOUT WHAT YOU'RE DOING AND TRY TO SCOUT OUT FOOD LEADS. WELL, LUCKILY, WENDY SPEAKS SPANISH, THOUGH, OR WE WOULDN'T HAVE TALKED TO ANYONE! EVERYONE THERE, PRETTY MUCH, HAS BEEN GLAD TO HELP, AND THAT'S WHERE WE GET MOST OF OUR FOOD.

RAFAEL FROM SPACE CADET HAD A BUNCH OF CANNED FOOD FROM A CAN DRIVE THAT THEY'D DONE AT A SHOW THERE, SO WE DECIDED TO GO OUT THE FIRST WEEK AND TRY OUT OUR LOT WITH CANNED FOOD AND A COOLER OF ICED TEA, AND IF IT WENT OK, WE'D GO BACK THE NEXT WEEK WITH COOKED FOOD. IT WENT FINE AND WE'VE BEEN OUT THERE NOW, EVERY SUNDAY AT 2:00 PM SINCE MAY 4th.

USUALLY, WE HAVE ONE BIG, HOT POT OF SOMETHING, SOME BREAD FROM A BAKERY, A COOLER OF ICED TEA FROM A MIX, AND, OF COURSE, THE ROCK HARD, DAY OLD BAGEL (THE BAGEL IS NOW STANDARD FARE AT FOOD NOT BOMBS ACROSS THE WORLD AND, ALONG WITH RAMEN, FOOD-FROM-A-FRIEND'S-WORK, AND DUMPSTERED FOOD, ONE OF THE 4 "PUNK ROCK FOOD GROUPS.") WHATEVER FRUIT, OR LEFTOVER VEGETABLES WE HAVE IS LEFT OUT WITH PLASTIC BAGS FOR PEOPLE TO TAKE HOME. WE'VE ALSO HAD TONS OF CANNED FOOD FROM THE FNB BENEFIT SHOW AND FROM A DRIVE THAT LIZ DID AT HER SCHOOL. SHE GOT HER TEACHER TO GIVE EXTRA CREDIT TO KIDS WHO BROUGHT CANS!

ACTUALLY, I'M SURPRISED AT HOW GOOD THE COOKING'S BEEN, AND HOW CREATIVE WE'VE BEEN WITH THESE HUGE CARLOADS OF SLIGHTLY ROTTING FOOD WE GET. WE MADE CHILI WITH CORN BREAD, BLACK BEAN SOUP, STUFFED PEPPERS, SPLIT PEA SOUP, AND EVEN STIR-FRY WITH RICE. I'VE BEEN LEARNING ALOT ABOUT COOKING. OF COURSE, I AM ALREADY ONE OF THE WORLD'S GREAT, UNDISCOVERED CHEFS. I'LL NEVER FORGET THAT HISTORIC DAY IN BILOXI WHEN ME, CINQUE, AND BRIAN TURD INVENTED THE FRIED LIMA BEAN SANDWHICH, WITH CHEESE. BUT, USUALLY, I LEAVE THE COOKING UP TO SHIRA AND IVY'S MOM.

LATELY, WE'VE BEEN BRANCHING OUT, BEYOND FOOD, TOO AS WE'VE BEEN GIVING OUT 2ND HAND CLOTHES, TOYS, BOOKS, AND EVEN BRAND, NEW TOOTHBRUSHES THAT JILL'S DAD HAD LEFT OVER FROM A HURRICANE ANDREW RELIEF PROJECT. IVY WENT TO ALL THE NEIGHBORHOOD THRIFT STORES AND CONVINCED THEM TO MAKE A WEEKLY DONATION OF CLOTHES, TOO.

I SUPPOSE IT WOULD BE NICE TO HAVE SOME PEOPLE INVOLVED WHO WERE OUTSIDE THE PUNK SCENE, BUT, AT LEAST THE PUNKS AREN'T AFRAID TO DO THE FUN STUFF. LIKE, AT THE 3rd FEEDING, WE FOUND THIS LADDER IN THE EMPTY LOT, AND MOLLY AND AMY FROM LAKE WORTH FNB USED IT TO TAKE OVER THE BILLBOARD AT THE EDGE OF OUR LOT AND PUT UP OUR FNB BANNER ON IT! OR, THERE WAS THE TIME WHEN THE YEARLY, WEST SIDE, STREET PARTY, THE GOOMBAY FESTIVAL HAPPENED ON GRAND AND OUR LOT WAS COVERED WITH CONCESSION STANDS. IVY, NATACHA, IAN, AND JILL TOOK OVER AN UNUSED BOOTH, NEXT TO THE HOT 105 BOOTH, PUT UP THE FNB BANNER, AND EVERYONE THOUGHT THEY WERE PART OF THE OFFICIAL FESTIVAL! AND WE DID GET OUR FIRST GOOD, BIG COOKING POT WHEN THE BONEHEADS WERE AT THIS KEG PARTY THAT GOT BUSTED, SO THEY GRABBED A HUGE POT FROM THE PARTY'S KITCHEN, FILLED IT WITH BEER FROM THE KEG AND SPLIT! JUSTO FOUND IT IN HIS CAR THE NEXT MORNING.

THERE'S BEEN SOME RAD, UNEXPECTED STUFF, LIKE HOW THIS ONE PLACE AT THE PRODUCE DISTRICT ALWAYS DELIBERATELY DAMAGES CANS SO THEY CAN GIVE THEM TO US! RYAN AND IAN AND ME WENT ONE TIME AND THE GUY GRABBED A COUPLE HUGE CANS OF TOMATO PASTE THAT WE NEEDED, TOLD US TO WAIT AND CAME BACK WITH THEM ALL DENTED UP! THIS CHURCH DOWN THE BLOCK HAS OFFERED SPACE TO STORE FOOD. ALOT OF YOUNG KIDS COME TO PLAY IN THE LOT AND EAT WITH US. AND, ODDLY ENOUGH, THE SEEDS FROM WATERMELONS AND OTHER STUFF WE'D CUT UP HAVE STARTED TO SPROUT ALL OVER IVY'S YARD!

THERE'S BEEN SOME PROBLEMS, TOO, OF COURSE. ALOT OF PEOPLE IN THE NEIGHBORHOOD TOLD US THEY DIDN'T WANT OUR FOOD, BECAUSE WE DIDN'T HAVE ANY MEAT. THIS SORT OF TOOK US BY SURPRISE AND LEFT US SPIRALLING INTO AN IDEOLOGICAL VOID, AS MANY OF OUR VOLUNTEERS AREN'T VEGETARIAN, EITHER, AND DIDN'T REALLY HAVE A READY RESPONSE FOR QUESTIONS ABOUT IT.

THERE'S BEEN ALOT OF CHAOS, TOO, OF COURSE, LIKE WE ALL WAKE UP, TOO LATE AND HUNG OVER, OR WE HAVE TO STEAL A BUNCH OF CUPS AT THE LAST MINUTE, OR A BUNCH OF PLASTIC SILVERWARE FROM TACO BELL AND MIAMI SUBS.

SOME OF US FELT THAT THERE WASN'T ENOUGH PEOPLE COMING ^TO EAT, OR THAT WE HAD TOO MUCH FOOD. WE'D HAVE TO WALK THE STREETS, FLYERING, EVERY WEEKEND TO GET A BIG CROWD, OR DRIVE DOWN TO PEACOCK PARK AT THE END TO GIVE THE LEFTOVERS TO THE ANNOYING HIPPIE DRUM CIRCLE CROWD. THEN I'D FEEL LIKE WE WERE CATERING TO PRIVELEGED STONERS AND WASTING OUR TIME, WHILE THE OLD MYSTIC BUMS LECTURED US ABOUT THE 60'S AND STARED HUNGRILY AT OUR TEENAGE GIRL VOLUNTEERS' BREASTS. WHAT A DRAG.

MAYBE THAT'S THE DRAWBACK OF BEING AFFILIATED WITH A NATIONAL GROUP, THIS FEELING THAT YOU'RE NOT DOING SOMETHING RIGHT, OR BY THE BOOK, OR THAT ITS BETTER SOMEWHERE ELSE. BUT I JUST THINK WE HAVE TO BE PATIENT. THE CROWDS HAVE BEEN PICKING UP. ALOT OF FAMILIES COME FOR THE TAKE-HOME PRODUCE AND CANS. THE LOT IS OBVIOUSLY SAFER WHEN WE'RE THERE FOR THE KIDS WHO PLAY AND GET HOT FOOD THERE. AND, ANYWAY, THERE'S NO AMOUNT OF PEOPLE SERVED THAT EQUALS "SUCCESS." AND BEING LATE AND HUNGOVER IS ONE THING US PUNKS ARE REALLY GOOD AT. WHY TAKE IT AWAY?

ONE WEIRD THING, THOUGH, IS THE EVERPRESENCE OF "THE END OF THE WORLD" AS A TOPIC OF CONVERSATION WITH THE FOLKS WE FEED. IT STARTS UP EVERYTIME. LIKE, THIS ONE GUY FROM THE MARINA WALKED UP TO ME ALL INNOCENTLY, PICKING AT HIS CUP OF CHILI WITH A PLASTIC SPOON. HE SAYS, "GREAT CHILI, REALLY GREAT..." AND, SUDDENLY, LAUNCHES INTO A 15-MINUTE LONG SUMMARY OF NOSTRADAMUS' THEORIES, ROUNDING UP WITH A FLOURISH OF NUMEROLOGY AND MASONIC CONSPIRACY THEORIES, THAT CONCLUSIVELY PROVE THAT THE WORLD IS ENDING IN 1998. "I'M NOT SAYING ITS ALL TRUE, BUT THAT'S ALOT OF COINCIDENCE, YOU HAVE TO ADMIT," HE FINISHES, ALMOST WHISPERING, HIS EYES BRIGHT WITH THAT MISSIONARY LOOK THAT SOMEONE FLASHES AS THEY HAND YOU A CHICK TRACT. HE'S A TRUE BELIEVER.

ANOTHER GUY TELLS ME WITH SOLEMN CONVICTION ABOUT NEW DISEASES THAT MEDICINE CAN'T CURE, THAT, IN FACT, GET STRONGER WHEN ANTIBIOTICS ARE USED. CURELESS DISEASES. EBOLA. DENGUE. "THIS MAKE OLE AIDS LOOK LIKE NOTHIN'!" HE DRAWLS, CONCLUSIVELY, BALLING UP HIS NAPKIN AND TOSSING IT TOWARDS THE TRASHBOX.

I'VE BEEN TRYING TO FIGURE OUT THIS SIMPLE FAITH IN SUCH A PROFOUND HOPELESSNESS. IS THIS "I TOLD YA SO" — A FAITH IN AN IRONY THAT CHAOS WILL DESTROY CIVILIZATION AND VINDICATE THE POOR AND HOMELESS? OR, IS IT JUST THE JOY AT FINDING SOMETHING TO BELIEVE IN THAT ACTUALLY SEEMS POSSIBLE? MAYBE ITS JUST A NEW VERSION OF CHRIST'S RETURN TO EARTH, OR "THE REVOLUTION." YOU KNOW; SOMETHING TO LOOK FORWARD TO. WHO KNOWS? COME JOIN US FOR FREE FOOD AT OUR WEEKLY FORUM ON THE APOCALYPSE, SUNDAYS AT 2:00 PM!

SO, SOME FRIENDS OF MINE HAVE ASKED ME WHY I'M INVOLVED IN A FOOD NOT BOMBS. REALLY, I'M INTERESTED IN KNOWING THE PEOPLE WHO LIVE IN MY NEIGHBORHOOD, IN MAKING IT A MORE ENJOYABLE PLACE TO LIVE, AND IN NOT FEELING SO HELPLESS TO CONTROL WHAT HAPPENS TO IT, WHETHER ITS ATTACKED BY COPS, OR DEVELOPERS, OR JUST POVERTY. BUT ON A DEEPER LEVEL, I CAN'T STAND THE THOUGHT THAT ALL THIS SHIT COULD JUST GO ON AND ON — LIKE, AT EVERY LEVEL. LIKE THE WHOLE WORLD'S WATCHING STAR WARS REISSUES AND LISTENING TO WHITNEY HOUSTON AND THINKS THE WORLD'S PROBABLY GOING TO END IN 2 OR 3 YEARS, AND YOUR FRIENDS ARE ON HEROIN, AND IT COULD ALL GO ON COMPLETELY UNCHALLENGED. NO FUCKIN' WAY!!! I WANT TO LIVE!

AS I GET READY TO LEAVE FOR THE SUMMER, THINGS LOOK PRETTY GOOD FOR THE SUNDAY AFTERNOON FEEDINGS. NEW PEOPLE ARE COMING IN TO TAKE THE PLACE OF ALOT OF US WITH SUMMER TRIPS PLANNED, AND THEIR BRINGING IN THEIR NEW IDEAS. ITS EXCITING; WE DON'T REALLY KNOW WHAT'S GOING TO HAPPEN WITH IT. I THINK OF THE

TOUGH, OLD BLACK LADIES AT THE L.R. MARCH YELLING AT THE COPS AND SINGING PROTEST SONGS. I THINK OF THE HUNGOVER PUNKS CUTTING VEGETABLES TO SERVE TO SOME TRULY NIHILISTIC EATERS. THIS TRAIN IS BOUND FOR GLORY? WELL, WHY NOT?

THE END!

SCAM PUNKS 1997

SCAM #4

"THE SECRET HISTORY ISSUE"

2 BUCKS APRIL 00

"NOT A VERY HIGH NUMBER!"

we're back

THIS ISSUE:

ATTEMPTS TO DESTROY STARBUCKS, SADAM HUSSEIN, THE STUN GUNS, NEEDLE EXCHANGE, U$KI, FILLED REVENGE, FREE PUNKSHOWS ON MISSION STREET, WHEATPASTING-ATTACK, AIDROW NEWSPAPERS, THE TURD, THE BIKE CHURCH, BIKES ON FREIGHTS, THE 90'S IN CRIME, CEMENT ETCHINGS, URBAN FISHERMEN, DRINKING IN PUBLIC TOILETS, AND MORE!

6.1: USING "THE ROCK" TO DESTROY MAJOR CITIES

BRING ON THE ZEROS!

981-2844

CAN U SPELL
FASCISM...YET?

SCAM #4

Con artists have showed u
in S.F. with a new scam. Page 3

WRITE ME:
PO BOX 4027:
SAN FRANCISC
CALIFORNIA
94140

☺ Society prepares the crime: The
criminal commits it. ☺

AT THE DEPARTMENT OF HUMAN SERVICES WE'RE YEAR 2000 READY, WHICH MEANS
THAT WHEN MIDNIGHT DECEMBER 31, 1999 ROLLS OVER, ALL OF OUR COMPUTER
SYSTEMS WILL DO WHAT THEY'RE SUPPOSED TO DO, SO THAT WE CAN CONTINUE
TO PROVIDE YOU WITH UNINTERRUPTED SERVICES ON JANUARY 3, 2000.

THE BIG NEW YEAR'S PLAN WAS TO GO TO HUNT'S DONUTS, SINCE THE SIGN
SAYS ITS "OPEN 25 HOURS", AND JUST SIT IN THERE, AT 20TH AND MISSION,
CHAMPAGNE AT MIDNIGHT, AND WATCH THE STREETS GO CRAZY THROUGH THE WINDOW.
IT REALLY WOULD BE THE 25TH HOUR! THE REST OF THE WORLD WOULD BE IN 2000,
BUT WE'D BE SOMEWHERE NO ONE HAD EVER BEEN BEFORE.

BUT THE STREETS WEREN'T GOING TO GO CRAZY. THE COPS WERE SHUTTING THE CITY
DOWN. WE RODE DOWNTOWN IN THE AFTERNOON TO WATCH THE FINANCIAL DISTRICT
WORKERS THROW ALL THEIR CALENDERS OUT OF THE SKYSCRAPER WINDOWS, LIKE THEY DO EVERY
YEAR, AND ALL THE WINDOWS ON MARKET STREET WERE BOARDED UP. IT LOOKED LIKE
AFTER A RIOT, BUT IT WAS BEFORE. BEFORE WHAT, I WONDERED. AS WE WATCHED THE
LITTLE PIECES OF CALENDER PAPER FLUTTER DOWN FROM TRANSAMERICA INTO THE ALMOST
DESERTED STREETS, IT SEEMED SO WEIRD TO ACTUALLY BE GOING INTO 2000. IT SEEMS LIKE
MY WHOLE LIFE, PEOPLE HAVE BEEN TELLING ME THE WORLD'S ABOUT TO END, FOR SOME
REASON, OR ANOTHER, BUT HERE IT WAS, ANOTHER YEAR'S DAYS FLUTTERING INTO THE PAST.

BY NIGHT TIME, THE COPS WERE EVERYWHERE AND THEY ALL HAD HUGE ROPES OF
THOSE PLASTIC HANDCUFFS HANGING OFF THEIR BELTS. MISSION STREET WAS DEAD. YOU KNOW
HOW WHEN YOU'RE IN A PROTEST AND IT FEELS WEIRD TO BE IN THE MIDDLE OF THE STREET
LOOKING OUT AT FAMILIAR BUILDINGS? YOU KNOW, THAT FEELING OF DISRUPTION OF THE USUAL
ORDER? STANDING ON MISSION, I FELT LIKE THAT. IT WAS LIKE THE NOT HAPPENING WAS
SO ACTIVELY HAPPENING. THE NON-EVENT WAS SO HEAVILY PLANNED.

WE HAD NO CHOICE BUT TO GO UNDERCOVER. WE, THE PUNKS, HAD OBTAINED SOME POLICE
RADIOS JUST FOR THIS NIGHT. NOT SCANNERS, BUT ACTUAL COP'S RADIOS THAT YOU COULD TALK ON.
I FELT LIKE A NARC GOING INTO THE PUNK SHOW WITH THE RADIO WELL CONCEALED
UNDER MY CLOTHES. WHAT IF IT FELL OUT, OR SOMEONE GRABBED ME TO DANCE AND FELT
IT? AND WHAT ABOUT THAT ANNOYING SQUAWKING BETWEEN SONGS?

IT WAS FINE, THOUGH. I KEPT THE VOLUME DOWN AND PLAYED HALF THE SHOW FOR THE
COPS OVER THE DISPATCH, ESPECIALLY THE BETWEEN SONG DEDICATIONS TO THE COPS.
SOON IT WAS MIDNIGHT, SO I HEADED TO HUNT'S WITH ANANDI TO MEET GRETA AND
BILL, WHO HAD THE CHAMPAGNE.

WE POPPED THE CORK AND WALKED AROUND. IT REALLY WAS DEAD. BILL SAID, "ITS THE
COMPLETE FUSION OF POLICE CONTROL AND THE MEDIA. THE COPS AND THE MEDIA SAY NOTHING'S
HAPPENING, SO NOTHING HAPPENS."

BUT I WASN'T SO SURE. THE NIGHT ENDED WITH ME AND ANANDI ON A ROOF, LISTENING TO
THE COP RADIO AND WATCHING MISSION. THE POWER WAS OUT AT THE SUNNYDALE PROJECTS. THERE
WERE FISTFIGHTS. A MAN WAS STANDING IN THE ROAD, SCREAMING ON GENEVA AVE. THERE WAS
DISCONTENT, CHAOS AS '99 ROLLED INTO '00. SCATTERED INCIDENTS.

AND THERE WAS US SAYING ON THE RADIO, "WE NEED BACKUP AT 24TH AND BALMY. 3 COPS ARE
PEPPER SPRAYING AN UNARMED LATINO MAN TO DEATH."

THIS IS SCAM #4, A LOOK BACK AT THE 90'S, A LOOK AHEAD AT THE ZEROS. IT STARTED WITH AN
ENORMOUS PILE OF FLYERS, TRAIN MAPS, OLD LETTERS, HITCH HIKING SIGNS, WHEATPASTED SCRAPS AND
ENDED UP HERE. A LOOK AT WHAT WORKED AND DIDN'T WORK. THINGS PUNKS INVENTED. I'M NOT
SURE WHAT IT ALL ADDED UP TO. BUT I KNOW WHEN THE COPS SAY "NOTHING'S HAPPENING," "THEY'RE
WRONG

SMALL STINKIN' PLANET, DEPT.
SOME LETTERS:

Hey Iggy:

Life is just a little too weird sometimes. I'd been reading SCAM #3 on the El trains all day, and then I went to Kinko's to print some flyers and, lo and behold, I found this fragment of a letter on the counter. I'd just been staring at your handwriting for a good chunk of time so I recognized it immediately. I thought you'd want your letter back... By the way, if you're really hopping trains in Late November like your letter says, I think you're crazy...

Erin McWilliams
Stuck in Chicago

PS. Was that you by chance, standing outside the tattoo place a block from The Kinks?

ED— NO. EVERYONE KNOWS ONLY JERKS STAND IN FRONT OF TATTOO PLACES.

Iggy:

It was weird to get your letter. My friend told me that day that he had given my zine with the picture of your graffiti im it to his friend, Pablo. Then, I get your letter right then, saying you got the zine from Pablo. Then, later that day, I'm hanging out byn the BNSF train yard and a yellow boxcar goes by with SCAM PUNKS graffiti on it! What's next? Am I going to come home and find CHICKENHEAD playing in my house?

Jesse/Stay Gold zine
Lawrence, KS

PS. Are you going to DC? I'm going, so I can beaten up and tear gassed again... Maybe I'll see you...

ED: YES, CHICKENHEAD IS REUNITING TO TRAVEL TO D.C. TO BEAT YOU UP AND SHOOT TEAR GAS AT YOU.

Iggy:

Remember me? I ran into you about a month ago, piss-drunk in the San Francisco MUNI tunnel, when I was on my way to take a Greyhound to Vancouver... Anyways, I'm back in SF, so I wanted to tell you a little about my trip. I got to East Vancouver in the early evening of Halloween where festivities were a go-go. The Commercial Drive Crusties had a huge shopping cart race which blocked traffic long enough for a spontaneous Food Not Bombs serving to materialize in the middle of a busy intersection! Once the shopping carts came back around the block, there were probably 50 kids milling about the intersection, enjoying delicious soup, potatoes, and muffins, with 10 shopping carts blocking all cars from entering! A few cops tried, unsuccessfull to move the blockades and fucked with a few people that they believed to be responsible for the race. They said they'd arrest people if the FNB table wasn't moved, so a couple of kids moved it, but only after someone suggested, "Hey! They can't do shit if we're all crossing the street!" which we did. There was a huge mob of kids walking back and forth on the crosswalk, slapping high-5's, post little league style! It was fucking awesome! More pigs showed up with a paddy wagon, but as long as we were "within the boundaries of the crosswalk and touching the curbs before recrossing" the kid was right; they couldn't do shit! Happy fuckin' Halloween! There was huge, crazy party and I got too drunk and passed out before midnight... —ANTHONY, CA LEUCADIA, CA

TO ORDER SCAM #4 SEND TWO DOLLARS TO:
~~RECORDS~~ THIS HERE! ~~RECESS~~
~~BOX 14088~~ PO BOX 481 ~~PO BOX 1112~~
~~KELEY, CA 97412~~ CHATTANOOGA, TN 37401 ~~TORRANCE, CA 90505~~
LATER NOTE: NOT available from recess!

O: LONG-AWAITED **MIAMI/SHOTWELL**, 17-SONG SPLIT LP WITH ~~PAGE~~ ZINE IS OUT NOW ON NO! RECORDS. EVEN LONGER AWAITED **TEEN RESENTMENTS 7"**, SCAM ISSUES 1-4, AND THE OLD **CHICKENHEAD 7"** ARE AVAILABLE FROM RECESS. CHAOS L.R. 7" LATER THIS YEAR, WE HOPE, ON THIS HERE!

Be Adventurous:

Expand your tastes to enjoy a variety of foods.

Eat foods everyday from **each** of the five major food groups, in the Food Guide Pyramid.

Choose a new fresh, canned or frozen vegetable or fruit each month. Pick one that is on sale.

Choose different types of canned, frozen or dried beans or peas each month.

GET FOOD STAMPS IN 3 STATES AT THE SAME TIME!

"THE LIGHT OF THE NEW AGE"

The light of the new age is dawning;
The light is the Messiah coming on his way;
to redeem men back unto himself.

There's no time to waste;
No time to play, for now is praying, meditation and thinking time.
Time to get out and work out our soul salvation;
Men, women, everyone running wildly, foolishly here and there
STOP!!!

Because it's time to prepare to meet "HIM", our Messiah;
He said almost two thousand years ago;
"2 thousand yrs underneath the law"; and
"2 thousand yrs under grace"

This is 1995, five more years before "2000", which is ushering in the new age of "Aquarius", where the Messiah is coming to establish "GODS" Kingdom on earth as he promised.

This will be the close of the Piscean Age. There will be no place to run and hide, no place to go.

Come to the Temple; Aquarian Ark Temple of Transformation;
Aquarian stands for new age, Ark is for the safety zone, Transformation means "change"; Change your thoughts, change your mind, and change your way of living and you can, you shall and you will be SAVED.
We must come and prepare to meet the MESSIAH, one and ALL!

AQUARIAN ARK TEMPLE OF TRANSFORMATION
4755 N.W. 2ND AVENUE
Miami, Florida

Teaching on Thursday evenings at: 7:00 p.m.
Sunday Morning Service at: 11:00 a.m.
For more information call: 756-3985 or 512-9610 Olleo her.

FIG. 1! FLYERS LIKE THIS ONE STARTED TO APPEAR MORE FREQUENTLY ON THE TELEPHONE POLES OF DOOMED BOULEVARDS LIKE MIAMI'S 79TH STREET AS THE YEAR 2000 APPROACHED.

FIG. 2: THEME SONG

RIDDLE OF THE 90'S

IN A DUMPSTER IN FT. LAUDERDALE
I WAS BORN AGAIN
(WITH A CAN OF PAINT, A TWELVE OF SCHLITZ
AND THE BOOD ON THE BASS!)
NOW I'M SNEAKING OUT OF TOWN ON A MIDNIGHT TRAIN
WONDERING WHEN I'LL SEE YOU AGAIN
(I KNOW WHERE I'M GOING, BUT
I'M NOT SURE WHERE I'VE BEEN...)
I REMEMBER THE BEERS, THE BASEMENTS
THE SHOWS AT I.B.P.
AND ALL THE TRAIN YARDS AND THE BROKEN HEARTS
AND ALL THE SHIT THAT WE GOT FOR FREE!
NOW I'M SNEAKING OUT OF TOWN ON A MIDNIGHT TRAIN
BUT I KNOW I'LL SEE YOU AGAIN
(I KNOW WHERE I'M GOING, BUT
I'M NOT SURE WHERE WE'VE BEEN...)
ASK THE COPS — ASK 'EM WHERE WE'VE BEEN!

I WROTE THIS SONG WHEN I PLAYED DRUMS LAST YEAR FOR A BAND CALLED "THE BREAKUPS". BUT WE BROKE UP. GO FIGURE. SO, LATER, IN 1999, I STARTED WORKING ON A NEW SONG "BRING ON THE ZEROS!" WHICH WAS KIND OF ABOUT THAT FEELING OF ENTERING AN UNCERTAIN NEW ERA, BEING REAL EXCITED ABOUT THE FUTURE, DESPITE BEING ABLE TO LOOK BACK AT THE RUINS OF ALL THE THINGS THAT DIDN'T WORK AND STILL FEELING SOME BITTERNESS ABOUT THAT. I WAS WORKING ON IT IN MY BAND WITH JIMMY AND THE KEY PART WAS THE PART WHERE HE WOULD GROWL, "ITS GONE, GONE, GONE.!!!" BUT, THEN, THAT BAND BROKE UP, TOO...

- 213 -

Short Fuse

By Erich Lyle

SEPT. 11, 1990 F.A.U. ATLANTIC SUN

For the past month, I've found my early morning adrenalin rush, not from a cup of coffee, but from a quick scan of the headlines. "Warnings... tough talk... more propaganda on both sides... but (sigh of relief) no actual war..." No surprise, early-morning, Bush-style invasion, no shots... but for how much longer? By now, every world leader of note who has been involved in negotiations has mysteriously walked away in disgust, resigned to publicly dismissing a non-violent solution as weak and irrational.

Now, the threat of war has invaded every aspect of our daily lives. The government reminds us daily to "sacrifice", and the papers are filled with letters home from our stationed troops. Abroad, Bush and Gobachev meet and promise to unite, and, if necessary, fight, under the premise that if the now-friendly suprpowers can just get rid of Hussein with a quick, tiny war, peace will reign. Traditionally, the Secretary of State's duty is to, at least, talk peace, but Baker is now the salesman, well known, but not well liked, going door to door in the Middle East begging for war money from countries that only a month ago called America "Great Satan." The preparations for war have begun.

— SEPT. 4. 1990 —

Against all reason and all hope, President Bush insists on leading us into war, under the premise that it will be a quick and painless surgery. He has refused to even try to talk with Saddam Hussein, and has instead, issued tough talk and ultimatums, while asking our allies, not for solutions, but for bomb money, and the American people, not for their approval, but for their "sacrifice."

Bush's mind is made up, but war is so ugly, and inhuman on the face of it, that the people who have to actually fight it have to be tricked into doing Bush's bidding. So now, the U.S. mass media that so rightously accuses Saddam Hussein of spreading propaganda, has been overrun by cabinet members, retired generals, defense contractors, and other hired hands, who are very carefully going about the business of selling war to the American people. Cheney and Scowcroft go on Sunday news shows to dazzle us with talk of superior firepower and patriotism, and, surprise, *Meet the Press* and the Brinkley show were brought to you by GE, the nuclear weapons maker, and McDonnel Douglas, the maker of fighter planes.

If That's the Way You Feel...

By Angela Kidd

The leaders of Iraq and America are supposed to have certain compromising skills, right? Well why can't they come up with an easier way to figure this out?

In elementary school, we are taught to not fight and share things. Have these so-called "Presidents" forgotten all of this? The basic rule of life, and two of the people that we are supposed to look up to and follow can't seem to remember it.

fighting isn't going to solve anything. But until we all figure this out, I guess we'll just have to live with the way this and other countries are run, and we'll just have to grin and bear it.

ABOVE: EXCERPTS OF MY COLUMN, PUBLISHED UNDER AN ASSUMED NAME, IN THE F.A.U. ATLANTIC SUN, FOLLOWED BY EXCERPT OF MY REPLACEMENT...

ME + SADDAM VERSUS THE GEORGE BUSH AMERICA!

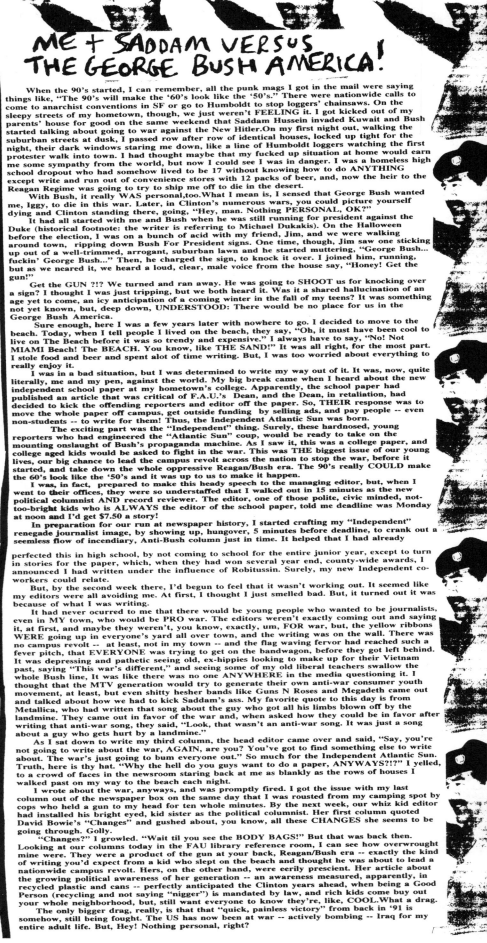

When the 90's started, I can remember, all the punk mags I got in the mail were saying things like, "The 90's will make the '60's look like the '50's." There were nationwide calls to come to anarchist conventions in SF or go to Humboldt to stop loggers' chainsaws. On the sleepy streets of my hometown, though, we just weren't FEELING it. I got kicked out of my parents' house for good on the same weekend that Saddam Hussein invaded Kuwait and Bush started talking about going to war against the New Hitler.On my first night out, walking the suburban streets at dusk, I passed row after row of identical houses, locked up tight for the night, their dark windows staring me down, like a line of Humboldt loggers watching the first protester walk into town. I had thought maybe that my fucked up situation at home would earn me some sympathy from the world, but now I could see I was in danger. I was a homeless high school dropout who had somehow lived to be 17 without knowing how to do ANYTHING except write and run out of convenience stores with 12 packs of beer, and, now the heir to the Reagan Regime was going to try to ship me off to die in the desert.

With Bush, it really WAS personal,too.What I mean is, I sensed that George Bush wanted me, Iggy, to die in this war. Later, in Clinton's numerous wars, you could picture yourself dying and Clinton standing there, going, "Hey, man. Nothing PERSONAL, OK?"

It had all started with me and Bush when he was still running for president against the Duke (historical footnote: the writer is referring to Michael Dukakis). On the Halloween before the election, I was on a bunch of acid with my friend, Jim, and we were walking around town, ripping down Bush For President signs. One time, though, Jim saw one sticking up out of a well-trimmed, arrogant, suburban lawn and he started muttering, "George Bush... fuckin' George Bush..." Then, he charged the sign, to knock it over. I joined him, running, but as we neared it, we heard a loud, clear, male voice from the house say, "Honey! Get the gun!"

Get the GUN ?!? We turned and ran away. He was going to SHOOT us for knocking over a sign? I thought I was just tripping, but we both heard it. Was it a shared hallucination of an age yet to come, an icy anticipation of a coming winter in the fall of my teens? It was something not yet known, but, deep down, UNDERSTOOD: There would be no place for us in the George Bush America.

Sure enough, here I was a few years later with nowhere to go. I decided to move to the beach. Today, when I tell people I lived on the beach, they say, "Oh, it must have been cool to live on The Beach before it was so trendy and expensive." I always have to say, "No! Not MIAMI Beach! The BEACH. You know, like THE SAND!" It was all right, for the most part. I stole food and beer and spent alot of time writing. But, I was too worried about everything to really enjoy it.

I was in a bad situation, but I was determined to write my way out of it. It was, now, quite literally, me and my pen, against the world. My big break came when I heard about the new independent school paper at my hometown's college. Apparently, the school paper had published an article that was critical of F.A.U.'s Dean, and the Dean, in retaliation, had decided to kick the offending reporters and editor off the paper. So, THEIR response was to move the whole paper off campus, get outside funding by selling ads, and pay people -- even non-students -- to write for them! Thus, the Independent Atlantic Sun was born.

The exciting part was the "Independent" thing. Surely, these hardnosed, young reporters who had engineered the "Atlantic Sun" coup, would be ready to take on the mounting onslaught of Bush's propaganda machine. As I saw it, this was a college paper, and college aged kids would be asked to fight in the war. This was THE biggest issue of our young lives, our big chance to lead the campus revolt across the nation to stop the war, before it started, and take down the whole oppressive Reagan/Bush era. The 90's really COULD make the 60's look like the '50's and it was up to us to make it happen.

I was, in fact, prepared to make this heady speech to the managing editor, but, when I went to their offices, they were so understaffed that I walked out in 15 minutes as the new political columnist AND record reviewer. The editor, one of those polite, civic minded, not-too-bright kids who is ALWAYS the editor of the school paper, told me deadline was Monday at noon and I'd get $7.50 a story!

In preparation for our run at newspaper history, I started crafting my "Independent" renegade journalist image, by showing up, hungover, 5 minutes before deadline, to crank out a seemless flow of incendiary, Anti-Bush column just in time. It helped that I had already perfected this in high school, by not coming to school for the entire junior year, except to turn in stories for the paper, which, when they had won several year end, county-wide awards, I announced I had written under the influence of Robitussin. Surely, my new Independent co-workers could relate.

But, by the second week there, I'd begun to feel that it wasn't working out. It seemed like my editors were all avoiding me. At first, I thought I just smelled bad. But, it turned out it was because of what I was writing.

It had never ocurred to me that there would be young people who wanted to be journalists, even in MY town, who would be PRO war. The editors weren't exactly coming out and saying it, at first, and maybe they weren't, you know, exactly, um, FOR war, but, the yellow ribbons WERE going up in everyone's yard all over town, and the writing was on the wall. There was no campus revolt -- at least, not in my town -- and the flag waving fervor had reached such a fever pitch, that EVERYONE was trying to get on the bandwagon, before they got left behind. It was depressing and pathetic seeing old, ex-hippies looking to make up for their Vietnam past, saying "This war's different," and seeing some of my old liberal teachers swallow the whole Bush line, It was like there was no one ANYWHERE in the media questioning it. I thought that the MTV generation would try to generate their own anti-war consumer youth movement, at least, but even shitty hesher bands like Guns N Roses and Megadeth came out and talked about how we had to kick Saddam's ass. My favorite quote to this day is from Metallica, who had written that song about the guy who got all his limbs blown off by the landmine. They came out in favor of the war and, when asked how they could be in favor after writing that anti-war song, they said, "Look, that wasn't an anti-war song. It was just a song about a guy who gets hurt by a landmine."

As I sat down to write my third column, the head editor came over and said, "Say, you're not going to write about the war, AGAIN, are you? You've got to find something else to write about. The war's just going to bum everyone out." So much for the Independent Atlantic Sun. Truth, here is thy hat. "Why the hell do you guys want to do a paper, ANYWAYS?!?" I yelled, to a crowd of faces in the newsroom staring back at me as blankly as the rows of houses I walked past on my way to the beach each night.

I wrote about the war, anyways, and was promptly fired. I got the issue with my last column out of the newspaper box on the same day that I was rousted from my camping spot by cops who held a gun to my head for ten whole minutes. By the next week, our whiz kid editor had installed his bright eyed, kid sister as the political columnist. Her first column quoted David Bowie's "Changes" and gushed about, you know, all these CHANGES she seems to be going through. Golly.

"Changes?" I growled. "Wait til you see the BODY BAGS!" But that was back then. Looking at our columns today in the FAU library reference room, I can see how overwrought mine were. They were a product of the gun at your back, Reagan/Bush era -- exactly the kind of writing you'd expect from a kid who slept on the beach and thought he was about to lead a nationwide campus revolt. Hers, on the other hand, were eerily prescient. Her article about the growing political awareness of her generation -- an awareness measured, apparently, in recycled plastic and cans -- perfectly anticipated the Clinton years ahead, when being a Good Person (recycling and not saying "nigger") is mandated by law, and rich kids come buy out your whole neighborhood, but, still want everyone to know they're, like, COOL.What a drag.

The only bigger drag, really, is that that "quick, painless victory" from back in '91 is somehow, still being fought. The US has now been at war -- actively bombing -- Iraq for my entire adult life. But, Hey! Nothing personal, right?

FINANCIAL DISTRICT FUN!

COULD THIS SHITTY HOMEMADE COUPON (BELOW) GET YOU AND 12,000 OF YOUR FRIENDS FREE COFFEE AT STARBUCKS? XEROX IT AT HOME AND TRY FOR YOURSELF! SCAM RECOMMENDS COLORED PAPER..

COME GET TO KNOW US!!!
STARBUCK'S is probably coming to a corner near you. Come try one *Venti* **"COFFEE OF THE DAY"**, or a *Solo* **Espresso** drink, **ABSOLUTELY FREE!**
No purchase necessary. Offer valid at any Starbuck's
(Expiration 01/01/01)

www.starbucks.com

THE "FAKE COUPON" SCAM HAS, OF COURSE, BEEN AROUND FOR A LONG TIME NOW. YOU KNOW — PEOPLE USING FAIRLY PRIMITIVE COMPUTER GRAPHICS PROGRAMS TO MAKE FAKE COUPONS THAT YOU CAN TRADE IN FOR COFFEE GROUNDS AND FREE ICE CREAM AND STUFF. SOMETIMES IT EVEN WORKS IF YOU JUST XEROX REAL ONES. ITS NOT HARD TO CONVINCE YOUR AVERAGE EMPLOYEE AT A CHAIN STORE THAT YOUR SHITTY HOMEMADE COUPON IS REAL AND TO GIVE YOU FREE SHIT.

BUT WHAT ABOUT CONVINCING EVERYONE IN DOWNTOWN SAN FRANCISCO THAT YOUR COUPON'S REAL? ANANDI AND I DECIDED TO SEE WHAT WOULD HAPPEN IF WE USED A COMPUTER AND A SCANNER TO MAKE COUPONS FOR STARBUCKS AND THEN XEROXED, OH, SAY, 12,000 OF THEM AND PASSED THEM OUT IN THE FINANCIAL DISTRICT.

OUR COUPONS, DESPITE BEING PRINTED ON COLOR PAPER, TURNED OUT PRETTY GHETTO LOOKING, BUT SOMEHOW THAT SEEMED EVEN BETTER. LIKE, HOW RIDICULOUSLY BAD COULD YOU MAKE THEM AND STILL HAVE THEM ACTUALLY WORK? AFTER ENDLESS DAYS OF HALF-ASSEDLY CUTTING OUT THE TINY STRIPS, WE WENT DOWNTOWN TO SEE.

ANTONIO TOOK A PILE TO POWELL AND MARKET AND SARAH WENT TO UNION SQUARE, LEAVING ME AND ANANDI AT MONTGOMERY AND MARKET, ABOVE THE MUNI STATION, JUST 2 BLOCKS FROM A STARBUCKS. ACTUALLY, EVERY CORNER DOWNTOWN IS ONLY 2 BLOCKS FROM A STARBUCKS. THAT WAS THE BEST PART.

WHEN WE SHOWED UP AT MONTGOMERY, LUCKILY, THERE WAS ALREADY SOME WOMEN PASSING OUT SAMPLE PACKETS OF EXCEDRIN WHICH ADDED LEGITIMACY TO OUR CAUSE. WHEN THE FIRST ODDLY CUT, IRREGULAR LOOKING COUPON WAS PASSED FROM MY HAND TO THE HANDS OF A PASSING SUIT, I WAS EXCITED. IT WAS STARTING!

MONTGOMERY STREET IS THE CAPITOL OF THE WHOLE FAKE ECONOMY. THE STOCK TRADING, INTERNET STOCKS, REAL ESTATE SPECULATION; THIS IS WHERE IT ALL GOES DOWN. AFTER A COUPLE MINUTES OF HANDING THEM OUT, PEOPLE IN SUITS WERE EXCITEDLY COMING BACK FOR MORE. PEOPLE WERE QUITE LITERALLY WALKING ONE WAY WITH THE COUPON, AND WALKING BACK BY A MINUTE LATER, HOLDING BIG, FREE COFFEE CUPS! ANANDI, HERSELF, DECIDED SHE NEEDED COFFEE, SO SHE WENT TO THE ONE 2 BLOCKS AWAY. SHE SAID THERE WAS A BIG PILE OF OUR COUPONS BY THE REGISTER AND EVERYONE IN LINE WAS GETTING FREE COFFEE! WHICH RAISES THE QUESTION, "IF I SAY ITS A COUPON FOR FREE COFFEE, AND THE CUSTOMER THINKS ITS A COUPON FOR FREE COFFEE, AND THE STORE GIVES THEM FREE COFFEE, IS IT STILL A FAKE COUPON?"

APPARENTLY SO. AFTER WE'D BEEN THERE CLOSE TO TWO HOURS AND HAD PROBABLY, AT ALL 3 SPOTS, PUT OVER 2,000 COUPONS ON THE STREET, A MAN CAME UP TO ME AND SAID, "I'M A STARBUCKS REPRESENTATIVE! YOU HAVE NO AUTHORIZATION TO PASS THOSE OUT! GIVE THOSE ALL TO ME!" HE WAS MAD. I SHRUGGED AND HANDED HIM THE 4, OR 5 LEFT IN MY HAND AND SAID, "LOOK, MAN, THIS GUY GAVE ME 20 BUCKS TO PASS THESE OUT FOR 4 HOURS, AND, IT LOOKS LIKE I'M DONE IN TWO!" AND STARTED WALKING AWAY, THE GUY TRIED TO INTERCEPT ANANDI AS SHE QUICKLY SPLIT THE OTHER WAY. HE SAID, "STOP! YOU'RE UNDER CITIZEN'S ARREST!" BUT SHE JUST SAID, "YEAH RIGHT!" AND KEPT GOING. NOW THAT WE CAN'T PASS THEM OUT IN THE STREET, I THINK WE'LL JUST LEAVE THE OTHER 10,000 IN STACKS AT LAUNDROMATS AND THRIFT STORES, AND MAIL THEM TO OTHER CITIES.

ON THE WAY HOME, I TRIED TO GET COFFEE AT THE STARBUCKS AT POWELL AND MARKET, BUT THE GIRL BEHIND THE COUNTER FLIPPED OUT AND YELLED, "WE DON'T TAKE THOSE! I DON'T KNOW WHO MADE THEM BUT WE'RE FLOODED WITH THEM. OUR COUPONS ALL HAVE UPC CODES TO SCAN!" THANKS FOR THE INFO. READERS OF SCAM #1 WILL REMEMBER THAT U.P.C. CODES STILL WORK WHEN YOU XEROX THEM!

THROWING SHIT OFF THE ROOF OF MACY'S!!!

MACY'S ISN'T EXACTLY THE FINANCIAL DISTRICT, BUT UNION SQUARE'S CLOSE ENOUGH... A COUPLE YEARS AGO, THE U.S. STARTED BOMBING IRAQ AGAIN. OR MAYBE IT WAS OUR LONG-TIME ENEMIES, SUDAN. OR, WAIT, WAS IT KOSOVO? I FORGET. ITS ALL BLURRED TOGETHER IN THE CLINTON YEARS. BUT I WAS PISSED AND BITTER. THE U.S. HAS BEEN AT WAR WITH IRAQ FOR MY ENTIRE ADULT LIFE, NOW, BUT ITS JUST BUSINESS AS USUAL. TO POINT THIS OUT, I MADE ABOUT 10,000 TINY STRIPS OF PAPER THAT SAID, "AREN'T YOU GLAD THIS A FALLING FLYER AND NOT A BOMB? NO WAR IN IRAQ!" AND THREW THEM OFF THE ROOF OF MACY'S ONTO RICH SHOPPERS AND TOURISTS BELOW! GRETA CAME WITH ME TO FILM THE SLOWLY FLUTTERING PAPER FROM BELOW. SHE SAID EVERYONE YELLED, "LOOK! TICKER TAPE!" AND GATHERED AROUND TO CATCH IT AND READ IT! WHEN I GOT OUT OF THE BUILDING, UNDETECTED, IT WAS STILL FALLING AND A CROWD WAS READING THEM. THEY DIDN'T LOOK AS HAPPY AS THE PEOPLE WHO GOT THE FREE COFFEE WOULD LATER LOOK, BUT, HEY, THAT'S JUST TOO BAD, HUH?

BIKES DURING

Previous to the Gulf War, the bike scene was politicized, but it was all exercising the right to have fun and be addicted to adrenaline. Then with the advent of a hugely unpopular, thinly-veiled oil war, bike riding took on a new urgency and relevance. There were always environmental bikeys, but we drunken bikers didn't hang out with them, really, and vice versa. Now we all had something in common.

During the war, the bicycle became the symbol of constructive protest. It was the opposite of a car. Cars, and the attendant oil-based economy, were the enemy of the people, and everyone finally admitted it. Protest rides swelled to mammoth numbers, and were a graceful, beautiful, leaderless current of riders, a quiet orchestra of free wheels spinning inevitably towards the Bay bridge, or some other vulnerable major artery, enormously successful at halting traffic, causing untold chaos, and almost always avoiding injury by the fuzz.

Like after the earthquake, though, there was a weird sense of, like, *power-outage*. This was because the riots and protests that we saw and caused each day were 100% blacked out of the broadcast news. My understanding was that during the Vietnam war, the news media were *VERY* interested in reporting protest and war footage, even if only to boost ratings. But conversely, in the IRAQ War, even the most sensational flagburning and street-lying-in and property destruction and fuzz-baiting failed to make it into the public information pool. The news just wasn't showing it.

This began as curious, but grew more and more eerie and distressing. It soon became apparent that the consolidation of the TV networks and defense industry was *more of a force than sensationalism*. That's what was really creepy. ALL THOSE PARANOID LEFTIES WERE RIGHT! It made you feel like the whole city could be reduced to ashes and the news would still be showing cockpit images of smart bombs via infrared, and flashing the president's approval rating...

Which in a way, is what happened. One of the fun things that people did were starting fires in the middle of Market Street, in front of the Chevron building, like EVERY NIGHT. I don't know where the rest of the populace was at that time...But no one seemed to want to drive on Market, or stop us. I'm not a big fan of hippie drumming, and in a weird way the appearance of a large fire in a crowd seems to signal the onset of some shirtless individuals with drums between their knees, so that would be my cue to leave.

During the nights, there were so many simultaneous protests that you could ride around downtown from one to the other, torchlit decentralized outbreaks of anger and indignation in the streets. From Folsom and First, or so, you could see the masses up on the Transbay Terminal overpass thing, in *mano a mano* combat with the overwhelmed riot police. There were a number of us below, stopped on our bikes with our cardboard signs, watching in wonder. It was really neat to see.

There must have just been HUGE numbers of us, though, because for most of it, the police just did nothing. They certainly did nothing effective. I remember being chased down U.N. Plaza by some fuzz, after defacing a federal building, but his pursuit was half hearted, and not really a threat.

After a day of holding signs and a night of breaking windows, we would head back to the Mission to regroup. Someone would turn on a TV, and once again we would be enraged by the boosterism. Even our own lame KQED got in on the censorship, by refusing to air any dissenting opinions.

So, in one of the coolest events of the resistance process, somebody put together a show where they projected video footage of protests from all over the country, on the side of the KQED building on York St.! (the flyer said something like, "see the real news on KQED!") There wasn't a sound system, but I think the organizer was narrating and commenting on a bullhorn. It was at night, and a huge crowd was there, and the KQED supposed-liberals were hunkered in their studios, sucking up to their corporate sponsors through the whole event (and the whole war, frankly). It was neat to see that people in all these other towns were as outraged as we were; I mean aside from that it was fun to have a movie party in the street in the Mission, it was really great to see the footage, and see people in Madison, Wisconsin and Butler, Pennsylvania, running onto basketball courts during games and laying down on the floorboards with protest signs (and more stuff that didn't make it to the major network news). Well, fuck KQED, we saw it ourselves!

WARTIME by GUERA

I don't like to write about stuff from long ago, because I've always prioritized imagination over accuracy. I just can't remember what really happened, it seems, because certain details seems really vivid to me, details which may be completely fictitious. That said, I remember going to a noontime bike ride/protest on a beautiful sunny day, by myself. There were a few hundred people there already. As usual, during massive protest rides, the bikes replaced the cars and spread out over all the lanes, and so an eerie quiet took over.

This was before Critical Mass, it's important to note. The bike riders didn't usually ride together, and many cyclists were sort of eyeing the others around them with appraisal, or even suspicion. There was no whooping, no bell-ringing. It was a tense anticipation, not a monolithic mob. Plus, it was daytime, downtown, so no one was hardly even drunk. There was a little chanting of anti-war slogans, and there was a half-assed police motorcycle escort. The ride started heading east on Market, and turned south on Second street. Soon enough, we were all at the foot of the on-ramp of the Bay Bridge, on Harrison and First. It seemed like there was no leader, just everybody heading towards the bridge in unison. The police were scurrying to head us off, but they were never fast enough. It was as if they couldn't bring themselves to believe that we would go there.

There was a sort of a wordless standoff at the edge of the ramp, where two sorry cops were standing alone at the head of it, trying to look big enough to intimidate what must have been 300 or 400 bikes by that time... After maybe twenty seconds, some biker said, "Fuck it, I'm going!" Then we all surged forward and the two fuzz had to step aside. We merged onto the bridge, more motorcycle cops showed up, and we pretty much used the west end of the bridge to block all the traffic.

Once on the bridge, the actual protest was fairly uneventful (except when Iraya kicked over the WHOLE ROW of cop motorcycles, achieving instant arrest and a "FREE IRAYA" campaign). The exciting thing was that we were successful, we effected the sneak attack, we were where we were not allowed, it was a rare view. It was spontaneous, energetic, dangerous, and not bogged down by bureaucracy. It was everything the Critical Mass is not.

My favorite thing, though, and a weird side effect of the IRAQ War, was the bike rides that took place after the initial anti-war effort. I mean, in retrospect, it was a fleeting moment. The first 49-mile ride, for example, was a bonanza of *both* spandex and beer - it seems to me that do-gooder cyclists and drunk punk bikers and messengers were like the peaceable kingdom (that painting where the jungle animals are all kickin it in harmony.) Guys in shiny shorts were sharing beers at each stop (well, at least they were waiting patiently while the rest of us shared beers) and we, for our part, were all more or less sticking to the route.

Now we have Critical Mass, and way more bikes in general. I guess that means progress. There are enough bikers that people have gone back to their separate cliques, and they have plenty of events to go to so they don't need to really intermingle. Maybe I don't even want to intermingle, to tell you the truth. But it was a cool thing while it lasted.

"NEW COLLEGE ON VALENCIA BOARDED UP THEIR WINDOWS WHEN THE GULF WAR STARTED"

ORGANIZE

RESIST

PHOTO   BILL DANIEL

I

In an old hotel, downtown. Off a small alley. It was a neighborhood where, if the cops came, no one ever saw anything. There were surveilance cameras everywhere. Some days, men on every corner would be talking to themselves, as if there was a radio station that only they got.

Rainy mornings. Lost under umbrellas, collecting cans. I walked in crowds between tall buildings. Everyday streets, walked deeper and deeper into a maze There were dead ends. Secret places. Hotel hallways and darkened bars. From my window, I could see a dumpster where a different man shot up every morning.

I did street outreach, passing out flyers about our services, to men in doorways. There were black guys with trash bags on their feet, men selling trash they'd found. Often, I'd see our clients in line at a corner store, or waiting to be buzzed in at a hotel, and I'd avoid eye contact, if they were with a non-client. I knew their biggest secret.

Secrets. Past lives. Hiding places. When we had sex, I'd remember the hum of old elevators coming to life. All I remembered was the murmur of pigeons in the airshaft between buildings, where the sun would never shine.

A man with a white mask over his mouth would empty trash into the dumpste across the alley every morning. Cops walked the streets with white, latex gloves on. I passed out condoms and lube to HIV positive clients, only.

On the 5th floor of the new Main Library, I found a book that said my hote was 62 years old. There were crowded days and old newspapers. Steaming coffee, waiting. She would stand in the alley and yell my name. Like a neon sign in a bar.

When I moved out, I still had her umbrella. Stuff was sad, the things you had owned. It lasted too long. Joseph Loya, apparently, died on Jones Street, but his stuff made it 2 blocks further up Turk. All of the letters were addressed to him. He hadn't been to the Russian Orthodox church in the Avenues since 1981. Someone named Buddy had sent him a postcard of the St. Louis arch in 1980 to his room at the YMCA in Houston. Someone was trying to sell it, but I just took it home and put it on my wall.

That night, I laid in bed, listening to the sounds in the alley. 62 years I would catch myself, sometimes, falling asleep, and sit bolt upright in bed.

Tenderloin

II

There was a mysterious smoke stack that I could see from my window, maybe 2 blocks from my place, and sometimes it gave off a steamy emission. I had always felt oddly drawn to it, and one day, I set out to once and for all, find its exact location. When I found it, in the center of a block, the fence in front of it was lined with men, smoking crack.

In my room, there was an ornamental strip of wood that ran around the perimeter of the room, about a foot and a half from the ceiling. After I'd liv there for about 6 months, I noticed a small orange dot out of the corner of my eye, just at the edge of this wood. I climbed up on a chair to see what it was. It was a clean, unused syringe with an orange safety tip. The last occupant, or the occupant before had hidden it up there. Holding it, I felt

time seemed to blur. This could be any of the hotel's 62 years. Dead ends and hiding places. Secrets and past lives. I put it back up there for the next guy to find when I moved out.

Our office was a converted storefront. The place was old, from before the world had ever heard of AIDS, or even the CIA. We had everyone's name on a list. I knew most of our clients by sight, but if I didn't know them, I'd have to look them up on the list. Everyone on the list had an incurable disease. But, day in and day out, they were surprisingly upbeat people. They only got upset if I had to get out the list. The very sight of it would enrage them. A 6 foot tall guy with a red wig on and a very ill fitting skirt would come in who I had never seen before, and I'd say, "Name please..." She'd say "Ginger". I'd pause. They could tell the list was coming. They'd start to quake with rage. "I come here every day!" they'd yell. But, finally, if they wanted their food bag, they would settle down and whisper, "Michael Ellis." The disease didn't seem to bother them, in a way, as much as their real names...

It seems we never get to control our real names in the library. We never get to see the list. The secret history might be in the old library, across the street from the new one, which spent much of the last few years surrounded by huge weeds and unmowed grass. I imagined the old history stacks covered in mold, surrounded by ten-foot fennel plants. There was a secret history inplaces where time stood still.

Sometimes, blackout drunk, she and I would have sex andshe would try to put it in without a condom. I'd think of elevator shafts and alleys, of hallways and hidden needles, and feel myself falling. And not wanting to catch myself.

In our office in the old storefront, a tranny sighed, "I wonder what this place used to BE..."

III

January turned to February. It was still raining. A girl at work told me about people who lived in tunnels under the Tenderloin and downtown. She said she'd found tunnel entrances in the basement of her old squat, and that her and her friends had gone in them and explored a little, but, basically, it was just too damn scary.

I became sort-of obsessed with finding the tunnels. I started by looking for entrances in the crater lots where buildings had been knocked down, downto There was one behind my hotel, full of weeds and broken TV's. With most of them, from the sidewalk, you just saw a fence, but if you snuck in, there'd be a huge field, walls covered with graffiti , and, sometimes, whole communities of people living just under the sidewalk. But there were no tunnel

An oldtimer in Chinatown told me, "Of course I know about the tunnels. People go in 'em down on Commerce Street, around the corner." Commerce turned out to be a one-block dead end on the other side of North Beach. Did he maybe mean "Commercial" which WAS right around the corner?

I checked every manhole cover on Commercial, but there was nothing.

I walked through a tent city in Civic Center to go check on finding some kind of old tunnel map in the new library. But, the new library with its huge unassailable looking walls, looked like it was built just to keep information from the streets out of it. I couldn't find anything. It seemed like they only had computers now, and no books.

Later, I read an article about the library that said they HAD thrown out tons of books. They had put them in storage... in a tunnel under Civic Center.

IV

Lately, I've had my own secret. I've been hiding stuff in the library. I started by putting stuff in the clipping files. I'd write stuff and just put it in. I put all my magazines in them, in the corresponding files. Then, I started making my own files. I took pictures of old bar signs in the Tenderloin and made a "Signs" file of my own and put it in. I started working on a punk flyer file. I go back and check and its all still there.

I've also made name tags for shelves so I could put my magazines up in the periodical section and make it look like the library ordered it. I mean, sure, they're already in the Special Collections, but whoever can find out when that room is even open? Now, I prefer just to get it right up on the shelf. Maybe I just still feel bad about stealing a couple books from the library when I was 15... But, piece by piece, I'm building a secret history collection.

THE SIDEWALKS OF SAN FRANCISCO

WHILE I WAS WORKING ON TAKING THE PHOTOS FOR THIS PROJECT,
I WAS OUT ON HAIGHT, NEAR FILLMORE, WHEN THIS GUY I'D MET AT
A SHOW A COUPLE NIGHTS BEFORE CAME UP AND ASKED WHAT I WAS
UP TO. I WAS TELLING HIM ABOUT HOW I WAS COMPILING CEMENT ETCHING
PHOTOS, BECAUSE I THOUGHT THEY WERE SORT-OF COOL AND MYSTERIOUS.
WHO WERE THESE PEOPLE ANYWAY, AND WHY DID THEY CHOOSE TO WRITE
WHAT THEY WROTE, WHEN THEY COULD HAVE WRITTEN ANYTHING? I WAS
TELLING HIM THIS WHEN I STOPPED TO TAKE A PICTURE OF ONE OF THE MANY
"SPEED RACER" TAGS IN THE CEMENT IN THE LOWER HAIGHT. HE ASKED, "YOU
KNOW ABOUT THAT GUY?" I DIDN'T, BUT I HAD ALWAYS WONDERED A LITTLE.
"WELL," HE SAID, "SPEED RACER WAS A BAND THAT LIVED HERE IN THE LOWER
HAIGHT, THE SINGER WAS THIS BIG, CRAZY, ATHLETIC GUY — JUST A REALLY FUN
GUY, THEY WERE SORT-OF PUNK, BUT THIS WAS THE LATE '80'S WHEN EVERYONE
WAS SORT-OF HEADING INTO THAT GUNS 'N' ROSES THING. WELL, THE
SINGER O.D.'D. IT WAS REALLY HEAVY. HE WASN'T EVEN A JUNKIE. HE JUST DID
IT A COUPLE TIMES AND DIED. VERY SAD..."

SO THAT WAS "SPEED RACER." I TOOK FOUR, OR FIVE SHOTS OF THOSE THAT DAY.
LOVE MESSAGES, BAND NAMES, POLITICAL SLOGANS, R.I.P.'S, HAND PRINTS
AND "FUCK YOU!"'S. I FOUND JUST ABOUT EVERYTHING IN THE CEMENT, A
SORT-OF SUBTLE DAY-IN, DAY-OUT HISTORY OF THE STREETS WE LIVE IN.
PLENTY OF DOGS AND PIGEONS WERE EVEN AROUND AT THE RIGHT TIME TO
LEAVE THEIR MARK ON OLE ESS EFF.
AFTER A COUPLE MONTHS OF TAKING PHOTOS, I BECAME OBSESSED WITH
STOPPING TO READ EVERY ETCHING I PASSED. I'D SEE ONE OF AN UNUSUAL
NAME, LIKE "ARIZONA JOE", OR SOMETHING, DATED FROM 1974 ON HAIGHT STREET
AND WONDER WHY OLE JOE CAME TO THE CITY. WAS HE JUST TOO LATE FOR THE
60'S IN THE HAIGHT? I'D LOOK AROUND TO SEE IF THERE WAS A CHURCH AROUND
WHERE JOE MIGHT HAVE PICKED UP SOME FREE MEALS BEFORE HE HEADED OFF
TO WHEREVER HE HEADED.

IT SEEMS LIKE A SILLY OBSESSION, MAYBE, BUT IT COULD BE REALLY
SATISFYING, TOO. LAST YEAR, I WAS RESEARCHING THE 1970 TRIAL OF LOS SIETE
DE LA RAZA. LOS SIETE WERE SEVEN LATINO YOUTHS FROM THE MISSION, ALL
SOMEWHAT ACTIVE IN NEIGHBORHOOD AND STUDENT POLITICS, WHO WERE DUBIOUSLY
CHARGED WITH THE MURDER OF A NOTORIOUSLY RACIST IRISH COP AND THE WOUNDING
OF HIS PARTNER IN A 1969 ALTERCATION. THEIR ARREST AND SUBSEQUENT TRIAL
BROUGHT A LOT OF ATTENTION TO THE POVERTY, LACK OF SERVICES, AND ROUTINE POLICE
BRUTALITY SUFFERED BY THE MISSION'S MAJORITY LATIN POPULATION. DURING THE
TRIAL A GRASSROOTS ORGANIZATION, ALSO NAMED LOS SIETE DE LA RAZA STARTED
OFFERING FREE LEGAL SERVICES, FREE BREAKFAST PROGRAMS AT NEIGHBORHOOD CHURCHES,
AND EVEN A NEIGHBORHOOD NEWSPAPER CALLED "¡BASTA YA!" (TRANSLATED LOOSELY
AS "WE'VE HAD ENOUGH OF THIS SHIT!") EVENTUALLY, THEY EVEN BRANCHED OUT INTO
RUNNING A RESTAURANT, ALSO CALLED "BASTA YA", NEAR THE LEVI-STRAUSS FACTORY
IN AN ATTEMPT TO PROVIDE CHEAP MEALS FOR AND TO POLITICALLY ORGANIZE THE
WOMEN IMMIGRANTS WHO WORKED THERE.
WELL, IT MAY HAVE JUST BEEN A BAD IDEA TO CALL A RESTAURANT "WE'VE
HAD ENOUGH OF THIS SHIT!" BUT FOR ONE REASON OR ANOTHER, THE RESTAURANT
FAILED. I'D ALWAYS READ ABOUT IT AS BEING "NEAR LEVI-STRAUSS", BUT I'D
WONDERED EXACTLY WHERE THE RESTAURANT HAD BEEN. USING AN OLD CITY
DIRECTORY, I FINALLY TRACED IT TO 260 VALENCIA, THE SIGHT OF TODAY'S

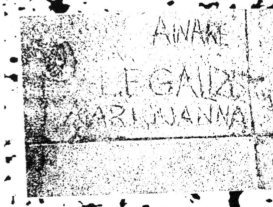

"PAULINE'S PIZZA" RIGHT NEXT TO THE LEVI-STRAUSS FACTORY.
BUT MY SEARCH DIDN'T SEEM COMPLETE UNTIL LATER. ONE DAY, WHILE
WALKING BY THE FACTORY, I FOUND IN THE CEMENT ON CLINTON PARK, AT
VALENCIA, "FREE LOS SIETE." THERE IT WAS, JUST AROUND THE CORNER
FROM EL BASTA YA, A KEY TO A VERY DIFFERENT MISSION DISTRICT. I COULD FEEL
THE 1970 SUMMER SUN AND IMAGINE LONG-HAIRED LATIN KIDS ON EVERY CORNER
AND "FREE HUEY!" RALLIES, AND, AS ALWAYS, THE WHITE COPS ON THE BEAT. I
COULD SEE THE SHIFTING LAYERS OF HISTORY, THE DISAPPOINTMENT AND STRUGGLE
WRITTEN IN THE CONCRETE WALKED SO CARELESSLY TODAY BY THE YOUNG, WHITE,
AND HIP. FOR GOOD MEASURE, SOMEONE HAD SCRAWLED NEXT TO IT, "IMPEACH
PIG NIXON!"

ANOTHER TIME, I WAS LISTENING TO THE "THESE PEOPLE" RECORD BY THE DICKS, WHICH FEATURES, ON THE BACK COVER, THE DICKS STANDING NEXT TO A NEWLY PLANTED "FRIENDS OF THE URBAN FOREST" TREE AND A SQUARE OF FRESH, WET CEMENT IN WHICH SOMEONE, PRESUMABLY THE DICKS THEMSELVES, HAD WRITTEN THE MIS-SPELLED "FIGHT FOR SOCIASM", JUST LIKE THAT, WITHOUT THE "L". LATER THAT NIGHT, I WALKED DOWN 15TH AND TO MY SURPRISE WALKED RIGHT BY THE VERY SAME ETCHING! IN THE 15 YEARS SINCE THE RECORD CAME OUT, THE TREE'S GROWN PRETTY HUGE! BUT "SOCIASM" WILL BE MIS-SPELLED FOREVER.

I GUESS I'LL NEVER KNOW IF IT WAS PAUL WESTERBERG HIMSELF WHO WROTE "THE REPLACEMENTS" IN THE CEMENT UP IN THE PANHANDLE. AND DID BLACK FLAG HIT THE CEMENT ON FILLMORE WHILE THEY WERE OUT WHEAT PASTIN FOR A SHOW HERE IN TOWN? MY THEORY ON BAND NAMES IS THAT ANY BAND THAT PEOPLE CARE ENOUGH ABOUT TO GET TATTOOS OF, LIKE FLIPPER OR BLACK FLAG, IS SO BIG THAT ANYBODY COULD HAVE WRITTEN THEIR NAMES IN CEMENT. BUT I DOUB EVEN THE GIRLFRIENDS OF THE BRIAN JONESTOWN MASSACRE WOULD HAVE WRITTEN THEIR NAME ON 3RD IN CHINA BASIN. IT HAD TO BE THE BAND.

BUT WHAT ABOUT THE LEWD, WRITTEN ON MISSION OVER BY THE WELFARE OFFICE WERE THEY GETTING THEIR CHECKS WHEN THEY TAGGED IT, WAY BACK WHEN? WERE THE THE FIRST S.F. PUNK ROCKERS ON WELFARE? OR WAS THE WELFARE OFFICE EVEN AT 8TH AND MISSION BACK THEN?

ON MY SEARCH I FOUND THAT NORTH BEACH HAD THE OLDEST STUFF, THE MISSION HAD ALL THE GANG STUFF, AND HAIGHT STREET HAD THE MOST ETCHINGS SAYING, "TAKE LSD!" I THOUGHT THAT WAS PRETTY CREEPY, IN A WAY, CONSIDER 50'S EARLY HISTORY AS CIA MIND CONTROL EXPERIMENT, AND HOW IT COULD THEN END UP AS THE FIRST THING THAT CROSSES SOME DROOLING HIPPY'S MIND T WRITE WHEN CONFRONTED WITH WET CEMENT. STILL, BESIDES "TAKE L.S.D."! HAIGHT STREET JUST HAD THE MOST ETCHINGS, PERIOD.

BUT MAYBE NOT FOR LONG. THE NEIGHBORHOOD HAS CLEARLY CHANGED TO MUCH. RECENTLY, I SAW ALMOST A WHOLE SIDEWALK OF WET CEMENT AT AGE AND SHRADER! I COULDN'T WAIT TO HIT IT WITH MY OWN ETCHING, BUT THERE WERE TWO THUG-LIKE BOUNCER-TYPES THAT WERE ACTUALLY GUARDING THE CEMENT! FUCK THAT! WE WANT THE SIDEWALKS!

SO I WENT DOWN TO THE PANHANDLE TO WAIT 'TIL THEY SPLIT. SURE NOUGH, IN A COUPLE MINUTES, THEY WERE GONE AND I RAN BACK UP THE LOCK, BENT OVER, DRUM KEY IN HAND, AND STARTED WRITING. I WAS HALFW ONE WHEN I HEARD A VOICE FROM ABOVE YELL, "HEY! YOU! CUT IT OUT.

I KEPT WRITING.

"HEY YOU! LEAVE THAT ALONE! WE JUST POURED IT!"

I IGNORED THEM. SOON, A COUPLE OF ANGRY CONSTRUCTION WORKERS WERE RUNNING OUT OF THE HOUSE AT ME WITH A WELL DRESSED MAN, APPARENTLY THE PROPERTY OWNER, IN TOW. "WE TOLD YOU TO STOP THAT!" ONE YELLED.

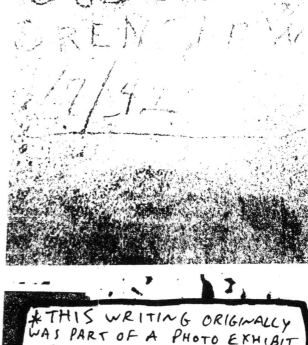

*THIS WRITING ORIGINALLY WAS PART OF A PHOTO EXHIBIT I DID AT THE BEARDED LADY CAFE IN S.F. OF OVER 200 PHOTOS OF CEMENT ETCHINGS IN THE CITY. THE SHOW WAS ON FROM 12/99 TO 2/00

"HE WANTS IT CLEAN!" YELLED THE OTHER, INDICATING THE OWNER.

I ARGUED. I SAID, "WHAT ABOUT THE TRADITION OF CEMENT ETCHING? WHAT ABOUT THE MYSTERY OF LONG LOST INITIALS, THE POETRY? WHAT ABOUT THE POIGNANCY OF PEOPLE WRITING 'SO AND SO PLUS SO AND SO FOREVER'?!?"

THEY STARED BLANKLY. THEY WEREN'T GETTING IT. THE OWNER FINALLY SPAT, "I WANT IT CLEAN." I SHRUGGED AND LEFT AND THEY WENT TO WORK, SMOOTHING OVER MY WRITING.

I THOUGHT THIS WAS THE END OF IT, BUT A COUPLE MINUTES LATER IN THE PANHANDLE, A COP CAR PULLED UP TO ME. THE COP YELLED, "ALLRIGH YOU! WHAT HAPPENED BACK THERE?!? GOT ANY I.D.?!?"

YES, A GROWN MAN HAD CALLED THE COPS ON ANOTHER GROWN MAN FOR WRITING IN THE CEMENT. PATHETIC. EVEN THE COP SEEMED A LITTLE EMBARRASS WHEN HE REALIZED WHAT IT WAS ALL ABOUT AND JUST SAID, "WELL, UH, DON'T DO IT AGAIN!" AND LET ME GO.

BUT I DID DO IT AGAIN. I CAN'T HELP IT. LAST DECEMBER I WAS RIDING MY BIKE BY CITY HALL WHEN I SAW MAYOR BROWN GIVING A PRESS CONFERENCE IN CIVIC CENTER, ONLY 30 FEET AWAY, ACROSS POLK STREET. APPARENTLY, IT WAS A DEDICATION CEREMONY FOR THE LIGHTING OF THE CHRISTMAS TREE IN THE NEWLY "CLEANED UP" CIVIC CENTER PARK. THE MAYOR, WITH HIS BACK TO ME, WAS TALKING AWAY TO A CREW OF NEWS CAMERAMEN.

I WATCHED FOR A MINUTE AND THEN I REALIZED THAT THE ENTIRE SIDEWALK IN FRONT OF CITY HALL HAD NEW, WET CEMENT! I BENT OVER, KEY IN HAND, DIRECTLY BEHIND THE MAYOR AND PROBABLY ON CAMERA, AND WHILE HE TALKED ABOUT HOW HE CLEANED UP AND REFURBISHED CITY HALL, I WENT TO WORK. I COULDN'T RESIST. I WROTE, "FUCK YOU, WILLIE BROWN!

P.S. THIS EXHIBIT IS DEDICATED TO THE MYSTERIOUS "NIKKO" WHO HA BY FAR, THE MOST ETCHINGS I HAVE SEEN BY ANY ONE INDIVIDUAL IN THE WHOLE CITY. HE'S MOSTLY UP IN NORTH BEACH AND CHINA TOWN, BUT I'VE SPOTTED HIS WORK IN THE TENDERLOIN, RUSSIAN HILL, TELEGRAPH HILL, SOUTH OF MARKET, AND EVEN ON SYCAMORE STREET IN THE MISSION! HOW DID HE DO SO MANY? WAS HE JUST IN THE RIGHT PLACE AT THE RIGHT TIME? WAS HE A WALKING MESSENGER, OR SOMETHING? MAYBE HE' 80, OR 90 YEARS OLD AND HE'S BEEN HITTING THEM HIS WHOLE LIFE. MAYB HE WORKS FOR THE CITY ACTUALLY LAYING CEMENT.

I'LL NEVER KNOW BUT I'LL ALWAYS WONDER.

INFAMOUS DRINKING EVENTS AND THE 21-TOILET RIDE

S.F. 2000

FORGET THE 49-MILE RIDE, HERE'S THE...

21 TOILET RIDE!!

COME JOIN US TO RIDE TO AND DRINK BEER INSIDE OF EACH OF THE JCDECAUX SPACE TOILETS!!!

FIG. 1: DRUNKEN REVELERS INSIDE TOILET AT 16/MISSION...

MEET BEHIND SAFEWAY AT THE...

WHERE: DAPHNE FUNERAL HOME · CHURCH/HERMAN

WHEN: **SATURDAY APRIL 1st 1:00PM**

LITTLE ROCK 1996

COME TO THE RICE STREET "DRUNK-LUCK"!

YOU BRING THE FOOD. THE BEER WE PROVIDE HOUSE!!!

200 THE

PROPERTY VALUE

CRIME RATE

AT 200 RICE STREET

FRIDAY JULY 19th

3:00PM we start cookin' 6:00PM we start drinkin'

CHICAGO 1997

HEY PUNKS! COME AND...

GET DRUNK AS HELL, ON THE EL!!

AT THE 1st ANNUAL "EL PARTY"

CTA

WE, THE PUNKS, WILL MEET AFTER THE CAVITY SHOW (AT THE FIRESIDE BOWL) TO JUST RIDE THE 'EL' BACK AND FORTH AND GET DRUNK ON IT! SHOW UP AT THE "LOGAN SQUARE" STOP ON THE BLUE LINE AND BRING YOUR OWN BEER AND TRANSFER

THURSDAY AUGUST 7TH @ MIDNIGHT

"THIS IS THE MORE DEGENERATE LESS ATHLETIC ALTERNATIVE TO THE FAMED 49-MILE SCENIC RIDE, SINCE AFTER THE TOILET ON TOP OF TWIN PEAKS, THE REST ARE ALL LIKE 2 BLOCKS FROM EACH OTHER... I DIDN'T KNOW WHAT TO EXPECT, BUT THEN PEOPLE CAME WITH COOL EXTRA-LONG FORKED BIKES AND BIKES THAT BREATHED FIRE, SO I KNEW IT WAS ON! WE GOT OFF TO A GOOD START, DRINKING AND MOSHING AROUND INSIDE THE TOILET AT STANYAN AND WALLER. SOMEONE BROUGHT A BAD BRAINS TAPE... IT WAS CLEAR, HOT, AND BEAUTIFUL AT THE TOP OF TWIN PEAKS, SO WE RESTED EXTRA LONG, WHILE WE WAITED TO SEE IF THE JC DECAUX REPRESENTATIVE COULD FIX THE BROKEN TOILET. HE COULDN'T, AND THIS WAS THE START OF A DISGRACEFUL TREND IN OLE ESS EFF, AS WE SAW THAT GUY 5 TIMES ON THE RIDE, CUZ ONLY LIKE 7 OUT OF 21 TOILETS ACTUALLY WORK. THE ONES THAT WERE BROKEN WE JUST SORT-OF DRANK NEAR. DRUNKEN FRISBEE BROKE OUT ON 6TH STREET WHILE I FIXED A FLAT, AND WE LOST HALF OUR CREW FOR GOOD TO GINA'S SHOW AND A BEER SPECIAL... AT BAY AND TAYLOR, A MIME DOING A FIRE SHOW AT THE CABLE CAR STOP, TRIED TO GET CHEAP LAUGHS FROM THE TOURISTS BY CHASING GRETA WITH HIS TORCH. SO SHE COMPLETELY SHOWED HIM UP BY MAKING HIS BIKE BREATH FIRE AND RIDING AT THE MIME! IT WAS HILARIOUS... IN THE END, THERE WERE 21 TOILETS, 4 SURVIVORS, COUNTLESS BEERS DRANK, AND ONLY ONE FISTFIGHT WITH A MUNI BUS DRIVER THAT RESULTED IN A SMASHED BUS WINDOW! NOT BAD... PHOTO BY RIDE FINISHER, CHRIS BECK.

SHEFF SAYS, "FIRST ANNUAL

ANOTHER SCAM EXPERIMENT...

IF YOU CONSIDER YOURSELF A PUNK...

COME HANG OUT ON THE STREETS!!!

THERE'S ALMOST NO SHOWS, BUT WE CAN STILL TAKE BACK THE STREETS! SHOW UP AND BRING BEER, OR SPRAYPAINT, OR WHATEVER YOU THINK YOU NEED TO HANG OUT...

GRAND

FROG MUCK <r

Punk in shopping cart drinking beer

WHERE? AT THE CLOCK IN FRONT OF COCOWALK ON GRAND AVE. IN THE GROVE

FRIDAY APRIL 9TH 9:00PM

I WAS BACK IN MY HOMETOWN FOR A SHORT VISIT, AND I COULDN'T SEEM TO FIND ANYTHING GOING ON. THERE WERE ALMOST NO SHOWS AND JUST A COUPLE DISMAL APARTMENTS WHERE THE LAST FEW PUNKS IN TOWN HID OUT AND DRANK. I COULDN'T EVEN FIND ANY PUNKS IN THE STREETS OF COCONUT GROVE WHERE WE ALWAYS USED TO HANG OUT AND PLAY MUSIC FOR MONEY AND STEAL BEER AND TABLE DIVE AND SPRAY PAINT AND EXPLORE THE ROOFS AND ALLEYS, ALL THE WHILE, OF COURSE, COMPLAINING ABOUT HOW BORING IT WAS AND HOW WE WISHED THERE WAS SOME OLD PUNK WHO HAD A DISMAL APARTMENT WE COULD HANG OUT IN.
     PUNK ROCK, THE MUSIC, IS NOW HERE TO STAY. THE INTELLECTUALS HAVE WEIGHED IN WITH THEIR EPIC OVER-ANALYSIS OF ITS DEEP, HIDDEN MEANINGS AND HAVE PATTED THEMSELVES ON THE BACK FOR GETTING THE JOKE 20 YEARS TOO LATE. PUNK IS, LIKE BLUES OR JAZZ, JUST ANOTHER TYPE OF MUSIC YOU COULD PLAY. BUT WHAT ABOUT "PUNK" — OR "THE PUNKS..."? MAYBE ITS BECAUSE, WHEN I GREW UP, PUNK'S EXISTENCE WAS SO FRAGILE AND WEEK-TO-WEEK, THAT I ALWAYS WORRY ABOUT THE SCENE JUST DISAPPEARING FOREVER. BUT WHEN I COULDN'T FIND PUNKS IN THE STREETS OF THE GROVE, I GOT WORRIED. I DECIDED, IN DESPERATION, TO PUT A FLYER OUT SAYING "IF YOU CONSIDER YOURSELF A PUNK, COME HANG OUT IN THE STREETS "AND SEE WHAT HAPPENED.
     THE FLYER SAID TO MEET AT THE CLOCK AT COCOWALK. WHEN I GOT THERE, IT WAS KIND OF AWKWARD. THERE WAS SOME KIDS AROUND BUT, DESPITE THE LINE-DRAWING NATURE OF THE FLYER, IT TOOK US ALL AWHILE TO REALIZE THAT WE WERE, IN FACT, THE PUNKS, AND WE HAD, IN FACT, ALREADY BEEN "HANGING OUT IN THE STREETS" FOR A COUPLE MINUTES. ONCE THE CONFUSION CLEARED, HOWEVER, THERE WERE 7 OF US WHO HAD CHOSEN TO IDENTIFY OURSELVES AS "PUNK" AND HAD COME TO HANG OUT IN THE STREETS. WE LEFT TOGETHER TO BUY CHEAP BEER AT KWIK-STOP.
     WE SOUGHT OUT THE TRADITIONAL PUNK DRINKING SPOT IN THE SHADOWS BY THE BENCHES OUT FRONT OF THE BARNACLE, AND POURED OUR BEER INTO CUPS. ALL MY OLD FRIENDS HAD STAYED HOME IN THEIR DISMAL APARTMENTS, SO I WAS MEETING THESE KIDS FOR THE FIRST TIME. WE TALKED ABOUT THE GROVE COPS. THEY STILL SUCKED. WE WONDERED IF THERE WERE ANY SHOWS COMING UP. THERE STILL WEREN'T ANY. ONE KID HAD BEEN TRAVELLING AND KNEW MY FRIENDS IN NORTH CAROLINA. IT WAS A PRETTY NICE NIGHT, BUT JUST WHEN WE FINISHED OUR FIRST CASE AND WE'RE GETTING WARMED UP, SUDDENLY THEY ALL STOOD UP TO LEAVE. "WAIT," I SAID. "SHOULDN'T WE GET MORE BEER? I KNOW A GOOD ROOF YOU CAN GET ON JUST BY GETTING A BOOST FROM THE TOP OF THE DUMPSTER IN THE ALLEY..."
     "NAH... THIS IS BEAT," ONE GUY SAID. "LET'S GO SEE IF WE CAN HANG OUT IN ROACH'S APARTMENT..."
     LATER, WHILE DRINKING MILWAUKEE'S BEST AND WATCHING THAT CLASH MOVIE AT ROACH'S APARTMENT, I DIMLY THOUGHT "HMM... MAYBE NOTHING HAS CHANGED..."
     I'M STILL WORRIED.

THE STORY OF THE HANGOVER!

BY ANANDI

SUN. cafe

the HANGOVER cafe
is open every sunday
from 11:00 am to 4:00 pm
we are a all vegan non-profit
collective (sorta) we want to
create a space for the kidz to
come meet eat drink and recove

IF YOUR STILL HUNGRY
WHEN YOUR DONE THEN
TELL US AND WHATEVER
ELSE YOU WANT WE'LL
GIVE YA IT FOR FREE!

The cafe started small: once a week in a storefront where some punks lived, a couple menu options, a few rickety card tables, a dumpstered waffle iron and lots of coffee and you'd have to wait an hour to eat cause there was only one little stove to cook everything and no one prepped cause they were hung over (!) and overslept.... But the way I remember it the best was after we moved into the warehouse space. This place was so amazing! It wasn't perfect (in fact it was eventually the achilles' heel that brought us down) (secretly funded by drug $ works better for the CIA than non-profit anarchist collectives I think) but it was free, it was huge, and it was ours! Not only were we still achieving the 3 biggest and clearest goals we'd had — getting the kids active and busy doing something, anything besides stealing beer (well, in addition to, anyway)), creating a community space/getting everyone in it, together, and serving cheap (food stamps or washing dishes as good as cash, always) tasty vegan food — we suddenly had enough room to do so much more! We opened an area as the lending library with all the materials we felt everyone should read, fully catalogued, and it spontaneously turned into a workhop area too, and we were able to have punk bands play (and some weird hippies too but I don't know whose fault that was).... And as many tables & chairs as we could get our hands on were full, every time! Everyone who came through town that summer got dragg out of bed and in to wash dishes and eat pancakes, it seemed. Bands would come in the morning after their shows and end up bringing the equipment in from the van to play and pass the hat for gas $... And every week the special was fancier, the library was bigger and more political, and we expanded to dinners, and food not bombs cooked in our kitchen, word spread further and wider... and then the collective imploded and all the money disappeared. But by then, we had done enough — the Hangover was a bridge from that slow, hopeless winter to a brighter, more promising year.

BISCUITS & GRAVY   2.00 $
home baked biscuits covered i
nutritional yeast gravy with a
side of soysage toast
and coffee

PEANUT SOUP
with veggies and tea   2.00$

TOFU QUICHE   2.00$
in a dill crust and a side
brown rice toast
and coffee

PANCAKES   2.00$
with maple syrup soysag
toast   and coffee

SKIP'S SUPRIZE   1.00$
it's a suprize stupid wit
toast   and coffe

DEAD MAN WAFFLES   2
with maple syrup soysage to
coffee

THE HIPPY   2.00$
miso soup with shitake mushroom
nori seaweed green onions tofu
and brown rice with tea

DESSERT(when available)
CIGARETTES(singles)
.0c

COFFEE(bottomless)   .75c
TEA   .25c
O.J.   .50c

THE HOMEFRY   2.00$
fried potatoes with tofu and veggies
toast   and coffee

PORTLAND OR.

soymilk and sugar are available
at the coffee station
ketchup salsa jam and margarine
are also available

JOHN SAYS:

"THERE'S A JOB OPENING FOR A LONE GUNMAN IN NEW YORK CITY... AND SOMEDAYS, I THINK I'LL TAKE IT!!!"

Column By JOHN DANIA

World
Bank
APPROVES
China's
Genocide
in Tibet

ABOVE: SCAM COLUMNIST, DANIA (ON THE LEFT) PICTURED HERE SCALING THE WORLD BANK HQ IN N.Y.C. MOMENTS BEFORE THE PRESIDENT OF THE WORLD BANK ACTUALLY INVITED THEM IN TO TALK. I SAW THIS PHOTO IN KING AD-ROCK'S MAGAZINE, BUT, JUST SO YOU KNOW, JOHN SENT IT TO SCAM FIRST!

The first version of this was scrawled on an inside-out barf bag, on an Air India flight back from speaking at a Tibet festival in Bombay. Unfortunately, I left it on the plane. Settled back in my Brooklyn apartment, I'm not sure I'll be able to recreate the feeling of the original, which was fueled by a mix of no sleep, free airplane rum, and a jumble of images and contradictions from my five days in India. So, it might help if you READ it when you've been up for two days and are just getting your caffeine-assisted third wind.

As a fulltime organizer for a mass movement, I firmly believe in the effectiveness and necessity of building grassroots opposition to the combined efforts of corporate criminals and governments to consolidate their power at the expense of people's freedom – here and around the world. Along the same lines, I've always had a lot of respect for the Positive Force kids, and all the punks who had the energy and the commitment it takes to work within the system. You know what I mean, the people who collect petitions and lobby City Hall to keep their all ages DIY club from getting shut down, organize anti-fur rallies at the mall, or even run for local office. That's great stuff, and it's completely necessary, but that's not what I want to talk about. I want to talk about what happens on those days when you've just had it, and you're in no mood for talking. Given that punks tend more often to be antisocial outsiders, loners, and anarchists than patient reformers or grassroots organizers, this is about the lone desperate acts, the rash attempts to make a point at all costs.

I was reading a great book on MLK a while ago, and it had lots of great background on the strategizing, planning, and painstaking organizing that made the civil rights movement a force to be reckoned with. Day after day, year after year, King found the strength to overcome slander, death threats, betrayal, and exhaustion. Reading about all that he accomplished and what it took to get there, I was left both inspired to try to be more like him, and feeling like there was no way in hell I had the patience to put up with all he went through. The book also mentioned the story of a guy who history has pretty much forgotten, who decided he'd had enough one day. With little fanfare and no organizational support he made some signs in support of race mixing and set off to march to Birmingham by himself. It came as a surprise to no one, most likely himself included, when he was shot dead on the side of the road less than two days into his walk. It would be hard to argue that his life or death changed much of anything, but I still found myself identifying much more closely with him than the tireless, "eyes on the prize" visionary, Dr. King.

Everybody's got their own pet peeves, so lets take "da cops" as an example. Seems appropriate, at the moment, yet another unarmed minority youth was killed by the police in NYC last week, this time right in front of my office. Yesterday, cops tear-gassed and beat down demonstrators and reporters alike in my neighborhood, making an angry funeral march even angrier. Eight million people in this city, and no one hates Giuliani enough to put a bullet in his head?!?!?. It's enough to destroy a person's faith in human nature.

OK, so what do you DO? First thing: clearly state your objective. What is it you are trying to accomplish? It might seem a little goofy, but it can be pretty helpful. Once you've done that, it is a lot easier to evaluate different ideas and see what makes the most sense. A few possible objectives might be to raise awareness about racist or violent cops, to stop police brutality in your community, to get one particular cop fired or suspended, to galvanize neighborhood support, or simply to get even and make yourself feel better. Blowing up a police car, for example, might be good for getting even and making yourself feel better, but might not work so well if you are trying to galvanize support in the neighborhood – especially if someone gets hurt.

Who has the power to get you what you want? Will it take elected or appointed officials, mass public support, the media, or celebrities? How much access or influence do you have? Can you get to someone who DOES have access and influence? Most public figures respond to the media, and we can definitely get in the media.

It's always good to put a face to your target. Is it one cop in particular, white cops in non-white neighborhoods, or is it a more systemic problem? If that's the case, you might want to go after the police chief, or maybe the mayor. Tone can be important, too. Personal attacks can embarrass someone into giving in, or they can cause them to get even more defensive, stubborn, and entrenched. Find out as much as you can about your target, and seek out their weaknesses. Do they go to church? Maybe they'd listen to

an appeal from their priest. Do you know where they live? What would they do if there were flyers all over their neighborhood letting everyone know that they beat up homeless people last week? How about if they came home to find that their house had been pelted with dumpstered donuts?

When possible, leave room to escalate the pressure if things don't change. Starting out with a phone call or a letter to the editor gives you a lot more room to maneuver later than if you start out bumrushing the police station.

Use your strengths. That could mean organizing a benefit concert to raise awareness and make some $ to support a local anti-police brutality or legal support organization, or it could be more about your willingness to risk arrest or blow off work to do what needs to be done. It might mean creating and duplicating art, like graffiti, comics, or banners.

Whatever you do, the main thing is to avoid letting them win. They win if you give up, if you don't try, if you kill yourself, or if you don't use your head at least a little bit. Being strategic doesn't mean you don't get to throw bricks through their windshields, it just means that there are SOME times (and some windows) where it won't make sense, and you'd be better off doing something else. Now put this down and go out and make something happen.

John Dania

ANOTHER DAY IN THE LIFE OF CRIME
BY IGGY SCAM

LATELY I'VE BEEN EXCITED ABOUT HOW YEARS OF PUNK ROCK SURVIVAL TECHNIQUES HAVE SEEMED TO PREPARE ME AND MY FRIENDS FOR ALMOST ANY SITUATION. I MEAN, HAS YEARS OF SCRAPING THE LAST DRY RAMEN OFF THE FLOOR OF THE TOUR VAN HELPED CREATE A MASTER RACE? THERE IS SOME EVIDENCE. I'M THINKING SPECIFICALLY OF THE TIME, RECENTLY, WHEN WADE AND HIS BROTHER WERE PLAYING AT THE TIP TOP AND THE WOMAN WHO LIVES UPSTAIRS FROM THE BAR THOUGHT IT WAS TOO LOUD SO SHE POURED AMMONIA THROUGH A HOLE IN HER FLOOR DOWN ONTO THEM TO MAKE THEM STOP.

BUT, THEY DIDN'T STOP. WADE CAUGHT THE AMMONIA IN A CUP AND DRANK IT DOWN. AFTER THE SHOW, HE SAID THAT NEXT TIME THEY PLAY THERE, THEY'LL PUT "COME WATCH US DRINK AMMONIA!" ON THE FLYER.

THIS REMINDS ME OF THE LAST TIME I WAS HANGING OUT WITH FOREST WHEN HE WAS VISITING MIAMI FROM CHATTANOOGA. IT WAS AFTER WE HAD ANOTHER PUNK MOVIE NIGHT ON MIAMI BEACH. IT HAD BEEN A PRETTY GREAT SHOW, WITH BANDS AND MOVIES. THE FUNYONS PLAYED AND SOMEONE'S 2-YEAR OLD KID CAME UP TO HELP SIR ROBERT PLAY THE TRASH PILE DRUM SET. WE SHOWED IAN'S ANIMATED FILM WHERE THE PUNKS BEAT UP THE COP WHILE AGAINST ALL AUTHORITY PLAYS ON THE SOUNDTRACK. WE ALWAYS SHOW THAT ONE. ITS ALWAYS GOOD.

BUT THE BEST PART OF THE SHOW WAS WE FINALLY HAD AN OCCASION TO DRINK THE KEG OF BEER THAT ME AND CINQUE HAD STOLEN A MONTH BEFORE FROM SOME YUPPIE BAR IN THE GROVE. THERE WAS SOME TROUBLE WHEN THE TAP BROKE, BUT CINQUE, HAVING STUDIED KEG MAINTENANCE IN MICHIGAN'S PUBLIC SCHOOLS, BENT OVER THE KEG FOR AWHILE, BUTT CRACK PROUDLY SHOWING, AND, FINALLY, SWEATING AND PANTING, HE WAS ABLE TO GET THE BEER FLOWING STRONG USING A RUSTY SCREWDRIVER WE FOUND. THE BEER, BUD LITE, HAD BEEN SITTING IN THE FLORIDA SUN ON MY PORCH FOR A WHOLE MONTH. IT WAS AWFUL. BUT IT WAS FREE!

AFTER THE SHOW, WHEN ME AND FOREST HAD CLEANED UP, WE STILL HAD ½ THE KEG. WE DECIDED TO DRIVE AROUND TOWN AND CATCH UP ON WHAT WE'D BEEN UP TO. SO WE LOADED UP THE KEG AND HIT I-95 NORTH.

DRIVING FAST AROUND MIAMI, DRUNK ON A FRIDAY NIGHT WITH A STOLEN KEG IN THE BACKSEAT AND THE STUN GUNS BLASTING ON THE RADIO — THIS WAS ABOUT AS FUN AS IT GETS. WE GOT OFF THE FREEWAY AND HEADED NORTH ON N.W. 7TH AVENUE, LOOKING FOR SOME DIVE TO EAT IN. WE WEREN'T REALLY LOOKING THAT HARD, THOUGH; JUST DRIVING. SOON THE GHETTO TURNED INTO SUBURBS AND WE WE WERE STILL DRIVING NORTH, JUST WHEN WE REALIZED WE WERE LOST IN SOME RICH NEIGHBORHOOD, THE COPS ROLLED UP BEHIND US AND PULLED US OVER.

YES, WE WERE DRUNK AND SPEEDING WITH A STOLEN KEG, PAST MIDNIGHT IN A QUIET SUBURB. WE WERE BREAKING MANY LAWS, BUT MOST IMPORTANTLY, WE WERE BREAKING THE LAW, THE WHOLE UNWRITTEN UNDERSTANDING BETWEEN COP AND CRIMINAL OF WHAT YOU SIMPLY CAN'T DO, THE VERY FABRIC OF SOCIETY. THE FIRST COP WALKED UP ANGRILY AND YELLED, "DO YOU KNOW HOW FAST YOU WERE GOING?!?" BUT WHEN HE SAW THE KEG ON THE BACKSEAT, HE STOPPED AND SMILED BROADLY, AND WALKED BACK TO TALK TO HIS PARTNER. THEY PRACTICALLY HI-FIVED EACH OTHER. THIS WOULD BE THE EASIEST BUST EVER!

OR SO THEY THOUGHT. THE COPS DID NOT YET KNOW WHO THEY WERE UP AGAINST. THEY CAME BACK TO OUR CAR CONFIDENTLY, LAUGHING, AND STARTED THREATENING US, SAYING "YOU GUYS ARE GOING STRAIGHT TO JAIL TONIGHT!"

JAIL? WAS THAT IT? THIS WAS HARDLY SCARY. MY OWN HOME WAS OVERRUN WITH ENORMOUS RATS AND HAD NO WINDOWS OR ELECTRICITY. FOREST'S HOME WAS WORSE THAN ANY JAIL. HE LIVED IN CHATTANOOGA WITH 20 PUNKS AND 20,000 ROACHES, SURVIVING OFF BEER AND WHATEVER LIQUOR STORE FOOD YOU HAD TO BUY TO BREAK FOOD STAMPS TO GET BEER MONEY. REDNECKS FROM THE SURROUNDING GREATER CHATTANOOGA AREA FLOCKED TO THEIR HOUSE WITH BASEBALL BATS TO TRY TO BEAT THE PUNKS UP IN THEIR OWN HOME. IF ONLY IT WERE A JAIL. THEN,

AMNESTY INTERNATIONAL WOULD HAVE PICTURES OF IT.

NEXT, THE COPS TOOK OUR I.D.'S AND HAD US GET OUT OF THE CAR, WHILE THEY CALLED US NAMES AND WAITED FOR OUR WARRANT CHECKS TO RUN. WE HAD HEARD WORSE AND WAITED LONGER. ANYONE WHO'D HAD TO WATCH THE STUN GUNS TRY TO TUNE BETWEEN SONGS HAD. THIS WAS NOTHING!

WHEN OUR RECORDS CAME UP CLEAN, THEY THEN WENT TO WORK TRYING TO GET FOREST BUSTED WITH THE D.U.I. TEST. SURE WE WERE DRUNK, BUT WE'D BEEN DOING EVERYTHING DRUNK FOR YEARS. FOREST WALKED THE STRAIGHT LINE AND TOUCHED HIS NOSE PERFECTLY. THE COPS WERE STARTING TO GET NERVOUS BUT THEY THOUGHT THEY'D BUST HIM FOR SURE BY MAKING FOREST RECITE THE ALPHABET BACKWARDS. FOREST, WITH A MIND WELL TRAINED FROM YEARS OF SPLIT SECOND GROCERY STORE CALCULATIONS OF WHAT WAS ACTUALLY THE CHEAPEST BEER PER OUNCE, EASILY RAN IT OFF FOR THEM. THE BALL WAS IN THE COPS' COURT.

THE COPS WERE FURIOUS. THEIR SEARCH OF THE CAR TURNED UP NOTHING, THE TAGGED KEG APPEARED TO BE UNTAPPED, AND WE WERE DRUNK AS HELL BUT THEY COULDN'T PROVE IT. THEY WERE, IN FACT, SO FURIOUS THAT THEIR EASY BUST WAS ABOUT TO WALK, THAT THEY CAME BACK AND YELLED AT FOREST, "OK, BUDDY HOLLY! LET'S RUN THROUGH THE TEST AGAIN — WITHOUT YOUR GLASSES ON!"

THIS WAS SO PATHETICALLY ILLEGAL, BUT WE WERE NOT SURPRISED. EVERY PUNK KNOWS THAT NO ONE HAS MORE CONTEMPT FOR THE LAW THAN A COP. IT WAS UNFAIR, BUT FOREST HAD NO CHOICE BUT TO TAKE OFF HIS GLASSES AND RUN THROUGH THE TEST AGAIN.

I HELD MY BREATH. COULD HE WALK THE LINE, NOW DRUNK AND BLIND? HE WALKED THE LINE WHILE THE ONE COP JUMPED AND MADE SUDDEN STARTLING NOISES TO THROW FOREST OFF! BUT FOREST DID IT!

THE COPS VISIBLY SAGGED, BUT GAVE THE BUST ONE LAST SHOT. THEY TOLD HIM TO RECITE THE ALPHABET BACKWARDS AND PUT HIS ARMS OUT AND THEN TOUCH HIS NOSE AT THE SAME TIME! THEN, WHEN HE STARTED, ONE COP LEAPED FORWARD AND TURNED ON HIS FLASHLIGHT IN FOREST'S EYES AND THE OTHER SHOUTED IN HIS FACE!

I CAN'T SPEAK FOR FOREST, BUT I CAN ONLY IMAGINE THAT THIS WAS SOMETHING LIKE TRYING TO DRUNKENLY PLAY AND REMEMBER ALL THE LYRICS TO SING ON STAGE AT CHURCHILL'S WITH THE STAGELIGHTS BLINDING YOU AND BRYAN MCKELLER TRYING TO HUG YOU AND POUR A FULL BEER DOWN YOUR THROAT. OF COURSE, FOREST PASSED THIS LAST TEST EASILY.

THE COPS WERE ENRAGED, BUT THEY KNEW THEY'D MET THEIR MATCH. AFTER THEY TALKED IT OVER, ONE CAME BACK AND SAID, "WELL, YOU GUYS BETTER GO BUY A LOTTO TICKET, BECAUSE YOU'RE THE LUCKIEST GUYS IN TOWN TONIGHT. I'M LETTING YOU GO."

WE TURNED AROUND AND DROVE THE KEG TO GEORGE'S AND HAD A PRETTY GOOD NIGHT AFTER THAT. BUT THAT LAST CRACK FROM THE COP STILL PISSES ME OFF TO THIS DAY. WHAT DID HE MEAN BY "LUCKY." WE STOLE THAT DAMN KEG FAIR AND SQUARE!

FEEDING THE POOR WITH...
THE MISSION

HOW COME NO ONE EVER TALKS ABOUT THE <u>GOOD</u> THINGS GRAFFITI WRITERS IN THE CITY DO, LIKE THEIR FREE BURRITO PROGRAM FOR STARVING CRACKHEADS AND PROSTITUTES?! THE **MISSION BURRITO PROJECT** WAS A GROUP OF GRAFFITI KIDS IN SAN FRANCISCO'S MISSION DISTRICT, WHO, WHEN THEY WEREN'T OUT DOING PIECES, FUCKING UP BILLBOARDS, AND DOING CRIMES WOULD MAKE HOMEMADE, VEGAN BURRITOS AND HAND THEM OUT, LATE AT NIGHT, AROUND THE DRUG-FILLED 16TH AND MISSION BART PLAZA! THEY ALSO MADE HOMEMADE HIP HOP TAPES WHICH THEY SOLD... TO BUY MORE BEANS AND RICE! AWHILE BACK, I WAS LUCKY ENOUGH TO CATCH UP WITH NOAH AND BEAVER OF M.B.P. IN THE TOP **SECRET WAREHOUSE** IN THE MISSION...

"HAVE YOU SEEN THEM?":

WELL-WORN M.B.P. STICKER, LIKE ONES SEEN ALL OVER MISSION...

IGGY: What is the MISSION BURRITO PROJECT?
NOAH: MBP is a group of people who...
BEAVER: ... Feed homeless people!
N: Yeah, MBP feeds homeless people, or anybody who is hungry.
B: Its burritos...
N: in the MIssion...
I: How many people usually make this up?
N: half a dozen, maybe 20...
B: its different every time. Sometimes, Noah does it by himself, sometimes 20 people... Usually about 5 focused people...
I: What gave you guys the idea to do this?
N: We did a mobile kitchen at the Rainbow Gathering and fed folks...
B: and Aaron Funk turned us on. He was one of the greatest dumpsterdivers that I ever met in my life...
N: ... a roadside vegetation hedonist!
B: I travelled with that guy. One of my first travelling experiences was being knee deep in a dumpster full of candy with him. He's the one who started the mobile kitchen known as the Granola Funk Express, that taught me andNoah so much about being on the road, and taking care of people... (editor's note: sure, this sounds like a load of hippie granola shit, but please, read on...)

GRAFFITI ON ERIE STREET, THE SO-CALLED "BURRITO ALLEY"

BURRITO PROJECT!

: With the mobile kitchen, we had the equipment, the pots, and pans... We just
ecided to travel and do it, to show up in new towns and feed...
: There's always one place in every town where kids hng out... We'd just show u
nd find some punks or skaters or hippies and go, "Hey, where do kids hang out her
: So, don't you think this is pretty unusual for the graffiti scene you guys are
oming from?
: I don't know ANYTHING about graffiti.
: Yeah! What are you trying to SAY, Mr. SCAM PUNKS?
: Yeah, its unusual but we're not just from that scene...
: Well, the graffiti scene here seems really kind-of selfish, and just self-
eferential...
: Yeah, but along with that you also have your political writers...
: Well, its about doing what you can with what you have at that exact moment. I
he situation is unacceptable and you can't express yourself, and your surrounding
ren't controlled by you, you're going to take whatever you have, like a pen, or
omething to scratch with, and do it, RIGHT NOW... But we have this kitchen now,
nd we can cook food so, we're doing what we can with what we have...
: We realize that we can't give every person a full, 10-course meal, but if we
n give 100 people an ill-ass dope burrito, that's fine... You can't just go out t
arket Street and do a block long, 20 color burner, and not get busted, so you do
 tag. You take that one step in the right direction... I tell my graffiti friend
hat I'm just trying to take it to the next level. I used to write graff every
ight. I like ATE it and SLEPT it, it was my life. I'm alot happier now that its
ot. I get alot less fame now, and people sucking my dick, but I feel like I'm
n my way now to doing good things and expressing myself, outside of a scene.
: I do graffiti because its a political action..
: So what usually happens when MBP goes out?
: We usually take 2 coolers of burritos around the 'hood, usually around 16th and
ission BART station. We take out about 130 on a night, and they're usually gon
one in about 20 minutes!
: Do the cops ever fuck with you, like they used to fuck with FOOD NOT BOMBS?
: No, never... We go out late at night, and we don't seek any media attention, so
obody knows about us.
: Not to mention that people are slinging crack and heroin and ass and rigs all
round us, so cops aint worried about burritos.

: Plus, we got our own secret spot.
: Yeah, Burrito Alley... When we only got a couple left, or if we're having a
ough night we go there. Burrito Alley's our happy place. We go there and every

ne's like, "Fuck Yeah! Its the burrito kids!" One time this maniac crackhead
tarted trying to fight me--this is the only time we had trouble-- because he
aid he didn't think my hands we're clean enough to serve food! Like, the guy
ants to get a crowd together to FIGHT me, and he's all spun, and other guys at
he BART are telling him to chill... So, we just went to Burrito Alley to forget
bout it...
TANK enters the room) TANK: Hey are you guys going out , later?
: no. Hey(to tape recorder) That's TANK!
: Yeah, The King of The Tenderloin!
: Iggy here is the king of the Turd-Filled Donut...
ank: Oh, you do that? I met Ivy out there the other night...

though it was funny that they left your huge TANK piece on the post office
101 Hyde, for like, a year, or whatever... Like the Tenderloin's so fucked
 they won't even bother to clean the Post Office!
k: well, there's still an area of that Post office that's like rolldowns cove
ered ith old tags. I'm just gonna cover the whole thing.
Shit, you could probably just go in there and tag the postal WORKERS!
k: there's this little cove there that provides good cover. I want to set up
e, a card board shack, like I'm homelessand sleeping, and hide behind that,
 when its chill "Pss! Pss!" (sound of spraying)...
Really? So, uh, what was your ADDRESS again?
OK, uh, Tank... Can you go away for a minute?
wait, now! That's the up and coming king of SF! Crushing toys!
k: you' recording this?
yeah, this is an interview for SCAM PUNKS, man. You're going to be FAMOUS!
 wait, let me ask you this: You're Iggy Scam, and then, what--- the zine is
M, and then, we're all, like, The SCAM PUNKS?
Shut up...
No, man, I'm interviewing YOU! Like, MSA told me to check out the Scam Punks
said that shit is SICK!

SHOPPING CARTS LOUNGE IN BURRITO ALLEY
WITH A BLOCK-LONG "MBP" PAINTED BEHIND...

FEED THE PEOPLE
BY ANY MEANS
NECESSARY.

I: So where do you get the food?
N: We buy it from Rainbow, or other locally owned and worker owned stores. The ingrediants are as locally produced as possible, and we use all organic food, except for the tortillas , which we buy mostly from corner stores.
I: The food is donated?
N: No. We buy it. We have shows in our Top Secret Warehouse to raise cash. We make hip hop tapes at home and sell 'emm, too. We use the money to make burritos
I: why buy the food?
N:Because, well, we're not down with the capitalist system. BY taking charity, we feel we'dbe justifying the system that put everyone in this position... By taking taking the spoils, we'd be taking something that's made BY keeping people down. It'd be hush money. We want something that supports itself, so we can say we're not part f the system, and that we don't take anything from it. We want our own system where the people can have what they need.
B: that's why we buy from worker owned stores. We use our own creative abilitie to make our system. It all pays for itself. We make the music that we love to support the food that inspires the music... We feel good about selling our music to support political action.I: How's the tape going?
B: We sold almost all 250!
N: I heard a Black Panther quote that said, "You can't be a revolutionary, unles you get up in the morning and serve food to the kids." We can talk about this all we want. We can go write it on the walls, and we can bug out all we want in our songs, but if we're not taking whatever concrete steps we can to do something RIGHT NOW, we're just talking...
I: But why Burritos?
N: Its portable. No waste. Perfect for the Mission. People hungry on the streets late at night love a steaming hot burrito.
B: and they don't have to stand there watching us wash dishes that some crackhead ate off just before them, either, like when we used to try to feed with stir-fry
I:N: Yeah, and its all set up, now! We've got the new rice recipe! We BAKE it,

instead, now so it doesn't burn on the bottom! Its at 450 degrees...
B: No, its 425, man!
N: you sautee the vegetables, garlic, and onions, and then throw in the rice, dry and brown it. The water's already preheated in another pan. Then you put the w water in and bake it.

I: What's next for you guys?
B: travelling... We're going on the oad this summer with the mobile kitchen. Build the empire, build the boat... Feed people, play music. I want to make movies...
I: I'm bummed that you're splitting town before we coild work on the rooftop tomato garden project in the mission (editor's note: we had a plan to grow tomatoes on the rooftops where they usually spraypaint, and use them IN the burritos!)
B: well, I'll show you that rooftop tonight.
I: Giant Value? On Mission?
B: Imagine how phat it'd be if you GREW the tomatoes for MBP!
I: Oh, yeah, did you ever find that tool to get the bus bench poster holders open?
B: Oh, uh... can you stop the tape?

SOON AFTER THIS INTERVIEW M.B.P. LEFT TOWN ON A CROSS COUNTRY TRIP WITH THEIR MOBILE KITCHEN, AND AFTER TRAVELLING AWHILE THEY MOVED TO PHILLY. BEAVER SAYS THEY'RE STILL GOING TO DO M.B.P.. "ONLY NOW IT MIGHT BE THE WEST PHILLY FELAFEL PROJECT...

GraffitiBlasters, Inc.
Graffiti removal
112 Shipl
415-882-

PHOTO BY BILL DANIE

dear Cindy...

...The whole staying-in-libraries thing started when I was having a real lousy trip in Gainsville. No one would put me up, so I came up with this idea to stay all night at U of F's library. I hid in a toilet on one of the upper floors and no one ever went into clean it, so I was in! But the next time, me and Ivy tried it at University of Miami and we got caught by a Cuban cleaning lady who totally lost her shit and started yelling 'I call the man! I call the man!' We were like, 'Uh...can we just leave him out of this!' Some male janitor let us out and we took off! The best time ever was at Humboldt State in Arcada. I was working on da SCAM and I found everything I was looking for and worked all night. I made tea in the toilet sink by putting duct tape over the drain and running hot water and I'd take breaks to drink tea and walk around the huge empty library in my socks, watching the rain fall and fog roll outside. I was not so lucky at the CAL Polytech library in tiny San Luis Obispo. I was so exhausted from travel that I fell asleep in the middle of reading this huge pile of books. Finally I got in my sleeping bag in what looked to be an unused storage room, and pulled sev- several book cart's in front of me. In the morning I was awakened by the flourescent light turning on and I could see a woman's feet walking towards me. 'Oh God,' I thought, 'She is gonna scream when she sees me.' Sure enough, she saw me and let out a piercing

shriek and all the library staff rushed to her aide. 'This is all a big misunderstanding!' I offered cheerfully, and I might add, somewhat cryptically... Quickly I packed my bag and was ready to go. I found some fire exit and took off. Moments later, campus security found me, shaving in a toilet. He was pretty cool about it. I told him I was a half dead vagrant, traveling by freight trains and that I'd fallen asleep in the library and woke up to find it closed; I paniced and figured I'd get in trouble if I called anyone and said I was in there, and I assumed the doors had alarms, so I figured I'd try and hide and wait. He said ok, whatever, just don't ever do it

again, ok?!? I wonder what he'd say if he caught me doing it again...The next time was at FSU in Talla- hassee (I had given serious though to ole Weber state in Ogden UT, but couldn't find a good hiding place)

In Tallassee I slept at the top of the flights of stairs, one full floor above where the library ended. This one was sort of weird, cuz I fell asleep waiting for the library to close, and woke up at 11:30 - like 4 hours after they opened! I slept through the whole thing! The Tallassee thing was remarkable, though, in that it was the first time I had traveled to a city specifically intending to live in it's collage library. (I've assumed that a college library is safer than a city library since they're sort of staffed entirely by students and have later hours and a more casual attitude towards people who are hanging out, i.e. "bums", who are sort of criminalized these days, often, at public libraries. I envision a day, not too far in the future, when cities, claiming fiscal crisis, turn the control of their libraries over to private comp- anies who will start to kick out "bums", open cafes inside, go for more internet shit, and launch a "come back to the new library, we now feature computers... and toilet paper!" campaign. They'll have Wackenhut go after Scoff laws to collect fines and late fees...)

So, as far as N.O., this was the most ambitious plan yet - to stay as long as possible! It sort of wasn't fun. The novelty of being in the library alone, gave way to the daily stress of the whole routine. Plus, I had to be in every night at ten! What a drag. Also, Tulane's in such a snobby, un-New Orleans, yupscale 'hood and, though there was easily scammed coffee and easy receipt scamming, being so far from town and being surrounded by frat boys started bumming me out. I was staying, once again, on the 6th flight of stairs of a 5 story library, by the locked door to the elevator machinery. I had sort of decided I was sick of it when I got caught by a cheerful black cleaning lady who in true N.O. style just said "Oh now, here you are studying so hard, ya don't know the library's been closed!" That sounded good to me. She let me out with out much fuss and that was that.

My real fantasy, of course, is to find an unused little room in the U of M library and stay in at night and put my own lock on it! That way I could go whenever I wanted and even give other people the key. But, for now things are going good at Ci...'s mom's, so I'll have to put it off.

love and puke, Iggy

XEROXED FROM DORIS #10.

TYPICAL, LAZY SCAM LAYOUTS ...

1) THE GATE

2) THE PATH

3) THE VIEW OF S.F.

4) THE SHACK

THE LANDFILL

BY IVY

Boo!

I remember the first time I set foot at the Albany Landfill, I was with Robin & Josh one night after a Gilman show. I remember thinking,"Wow! I wanna live here...I'll build a pirate shack right here on the beach, grow my own garden, and I'll have a bench in front where my friends can hang out!" So over free Just Desserts coffee I started making a blue print for my shack. At the same time my pals Faith & Kerb were plotting the same thing. We decided to help each other by first buiding one house together and then another one down the road. That never happened but we did successfully build a fine lookin' shack! Kerb & Faith had a van we would use in heists of wood and building supplies thanks to various stores and construction sites. Then we'd drag the wood down the dirt trail a half mile to the site we carefully picked.

The Albany Landfill was shut down for dumping Jan.1,1984 and had become a wilderness of trees, shrubs, and concrete rubble. Over the years it became an unofficial park of sorts where Albany residents would come to walk their dogs and teenagers would build bonfires and get drunk. I've also heard accounts of people going on dates there...But we weren't the first ones to have caught our eye on the idea of landfill life.

There was the writer guy who had lived in a tent in the landfill for a few years to write in peace. He made a living by collecting winning tickets dropped in the nearby horse racetrack, Golden Gate Fields' parking lot.

Then there was J.P. the speed freak who tweaked endlessly in the bushes whose dwelling had a fence made of flattened trash cans left from the landfill's active days. He also had this ENORMOUS_CAULDRON in his yard where he would try to conjure up speed induced spells. He was the embodiment of Mystic Tweaker! Once when there was a threat that we could be kicked out of the landfill he jabbered onto me and Anandi about how we should <u>wheel</u> the cauldron to Albany City Hall, fill it with some potion, and beat drums in protest of our expulsion. Like I said Mystic Tweaker.

It was the fall of '93 that Faith, myself, Lil Mike, Brad, and Bill from Radon all helped build the shack, but it was really Kerb's master building skills that kept it together.He designed the walls so that there was one inside layer of plywood, then a palette stuffed with newspaper sealed by an outside layer of plywood.It kept the place pretty damn warm.We were able to make the shack very homey. Our front door belonged to a dear friend of mine, Charlene Paul, who had passed away. I sprinkled some of her ashes into the bay right there on the shore of the landfill. Years later when the shack was destroyed I managed to pull her door from the rubble and write an obituary to Charlene and the shack and send it to sea...

Soon after the shack was built Christmas '93 rolled around and Kerb and Faith were going to take off travelling the U.S. in their van. Right before they left we had a get together at the shack on Christmas eve. We awoke to a gift of

fresh baked chocolate chip cookies with a note from a sweet dog walker lady that wished us all well.

Brad, Lil Mike, and I were the first longterm occupants. It was quite a trudge from town to house and especially at night. I believe living in the landfill helped me overcome some of my fears of the unknown. There were times I would have to walk or bike back alone at night.Your imagination could run rampant going down a pitch black path in the woods. There were 2 particular bushes that scared me the most. When passing them I would act all crazy & yell & sing ridiculous songs I made up to ward off the monsters waiting to kill me! You see the landfill was located on the edge town on the bay. It was a peninsula past the I-80, a no-man's land.The parking lot in between the landfill and the horse racetrack was used for kite flying, hang gliding, remote control cars, and people either doing donuts or learning how to drive a car. Our closest water source was a spigot at the racetrack that we'd get water from and lug a good mile to the shack every few days.

I remember one night my friend Jessica & I snuck into the Albany Theater to see a winona Ryder movie with a bottle of whiskey. The movie sucked so bad we ran out of there drunk and yelling and spilling whiskey on the theater seats! As we trudged down Solano passing all those fancy houses I said,"Hey! All these houses have numbers...Our house needs a number!!" So we proceeded to steal "1235" from some apartment building and screwed it right into the shack(address:1235 Landfill Way!). Yeah, it was our home.

5) MYSTIC TWEAKER

EXPLAINS EVERYTHING

Dog walkers and campers weren't the only inhabitants of
he landfill... There was the old naked guy who liked to get
ack to nature by rolling around in the mud on the beach!
esus what a sight! There was more than one occasion when I'd
ake up to see the naked guy up on the hill staring into the
un. One Sunday morning I was hangin' out on our porch when I
eard something rustling in the bushes I looked over to find
ome kid wearing a duct tape suit complete with a duct tape
word hiding in the bushes!! I followed this kid around to
nd there more of them! I watched these kids battle each
ther with duct tape armour. Finally they noticed me hiding
n the bushes and got all scared and asked,"Uh...Can we help
ou?" I said,"Yeah! What are you doing?!" They replied,"Wer'e
laying Archery Tag, a medieval combat game!" Hmmmmm.
    At the time none of us were employed so we would find
reative ways to get by. My favorite was walking into Safeway
r Lucky and filling their handbaskets with food and booze
nd walking out the door. Brad, Mike, and I would cook up
easton our propane stove. We were lucky kids, lots of our
riends worked in either coffee or bagel shops.Our friend,
chie Bucher worked at Grace Baking on Solono and would
resent me with the most lavish fruit cheese cakes, which
me in handy at our periodical dinner parties.
    I can't forget to mention my sweetheart, Sadie. She was
r cat that I found in the MUNI graveyard in San Francisco in
e Fall of 93.When Brad and Little Mike left to hop trains

1235

n the northwest, I was left alone at the shack. I would
enture down the dark path, terrified, but luckily, I knew
adie would be waiting for me at the homefront, and would
ook forward to getting home to her.Sadie was just a kitten
t the time and was VERY playful. the landfill is like a cats
aradise with bugs and rodents abound. Every so often I would
ake up in the morning to a present she would leave at my
eet, which was usually some rodent that was bigger than her!
    Towards the end of my stay at the landfill, when it was
ust me and Sadie, a cop was shot by someone he chased into
he landfill. What ensued was a massive manhunt. At dawn,
ith infrared cameras, helicopters, boats, submachine guns,
d TONS of cops and dogs all landfill residents, including
e, were found and brought to the police station for
uestioning. In that interview, the landfill residents got a
lessing from the Chief of Police and the City of Albany to
 ahead and live there. The Chief said, "If I wasn't a cop,
'd live there, too!" Whatever. On the front page of the next
ay's Oakland Tribune was a picture of our shack and some
idiculous article about "landfill life."
    Soon, it was time for me to go and I decided to move
ack to Florida. Before I left, I wanted to leave one lasting
ift for the landfill. I was inspired by the movie, "The
iano", and became obsessed with pianos, so I decided I would
ring a piano out to the landfill. I heard Pheonix Iron
orks, this huge artist warehouse in West Oakland, was
hutting down and they had alot of pianos, so I went there to
sk them if I could have one. They said, "Sure. Take any one
f these three!" So I picked one out. That was the easy part.
etting my friends to drive it out to the landfill was the
ard part! By the time I found a ride, the Pheonix Iron works
uy had given my piano away to become part of a sculpture!
uckily, I remembered there was a piano sitting on the porch
f my old squat in Emeryville. I swear, its true! It took 6
 us to slide it down the stairs into the back of Celia's
ncle's truck! Celia's uncle turned out to be sort-of wild.
e got really into the offroading, and just forged his own
th through the landfill, with us screaming in the back,
hile he flattened all these bushes, until we reached the
iano's final destination. At a beautiful cliff overlooking
e Bay, we pushed the piano off the truck to its new home in
e wilderness.
    Two days later Sadie and I were on a plane to Miami.

6)THE PIANO

"I TOOK MY BIKE ON FREIGHT TRAINS!!!"

... YET ANOTHER GRIPPING, TRUE-TO-LIFE DRAMA OF MAN AND BIKE ON THE OPEN ROAD.

I LOVE BIKES AND, BY NOW, I'VE MANAGED TO TAKE THE VARIOUS BIKES I'VE OWNED OVER THE YEARS TO JUST ABOUT EVERYWHERE. I'VE TAKEN THEM ON ROWBOATS, CARRIED THEM ACROSS SOUTH FLORIDA SWAMPS, RIDDEN ON INTERSTATES ALONGSIDE 65 MPH TRAFFIC, AND EVEN HAD A BIKE ON TOP OF THE VAN ON MY OLD BAND'S LAST TOUR. LAST SUMMER, I FINALLY FOUND THE COOLEST THING YET: TAKING MY BIKE WITH ME ON MY CROSS COUNTRY FREIGHT HOPPING TRIP.

HERE ARE SOME OF THE ADVANTAGES TO TAKING YOUR BIKE ON YOUR NEXT TRAIN TRIP:

#1) INSTEAD OF TRUDGING THE COUNTLESS MILES FROM ONE END OF THE TRAIN YARD TO THE OTHER WITH YOUR ENORMOUS PACK ON, YOU CAN JUST RIDE!

#2) YOU CAN TELL THE YARD BULL, IF YOU'RE CAUGHT, THAT YOU ARE "JUST REALLY LOST." WHO WOULD HOP A TRAIN WITH A BIKE, RIGHT?

#3) TRAIN YARDS ARE USUALLY REALLY FAR FROM ANY REAL PART OF TOWN, SO WITH A BIKE, YOU DON'T HAVE TO WALK TEN MILES TO FIND A STORE THAT TAKES FOODSTAMPS, OR DO COOL STUFF. WITHOUT MY BIKE, I NEVER WOULD HAVE FOUND THE FREE ZOO IN ROSEVILLE, THE FOUNTAIN I SWAM IN IN KANSAS CITY, OR THE YUPPIE CAFE IN OLD TOWN PUEBLO WHERE I PERFECTED THE "RIDE-BY TABLE DIVE."

#4) YOU MAY CATCH SOME TRAINS THAT YOU NEVER WOULD HAVE CAUGHT ON FOOT. FOR INSTANCE, A BRAKEMAN IN ROSEVILLE TOLD ME IT'D BE A "REAL LONG WHILE" UNTIL THE NEXT TRAIN WENT OUT TO OGDEN, UTAH, SO I WENT AND RODE AROUND TOWN AND SCAMMED REFILLS AT THAT BAD CAFE BY THE YARD. MAYBE TWO SHORT HOURS LATER, I RODE BY THE YARD AND HAPPENED TO NOTICE MY TRAIN TO OGDEN PULLING OUT, GOING TOO FAST TO CATCH! FUCK! HOWEVER, I WAS, LUCKILY, ON A BIKE, SO I RODE UP TO THE HEAD OF THE TRAIN AS FAST AS I COULD, MATCHING ITS SPEED, HOPING THAT IT'D STOP, OR SLOW AROUND A CURVE UP AHEAD.

SURE THIS WAS PRETTY BRAZEN, ME CHASING THIS TRAIN THROUGH TOWN IN BROAD DAYLIGHT; IT FELT LIKE WHEN I RODE MY BIKE ON THE MOVING SIDEWALK AT MIAMI INTERNATIONAL AIRPORT, AND I THOUGHT AN ARMY OF COPS WOULD SWOOP DOWN ON ME AT ANY SECOND, BUT IT WAS ONE OF THOSE RAD MOMENTS WHEN THE REST OF THE WORLD'S NOT THERE AND ITS JUST YOU AND THE TRAIN.

FINALLY, WAY OUTSIDE THE YARD, THE TRAIN SLOWED AND I MANAGED TO GET OFF THE BIKE AND GET IT AND ME UP ON THE TRAIN. WITHOUT THE BIKE, I NEVER WOULD HAVE CAUGHT UP TO IT!

#5) LAST, BUT NOT LEAST, YOU CAN RIDE YOUR BIKE AROUND INSIDE BOXCARS! YO!

HERE ARE SOME THINGS TO WATCH OUT FOR ⟶

One the most influential books in th punk scene in the 90's wasn't even real a book, and almost no one knows wh really wrote it. I'm talking about th famous "Crew Change Guide" that ha been xeroxed and re-xeroxed and update and handed back and forth from punk punk countless times over the years Somehow, almost everyone has it, or use to. Its a state-by-state listing of wher every train yard in the country is, wher trains stop to do crew changes, and wher you can catch out. I had always wanted t hop trains, but it wasn't until Greta gav me a faded, tattered copy of this back i '92 that I became obsessed with it. Wh made this? How many people were reall out there on the rails? The whole thing was so mysterious.

It turns out that the crew change guide was made mostly by this weird obsesse railfan/part-time hobo from Chicago named Paul G. Norton, who was not in any way a punk, but was a nurse in "rea life". I've never met him, but I heard he turned up at some anarchist youth gathering in Chicago a couple years back to give a "workshop" on train hopping. I thought he was in retirement, or something, until the masterful 1997 update started making the rounds late that year, when I was out on the rails myself. It included this new brilliant entry for the Conrail yard on the southside of Chicago, where Norton, in razor sharp, Hammett-like prose, details how he found the one spot in the entire yard where you can wait for the eastbound trains and the train cop's car's headlights can't see you. He gives detailed instructions to where he had hung two keys from a tree, and layed two mats on the ground where you are to wait. I went down there with Mitchell to check it out, once. We had the guide out and were pacing off the steps, all treasure map style. The key wasn't there anymore, but it was pretty exciting.

#1) WATCH OUT FOR MTV VIDEO CREWS IN THE TRAINYARD! THE FIRST TIME I EVER TOOK MY BIKE ON A TRAIN WAS ON A PERFECT SPRING DAY IN BERKELEY, WHEN I WAS ON MY WAY UP TO SACRAMENTO TO SEE MY FRIEND, THE GAMBINO. I RODE OUT TO THE WEST OAKLAND WASTELAND WHERE THE NORTHBOUNDS STOP AT A LIGHT. BELIEVE IT, OR NOT, RANCID WAS THERE FILMING A VIDEO FOR MTV! IT WAS SO "ONLY IN BERKELEY" THAT I WAS SURPRISED IT HAPPENED IN WEST OAKLAND. WHEN MY BIKE AND I FINALLY LEFT THE YARD ON THE PORCH OF A GRAINER, RANCID WAS

SWERVING DOWN THE SERVICE ROAD IN A GREEN MUSTANG WHILE A CAR WITH A CAMERAMAN HANGING OUT THE WINDOW FOLLOWED THEM. SHEESH!

OF COURSE, AT THE TIME I THOUGHT THOSE GUYS WERE SELL-OUTS, FOR MAKING A VIDEO, BUT THEIR SUCCESS HAS CONVINCED ME TO PUT OUT MY OWN "VIDEO SINGLE" FEATURING A CUT FROM MY UPCOMING SPOKEN WORD 8 CD BOX SET. THE FOOTAGE IS CULLED MOSTLY FROM STORE SURVEILANCE CAMERA FILMS OF ME STEALING SHIT, WITH FOOTAGE OF DANCING, FEMALE FASHION MODELS SPLICED IN. ITS ONLY $101.50 FROM THE ADDRESS AT THE END OF THE ZINE, AND IS TOTALLY WORTH IT CUZ IT SHOWS LOTS OF ASS!

2) YOU NEED THE RIGHT BIKE: THE ZO-BAG GUY TOLD ME HIS FRIEND HAD A SPECIALLY MADE, FOLD-UP BIKE THAT YOU COULD THROW RIGHT ON THE TRAIN. WELL, I DON'T KNOW ABOUT THAT SHIT. I HAD A LOW-TECH, 3-SPEED SEARS STORMY ARCHER THAT WAS LIGHTER AND EASIER TO LIFT THAN THE CLUNKY SCHWINN "EAST BAY SPECIALS" THAT ARE ALL OVER TOWN. MOST IMPORTANTLY, THE BIKE WAS A BEAUTIFUL, CHERRY RED COLOR AND IT RODE REAL FAST. IT WAS JUST SO "SUMMERTIME" THAT THE BIKE ITSELF INSPIRED THE WHOLE IDEA OF THE TRIP AND NOT THE OTHER WAY AROUND. I REALLY WANTED TO RIDE THAT BIKE, SAY, UNDER THE ARCH IN ST. LOUIS ON A BREEZY, WARM, SUMMER DAY.

OLE CHERRY RED WAS JUST THE FINEST BIKE IN S.F., EXCEPT MAYBE A SIMILAR CHERRY RED, GIRLS' MODEL THAT I ALWAYS USED TO SEE PARKED OVER ON LEXINGTON. I THINK MY BIKE HAD A CRUSH ON THAT ONE...

ONE PROBLEM, THOUGH, WAS THAT TRAIN YARD GRAVEL DESTROYED MY BEARINGS IN THE BACK WHEEL, PRETTY FAST, AND I WENT THROUGH 3 BACK WHEELS ON THE TRIP! SO, YOU MAY WANT A GOOD ALL-TERRAIN, FAT WHEELED OFF ROADER THAT CAN TAKE THE ABUSE. THEN AGAIN, YOU'RE PROBABLY BETTER OFF WITH A THRIFT STORE JUNKER THAT YOU WOULDN'T MIND LOSING FOREVER... ANYWAY, MUCH THANKS ON THIS LAST TRIP TO THE WISE, OLD BIKE MECHANIC WHO LOOKED LIKE STEINBECK IN ST. LOUIS AND THE BIKER PRIDE GUY IN MILWAUKEE FOR MAINTENANCE AND TO THE UNIVERSITY CITY PUNK HOUSE AND SCOOBY DON'T FOR THEIR UNUSED, BASEMENT WHEELS.

3) HOPPING TRAINS ON THE RUN IS MORE TRICKY WITH A BIKE, BUT IT CAN BE DONE: IN OGDEN, AFTER WAITING ALL DAY WHERE THE TRAINS SUPPOSEDLY STOP AND WATCHING ABOUT 5 OR 6 GO BY WITHOUT STOPPING, I DECIDED TO START GETTING THE TRAINS ON THE RUN, NO MATTER WHAT. SO I DEVELOPED THIS RAD MANOEVER WHERE YOU RAISE THE BIKE OVER YOUR HEAD AND CHASE THE TRAIN. THEN YOU STAB THE BIKE, BACK-WHEEL FIRST, BETWEEN THE GRAIN CAR'S LADDER AND BODY, SO THAT IT STICKS IN THERE AND HANGS OUT. THEN, YOU CLIMB UP ONTO THE TRAIN AND PULL THE REST OF THE BIKE UP. ITS SORT-OF LIKE HUNTING THE TRAIN WITH THE BIKE AS A SPEAR... YEAH, I GUESS THIS WHOLE THING CONSIDERRED AS A SPORT IS KIND OF WEIRD, I GUESS, BUT I HAD FUN...

WHEN THE SUMMER WAS OVER, AFTER 6396 MILES TOGETHER, I GAVE OLD CHERRY RED AWAY, BUT THE NEW OWNER, THEO, LETS ME RIDE THE BIKE WHENEVER I'M IN TOWN. LAST TIME I WAS IN BERKELEY, WE WENT AND RODE THROUGH THE LANDFILL AND HOPPED BART TOGETHER FOR OLD TIME'S SAKE. I THINK THE COOLEST STORY THOUGH WAS ABOUT THE BIKE'S OLD OWNER BEFORE ME. THIS GUY, HEN, GAVE THE BIKE TO IVY WITH NO BRAKES, OR GEARS AND TWO FLAT TIRES. LITTLE MIKE ENDED UP FIXING IT UP, BUT THEN HE LEFT TOWN, AND I ENDED UP WITH THE BIKE. MANY MONTHS AND MILES AND TRAINS LATER, ON THE STREETS OF MINNEAPOLIS, WHO DO I ALMOST RUN OVER WITH THE BIKE? HEN! HE WAS PRETTY STOKED TO SEE OLE CHERRY RED IN ITS NEW GLORY. IT TURNS OUT, HE'D MOVED TO MINNEAPOLIS AND NOW HAD A WIFE AND A KID. HE HAD SETTLED DOWN — BUT NOT HIS OLD BIKE!

Since I first read Norton, I've hopped over a hundred trains myself, and have compiled alot of info. from me and Brad's trips to go along with the Norton guide. One winter night in Ann Arbor, a couple years ago, I tried to edit it all together.

It was very strange, re-typing Norton's trademark, clipped prose, thinking of the places he described, and considerring his unlikely impact on the punk scene, and how everyone took to the rails in the '90's. I started with the "A"'s. It was all there. Alberta with its tiny "c-c"'s, breathlessly waiting in the trainless night. Arizona. Tiny Field, British Columbia where they put the helper engines on. When will I be by the depot in Field again?

I could picture the ATSF depot baking in the Needles, CA sun so clearly. The donut shop by the tracks in West Colton, and the "La Villa Restaurant". Places I'd never exactly been. Embankments, gates, bridges, and holes in fences in the dark, dirty, forgotten corners of every town in the U.S. and Canada and the trains that are always there...

I finally broke down in the Mt. Shasta entry for the McCloud River Railroad. Norton writes simply, "Trains to McCloud as business requires." It was too much. Would you "edit" Hemingway? Would you retype Dosteovsky? Norton had created a truly singular vision in his work -- the lonely, heartbreaking, obsessive mapping of America's subconscious geography. There's an unlocked gate 300 feet behind the "Lamplighter Tavern" in Worcestor, Massachussetts. You always knew it was there...

AN INTERVIEW WITH MONICA FROM WEST PHILLY'S...

BIKE CHURCH!!!

IT SEEMS LIKE ALL MY FRIENDS HAVE BEEN MOVING TO WEST PHILLY LATELY, AND ONE THING THEY ALL TELL ME ABOUT BESIDES THE RAD MILES OF CRUMBLING NEIGHBORHOODS TO RIDE YOUR BIKE IN AND THE SCORES OF PUNKS LIVING IN ABANDONED BUILDINGS, IS THE BIKE CHURCH. SO, WHEN MONICA FROM THE BIKE CHURCH WAS HERE IN TOWN, RECENTLY, I INVITED HER TO THE SCAM OFFICE AT HUNT'S DONUTS ON 20TH AND MISSION TO TELL US ABOUT IT...

SCAM: WHAT IS "THE BIKE CHURCH?"

Monica: The bike church is a place where people can fix up their bikes, or buy and borrow already fixed up bikes. There's access to tools and recycled parts and there's always someone there to help you fix stuff. Its a big, open space with buckets and buckets of donated bbb parts and tool stations. There's also a library of books, like bike repair books that people can use to fix stuff, and source books for appropriate technology, like pedal powered tools and bike history stuff. We also use the space to just hang out and listen to records and watch movies and stuff.

HOW DID IT START? WHERE IS IT?

Monica: Well, me and Jarrivel started it. We'd always wanted to do a bike co-op. We'd heard about this after school program for kids that was run out of the basement of this church in West Philly, where kids could learn about bike repair, and, at the end of the program, when they graduated, they'd earn a free bike. I started volunteering there, and eventually asked them if we could use their space in the evenings. It was fun; we'd sneak into the church, upstairs. It was this big space with all the pews removed, and we'd ride our bikes around in it all night.

It turned out that our programs helped each other. We used their tools and parts to build bikes that we sold to raise money for them. Since then, they've started getting money from grants and we've moved to a space in another church in West Philly, but their program's still there. I haven't seen the new space yet, because I've been travelling, but I called home today, and heard its been pretty busy. Its easy to find churches, byt the way, to do kids programs in in Philly...

HOW IS THE BIKE CHURCH FUNDED?

Monica: Well, we don't really need money. We just recycle the parts. Its easy to get a bike co-op started, because all you have to do is put out some flyers asking for donations, and it turns out, everyone's got some old bike rusting in their basement that they'll give you.

AND REPAIRS ARE FREE?

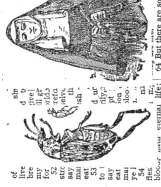

the bicycle church

bike church

Monica: Yeah. We're volunteers. We just kind build... have at least one person there when the Bike Church is open. When people come in, we help them find tools and parts and help instruct them. That's the thing, we don't do it for them, but we try to help them learn how to do it themselves with the tools and repair manuals. Besides me and Jarrivel, there's a bunch of other folks who work there, so its pretty staffed. Rebecca's a big part of it, and, of course, Dr. Solar, the master genius of bike mechanics...

WHERE'D YOU GET THE IDEA?

Monica: We'd heard about alot of other bike co-ops. In Austin, TX there's a yellow bike project, that, as far as I've heard, works alot like our project. That's where they have bikes painted yellow that are parked all over town, and anyone who comes across one is free to ride it. You're supposed to just leave it when you're finished with it, so someone else can use it. I heard they tried that in Portland

SCAM: I heard they tried that in Portland, too, but it didn't work...

Monica: Yeah, I heard of that. They tried it in this small town in NorthWest Pennsylvania, to that I went to... I can't remember what it was called, but it didn't work there either. Peopl just stole the bikes, or they'd break 'em. But, I heard it works in Austin and they're doing it in Montreal, too, and its going good. I don't think it'd work too good in Philly. The way The Bike Church lends out bikes is that we always have bikes ready to rent, or sell. If someone comes into town and needs a bike, they can leave their I.D. with us and borrow the bike as long as they need it. That way, we usually get the bikes back.. We usually try to charge $5 for rental, too, but we don't always stick to it...

THAT SEEMS FAIR... HOW MANY DO YOU SELL?!

Monica: Alot, actually. It first the Bike Church was pretty word-of-mouth and just our West Philly friends knew about us, but now lots of people know about us. Whenever SEPTA goes on strike, we get alot of people on bikes! Older folks, students, young kids... everybody. We have bike sales sometimes where we line up all the bikes on the street, and sell 'em cheap. On the average they go for $40 or $50, but you can buy a junky 10-speed for $10 or $15....

DO YOU GUYS ORGANIZE BIKE EVENTS, TOO?

Monica: Nah, not really. We had some potlucks and showed some movies to raise money for the kids program. Of course, there is a side scene of people working on weird, tall bikes and choppers, for a bike circus. Unicycles, and stuff. And there's Critical Mass...

ANYTHING ELSE?

Monica: Its pretty easy to set up a bike co-op. All you need is space and some donations. You could probably fix up a couple bikes to sell to get tools... There's a bike co-op in Oakland at The Bat Cave that's a good example of a simple, succesful co-op. They have one set of every tool, a garge behind a house, and there's always at least one person there. I think their phone number is 510-595-1803...

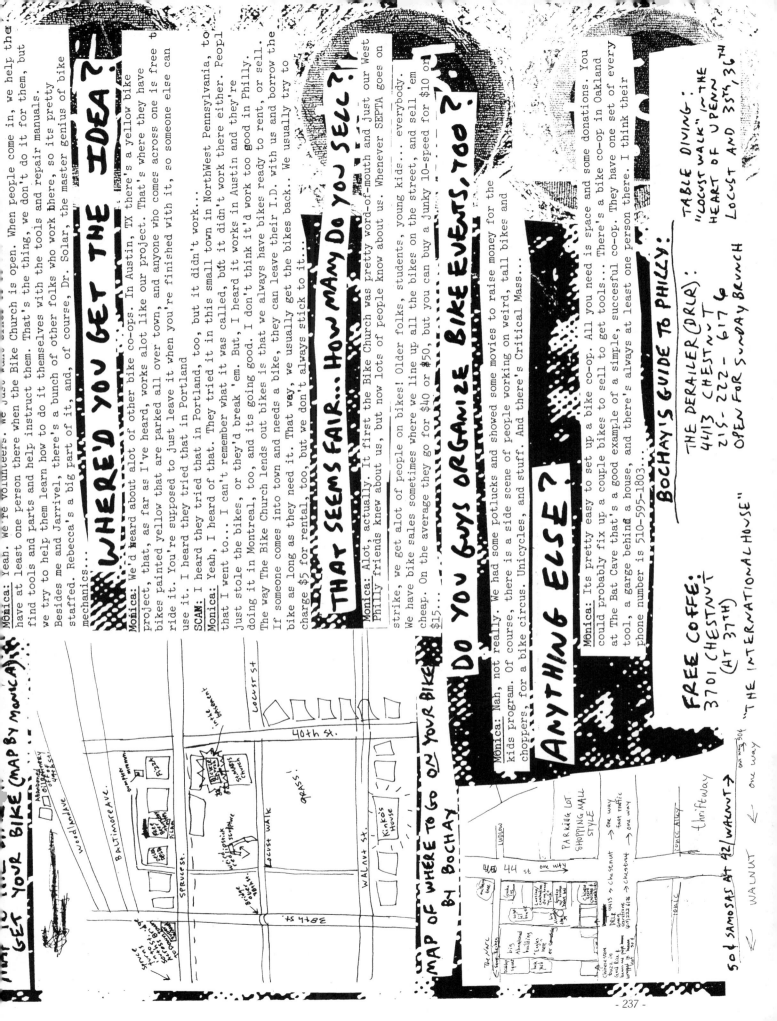

GET YOUR BIKE (MAP BY MONICA)!!

Woodland Ave.
Baltimore Ave.
Spruce St.
Locust Walk
Locust St.
Walnut St.
40th St.
38th St.
Kinkos House
GRASS!
in the basement
weird religious sculpture
Pizza
St. Marys Church
abandoned gymnasium
Abandoned Cliffords of 42nd St.

MAP OF WHERE TO GO ON YOUR BIKE BY BOCHAY

44 st
Ludlow
one way
Peace Alley
thriftway
Walnut
one way
one way fast traffic
one way
one way
PARKING LOT SHOPPING MALL STYLE
DRLR 4413 → chestnut → chestnut
(215)222-6176

5 0l SAMOSAS AT 42 WALNUT →

BOCHAY'S GUIDE TO PHILLY:

FREE COFFE:
3701 CHESTNUT
(AT 37TH)
"THE INTERNATIONAL HOUSE"

THE DERAILER (DRLR):
4413 CHESTNUT
215 - 222 - 6176
OPEN FOR SUNDAY BRUNCH

TABLE DIVING:
"LOCUST WALK" IN THE
HEART OF UPENN
LOCUST AND 35TH, 36TH

EL JORNADA DEL MUERTE

IGGY SCAM'S DOOMED TRIP TO MEXICO

ONE TIME, I TRIED TO HITCH HIKE TO MEXICO CITY WITH ONLY 20 BUCKS, SOME JUST-ADD-WATER-FOOD, MY SPANISH/ENGLISH DICTIONARY, A GALLON OF WATER AND MY X TAPE. I'M STILL NOT SURE WHAT I WAS THINKING BUT, THE PLAN, AS I REMEMBER, WAS SOMETHING LIKE THIS: FIRST, I'D HITCH DOWN THE BAJA CALIFORNIA. I KNEW THAT LOTS OF AMERICAN SURFERS HUNG OUT ON THE PENINSULA, AND I FIGURED IT'D BE EASY TO GET RIDES WITH THEM. MAYBE WE'D EVEN STOP AT SOME SECRET HIDDEN BEACH SPOT AND SURF. I'VE NEVER SURFED BEFORE, BUT, IN THE PLAN, I WOULD SHOW AMAZING SKILL FOR A BEGINNER AND THE SURFERS WOULD ACCEPT ME AS THEIR OWN, MAYBE SHARE THEIR DRUGS WITH ME, OR WHATEVER. THEN, I'D GET TO LA PAZ, AT THE TIP, WHERE I'D HIT UP RICH, AMERICAN TOURISTS WITH SOME LOST, ROBBED COLLEGE STUDENT S.O.B STORY, AND GET CASH TO TAKE THE "CHEAP" FERRY TO MAZATLAN, ON THE MAINLAND. ON THE BOAT, OF COURSE, I WOULD MEET AND FALL IN LOVE WITH SOME AMAZING, TRAVELLING PUNK WOMAN. WE WOULD EXPLORE MAZATLAN TOGETHER, NARROWLY AVOIDING ARREST AND INTERNATIONAL INCIDENTS AT EVERY TURN, S,HE'D HAVE TO LEAVE, AND I HEAD TO MEXICO CITY, ALONE, ON THE "CHEAP" PASSENGER TRAINS. IN MEXICO CITY, I'D WALK AROUND ALOT, LOOK AT ALOT OF OLD SHIT, AND HANG OUT WITH THE PUNKS OF MEXICO CITY, WHO'D TAKE ME TO ALL THE RAD SPOTS WHERE THEY SNIFF GLUE, OR HIDE FROM THE SECRET POLICE, OR WHATEVER. THEN I'D SHOW UP AT THE AMERICAN EMBASSY, PENILESS, WITH ANOTHER LOST, ROBBED STORY, IN ORDER TO GET SENT HOME. ONE PROBLEM, I GUESS, WITH BEING USED TO GETTING EVERYTHING FREE BEING USED TO MIRACLES HAPPENING, IS THAT YOU KINDA START TO EXPECT THEM. LESS THAN 48 HOURS AFTER I CONCEIVED THIS PLAN I WAS LEAVING OAKLAND ON A FREIGHT TRAIN SOUTH TO L.A. AND BEYOND...

EVERYTHING WAS WRONG FROM THE START. THE GIRL I HAD A BIG CRUSH ON WAS SUPPOSED TO SEE ME OFF AT THE DIVE COFFEE SHOP BY THE TRACKS. BUT SHE STOOD ME UP. IF SHE WOULDN'T SEE ME BEFORE I LEFT, IT SEEMED UNLIKELY THAT SHE WOULD BE WON OVER AT ALL BY MY BRAVERY AND HEROISM IN GOING. I CONSIDERED NOT GOING AT ALL, BUT, FINALLY, LEFT HER A PATHETIC NOTE ON A TELEPHONE POLE BY THE TRACKS, AND CAUGHT MY TRAIN SOUTH.

MUERTE ←

The Thumb (ignore it)

The water (Don't drink it)

HELP!

ONE OF THE MAJOR FLAWS OF MY PLAN WAS THAT I HAD TO GO THROUGH TWO OF THE MOST MISERABLE CITIES IN AMERICA - L.A. AND SAN DIEGO - TO EVEN GET TO THE BEGINNING OF MEXICO. IN L.A. I SLEPT UNDER A BRIDGE AND STARTED HITCH HIKING TO SAN DIEGO IN THE MORNING. IT WAS TERRIBLE. TWELVE HOURS OF BEING PASSED BY FIVE LANES OF 65 MPH TRAFFIC AND NO RIDES! I GOT ALL THE USUAL SHIT - PEOPLE GIVING ME THE THUMBS UP, PEOPLE GIVIN'T ME THE FINGER, PEOPLE SWERVING TO PRETEND THEY WERE GOING TO RUN ME OVER, PEOPLE YELLING "HEY FAGGOT!" PEOPLE STOPPING AND THEN SCREECHING AWAY JUST AS I RAN UP TO THEIR DOOR. EITHER YOU PICK UP HITCH HIKERS OR YOU FUCKIN' SUCK, THAT IS IT. I SLEPT UNDER A BRIDGE AGAIN AND, THE NEXT DAY, I TOOK A CITY BUSSES TO SAN DIEGO FOR ABOUT $2.15. I WASN'T EXPECTING SAN DIEGO TO BE SO CONSERVATIVE AND RACIST AND UPTIGHT, BUT ITS A BIG NAVY TOWN AND A BORDER TOWN, SO IT MAKES SENSE. I WALKED AROUND AND GOT KICKED OUT OF WHOLE REGIONS OF TOWN FOR BEING SCUMMY. LIKE, "SIR, WOULD YOU PLEASE LEAVE THE WATERFRONT. YOU SMELL." TWO TERRIBLE SAN DIEGO DAYS FINALLY CAME TO A HEAD WHEN, IN A 25¢ COFFEE FRENZY, I YELLED, "FUCK YOU, SAN DIEGO!" AND TOOK A PISS OFF THE NORDSTROM'S CAFE BALCONY, ONTO DOWNTOWN BELOW. BUT, I'M GETTING AHEAD OF MYSELF, BECAUSE FIRST I TRIED TO RAISE MONEY IN SAN DIEGO.

~~I HAD FINALLY LOOKED AT A MAP AND FOUND THAT MEXICO CITY WAS ALMOST~~

I HAD FINALLY LOOKED AT A MAP AND FOUND THAT MEXICO CITY WAS ALMOST A FULL 3,000 MILES FROM SAN DIEGO! SHIT! MAYBE I'D NEED MORE THAN 20 BUCKS. SO, MY FRIEND, FREUD, AND I TRIED TO OPEN A LEMONADE STAND, DOWNTOWN.

I STOLE THE FROZEN JUICE CONCENTRATE AND LUGGED A HUGE TABLE FROM THE DOWNTOWN PUNK HOUSE TO THE MAIN DRAG. I TAPED A HUGE MAP OF MEXICO BEHIND ME ON A BANK'S WALL, WITH A BIG SIGN THAT SAID, "SEND THIS BOY TO MEXICO!" IT WAS A HOT DAY, IN THE 80'S, AND I FIGURED THAT IF THE COLD DRINKS DIDN'T SELL, THAT, AT LEAST, MY STORY MIGHT KINDA CAPTURE DOWNTOWN SAN DIEGO'S IMAGINATION A BIT. BUT THE END RESULTS WERE PRETTY DISCOURAGING - ABOUT 6 BUCKS IN 3 HOURS. FINALLY, WE GAVE UP AND I ENDED UP POURING MOST OF THE LEMONADE OUT ON THE STREET IN FRONT OF THIS TACO BELL, AFTER THEY WOULDN'T LET ME USE THEIR BATHROOM FUCKERS...

BY NOW, I DIDN'T EVEN REALLY WANT TO GO ANYMORE, BUT, I FIGURED, I'D GO AHEAD WITH THE PLAN. AND IT WOULD EITHER START TO WORK REALLY QUICKLY, OR I'D GIVE UP. I WALKED OVER THE BORDER INTO TIJAUNA AND FIGURED I SHOULD AVOID SLEEPING OUTSIDE IN TOWN. SO I TOOK A CHEAP BUS TO ENSENADA, ABOUT 100 MILES DOWN THE COAST. ON THE BUS, I READ MY SPANISH/ENGLISH DICTIONARY. THE WHOLE TRIP JUST SEEMED SO DOOMED. I OPENED RIGHT UP TO THIS ONE PAGE WITH ALL THESE EMERGENCY PHRASES. "ME HA ROBADO (I HAVE BEEN ROBBED)" AND "HAY OCURRIDO UN ACCIDENTE (THERE HAS BEEN AN ACCIDENT)". WHAT IN THE HELL WAS I DOING HERE? "I AM LOST (ESTOY PERDIDO)". "I WANT TO GO TO THE EMBASSY (QUIERO IR AL CONSULADO)". "SOY INNOCENTE." I AM INNOCENT.

ENSENADA HAD A MAIN TOURIST DRAG, BUT WAS A LOT QUIETER AND MORE LIKE A REAL TOWN THAN TIJAUNA. THERE WERE MORE HOMES THAN BARS. THE CITY'S KNOWN FOR ITS BEACHES, SO I DECIDED TO GO SLEEP ON 'EM, AND THEN HITCH FIRST THING IN THE MORNING. IN THE MORNING I WAS AWAKENED BY PEOPLE TALKING AROUND ME. I POKED MY HEAD OUT OF MY SLEEPING BAG AND SAW A DONKEY STARING AT ME FROM ABOUT 5 FEET AWAY! I STARTED LAUGHING. WOW. GOOD MORNING, MEXICO. THE PEOPLE TALKING WERE BEHIND ME. THEY WERE THE MILITARY POLICE, AND AFTER MANY MINUTES OF ATTEPTED CONVERSATION, I GATHERED THAT I WAS IN A MILITARY HELICOPTER LANDING AREA AND THAT I COULD GO BACK TO SLEEP ABOUT 1½ FEET AWAY, ON THE OTHER SIDE OF THIS CRUMBLING WALL. THE MP'S WERE FRIENDLY AND APOLOGETIC AND I DIDN'T HAVE TO BRIBE THEM TO LEAVE. I WENT OVER BY THE DONKEY AND STARTED TO HEAT UP WATER FOR TEA WITH STERNO. THESE TWO KIDS, ONE A TEENAGER, AND ONE ABOUT 8 YEARS OLD, WERE WATCHING ME WITH GREAT INTEREST FROM THEIR DOORWAY. I WAVED AND THEY CAME OVER. I USED THE DICTIONARY TO TALK TO 'EM. APPARENTLY, THEIR FAMILY OWNED THE DONKEY AND CHARGED PEOPLE FOR DONKEY RIDES ON THE BEACH. BUT, NOW, THE SUN WAS UP AND THE BEACH WAS STILL DESERTED, SO THE DONKEY WAS JUST HANGIN' OUT. THEY HAD NEVER SEEN STERNO BEFORE AND WERE REALLY EXCITED BY IT, AS I STILL AM. LET'S FACE IT, STERNO IS JUST PLAIN RAD. ITS NOT MAGIC — IT'S SCIENCE! I GUESS THEY DON'T HAVE STERNO IN MEXICO. ACTUALLY, THEY DON'T HAVE A LOT OF THINGS, LIKE GOOD DUMPSTERS, FREE REFILLS, OR FOOD STAMPS, OR SOY MILK. THERE IS NO SOY MILK IN MEXICO.

I WALKED TO MEXICO HIGHWAY 1 AND PUT MY THUMB OUT. FROM THE WAY PEOPLE WERE STARING AT ME, I GUESSED THAT NO ONE HAD EVER DONE THIS BEFORE. OH WELL. A GUY PUSHING A HOT DOG CART CAME OVER TO TALK TO ME. AGAIN, I HAD TO USE THE DICTIONARY, BUT THIS WAS FUN. NOT KNOWING THE LANGUAGE MADE ME FEEL PRETTY LONELY AND I WAS STARTING TO FEEL LIKE MAYBE AMERICANS SHOULDN'T GO TO MEXICO, AT ALL — LIKE THERE'S NO HONEST, UNEXPLOITIVE WAY, LIKE AMERICA JUST RENTS MEXICO AND RIDES IT LIKE A DONKEY ON THE BEACH. BUT, ACTUALLY PIECING TOGETHER A 15-MINUTE TALK WITH THIS HOT DOG GUY AND THE TWO BROTHERS, BEFORE, WAS COOL. THE HOT DOG GUY, WANTED TO KNOW WHY I HAD COME TO MEXICO. "TRABAJO? (WORK)". "NO," I GRINNED. "AVENTURA! (ADVENTURE)".

I WASN'T GRINNING FOR LONG. IT WAS OVER 90° OUT. AND I WAS TRYING TO RATION MY SAN DIEGO TAP WATER CAREFULLY, CUZ WHEN IT RAN OUT, I'D HAVE TO BUY BOTTLES OF PURE WATER, AND I ONLY HAD 18 BUCKS. PEOPLE JUST DROVE RIGHT PAST ME FOR HOURS. WHERE WERE THE SURFERS? I WOULD LATER LEARN THAT NOT ONLY IS IT UNCOMMON FOR MEXICANS TO PICK UP AMERICAN HITCH HIKERS, BUT IF THEY DO, ACCORDING TO CUSTOM, THEY EXPECT MONEY IN EXCHANGE FOR THE RIDE. AFTER TEN HEARTBREAKING HOURS, I WAS VERY SICK AND VERY SUNBURNED. FINALLY, SOME MIDDLE AGED AMERICAN GUY STOPPED, JUST OUT OF CURIOSITY. I DIDN'T REALIZE HOW WEAK AND OUT OF IT I WAS UNTIL I FOUND I COULD BARELY TALK TO HIM. HE LIVED IN ENSENADA AND OFFERED ME DINNER AND A FLOOR TO CRASH ON, AND, IN MY POSITION, I COULD NOT REFUSE. AT HIS HOUSE, I ATE BEANS AND INSTANTLY PASSED OUT.

WHEN I WOKE UP THE NEXT DAY, THE GUY WAS STOCKING HIS FRIDGE WITH CASES AND CASES OF TECATE AND BLASTING MEXICAN DISCO. HIM AND HIS ROOMMATE WERE TRANSFERRED TO MEXICO TO RUN THIS BAIT AND TACKLE FACTORY, AFTER NAFTA, AND, NOW, HE WAS HAVING A BIG PARTY FOR THE PEOPLE WHO WORKED IN THE FACTORY. HE TOLD ME HE "HAD HIS EYE ON THIS ONE CUTE LITTLE THING FROM THE ASSEMBLY LINE" AND THEN HIM AND HIS ROOMMATE STARTED TO ARGUE OVER WHO SHOULD "GET" HER. WELL, THEY WERE BOTH COMPLETELY INSANE, I DECIDED. BUT, THERE WAS FREE BEER, SO I STAYED.

I GOT DRUNKER AND DRUNKER AND MET MORE AND MORE PEOPLE. I'D GET INTRODUCED TO SOMEONE, WE'D HOPELESSLY TRY AND TALK VIA THE DICTIONARY, FOR ABOUT 5 MINUTES 'TIL WE BOTH STARTED LAUGHING AND GAVE UP AND RAISED OUR BEERS IN A DRUNKEN TOAST. AH YES, THE TRUE INTERNATIONAL LANGUAGE: PROBLEM DRINKING. IT WAS FUN. ONE REAL COOL LOOKIN' GUY, WITH SHADES, WHO, FOR SOME REASON, WAS CALLED "THE COWBOY" KEPT COMING OVER TO ME EVERY 15 MINUTES TO LEAD ME THROUGH A COMPLICATED SERIES OF HAND SHAKES. WHEN IT WAS DONE HE'D HIT HIS CHEST AND SAY "AMIGO." ALL THE GIRLS KEPT TRYING TO GET ME TO DANCE WITH THEM. THIS WAS JUST TOO WEIRD, FINALLY, THOUGH, AND I WENT AND PASSED OUT IN ANOTHER ROOM.

IN THE MORNING, IT MADE SENSE TO LEAVE MEXICO. I SAW ALL THE HOLES IN MY PLAN PRETTY CLEARLY, AND IT SEEMED KINDA COOL JUST TO COME TO MEXICO, GO TO SOME WEIRD PARTY AND LEAVE. IT WAS 100 MILES TO THE BORDER, AND THE AMERICAN GUY OFFERED A RIDE TO THE BUS STATION, BUT I WANTED TO GIVE THE UNEXPECTED ONE MORE CHANCE. SO I DECIDED TO WALK BACK TO AMERICA. WELL, I FOUND SOME TRULY AMAZING BEACH AND CLIFF SPOTS ON THE WAY, BUT, MOSTLY, THE HIGHWAY WAS TOO FAR FROM THE WATER. I WALKED 33 MILES THAT DAY, AND, FINALLY, WHEN I'D HAD ENOUGH, THE UNEXPECTED DID HAPPEN. SOMEONE ACTUALLY STOPPED AND OFFERED ME A RIDE. A RIDE, ONCE AND FOR ALL, OUT OF MEXICO.

"GET IN THE POOL!" OR...
SWIMMING ACROSS THE USA with CHICKENHEAD!

by Iggy Scam

TWO GREAT SUMMER PAST TIMES ARE SWIMMING AND BAND TOURS AND THAT'S WHAT THIS IS ABOUT. A COUPLE SUMMERS BACK, MY OLD BAND, CHICKENHEAD WENT ON OUR LAST TOUR. WE HAD SOME GREAT SHOWS, SOME CANCELED SHOWS, SOME PANHANDLING FOR GAS MONEY IN SOUTH DAKOTA — MOST OF THE USUAL BAND TOUR SHIT — AND ALSO SOME GREAT SWIMMING. THE FIRST SWIMMING WAS IN SOME SMALL TOWN IN CONNECTICUT. THE KID WHO BOOKED THE SHOW SAID, "OH, DUDE, I WAS SO STONED WHEN YOU GUYS CALLED TO BOOK A SHOW THAT I FORGOT ALL ABOUT IT..." AH YES, ANOTHER "BOOK YOUR OWN FUCKIN' LIFE" MOMENT. WE HAD A GREAT TIME WITHOUT THE SHOW, THOUGH. I STOLE A WATERMELON FROM A SUPERMARKET AND WE PICNICKED AND SWAM IN THIS ICE COLD, BEAUTIFUL, CLEAR LAKE ON THE EDGE OF THIS FOREST AREA WITH HUGE GREEN TREES ROLLIN' UP THE HILL. I DOZED IN THE SHADE WHILE CHUCK LOOSE WENT AND STOLE SOME GUMBALL MACHINES FROM THIS LAUNDROMAT IN TOWN. WE FIGURED WE'D MAKE UP FOR THE CANCELLATION BY SELLING GUM FOR GAS AT ABC-NORIO THE NEXT DAY. NEW YORK CITY — I GOT TO BORROW SABU'S BIKE AND RIDE AROUND TOWN ALL DAY, BUT THEN I WAS ALL SWEATY WITH NO PLACE TO SWIM AT ALL! FUK! AS IF THIS WASN'T BAD ENOUGH, I HAD BEEN CHASED OUT OF A JERSEY CITY SUPER-MARKET THAT MORNING BY STORE SECURITY. THE COPS STOPPED US BEFORE WE GOT TO THE LINCOLN TUNNEL. THEY LET ME GO, BUT THEY TOOK AWAY OUR GUMBALL MACHINES! FASCISTS!! BALTIMORE — AS USUAL, WE TOTALLY ROCKED BALTIMORE AND THE SWIMMING WAS INCREDIBLE, TOO! AFTER THE SHOW, 15 PUNKS DRAGGED US AN HOUR OUT OF TOWN AND UP THE SIDE OF A MOUNTAIN TO DIVE OFF HUGE CLIFFS INTO THE CITY'S WATER RESERVOIR! THE NEXT DAY I WENT SWIMMING IN THE FOUNTAINS BY THE HARBOR WITH THERE RAD, CRAZY 8-YEAR OLD KIDS FROM THE NEIGHBORHOOD. THE KIDS TRIED TO GIVE ME MONEY FROM THE BOTTOM OF THE FOUNTAIN AND CONVINCED ME TO PICK THEM UP AND THROW THEM INTO THE FOUNTAIN, ALL WHILE TONS OF TOURISTS AND SAPS WALKED BY. KIDS RULE, SOMETIMES. BUT FINALLY, THE COPS CAME AND WE ALL RAN AWAY LAUGHING. KENT, OHIO. THIS WAS LOOKING TO BE THE MOST EXCITING SWIMMING YET, CUZ IT WAS A DREARY DAY AND I KNEW ALL THE POSERS WOULD STAY HOME AND I'D HAVE A POOL ALONE FOR TRUE INNER PEACE. I FOUND AN APARTMENT BUILDING WITH A POOL AND SAW THAT A SIGN THERE WARNED THAT THE POOL HAD THAT CHEMICAL IN IT THAT TURNS RED IF YOU PISS! YO! I COULDN'T WAIT TO SEE IF IT WORKED, BUT THE APARTMENT MANAGER YELLED AT ME AND DROVE ME AWAY BEFORE I COULD EVEN GET IN THE POOL. WHAT A MISSED OPPORTUNITY... CHICAGO — I WANTED TO SWIM IN THE LAKE, BUT SHANE AND VAPID WARNED ME THAT THE LAST GUY THEY KNEW WHO SWAM IN THE LAKE HAD COME OUT WITH A NOSEBLEED! FUCK THAT S#!T! MINNEAPOLIS — 10,000 LAKES SHOULD MEAN NO END OF SWIMMING BLISS, BUT ON THE 1ST DAY, WE "CRUISED TO THE LAKE, FUN, FUN, FUN" LIKE THE REPLACEMENTS SONG, AND I WAS THE ONLY CHICKENHEAD TO DARE SWIM IN THE GREEN, FOUL SMELLING PIT. THE NEXT DAY, I DESPARATELY FOUND A KIDDIE POOL AN HOUR BEFORE THE SHOW. A CROWD OF BEMUSED PARENTS, CONFUSED KINDERGARDENERS AND BUDDHA, OUR BASS PLAYER, LOOKED ON AS I, FIRST, LAID ON MY BACK AND THEN ROLLED AROUND, BARELY UNDERWATER, FOR A COUPLE MINUTES, WHATEVER IT TAKES! PORTLAND — I LOOKED ALL DAY ONLY TO FIND SOME YMCA-STYLE, INDOOR SHIT. THE LADY AGREED TO LET ME SWIM FOR FREE ONLY AFTER SHE REALIZED I WAS GOING TO JUMP IN THE POOL, WHETHER SHE LIKED IT OR NOT. UNFORTUNATELY, IT WAS LAP HOUR, OR SOME SUCH SHIT, AND THE POOL WAS PACKED WITH PEOPLE SWIMMING LAPS IN ROWS. I KEPT GETTING OUT OF THE ROWS AND, BASICALLY FUCKIN' SHIT UP. IT SUCKED, SO I LEFT BEFORE THE GERIATRIC SWIMMERS COULD GET IT TOGETHER TO LYNCH ME. BERKELEY — THIS IS A SWIMMING PUNK ROCK LOVE STORY, UH... SORT OF. ME AND THIS RAD GIRL WENT SWIMMING IN A MOTEL'S POOL, DRANK ON THE DOCK, WALKED AND SPRAY PAINTED THE TRACKS AND CAMPED OUT IN SLEEPING BAGS. DRUNKENLY, WE KISSED... AND THEN SHE THREW UP! TOO MUCH MALT LIQUOUR, I GUESS. THAT POOL ALWAYS SEEMS KINDA LONELY NOW, AND I HARDLY EVER GO THERE... SAN FRANCISCO — ME AND GRETA WALKED ALL DAY AND THEN WENT TO SWIM IN THE SAN FRANCISCO BAY. SHE SAID IT WAS SAFE. I KNEW SHE WAS LYING, BUT WENT ANYWAYS. THE WATER WAS KINDA GREASY AND COLD AND WE WERE BOTH BLEEDING WHEN WE CAME OUT. LIKE THE WATER WAS SHARP. UGH. THIS IS WHERE THE TOUR ENDED AND I HAD TO CHOOSE BETWEEN MY LOVE OF PUNK ROCK AND MY GOAL TO BE THE 1ST PUNK TO SWIM ACROSS THE ENGLISH CHANNEL. CHICKENHEAD BROKE UP, BUT THIS SUMMER YOU'LL STILL FIND ME AT THE POOL. SEE YA THERE!

THE ROCK 'N' ROLL LIFESTYLE!

BLOOD MOP GOES ON TOUR WITH THE SPAWN SACS AND CHAOS L.R.   by IGGY SCAM

IN PUNK ROCK, OVER THE YEARS, HOW HARD A BAND ROCKS HAS COME TO BE MOST EASILY MEASURED BY THE AMOUNT OF GROSS BODY FLUIDS A BAND RELEASES ONSTAGE. THERE'S THE HISTORY, THE LORE — IGGY AND DARBY COVERED IN BLOOD, THE CLASH COVERED IN A WHOLE AUDIENCE'S SPIT. IT STILL HOLDS TRUE TODAY. A COUPLE WEEKS AGO, I BORROWED THIS GUY'S GUITAR FOR A SHOW AND, WHEN I HANDED IT BACK, A BLURRY 15 MINUTES LATER, THE GUITAR AND MY HAND WERE SPLATTERED WITH BLOOD. WE BOTH JUST STARED AT IT FOR A MINUTE, SORT-OF IN AWE, LIKE, "FUCK YEAH! THAT'S COOL!"

IT REMINDED ME OF WHEN I LIVED WITH CHICKEN JOHN IN A CLOSET FULL OF HIS STUFF. ONE DAY, AFTER MONTHS OF LIVING THERE, HE SHOWED ME A NON-DESCRIPT SHOE BOX THAT HAD BEEN SITTING NEAR MY PILLOW, THE WHOLE TIME I'D LIVED THERE. IT TURNED OUT THAT IT WAS FULL OF SHIT-ENCRUSTED MICROPHONES THAT HE'D SAVED FROM HIS TOURS WITH G.G. ALLIN! IT WAS A REAL MUSEUM PIECE OF PUNK. HOLDING THE BOX, I COULD CLOSE MY EYES AND SEE THE SWEATY CLUBS, THE BROKEN BEER BOTTLES, THE FLAILING, SHIT-SMEARED SINGER... IT WAS REAL HISTORY.

BUT WHAT IF THE PUKING AND SHITTING ISN'T ON STAGE AT ALL, AND JUST SORT-OF HAPPENS EVERYWHERE YOU GO? IS IT STILL THE ROCK?!? THIS MAY BE THE QUESTION THAT THE SPAWN SACS ARE TRYING TO ANSWER.

I HAD BEEN WAITING FOR THE SACS TO ROLL INTO SAN FRANCISCO, EVER SINCE I GOT THEIR GREAT RECORD, "WE ARE THE ASSHOLES OF THE NIGHT" IN THE MAIL. FITTINGLY, THE FIRST OF THEIR THREE SHOWS WAS AT THE OLD MISSION RECORDS STORE ON MISSION STREET. IN BODY FLUIDS ALONE, MISSION RECORDS HAD HAD SOME OF HARDEST ROCKING SHOWS OF ALL TIME. THE SHOWS ALWAYS STARTED LATE, AROUND 11:00 PM. BY MIDNIGHT, THERE WOULD BE WHOLE SQUAT-LOADS OF CRUSTIES, SLIPPIN' IN THEIR BLOOD AND VOMIT. THE OWNER STARTED, THOUGHTFULLY, PROVIDING BUCKETS TO PUKE IN, BUT THEY'D INEVITABLY BE KICKED OVER BY THE CURIOUS MOSHERS FROM REDWOOD CITY. BY 1:00 AM, THE PLACE WAS PART OVEN AND PART ASHTRAY, JAMPACKED WITH UNDERAGE DRINKERS, SWEATSOAKED BANDS, AND PUKING DRUMMERS. BY 2:00 AM, THERE'D BE A WHOLE ROW OF PASSED-OUT PUNKS AND THEIR DOGS, OUT IN FRONT OF THE STORE, SLEEPING IT OFF ON MISSION STREET. BY 4:00 AM, AFTER CLEANUP, YOU'D LOOK AT THE CRATES OF EMPTY BEER CANS AND BOTTLES AND THE PASSED OUT PUNKS, AND SAY, "NOW THAT'S A PUNK SHOW!"

FUELED BY SEVERAL JUGS OF STOLEN WHISKEY, THE SACS ROCKED MISH REX ABOUT AS HARD AS YOU CAN, AND, WHEN IT WAS OVER, WE ALL WALKED, DRUNKENLY, AND HAPPILY AROUND THE CORNER TO JIMMY'S PLACE, WHERE THEY WERE STAYING. JUST AS WE GET THERE, ONE OF THE GUYS FROM MISSION RECORDS PULLS UP IN A CAR, AND SAYS, "THIS GUY'S WITH YOU, RIGHT?" IN THE PASSENGER SEAT SOAKED IN SWEAT AND SNORING AWAY, IS THE SPAWN SACS' SINGER, TOM, COMPLETELY DEAD DRUNK AND PASSED OUT. "I FOUND HIM IN THE BATHROOM."

TOM, BORN AND RAISED IN A RURAL, MICHIGAN, FARM TOWN, IS JUST PLAIN BIG. IT TOOK SIX OF US TO GET HIM OUT OF THE CAR AND UP THE TWO FLIGHTS OF STAIRS TO THE KITCHEN. FROM MY POSITION AT THE THIGH OF HIS LEFT LEG, I PROBABLY WAS THE ONE WHO HAD THE MOST OF TOM'S ASS IN MY FACE. HALFWAY UP THE STAIRS I BECAME CURIOUS ABOUT THE STRANGE AND TERRIBLE ODOR I WAS SUDDENLY SURROUNDED BY. I TOOK A COUPLE MORE SNIFFS AND I KNEW. "HEY GUYS," I SAID. "I THINK TOM SHIT HIS PANTS."

AND, SURE ENOUGH, WHEN TOM AWOKE THE NEXT MORNING, WITH WITTICISMS LIKE "I LOVE COPS" AND "I SHIT MY PANTS" SCRAWLED ACROSS HIS FACE, HE ADMITTED IT, OVER THE MORNING'S FIRST BEERS. MOST PEOPLE'S STORIES ABOUT THEIR PATHETIC ATTEMPTS AT THE ROCK 'N' ROLL LIFESTYLE END HERE: "ONCE WHEN I WAS YOUNG AND CRAZY AND IN A PUNK BAND, I WENT ON TOUR AND GOT SO DRUNK

THAT I SHIT MY PANTS." BUT IN THE WEEK THE SPAWN SACS SPENT ON JIMMY'S FLOOR, THE TURDS KEPT COMING!

BY THE END OF THE WEEK, WE WERE TRULY IMPRESSED. JIMMY HAPPENED TO RUN INTO JELLO BIAFRA OUT ON MISSION STREET. HE SAID "HEY JELLO, CHECK THIS OUT: I GOT THIS BAND FROM FLORIDA STAYING AT MY PLACE. EVERY NIGHT THEY GET SO DRUNK THAT THEY SHIT THEIR PANTS. HAVE YOU EVER HEARD OF THAT?"

JELLO THOUGHT IT OVER FOR A LONG MINUTE AND FINALLY SAID NO, HE HADN'T! AS PUNK HEADS INTO ITS THIRD DECADE, THE SACS INVENTED A NEW STYLE!

BUT, STILL, DOESN'T THAT SORT-OF RUIN "THE OLD DAYS" FOR YOU A LITTLE? I WOULD HAVE THOUGHT THE SHOWS THEN WERE SO CRAZY THAT GUYS WERE CRAPPING THEMSELVES ALL OVER THE PLACE, BACK THEN. I'M SORT-OF BUMMED THAT JELLO DIDN'T BUST INTO A LONG WINDED STORY ABOUT THE TIME THE GUY FROM THE DILS CRAPPED HIS PANTS AND THEN, AS A JOKE, ROLLED HIS TURD UP IN A TORTILLA AND GAVE IT TO WILL SHATTER TO EAT. OH WELL. SO MUCH FOR LIVING IN THE PAST.

I WAS SO INSPIRED BY THE SACS' TURD-FILLED VISIT, THAT I DECIDED TO TRY AND GET MY OLD BAND FROM LITTLE ROCK, CHAOS L.R., BACK TOGETHER FOR A SHORT SUMMER TOUR. IT WASN'T GOING TO BE EASY, BECAUSE I NOW LIVED IN SAN FRANCISCO, THE SINGER LIVED IN CHICAGO, AM GUITARIST WAS IN PORTLAND, AND OUR BASSIST DIDN'T EVEN WANT TO GO. BUT, SOON, WE HOOKED IT UP. THE SINGER HAD THE TRUCK, THE GUITARIST GOT US EQUIPMENT TO USE, I BOOKED THE SHOWS, AND WE RECRUITED A NEW BASSIST — A THEN YOUNG AND STILL UNKNOWN ALAN DISASTER. WHO KNEW THAT WHEN ALAN BORROWED A BASS AND STARTED HITCHING NORTH TO CHICAGO TO MEET HIS RIDE TO CALIFORNIA FOR TOUR THAT HE WAS THUMBING HIS WAY INTO PUNK SEMI-HISTORY

THE TOUR SOMEHOW CAME TOGETHER REAL WELL. WE HAD NEW SONGS, WE PLAYED GOOD, PEOPLE ACTUALLY SHOWED UP TO WATCH, AND WE EVEN GOT PAID SOMETIMES! BUT THE ACTUAL SHOWS SOON TOOK A BACKSEAT TO THE REAL DRAMA OF THE TOUR: AGAINST EVEN THEIR OWN WILLS, ALAN DISASTER AND THE SINGER, MITCH, HAD EMBARKED ON AN UNFORTUNATE AND SHAMEFUL RACE TO SEE WHO WOULD PASS OUT DRUNK AND WET THE MOST BEDS IN THEIR SLEEP. AT FIRST, IT LOOKED LIKE A TIGHT RACE, AND I EVEN SORT-OF ASSUMED THAT WITH THE AMOUNT OF BEER WE ALWAYS HAD ON HAND THAT ME AND THE GUITARIST, MATT, WOULD PROBABLY CATCH UP. BUT, ON THE MORNING AFTER OUR SHOW IN BELLINGHAM, WHEN ALAN PROUDLY ANNOUNCED, "I'M UP TO #3!" AND THEN MODESTLY ADDED, "AND THERE WAS A GIRL WITH ME, TOO.." WE KNEW ALAN WAS ON HIS WAY TO A BRIGHTER FUTURE, MAYBE EVEN A SOLO CAREER. SURE ENOUGH, AT THE END OF A MERE WEEK LONG TOUR, ALAN DISASTER HAD OUTPEED MITCHELL, 5 BEDS TO 3, AND HAD EVEN MANAGED TO PEE ON 2 GIRLS WHO HE'D LURED INTO BED WITH HIS DISARMING SOUTHERN CHARM. MATT AND I HADN'T PEED EVEN ONCE! CHAOS L.R. MANAGED TO RECORD BUT ALAN WAS SIMPLY OUTGROWING THE BAND. WE ALL WENT BACK TO OUR SEPARATE CITIES, BUT ALAN DISASTER WENT ON HIS OWN SUMMER WEST COAST TOUR, THUMBING IT FROM TOWN TO TOWN, BORROWED BASS IN HAND. EXCESS IS THE STUFF OF ROCK 'N' ROLL LEGEND. WAS IT MICK JAGGER, OR ROD STEWART WHO HAD 10 GALLONS OF SPERM PUMPED OUT OF HIS STOMACH? WHO KNOWS? BUT I DID SEE WITH MY OWN EYES, 10 GALLONS OF BEER AND PISS PUMPED OUT OF ALAN DISASTER'S MATTRESS!

more letters:

Iggy:

I'm in Raleigh, hiding from cops, stupid people, college students,etc. I've just been drinking on plasma cash, smoking opium, trying to find a drug study to do for some money to get out of here... We had to leave Greensboro. We had moved out of our house into the abandoned house 2 doors down, and the owner came and said we could live there for awhile! The reason being "I don't want you sleeping on the streets, cuz the fucking cops might mess with you..." Then, we got a note on our door, one day:"Hi! We are the cops! No more parties or we'll kick you out! Signed, Officer so-and-so, GPD #713" We had ripped off this gas station for 10 cases of beer and it was all in there, so they thought 20 people were drinking what just us 2 were drinking every night. That day, we went dumpster diving. This cop pulled up and gave us $10 cause he felt bad for us. It turned out, the cop was the brother of our arch nemesis, Officer C.L. Combs of the Greensboro PD. The cop said, "My brother and I are very different kk people," with a sigh... Anyways, I'm kind of sick and out of it and rambling... write back. Oh yeah,me and my girlfriend Sarah, went and saw The new Misfits. That was fucking weird... She got us all in for free, but then she got kicked out of the club for "biting 10 people" during "We Bite."...
You know of any good boats to squat on the Bay in Miami?
Brain
Raleigh, NC

EDITOR'S NOTE: BRAIN'S MISSING AGAIN... ANYONE WHO RUNS INTO HIM, TELL 'EM TO DROP A LINE...

SHED No TEARS

IT WAS AN OFF NIGHT ON TOUR AND WE WERE STUCK IN SEATTLE, AGAIN. IT WASN'T SUPPOSED TO BE AN OFF NIGHT, BUT THE COPS AT THE BORDER WEREN'T ABOUT TO LET US INTO CANADA, SO WE HAD TO DRIVE BACK. SOME TOUR. THE NIGHT BEFORE, WE'D PLAYED, MORE OR LESS, TO THE GUITARIST'S BROTHER AND SISTER, AND THE GUY WHO BOOKED THE SHOW'S GIRLFRIEND, AT A DISMAL, NEAR EMPTY CAFE. STILL, WE PLAYED AS HARD AS WE COULD, AND SOUNDED GREAT. IT WAS ONLY AFTER THE BROTHER AND SISTER LEFT THAT WE GOT BORED, AND, BETWEEN SONGS, TOOK TURNS YELLING OUT THE WINDOW OF THE 2ND STORY CAFE THROUGH A BULL HORN AT PASSING HIPSTERS BELOW.

NOW, WE WERE PARKED IN FRONT OF AN UPSCALE MICROBREWERY, DOWN THE BLOCK, WHERE WE WERE WAITING TO SEE IF THE MANAGER WOULD LET US PLAY AFTER THE JAZZ BAND THAT WAS IN THERE. ALOT WAS RIDING ON IT, IT MEANT NOT ONLY FREE BEER, BUT A RARE CHANCE TO PLAY OUR ANTI-YUPPY ANTHEMS TO AN ACTUAL ROOM FULL OF YUPPIES. I GRINNED BROADLY AND SAID, "TOUR... IS... GREAT!"

THE GUITARIST SAID, "THIS IS PROBABLY THE WORST TOUR I'VE BEEN ON IN THE 15 YEARS I'VE BEEN TOURING."

THE BASSIST SAID, "I THOUGHT YOU SAID THE ONE BEFORE THIS WAS THE WORST, BEFORE WE STARTED."

"WE ARE GETTING BETTER," I SAID. "BETTER AT GETTING WORSE AND WORSE!" IT WAS TRUE, TOO. COULD THIS BE HOW WE LIKE IT? WE SING SONGS ABOUT HOW THE COPS FUCK WITH US AND WE'RE DOWN AND OUT AND THEN THE COPS FUCK WITH US AND WE'RE DOWN AND OUT. IS IT A SELF-FULFILLING PROPHECY? WHAT CAME FIRST, THE LYRICS OR THE LIFESTYLE? WHO KNOWS? IT WAS THE GUITARIST'S TURN TO KEEP THE BASSIST FROM GETTING TOO DRUNK TO PLAY SO I GAVE THE BASSIST MY BEER AND TOOK OFF FOR A SHORT WALK AROUND THE NEIGHBORHOOD.

WE'RE DESPERATE. STRANDED. TREATMENT BOUND. I WAS WALKING ON PIKE MAKING A LIST OF SONGS THAT WERE WRITTEN UP TO 20 YEARS AGO, BUT WERE, NOW, ABOUT US, TONIGHT. ITS FUNNY HOW YOU SORT-OF GROW INTO PUNK LYRICS OVER THE YEARS. FUNNY AND A LITTLE SAD. LIKE WHEN YOU'RE A KID, YOU THINK "HA HA! 'DEAD COPS'! FUCK YEAH!" BUT BY THE TIME YOU'VE FELT ENOUGH COPS PUTTING HANDCUFFS ON YOU, YOU KNOW THAT "BEYOND AND BACK" REALLY IS A SONG ABOUT A DEAD END LIFE, "ALTERNATIVE ULSTER" REALLY IS ABOUT PEOPLE TRYING TO BE FREE, AND "DEAD COPS" IS MORE THAN A CHORUS; ITS SOMETHING YOU FEEL IN YOUR BONES, AND SING WITH PRIDE. THIS IS OUR SHITTY TOUR!

ALONG THE WALK, I PASSED A PUNK GIRL WHO WAS CRYING INTO A PAYPHONE. SHE WAS TELLING THE PERSON ON THE OTHER END, "THEY LOCKED MY SQUAT UP WITH ALL MY STUFF INSIDE OF IT! I DON'T KNOW WHAT I'LL DO!" I STOPPED AND WAITED. IT WAS LIKE LOOKING AT SOMETHING OUT OF MY OWN PAST. I CAN'T EVEN COUNT HOW MANY TIMES I STOOD AT A PAYPHONE, DESPERATELY LOOKING FOR A PLACE TO STAY BECAUSE MY SQUAT GOT BUSTED. WHEN SHE HUNG UP, I GAVE HER SOME OF MY FOOD STAMPS AND ASKED IF THERE WAS ANYTHING I COULD DO TO HELP.

SHE CALMED DOWN A LITTLE AND SAID, "WHAT I REALLY NEED IS A CROWBAR, SO I CAN GET THE LOCK OFF AND GET MY STUFF OUT." I KNEW WE HAD TOOLS BACK AT THE VAN, SO WE WALKED OVER TO CHECK IT OUT. THE GUITARIST GAVE US A CROWBAR AND A HAMMER, AND AS WE HEADED TOWARDS HER SQUAT, HE CALLED OUT "GO AHEAD AND KEEP THE CROWBAR. JUST BRING BACK THE HAMMER. IT USED TO BELONG TO A FRIEND OF MINE!"

ON THE WALK TO HER SQUAT, I FOUND OUT MORE ABOUT HER STORY. SHE HAD BEEN KICKED OUT OF 3 SQUATS THIS MONTH, AND THE COPS FUCKED WITH HER EVERYWHERE SHE WENT. A HOMELESS KID STOPPED US AND ASKED IF WE HAD ANY POINTS. SHE SAID, NO, HER NEEDLES WERE LOCKED UP IN THE SQUAT, TOO, AND SHE WAS SICK, HANGING OUT WITH HER MADE ME THINK BACK TO HOW, AFTER I'D WRITTEN SEVERAL ZINES ABOUT SCAMMING AND SQUATTING, I'D SEE KIDS WHO WERE ALL STRUNG OUT ON DRUGS ON THE STREET AND WONDER IF I'D SOMEHOW CONTRIBUTED TO IT BY WRITING STORIES THAT MADE IT ALL SEEM SO EASY AND FUN. BUT, WHEN I RE-READ THEM, I FOUND THAT, IN THE ZINES, I WAS GETTING KICKED OUT OF SQUATS, BANNED FROM PUBLIC PLACES FOR BEING A BUM, AND, EVEN, GETTING ARRESTED, ON PRACTICALLY EVERY PAGE. THE WARNINGS WERE ALL THERE. I MEAN, WHEN PUNK HEROS O.D., DO KIDS QUIT USING HEROIN?

WHEN WE GOT TO HER OLD PLACE, THE LOCK TURNED OUT TO BE EASY TO GET OFF. IT WAS SO SMALL THAT I ONLY NEEDED THE HAMMER TO REACH UNDER AND RIP OFF THE HASP IN A FEW TUGS. THEN, WE HURRIED IN, LIT A CANDLE AND STARTED TRYING TO STUFF ALL HER BELONGINGS INTO HER BACKPACKS. WHEN WE THOUGHT WE HAD IT ALL, WE HEARD VOICES, SO WE GRABBED EVERYTHING, BLEW OUT THE CANDLE, AND RAN.

I LEFT HER AT THE CORNER. SHE SAID SHE'D BE ALLRIGHT. SHE KNEW ANOTHER PLACE SHE COULD PROBABLY SQUAT, AND SHE WALKED OFF, LOOKING PRETTY BAD ASS, CROWBAR IN HAND.

BACK AT THE VAN, THE SHOW WAS ON BUT THE BASSIST WAS ASLEEP. IT WAS JUST ANOTHER NIGHT ON TOUR, BUT IT FELT LIKE ALL THE TOURS AND ALL THE SQUATS AND EVERYTHING HAD BEEN GOING ON FOREVER. I SAID, "WHEN DO WE GO HOME, AGAIN?" BUT THE GUITARIST, ON HIS WORST TOUR IN 15 YEARS, JUST HANDED ME THE BASSIST'S BEER AND SAID, "THANKS FOR BRINGING THAT HAMMER BACK. I'VE BEEN CARRYING IT AROUND FOR YEARS."

HE SAID, "WILL SHATTER LEFT IT AT MY HOUSE A MONTH BEFORE HE DIED."

STUN GUNS

Hoo boy, the Stun Guns are miami, Fla's long favored ROCK GODS! yeow! Here, they are interviewed by Iggy Scam (henceforth, SCAM) and Mr. Chuck Loose (likewise, MRR). If you care, and you should, because it's good and I wouldn't shit you 'cause I'm your pal, you can get their seven inch record "I Can't Believe It's Not Murder" from Starcrunch Records at PO Box 9152 Miami, FL 33124. Send three dollars and tell 'em Chuck Loose sent ya, Anyway, this interview was conducted with Mr. Paul Enema (who I have chosen to call Enema), "Hurricaine" Andrew Guns (call him Pandy), George "Machine Gun" Kelly (George) and the bionic Mr. Buddha (who shall be referred to as Bood) at "Machine Gun" Kelly's squalish flat in historic El Portal, Florida.

Enema: First off, we want to play in Cuba.

Bood: Yeah, anyone who can help us get a show, like Fidel Castro, if you're reading this, let us know.

Enema: Be careful what you say about Castro, In Miami, they'll kill ya!

MRR: George, when are you gonna run for El Portal city commissioner? *(El Portal- the hamlet, nay, the municipality, of El Portal is located within the confines of "old miami", and, believe it or not, the entire burg is a bird sanctuary!! Indeed! In fact, vistors to the historic "EL" have been publicly flogged or set afire for daring to harm to local flora and fauna!)*

George: I should soon! It only takes 26 votes to win!

Scam: Oh, so that's why you let Buddha and Paul live on your floor, so they can establish residency and vote for you.

MRR: Have you ever seen a riot in Miami?

George: Anyone can see a riot in Miami!

Pandy: Yeah, I saw a riot one time with my mom, there was a buncha people running towards us and then some guy came up and put his penis on my mom's car!!

Scam: No way!

MRR: Wow, it really was a riot!, .so, you just got back from tour with The Schaeffers *(The Schaeffers- Dalton, Georgia's last great punk hope! possibly the only band with enough gumption to faithfully render a cover of "The Crue's" 'Livewire', .OOOOOOGGG GAAAAHHHHH!!)* , how was New Orleans? Weren't you excited to be in a town where you can drink 24 hours a day?

En-

ma: we can drink 24 hours a day right here!

George: It was cool, except for the asshole who wrote on our van.

MRR: Who wrote on your van?

George: Well, the guys at the place we played at said they wrote on our van 'cause we spray painted on the front of their building.

Enema: But we did.

George: Oh.

Bood: All I know is, we played the show and in the middle of the night, someone wrote "the Stun Guns", "hey shmecky" and "the Schaeffers" on the club,

Scam: It was Paul! you dick, me and Mike Schaeffers had to clean it up at 5:00 A.M., when I was too drunk to even stand!

Pandy: Well, we don't know who did it, um, we never will, but then the guy wrote shit on our van, blah blah blah, but the cool thing was in New Orleans, I made money for playing drums in the street!

MRR: Really?

Pandy: yeah, we were drinking by the river and there was this guy playing drums, who, as it turns out, was from West Palm Beach *(West*

Palm Beach-or 'WPB' locally, although a scant 70 miles from miami, it is removed by, um, light years socially, like, not only can you not get cuban coffee or malta, ya can't even get a good guayabara there, sheeesh), he let me and Ivy (close Stun Guns confident and associate) play drums and we got "tons" of change.

Scam: What did you buy with it?

Pandy: More, uh, alcohol! wait, my mom's gonna read this!

Scam: Hi, Andy's mom!

Pandy: Actually, if you're reading this mom, send me a new pair of shoes!

MRR: What else happened on tour?

Pandy: Uh, .we walked around the Grand Canyon with our guitars, and let all these tourists take pictures holding our guitars.

Enema: See, anybody can be in this band, (editing note: here the Stun Guns took 20 minutes trying to remember anything from the 2-month tour, and only vaguely remember drinking pitchers of beer and singing James Brown songs in a bar in California, 'the "something" duck')

MRR: Have you ever been to the Police Hall of Fame in Miami? (Miami Police Hall Of Fame-Miami's Police Hall of Fame, there, ya rock-et scientist. duh.)

George: Yes! why I "sat in the electric chair" and everything!

Enema: They have a great adult crime scene set up with plastic cops to shoot at!

MRR: Wow! Did they have any John Dillinger stuff?

Enema: No! it's a police hall of fame, not a cool old gangster's hall of fame!

Scam: OK, Paul, how about I name some Stun Guns lyrics and you see if you can tell me what song you sing them in, .what about "we hide fugitive thoughts behind cold beers"?

Enema: That's in "TV Tan", .I got it right? What do I win?

Scam: What about "don't hang around if you can't take it"?

Enema: Alright! That's enough outta you!!

Scam: I don't think he knows.

MRR: When did people start throwing stuff at you guys while you play?

Enema: It was our first show at Churchill's with Chickenhead, (Churchill's Hideaway-Miami's own quasi-legendary rock-and-roll-British-pub-smack-in-the-middle-of-little-Haiti.)

Scam: No, that was both bands second show, it wasn't then, it was the Friday the 13th show in September '91 with the prom sluts, the human oddities, chickenhead and the methadone actors, (Friday the 13th Show-traditionally this is the day that Dave, the crazy British owner of Churchill's allows the punks to grace his stage and play the Hideaway.)

Enema: Wow, you remember all that? I just have this vague memory of chairs and bottles flyin' at me, shit!

Scam: What was the worst thing that's been thrown at you on stage?

Pandy: Oh, the firecrackers! it was on the 3rd, not the 4th of July.

Bood: In Texas, somewhere.

Pandy: Yeah, it was one of the best shows of the tour, these people where just totally goin' crazy, throwin' firecrackers at us while we played in their living room!

Enema: I'm glad we didn't play at Calle Punk-O! (Calle Punk-O! (Ky-ay-punk-oh!) loosly translates as "punk street", an all day punk rock show in "Jose Marti Park", Little Havana, Miami, near Calle Ocho (Eighth Street) I looked around before we were supposed to play and there was nothing for people to throw but rocks!!

MRR: Have you ever attacked anyone with an axe handle?

Enema: Why do people always ask us that?

"CLEANING UP THE MISSION:

One of the most often repeated and least questioned statements about gentrification is that we, the punks, can't do anything about it because its our fault. This line of reasoning, widely belived by even the punks themselves, goes that gentrification, like other economic forces, is somehow a "natural" process, like the weather, and that it "naturally" occurs when punks and artists move into a ghetto for the cheap rents. After we arrive, the rents "naturally" rise, the poor are "naturally" kicked out.

While I'm sure that such traditional punk contributions to Mission District life as providing warehouse space for teenagers to drink at punk shows, buying pills at Evergreen, doing graffiti, and dealing speed have caused the Mission real estate values to skyrocket, sometimes these "natural" economic forces need a more sinister kickstart to help get the process going. Long before the punks and artists arrived, the "cleaning up" of the Mission campaign, as we now know it, probably started in earnest on the night of December 12, 1975 when a still unknown person or persons entered the cheap and rundown Gartland Apartments at 16th and Valencia, soaked the stairwell with gasoline, and dropped a lit match.

At least 12 people died in the confirmed arson. A temporary morgue was established on 16th in front of the Wells Fargo bank. The hotel was not rebuilt. The people who lived there had to go somewhere else, while the "Gartland Pit" remained empty until the early '90's. No one was ever arrested for starting the fire.

By the mid-80's, punks, artists, and activists had shown up in The Mission and the Gartland Pit was often used as a sight for protest, film showings, even punk shows. This may be gentrification, but it is a gentrification that was started, not by "the yuppies taking over", but by straight up violence against poor people's homes.

The Mission cleanup was devised by city planners, though, long before the Gartland burned. In the 60's, after urban renewal had sucessfully removed most of the housing where black people lived in the Fillmore, and was clearing out the SRO hotels of South of Market, The City planned to use BART to drive the Latino concentration out of the Mission. Following the lead of Manhattan, SF planned to deindustrialize and base its economy on stock trading, insurance and real estate. The idea was to level the Mission and build new apartment towers to house the young office workers that would work in the Financial District and build BART to provide easy access to Montgomery Street. Despite massive opposition the BART was built under Mission Street, but the gleaming offices and apartments planned for 16th and Mission BART plaza obviously never materialized.

So much for urban planning. Today, 16th and Mission is the sight of a foul smelling market that sells boar and ostrich meat, a donut/pornography store called "The Fun Spot", and the largest open air heroin market between LA and Vancouver.

And the guy who designed 16th/Mission BART plaza for the City was last seen, penniless and insane, trying to sell a late night transfer to Wolf Boy.

But from the late 60's on, The Mission was under attack, when landlords realized how much their property would be worth if they could just get rid of the people who lived in it. The message was often beaten home by SFPD. Officers Brodnik and McGoran, code named "Mission 11" walked the beat on Mission Street, a couple of old time, racist Irish cops from The Mission with a special hatred for Mexicans. When they weren't getting drunk on duty and hitting on waitresses at Bruno's, they were out cruising the strip in their trademark unmarked white pickup truck. They'd jam up the longhaired Latin kids hanging out at the Doggie Diner on 18th and Mission, rough 'em up, and then drop them off way up in Noe Valley and make them walk home. Brodnik's infamous 2-foot rubber hose that he carried to work over uncooperative kids is the stuff of subconscious Mission Street history; you can feel it in the street. But it didn't do him any good on May 1, 1969 when Mission Eleven stopped some kids in Noe Valley and a scuffle broke out, during which McGoran's gun was discharged and Brodnik was shot down dead.

The seven youths present at the shooting, incredibly, were all charged with Brodnik's murder, and they became known as "Los Siete De La raza". The massive organization in the Mission for their legal defense proved that the neighborhood was going to be harder to put down than the cops thought. Out of their defense grew a Mission newspaper, "Basta Ya", free legal defense programs for poor Latinos hassled by The Man, a free breakfast program at St. Peter's church on Alabama Street, and a worker run restaurant next to the Levi-Strauss factory on Valencia, that provided cheap food and attempted to organize the latin women who worked at Levi's. A year after the shooting, in a trial that put the SFPD and Mission ghetto conditions on trial, Los Siete were found not guilty of the murder.

A couple years later, in 1973, activist attorney Oscar Acosta came back to SF to write "Revolt Of The Cockroach People", the classic of the Chicano movement, at the Royan Hotel, "The Mission's Finest" on Valencia, down the block from the still unburned Gartland. I have an old Chronicle clipping that shows a big, heavy-set, long haired Latin guy, identified in the caption as "Walter Acosta", but obviously The Brown Buffalo, himself, walking on 24th at South Van Ness, by an old mural that shows cartoon pigs in SFPD uniforms herding cartoon rats with Latin features and work clothes into a paddy wagon.

The mural is gone today. Those were different times. But it still says, "Free Los Siete" in the cement on Clinton Park next to the Levi's factory.

PhotoBill: "Breasts downtown... Latins For Life..." Heart 101: "I Really DID get evicted, so I wheatpasted all my art up since I had nowhere to put it.."

MY LIFE ON MISSION STREET"

PT. I

Mission Street today looks surprisingly similar to photos of Mission Street 30 years ago. The theater signs are all still there, as is the Leed's sign. The front door at Hunt's has been "Open 25 Hours" the whole time. I have squatted in one abandoned theater, played punk shows in every boarded up doorway on Mission, and marched down the middle of the street with hundreds of angry protestors. But it is in just walking down the old main drag every day past these same old signs and produce stands that I've felt smaller memories of my own life --making out on the roof of El Capitan, walking home in rain drunk, spending the night in Mission Station -- blur into something larger, the memory of the street, something sweet and sad that won't go away. A history flowing continuously, but buried deep beneath the street, like Mission Creek.

Against this backdrop, history has come back to the Mission to repeat itself again and again. The Thor Hotel, a dive at 17th and Mission, burned down in the '70's, and was remodeled in the '80s. The new tenants organized a tenants union to demand that the new owners make the hotel cleaner and safer. The owners responded by calling the cops to break up their union meetings and hiring thugs to beat the organizers in their rooms. The union was effectively destroyed.

In 1999 the Thor Hotel once again suffered a mysterious fire, and this time, burned down for good. The hotel and storefront it was built over still loom, creepy and burnt out, over the nightly crowds of hipsters who now come to the Mission, and the cops who cruise alongside, to safely escort their wallets into The Beauty Bar.

In the last couple years, the unprecedented flow of young computer cash into the Mission from the booming Silicon Valley economy has completely rewritten the "natural" rules of gentrification. Forget the punks and artists.; the computer crowd is ready and completely willing to pay $2500 a month for an apartment and they will gladly rent it, not just in the hip Mission, but anywhere in the City, even if its a cookie-cutter loft space in an ugly green box-like building that took only 4 months to build, and sits next to the Muni yard with 101 South running right outside the 2nd story window! They will pay any amount to make the City the way they want it, and the landlords and cops will, apparently, do ANYTHING to help them. In late 1998, in a still unsolved case,

an old abandoned warehouse on Hoff Street, just off 16th and Mission, burned spectacularly to the ground as the tenants from the nearby Thor and King hotels watched anxiously in the blocked off streets. The police believed it to be arson and immediately searched for "an unidentified homeless man" they claimed may have started it. The investigation, however, didn't in any way stop the owner from building a brand new Live/Work space on the property in one short year.

And by the time the Hoff Street live/work was completed, the King Hotel, too, had burned to the ground.

Ironically, the most visible product of the new booming economy on Mission Street itself seems to be vacancies like the Thor. The economy is so based upon pure speculative value that property in San Francisco has apparently limitless value as long as no people actually live or work on it. The property sits vacant, a black hole sucking up new worth, as whispers of rumours about who might buy it circulate.

Back when Mission Records was still by my old squat, the New Mission Theater, a seedy video store down the block at 21st burned down. The guys from Mish Rex said that the video store owner, who owned Mish Rex and half the block, too, showed up with the property manager and the video store owner to stand on Mission with the huge crowd that had assembled to watch the place burn down. You might think they'd be bummed out, but no, they were laughing hysterically, and making jokes about how lucky they were. Now, the property manager, who'd been trying unsuccessfully to sell the dive for years would get full insurance AND be able to sell the now vacant property. And the video store owner was lucky, too, because he was watching all these crappy old ten year old videos and suspect porn get burned up that was insured like it was brand new.

He really WAS lucky, it turns out. His OTHER seedy video store on Mission had burned down earlier that year.

The video store is still burnt out and empty, even with the upscale Foreign Cinema with its valet parking going in next door. I walk by it and think, "Community center, neighborhood newspaper, needle exchange, junk store, practice space, art studios, art gallery, bike repair shop, collectively run coffee shop, book store, punk club." There is almost anything we could do with that space. Everyone in town wants a space to do SOMETHING with, and we're not even exactly sure what we want to do, because we haven't even invented it yet. I walk by it and get a bitter taste in my mouth everytime.

PhotoBill: "What everhappened to Mr. Element? The person who drew the cakes? The horses?

Where'd they go?"

Where landlords haven't taken the matter into their own hands to force tenants out, the police have. History repeats itself in the Mission, again, as Officer Jim Ludlow walks Mission 11's old beat. Ludlow, like Brodnik and McGoran, is an old-time, racist Irish cop, out of Mission High School. His father and his father's father worked out of Mission Station, and his dad served alongside Brodnik and McGoran. Ludlow, too, apparently never got over the Mission's change from an Irish neighborhood into a Latino neighborhood. Picking up where Mission11 left off, Ludlow launched his own one man crusade to clean up the Mission.

Ludlow invented for himself the position of "Mission Permit Enforcement Officer", and went to work. In the media, especially the easily-duped and supposedly anti-yuppie New Mission News, Ludlow represented himself as a servant of the community, one officer dedicated to driving out the seedy, often drug ridden Latino working class bars, that, supposedly, all the "good people" in the neighborhood felt terrorized by. In reality, Ludlow's scam worked like this: Ludlow knew there was a moratorium on new liquour licenses in The Mission, and that if someone with alot of new money wanted to open a club in the Mission, the only way would be to buy an existing license, or wait for another club to go out of business. But, since, Ludlow was now the "Mission Permit Enforcement Officer", someone who wanted a bar would have to go through Ludlow. Ludlow, it turns out, would let a potential buyer approach him, and then he'd simply ask them, "Which bar do you want?" Then, Ludlow would mercilessly go after the bar the buyer wanted, citing them again and again for every possible health violation possible and setting up drug stings on the premises, until the bar owner was so harrassed and owed so many fines that they might have to go out of business.

Then Ludlow would say, "Well, if you want to sell the bar, I think I know a buyer..."

It is unknown whether Ludlow's work as a real estate broker was entirely public service, or whether he received a, uh, stipend, for his work. But, either way, in a short couple years, Ludlow had run out not just a couple punk clubs, but EVERY SINGLE LATIN BAR IN TOWN, and installed in their place, a playground for rich hipsters and out-of-town yuppies. Many, like Doc's Clock and McCarthy's, in a sort-of cruel Invasion-Of-The-Neighborhood-Snatchers twist have even kept the same names and signs they've had for over 30 years, even though the day laborers and neighborhood guys who drank there just a couple years ago have been completely replaced with cab-hailing white folks.

How do we know all this about Ludlow? Because he TOLD us. Ludlow, like Brodnik and McGoran also has a thing for getting drunk and hitting on barmaids, though Ludlow preferred Doc's to Bruno's. All through 1998 it was possible to go into one of a couple of new Mission bars and find Ludlow bragging loudly and drunkenly to anyone who would listen that this was HIS place, that he MADE it happen. And when Mission Records looked at their new space, the old "Seven Coins Of Gold", Ludlow showed up with a crew of coked out twenty-somethings to look at the space at the same time, and launched into an impromptu speech to the landlord about how exactly went about "going after" these old bars. When Ludlow in a fit of possibly coke-fueled hubris went on to say he was "going after" the corner store at 26th and Mission, the landlord stiffened. He was the landlord of that place, too! When Ludlow split, the landlord gladly gave Mission Records the space.

Eventually, Ludlow's false identity as "Permit Officer" was discovered. Too many people knew. He was transfered out of the neighborhood, and today, not even a plaque is there to commemorate Ludlow's efforts. Where Ludlow walked in Mission 11's footsteps, past the old Thor, past the kids selling heroin to hipsters at 16th and Valencia where the Gartland burned, where the Gartland Pit yawned, today, there is only vacancy. New Mission computer workers, trading stocks and creating cyberspace to get money to drive up the value of burnt out storefronts and empty lots, and then buying heroin on the way out to party. There is still something in these old streets, something sweet and sad that won't go away. A dark history, flowing deep beneath the street, like Mission Creek. The most fitting tribute left to Ludlow's efforts to clean up the Mission may just be the used needles in The Beauty Bar toilet.

SOURCES: "STRICTLY GHETTO PROPERTY" · RAMPARTS PRESS 1972.
"BASTA YA! THE STORY OF LOS SIETE DE LA RAZA" MAGAZINE 1972
INTERVIEW WITH MISSION RECORDS IN OCTOBER 1999 ISSUE OF "THE PROBE"
"SAN FRANCISCO BAY AREA MURALS" BY TIMOTHY DRESCHER

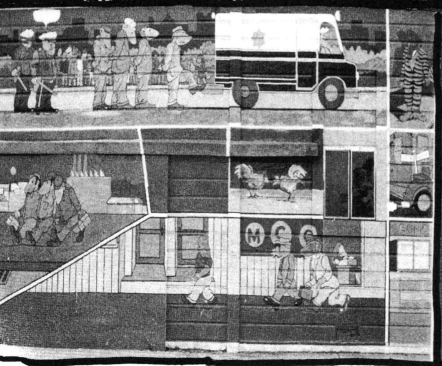

"MCO" BY MICHAEL RIOS
MURAL AT 23RD AND FOLSOM
MISSION DISTRICT 1972

ANONYMOUS CEMENT ETCHING
AT 19TH/ ALABAMA
MISSION DISTRICT 2000

"BOTH WAYS AT ONCE"

I always find it amazing how I can go from being so 100% wide awake, can't sleep at night inspired to being completely embittered and discouraged, and back again, all in, like, a week. Things can seem so bleak, and, all of a sudden, out of the ruins comes a new plan, and I'm all excited again. In reality, of course, things are usually going both ways at once.

A couple years ago, I was feeling pretty hopeful when I rolled into Portland on a train on my way to moving back to San Francisco. I still had all the good stuff from the trip stuck in my head -- the all night bike riding and spray painting in Ann Arbor, the squats in Philly -- and now I was looking forward to getting back to the City. Ivy had just moved there, too, and I was expecting a whole new era of crime.

My first night in Portlnad, I hooked up with my old friend, Ol' JB, and we found a good spot overlooking the city to drink some beers and catch up. He was pretty hopeful about the future, too. He was living in a new place -- a trailer that he got to park, rent free, in his friend's back yard. He only had to wash dishes a couple hours a week for beer and smokes money, and he had time to work on his new band and some of the different stencil and wheatpasting stuff he'd been trying to do around town.

He said, "I want to stick it outnhere. I've always moved places just after they've been 'discovered", and then flee when the good times are spent. " He had decided to stay and make it work there, no matter what.

I knew what he meant. On my travels, as much fun as I'd had, I'd come to see that being the guy just off the train, holding up the end of the Mumia puppet, just wasn't going to cut it. I had started to feel that if we, the punks really wanted to be taken seriouslywe were going to have to stay in one place and pay some dues for awhile and really make an effort to find out how we can be part of the community. I was thinking, specifically, of the October 22 Anti-Police Brutality march I'd been to in Philly. On the one hand, it had been pretty inspiring that the punks could pull off a fairly credible march like that in a major city. It had been good at parts. At one time, we had broke out of the march and started writing RIP's of people killed by cops in chalk all over the SEPTA station sidewalks, and passersby had stopped to read flyers and actually find out what we were doing. But, on the other hand, the march was almost exclusively white, punk kids who lived in abandoned buildings in the ghetto, but were, apparently, unable to convince any of their black neighbors to come march with them about an issue that certainly affects them the most. The march was a good start, but we were going to have to start making solid connections and explaining ourselves better to people we usually don't talk to-- the people who aren't the punks.

Since JB readily agreed, I rewarded myself for this succint political analysis with another beer. Now that I was going to take over SF and he was going to make it happen in POrtland, we had it all figured out. It was one of those great nights talking with a friend where everything seems real clear, and we drank awhile, talking not about all the cities we wanted to go to, but about ideas we had for where wer were at. I think, by the end of the beer, we had figured out how to stop gentrification, devised a free bike program, and, I swear, invented a plan to get grants to start a program to teach inner city kids how to fix up abandoned buildings so they could learn a trade, get paid, and own a house. It was alot of beer.

Maybe it was because the reality of Portland wasn't living up to my new, idealized version of the world, but, by the time I hooked up with JB again, a few days later, I was in a much worse mood. He wanted to see if I wanted to go drink wine and build a fire by the tracks, our usual tradition, which sounds enjoyable enough, except his mood had darkened, too. He said, "I know a great spot... if the FUCKIN' YUPPIES haven'T PAVED OVER it and built a GATED CONDO there, yet!"

I said, "It doesn't matter. All it does is rain in this stupid town anyways. I'll meet you there, if I can even convince any of these fucked up convenience stores to sell to me with my out of state ID!"

When JB showed up, he had a big box in his arms and alot of wine. "THIS... This is a box of every shitty fanzine I ever got!" he snarled. "And tonight, I'm putting them out of their misery!" So THIS was the fire. It was going to be alon night.

We got the fire going and started drinking. One by one, the zines went into the fire. I was shocked. Here was a whole decade's worth of hope and hard work and sweat and inspiration going up in flames. Small town scene reports, tour diaries, youthful enthusiasm, and traditional hatred of The Man, all GONE!

But, when I saw there was no talking him out of it, I gladly started to help. Yes, there it went: Awhole decade's worth of excruciating accounts of 3 month Greyhound trips, letters kids wrote to their ex-girlfriends and PRINTED, puzzling reviews of dumb shit like the editor's pets and shoes, and articles on why meat is murder. Let it burn!

But, then, next, came JB's wheatpasting campaign flyers. "But, I thought you wanted to put those up..." I said.

"No one cares!" He shouted. "No one even walks around in this town except homeless people, and if a homeless guy stopped to read it the fucking COPS would come tell him to move along, so they can make this town safe for rich jerks!"

I saw his point. "You're right. I heard San Francisco's been taken over by yuppies, too. Why am I going there? I probably won't even recognize my old neigh neighborhood. I heard they built a sushi place in my old squat!" I looked off in the distance, trying to figure out which one of Portland's lovely bridges I would throw myself off of.

Soon there was only one thing left to burn. "This was my last attempt at a zine!" he declared, producing a folder. "I thought it was the best one I'd ever done. But my trailer roof leaked on it, and the pages are all soaked and stuck together."

"But , you can't salvage ANY of it?!?" Now I was worried. I'd never seen him so bummed.

"No. Fuck it! Its OVER!" And the originals went on the fire.

Studying JB through the fire, I couldn't tell if he was just momentarily discouraged, or if he was that rare person who has the guts to admit when something's through, its really through, and its time to move on. But, when he turned his back to get more wine, I grabbed the magazine off the fire and hid it in my bag, anyways. Maybe it would be the best zine he ever did again, someday. Maybe, just in two days.

FIG. 1: JUST A SMALL SAMPLING OF BACK PAGE ADS

FIG. 2: I SWEAR THIS DRAWING CAME WITH THE STUDY'S CONDOMS!

SAFE SEX, GET PAID?

A SCAM TOUR OF THE MURKY WORLD OF THE FREE WEEKLY'S BACK PAGE ADS   BY IGGY SCAM

AH YES, THE BACK PAGE OF THE FREE WEEKLY... A CATCH-ALL FOR HUMAN MISERY. WEEK AFTER WEEK, THE SAME LONELY ADS BLOW ON TATTERED SCRAPS THROUGH WINDY ALLEYS AND RIDE TO ALL CORNERS OF THE BIG CITY, CRUMPLED IN THE BACK SEATS OF BUSSES, LOOKING FOR A HOME. ARE YOU UNEMPLOYED? WORRIED ABOUT S.T.D.'S? THINKING ABOUT PENILE ENLARGEMENT? OR MAYBE YOU NEED SOMETHING TO CHANGE YOUR LIFE. YOGA. SPANISH LESSONS. ARE YOU CURIOUS ABOUT "VIBRATIONAL HEALING"?

I DON'T THINK THERE'S EVER BEEN A TIME IN MY LIFE WHEN I WAS DOWN AND OUT ENOUGH TO SCAN THE BACK PAGE AND WONDER, "CAN I REALLY MAKE MONEY IN VOICEOVERS?!?" BUT EVERY GUY, AT ONE TIME OR ANOTHER, HAS CERTAINLY SEEN THE "SPERM BANK NEEDS DONORS" AD AND THOUGHT, "THAT'S IT! I'M RICH! I'LL NEVER WORK AGAIN IN MY LIFE!"

ITS JUST ANOTHER TRICK. LIKE THE BLOODBANK, YOU CAN'T JUST SHOW UP WITH A BIG BAG OF SPERM AND EXPECT TO GET PAID. THERE'S ALL THIS SCREENING AND PAPERWORK. BUT WITH SPERM BANKS ITS WAY HARDER TO GET ACCEPTED, CUZ THEY WANT YOU TO BE, LIKE, A GENIUS AND A FOOTBALL PLAYER, WHERE, WITH THE BLOOD BANK, YOU JUST HAVE TO SWEAR YOU HAVEN'T BEEN PAID TO HAVE SEX WITH AN H.I.V.+, INJECTION DRUG USING HAITIAN MAN WITH A TATTOO SINCE 1979. EASY.

WHEN MY SPERM GOT REJECTED FROM A SPERM BANK IN MILWAUKEE, IT WAS BECAUSE I COULDN'T PROVIDE A MEDICAL HISTORY OF MY PARENTS AND GRANDPARENTS. BUT IT STILL LEFT ME FEELING STRANGELY INADEQUATE, AS IF MY LIFE WAS SPIRALLING DOWN TO THE BOTTOM, AMONGST THE DESPERATION OF THE OTHER BACK PAGE ADS. OH WELL. AT LEAST I NEVER CALLED "SMOKE POT, GET PAID."

BUT WHAT ABOUT "SAFE SEX, GET PAID"? IS IT A MYTH? I'D ALWAYS WONDERED, UNTIL I STARTED GOING OUT WITH A GIRL WHO, POSSIBLY, IS EVEN MORE INTO FREE STUFF AND SCAMMING THEN I AM. WHEN AN AD LOOKING FOR COUPLES TO TRY OUT A NEW CONDOM FOR $100 RAN ON THE BACK PAGE, SHE SIGNED US UP. ACTUALLY, IT WAS VERY SWEET. WE'D ONLY BEEN GOING OUT FOR A COUPLE MONTHS, SO SIGNING UP FOR A 6 MONTH CONDOM STUDY SEEM LIKE A BIG STEP FOR US. WE HELD HANDS ON THE BUS TO THE CLINIC.

BUT, IT TURNED OUT TO BE TOO MUCH HASSLE TO REALLY BE A SCAM. THEY WANTED US TO MAKE DAILY ENTRIES IN A LOG BOOK AND SHOW UP BACK AT THE CLINIC TO BE INTERVIEWED TWICE A MONTH. FUCK THAT!

AS THE NURSE TOLD US MORE ABOUT THE CONDOMS WE WERE SUPPOSED TO BE TESTING, IT ALSO STARTED TO SEEM MORE LIKE ONE OF THOSE SKETCHY MEDICAL RESEARCH STUDIES THAT YOU HEAR ABOUT SO MANY PUNKS DOING THESE DAYS, LIKE WHERE YOU GET $700 TO STAY AWAKE FOR A WEEK, OR CUT OFF YOUR SMALLEST TOE. BY THE WAY, DID YOU EVER NOTICE HOW NO MATTER HOW ANTI-GOVERNMENT, FREE-MUMIA, WE-NEVER-WENT-TO-THE-MOON SOMEONE IS, THEY'LL ALWAYS BELIEVE SOME BIG PHARMA-CEUTICAL COMPANY WHEN THEY SAY THE WEIRD PILLS THEY'RE PAYING YOU $1,000 TO TAKE ARE "TOTALLY HARMLESS"? ANYWAY, THE NURSE TOLD US THE CONDOMS "BROKE A LOT" EVEN THOUGH THEY WERE REALLY BIG AND WEIRD AND LOOKED LIKE ZIPLOC BAGS. WHEN WE GOT HOME WITH THEIR LOGBOOK, WE DECIDED $100 WASN'T MUCH TO START A FAMILY ON, SO WE NEVER CALLED 'EM BACK.

BUT, BELIEVE IT OR NOT, IT WAS A SCAM. EVENTUALLY THEY CALLED US AND OFFERED US $100 FOR ANY PART OF THE LOG WE MAY HAVE FINISHED. WE QUICKLY FAKED SOME ENTRIES AND SENT IT IN FOR 50 BUCKS EACH FOR ABOUT AN HOUR'S WORK. IT DOESN'T WORK FOR EVERYONE, THOUGH. A FRIEND OF MINE WHO ALSO TRIED IT GOT DUMPED BY HIS GIRLFRIEND DURING THE STUDY! IT WAS SAD. HE WENT FROM "SAFE SEX GET PAID" RIGHT BACK TO "SPERM DONOR" IN ONE NIGHT

THERE'S NOTHING MORE SATISFYING THAN...
A TURD-FILLED REVENGE!!!

STORY AND "ART" BY IGGY SCAM

FIG. A: A voodoo doll of an asshole store owner being mashed into a steaming TURD!!!

YOU MAY HAVE NOTICED THAT ITS GETTING PRETTY HARD TO USE THE BATHROOM ANYWHERE IN PUBLIC THESE DAYS. EVERYWHERE YOU GO, ITS "FOR CUSTOMERS ONLY!" WHAT'S UP WITH THAT SHIT?!? EVEN IN NEW YORK CITY, WHERE YOU USED TO BE ABLE TO JUST SPRAY IT ANYWHERE, LIKE IN DOORWAYS, ITS NOW HARDER. THE BIG CRAPPLE USED TO BE THE KIND OF TOWN WHERE ANYONE WITH THE INCLINATION — RICH, POOR, OR WHATEVER — COULD JUST CRACK A BEER, SHOOT UP, AND SHIT ON A WALL — EVEN ALL AT THE SAME TIME — RIGHT THERE ON THE SIDEWALK AND NO ONE WOULD LOOK AT YOU TWICE! WELL, NOT ANYMORE. MAYOR GIULIANI'S GOT THE COPS OUT, CRACKING DOWN, GIVING OUT THE SO-CALLED "QUALITY OF LIFE"

TICKETS FOR STUFF LIKE THAT. QUALITY OF WHOSE LIFE, RUDY?!? WHERE HAVE THEY GONE, THE PUKES OF FLATBUSH, THE BATHROOM BOYS OF SUMMER? CERTAINLY NOT TO THE BATHROOM!

I USED TO HAVE A DAILY BATTLE IN SAN FRANCISCO WITH THE MANAGER OF THIS PLACE ON MARKET AND 4TH, THE "S.F. STYLE PIZZA PLACE." HE WOULDN'T LET ME ANYWHERE NEAR THE TOILET, EVEN THOUGH THE PLACE WAS ALWAYS EMPTY. IT WAS ALWAYS THE SAME: I'D WALK IN AND STEADILY WALK, AS FAST AS POSSIBLE, WITHOUT LOOKING AT THE MANAGER BEHIND THE COUNTER, TOWARDS THE BATHROOM, WAY BACK AT THE REAR OF THE PLACE. HE'D YELL, "HEY!" I'D KEEP GOING, WITHOUT LOOKING. HE'D YELL, "HEY!" AND, REALIZING WHERE I WAS HEADED, "THE RESTROOM'S FOR CUSTOMERS ONLY!"

I'D KEEP WALKING, HEAD DOWN.
HE'D ACTUALLY LEAP OVER THE COUNTER!
I'D START TO RUN.

THE REST WAS A RACE TO SEE WHO MADE IT TO THE DOOR FIRST. MAYBE IF HE'D EVER HAD ANY CUSTOMERS, HE WOULD HAVE BEEN EMBARRASSED, BUT IT WAS ALWAYS JUST ME AND HIM, RUNNING SILENTLY TO THE TOILET.

ONE TIME I BEAT HIM TO THE DOOR, BUT ONLY ONCE. I RAN INSIDE, LAUGHING HARD, THINKING, "I WON!" BUT THE DOOR TO THE STALL WAS BROKEN AND COULDN'T BE LOCKED, AND BEFORE I COULD EVEN GET MY ZIPPER DOWN, HE WAS THERE, ACTUALLY PULLING ME OUT OF THE STALL! HERE WAS A GROWN MAN, READY TO FIST FIGHT TO KEEP ME OUT OF HIS TOILET. HE YELLED, "FOR CUSTOMERS ONLY!" I YELLED, "I'M GOING TO SHIT IN A BAG AND THROW IT AT YOU!" I HAD TO GO THERE EVERY DAY, JUST TO PISS HIM OFF...

I NEVER MADE IT INTO THAT TOILET, OR A LOT OF OTHERS IN SF, AND I STILL FEEL THAT IF YOU'RE DENIED THE SIMPLE RIGHT TO A TOILET BY SOMEONE, YOU HAVE THE FULL RIGHT TO PISS AND SHIT ON ANYTHING THEY OWN!

WHEN YOU'RE TRAVELLING, YOU'RE EVEN MORE AT STRANGER'S TOILET MERCY. ONCE, I WAS STUCK IN THE SUPPOSEDLY FRIENDLY, HIPPY, COLLEGE TOWN OF EUGENE, OREGON. IT WAS LATE AT NIGHT, I NEEDED TO CRAP AND THE ONLY PLACE OPEN WAS THE GREYHOUND STATION. BUT WHEN I WENT IN, THE TICKET AGENT RAN OUT AND BLOCKED THE TOILET DOOR, SAYING YOU COULD ONLY USE THE BATHROOM IF YOU WERE BUYING A GREYHOUND TICKET. I SAID, WELL, I WANT TO BUY A TICKET TO MIAMI, BUT I HAVE TO GO TO THE BATHROOM REAL BAD FIRST. HE SAID, "NO, YOU BUY THE TICKET FIRST." I WAS LYING, OF COURSE, BUT I CAN'T BELIEVE THAT HE REALLY ARGUED WITH ME ABOUT IT FOR FIVE MINUTES! I FINALLY YELLED AT HIM "I WAS GOING TO GO TO MIAMI, BUT NOW, I'M SO INSULTED BY YOU THAT I'LL JUST STAY HOME!"

BUT IN PROVIDENCE, I GOT REVENGE, FOR TOILET-DENIED TRAVELLERS EVERYWHERE. I WAS HOPELESSLY LOST IN A RESIDENTIAL AREA, LIMPING AROUND WITH A TERRIBLE CASE OF THE RUNS, AND I COULDN'T FIND ANY STORES! FINALLY I FOUND A SCHOOL AND HEARD AN AFTERSCHOOL SPORTS PRACTICE IN THEIR GYM. I KNOCKED ON THE LOCKED DOOR, EXPLAINED MY SITUATION HUMBLY, AND BEGGED TO USE THE TOILET. THEY COLDLY, FLAT OUT SAID NO. I WAS IN SHOCK, AND COULD ONLY LIMP INTO A BUSH AND TRY TO GO. I HAD ALREADY, UH, LOST A LITTLE OF IT AND COULD BARELY HOLD IT ANYMORE. IT WAS JUST SO MEAN AND TERRIBLE, STUCK, SICK, TRAVELLING, AND RUINING MY ONLY BOXERS WITH NO SHOWER OR LAUNDRY IN MY FUTURE. I MEAN, WHY COULDN'T I JUST USE THE TOILET?

SO, I TOOK OFF THE BOXERS, CRAPPED ON 'EM, WENT BACK TO THE SCHOOL, STUCK THE FILTHY THINGS ON THE DOOR AND LEFT A NOTE, "FOR ASSHOLES ONLY!!!" I'M NOT EXACTLY PROUD OF IT. NO ONE LIKES TO HAVE TO LEAVE A PAIR OF SHIT SMEARED PANTS FOR A GYM TEACHER AND A MIDDLE SCHOOL BASKETBALL TEAM TO DISCOVER. BUT IT DID FEEL GOOD, AND I AM PROUD THAT I, PERSONALLY, HAVE NEVER DENIED A SICK, HOMELESS PERSON THE USE OF A TOILET.

AS FOR THE GUY AT "S.F. STYLE PIZZA", WHO KNOWS? THEY STRUGGLED, CHANGED THE NAME TO "CAPISTRANO PIZZA", AND FINALLY WENT UNDER. THE SWALLOWS WILL NEVER RETURN TO THE CAPISTRANO PIZZA PLACE AND NEITHER WILL I. I GUESS THEIR UNUSED TOILET FOUND TOO FEW "CUSTOMERS", HUH? I CAN'T SAY I GIVE A SHIT. THEY WOULDN'T LET ME, ANYWAYS!

MIAMI/SHOTWELL at LEED'S MAY 21, 1998

THE COPS SHUT DOWN ALL THE PLACES TO PLAY, EXCEPT A COUPLE AWFUL DIVE BARS SO, WE, THE PUNKS, DECIDED TO JUST GET A GENERATOR AND HAVE FREE SHOWS IN THE STREETS! A COUPLE FOLKS AROUND TOWN, LIKE JOHN GEEK AND MARCUS THE ANARCHIST, WERE ALREADY HAVING FREE, ILLEGAL SHOWS OUT IN ABANDONED INDUSTRIAL AREAS LIKE THE TOXIC GOLF COURSE (AKA "TIRE BEACH"), BUT WE THOUGHT SHOWS SHOULD BE RIGHT THERE ON MISSION STREET IN THE HEART OF OUR NEIGHBORHOOD, AND, AFTER SEEING HOW HUGE THE CROWD WAS AT THE MAY DAY MARCH, I FIGURED WE HAD A BIG ENOUGH CROWD TO DO WHATEVER THE FUCK WE WANTED.

WE DECIDED TO HAVE OUR FIRST SHOW IN THE SPACIOUS DOORWAY OF THE ABANDONED LEED'S SHOE STORE AT 22ND AND MISSION, SINCE WE HAD HEARD THAT THE BAND RUBE WADDELL HAD HAD BIG CROWDS THERE BEFORE FOR QUIETER ACOUSTIC SHOWS. AFTER WE GOT THE FLYERS OUT, PEOPLE WERE ASKING ME ALL WEEK IF THE SHOW WAS REALLY GOING TO HAPPEN. I WAS STARTING TO WONDER MYSELF. WE COULDN'T FIND JOHN GEEK TO BORROW HIS GENERATOR UNTIL HOURS BEFORE THE SHOW AND WHEN ME AND JIMMY FINALLY PULLED UP TO LEED'S, ON TIME, WITH THE P.A. AND AMPS AND GENERATOR, THERE WAS ALMOST NO ONE THERE. WOULD ANYONE SHOW? WHAT IF WE PLAYED, GOT BUSTED, AND NO ONE EVEN CAME? FUCK!

BUT THEN I SPOTTED THE UNMISTAKABLE PROFILE OF A LONE PUNK ROCKER, BOTTLE IN HAND, STRIDING TRIUMPHANTLY PAST THE FRUIT STANDS AND TAQUERIAS ON MISSION, AND I KNEW THE SHIT WAS ON!

WITHIN MINUTES, THERE WAS 50, OR 60 PUNKS JAMMING THE SIDEWALK, BUS STOP, AND DOORWAY IN FRONT OF LEED'S. EVERYONE WAS THERE — THE PUNKS WHO LIVED IN THE LAUNDROMAT IN OAKLAND, THE GIRLS WHO WORKED AT TOM'S GROCERY ON 6TH, THE KIDS WHO PANHANDLE AT FISHERMEN'S WHARF... FLOYD SHOWED UP WITH A HUGE CARTON OF NACHOS. TOMMY STRANGE CAME WITH HIS DOG, FLIPPER. YES, EVERYONE WAS THERE EXCEPT SHOTWELL'S BASSIST AND DRUMMER WHO WERE AFRAID TO PLAY, BECAUSE THEY DIDN'T WANT TO GET ARRESTED. LUCKILY, EVERYONE IN THE MISSION HAS PLAYED DRUMS IN SHOTWELL, AND PETE, THE LAST EX-DRUMMER HAPPENED TO WALK BY TO CHECK OUT THE SHOW AND WAS QUICKLY ENLISTED TO PLAY DRUMS AND SAVE THE ROCK!

ANTICIPATION FILLED THE AIR. WOULD THE COPS SHOW UP? WOULD WE GET ARRESTED? AND, MOST IMPORTANTLY, WHERE WAS IVY?!? SHE WAS LATE, THE STREET WAS FILLED WITH DRINKING PUNKS, AND THE COPS WERE ALREADY CIRCLING. WHAT IF WE GOT BUSTED BEFORE WE EVEN PLAYED A CHORD?

THEN WE REALIZED THE BASS AMP WAS MISSING! I WAS ABOUT TO RUN DOWN TO HUNT'S DONUTS AT 20TH TO SEE IF SOMEONE HAD STOLEN IT AND WAS TRYING TO SELL IT, BUT THEN RAVI, JEFF, AND SEAN-THE-DEAD-GUY FROM THE LAUNDROMAT IN OAKLAND CAME UP AND PRESENTED ME A RANSOM NOTE. IT READ, "GIVE US BEER AND WE GIVE YOU YOUR AMP." THEY WERE TRASHED AND COULD BAREL

SPEAK. GRADUALLY I CAME TO REALIZE THEY HAD WHEELED THE AMP AROUND THE CORNER TO SAN CARLOS STREET. BARELY CONTAINING MY RAGE AND EXASPERATION, I GRABBED SEAN AND GROWLED THAT HE REALLY WOULD BE DEAD IF HE DIDN'T RUN BACK WITH THE AMP.

THEY SPLIT, AND, A MOMENT LATER, JEFF WHEELED THE AMP UP. "WE'VE DECIDED TO RETURN THE AMP," HE BURPED, GRAVELY.

FINALLY, SHOTWELL STARTED THE SHOW. IT WAS SO RAD! JIM STRUCK THE OPENING NOTES OF "LIBERTYVILLE ON THE ROCKS" AND THE DANCING STARTED RIGHT THERE ON MISSION STREET! IVY RAN UP, SOMEONE HANDED ME AN ICE COLD 40, AND THE GIRL I HAD A CRUSH ON FLASHED ME THE KIND OF LOOK FROM ACROSS THE CROWD THAT ONLY A GIRL WHO HAS A CRUSH ON YOU CAN FLASH. WE PLAYED TAG-TEAM STYLE, EACH BAND PLAYING A COUPLE SONGS AND THEN SWITCHING OFF, SO THAT EVERYONE WOULD GET A CHANCE TO PLAY IN CASE THE SHOW WAS STOPPED. EVERY TIME JIMMY WOULD INTRO A SONG ALL BITTER AND CONVINCING LIKE, "THIS IS FOR THE PEOPLE WHO WORK ALL THEIR LIVES FOR SHIT AND GET SENT OFF TO DIE IN WARS," THE COPS WOULD DRIVE BY AT THAT MOMENT AND EVERYONE WOULD TURN AND LOOK AT THEM, LIKE, "YEAH! FUCK YOU!" AND MISSION STREET LATIN GUYS, STOPPING TO CHECK OUT THE SHOW WOULD NOD IN AGREEMENT. IT WAS A GREAT SHOW.

SOMEWHERE IN ALL THIS, EX-SHOTWELL BASSIST, GREG, SHOWED UP. HE WAS WALKING BY AND SAW SHOTWELL PLAYING WITHOUT A BASSIST, SO SOMEONE HANDED HIM A BASS AND HE FINISHED OUT THE SET. IVY DEDICATED MIAMI'S LAST SONG "THE CITY THAT NEVER SLEEPS" TO THE ALL NIGHT #14 MISSION BUS AND THEN, AS THE SONG ENDED, IT ACTUALLY PULLED UP TO THE STOP AND EVERYONE CHEERED. THE BUS DRIVER LOOKED SORT-OF STARTLED, BUT HE TOOK IT IN STRIDE AND WAVED.

FINALLY, JIM ANNOUNCED THE LAST SONG, THE HIT "GHACKED", THE ODE TO SUMMERTIME AND PILLS AND DRINKING IN THE STREETS. JUST THEN, A COP PULLED UP, BUT EVERYONE KEPT DANCING AND DRINKING. BEFORE HE COULD DO ANYTHING, THE SHOW WAS OVER, AND THERE WAS NOTHING HE COULD DO! AND THAT WAS IT — A HUGE CROWD OF PUNKS, 2 BANDS, BEER, AN HOUR OF ROCK, AND NO COP HASSLE! I WENT HOME AND I COULDN'T SLEEP!

SHOTWELL AT "STOP NATO BOMBING" PROTEST. UN PLAZA. 5/99   PHOTO BY CHRIS BECKER

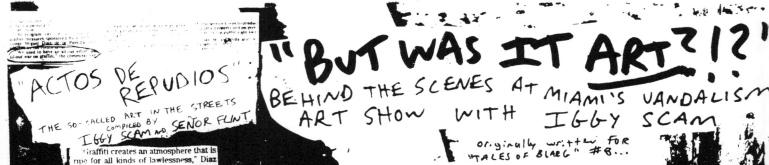

"ACTOS DE REPUDIOS":
THE SO-CALLED ART IN THE STREETS
COMPILED BY
IGGY SCAM AND SEÑOR FLINT

"Graffiti creates an atmosphere that is ripe for all kinds of lawlessness," Diaz de la Portilla says. "It makes residents feel things are out of control."

"BUT WAS IT ART?!?"
BEHIND THE SCENES AT MIAMI'S VANDALISM
ART SHOW WITH IGGY SCAM

originally written for "TALES OF BLARG" #8...

As close as most poor Tales of Blarg readers will come to the World Of Art is trying to sneak a bottle of wine into their backpack at some snooty gallery's opening night. But, I remember now I got my big break and stormed the gates of Big-Time Art like it was yesterday: I was at this warehouse in Miami that had "art openings" while bands played, and I was puzzling over the stoned doodlings of some kid who didn't have the sense to DROPOUT of art school, when I thought, "I can do that--- except I'll be DRUNK!" And, so, the Vandalism Art Show was born.

My goal was to finally get around to doing all the billboard alterations, spraypaint attacks, and wheatpasting poster campaigns that I had always meant to do in Miami, and to do them ALL AT ONCE. I would then photograph the evidence and show it at the warehouse space while The Stun Guns played.

There actually were a couple serious points I was trying to make with this show. I wanted to point out that "art", removed from the museums and galleries and displayed in the streets might be more relevant to people. There were certain political ideas about what was happening in Miami that I wanted to get across to the people who saw the "art" in the streets, and, then, later, to the punks when it was re-presented at the warehouse. But, I also wanted to do something fun,too, which is why I started off with the gay cop flyers in Little Havana.

ONE NIGHT WHILE WALKING IN

Little Havana, I found 8th Street was plastered with tons of yellow bumper stickers reading, "Support Mayor Penelas! Stop Crime!" paid for by the mysterious "Comite Dominicano." I wanted to help the mayor get the word out, too. I called up Chuck Loose, an artist in his own right who possesses an extensive collection of Tom Of Finland books, and asked him to find me one of Tom of Finland's best drawings of a muscle-bound-gay-cop-with-the-enormous-porno-cock. Then, I cut out the lettering of the bumper sticker and glud it on to an 8½ by 11' blow-up of the cop drawing, so that it read "Support Mayor Penil-as! Stop Crime!" with this cop with the huge dick lewdly grinning at you. It still was "paid for by the comite dominicano", too.

I went out and glued them up with 3M Spray Glue all over Little Havana and downtown, wishing I'd be around in the morning to see The Comite's reaction to MY support. They wouldn't like it.

I used a similar technique -- what we artists call "cut and paste" --- for my next idea. I wanted to point out some of the huge differences between Miami's official image of sun and fun and beaches, largely disseminated to the world through postcards, and the real city we live in, which is consistently ranked as one of the two, or three poorest cities in the nation. I wanted to do this AND offend tourists at the same time. Between the time the average tourist arrives in Miami and the time that they are robbed and forced into the trunk of their own rental car at gunpoint, they are bound to buy some postcards for the folks back home. So, I made fake postcards to put in giftshop postcard racks across town.

The first card was based on a real one I found. It said, "Miami on the rocks" and featured a blonde in a bikini who apparently had nothing better to do than lounge around on this big rock near the ocean. I took the lettering and put it onto this picture I had taken of a burned out crack house in Little Haiti. How do I know, you ask, that it was a crack house? Because it had "Crack house" spray painted in huge letters across the front!

My next card was easier. I just took a simple beach card that depicted two girls in bikinis with the caption "Hello Again", and pasted two enormous penises that I cut out of a porno mag over their crotches. Chuck Loose took the two cards, fine tuned them a little on the computer, and then scammed me hundreds of copies on real cardstock at the copy shop he worked at. Soon, I had snuck them into card racks all over South Beach and The Grove! I still wonder if anyone sent any of those back home...

SAVING YOUR NEIGHBORHOOD WITH GRAFFITI!?

The main thing about Miami that was breaking my heart was how, all across town, developers were bulldozing old trees, old houses, ENTIRE HISTORIC NEIGHBORHOODS and replacing them with brand, new chain stores and condos that seemed to take only a couple weeks to build. All my old neighborhoods were disappearing before my eyes, especially East Little Havana, and the developers were completely unaccountable to anyone. In East Little Havana, where a shiny, new "Financial District" was being mercilessly erected on top of the vacant lots full of roosters,a whole block of apartment complexes was evicted and tore down just before Christmas and in its place appeared a sign that read, "Coming Soon: Publix, Where shopping is a pleasure!" This,even though there was another grocery store, nearly brand new,only one block away!

I changed that sign to read, "Publix, Where Eviction Is A Pleasure," at least once a week, until that store was completed, and now I steal everything I can from it. Down the block, a formerly vacant lot of trees now had a sign that said, "Coming Soon, Walgreen's Drug Store." I changed it to read, "Coming Soon, Shiny, Sterile Building." And the "For Sale" sign in the neighboring empty lot that said, "zoned for commercial development," was changed to read, "Zoned for rich, all white neighborhood." I have no illusions that this would stop these lots from being developed, but I was hoping to, at least, get the people who saw the signs, and, later, the people at my show to think about that.

Coconut Grove, the other neighborhood I spent most of my years in Miami living in, was even more overrun with new, ugly, gated condos and chain stores. In the heart of the Grove, where a small bar and restaurant once stood, a sign announced, "Coming soon: Just For Feet, The World's Largest Indoor Shoe Store!" for awhile, 'til someone (...uh,me) changed it to read, "Just For Idiots". I did it real crudely, with just white sticker paper over "feet" and a red marker for "Idiot", too, so that you could easily tell that someone hated it enough to take the time to change it.

Everyday it seemed like a rickety old, wood, Florida-style house was leveled to make way for a flourescent pink, or aqua gated condo. Out of pure spite, I started spray painting, "No more ugly pink buildings!" on all the new ones. The question at the heart of this is, really, "Do we, the people who live in a place all our lives have any right to decide what our streets are going to look like?!?"

I thought so. I made a stencil of a completely round circle
and, at 4:00 AM, went to the new, flourescent yellow condo on
Bird Avenue, where I spray painted big, blue polka dots on the
outer wall of the yellow compund. It looked great! This was
clearly an innovation. Instead of VANDALIZING, per se, I was just
REDECORATING. I thought the polka dots looked so cool that I was
sure the owner would just leave them up. I envisioned an up-from-
the-streets art career, like Keith Haring. "Gritty , street
level polka dot artist" turned famous designer of (tasteful)
polka dot houses. The MOMA would give me a show, and I would
shock the art world by putting polka dots on the OUTSIDE of the
museum.
      Well, I was wrong. When I went to get a photo at 9:00 AM for
the eventual art show, they were already out there painting over
my blue dots. Another sad triumph for the enemies of Truth and
Beauty.

NOT CREME-FILLED! CRIME-FILLED!

      Even though I spent all night and day thinking of my work, I
didn't become a Young Starving Artist for real, until the
dumpsters at the Dunkin' Donuts at 79th and Biscayne and the
grocery store on 79th by my house were cruelly locked, cutting
off ½ of my food supply. I went to work on one of my most
ambitious pieces yet. I cut the locks with bolt cutters and left
neatly typed notes from "The 79th Street Homeless Neighbors
Association" taped to the dumpsters instructing the merchants
that the "association preferred that the dumpsters remain
unlocked." It worked! They left them unlocked after that.

WILL CADDY FOR FOOD

      But this was all just building up to the project that almost
put me over the edge, my installation at the Miami Shores Golf
Course and Country Club. Wouldn't it be funny, I thought, late
one night while riding through the course, if you could write
"Got any spare change?" really huge on the golf course, somehow,
so that early morning, rich, golfer types would be FORCED to see
it? But, how would you do it?
      With a shovel, of course! On the little hill of grass where
the sand trap at Hole 9 was, I used a shovel to DIG OUT the words
"Got Any Spare Change?" really huge, so that, because they were
elevated, you could see them from many yards away. It was hard.
It may have taken me two hours of digging out the sod, at 10:00PM
on a Saturday, sweating profusely, and thinking, "What in the
hell am I DOING?" I still think, years later, that this was,
quite possibly, the STRANGEST thing I have ever done. But I did
it, as I did everything in those days, for ART!

STILL LIFE WITH PENIS

      For my final piece, I had my eye on this blank, white
billboard that it looked like it would be easy to climb up on.
It was right on Flagler, coming into downtown, and there would be
lots of traffic there all day to read anything you wrote on
it. But what could you write? I figured that any slogan you wrote
like "Free Mumia!" would be pretty feeble, and would be ignored
by most passing motorists. The billboard called out for something
really huge that would capture the city's imagination, something
big, like when that freak wrapped all those islands in Biscayne
Bay in weird, pink plastic. What that blank billboard called out
for, I decided, was a huge, full color, 15 foot tall penis !
      I wasn't sure if it was even possible, but then Chuck Loose
told me that at his work, he had access to a machine that would
ake an image and print it out on 32 big pieces of paper in such a
way that, when assembled properly, the 32 pages would be a blow
up of the image. Now, all we needed was the perfect photo.
      I asked Sir Robert to find me one of his pornos that had
pictures dicks in it. He vehemently denied owning any pornos, let
alone any that had male organs in it. Nevertheless, a week

later, he presented me with some crude porno mag that he had, he said, "stolen from Border's." The porno had most of the usual unimaginable filth, but then, near the middle I found IT, the perfect penis for the billboard. Its gentle curve suggested the lines of Miami's famous Art Deco architecture style. The visible veins brought to mind Miami's tangled mess of freeways. The hardness of the erection seemed to invite comparisons to the confidence and aggression in the forms of the skyscrapers of the new financial district, nearby. Yet, it also mocked their ambition, as if to say, "You can't keep it up forever." Most tellingly, the penis itself pointed to nowhere, calling to mind the lack of a city center in Miami's vast, increasingly faceless, urban sprawl. Yes, this dick was ART!

Now I was ready to go to work, but, like the production of most great works of art, there was a cloud of doom hanging over the creation process. While working on the project, I broke my collar bone in a Freak Bike Accident, and was had to complete the piece with my right arm immobilized in a sling. I was forced to rely heavily on my assistant, Cinque, as well as copious amounts of St. Ide's Special Brew-- the only thing that would dull the horrible pain! Nonetheless, with Art Immortality in our sights, we enlisted George "Machine Gun" Kelley as our getaway driver, and the night before the show, headed out to the billboard at 2:00 AM.

Everything went wrong. First of all, when we actually assembled the paper that Chuck had given us, the penis was only about 3 feet tall. Certainly big for a penis, but hardly the grand statement we had envisioned. Then, we got to the billboard, it was no longer blank! It was now covered with a cigarette ad, and it was in Spanish, so we weren't sure if the penis would be funny on it, or not. The wheatpaste was making the pages soggy and we had to struggle to keep them from

ripping. Then, we realized the pages were out of order and we weren't sure if we knew how to get them back together. It was an ugly scene.

We decided to put the penis up on the blank wall under the billboard, so Cinque leaned precariously off the edge of the bridge railing, gluing up the pages, hoping we were getting it right, while I yelled instructions and motioned with my one good arm. Then, Cinque fell OFF the bridge! Luckily, it was only 4, or 5 feet down into a thorn bush. Bleeding only slightly, I helped pull him up as best I could, and we finished.

Back at the car, our getaway driver, George, was snoring heavily, but woke with a startled yell, when we got in. "I thought you were the cops!" he yelled. The whole thing seemed like a disaster. If only I had been able to get an NEA grant to do this, I thought, disgustedly. Then I'd at least be famous like that guy who got paid by the government to pee on crucifixes.

But, still, driving by it on our way home, you could see, it really was a big penis. It actually WAS sort-of unnerving, hanging there.. It had a certain shock appeal, and I could see Cuban Exile groups blaming its appearance there near Little Havana on the usual "Agents of Castro."

The next day I got the photos all developed and copied and put up at the space just minutes before show time. People seemed to like it, but I didn't even care what people thought anymore. I was just glad that my art career was over so I could relax and get drunk at the punk show.

But, wouldn't you know it--- the punks had already snuck off with all the opening night bottles of free wine!

MIAMI/SHOTWELL/YOGURT/ MANY OTHERS AT 1ST ANNUAL CLARION ALLEY BLOCK PARTY BY IGGY

A PUNK SHOW? IN THE GROSSEST, MOST TURD-FILLED ALLEY IN ALL OF ESS EFF? AND, IT WASN'T EVEN ILLEGAL, THE FOLKS SETTING IT UP GOT A PERMIT! VERY EXCITING, EXCEPT I CAN'T REMEMBER MUCH ABOUT PLAYING. I DO REMEMBER THAT WHEN ME AND IVY WERE OUT WHEATPASTING UP POSTERS FOR THE SHOW, ONE OF THOSE JERKS WHO GETS PAID TO WHEATPASTE CORPORATE ADS ON MISSION STREET'S BURNT-OUT STOREFRONTS SHOWED UP JUST AS WE FINISHED RIPPING HIS SHIT DOWN, AND GOT IN A FIGHT WITH US CLAIMING IT WAS "HIS" WALL. HIS?!? FUCK THAT! IN THE END, WE PUT UP OUR SHIT AND, WHEN HE LEFT HIS GLUE UNGUARDED IVY STOLE A BUNCH OF IT! CORPORATE WHEATPASTE STILL SUCKS!

MUSIC! MURALS! TURDS! RIGS! ITS THE... FIRST EVER
CLARION ALLEY STREET FAIR!
LIVE PUNK IN CLARION ALLEY, ABSOLUTELY FREE WITH...
SHOTWELL   YOGURT
MIAMI AND TINA, AGE 13

SUNDAY OCT. 25TH 6:00PM
CLARION RUNS FROM MISSION TO VALENCIA, BETWEEN 17TH AND 18TH

the PUNKS, the DOMINO THEORY, and YOU...

Story by Iggy, picture of punk controlling world by AAT

WHEN I'M NOT STRUGGLING TO PUT OUT MY OWN BI-YEARLY ZINE, I DEVOTE MOST OF MY TIME TO MY OTHER MAJOR CONCERN WHICH IS PREPARING THE EARTH FOR ITS EVENTUAL TOTAL DOMINATION AND CONTROL BY THE PUNKS. JUST STARTING RIGHT HERE IN BERKELEY, A LOT OF THINGS WOULD BE DIFFERENT IF THE PUNKS WERE IN CONTROL. LIKE UNIVERSITY AVENUE, THE TRUE EPICENTER OF MEDIOCRITY IN THE WHOLE BAY AREA. CREPES A GO GO? THE LEANING TOWER OF PIZZA? VIDEO MANIACS? WHAT'S UP WITH THAT SHIT?!? "BERKELEY'S BURNIN' WITH BOREDOM NOW! NAH NAH NAH NAH NAH NA NAH..."

A BIG VICTORY RECENTLY WAS WHEN THE PUNKS TOOK OVER BROTHERS' BAGELS IN NORTH BERKELEY. WHEN I MOVED HERE, ME AND DR. SICKLY WOULD CRAWL UP THE BLOCK EVERY DAY FOR THESE OVERPRICED BAGELS, BURNT COFFEE AND SNEERING CONTEMPT FROM THE COUNTER GIRLS — THESE TWO MEAN, FAT SISTERS WHO WERE STUDENTS AT U.C.B. WHEN THEY WEREN'T WORKING THE BAGEL SHOP. WE ALWAYS WHINED TO EACH OTHER ABOUT IT. IT WAS HIS DAILY RITUAL, THOUGH. COFFEE, SALT BAGEL AND A SNEER. FINALLY, I HIT ON THE IDEA OF A PROTEST, AND ONE SATURDAY MORNING, ME, DR. SICKLY, THE PIRATE GIRL, AND MR. STARCHY BROUGHT DRUMS, AN ACOUSTIC GUITAR AND A TROMBONE UP TO BROS. WE SET UP IN THEIR PATIO AREA AND PLAYED LOUD SONGS, MADE UP ON THE SPOT, ABOUT OUR LOVE OF SALT BAGELS AND OUR HATRED OF THE COUNTER GIRLS. AFTER 15 MINUTES, NOTHING REALLY HAPPENED, SO WE DECIDED TO STEP UP OUR ATTACK. WE MOVED OUR INSTRUMENTS INSIDE THE STORE AND STARTED PLAYING TO A VERY SURPRISED GROUP OF BAGEL BUYERS. ONE OF THE COUNTER GIRLS WAS THERE AND SHE SCREAMED HYSTERICALLY FOR US TO STOP. SHE WAS REALLY UPSET, BUT WE WOULD NOT GIVE UP UNTIL OUR DEMANDS WERE MET. ACTUALLY, WE SOUNDED REALLY GOOD. MR. STARCHY'S TROMBONE REALLY MADE IT ROCKIN'. ANYWAY, SHE SCREAMED "WHAT DO YOU WANT?!!?" AND WE STOPPED AND SAID, "A BIG

ALL NAMES ARE CHANGED TO PROTECT THE FUCKIN' PUNKS!

CONTINUED ON NEXT PAGE ——→

WHEAT PASTING

EARLY 1997, MIAMI

SUPPORT MAYOR PENILAS

STOP CRIME!

COMITE DOMINICANO

SUMMER 1998, SAN FRANCISCO

think different.

CAMPAIGN →

BAG OF BAGELS." SHE STARTED FILLING UP A BIG BAG OF BAGELS! IT WORKED! OR SO WE THOUGHT... SHE RANG IT UP AND SAID, "THAT'LL BE 5 BUCKS." FIVE BUCKS?!? WE ALL LOOKED AT EACH OTHER AND STARTED PLAYING AGAIN, WITHOUT SAYING A WORD. NO STOP 'TIL FREE BAGELS! AFTER A COUPLE MINUTES OF US PLAYING AND HER YELLING, SHE CALLED THE POLICE AND WE DECIDED TO LOAD THE DRUMS ON THE SHOPPING CART AND HEAD HOME. SHE WOULDN'T GIVE US ONE SINGLE BAGEL, EVEN THE DUMPSTER WAS EMPTY. WE LOST...

BUT THEN, A WEEK LATER, BROTHERS HIRED OUR FRIEND, ARKANSAS. HE COULDN'T KICK DOWN FREE FOOD CUZ OF THE EVER PRESENT COUNTER GIRLS. BUT, WHEN THE GIRLS SOMEHOW FOUND OUT THAT HE KNEW US, THEY WERE STILL SO UPSET AT OUR PERFORMANCE THAT THEY CONSPIRED TO HAVE ARKANSAS FIRED. WELL, IT TOTALLY BACKFIRED! THE OWNER HAD ALWAYS KINDA HATED THOSE GIRLS, TOO, AND WHEN SHE CAUGHT THEM TRYING TO HAVE HIM FIRED, THE OWNER FIRED THEM! SOON AFTER, MORE PUNKS WERE HIRED IN THEIR PLACE AND THE PUNKS HAVE HAD FREE BAGELS, CREAM CHEESE, JUICE AND COFFEE EVER SINCE. INEVITABLY, THE DESERT SHOP THAT SHARED THE BUILDING WITH BROS. HIRED AN ALL PUNK STAFF AND THERE WAS FREE PASTRIES AND CHEESE CAKE AND NICELY MADE PUNK BIRTHDAY CAKES. IT WAS THE DOMINO THEORY AT WORK! ONCE BROTHERS FELL, SO WENT THE WHOLE BLOCK!

SOLANO AVENUE TOOK A BIG HIT FROM THE PUNKS, TOO. DR. SICKLY AND H. USED TO SNEAK INTO THE OAKS THEATER A COUPLE TIMES A WEEK, THROUGH A SECRET BACK ENTRANCE, JUST FOR THE THRILL OF BEING KICKED OUT ALL THE TIME BY THE SAME ENRAGED MANAGER. DR. SICKLY EVEN DESTROYED THEIR SECURITY ALARM ONCE, JUST FOR KICKS. SOON AFTER, THE THEATER MYSTERIOUSLY CLOSED, ONLY TO OPEN UNDER "NEW MANAGEMENT" WITH PUNKS IN THE TICKET BOOTH! FREE MOVIES! SOON AFTER, JUST DESERTS DOWN THE BLOCK HIRED SEVERAL PUNKS, TOO, AND THERE WAS GOOD FREE COFFEE AND CAKE FOR ALL..

ALL THIS SUCCESS GOT US KIND OF COCKY. THIS UNIVERSITY AVENUE LIQUOR STORE CARDED ME. THE GUY SAID "DO YOU HAVE I.D.?" I SMILED, "NOPE!" AND RAN OUT THE DOOR WITH MY BEER. THE GUY FEEBLY WAVED HIS ARMS AND WENT "POLICE! POLICE!" SOMETIMES, I STILL WALK BY THERE AND SEE THE GUY AND MIMIC "POLICE! POLICE!" AND LAUGH. EMBOLDENED, THE PUNKS SET THEIR SIGHTS ON THE EVIL RASPUTINS GUY ON TELEGRAPH, BUT NO ONE KNEW WHAT TO DO ABOUT IT. THEN, LEFTY WAS DRUNK ON THE AVENUE, GETTING HIS FREE SLICE OF PIZZA AT BLONDIE'S ON HIS BIRTHDAY. THE OWNER OF 1/2 OF TELEGRAPH, INCLUDING RASPUTINS, KEN S. WAS OUTSIDE ORDERING SOME GUY AROUND. LEFTY LOOKED AT HIS SLICE, LOOKED AT KEN. STEPPED UP AND KICKED KEN IN THE BUTT...!!! HEY KEN, WATCH YOUR BACK, OR, UH, BUTT! THE PUNKS ARE COMING

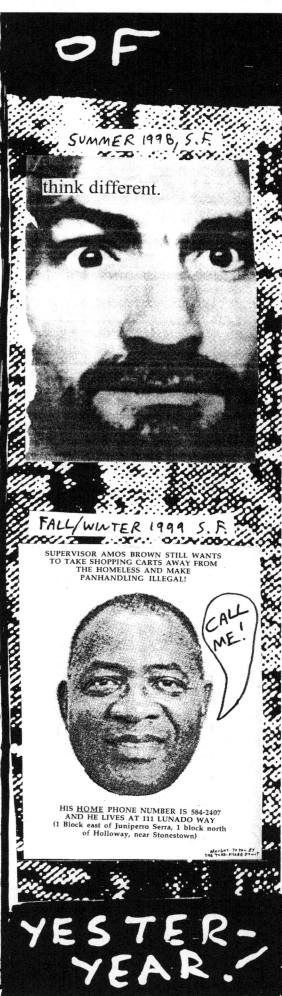

OF

SUMMER 1998, S.F.

think different.

FALL/WINTER 1999 S.F.

SUPERVISOR AMOS BROWN STILL WANTS
TO TAKE SHOPPING CARTS AWAY FROM
THE HOMELESS AND MAKE
PANHANDLING ILLEGAL!

CALL ME!

HIS HOME PHONE NUMBER IS 584-2407
AND HE LIVES AT 111 LUNADO WAY
(1 Block east of Juniperro Serra, 1 block north
of Holloway, near Stonestown)

BROUGHT TO YOU BY
THE THREE-FINGERED DONUT

YES TER-
YEAR!

LEGAL ART AND

A TALK WITH SF PAINTER, RIGO AND...

JUST ABOUT EVERYONE IN SAN FRANCISCO HAS SEEN THE WORKS OF **RIGO**, IF ONLY BECAUSE THEY'RE SO DAMN BIG! SOMEHOW RIGO CONVINCES PEOPLE TO LET HIM DO THESE HUGE, RAD PAINTINGS ON THE ENTIRE SIDES OF BUILDINGS ALL OVER TOWN. MY FAVORITE IS "ONE TREE" DOWN IN A SORT-OF RUNDOWN PART OF SOUTH OF MARKET, AT THE FREEWA ON RAMP, MOTORISTS STUCK IN TRAFFIC GET TO SEE IT EVERYDAY. I TALKED WITH RIGO FOR 15 MINUTES LAST WEEK BEFOR HE SPLIT TOWN TO FIND OUT HOW HE DOES I

SCAM: So, I guess my main question is about how you manage to do these huge pieces on the entire sides of buildings. I mean, I go out and lurk around and do graffiti and posters, and have to hide from the cops, and then they take it down right away, but you do this huge shit...
RIGO: Well, there's different ways. It varies. When I lived in the Clarion Alley, we wanted to start the Clarion Alley Mural Project, so we went to City Hall and looked up who all the building owners were. Then we contacted them, one by one, and asked them if they'd mind if we put some art on their buildings. Some of them were really hard to find, or they wouldn't even reply. But alot said "Yes!" and that's how it started.
Sometimes, the City will have a site where they want to put some artwork, and they'll put out a call for applications. But, usually, I just see a building and decide I want to do something on it. Then, I try to find out who owns it, and figure out how to convince them to have some artwork in their building, and I tell them it won't cost them anything. Then, once I have their permission, I have to go out and raise the money somehow...
S: How'd you do the "One tree" piece, though? Isn't that CalTrans state property?
R: Well, the LAND is, but the building is this electric supply company. This art group, The Capp Street Art Project, which is no longer around, was paying for it, so I got the director of Capp Street to call the building owners for me. They were these really cool, Norwegian-American guys who were just like, "yah! Do it!" They didn't even want to see a sketch.
S: Then, when you have permission, though, how do you, being just one person, actually physically paint the whole buildings?
R: I paint them myself with another person, but there is alot of money spent on labor and equipment rental. With "One Tree", "Extinct", and "Inner City Homes", the money came from a big grant to Capp Street. They got a huge grant to set up this "Art In the Urban Landscape" program. A bunch of people applied, and I was one of 6 people or groups chosen. I had never had that much financial support before, so I ended up splitting the money up into 3 big projects. The grant was $35,000!
S: Which ones did you do without Capp Street?
R: I did "Sky/Ground". I saw that building (at 3rd/Mission) and was like, "Oh, man... I got to do something there..." There was already a mural on one side by Johanna Kosig. I saw the credits that said, "Funded by the Redevelopment Agency", so i figured they owned it. I called Johanna and asked her if she'd mind having me do something on the other walls. She said, No, go ahead... So I called the Redevelopment Agency and set up an appointment I told 'em, "You have these huge, blank walls, and there's already some art on the other side... Would you consider haveing me do something?" They were like, "well, we don't really have any money for that..." I said, "No! I just need PERMISSION!"
S: How'd you get money for that one?
R: Well, 3 years before that, this guy Stanley Gatti, who was a florest and party caterer/designer called me up and said, "You know, I really like what you do." He was working to elect Willie Brown when Willie was running for Mayor the first time, and he was like, "Oh, if Brown wins, I think it will be really good for the arts in San Francisco," and all this crap. But, he said, if you ever need any funding, call me up and I'll see what I can do. So, 3 years later, he's Brown's President of the city Art's Commission. I called him up and it was just incredible. he footed the whole bill, and, you know, he never like asked for anything in return.
S: So, it seems like you manage to avoid political pressures and just sneak this stuff by people...
R: No, I run up against tons of that. There's too many stories to tell. Most recently, these guys came into the Mission and bought a building. They wanted me to do something on it. So, I thought I'd do a tribute to Chuy Campesano (editor's note: the late Campesano was a well-known Mission District muralist, whose name was back in the news in 1998 when this notoriously slimy family, the Cort family, who'd been buying up property and illegally evicting people all over the Mission, bought the building at 16th/Treat where Campesano had a huge mural across the entire building. Without consulting the estate of the artist, or the community, they whitewashed the mural so they could sell the space to advertisers. There was a huge public uproar, and, though I personally had always hated that hideous mural and secretly wished it would disappear, it was yet another horrible example of yuppie shit taking

over the Mission...)They were like, "Oh, um, sounds great..." but, then, when it came down to it, they backed out of it. They told me they didn't want it to be anything that involved any specific community figure or event in the Mission District.
So, usually I try to make something good happen, even when the people aren't so good, but I haven't even been back in touch with them. I was really into it, though. The building was at 18th and Folsom, a couple blocks from where the whitewashed mural was, and I was going to draw Chuy, larger than life, looking towards the building with a sketch of the mural in his hand...
S: Nice...
R: Yeah, but they were totally hypocritical. They said they wanted to respect tradition and set themselves apart from the Cort family..
S: But they really just wanted to buy up your shit for their own credibility...
R: Exactly.
S: What are you working on now?
R: I put a show together at the DeYoung Mueum in Golden Gate Park to show paintings by the political prisoner, Leonard Peltier. Now, I'm taking that show to London, and I'm making a zine with info on Peltier's case and his art, and writing about him. The show is 10 paintings, original oil, that he's painted in prison since 1976. Some of the stuff he's saying is really right on. I was just writing down this letter that Subcomandante Marcos wrote to him, and it was rad. Really nice stuff
S: Did you get your start in graffiti?
R: No. I never did alot, but some. I did posters and some big walls, but I'm not from this country, so I can't spend too much time running from the cops. I could get deported. With my way, you have to deal with some bullshit and be able to articulate what you want really well, but its good to not have to run from the cops. I remember, one time, we were doing a banner with this young graffiti kid in Clarion Alley, late at night, for the Block party. This cop car comes up, heading towards Mission, so I had to move the banner a little. He still couldn't get by, so I had to move the ladder. Then, the cops goes, "Sorry to make you move!" and drives on! I was SO stoked that the cops were apologizing to US!

ILLEGAL ART!

SOME PHOTOS AND STORIES BY HEART 101.

← THIS IS NOT HEART 101, OF COURSE

"I Found out what size the bit that opens the MUNI bus shelter poster holders is, by sticking some chewing gum on the bolt and making a mold. I took the gum to a hardware store on Mission Street and asked, 'What size is this?'"

"When you take out the poster and paint on the plastic board its mounted on, they'll usually just put a new poster in, without cleaning the plastic. Then, at night, when the bus shelter light comes on, your painting shines through it, and looks all rad and ghostly...GRACE and I put up this anti-yuppie poster she painted in Noe Valley, and it ended up making the Noe Valley neighborhood paper! Only, they captioned it, "Local artists express their outrage over phone company rates," or something like that. That's not what we meant! We meant Noe Valley's full of yuppie assholes!"

"I have this theory that once you write your name so many times, you just burn it out, and people don't even see it anymore. So I wanted to start other stuff instead of HEART, as if to say, 'HEART 101 says this...' I wrote RESPONSIBLE in 4 specific sites in the Mission, just to point out the horrendous lack of respect these dot.com rich fucker kids have when they come into the neighborhood. Its just a call to responsibility... To people who say graffiti isn't responsible, and I should volunteer at a soup kitchen, or something, I say, fuck it, I already do both..."

William Upski Wimsatt
author of *Bomb the Suburbs*

NO MORE PRISONS.

URBAN LIFE,
HOMESCHOOLING,
HIP-HOP LEADERSHIP,
THE COOL RICH KIDS MOVEMENT, .
A HITCHHIKER'S GUIDE TO COMMUNITY ORGANIZING,
AND WHY PHILANTHROPY IS THE GREATEST ART FORM OF THE 21ST CENTURY

"ISLAIS CREEK HEARTBREAK"
A STORY OF DOOM...

When MSA moved back to San Francisco, he said he only came back because he thought it'd be a good place to work on his big project. He wanted to put on illegal art shows inside of abandoned buildings. At the time, he was living in this old, forgotten grain silo on SF Port property. You had to climb all these sketchy ladders up a bunch of flights to get up there, but that, apparently hadn't stopped anybody before, because the inside of the place was covered in graffiti. You could paint there and sleep there. He called it the "Live/Work". he'd leave there and spend all his time riding around SF, looking for a new space, sort-of like it, where he could break in and work. Just cover the walls and then, when it was ready, have a big party and invite people to come check it out.

Eventually, he thought he'd found a good spot – this enormous, 5-story warehouse right on Islais Creek-- and he asked me if I wanted to come check it out with him. I said, "Fuck Yeah!" I'd always wondered about that place, too. Bochay and I had rode by it a couple times when we were looking for squats last fall. It WAS the perfect size and the neighborhood was suitably deserted. The whole rest of the block was taken up by junk yards and auto wreckers.

When we first rode down there, it was pretty funny. We couldn't find a way in! We looked for well over an hour, until MSA finally found this small hole in the corrugated metal back wall that some madman had punched out somehow. It was really narrow and the edges were razor sharp, but we were able to squeeze in.

So, wouldn't you know it, when we get inside, there's at least 5 kids, with fucking OXYGEN masks on, painting huge pieces in different parts of the ground floor. We were like the last people in town to get inside. MSA said, "I feel like I just walked into 'Beat Street'".

The building turned out to be so rad, though. It just went on and on. There was so much space, and the higher up in it you went, the less tagged up it was. There was just room after room, waiting to be painted in!

We started getting more and more excited, and making crazy plans, the further in we went. MSA wanted to line the stairways with torches, and have a room people could roller skate around in. I said we could use Anandi's rowboat, and have people show up to a spot on the creek, where we'd meet them and ROW them to the secret show in the building. MSA said, Yeah! And we could paint the rooms with some boat or sea theme. Is said, yeah! But where do we put the rope swing? We could have it in here!

By the time we got on the roof, we had made a HUGE plan: We wanted to invite 5, or so people we knew who did graffiti to help out, and then we'd have meetings to plan out who was going to do what and in what room, so it just wasn't a big mess. The whole thing would be a big

THE SCAM INTERVIEW WITH... GOOD OL'
UPPSKI!!!
whoops! I mis-spelled ya you

ONE OF THE THINGS I LIKE ABOUT UPSKI'S BOOK (BOMB THE SUBURBS, NO MORE PRISONS) IS THAT HE'S NOT AFRAID TO ATTEMPT RIDICULOUS STUNTS AND GRAND PUBLIC EXPERIMENTS IN ORDER TO GET PEOPLE TO THINK ABOUT HIS IDEAS. LIKE, THERE'S HIS "BET WITH AMERICA." AFTER BOMB THE SUBURBS CAME OUT, UPSKI ANNOUNCED HE WAS MAKING A BET WITH AMERICA: HE WOULD HITCHHIKE AROUND THE COUNTRY TO EVERY MAJOR CITY, WHERE HE WOULD GO STRAIGHT TO THE HARDEST, MOST INFAMOUS GHETTO IN TOWN TO PUT UP POSTERS FOR THE BOOK AND SELL IT, OR GIVE IT AWAY ON THE STREETS. IF HE DIDN'T GET HIS WHITE ASS KICKED, HE'D WIN THE BET BY PROVING HIS POINT THAT THE STREETS AREN'T AS DANGEROUS AS THE MEDIA AND THE PRISON BUILDERS WANT US TO THINK AND THAT WE DON'T NEED ALL THE NEW COPS AND GATED COMMUNIT AND IF HE GOT KILLED, WELL, THAN HE LOST... OF COURS HE WON; YOU DON'T GET KILLED FOR WALKING THROUGH THE GHETTO, YOU GET KILLED FOR BEING AN ASSHOLE OR HAVING SOMETHING SOMEONE WANTS. BUT, STILL, IT TURNED OUT TO BE A GOOD WAY TO DRAW LOTS OF ATTENTION TO BOMB THE SUBURBS AND ITS CENTRAL THEME THAT FEAR OF DIVERSITY IS RUININ AMERICA... THE LAST TIME I TALKED TO UPPSKI, A COUPLE YEARS BACK IN CHICAGO, THOUGH, HE WAS DISCOURAGED TH HIS MESSAGE WAS GETTING LESS ATTENTION THAN HIS PERSONAL AND ALL HIS PUBLICITY WAS BACKFIRING. NOW HE'S BACK WIT A NEWER, LOW-KEY APPROACH. HE'S QUIT HITCH HIKING AN DEVOTED HIS TIME TO STARTING ORGANIZATIONS TO TAKE DOWN THE PRISON INDUSTRIAL COMPLEX. HIS NEW BOOK NO MORE PRISONS PICKS UP THE ANTI-SUBURBANIZATI THEME WHERE THE LAST ONE LEFT OFF, BUT MUCH OF I DETAILS UPSKI'S ALARMING ASSERTION THAT WHAT THE UNDERGROUND PRINCIPALLY NEEDS IS MORE MONE I CALLED HIM UP TO SEE WHAT HE'S BEEN UP TO LATELY AND WHAT HE'S TRYING TO SAY:

SCAM: Hey, I don't have ALOT of questions prepared, but I wanted to check in and see what you've been working on, lately...

UP: Well, I have an organization called the Prison Moratorium Project that's trying to start anti-prison organizations on 40 college campuses. We're trying to get people to think about why there's 2 MILLION people in prison in the U.S. We want them to see how the prison industrial complex feeds on people's fears, and how the media keeps pumping up that fear, always spreading this crime hysteria, even though the crime rate has GONE down. We want this to be THE biggest issue on campus, cuz its already the biggest issue for a lot of poor kids.

S: On campus... like the Stop Apartheid or US OUT OF EL SALVADOR of the 00's...

UP: Exactly! The good thing is its an issue that people really understand. They see how much funding goes to prisons and cops and how little goes to schools. Even my dad, who is a college professor, was whining to me about how there's all these budget cuts at the school. I said, "Dad! Guess WHY you're having these budget cuts. Its the PRISONS!" He was like, "Hmm... I see your point..."

S: Maybe you need to actually GO to prison to help him see...

UP: Yeah, no shit, I'll GO... But I think there's already someone who is black holding my place in line...

S: Well, one of the criticisms that I have and other punks I know have of your latest book is the whole "Cool Rich Kids Movement" part. In much of the book, you seem more concerned with fund raising than any kind of direct action. There seems to be a lot of emphasis on raising money to start organizations to raise more money. Traditionally, I think, in the punk scene, we've always tried to just go with what you have and not be held back by waiting for more money.

UP: Like, I LOVE the Kensington Welfare Rights Union. They kick ass. But, they're like these world famous anarchists and they're barely scraping by. And there's ABC NO RIO, which is like this MECCA of punk and anarchist cats who've taken back this abandoned building, for, like, the whole Lower East Side. And now... they need 100-something grand to keep it. So, secret, while we were working on it, so that when it was finally done, it'd really blow people away. It was exciting. This was a chance to try to organize a bunch of people to work together on a big, bad ass, fun project. And, to top it off, on the roof, there was the metal remains of the scaffolding of a big neon sign, facing the nearby freeway. We could put our own sign up there for the cars on the 101 and change it as much as we wanted to!

We started going to the building alot to walk around in it and get a clearer idea of what we were going to do in there. We found a better way in , too, using a pallet to climb up to a broken window. Walking around inside it at night with candles, I was starting to get really into the place, and I was thinking of maybe trying to squat it, after all. In preparation, I stole a propane stove from a camping supply store in Berkeley and took some chain and a lock down there. I picked out a large room with a nice view of the train tracks.

Well, as the saying goes, "It would've been fine if it wasn't for those meddling kids!" Except, in this case, it was the meddling tweaker. A couple times, when we were outside the building we had noticed this sketchy, scruffy, white guy scoping us out. He appeared to be living in this trailer that was parked in front of the junkyard, and he looked like your average toothless and bearded wasteland dweller-- one of those guys you see in all the seedier, more dimly lit parts of California, riding a stolen mountain bike around in circles around the block at 3:00 AM. So we ignored him. How much trouble could one lone speed freak really cause us?

It turns out, ALOT. That's the problem with tweakers. If they're already assholes, then they have so much more EXTRA time to fuck with you. One night, we were in the building with Ivy and Monica, when the cops surrounded the building, shining their search lights up into the open windows. They even came over their PA and said, "Allright! Come out of the building, NOW!" We said, Yeah right! They wanted us to come out, of course, because there was NO WAY they were going to come in. Ivy pulled out a beer and we drank and waited until they finally went away. We didn't get in trouble, of course, but we were pretty bummed. If we couldn't sneak around in there with 4 people, how could we have a big, crazy party with 100?

Our plan was officially off. It still sounded fun, as MSA suggested, to have a small painting party with a couple folks, some beers, and a bar-b-q. But, everytime we tried to go back, we ran into the damn trailer tweaker, who would ride his bike over to us and just start screaming at us about how he was going to go call the cops. It was awful, and pathetic. He was the god damned one man, "Wasteland and Toxic Sewage Creek Civic Improvement Society"!

The building project was starting to seem like a version, in miniature, of the whole problem in the City in general. There was just no space! Everyone was getting evicted or priced out. Ivy and I lost our band practice space. There was no place to have punk shows. It was just so depressing. I gave up on the squat and moved back into my old hotel. MSA got a bike messenger job, so he could save up money to leave town, and start over somewhere else. But, there was still that scaffolding on the roof. I wondered if we could put a good banner up there and, at least, salvage something good out of this experience...

With the election coming up in a few weeks, it seemed like a good time to put up a huge "NO ON 21" banner facing the freeway. Proposition 21 was this really California-style, cutting edge of fascism law that was on the ballot, statewide. If it passed it would make it easier for kids as young as 14 to get tried as adults, it would make just about anything 3 or more kids did together a "gang" crime, and would've made "gang" crimes all felonies, making it easier to go ahead and pick up your 3 strikes and be out before you were even 18! It also would make all graffiti that was over $400 in damages --which is practically all of it - a felony. Get caught writing your name on MUNI 3 times and, by law, the judge would have to send you to an adult prison FOR LIFE! Prop 21 was so obviously targeted at poor and ghetto minority kids, and so obviously fucked up, but a huge protest movement of ghetto kids had organized to fight it and alot of hip-hop type organizations were working hard against it. It seemed like a good issue for graffiti writers to take on.

---

what I'm saying is, you have to grab power and do rightous things with it any way you can, and if you have access to MORE power and you turn up your nose at it...
S: well, I don't turn up my nose at it. What I think IS cool is that what you're talking about might broaden the horizons of the punks a little since we are so stubbornly against using, charging, or even talking about money. It seems though that the hip-hop crowd would want some encouragement from examples of things that we do all the time without ANY cash. It might seem a little much to read your book, and think, whoah, I got to go start all these organizations and talk to all these rich jerks and get the cash before I can even START to do anything...
UP: Well, OK, I agree with you... There's alot of examples of stuff done without money. In the Bay Area, take OLIN, the latino high school organization. They've organized these huge 4,000 kid high school student walkouts...

S: Yeah! High school shit is TIGHT here!
UP: Those kids are so on point. They got cell phones, they hop the BART, and then they go protest at a prison. As far as I know, they've never gotten a single grant, so that's a dope-ass example. But they're fighting Prop 21, and the organization I roll with, Active Element, which my book is going to fund, just raised like $25,000 and we're sending 23 of it to grassroots, hip-hop related organizations in California. I think almost half of them have never gotten a grant before. Gita, who runs Active Element, calls up OLIN yesterday to tell 'em they're getting a grant, and they're like, "What ?!? $2,000 ?!?!" They went crazy!

What I'm saying is, to be sustainable and to involve more people – and face it, we need more people – and to make it possible for more people who have less resources, and less education, and less opportunity,and, even... who have less ambition and politics than you, or I might have... we need more money to support them to become kick-ass organizers. That's obvious. You say, "Rich jerks..." Well, there's enough rich people now, and enough have kids, and enough are young, and enough have come into their money without being super money hungry, that there's a certain minority who aren't jerks... They're certainly not going to renounce capitalism, but they might be willing to support grassroots, bottom-up, strategic political organizing to change the system. We're trying to find these people.
S: They may not be reading this magazine...
UP: Well, there's 5 million millionaires in the US. Chances are good someone reading this knows someone... All I'm saying is we want the most privelaged among us to know that, even though it may not be fashionable to talk about, they have something that can be used for transformation. For example, since I've known you, you've wanted to do a book. You could do a great book. I mean, you helped start this whole Scam lifestyle -- hopping trains, stealing everything. You could do a book where I printed mine, for like $2,000. You don't have that. But one of your readers might...
S: I'm DEFINITELY printing that... So you think, in general, you're not putting more time and money into RAISING money, than some direct action. You come out ahead?
UP; Yeah. We don't do "benefit shows". I mean, most of the money we get is donors giving $5,000 or more. We network with people with wealth and people with connections to wealth.
S: How are you getting around right now? Hitch hiking?
UP: No, I'm not. I LOVE hitch hiking, but now I get paid like $1,000 to come speak at a college, so I have to make sure I get there on time. I'm accountable to dozens and dozens of people. In alot of ways its a sacrifice, cuz I used to hitch hike EVERYWHERE. This whole having money thing is weird. In a way, its a thrill, being a well known writer/activist and having peopole want to hear what the fuck I have to say, and having access to money for my organization. But, in a way I HATE it, cuz I used to do crazy shit... like I used to shoplift alot. Now, if I get caught stealing, it would discredit everything we're trying to do...
S: Well.... I hope you just get paid enough to make up for losing that...
UP: Well, its about more than my ENJOYMENT. We're trying to build something.
S: Do you still do graffiti?
UP: Yes! This is something I won't give up ever! Actually, after almost 10 years of just doing graffiti sporadically, now, I'm embarking on the biggest graff campaign of my life. I'm writing "NO MORE PRISONS" on sidewalks across the USA. Me and some other people have been doing it. We hit New York, Philly, Chicago...
S: You using Griffin's?
UP: No,no... Spraypaint.
S: I had just finished your new book, so I hit a couple No More Prison tags for you when I was on my last trip back to SF.
UP: On the freights?
S: Yeah... Knoxville. Asheville. St. Louis. Just a couple.
UP: No shit... So you be bombin', huh?
S: Well, I'm usually into more political or site specific stuff, though. Like there was a famous residential hotel arson in '75 right at what is now the hippest corner in town, 16th and Valencia, and I've written stuff there about it...

First, we needed a huge banner. We went and, somehow, managed to sneak back into the building and took measurements of the scaffolding. It was 12 feet high and 50 feet long! That was alot of banner. But MSA had an idea.

We borrowed some wire cutters from Jimmy's garage and headed to 7th and Mission, where, a black, plastic tarp, the length of a city block, was lining the fence around a construction site by the old Greyhound station. A tape measure revealed that it was 6 feet tall. Two lengths of it, attached together, would be perfect! It was really the best stuff for banner hanging, because it had metal ringlets inset into the tarp, where you could tie it onto things, without it ripping. We cut the wire holding the tarp to the fence, while crackheads and cops circled in ever tighter rings. It took forever, but we finally got 60 feet of the damn stuff off. It was pretty absurd. You couldn't roll it up anyway, really. It was too slippery. We had tons of plastic and no way to move it!

I spotted what could have been our salvation, a shopping cart down the block. But it was locked with a kryptonite to a parking meter! Times really ARE tough.

Finally, we started pushing the huge pile of plastic up Mission, using our bikes to balance it. It was just WRONG. You know what I mean? Cops kept going by, slower and slower, and looking at us in this way that suggested the only reason they didn't stop and run us in on general principle, was because we looked so pathetic, that our feeble criminal effort was almost POIGNANT. Finally, we found another cart and stuffed it in, and made it home, safe.

We got it down to the building in a car, and MSA painted it, white on black, with a roller, up on the 3rd floor. It said "NO ON 21", 30 feet long and 12 feet tall!

When it dried, the next day, we went back to put it up, with Heart 101 along to help. We were tying it to the scaffolding with those plastic handcuff things that cops use these days, because there was a bunch laying around our house. You could find them out on Mission all the time. I liked the irony of that. Heart and MSA did the climbing, because I suck at that, and I tied the bottom down with heavy twine. In a half-hour it was up! Riding home, me and Heart looked back, and couldn't believe it. It was just SO huge! You could see it everywhere!

We were so happy to finally have some victory at that building that had turned into such a headache. Heart and I stayed out at Hunt's Donuts all night making plans to do huge poster attacks on the bus lines all summer.

But, the next morning, when I went out to get a photo of the banner and show it to Caty, who was in town, it was already gone! I couldn't believe it! It had lasted less than 12 hours!

I knew we were doomed. We would always have to sleep, and that tweaker would always be awake. I didn't want to see that building again as long as I lived.

But, we went back one more time. MSA and I figured that they probably just cut the banner down and left it on the roof, because it was such a pain in the ass to move. So we went back to get it, so we could, at least, hang it on the pedestrian bridge OVER the freeway.

Well, when we got there, it just wasn't there. It had disappeared. We hung out on the roof, looking around at the great view of the City. A big ship was leaving the Port at the end of the Creek. It was such a great roof. There was so much you could do with that space. But it just wasn't to be.

MSA said,"Well, at least its still a great DRINKING spot," and pulled a 40 out of his bag. I didn't say anything. I didn't say anything until I felt the first rain drops less than a minute later. Then, I said, "Let's get the hell out of here..."

I FINALLY GOT THIS SMALLER BANNER UP OVER → 101 (SOUTH) ON MY OWN, ON THE NIGHT BEFORE THE ELECTION

UPSKI INTERVIEW COMPLETED:

UP: I love that! That's the shit... You didn't see NO MORE PRISONS on upper Haight Street? Just all over the sidewalk? There's alittle out in the Bay Area... Cleveland got bombed. Vancouver got bombed. Minneapolis got a little. Whichita, Kansas got totally bombed. I been hearing Berlin got it. Over the course of the year, me and anyone I can get to help are doing it. Its up, though. If you say, "No More Prisons," in New York City, they seen it. But, I only do sidewalks, because we need allies. We don't want to alienate anyone who would be on our side by writing on their storefront...

S: What do you think a better way of getting your point across is, then. Graffiti that everyone sees, or a book.

UP: Well, we're trying to stop the prison industrial complex, and we'll do it any way we can. They're both good.

S: In Bomb the Suburbs, you wrote about people trying to organize graff writers in Chicago and other cities, and have all-city graff meetings to try to get people to work together and really pull off some big shit. In the book, it always failed. Did writing about it cause any good to come out of further organizing efforts?

UP: No! not at all! Its wack... That's why I've changed my strategy, because the organizing hasn't worked. I feel it CAN be done. You can organize punks and criminals and graff kids and hipsters and b-boys. It'd take alot of money and someone with alot of experience to do it right, though, because A) People are not thinking imaginatively about their possibilities, B) Those few that are are always infighting, and C) everyone's just trying to survive day to day, anyway. My friends in Chicago still talk about it, but that's as far as its got... And even with No More Prisons, as influential as I supposedly am, I've inspired less than 10 people across the country to go write No More Prisons everywhere...

EDITOR'S NOTE: I TALKED TO UPSKI ABOUT A MILLION OTHER THIN[G] LIKE DIFFERENCES IN PUNK AND HIP HOP ACTIVISM, BUT THIS IS WHE[RE] MY TAPE GOT FUCKED UP! SORRY UPSKI AND READERS...

PROTEST REVIEW   2/28/00

3RD EYE MOVEMENT SCHOOL TAKEOVER (2/3/00): PRISON AND COP ISSUES WERE FRONT PAGE NEWS ALL WEEK. THERE WAS THE PELICAN BAY PRISON RIOT, THE MASS ARRESTS AT THE MUMIA MARCH AT SF'S FEDERAL COURTHOUSE. WHEN THE GOVERNOR OF ILLINOIS DECLARED A MORATORIUM ON EXECUTIONS IT LOOKED LIKE WE MIGHT WIN THIS SOMEDAY. WHEN THE DIALLO VERDICT CAME IN, IT WAS BACK TO LOS[ING]. MEANWHILE, 3RD EYE WAS DOING THEIR "WEEK OF RAGE" OF BADASS EVENTS, ORGANIZING AGAINST PROP. 21. THEY STARTED BY DOING AN OCCUPATION OF THE JAIL IN DOWNTOWN OAKLAND! THESE WERE HUGE FRONT PAGE NEWS EVENTS COMPLETELY RUN BY HIGH SCHOOL KIDS! FOR THE LAST DAY, ORGANIZERS WERE SAYING TO SHOW UP AT THE RALLY AT DOLORES PARK IN S.F. AND BRING A SLEEPING BAG, BECAUSE THEY WERE GOING TO MARCH TO A SECRET SPOT AND OCCUPY IT ALL NIGHT. FOR SOME REASON, I THOUGHT WE WERE GOING TO END UP MARCHING TO JUVENILE HALL, WHICH I FIGURED WOULD BE A MASS ARREST, SO I BROUGHT BOXCUTTERS TO CUT HANDCUFFS OFF WITH. BUT, THE MARCH LUCKILY ONLY WENT TO THE TECH HIGH SCHOOL AT 15TH AND MISSIO[N] WHERE THE KIDS CUT THE LOCK, PULLED IN A SOUNDTRUCK, AND KIC[KED] OFF AN ALL NIGHT PARTY/DANCE PROTEST! THEY BROKE INTO THE TOILETS AND OPENED THEM UP AND BROUGHT OUT FOOD TO SERVE. THE COPS WERE EVERYWHERE ON THE STREETS, BUT THE KIDS 'SECURITY STA[FF]' WAS KEEPING THEM OUT. THE COPS HAD BEEN CAUGHT OFF GUARD, AND THEY NOW REALIZED THAT IT WOULD BE BAD TO ATTACK AND ARREST A COUPLE HUNDRED WELL ORGANIZED, ORDERLY KIDS WHO WERE CHANTING, LIVE ON ALL NETWORKS, "WE WANT SCHOOLS, NOT JAILS!" SO THE COPS MEEKLY ASKED IF THE KIDS COULD TURN IT DOWN AT 1:30 AM AN[D] SPLIT! WE WON! THERE WAS A GRAFFITI SLIDESHOW ON A WALL AND A BILLBOARD TAKEOVER, ALOT OF BORING RAP, AND... COFFEE IN THE MOR[NING]

INTERVIEW BY IGGY AND IVY, REPRINTED FROM TURD-FILLED DONUT #4...

TURD-FILLED DONUT: Could you just start off by telling us a little about the Biotic Baking Brigade's history?

Biotic Baking Brigade: The first time we pied anyone was Charles Hurwitz, the CEO of Maxxam. They bought out Pacific Lumber and are the one's cutting down the Headwaters. He's just totally evil. Then we got Milton Friedman, the economist. He was speaking at a conference on privatizing education, so he got a pie. Then there was Robert Shapiro, the head of Monsanto Corporation. They produce Round Up, the herbicide, and they made other fucked up stuff like Agent Orange. Their new thing is Agricultural Biotechnology. Basically, they're altering the genetic makeup of plants. Farmers in India are burning Monsanto fields in protest now, because Monsanto is creating plants that will not grow without chemicals, and, of course, you have to buy the chemicals from Monsanto! Then, we got Gavin Newsom from the Board of Supervisors. We did that one at the party he had at his restaurant on election night. All the people there were wasted, just well-dressed people totally sloshed. There were girls with 3-inch heels puking in the toilet. Newsom's always been pretty anti-tenant, so we hit him with two pies.

TFD: Did you get arrested?

BBB: No, he didn't want to press charges. He just laughed it off.

TFD: Was he loaded?

BBB: I'm not sure. He said, "Are you guys from the tenants union?" And we said, "Why? Do you have a guilty conscience, or something?"

TFD: So next up was Willie Brown...

BBB: Yeah. We got the Mayor with 3 pies when he was having a press conference at City Hall to announce his Great Sweep program, where he gets a bunch of volunteers to go out and pick up trash in different neighborhoods. We did it because at the same time that he was announcing that he was also coming out with these other programs against the homeless that don't really do anything but sweep people out of different areas like The Castro, or Union Square, or The Haight. A couple weeks before he had been quoted in the paper as saaying he was to the point where he just wanted to see people "swept off the streets" and that was really offensive to me. I mean, no matter how down and out people get, they're still people, yua know? They're not just trash or a hamburger wrapper, or something you can sweep up.

So, we figured we could just go out with signs and picket, or something, and no one would notice, but pies are sexier and make better news stories. He was about to announce a surprise deal for the '49ers stadium at the Great Sweep press conference. He said, "I have something more dramatic to announce..." and that's when we got him!

TFD: What happened after you threw the pies?

BBB: Brown tried to tackle one of us. He got one of us in a headlock. Some bodyguard tackled me and broke my collarbone. I was screaming in pain! We all got arrested. An ambulance took me to the hospital first and all the doctors and nurses were all so cool to me. They were all like, "Good job! Way to go!" Then, everyone in jail was totally glad we did it, too.

TFD: Of course! Everyone in town thinks its cool except like 5 people who write for The Chronicle...

BBB: Right. Well, the people who don't like what we have to say are never going to like the way we say it. People have said that it was violent, but, I mean, its a pie. Its not non-violent in the same way that a sit-in is, but the whole point is that no one gets hurt. I Do feel a little bad, because, it turns out that Brown has glaucoma and he can't see too well, so he didn't actually know what hit him.

TFD: Yeah, when I interviewed him, I noticed he has these wandering eyes. I tried to look him in the eye but It was impossible. I thought he was a robot, or something.

BBB: Yeah. I don't think any jury in S.F. will convict us.

TFD: What's next for the Biotic Baking Brigade?

BBB: Well, personally, with my broken shoulder, I will only be BAKING pies for awhile. But, I believe the pastry uprising will continue. There's a lot of people out there who deserve a pie, and alot of people who are capable of delivering them. To be in the Biotic Baking Brigade, all you need is a pie and a vision of a better world.

TFD: Do you have anything else you want to say to our readers on 6th Street?

BBB: Well, we really hope that people enjoyed this. Things get bleak sometimes, but we choose to get our politics across this way, because its funny. People-- especially the people mosty affected by Brown's lack of action and lack of compassion, need a good laugh sometimes.

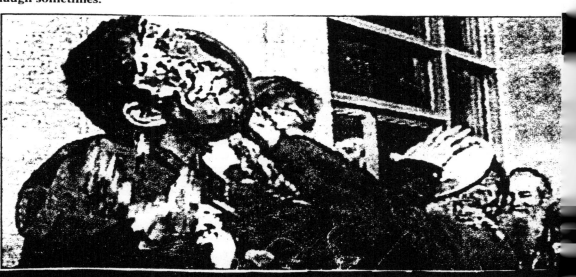

Take that!

Biotic Baking *Brigade members smash pies into each other's faces Friday after a court hearing for three members accused in a pie attack Saturday on Mayor Brown. Defendant Gerard Livernois is being pied at right; the other two are brigade members but not defendants in the case.* [A-4]

THE TURD-FILLED Donut

WHILE YOU'RE WAITING FOR CHECK DAY, IT'S... MARCH '98

ISSUE #2 "BEWARE THE DONUT THAT CONCEALS A TURD!" FREE

THIS ISSUE: SHOPPING CARTS, BEER, LOVE...

Stop the City from Taking Our Carts !!!

SUPERVISOR AMOS BROWN HAS CALLED FOR A "CRACKDOWN" ON SHOPPING CARTS IN THE CITY, AND WILL BE SPEAKING ABOUT HIS PROPOSAL AT AN UPCOMING PUBLIC HEARING. THE POLICE AND THE PARKS AND RECREATION DEPARTMENT CONTINUE TO ILLEGALLY CONFISCATE HOMELESS PEOPLE'S SHOPPING CARTS AND PERSONAL BELONGINGS.

COME SPEAK OUT AGAINST THIS CRACKDOWN
**THURSDAY, MARCH 5
10:00 AM
401 VAN NESS AVENUE, ROOM 410**

TOP: COVER, TFD #2 BY GRETA
MID: COVER, TFD #3 BY AESOP
BOTTOM: BACK COVER, ISSUE #2

ITS THE...

TURD-FILLED DONUT STORY!!!

BEHIND THE SCENES LOOK AT A 6TH STREET PUBLISHING EMPIRE!

IT SEEMS LIKE PEOPLE ALWAYS GIVE ME SHIT AND ASK WHY I HAVEN'T DONE A FANZINE IN A COUPLE YEARS, BUT IF THEY LIVED IN SAN FRANCISCO, THEY'D KNOW THAT I HAVE BEEN DOING A ZINE EVERY COUPLE MONTHS FOR 2 YEARS. SINCE DECEMBER 1997, ME AND IVY HAVE BEEN DOING THE SKIDROW NEWSPAPER THAT WE CALL THE TURD-FILLED DONUT.

HERE'S HOW IT STARTED: WHEN I MOVED BACK TO S.F., IVY WAS LIVING HERE, ALREADY, IN A WELFARE HOTEL ON S.F.'S SKIDROW, 6TH STREET, AND WORKING WITH TEEN RUNAWAYS AND STREET KIDS ON HAIGHT STREET, PASSING OUT CONDOMS AND CLOTHES AND DOING NEEDLE EXCHANGE. BY MY 3RD DAY BACK, I'M PROUD TO SAY, I WAS BACK ON WELFARE, MYSELF, AND HAD MY OWN HOTEL ROOM A BLOCK UP 6TH FROM HERS. AT THE END OF A WEEK, I'D STARTED DOING MY "ALTERNATIVE WORKFARE", A REQUIREMENT OF "WORK" TO RECEIVE MY WELFARE AT THE TENDERLOIN AIDS RESOURCE CENTER. I PASSED OUT CONDOMS AND BAGS OF SNACKS AND CLEAN WATER TO H.I.V. POSITIVE CLIENTS, TWO DAYS A WEEK.

AS FAR AS I WAS CONCERNED, THIS WAS THE SCAM LIFESTYLE. I HAD A PLACE TO LIVE, FOODSTAMPS, AND SPENDING MONEY LEFT OVER AND ALL I HAD TO DO WAS A COUPLE HOURS OF SOCIAL SERVICE WORK, WHICH I'D DO ANYWAYS. I HAD PLENTY OF TIME TO RIDE MY BIKE ALL OVER TOWN, HOP SWIMMING POOLS, AND HANG OUT AT DONUT SHOPS, DRINKING TOO MUCH COFFEE. MY HOTEL WAS CLEAN, FRIENDLY OLDTIMERS DRANK BEER AND LISTENED TO BALLGAMES ON AM RADIO ON THE STEPS, AND I HAD A WINDOW FACING THE STREETS AND A GIRLFRIEND WHO CAME OVER TO YELL UP AT IT. LIFE WAS GOOD.

BUT YOU WOULDN'T KNOW IT WAS POSSIBLE FOR LIFE TO BE GOOD IN THE TENDERLOIN FROM READING ANY PAPERS IN TOWN. IN THE LIBERAL, FREE WEEKLY BAY GUARDIAN, HOTELS WERE NEVER CLEAN AND FRIENDLY; THEY WERE ALWAYS RAT-INFESTED, DISEASE FILLED FIRE TRAPS FULL OF IMPOVERISHED VICTIMS. THE MAINSTREAM PAPERS ONLY CAME TO 6TH STREET WHEN THE POLICE TALKED ABOUT "CLEANING IT UP." EVEN THE STREET SHEET, THE HOMELESS NEWSPAPER, ONLY DEPICTS THE HOMELESS IN THEIR GRAPHICS IN THE SHADOWS, COWERING FROM IMPENDING ATTACK OF A POLICE-MAN. TO READ THE STREET SHEET, YOU'D THINK NOTHING EVER HAPPENS TO HOMELESS PEOPLE EXCEPT GETTING HASSLED BY COPS AND LIT ON FIRE BY FRAT BOYS.

THIS COMPLETELY DENIED THE REALITY I SAW EVERYDAY IN THE NEIGHBORHOOD: THE SWEETNESS AMONG THE DAY-IN/DAY-OUT REGULARS AT THE DONUT SHOP, THE HUMOUR OF THE DIVE BAR BARTENDERS AND TENDERLOIN JUNK STORE OWNERS, THE BRAVERY OF THE DRAG QUEENS WHO CAME INTO MY WORK FOR THE BAG LUNCH... I WANTED TO DO A PAPER THAT WROTE ABOUT THE SWEET STUFF ALL MIXED INTO WITH THE DESPERATION, THAT COULD GIVE FOLKS ON MY STREET SOMETHING TO LAUGH ABOUT AND ALSO SHOW POOR PEOPLE FIGHTING BACK FOR A CHANGE. SO, AT A TIME WHEN SUPPOSEDLY-LIBERAL MAYOR WILLIE BROWN WAS TRYING TO LAUNCH THE BIGGEST ANTI-HOMELESS POLICE SWEEPS IN THE CITY'S HISTORY, TURD-FILLED DONUT #1, A 6 PAGE "X-MAS ISSUE" CAME OUT, OUR MASTHEAD READING, "THIS IS ISSUE #1 OF THE TURD FILLED DONUT. WE COVER THE TENDERLOIN, 6TH STREET, THE MISSION AND ANY OTHER PART OF S.F. THAT THE CITY WISHES WOULD JUST DISAPPEAR!"

TILL ON WELFARE, EH, IGGY?

EXCEPT UNDER CO

SAY TO PEOPLE
O ARE POVERTY STRICKEN
ARE BETTER OFF
NG POVERTY STRICKEN
ERE THE COST OF LIVING
; NOT SO
GREAT...

WILLIE BROWN

THE FIRST ISSUE, WITH ITS LISTINGS OF FREE X-MAS MEALS AND THE DEBUT OF "TURD CAEN", THE 6TH STREET GOSSIP COLUMN BASED ON SF LEGEND HERB CAEN, DID FAIRLY WELL. WE PRINTED AROUND 400, AND, OF COURSE, STOLE 'EM FROM KINKO'S. WE PASSED 'EM OUT ON THE STREET, AT THE WELFARE OFFICE, AND AT A COUPLE SOCIAL SERVICE AGENCIES. WE ALSO SNUCK SOME INTO COPIES OF THE GUARDIAN AND THE WEEKLY, AND WHEAT PASTED THE ISSUE, IN ITS ENTIRETY, AROUND THE ALLEYS OFF 6TH, AND DOWN IN CHINA BASIN, WHERE PEOPLE LIVE IN THEIR CARS. IT SEEMED TO BE A BIG HIT AMONG THE SOMEWHAT JADED T.L. OUTREACH WORKERS, AND I STARTED SEEING FAXED COPIES OF OUR BACK COVER, A SHOPPING CART WITH A SIGN READING "FUCK YOU, WILLIE BROWN!" TAPED TO IT APPEARING IN VARIOUS SOCIAL SERVICE AGENCIES AND NON-PROFITS. I EVEN HEARD SOME CRUSTIES THOUGHT OUR JOKE ANNOUNCEMENT OF "THE CRITICAL PISS" ("WE'RE NOT BLOCKING TRAFFIC! WE'RE PISSING!") TO BE HELD IN THE FILTHY STEVENSON ALLEY, WAS REAL AND SHOWED UP!

BUT I WAS STILL SORT-OF BUMMED THAT NO ONE WROTE, OR CALLED US ABOUT IT AND NO ONE ANSWERED OUR AD AT THE END ASKING FOR ANYONE WHO WANTED TO WRITE FOR US TO CALL US UP. OUR DISTRIBUTION SUCKED. I FIGURED OUR ONLY HOPE WAS TO GET OUR OWN TURD-FILLED DONUT NEWSPAPER BOX AND PUT IT ON 6TH ST.

IVY SUGGESTED A SPOT SHE'D SCOPED OUT, AROUND 4TH AND MARKET, WHERE THERE WAS ABOUT 10 NEWSPAPER BOXES IN A LONG LINE. WHO'D MISS JUST ONE? WE PUSHED A SHOPPING CART OVER THERE AND SELECTED THE BOX OF THE MYSTERIOUS PUBLICATION, "DOWNTOWN S.F." THE BOX WAS EMPTY, AND NEITHER OF US HAD EITHER SEEN "DOWNTOWN S.F." OR EVEN HEARD OF IT. WHEN THE SIDEWALK SEEMED RELATIVELY FREE OF TRAFFIC, WE GOT IT UP AND IN THE CART, AND HEADED TO 6TH. IT WAS A PRETTY SKETCHY SCENE, US JUST PUSHING THIS BIG, OLD NEWS BOX DOWN THE STREET, BUT I KNEW IF WE COULD JUST GET IT THE COUPLE BLOCKS TO 6TH, IT WOULD, LIKE ALL STOLEN PROPERTY THERE, MAGICALLY DISAPPEAR FOREVER. SURE ENOUGH, WE STOPPED TO PAINT IT ON NATOMA, WHILE SOME CRUSTIES WE KNEW HUNG OUT WITH US AND DRANK. A COP ROLLED BY US AND, SEEING 6 DIRTY PUNKS WITH A DOG, DRINKING BEER IN THE STREET, BLASTING A RADIO, AND SPRAYPAINTING A NEWSPAPER BOX, THE COP SMILED, WAVED, AND SAID, "NICE DOG!"

I STORED THE BOX IN MY HOTEL ROOM 'TIL ISSUE #2 WAS DONE. WHEN I BROUGHT IT UP THE STAIRS, STRUGGLING TO CARRY IT, THE NIGHT DOORMAN, A MIDDLE AGED BLACK GUY WHO ALWAYS WORE MIRRORED SUNGLASSES AT NIGHT, GREETED ME WITH THE SAME INSCRUTABLE EXPRESSION HE ALWAYS WORE, WHETHER I CAME IN WITH 2-12 PACKS, COVERED IN SPRAY PAINT, OR WITH A GIRL WITH BLUE HAIR. HE'D SEEN IT ALL.

ISSUE #2 FINALLY CAME OUT WITH A COVER BY GRETA MUDFLAP, MORE TURDCAEN, A CELEBRATION OF DRINKING IN PARKS OF S.F., AND

1: A TFD READER NAPS BY OUR 2ND NEWSBOX AT JONES AND GOLDEN GATE

TURD FILLED DONUT

FIG. 2: THE MAP OF THE 6TH STREET BEER HUNT...

ALL THE CLUES ARE ON 6TH STREET BETWEEN MARKET AND MISSION. SEEMS LIKE A LOT OF WORK FOR BEER...

IT'S A GAME, STUPID!

CLUE #6 IS THE MOST IMPORTANT, WHERE THE BEER ACTUALLY IS. WHEN YOU GET TO THERE, USE CLUES 1-5 FOR DIRECTIONS TO THE BEER! CLUE #6 IS A TWO-PARTER. YOU USE THE #'S TO FIND OUT THE LETTERS TO WRITE IN THE BLANKS.

the FIRST ANNUAL

6th Street TREASURE HUNT for BEER!

① Go to GINGER*s TOO
Step back from the shamrock and look up!

② you might need some thing from there!

③ STANDING IN FRONT OF THE "TURD FILLED DONUT" DISPENSER, READ THE CIRCLED LETTERS ABOVE!

④ what can't you get at GRAND CAFE without purchase, and it costs 50¢ at BELL DONUT, hot?

⑤ when leaving the bar, where you are the STAR, clue #5 is on the street sign...

⑥ TO SPELL OUT CLUE SIX--- the letters are ALL INSIDE the TOILET at 6th + MISSION— SIT ON THE CAN, and COUNT FROM THE TOP OF THE SIGN! GET THE NUMBERS TO COUNT BEFORE you go in there, hints below, it's a FOUR letter word.

FOR EACH LETTER, COUNT THE ADDRESS NUMBER OF...

BELL'S DONUT | BEST COLLATERAL | CHIK-N-GRILL | JACK'S BUY SELL TRADE | this one is just a number, "PHO BO at TU LAN"

" "

keep track of your clues to find the prize!

1. _____
2. _____
3. _____
4. _____
5. _____
6. _____

BEER

IT'LL BE COLD TOO!

IVY'S ARTICLE ON CHEAP AND FREE, COOL SPOTS TO GO ON DATES, MOSTLY DOWNTOWN AND IN THE NEIGHBORHOOD. WE LOCKED UP OUR BOX TO A SIGN TELLING PEOPLE NOT TO PEE IN THE ALLEY AT 6TH AND JESSIE. WE WERE SO EXCITED TO GET IT OUT, THAT WE WEREN'T PAYING ATTENTION, AND DIDN'T SEE THE COPS ROLLING UP WHILE WE'RE DRINKING BEER AND COALLATING IN THE ALLEY BEHIND IVY'S HOTEL. WE GOT DRINKING IN PUBLIC TICKETS! HOW IRONIC. LUCKILY, OUR ARTICLE ON DRINKING IN PARKS ALSO HAD LEGAL ADVICE ON WHAT TO DO IF YOU GOT CAUGHT. WE TOOK OUR TICKETS TO THE COALITION ON HOMELESSNESS LIKE THE ARTICLE SAID, AND THEIR LEGAL REPRESENTATIVES GOT 'EM THROWN OUT OF COURT!

WITH ISSUE #2, WE FINALLY GOT SOME RESPONSE. THE WEIRD, CRACKHEAD BIKE MECHANIC AT FIXED GEAR, THE BIKE SHOP AROUND THE CORNER FROM MY PLACE CALLED TO TELL US THEY LOVED US AND WANTED US TO DO A STORY ON THEM. YEAH RIGHT. THEN, A MIDDLE-AGED DRAG QUEEN NAMED QUEEN ANTOINETTA, WHO WAS THE TENANT REP AT BALDWIN HOUSE CALLED US EVERY DAY FOR AWHILE TO SEE IF WE'D INTERVIEW HER. THEN, ONE DAY, I WOKE UP TO HER BANGING ON MY DOOR! SHE GAVE ME HER CARD WHICH READ "THE QUEEN OF 6TH STREET." SHE NEVER ENDED UP WRITING FOR US, THOUGH. BUT, FOR AWHILE, THE GUYS IN MY HOTEL WOULD JOKE WITH ME, "HEY IGGY! THERE WAS A DUDE HERE LOOKIN' FOR YA... IN A DRESS! IS THAT YOUR OLD LADY? YOUR OLD MAN?"

SOON, HOWEVER, WE GOT A NEW NEWSPAPER BOX AND A COUPLE NEW COLUMNISTS. TWIST GAVE US THE BOX AND WE PUT IT OVER BY ST. ANTHONY'S SOUP KITCHEN AT JONES AND GOLDEN GATE, THE DONUT'S FIRST MARCH NORTH OF MARKET. RG (PRONOUNCED "URG") AN ORGANIZER AT THE WORKFARE RIGHTS UNION, P.O.W.E.R., STARTED DOING A "WORKFARE DIARY" ABOUT HIS EXPERIENCES CLEANING CITY BUSSES FOR HIS WELFARE CHECK. HIS FIRST COLUMN WAS ABOUT THE FINE ART OF MAKING FAKE BUS TRANSFERS FOR FREE RIDES. JIMMY SHOTWELL, WHO WORKS AS A HAULER AND FLEA MARKET SALESMAN, ALSO STARTED WRITING "THE WANDERING SCAVENGER" COLUMN, DIRECTING PEOPLE TO WHERE TRASH MIGHT WOULD BE IN DIFFERENT NEIGHBORHOODS ACROSS TOWN, SO THEY COULD GO DIG THROUGH RICH FOLKS' TRASH FOR FREE STUFF!

THE PROBLEM WITH THE NEWSPAPER BOXES TURNED OUT TO BE THAT THE COPS KEPT TAKING THEM. THE GIRLS FROM TOM'S GROCERY SAID THEY SAW A COP BORROW BOLT CUTTERS FROM A PAWN SHOP, CUT OUR LOCK, AND TAKE OUR BOX! HOWEVER, WE FOUND A NEWSBOX SUPPLY PLACE IN CHINA BASIN THAT ALWAYS HAS 5, OR 10 OUTSIDE. WHENEVER THE COPS TAKE ONE, WE GO GET ANOTHER ONE AND REPAINT IT. IT SEEMS, NOW, THEY'VE QUIT, AS WE'VE HAD THE SAME BOX NOW FOR A RECORD 5 MONTHS! THE ISSUES FLOW FAST OUT OF THE BOX AND, ON MANY DAYS, IT SERVES AS A BENCH FOR STREET DRINKERS...

OUR BIGGEST BREAKTHROUGH, THOUGH TOWARDS BECOMING A CREDIBLE PAPER HAPPENED WHEN IVY ACTUALLY SCORED A TURD-FILLED DONUT INTERVIEW WITH S.F. MAYOR, WILLIE BROWN! ONCE A MONTH, BROWN HAS AN EVENT WHERE HE MEETS, INDIVIDUALLY, WITH 25 S.F. CITIZENS, ONE AT A TIME, FOR 15 MINUTES EACH. THE PRESS LOVES IT AND ALWAYS SHOWS UP TO GET PICTURES OF WILLIE LISTENING ATTENTIVELY TO HIS POOR CITIZENS GRIEVANCES. IN ORDER TO SEE THE MAYOR, YOU HAVE TO LINE UP ON A CERTAIN DAY AT CITY HALL AT 5:00 AM AND BE ONE THE FIRST 25 PEOPLE IN LINE, SO IVY WENT DOWN THERE AT 5:00 AM AND MANAGED TO GET A TICKET THEN WE ASKED PEOPLE ON 6TH STREET WHAT QUESTIONS THEY WISHED THEY COULD ASK

Willie to poor people: Leave town

ONE OF THE NICE THINGS about Willie Brown's monthly public-availability sessions is that the mayor gets to relax and speak his mind. How else to explain the astonishing candor with which he answered zine writer Ivy McClelland's tough questions about living poor in San Francisco?

McClelland lined up for a ticket to meet the mayor, then conducted a brief interview that ran in her zine *Turd-Filled Donut*. Our subscription to *TFD* seems to have lapsed, but we spotted her interview when it was reprinted in the venerable hardcore rag *Maximumrocknroll*. An excerpt:

Willie Brown: We do pay the highest welfare grant in the state.

Ivy McClelland: *Right, but it's also the most expensive place to live, possibly, in the whole country.*

Brown: And that's why I say to people who are poverty-stricken, I know how much you love San Francisco, but because of the nature of the cost of living here, you are better off being poverty-stricken where the cost of living is not so great.

McClelland: *But that would mean displacing people who have lived here their whole lives, just because they're poor.*

Brown: Yeah, but you got to.

We called the Mayor's Office to ask if Brown really said that, and if he really meant it. (A volunteer at *Maximumrocknroll* told us McClelland had gotten the interview on tape, and there is indeed a tape recorder in the photograph of the two talking, but we couldn't get a copy by press time.)

Brown spokesperson Ron Vinson asked us to fax him the interview. He didn't deny that Brown had made those comments, but said, "I can't really respond to that because I wasn't there." He described Brown's conversation with McClelland as "kind of inconclusive."

All the people struggling to pay their rent in San Francisco might see it a little differently.

> 'I say to people who are poverty-stricken, you are better off being poverty-stricken where the cost of living is not so great.'
>
> *Mayor Willie Brown*

← GUARDIAN REPRINT. (BELOW) COVER OF #4 BY CHRIS JOHANSEN

THE TURD FILLED DONUT

DECEMBER ISSUE NO. [?]

THIS ISSUE: SPECIAL INTERVIEW WITH MAYOR WILLIE BROWN AND THE PEOPLE WHO PIED HIM!

THE MAYOR IF THEY HAD A CHANCE TO TALK TO HIM.

APPARENTLY, BROWN DIDN'T TAKE TALK WITH THE LOWLY TURD-FILLED DONUT VERY IMPORTANT, BECAUSE, DESPITE A VERY VISIBLE TAPE RECORDER THAT IVY HAD TOLD HIM WAS RECORDING, HE MADE SLIP-UP AFTER SLIP-UP. MANY OF THE QUESTIONS FROM THE STREET CONCERNED THE SAFETY, UPKEEP, AND CLEANLINESS OF THE RESIDENTIAL HOTELS THAT WE AND MANY OF OUR READERS LIVED IN ON 6TH. BROWN WAS SURPRISED TO LEARN THAT THERE ARE NO KITCHENS IN S.R.O. HOTEL ROOMS AND THAT YOU CAN'T BUY HOT MEALS WITH FOOD STAMPS. HE WAS JUST SO OUT OF TOUCH. HE TOLD HIS AIDE, "NO KITCHENS? LET'S GET RIGHT ON THIS, FIRST THING, MONDAY MORNING!" AS IF THEY COULD START BUILDING KITCHENS IN 70 YEAR OLD ROOMS, JUST LIKE THAT.

BUT BROWN'S BIGGEST FUCK-UP CAME WHEN, TALKING ABOUT THE CONTROVERSIES RAGING IN THE CITY OVER ILLEGAL EVICTIONS AND WELFARE CUTS AND ALL THE OTHER POLICIES THAT ARE WORKING TO COMPLETELY REMOVE THE POOR FROM S.F. WHICH ALREADY HAS THE U.S.' HIGHEST RENTS. HE ACTUALLY CAME OUT AND SAID, "I SAY TO PEOPLE WHO ARE POVERTY STRICKEN, YOU ARE BETTER OFF GOING WHERE THE COST OF LIVING IS NOT SO GREAT..." HE HAD COME RIGHT OUT AND SAID IT! "IF YOU'RE POOR, GET LOST!"

THIS INTERVIEW ENDED BEING REPRINTED IN THE GUARDIAN UNDER THE TELLING HEADLINE "██ ~ TO POOR: "LEAVE TOWN!" KUSF BORROWED THE TAPE SO THEY COULD BURN A CD OF IT TO PLAY ON THE AIR REPEATEDLY. AND, A YEAR LATER, DURING BROWN'S RUN FOR RE-ELECTION, THIS OFFHAND REMARK TO THE T.F.D. WAS USED AGAINST HIM IN THE CHRONICLE, EXAMINER, AND THE GUARDIAN, AS WELL AS BEING CITED IN HIS OPPONENT, TOM AMMIANO'S LITERATURE, AND APPEARING ON COUNTLESS ANTI-BROWN STICKERS AND WHEATPASTINGS ALL OVER TOWN. THE MOST EXCITING THING, FOR ME PERSONALLY, WAS HEARING THAT OUR ELECTION ISSUE FROM NOVEMBER '99, WAS ENDORSED AMMIANO, WAS SPOTTED TACKED TO A WALL AT AMMIANO'S ELECTION HEADQUARTERS!

THE T.F.D.'S PRINTED A WIDE VARIETY OF ARTICLES OVER THE 2 YEARS. WE'VE WROTE ABOUT PEOPLE WINNING LAWSUITS AGAINST THEIR SLUMLORD HOTEL OWNERS, WE'VE COVERED COALITION ON HOMELESS DEMOS DEMANDING CIVIL RIGHTS FOR THE HOMELESS, AND WE INTERVIEWED THE UN PLAZA HOMELESS PROJECT, A GROUP OF HOMELESS PEOPLE WHO WERE DOING ACTIONS IN CITY HALL AND DEMANDING THAT THE CITY GIVE THEM AN ABANDONED BUILDING TO FIX UP AND LIVE IN. WE WROTE ABOUT TRANNY HISTORY IN THE TENDERLOIN AND THE ACTIVISTS WHO ATTACKED MAYOR BROWN WITH A PIE AT A PRESS CONFERENCE, THE BIOTIC BAKING BRIGADE. BUT, I THINK, OUR MOST WELL KNOWN STORY, BESIDES THE BROWN INTERVIEW, WAS THE ONE WITH NO MORALLY, OR POLITICALLY UPGRADING BENEFITS "THE 6TH STREET TREASURE HUNT FOR BEER." GRETA AND I HID A 6-PACK AND MADE A MAP, THE CENTERFOLD TO ISSUE #5, TO FIND IT. IT WAS ACTUALLY PRETTY HARD, BUT IF YOU SOLVED IT — AND ALL THE CLUES WERE RIGHT ON 6TH STREET — THEN YOU WOULD'VE FOUND THE BEER IN A SUITCASE, FLOATING IN THE BAY, AT THE END OF A ROPE TIED TO A LADDER ON PIER 7! THAT'S HOW THE BEER WAS GUARANTEED TO BE COLD; IT WAS IN THE BAY! IT TURNED OUT MY FRIENDS, RAVI AND SEAN, FOUND THE BEER, SO WE PUT MORE OUT THERE. ONE DAY, I WENT TO CHECK ON THE SECOND 6-PAK AND I FOUND THE ROPE UP ON THE DOCK NEXT TO A BUNCH OF CRUSHED TECATE CANS! SOMEONE FOUND THAT, TOO. PEOPLE STILL STOP ME AND ASK ME WHEN I'M GOING TO HIDE SOME MORE BEER!

NOW, AFTER A COUPLE YEARS OF DOING THE T.F.D. SPORADICALLY, I THINK ITS COME A LONG WAY, BUT IS STILL VERY MUCH AN EXPERIMENT IN PROGRESS. I WANT TO MAKE IT COME OUT MORE OFTEN, SO THE REPORTING'S MORE CONSISTENTLY RELEVENT. WITH THE NEWEST ISSUE, I'M LEARNING TO USE "PUBLIC RECORDS REQUESTS" TO DIG UP DIRT ON PUBLIC OFFICIALS. OUR GOAL IS TO GET A GRANT SO WE CAN PAY PEOPLE TO WRITE FOR US AND GET MORE PEOPLE INVOLVED. IT'LL BE SO FUN; WE CAN PUT OUT FLYERS LOOKING FOR WRITERS, AND WHEN PEOPLE NEED 20 BUCKS FOR BEER, THEY CAN COME WORK ON A STORY FOR TURD-FILLED DONUT. IT'LL BE JUST LIKE THE BLOOD BANK!

WE'RE THE ONLY PUNK RUN NEEDLE EXCHANGE IN THE COUNTRY! WE SNUCK NEEDLE EXCHANGE INTO THE HAIGHT, BY BEING THERE AND DOING IT 3 DAYS A WEEK, NO MATTER WHAT. THE COPS COULDN'T KEEP ARRESTING US...

"SHARE DRUGS, NOT NEEDLES..."
AN INTERVIEW WITH...
SAN FRANCISCO NEEDLE EXCHANGE.

I'M ALWAYS INTERESTED IN WHAT KIND OF PUNK SKILLS AND ATTITUDES AND IDEAS PUNKS BRING WITH THEM WHEN THEY GET INVOLVED IN ACTIVISM. HOW DOES BEING A PUNK AFFECT THEIR GOALS OR TACTICS? WHAT WILL WE CREATE IN THE WORLD BESIDES MUSIC? THE SAN FRANCISCO NEEDLE EXCHANGE GOT STARTED THE PUNK WAY — BY FIGHTING THE COPS! WHEN THE SAN FRANCISCO DEPARTMENT OF HEALTH DECIDED NEEDLE EXCHANGE WAS TOO CONTROVERSIAL FOR THE HAIGHT, SFNE GOT INDEPENDENT FUNDING TO START THEIR OWN EXCHANGE. AND WHEN THE COPS SHUT 'EM DOWN THEY KEPT GOING BACK!
NOT ONLY IS THIS COUNTRY'S RIGHT WING DRUG WAR FILLING PRISONS WITH NON-VIOLENT OFFENDERS, AND FILLING THE POCKETS OF POLICE DEPARTMENTS AND PRISON BUILDERS WITH TAXPAYER MONEY, BUT IT ALSO KEEPS SENSIBLE HARM REDUCTION DRUG POLICIES FROM BEING IMPLEMENTED. THE SPREAD OF H.I.V. AND HEPATITIS IS A PUBLIC HEALTH EMERGENCY THAT COULD BE SLOWED BY NEEDLE EXCHANGE, BUT EVEN COMPARATIVELY LIBERAL CITIES LIKE S.F. LET ANTI-DRUG HYSTERIA DICTATE PUBLIC HEALTH POLICY. IN THE EARLY PART OF THIS CENTURY, IT WAS ILLEGAL TO PUBLICLY ADVOCATE BIRTH CONTROL. IF YOU READ EMMA GOLDMAN'S BOOKS, HER AND REITMAN AND THEIR CONTEMPORARIES WERE ALWAYS GETTING ARRESTED OR HAVING COPS RAID THEIR HALLS AND SHUT DOWN THEIR SPEECHES ABOUT CONDOMS. TODAY, SFNE AND THE NEEDLE ARE FIGHTING THE SAME UPHILL BATTLE... I TALKED WITH SFNE'S RO GIULIANO AND MATTY LUV (WHO MANY SCAM READERS KNOW FROM HIS OLD BAND, HICKEY...)

MATTY LUV

SPARE SOME XCHANGE?

430-530 MON WED FRI
OAKNSHRADER

MON WED FRI
PAN 430 - 530pm HANDLE
OAKNSHRADER

SCAM: OK, you might just want to start off with a brief rundown of the idea behind needle exchange, and just what the basic idea of "Harm Reduction" is, for some of our readers who may not know much about it…
MATTY LUV: Harm reduction is non-judgemental medical treatment around issues of drug use. Rather than saying abstinence from drugs is best, we take the position that people use drugs and always have used drugs, no matter what the law is. Instead of treating drug use as immoral, the idea is that any positive change in drug use is good, is a step towards greater health. By using clean needles, you can stop the spread of HIV and Hepatitis. By teaching people what to do if someone OD's, you can save lives. Abstinence is not the issue, but, if people stay alive and healthy, maybe, one day, down the road, they might be interested in that.
RO: In San Francisco, there's 4 overdoses a day, and soft tissue abscesses are the #1 cause of visits to the emergency room at SF General. The City spends $18 million on abscess care, when its easily preventable, because they're more interested in trying to ARREST users.

LIFE ON HATE STREET

SCAM: OK, so what events led to the formation of the SF Needle Exchange?
ML: OK, well some background on the Haight… The Haight is pretty much a police state. If you're on the streets and you don't look like you own property, or shop there, you're liable to get stopped by the cops and shaken down for no reason.
RO: Mayor Brown shut down the east end of Golden Gate Park in the Haight in October… November 1997, basically, because he didn't want the kids there. Teenage runaways from all over the country still come to the Haight. Brown had this whole ruse about building a children's playground and a skating rink…
ML: But, now its over two years later, and there's still just a fence there…
SCAM: Right, I remember that was when I moved back to SF, and I was shocked. Here was Brown talking about using helicopters with night vision to root out sleeping homeless people in the park… I went to these real crazy HANC (Haight Ashbury Neighborhood Council) public forums about it. People were at each other's throats…
ML: ,Yeah, it was a very politically charged environment we started in…
RO: I had a job as an outreach worker in the Haight at that time, working with the street kids.
ML: And I had just got back from Hickey tour, with Ivy, who we brought back to SF with us. We got on GA (SF welfare) and got our GA workfare jobs at the AIDS Foundation. We were supposed to be helping street kids in the Haight do a fanzine and a leather workshop. We weren't supposed to be doing needle exchange at all…
RO: But, when Golden Gate Park closed, the Department of Health stopped all their needle exchange in the Haight, because it was just too politically hot. This left this huge gap in services. They expected the kids to go all the way past the Castro to the Department of Health site behind the Safeway on DuBoce, but these kids never even go past Masonic, or even Ashbury! So, the outreach worker who was doing exchange before supplied me with needles and I started doing the exchange myself, VERY covertly… Then, Matty and Ivy started helping me.

- 270 -

THE 911 SITUATION

STAY CALM... DON'T FREAK THE FUCK OUT. CALL 911 AND TELL 'EM THAT THE PERSON OD'D AND WHAT DRUG THEY'RE ON. WAIT WITH THEM TILL THE AMBULANCE ARRIVES. CONTINUE TO SHAKE THEM AND SHOUT THEIR NAME. IF YOU THINK THE PERSON HAS WARRANTS YOU CAN TAKE THEIR ID BEFORE THE PIGS SHOW UP. PUT THE PERSON IN THE RECOVERY POSITION SO IF THEY PUKE THEY WON'T CHOKE ON THEIR OWN VOMIT:

The recovery position

IT'S REAL IMPORTANT TO HAVE SOMEONE STAY WITH THE PERSON AND TRY TO WAKE THEM UP OR KEEP THEM AWAKE. SO STICK AROUND, EVEN IF IT MEANS HAVIN' TO DRAG THE PERSON OUT FROM YER SQUAT OR APARTMENT. STASH YER SHIT, DISPOSE OF YER RIGS AND COOKERS. IF YA HAVE NO CHOICE AND HAVE TO LEAVE THE SCENE TRY TO GET SOMEONE ELSE TO STAY UNTIL THE PARAMEDICS ARRIVE.

SAN FRANCISCO

NEEDLE EXCHANGE

ML: For a long time, we did a roving exchange, handing out needles out of our Zo bags... ← "ZO BAGS"

RO: I'd be doing outreach, you know... handing out condoms and socks, and I'd just ask if anyone needed any clean points.

ML: We were, quite literally on our own. We only had 300 needles. We had to take the dirties to other exchange sites to exchange them, as if we had used them all ourselves...

SCAM: How'd you get 300 needles?

ML: "Somebody", um... GAVE them to us...

SCAM: Did you guys have prior needle exchange experience?

RO: Oh, yeah. I went to college for this. Since 1993, I've done needle exchange, here and back in New York City. I worked at the Department of Health site here for awhile. When the park closed, I just wanted to try to fill the gap.

ML: I had no experience. Since I got out of high school, I've pretty much only had shitty jobs and played in bands. My first real involvement in anything like this was, one time, between tours, I needed a job. Through an, uh, embellished resume, I got a job at UCSF doing survey work, interviewing injection drug users about their habits and testing them for HIV and TB. So, I received a brief HIV counseling training. But, basically, I didn't have anything to do between tours, so I threw myself into this. Later on, when we'd be going to meetings with the cops, or neighborhood groups, I didn't even own a pair of long pants to wear to them. I'd be on my way there, hoping I could find a long pair of Ben Davis pants on the fuckin' STREET!

SCAM: How did the roving exchange lead to an actual exchange site?

RO: I got stuck with a dirty point. We had to do everyting so clandestinely with the bio bucket in the Zo bag and all these people shiftily putting in dirties and reaching in. We were out there after dark a lot... Finally, one time I got stuck. It was getting pretty sketchy. So we tried to use the side of the Cala Supermarket at Haight and Stanyan as a fixed site, because kids panhandled there.

ML: But, then one time, we told like 4 people to meet us there, and, like, 50 kids came.

RO: Right, so obviously we needed something less conspicuous than the side of the Cala on Haight!

ML: Different agencies... that shall remain nameless... helped us out by flowing us needles for awhile, and we started doing 2 hour shifts, 3 days a week at the corner of Oak and Shrader in Panhandle park. It started real slow. I can remember days where I'd sit there for, like, 1 and a half hours in the pouring rain, until someone finally showed up, and it'd be a homeless kid in a rainsuit, who'd say something like, "Dude! You should get an umbrella! You're soaked..."

RO: After that, when the AIDS Foundation found out we'd been doing exchange the whole time, they declared us a secondary site for exchange.

SCAM: What's that?

RO: Well, we got the right to be there, sort-of, but they wouldn't give us any legal backing at all...

ML: OR any needles. We still had to turn in all our dirties to get clean ones. I'd always be riding my bike around on Oak Street with, oh, a THOUSAND dirty needles in my bag... But they just didn't give us any support, because it was too controversial.

SCAM: This is the AIDS Foundation, too... You'd think they'd have an interest in stopping the spread of HIV...

ML: Well, we were getting harrassed by the cops all the time, and the AIDS Foundation's brilliant response was "Get out of the Panhandle then! Quit doing it!" Fuck that!

S. F. N. E. VERSUS S. F. P. D

RO: So, then the Foundation cut off their funding for the youth program, because they didn' t want anything in the Haight. I'd heard through the grapevine that that was going to happen, so I had already started getting funding together so we could become the first independent needle exchange in SF. We had a fiscal sponsor, other funding, and tons of backers. We had a small, start-up grant of 10,000 needles from the North American Syringe Exchange Network, which was matched by my friend, Rene, from New Needles Now! Down in LA. That was enough needles to carry us for awhile until we could write more grants and get more cash.

Now, we were independent. We had no legal backing at all, and no organization behind us. Our last day with the AIDS Foundation, officially, was June 30, 1998 and then, our first day on our own was July 1st. On our first day, Officer McGloughlin came to shut us down.

SCAM: Ah, yes... Good old McGloughlin. He was, I think, according to the Turd-Filled Donut story I did, #5 on the list in the whole city of cops who wrote the most "Quality Of Life" citations to fuck with homeless people...

ML: Yeah, he'd been by the exchange to fuck with us before, and he and I had argued. He's just your basic conservative, Republican dickhead.

RO: One of our HIV+ participants tried to tell McGloughlin that if there had been a needle exchange for him a couple years ago, he wouldn't have contracted HIV. He asked McGloughlin, "What would you do if it was one of YOUR kids who was addicted to heroin, or got AIDS?" Officer McGloughlin's brilliant response was, "None of my kids would get addicted to heroin or get AIDS!"

SCAM: What is the exact law, anyways? Needle Exchange IS legal, right?

ML: Needle Exchange is legal in a declared Public Health State Of Emergency. The State of Emergency is in effect, now, in SF, because of the AIDS epidemic, so exchange is legal, and SFPD policy is to leave exchange sites alone. One time, I was wearing this "Fuck Bush!" button that one of the kids gave me, and Officer McGloughlin rode by. Then he stopped and said, "That button is obscene! There's kids in this park!" I said, "Look, if you're close enough to read my button, by SFPD policy, you're too close to our site...

RO: So, the first day, he gave us a warning. Of course, we went back, and the next day he came back and arrested us. He took us away in cuffs in front of the whole exchange...

ML: Ro went to Park Station and got sited out. I, unfortunately, had a knife on me which is considerred an illegal, dangerous weapon in the state of California...

(We all stop to laugh at Matty having a knife)

RO: He used it to pop the lids off bio buckets!

ML: Look, it was a real weapon! It was teak handled, double edged, serrated, and over 6 inches in length. GUARANTEED penetration!

SCAM: Well, if you live on 24th Street and sometimes you got to walk down by 16th...

ML: So, I got a felony for that and spenty the night at 850 Bryant...

OVERDOSE AWARENESS

HOW CAN YOU TELL IF SOMEONE OD'D?

THEY TURN BLUE OR KINDA GREYISH

THEY MAY HAVE SLOW, SHALLOW, BREATHING (OR NONE AT ALL)

THEY MAY HAVE A SLOW PULSE (OR NO PULSE AT ALL)

THEY MAY VOMIT

THEY MAY HAVE A SEIZURE

WHAT SHOULD YOU DO?

CALL THEIR NAME AND SHAKE 'EM. CHECK FOR PULSE AND BREATHING. SPLASH WATER ON THEIR FACE. IF THERE IS NO RESPONSE OR THEY'RE NOT BREATHIN'

CALL FUCKIN' 911

RO: The actual charges for what we're doing aren't even criminal. They're misdemeanor violations of business codes. "Possessing medical equipment without a proper license." "Dispensing medical equipment without a prescription". California is one of only 9 states where buying syringes over the counter is illegal, anyway... So, we just bailed Matty out the next day.

ML: We called the Linda Smith Center, a think-tank on drug policy, and they helped me out with a real good lawyer who got all the charges dropped. Next time I saw McGloughlin, he was pissed. "What happened to that felony weapons charge?"

I said, "It got dropped, dude. It was harrassment." So... he arrested us again!

RO: (laughing) Yeah, we had SO MUCH backup. People from the Harm Reduction Coalition and the Linda Smith Center came to exchange, willing to get arrested... YOU were there from the Coalition On Homelessness. Tim from the Coalition had the video camera... And then McGloughlin left us alone for 3 weeks. We thought everything was cool, so people quit coming. Then, McGloughlin showed up and arrested us again. It turns out he had been ON VACATION for 3 weeks!

ML: The day he got back to town, he arrested us.

RO: That time, we both had to go to 850 Bryant because he considerred us "Repeat and Dangerous Offenders". We spent 9 hours there, just to get cited out again.

ML: It was cute, though. She was in the girls' cell across the hall from me, and we could wave at each other...

ML: Yeah, but Matty's cell had the phone!

SCAM: Where do you think McGloughlin GOES on vacation?

RO: I think he has a cabin up north...

ML: I actually got sort-of friendly with him that time. We talked about bicycles. I asked him how come a pig never rides his bike in the rain. Because I CERTAINLY ride MINE in the rain...

RO: After that arrest, the Haight Ashbury Free Clinic and HANC were up in arms, because they'd seen less needles on the street because of us. They said, look, we can't have the Haight without needle exchange, because there's tons of young injection users and the Hep C rate's throught the roof!

ML: So that arrest led to our meeting with the head of Park Station, Captain Newland.

It was supposed to be just a small meeting with me and Ro, an outreach worker from the Haight Ashbury Youth Outreach Team and a couple cops, but we packed it with our supporters. We brought 13 people. We had to to try to legitimize ourselves with the cops. They just looked at us and thought we were just the kids on the street.

RO: We had representatives from the Harm Reduction Coalition there. ALL the Haight outreach workers. Legal people from the Linda Smith center came all the way from NEW YORK. You came there from the Coalition On Homelessness. The DIRECTOR of the Hight Ashbury Free Clinic was there. The president of HANC...

SCAM: Wasn't that the meeting where Newland had to split to go bowling, and we were saying we should get a crusty bowling team together to settle this once and for all, ON THE LANES!

RO: Well, actually, we found out a lot about the arrests BEFORE they would happen from someone we know who is Newland's bowling partner!

ML: Its true. We're oddly well-connected. They bowl together every Tuesday night at Japantown Bowl on Geary. When there was the threat of impending arrest, the bowling contact would warn us before it happened. Then one of us would stand at Oak and Shrader with no needles or anything and just tell the kids to go to another secret spot where one of us would be waiting with needles. During the Haight Street Fair, we actually did exchange INSIDE of a porta-pottie at Haight and Cole!

RO: You see, Newland wasn't really against us. He just had this one officer, McGloughlin, who was making this his pet peeve issue. Once Newland saw that first hand, we were OK. McGloughlin was at this meeting, yelling at 50 year old homeowners who were saying they WANTED there to be a needle exchange. These are the constituents he's supposed to please. Newland actually told him to shut up a couple of times. At that meeting, Newland said he'll leave us alone, if we found an indoors space. Then 409 Clayton let us start doing exchange in their space on a trial basis.

We set up strategical planning on how to keep the space. That's why we have a door person. We're responsible for making sure the whole 400 block of Clayton is clean. We have to rake the children's playground in the Panhandle every night for needles, not that we've EVER found a needle in the children's playground. We've been there almost 2 years without a single complaint.

"THE ONLY PUNK RUN NEEDLE EXCHANGE"

SCAM: How has punk rock experience helped you start SFNE?

ML: We're the only punk-run needle exchange in the country. I mean, me, Ro, and Ivy started it, and our volunteers are mostly punks. And, basically, we snuck needle exchange into the Haight, based on the fact that we were going to be there and doing it in the Panhandle, 3 days a week, no matter what. The cops just couldn't keep arresting us.

We've been very dilligent about the way we run the space. That's one thing I learned from putting on punk shows over the years, is how to keep things cool on the outside so as not to attract the cops.

RO: "No drinking outside the show", became "No smoking and hanging out on the steps", or, "No doing drug business on the steps of 409 Clayton".

ML: We culturally identify with the kids we serve, which helped gain their trust, and they're hard kids to reach. Then, there's the organizational skills I learned from booking tours and that problem solving.

One of the first things we did to advertise the exchange was make a series of stickers that had the logo of a punk band on it and the exchange days and times and location written real small at the botoom. So, if the kids put it on

BLACK FLAG

MON WED FRI
430 - 530pm
PANHANDLE

FIG 3: BOBBY SEALE + HUEY NEWTON

"CARRIED GUNS TO 'POP' PIGS"

FIG. 4: EX-HICKEY SINGER/GUITAR

I ♥ H KILL!

"CARRIED KNIFE TO POP LID OFF BUCKET OF RIGS..."

their skate or on their jacket, they'd always have the schedule, and if a cop happened to see it, he'd just think it was a band. There was a Black Flag one, The Misfits...

SCAM: I had The Descendents one!

ML: That was super effective, because they weren't flyers left laying around for cops and angry citizens to find. They got stuck on.

We also made these pamphlets, Alien Meth Fiend. In any outreach situation, there's all these really dull pamphlets full of HIV or OD prevention info. So we started making punk-style pamphlets with info in an easy to understand language and punk style layouts. The kids actually read them.

RO: Also, the kids, having seen us go to jail for this, earned a lot of respect for us and the program. They knew we were there for them. It gave them a real ownership of the program. After the program survived the arrests, they felt like they didn't want to fuck it up...

ML: Also, this is the first interview we've ever done for SFNE, which is another thing I learned from punk: Most "exposure" and media coverage sucks. People just want to distort what you're doing because they have their own agenda. Back when we were getting arrested, The Guardian, Frontlines, The Independent... they all wanted to talk to us. But we thought it would just make it worse. This guy wanted to put us in his real pro documentary on the lives of down and out people. We turned them all down. We just didn't see any benefit to it...

SCAM: Yeah, I was writing a thing about the Turd-Filled Donut in this issue and I realized it was the first time I'd tried to tell our story, because we'd turned down a lot of papers, too. The stories wouldn't help us serve the people we were trying to serve... Publicity is more likely to get you shut down than get funding.

HOW IS S.F.N.E. INDEPENDENTLY FUNDED?

RO: I write grants constantly!

ML: Its hard to get funding, obviously, for something that's illegal... Our first grant was just needles, and then we had to scam supplies. Other exchanges helped out. Our paramedic friend would just "get" us supplies... We worked every day for at least a full year without getting paid...

RO: There's foundations. The Comer Foundation gives harm reduction grants specifically to controverrsial programs that can't get funding anywhere else. There's the Tides Foundation, which is run by George Soros, this billionaire who gives to needle exchanges.

ML: Basically, we're funded by philanthropy.

RO: When the Beastie Boys came around last time, they had this thing where a buck from every ticket they sold would get donated to this non-profit, Millarepa, that would give small grants in every city to groups who were doing stuff that the Beasties were down with... They gave us $3,000 to help the kids put out a zine called "War On Sleep".

HICKEY, NEEDLE EXCHANGE, AND YOU...

SCAM: Why did Hickey break up, Matty, and what was the initial appeal for you of doing this kind of work?

ML: I don't really know why Hickey broke up. When we came back from what turned out to be the last tour, it was just apparent that we weren't going to do it anymore. Hickey

was a fairly intense experience: 4 years, 7 US tours, 2 full records of stuff. I was looking forward to not being in a structured band for awhile, but I was looking for a way to stay in touch with the punk community. A lot of the kids from the exchange were kids who went to our warehouse shows at 17th and Capp. Its cliched, "Doing it for the kids," but I like the kids. The kids are a lot nicer than a lot of my peers who grew up and turned out to be real fucking drags.

RO: Punk's been integrated into our program a lot. We've done lots of benefit punk shows.

ML: When I got arrested, we did a benefit at Mission Records to pay the bail off..

RO: And we did that big New Year's show in 98 at Mission Records. We got Thrasher to donate skateboards and clothes for presents to the kids and we served food. FuckFace and Chinese Love Beads played...

SCAM: That was a great show! There were just kids passed out ALL OVER Mission Street!

ML: Puke everywhere...

RO: Whenever we do benefits, we get the kids in free.

ML: Even at the last Hickey show before that tour, I made up 20 passes and gave them out at the exchange.

RO: kids at the exchange travel a lot. A lot of them saw Hickey in different spots all over the US.

ML: At exchange, I'll see kids with Hickey patches and I'll be like, "Which show did you get that at? Arkansas in '95?"

SCAM: Does it bum you out to give a bunch of needles to a kid with a Hickey patch who is all strung out and not doing so great?

ML" Not at all...

RO: Hickey was pretty fucked up, too.

ML: Well, I think its beneficial for the kids that are really down and out to be involved in the punk scene and to be able to go inside of shows and to have a community.

SCAM: Yeah, its always sad to me to see when people lose all connection to punk, like if some young kid gets kicked out of the scene. Suddenly, they're not part of the nation of freaks. They're just some dude on the street... In this decade there was such a huge crusty backlash...

ML: Yeah, I used to adhere to that, too, but then, somewhere along the way, after running into enough of them on Hickey tours, I started thinking they were cool.

SCAM: Yeah. Me, too. At first I thought they were just like hippies.

ML: Exactly!

SCAM: But then I was like, "What's wrong with sitting on the sidewalk and drinking beer all day, anyways?" I have a long, proud history of that.

ML: Sure. That's how I spent the better part of my youth.

RO: That shows kids what they can do or what they could become. We're punks who started an exchange. We can help them get involved in SFNE. We can get them into paid posotions at some of the user studies in the Haight where they'll hire homeless kids, and then, maybe, they can get a pay check and a more stable living situation, and still stay true to hat they want to do.

SCAM: Right! If they stay healthy, they can quit panhandling and get on WELFARE, like me!

ML: Once people have been truly marginalized its hard to come back...

DESCENDENTS

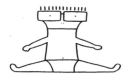

MON WED FRI
PAN   4:30 - 5:30   HANDLE
       OAK N SHRADER

AT THIS POINT, I WAS GOING TO AGREE THAT ITS IMPORTANT TO USE PUNK AS A LIFELINE FOR KIDS WHO ARE SO UNDER ATTACK FROM THE COPS AND EVERYBODY, BUT THEN THE PHONE RANG, AND MATTY HAD TO SPEND 10 MINUTES HELPING THE CALLER FIND A VEIN IN THEIR ANKLE TO SHOOT UP IN, CUZ ALL THEIR VEINS WERE COLLAPSED, AND THAT SEEMED TO MAKE MY POINT NICE ENOUGH FOR ME...

THE PARTS THEY'LL LEAVE OUT OF THE MOVIE...

ONE BROKE AND HUNGRY MAN'S RACE AGAINST TIME TO MAKE IT ACROSS THE COUNTRY FOR... A WEDDING! BY IGGY SCAM

"IS THERE ANYBODY HERE TONIGHT DRIVING TOWARDS...UH... MINNESOTA? A GUY HERE REALLY NEEDS A RIDE AFTER THE SHOW..." I HAD FINALLY GOT THE GUITARIST OF THE OPENING BAND TO HELP ME FIND A RIDE OUT OF TOWN, BETWEEN SONGS. SOMEHOW, AFTER A MONTH ON THE ROAD, I'D ENDED UP STUCK AT THIS SHOW IN MADISON, WISCONSIN AND ONLY WHEN I SAW THE FLYER DID I REALIZE I'D TOTALLY LOST TRACK OF TIME AND HAD ONLY 9 DAYS TO BE BACK HOME IN SAN FRANCISCO FOR A GOOD FRIEND'S WEDDING. I WAS TOTALLY BROKE AND HAD NO WAY BACK EXCEPT TO HOP FREIGHT TRAINS, AND — I HAD A BEAT UP, ONE SPEED BICYCLE NAMED "OLE CHERRY RED" WITH ME THAT I'D BEEN HOPPING TRAINS WITH. I WAS TRYING TO WIN A BET THAT I COULD MAKE IT ALL THE WAY AROUND THE COUNTRY WITH THE BIKE. ME AND MY BIKE HAD TO BE AT THE WEDDING. THE WHOLE TRIP WAS ON THE LINE: COULD ME AND MY BIKE MAKE IT 2000 MILES IN 9 DAYS WITH NO MONEY? MY FINGERS WERE CROSSED. AT LEAST IT WASN'T MY WEDDING.

AFTER THE SHOW, MY FRIENDS FROM MILWAUKEE WHO'D DRIVEN UP TO THE SHOW IN MADISON, OFFERED TO DRIVE ME 20 MILES WEST TO THE TINY RAILROAD TOWN OF PORTAGE, WISCONSIN, WHERE THE CHICAGO TO MINNEAPPOLIS TRAINS STOP TO CHANGE CREWS. I KNEW IT'D BE EASY TO GET ON A WESTBOUND TRAIN THERE. WE PULLED INTO PORTAGE, PAST 2:00AM AND SAID OUR GOODBYES DOWN THE STREET FROM THE YARD. THE GIRL WHO WAS DRIVING EVEN GAVE ME A KISS GOODBYE ON THE CHEEK! IT WAS VERY SWEET, LIKE A MOVIE, AND I RODE OFF TO THE YARD ON OLE CHERRY RED FEELING GREAT AND THINKING HOW GREAT MY LUCK HAD BEEN ON THE WHOLE TRIP. LIKE, I'D SOMEHOW MANAGED TO OUTRUN THAT COP THAT CHASED ME OUT OF THAT GROCERY STORE IN OGDEN, UTAH. I'D FOUND A BROKEN COPY MACHINE AT A MEMPHIS KINKO'S THAT DIDN'T TAKE MONEY OFF YOUR CARD AND HAD USED IT TO SCAM HUNDREDS OF COPIES OF MY ZINE. I'D LUCKED INTO LAST MINUTE RIDES TO CHICAGO, MILWAUKEE, AND MADISON, AND NOW I WAS HERE, FEELING LIKE I WAS IN A MOVIE AS THE STARVING, YOUNG WRITER TAKING HIS ZINE ACROSS THE COUNTRY, GETTING KISSES GOODBYE AND DASHING OFF TO HOP LATE-NIGHT TRAINS OUTTA TOWN. I'D GET THIS TRAIN OUT OF PORTAGE, EASY, AND THEN CALIFORNIA, HERE I COME!!! RIGHT?

AT THE TRAIN YARD, I KNEW SOMETHING WAS WRONG, RIGHT AWAY. ABOUT 8 TRAIN WORKERS WERE AT THE ENTRANCE, SITTING AROUND A TABLE, LAUGHING AND PLAYING CARDS. THEY LOOKED VERY... UH... RELAXED. I RODE UP AND SAID, "GOOD EVENING... CAN ANY OF YOU GUYS TELL ME WHEN THE NEXT TRAIN TO MINNEAPPOLIS IS GONNA STOP HERE?" THEY ALL LOOKED AT EACH OTHER AND LAUGHED. ONE OLDER GUY SAID, "THERE'S NO TRAINS STOPPING HERE..." "WHY NOT?" "WE'RE ON STRIKE! WE SHUT DOWN THE RAILROAD!" THEY ALL ANSWERED, AND POINTED AT THEIR PICKET SIGNS SCATTERED AROUND THE TABLE ON THE GROUND. "THE SOO LINE RAILROAD CAN ONLY RUN ONE TRAIN A DAY NOW WITH SCABS FROM CHICAGO AND IT DOESN'T DO CREW CHANGES, CUZ THERE'S NO CREWS!" THEY ALL LAUGHED HARDER. I SAW A BOTTLE ON THE TABLE. THEY'D BEEN DRINKING. UNLESS THEIR DEMANDS WERE MIRACULOUSLY MET IN THE MIDDLE OF THE NIGHT I WAS GOING TO HAVE TO HITCH HIKE TO THE NEXT WORKING RAILROAD IN MINNEAPPOLIS. I WISHED 'EM LUCK ON THE STRIKE AND DASHED OFF TO FIND A DITCH TO SLEEP IN.

I MADE DECENT TIME AND GOT TO MINNEAPPOLIS ON 4 RIDES, LATE IN THE AFTERNOON. BUT THEN MY BIKE INSTANTLY QUIT WORKING. THE BACK WHEEL FROZE UP AND WOULD NOT MOVE. BASICALLY, THE BEARINGS INSIDE THE WHEEL WERE TOTALLY TRASHED FROM RIDING ON THE GRAVEL IN TRAIN YARDS. I FOUND A REAL COOL BIKE MECHANIC — THIS LARGE, CHEERFUL MIDWEST GUY IN HIS 40'S WHO LOOKED LIKE STEINBECK — IN THE FIRST BIKE SHOP I WENT TO. HE UNDERSTOOD MY SITUATION CLEARLY — DAYS, 2,000 MILES TO GO, AND NO CASH — AND HE TRIED EVERYTHING POSSIBLE TO GET THE BIKE TO WORK. YOU COULD TELL HE REALLY CARED, THAT HE WAS ONE OF THE TRUE SAINTS OF BIKE REPAIR WHO ARE MOTIVATED ONLY BY THE LOVE OF BIKES - NOT LIKE THE NEW-SCHOOL GEAR HEADS WHO JUST WANT TO SELL YOU FANCY PARTS AND SPANDEX SHORTS. HE WAS SURE IT WAS GONNA WORK EVERYTIME HE TRIED SOMETHING, BUT I HAD A FEELING IT WAS HOPELESS. I RECOGNIZED THIS BIKE TROUBLE AS PART OF A RUNNING JOKE BETWEEN ME AND GOD. MY LUCK HAD TURNED BAD, AND I'D JUST HAVE TO TRY AND WAIT IT OUT. IN THE END, HE SAID ALL HE COULD DO WAS ORDER A NEW WHEEL FOR 60 BUCKS. NONE OF THE OTHER SHOPS HE CALLED FOR ME HAD A USED WHEEL LAYING AROUND, EITHER. I HAD SPENT ALL DAY HITCHING AND AT THE SHOP. I HAD 8 DAYS LEFT TO GET HOME...

IT LOOKED BAD, BUT I COULDN'T JUST LEAVE MY TRUSTY OLE BIKE BEHIND, RIGHT? WE'D OUTRUN A TRAIN COP IN PUEBLO TOGETHER, SLEPT ON A ROOF IN KANSAS CITY TOGETHER... I HATCHED A PLAN TO GET THE 60 BUCKS, AND KNEW IT COULD NOT FAIL. FIRST, I STOLE A COUPLE OF BIG, EXPENSIVE, HARD COVER BOOKS FROM THIS BOOKSTORE AND THEN I "RETURNED" THEM. IT WAS EASY AND THEY ACCEPTED THE BOOKS, NO PROBLEM! I WAS SO EXCITED. THEN, THEY HANDED ME MY $120... IN STORE CREDIT. I WENT TO EVERY PUNK HOUSE IN TOWN TRYING TO FIND ANYONE WHO'D GIVE ME ANY MONEY FOR IT, BUT EVERYONE WAS BROKE LIKE ME. IT WAS USELESS TO ME. I HIT BOTTOM WHEN I WAS CARRYING MY BIKE TO YET ANOTHER SHOP AND SAW A BLACK CAT UP AHEAD, ABOUT TO CROSS MY PATH. "OH NO YOU DON'T, FUCKER!" I YELLED AND STARTED RUNNING TO BEAT THE CAT TO THE SPOT. THE CAT STARTED RUNNING, TOO. IT WAS A RACE TO THE FINISH, BUT I WON! NOW, MY LUCK WOULD CHANGE, RIGHT? SURE ENOUGH, MY FRIEND, MAGIC MIKE, FOUND A WHEEL IN HIS GARAGE AND IT FIT MY BIKE! IT WAS RUSTY, BUT IT WORKED! I WAS READY TO SPLIT MINNEAPPOLIS, BUT THEN I REMEMBERED SOMETHING. I RODE TO THE BIKE SHOP AND ASKED THE STEINBECK-GUY, "DO YOU READ?" HE SAID, "UH... YEAH." I GAVE HIM THE STORE CREDIT AND HEADED TO THE BURLINGTON NORTHERN TRAIN YARD AT THE EDGE OF TOWN, STOPPING ONLY ONE MORE TIME IN TOWN, TO SAY "HI" TO THE STRIKING WORKERS IN FRONT OF THE SOO LINE YARD ON THE WAY...

I HAD GIVEN THIS GUTTER PUNK IN FRONT OF THE TACO BELL IN UPTOWN A COPY OF MY ZINE IN EXCHANGE FOR INFO. ON WHERE TO CATCH THE ONE TRAIN THAT GOES ALL THE WAY FROM MINNEAPPOLIS TO PORTLAND, SO WHEN I DID WHAT HE SAID, HOW COME MY TRAIN STOPPED AND WENT NO FURTHER THAN STAPLES, MN - ANOTHER TINY RAIL- ROAD TOWN? I WANT MY ZINE BACK! HE SCAMMED THE SCAM! I RODE MY BIKE UP THE TRACKS IN A GLOOMY, PRE-DAWN DRIZZLE TO THE DESERTED AMTRAK STATION/ BN CREW OFFICE AND FOUND AN EMPTY ROOM UPSTAIRS TO SLEEP IN. WHEN I WOKE UP, I CONSULTED MY MAPS AND TRAIN INFORMATION THAT MY FRIEND, BRAD, GAVE ME AND FOUND OUT THE PORTLAND TRAIN WOULD STOP AND CREW CHANGE IN STAPLES AND IT'D BE EASY TO CATCH IT. SINCE I WAS IN POSITION TO CATCH A RIDE ALL THE WAY TO THE WEST COAST, AND WAS ONLY 1½ HOURS FROM FARGO, I DECIDED TO LOCK UP OLE CHERRY RED AND HITCH OVER AND GET DRUNK WITH THE FARGO PUNKS AND THEN HITCH BACK TO MY TRAIN THE NEXT DAY. HIGHWAY 10, A NEARLY DESERTED 2-LANER THROUGH THE HEART OF MINNESOTA PRAIRIE LAND, PROVED TO BE EASY TO HITCH ON. 2 HOURS, AND 3 RIDES LATER I WAS IN FARGO.

THE FARGO PUNKS ARE ALWAYS GLAD TO HAVE VISITORS. WE DRANK LOTS OF BEER AND TALKED SHIT ALL NIGHT AND CRASHED. IT WAS WORTH THE TRIP. THE NEXT MORNING, I DECIDED I'D GO FIND A PLACE TO SWIM AND THEN START THE HITCH BACK TO MY BIKE. IT WAS ALMOST THE END OF MY TRIP...

THERE'S A BIG PUBLIC POOL IN THE PARK BY THE PUNK HOUSE. IT WAS CLOSED SO I HOPPED THE FENCE TO SWIM. AFTER A COUPLE MINUTES, I LOOKED UP TO SEE 5 OR 6 LITTLE KIDS WATCHING ME FROM THE FENCE. WHEN THEY SEE THAT I NOTICE THEM, THEY RUN AWAY. SOMEHOW I JUST KNEW THEY WERE GOING TO GO TELL ON ME, THE MISERABLE LITTLE FARGO RATS. SO I TOOK ONE MORE LAP AND GOT UP TO LEAVE. AS I CAME DOWN THE FENCE, THIS GUY, ABOUT MY AGE WITH A LOLLAPALOOZA SHIRT ON, COMES UP AND SAYS, "YOU CAN'T SWIM NOW. THE POOL'S CLOSED." DUH. I SAY, BRIGHTLY, "I KNOW, THAT'S WHY I'M LEAVING!" AND

HEAD OUT. HE SAYS, "OH, I WOULDN'T LEAVE NOW. THE COPS JUST GOT HERE." WHAT A PRICK. BUT, WHAT DO YA KNOW? THE COPS WERE THERE! I STARTED RUNNING. THE PUNK HOUSE WASN'T FAR. BUT SEVERAL COP CARS SPED THROUGH THE PARK AND CORNERED ME BY THE MONUMENT TO FARGO'S FOUNDERS. THIS LED TO AN ENORMOUS HASSLE. I.D.? WHAT? IN MY SWIMMING TRUNKS? SHEESH. APPARENTLY, THE LOLLAPALOOZA GUY, WHO IS NOW STANDING TO THE SIDE WEARING A SORT-OF "NANNY NANNY BOO-BOO, YOU GOT CAUGHT!" CHILDISH GRIN, IS SOMEHOW EMPLOYED AT THE POOL AND THE COP SAYS, IF THE KID WANTS TO PRESS CHARGES, I'LL GO TO JAIL! I QUICKLY CALCULATE THAT THIS IS SATURDAY AND I PROBABLY WOULDN'T BE ABLE TO GET OUT OF JAIL 'TIL MONDAY MORNING. 5 DAYS FROM THE WEDDING, AND I'D STILL HAVE TO GET BACK TO MY BIKE IN STAPLES... NO, JAIL WAS CLEARLY UNACCEPTABLE HERE OFFICER, DID I MENTION I HAD TO GET TO A WEDDING?

I GUESS LOLLAPALOOZA HAD RAISED THE KID'S CONSCIOUSNESS ENOUGH FOR HIM TO LET ME GO. BUT THEN THE COP WANTS TO DRIVE TO THE PUNK HOUSE AND SEE MY I.D. BEFORE I CAN GO! STILL DRIPPING WET, I GET IN THE COP CAR AND FIRST, WE DRIVE TO THE FAKE ADDRESS I HAD ORIGINALLY GIVEN HIM. I GRIN, "WHOOPS! WRONG ADDRESS," AND SHRUG. THE COP IS TOTALLY PISSED. "YOU THINK WE FUCK AROUND IN FARGO!?" YOU SHOULD NEVER BRING THE COPS TO YOUR FRIENDS' HOUSE BUT I HAD NO CHOICE BUT TO CONVINCE HIM I'D REMEMBERED IT WRONG AND GET HIM TO DRIVE TO THE PUNK HOUSE. HE SAW MY I.D. AND FINALLY SPLIT, AND THEN I VERY CAREFULLY WALKED OUTTA TOWN AND STARTED HITCHING ACROSS THE BORDER IN MINNESOTA...

THE HITCH BACK TO STAPLES WASN'T AS EASY — 4 RIDES, 4 HOURS — BUT I AT LEAST I KNEW I'D BE ON THAT LONG RIDE WEST THAT NIGHT. IN STAPLES, I WALKED CONFIDENTLY INTO THE CREW SHACK AND SAID TO A WORKER, "SAY, WHEN'S THAT OLD PORTLAND HOTSHOT GONNA STOP HERE TONIGHT?" HE SAYS, "WELL... THOSE TRAINS DON'T STOP HERE ANYMORE... THEY MOVED MOST OF THE WORK UP TO DILWORTH,

MN A COUPLE MONTHS AGO..." I COULDN'T BELIEVE IT. THE PUNCHLINE? DILWORTH WAS THE TINY TOWN 2 MILES OUTSIDE OF FARGO WHERE I'D STARTED HITCHING THAT DAY! HA HA HA HA!

I HAD NO CHOICE TO TAKE MY BIKE RIGHT BACK OUT TO HIGHWAY 10 AND START BACK TOWARDS DILWORTH. THERE WERE 2 HOURS LEFT OF DAYLIGHT TO MAKE A ONE AND A HALF HOUR DRIVE. IF IT GOT DARK, I'D PROBABLY LOSE A WHOLE DAY, CAUSE IT'D BE HARD TO HITCH AT NIGHT ON THAT DARK EMPTY ROAD. IT TOOK AWHILE TO GET A RIDE. A BIKE ISN'T SO HARD TO TAKE ON TRAINS, CUZ EVEN IF YOU CATCH ONE ON THE RUN, ITS STILL JUST SOMETHING ELSE TO PUT ON THE TRAIN, BUT IT

KIND OF AN AWKWARD THING TO GET A TOTAL STRANGER TO MAKE ROOM FOR
THEIR CAR. I HIDE THE BIKE, AND FINALLY GET A RIDE IN A PICK-UP TRUCK
WAY THERE, WHERE I GET DITCHED BY THIS DESERTED CONOCO STATION. I'M
ERE FOR AWHILE BEFORE I NOTICE ONE OF THOSE "25¢ A MINUTE, ANYWHERE
= THE U.S." PHONES OUT FRONT. I FIND, IN MY POCKET, ONE QUARTER, I DECIDE TO
LL MY FRIEND, LEFTY, IN BERKELEY FOR INSPIRATION. HE ANSWERS. I SAY LOOK,
ONLY HAVE EXACTLY ONE MINUTE, AND I JUST WANTED TO SAY HI. HE SAYS,
HERE ARE YOU?" MINNESOTA. I HAVEN'T TALKED TO HIM IN 2 MONTHS, BUT
DOESN'T SEEM SURPRISED TO HEAR FROM ME, AND, INSTEAD GETS RIGHT TO THE
INT. "THE WEDDING IS NEXT WEEKEND. YOU HAVE TO WEAR A SUIT, OK?"

A SUIT? "YEAH." I WATCH AS THE SUN STARTS TO SET ON THE ENDLESS EXPANSE
= PRARIE. "I'LL TRY AND COME UP WITH ONE..." THEN, MY MINUTE'S UP. BUT I STILL
AVE 6 DAYS TO GET HOME, AND, NOW, TO GET A SUIT.
BELIEVE IT, OR NOT, I FINALLY GET A RIDE TO DILWORTH FROM A GUY WHO HAS
ME OF THOSE BIKE RACKS ON TOP OF HIS CAR. WHEN I GET TO THE YARD, MY TRAIN,
HE ONLY ONE OF THE DAY, IS THERE AND LEAVING! SOMEHOW, I CATCH IT ON THE
RUN, THROWING MY BIKE INTO THE OPEN TOP OF THE CONTAINER CAR AND THEN CLIMBING
UP WITH MY WATERBOTTLE IN MY TEETH. I DON'T KNOW. I STILL THINK THIS
IS BETTER THAN GREYHOUND. I'M SO HAPPY AS WE RACE ONCE AND FOR ALL AWAY
FROM THESE TINY LITTLE TOWNS, WE PASS A CLOCK IN FARGO THAT SAYS "9:30 PM".
I WOULDN'T SEE ANOTHER CLOCK FOR 48 HOURS...
HE NIGHT WAS FREEZING, AND WHEN DAY CAME, IT ALTERNATED BETWEEN BRUTAL
AT AND BEATING RAIN. I STILL HAD ABOUT 30 HOURS TO GO, SO WHEN WE STOPPED
A LIGHT IN MONTANA, I DECIDED TO LEAVE OLE CHERRY RED BACK IN THE CONTAINER
O RUN AHEAD TO RIDE INDOORS IN THE UNMANNED, REAR ENGINE AT THE FRONT
THE TRAIN. THE ENGINEERS ONLY RIDE THE FRONT ONE AND DON'T CARE IF YOU RIDE
E OTHER ONES, ESPECIALLY IN BAD WEATHER. I MOSTLY SLEPT, BUT STILL, I GUESS
MEONE SAW ME, 'CAUSE WHEN WE STOPPED IN HAVRE, MT TO FUEL UP THE ENGINES,
CREWMAN GOT ON MY LOCOMOTIVE AND SAID, "SO YOU'RE THE ONE THE GESTAPO'S
OKING FOR! THEY GOT RAILROAD POLICE AND A CITY COP OUT HERE LOOKING FOR
ME BLONDE DUDE GETTING OFF THE TRAIN! YOU BETTER STAY DOWN 'TIL WE GET
T OF HERE, AND... I DIDN'T SEE YA, RIGHT!" RAILROAD WORKERS ARE COOL LIKE THAT.
LL, I COULDN'T RESIST A LOOK OUT THE WINDOW AND ALMOST RAN OFF THE
AIN WHEN I SAW THE ENGINES WERE UNHOOKED FROM THE TRAIN TO FUEL AND A
ILDER ENGINE WAS ADDING AND REMOVING CARS FROM THE TRAIN WE WERE
ULING — THE TRAIN WITH MY BIKE ON IT! I HAD NO WAY OF KNOWING IF MY
IKE WAS GOING TO PORTLAND, TOO, AND COULDN'T CHECK CUZ THE COPS WERE OUT
HERE! IT'D BE ANOTHER FULL 24 HOURS 'TIL I FOUND OUT...

LUCKILY, ME AND MY BIKE MADE IT TO PORTLAND, WHERE I CRASHED AT A FRIEND'S
SE AND THEN CAUGHT OUT SOUTH TO ROSEVILLE, CA THE NEXT AFTERNOON. WHEN I
ED INTO ROSEVILLE THE BIGGEST YARD ON THE WEST COAST, NEAR SACRAMENTO, A FULL
HOURS LATER, I HAD BEEN ON TRAINS 75 OUT OF 100 HOURS! I WAS TIRED. I PASSED
BEHIND A CREW SHACK. IN THE MORNING, A WORKER DIRECTED ME TOWARDS
CK #53 WHERE MY VERY LAST TRAIN, THE TRAIN TO OAKLAND AWAITED. I PASSED
T ON THAT, TOO. THE TRAIN LEFT 24 HOURS BEFORE THE WEDDING AND I SMILED
MY HALF SLEEP. AH... HOME. WHERE WOULD I GO FIRST? WOULD I GO DRINK
TH IVY AT THE LANDFILL? GO GET COFFEE WITH LEFTY? OR JUST SLEEP...
THE TRAIN STARTED TO SLOW AND I FIGURED WE WERE CROSSING THE BRIDGE
ER THE SACRAMENTO RIVER IN DOWNTOWN SACRAMENTO WHERE ALL THE TRAINS
SLOW. I LOVE THAT BRIDGE CUZ ONE TIME I WAS READING THIS JACK LONDON
OK AT THE BRIDGE AND WAITING TO CATCH A SLOW ONE TO OAKLAND, WHEN, IN THE
OK, JACK SAYS HE CAUGHT HIS FIRST TRAIN EVER AT... THE BRIDGE OVER THE SACTO RIVER!
WAS LIKE BEING IN THE BOOK! BUT WHEN I LOOKED OUT OF MY SLEEPING BAG, I
W NO BRIDGE. INSTEAD, I KNEW I WAS ON THE WRONG TRAIN, CUZ WE PASSED
U UNRECOGNIZABLE TOWN, AND I'D GONE THIS ROUTE A BUNCH OF TIMES WE SLOWED NEARLY
A STOP AND I SCRAMBLED TO THROW MY BIKE AND BAGS OFF. WHEN I FINALLY
ODE INTO TOWN, I SAW THE SIGN ON THE AMTRAK STATION — "LODI, CA"!
ALMOST DIED LAUGHING! NOW I WAS "STUCK IN LODI"! "LODI, CA"! THIS TIME, I
A'S IN A CCR SONG! I HAD NO CHOICE BUT TO RIDE OUT TO I-5 AND
T OUT THE OLE THUMB ONE MORE TIME. I HAD ONE FULL DAY LEFT...

-5, AN IMPROBABLE LOOKING, DOOMED SPAN OF BLACKTOP IN THE MIDDLE OF
IFORNIA'S DRY GRAPE COUNTRY STRETCHES ON AND ON TO THE HORIZON, LIKE A
RAGE, CARRYING MODERN, AIR CONDITIONED TRAFFIC AT 85 MPH PAST DUSTY,
NCIENT GRAPE ORCHARDS WHERE LITTLE HAS CHANGED FOR DECADES. THERE ARE
EW TOWNS AND NO ONE STOPS. IT IS HOPELESS, BUT SOMEHOW FUNNY: I MAKE
ECORD TIME ACROSS THE COUNTRY ONLY TO GET STUMPED LIKE A GRAPE BY THE
ENTRAL VALLEY SUN, A MERE 120 MILES FROM HOME, LOVE, HOPE, ETC. THAT IS
E ESSENCE OF I-5. IT IS INDESCRIBABLY MISERABLE AS THE HEAT RISES TOWARDS
AND I AM NOT SURPRISED WHEN A COUNTY SHERIFF PULLS UP...
I AM SURPRISED, THOUGH, WHEN HE OFFERS ME A RIDE! HE SAYS, "I CAN TAKE YOU
P THE ROAD 15 MILES." AND I THINK, THIS IS COP HUMOR, LIKE THE CONCENTRATION
MP IS 15 MILES UP THE ROAD, OR SOME THING... BUT HE PATS ME DOWN FOR
EAPONS AND THE NEXT THING YOU KNOW, I'M IN THE FRONT SEAT WITH THE COP.
E DRIVE MOSTLY IN SILENCE, EXCEPT WHEN THE COP SAYS, "NOTHING PERSONAL, BUT
'M GONNA ROLL DOWN THE WINDOWS. YOU SURE SMELL BAD..."
THE NEXT SPOT WAS SOMEHOW WORSE. I MADE A BIG SIGN THAT SAID, "PLEASE?!?"
D STILL SWEATED IT OUT FOR 4 HOURS 'TIL I GOT A RIDE TO SACTO. IT TURNED
T TO BE THE LAST RIDE OF THE TRIP...
EN SACTO, I STOPPED AT THE PUNK RECORD STORE AND RAN INTO MY FRIEND, ERIN,
O WAS DRIVING TO THE SAME WEDDING! SHE GAVE ME AND OLE CHERRY RED A
DE. BUT, FIRST, THAT NIGHT WE STOPPED TO DRINK BEER WITH THE BENICIA PUNKS.
PUNKS OF BENICIA SAID I COULDN'T GO TO A WEDDING WITHOUT A SUIT, AND THEY
G OUT ENOUGH STUFF FROM THEIR CLOSETS TO MAKE A NICE TUX. WE DROVE
THE WEDDING AND MADE IT AN HOUR BEFORE IT STARTED! I WAS CLEAN, I
D A SUIT... IT WAS ALMOST THE PERFECT ENDING, LIKE I'D PLANNED, I
IT WASN'T OVER YET. I GOT ERIN TO DROP ME OFF A BLOCK AWAY SO I COULD
DE UP ON MY BIKE AT THE LAST MINUTE... JUST LIKE IN A MOVIE...

KINGS OF THE GRAFFITI ROAD?

I FINALLY MET THE COLLOSSUS. HE SIGNED
MY NOTEBOOK! ME AND TWIST AND MARGARET
STOOD AROUND HIM IN AWE AT AN S.F. PARTY...

TRUST JESUS

BUT WHO'S "TRUST JESUS"? I PICTURE A PRETTY
CLEAN GUY WITH A BACKPACK, WALKING BACK AND
FURTH FROM ST. LOUIS TO NASHVILLE TO IOWA, ETC.

OCTOBER IN
THE RAILROAD
EARTH

BILL SAYS, "DIRTY GUY LIVING OUT OF AN OLD
70'S CAR..." WHO KNOWS?

97

KREAMY 'LECTRIC SANTA
ONE MIAMI BAND'S STRUGGLE WITH VOODOO, KRISHNAS, AND UNEMPLOYMENT!

😊 SATISFECHO ☐   ☹ NO SATISFECHO ☐

From left to right Priya,
Bo, Intimadator, Jan 9
lower center Andy (hurricane)
powell

by IGGY SCAM

I THINK I GOT TO DO THIS INTERVIEW WITH KREAMY 'LECTRIC SANTA 'CUZ I'M PROBABLY THE ONLY PERSON THEY KNOW WHO HASN'T BEEN IN THE BAND. AND THE ONLY REASON FOR THAT, PROBABLY, IS BECAUSE I WAS AWAY FROM MIAMI FOR 1½ YEARS. IN THAT TIME, A LOT HAS CHANGED AND A LOT HAS STAYED THE SAME FOR K.L.S. LIKE THEY'VE GONE THROUGH A LOT OF BAND MEMBERS, BAD JOBS, AND APARTMENTS, BUT THEY STILL MANAGE TO PLAY GREAT SHOWS AND THEY'RE STILL PLAYING AT CHURCHILL'S, THIS DIVE BAR IN LITTLE HAITI. I'VE SEEN SOME OF THE GREATEST SHOWS AT CHURCHILL'S LIKE THE 1st TIME I SAW K.L.S. THEY HAD LIKE 5 PEOPLE SINGING, A VIOLIN PLAYER, AND A RAPPER! IT WAS CRAZY. THE BAR ERUPTED IN A DRUNKEN TRASH FIGHT DURING THE LAST BAND'S SET. I DON'T THINK ANYONE BOTHERED TO CHARGE AT THE DOOR. THAT'S USUALLY HOW THE BEST SHOWS ARE AT CHURCHILL'S, OR THE BEST K.L.S. SHOWS. THE OTHER NIGHT, I SAW K.L.S. FOR THE 1st TIME IN 20 MONTHS AND THEY WERE BETTER THAN EVER. WHAT WAS FUNNY, WAS IT WAS PART OF THIS STUPID 2-DAY "WAKE UP MIAMI" FESTIVAL WHERE ALL THE SHITTY PRO-ROCK AND "ALTERNATIVE" POSERS WERE TRYING TO "SHOWCASE THEIR TALENT", OR SOME SUCH SHIT, SO A LOT OF PEOPLE WERE AT CHURCHILL'S WHO'D NORMALLY ONLY BE AT "SERIOUS" CLUBS. DURING K.C.S.'S SET MORE AND MORE PEOPLE CAME UP TO SING ALONG, AND DANCE, AND GUZZLE BEER, AND STAND ON THEIR HEADS ON STAGE, WHILE SOMEONE THREW OUT THIS ENTIRE BOX OF CHEAP CIGARS, SO THERE WAS SMOKE AND CIGARS EVERYWHERE! THE CROWD DIDN'T REALLY KNOW WHAT TO DO, EXCEPT THE HALF THAT CROWDED THE STAGE...

WELL, IT'S HARD TO FIND OUT WHAT A BAND SOUNDS LIKE FROM AN INTERVIEW. I'D SAY, THESE DAYS, KREAMY 'LECTRIC SANTA IS SOMEWHERE BETWEEN RICHARD HELL AND BIKINI KILL WITH GUY AND GIRL SINGING. BUT WHAT I WANTED TO GET ACROSS HERE IS THAT WHILE MOST MIAMI BANDS HAVE A MANAGER AND ARE WILLING TO DO ANYTHING TO "MAKE IT" K.L.S. STILL IS NOT HIP, ARTY, SMUG, OR "INDIE ROCK". THEY'RE REAL DOWN TO EARTH. SO, I ASKED SIR ROBERT, PRIYA, ANDY, AND TIM A COUPLE QUESTIONS EACH AT THEIR APARTMENT IN COCONUT GROVE. SINGER, JAN, ISN'T INTERVIEWED HERE CUZ SHE WASN'T AROUND...

SIR ROBERT IS K.L.S.' SINGER/GUITARIST. HIM AND PRIYA STARTED K.L.S. 4½ YEARS AGO. USUALLY HE'S ALL STRUNG OUT ON CUBAN COFFEE, BUT HERE, HE WAS TIRED OUT AFTER 12-HOURS AT WORK. Q: HOW MANY BASS PLAYERS HAVE YOU HAD? A: TOO MANY. PRETTY MUCH EVERYONE WERE HANGIN' OUT WITH AT THE TIME ENDS UP IN THE BAND. OUR OLD BASSIST, TIMMY, LIVED ON OUR COUCH FIRST. Q: WHAT HAPPENED TO THE RAPPER? A: HE HAS A KID, HE WORKS IN A HOTEL, BUT HE'S STILL THE KING OF RAP. WHAT'S THE WEIRDEST SHOW YOU'VE EVER PLAYED? I WAS PLAYING ONE NIGHT AT CHURCHILL'S AND THESE HAITIAN GUYS REALLY LIKED US, SO THEY ASKED ME TO COME JAM WITH THEM THE NEXT WEEKEND, At THIS HALL THEY RENTED IN LITTLE HAITI. SO I WENT THERE TO CHECK 'EM OUT. IT WAS REALLY STRANGE CUZ THEY WERE ALL WEARING WHITE SUITS AND PUTTING CHALK ON THE FLOOR LIKE SOME VOODOO CEREMONY! THEY READ HAITIAN POETRY FOR AWHILE AND THEN

ASKED ME UP ON STAGE. I PLAYED THIS RIDICULOUSLY TUNED, BROKEN, ACOUSTIC GUITAR THAT I CALL THE "LES PALSEY" AND I THINK IT REALLY ANNOYED THEM, THEY MADE ME STOP. BUT LATER ON, IT WAS COOL, I GOT TO JAM WITH THESE PERCUSSIONIST GUYS THERE AND THAT WAS FUN. Q: WHAT'S CHANGED SINCE YOU GOT STARTED PLAYING IN BANDS? WELL, PUNK ROCK IS MORE ACCESSIBLE. JOCKS COME TO OUR SHOWS, NOW — PEOPLE WHO WERE NEVER A PART OF IT BEFORE. ITS ABOUT TIME FOR SHIT TO MOVE ON. PUNK ROCK'S ALWAYS BEEN SOMETHING TO EXPAND UPON, BUT NOW MORE BANDS JUST WANT TO BE ACCEPTED OR NOTICED. EVERYONE'S SAFE!

PRIYA IS THE SINGER AND VIOLINIST OF K.L.S. I ASKED HER TO TELL ME A BAD LANDLORD STORY — HERE IT IS: "WE USED TO GET NASTY LETTERS FROM THE OWNERS OF THIS ONE APARTMENT WE LIVED IN, ON THE OTHER SIDE OF THE GROVE. IT WAS REALLY SMALL AND ONE BEDROOM, AND REALLY HOT, LIKE JUST A HOT LITTLE BOX WITH NO AIR CONDITIONING. WE HAD THIS REALLY HIGH LOFT WITH OUR BED ON TOP, AND WE'D HAVE BAND PRACTICE — THIS WAS WHEN MARCEL PLAYED DRUMS — AND WE'D PUT MARCEL'S DRUMS UP ON THE BED SO THAT HE WAS PLAYING RIGHT UP AGAINST THE CEILING, AND WE'D PLAY UNDER HIM ON THE FLOOR. IT WAS REAL FUN, BUT WE HAD TO MOVE OUT AFTER A COUPLE MONTHS. THE COPS CAME SOMETIMES, AND WE GOT THIS LETTER FROM THE LANDLORD ABOUT HOW THE NEIGHBORS HAD CALLED HER AND HELD THE PHONE UP TO OUR WALL AND ALL THE LANDLORD COULD HEAR WAS THIS "LOUD, ABRASIVE NOISE..." AND THEN THERE WAS THAT TIME THAT DOTTIE (PSYCHO OLD LAND LADY) CHASED YOU OUT OF THE POOL AND INTO OUR APARTMENT AND YOU TRIED TO SHUT THE DOOR ON HER, BUT SHE BARGED RIGHT IN... Q: OH, AND YOU HAD ALL THE DRUGS ON THE TABLE... A: YEAH... THAT WAS PRETTY BAD.

ANDY — IS THE NEW BASSIST, AND LOCALLY LEGENDARY FOR NOT BEING ABLE TO GET A JOB. NOW, NOT ONLY IS HE IN KLS BUT HE GOT A JOB AT A YOGURT PLACE IN THE GROVE. Q: ANDY, HOW THE HELL DID YOU GET A JOB? A: WELL, YOU REMEMBER HOW THEY STOPPED LETTING US PLAY GUITARS IN THE STREETS IN COCONUT GROVE? THEN I HAD NOTHING TO DO AND NO MONEY-MAKING MUSIC, SO I HAD TO GET A JOB. MY BOSS HIRED ME CUZ HE'S IN A BAND, TOO. HE LETS ME MAKE MY SCHEDULE AROUND THE BAND. HOW IS IT? OK. LET ME TELL YOU ABOUT THE KRISHNAS. THE BOSS USUALLY HAS ME WORKING DURING ALL THE BIG FESTIVALS, LIKE THE COCONUT GROVE ARTS FESTIVAL AND THE KING MANGO STRUT. DURING KING MANGO, I WAS OUT GETTING THE TRASH WHEN I SAW ALL THE KRISHNAS FROM THE TEMPLE DANCING, LIKE "BOING!"-ING DOWN THE STREET, SO I SAID "COME ON IN!" AND THEY RAN IN THE YOGURT SHOP! THEY WERE DANCING WITH THEIR TAMBOURINES IN THIS TINY SHOP AND THE YUPPIES INSIDE WERE TERRIFIED! FINALLY, I STARTED DANCING WITH THEM. IT SEEMED LIKE THE THING TO DO. I WAS MANTRA-ING OUT. Q: WAS IT YOUR LIFELONG DREAM TO JOIN KLS? A: ITS A BIG SURPRISE, BUT I ALWAYS LOVED 'EM. LAST TIME I SAW 'EM BEFORE I JOINED, JAN PUNCHED THIS GUY WHO WAS BEING A CREEP AND GAVE 'EM A BLACK EYE! THEY WERE ALL TRIPPING AND THEY PLAYED THE "DIFFERENT STROKES" THEME SONG SO FUCKED UP THAT I HAD TO RUN OUT OF THE CLUB. NOW I'M IN THE BAND...

TIM IS THE DRUMMER, HE'S BEEN IN BANDS WITH ROBERT SINCE THE PROM SLUTS IN 1986. HE'S ALSO MAKING A MOVIE... Q: TIM, WHAT'S THE MOVIE ABOUT? ITS KINDA HARD TO EXPLAIN — NOT THAT ITS UNUSUALLY CLEVER OR AMAZING — ITS JUST IN THE WORKS. ITS ABOUT OUR FRIEND, DAVE, WHO SOMETIMES DOES PROJECTIONS AND VISUAL STUFF FOR THE BAND. HE'S A CROSS DRESSER. IN THE MOVIE HE'LL BE A DRAG QUEEN NAMED "KUMQUAT" — THAT'S THE MOVIE'S NAME — AND I WAS THINKING I'D GET OUR OLD BASS PLAYER, TIMMY, TO SHAVE HIS HEAD AND EYEBROWS AND PLAY A TOUGH GUY WHO FALLS IN LOVE WITH KUMQUAT. KUMQUAT'S NOT DOWN WITH THAT. THERE'LL BE GUN BATTLES AND SHIT. ITS BASICALLY TWISTED TV CRIME DRAMA... Q: HOW MANY TIMES HAVE YOU PLAYED AT CHURCHILL'S? A: I'VE PLAYED THERE OVER 100 TIMES, SINCE THEY STARTED DOING SHOWS IN 1986. I'VE PLAYED WITH MORBID OPERA, THE PROM SLUTS, KLS. I JUST LIKE PLAYING MUSIC. I NEVER THOUGHT WE'D BE ON TOUR BUSSES, SCREWING GROUPIES, BEING ROCKSTARS, SO I'D PLAY CHURCHILL'S EVERY NIGHT OF THE WEEK. PLUS, ALL THE OTHER CLUBS COME AND GO BUT CHURCHILL'S IS ALWAYS THERE. LIKE, ROACHES AND MAGGOTS... ITS ALWAYS THERE...

K.L.S. IS ALWAYS THERE, TOO, AND FINALLY HAVE RECORDINGS COMING OUT. WRITE KREAMY 'LECTRIC SANTA FOR INFO. P.O. BOX 1224, MIAMI, FL 33133

STORIES ABOUT... 50 MILLION!!!
AS TOLD TO IGGY SCAM

    50 MILLION has been my favorite band since I moved back to San Francisco a couple years ago, not just because they're so good, but because they're always changing and trying new stuff, and every show's completely different. 50 Million is the two brothers, Wade and ShellHead and anyone else they can get to play with them, which, over the years has been Noah and Scottzie from THE FAGGZ, Jen from STARCLEANERS, Aesop and Matty from HICKEY, and even yours truly on drums last summer. Their first couple records, not reviewed in many punk mags like this one, were just Wade and Shell on guitar, singing some of the sweetest, most sincere pop songs that you've ever heard into their 4-track. Then, Wade moved to drums, with Noah on bass and they put out a couple loud, tough punk records. But, I've played with them with 2 guitars and NO bass, and booked 'em for shows where they just showed up with a bunch of guitars and made a lot of noise... I remember, to raise cash before they went on tour a couple years ago, they announced that they'd play 5 shows in a week and not repeat a single song...

    Last month, things seemed to be looking up for the 50 Million. They were back playing and writing new songs as a 2-piece after Noah quit and moved to New York City. They were getting ready to release a new double record they'd been working on, tentatively titled THE SONG REMAINS INSANE. And, their landlord had agreed to give them several months to pay back the rent they owed him on the famed 50 Million storefront on Valencia. I went and saw them play a show where they played in the storefront window and the audience drank beer and watched out on the sidewalk by the #26 stop, occasionally writing requests on scraps of trash and holding them up to the window. Later, Shell excitedly told me about their plans to tour as a 2-piece and do more shows in the storefront.

Wade told me how they'd been playing an endless loop of 50 Million records, CD's, and practice tapes OUT the window onto the street, 24 hours a day, so people walking by heard 50 Million muzak. Sure enough, there was a sign in the window that said, "You are listening to 50 Million"...

I wanted to interview them, but since then, Wade beat up Shell, they quit playing, the landlord broke off talks, and, it turns out, other, lesser bands already HAVE records called THE SONG REMAINS INSANE... So, instead, I had to ask other people to tell me 50 Million stories. Everyone in town's got a 50 Million story. I remember when they played at The Build and made the money they spent to rent the space back by selling Wade's prescription drugs from the stage. I remember when my old band, MIAMI, played with them and on the way to the show, we drove by 50 Million who were walking down the street with sandwich boards on, announcing the show. I remember stealing eyeliner with Shell when we played at the tranny bar and had to play in drag... Here's more 50 Million stories! compiled by Iggy Scam

Matty Luv (from Yogurt/Hickey/Miami who recorded 50 Million's "Bust The Action" LP...): " Well, normally when I record a band, I do it pretty cheap, so its customary for them to get me drunk and give me drugs and stuff, but I remember 50 Million were so broke that they were bumming smokes off ME and trying to get beer from me the whole time... A lot of 50 Million stories end in jail or the hospital. I can still remember one night at the Nightbreak. John and Wade got in a fight with a 2 by 4 with a nail in it. I think they wanted to kill Scottzie, too. I just remember that feeling, that SOMEBODY was going to die, either from that scene, that house, maybe even OUR house... I remember when I first saw them when Hickey played with them at the Chameleon... Shell had just got in from Texas that day. We had heard "Carpet Technician" on KUSF a lot, so we expected this small, poppy, wimpy thing, but somehow they practiced a bunch of songs with Noah and Scottzie from The Faggz on bass and drums. Shell came out in a Superman suit and we were all like, "Who is THIS guy?"

Ivy: (singer of Miami):"I remember when Wade drank ammonia at the Tip-Top. There was this hole in the ceiling directly above the stage and, if the band was too loud, the woman who lived upstairs would pour water on the band. That night she poured water on the opening band. But then 50 Million played. I don't even think they had drums that night. It was just Wade and Noah and Shell, all FUCKED UP, making all kinds of feedback and jumping around. Well, the lady upstairs started pouring AMMONIA through the hole! Wade caught it in a cup and drank it, and started yelling, "Go ahead and pour more! We'll drink it!"

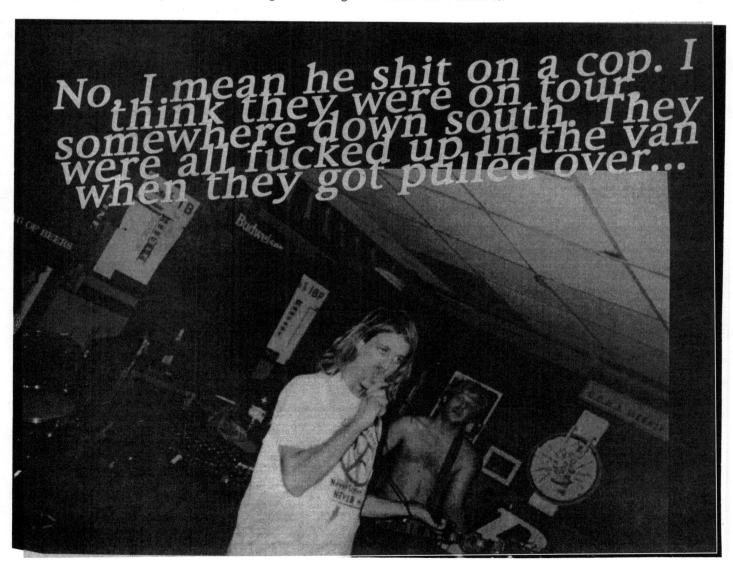

No, I mean he shit on a cop. I think they were on tour somewhere down south. They were all fucked up in the van when they got pulled over...

Iggy: "Oh yeah, when they went to play there again, Wade said he was going to put on the flyer, 'Come watch us drink ammonia!'"

Pablo Roman (editor Letters From Mike fanzine): "One time, I was at this party with Wade and we found this can of gold spray paint. He read the can to make sure it had stuff in it that could fuck you up, and said he wanted to huff it, but he couldn't find anything to put it in. Then, some guy who overheard us talking about it, pointed to this clown nose on the ground. Without a word, Wade picked up the rubber clown nose, sprayed the paint inside it, and put it on his face. I remember seeing him later that night with a big, gold streak running down his face..."

Buddha (guitarist Jack Palance Band. ex-Chickenhead, Stun Guns, Los Canadians, Cavity, etc..): "When 50 Million came to Miami, I'd never heard them before, but I knew who they were on sight. "Oh, that must be the band from SF," I thought. They were crazy looking weirdos, and stood out from the normal looking Miami punks. They played an outdoor show with my band the Street Drinkers. After the show, they stayed at my house. Everything was pretty blurry. There was a lot of beer and pills. Shell, at one point, kept me from throwing chairs at people. There was some emotional scene where Monica called one of the 50 Million guys an asshole and he started crying. In the morning, ten hits of acid and some weed were missing from my house, and people were blaming 50 Million for destroying the scene. Now I listen to 50 Million at least once a week...

Jason Bean (singer of Human Beans): "As much as they've pissed me off, 50 Million's always been there for me, even when its just been a CD when I was sad. They've beaten me up, gotten me high, and written songs that creepily echoed what was going on in my own head... I heard one time Wade shit on a cop..."

Iggy: "Wait, you mean when he got caught putting the "Off Da Pigs" sticker on that cop's back in front of Mission Station, and the cops beat him up?"

Jason: "No, I mean he shit on a cop. I think they were on tour, somewhere down south. They were all fucked up in the van when they got pulled over The cops were tripping on Wade. I don't know if they found his pot, or what. They wanted to search him, but Wade was saying, "Listen, I don't think you want to do that right now...""

But they wouldn't listen. He was trying to tell them that he had diarrhea and he'd shit his pants, and the ass of his pants was ripped out. Well... They searched him... Wade said he was afraid, after that, that they were going to KILL him. They had their guns out and shit. They didn't know WHAT to make of these guys. They were going to take him in, but finally Wade said, "Look, do you REALLY want ME in the back of your car right now?" The cops thought it over, and finally told Noah, "You take care of this guy, OK?!?" and went away.

Matty: I also have one sort-of nice 50 Million memory. On one Hickey tour, we stayed with them when they'd moved back to Austin. They had this real beat-up house in South Austin, just this real desperate, white trash neighborhood. We stayed there on Christmas. I remember they had just quit drinking, so they were smoking their weight in pot. Me and Caroline drank a bottle of Boone's Farm in a drainage ditch and then we all made Christmas Ramen..."

Iggy: "What's your favorite 50 Million song?"

Matty: "My 3 favorites are 'Evergreen', 'Sunday To Monday', and 'Blackout', because they just really well-written songs, flawless lyrically and melodically. Oh yeah, there's 'Amy Jahn', too, which is probably the best adolescent sex song ever written...

Jason: "My favorite is 'We'll Run Away'. I can't hear it without getting all choked up, not because its too sad, but because its too real..."

Greg Harvester (editor Rice Harvester fanzine, drummer of Grumpies and Forced Vengeance): "When I first met 50 Million, I could hear Shell's voice from a block away (and he was talking at normal volume). He was telling this girl that she had beautiful eyes. When they played, Shell tackled me in mid-song and rolled around on the floor with me in a faux wrestling match. Everyone else thought it was real, though, and wanted to kick his ass. Later, the boyfriend of the girl with the beautiful eyes wanted to kill Shell, too. Shell tried to calm him down, while Wade jumped around telling him, "I don't want to kill you, but I should!" I didn't know until later that Wade had a machete in his pants the whole time. I left with them, unharmed, in their van as Wade calmly said, "I'm glad we didn't have to blow his head off with the shotgun." I turned around and the shotgun was right behind me...

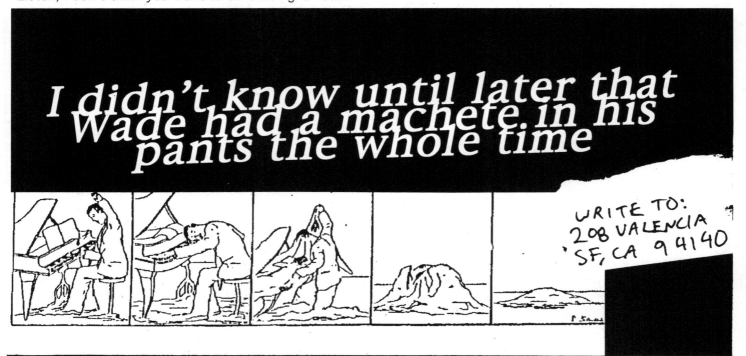

I didn't know until later that Wade had a machete in his pants the whole time

WRITE TO:
208 VALENCIA
SF, CA 94140

ITS NOT THE OLD MAN AND THE SEA. ITS...
"THE YOUNG MAN AND THE FOUL, POLLUTED INNER CITY WATERWAY"
OR..."THE SEARCH FOR THE URBAN FISHERMEN."

Take the 22 Fillmore bus in San Francisco, south, away from downtown to the end of the line. Get off on a street of dead-end railroad tracks, where shopping carts drag in the fog. go down the hill at 20th, past the empty lot on your right, past the old port complex on your left, past the people living in their cars. When you get to the impound lot, you can see the Bay. A walkway takes you past some abandoned warehouses, then abruptly stops at a fence and a NO TRESPASSING sign.

There is a hole in the fence.

On the other side is a rotten dock, where, on many nights you can find a mysteriious group of men. They're not loading smuggled drugs or dumping bodies; they're fishing.

The EPA says this rotten dock is one of the most polluted parts of the entire San Francisco Bay. The fishermen say its a great place to catch halibut.

It never fails: the more filth and polluted a body of water in a city is, and the harder it is to access, the more guys you'll see fishing in it. There can be a 15-foot high fence, topped with razor wire, and just under the sign that says DANGER: HAZARDOUS MATERIAL, you'll see the torn apart metal, all pushed out, where they sneak in. And, it isn't exactly scientific, but it seems like I'm seeing these urban fishermen more and more, hearing tales about them as I travel across the country. Men with poles camped out on a railroad bridge over the Sacramento River. Dark figures with nets in a creek behind a Florida strip mall. The guys that hang out at the lake in Cleveland, where warm water from an electrical plant guarantees good fishing, even in thedead of winter... Once, a trucker who picked me up when I was hitchhiking on I-75 spent the whole drive excitedly pointing out the roadside ditches where he'd often pull over his rig and fish.

Wherever a ripple breaks the placid, smooth surface of the modern world, the urban fishermen are there to stick a hook in.

Last year, I went out on the road, looking for them.

Part One: Miami, Florida

According to the WPA Guide To Florida, early settlers to Biscayne Bay described waters "of every delicate shade of blue and green, tinged with every color of the spectrum... a sort-of liquid light, rather than water, so limpid and brilliant is it." By all accounts, the fish were practically jumping into the boat.

Today in Miami, it is still possible to live that early, pioneer life. Orange, mango, and avocado trees, their branches heavy with fruit, line many residential streets, and anyone with a machete can harvest the coconuts that grow wild, even on Flagler Sreet in the heart of downtown. Roosters run free in the streets around Little Havana and Little Haiti and in the empty lots around the River. And, of course, despite the official health warnings, posted in 3 languages, and the occasional raw sewage leak into the Bay, there's still plenty of fish.

Most of the Miami River isn't publicly accessible -- it runs through boat yards and the back yards of residences -- but I still found a group of Latin guys behind the old Shriner's temple. They had no fishing poles, but they'd rigged up some pretty inspired Do-It-Yourself gear. They'd tied their lines through holes they had punched through empty tall cans of malt liquour, then wrapped the slack line around the cans. Then, they unravelled their lines, held their cans with two hands, and waited.

I walked up and said, "Coges algo?" One guy, rapidly rolling up his line said in a thick Spanish accent, "Yeah! I got one now!" and, sure enough, he pulled up a small, black and white spotted fish, and laid it on the concrete sea wal. All five of us gathered around it for a couple of excited moments, as a ripple of joy spread among us, strangers. The guy who caught it declared, "Ees for fry pan!" and dropped it in the bucket.

But even more sought after in Miami than the free, spotted fish dinner are "pink gold": Biscayne Bay shrimp. I used to live on an abandoned boat, just off the shore and out of the neon of Coconut Grove. My neighbors were mostly shrimpers who, like me, would row back and forth every day to our various salvaged, patched, and varely floating boats. Shrimiping works\like this: first you drive the boat to where you think the shrimp are going to be, which was often in the warm waters around the Turkey Point Nuclear Reactor, south of Miami. You put the huge net in the water and drive the boat in a circle. Guys called "pickers" sort

the stuff the net brings in: shrimp go into buckets; broken glass and tires go back into the water. Its illegal to sell the shrimp for anything but bait. But, back on the docks, shrimp are like money. In Miami, it is still possible to buy car parts, new shoes, and tickets to basketball games with a bucket of shrimp.

Part 2: Chicago

My friend, Joaquin and I arrived in Chicago and decided to test my theory that the urban fishermen will instinctively find the most polluted waterway in any city. We got out a city map and traced the course of the Chicago River, south, into Lake Calumet, near the Indiana border. Lake Calumet has been used as a garbage dump, and now serves as the southernmost port for ships navigating the St. Lawrence Seaway. On the map, its surrounded by huge, mysterious, blank white spaces: the real\life home of a sewage treatment facility, railyards, a Ford Motor Company assembly plant, and the now mostly unused sites of an entire century's steel production. The blank white space was exciting; it was like the "Ye Dragons Here" of ancient maps. We hit I-94 and headed south.

Despite the best efforts of man, fish still swim in the Chicago River and its tributaries. It has been dredged, widened, and dredged some more. It carried sewage and pollutants. The South Fork of the South Branch of the river is called Bubbly Creek, and not because it resembles a natural, clear, bubbling spring. The slaughterhouses on the creek used to throw carcasses and manure right into it. Decaying matter on the bottom caused bubbles to rise to the surface. Sometimes the river just crusted over, and chickens were seen walking across its surface.

Today, the river's path through a landscape of dead steelmills and abandoned factories and into man-made canals is, in itself, this century's history written into the land, testament to the idea that man would make an entirely better world with machines.

Nearing Lake Calumet, we passes blackened smokestacks and iron pipes belching sick, blue flame, and came to a dead end at the base of the lake. getting out of the car, we saw that the road appeared to crumble directly into a river of thick, black muck. The stench of sewage was overwhelming. On a fence was a sign that said SLUDGE DRYING TROUGH. Looking around at what appeared to be miles of such troughs, I though, here we are: the blank, white space on the map.

And, of course, at the tip of the dead end was a parked car and two black guys, fishing. The two guys Joaquin went over and did the talking. It wasn't much of an exchange. The two guys seemed nervous that we were going to try to steal their secret spot. "Anything you can catch in Lake Michigan, you can catch here," one said, as if that explained everything. Sure, why go all the way to Lake Michigan, when you can just mosey on down to your neighborhood sludge drying trough?

Driving home, we could see why they'd be nervous. The blank, white space on the map might just wind up being Chicago's next hip, up and coming neighborhood. Passing the old Lake Calumet garbage dump, we saw that its been turned into a golf course. Its weird:\you pass the old trash incinerator, and then there's this course, with all these yuppies, driving their golf carts right over a hundred years of trash. And, because of all the nitrogen in he water, its the greenest grass you ever saw.

Part 3: Detroit

The best way to see Detroit in all its glorious decay, is to hop a fence and climb 14 stories up to the roof of the abandoned train station, just west of downtown. From this height, the city appears oddly green as empty lots and wilderness slowly overtake the old metropolis. Trees grow out of the remains of crumbled houses. Seeing how nature has begun to reclaim the Motor city, I could only think of Henry Ford's famous line, "History is bunk."

My friend, Mitchell, and I drove into Detroit on a bitterly cold morning. It was a lonely day in a lonely town. We went over to Riverside Park. I had been there, once, last summer, when the seawall was lined with guys drinking beer and tossing lines. On one side of the park was the oldtimers, listening to radios playing soul tunes, and on the other side there were kids who had pulled up and left their car radios on, blasting bass. But, today the park was cold and empty. Mitchell and I took turns, half-heartedly tossing our lines into the slushy river. I wondered what kind of history you would find at the bottom.

Detroit makes today's obsession with the milennium and the End Of The World seem even more absurd. What are people talking about when they talk about the "End Of The World", anyway? I've begun to realize that they're not talking about the actual physical destruction of the planet, anymore; they're talking about something more like detroit: the end of a certain way of life. The End Of The World means no more CNN, no more air conditioning, no more ATM machines. And what do the scattered survivors who are ALREADY pushing their shopping carts around toxic, devestated cities do while they wait for this End Of The World? Go fishing, of course.

NEXT MORNING

OK, DR. MORSE, I UNDERSTAND ABOUT THE RAPTURE AND WHAT HAPPENS IN HEAVEN......

NOW TELL ME, WHAT HAPPENS TO THOSE LEFT DOWN HERE?

Part 4. Fishing in my Hometown

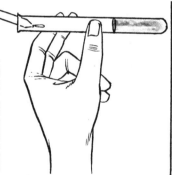

WATER), LIQUID WILL TURN REDDISH-VIOLET.

I first encountered the forerunners of today's urban fishermen while growing up in my hometown in South Florida. There was a canal that ran along the edge of my neighborhood. At places its foamy, brown waters were no more than 2 feet deep, and filled with cans, bottles, and even the occasional shopping cart. Still, whole black families sat out on the canal, fishing all day.

As our shabby, seaside town made a push to become more affluent and suburban, the fishing families were kicked off the main drag, but they kept fishing, a mile down the canal, behind a faded, pink apartment building.

The town was on the way up. A shopping center went up nearby, the university campus was improved, and a brand, new mall even went up at the edge of our town. Still, this weedy, toxic strip flowed along at the edge of our neighborhood, in apparent defiance of this new, sanitized version of our town. Kids were told not to play near it and my mother told me that if I even TOUCHED the canal's waters, I might get polio or cancer. Looking at it today, I think how strange it is that the very definition of the word "Water" has changed in my lifetime. "Water" comes in bottles. But THIS stuff? You can't drink it. You can't touch it. Its not "water". Its "the canal".

These days, when I'm back home, I like to walk through town, following the course of the canal, as much as possible. Past the old graveyard, past the old, hidden tree houses that I think only I know about, past some old, rundown apartments, and under Glades Road. When you get past the campus, the canal finally takes you near enough to see the old IBM compund where my father worked, and where the IBM PC was invented.

Growing up, everyone's dad worked for IBM, and there was always this not-so-subtle subtext to our math and science lessons that we had to study hard to "keep up with the Japanese". This was an irony that I would savor during many underage drinking binges, years later, when many of us IBM kids had dropped out of school, and IBM itself had fallen so far behind APPLE, that it was forced to leave the compund abandoned and mov to North Carolina. And, as for the PC itself -- once named TIME Magazine's 1982 "Man Of The Year", -- it is now woefully outdated, thrift-store technology, but the man who designed its software, one Bill gates, is the richest man in history. A history that many claim COMPUTERS THEMSELVES will negate at the very second the clock strikes Jan 1, 2000.

Walking along the canal to where the old brown and grey, 1970's IBM buildings brood today, alongside I-95, I think how strange it seems to be standing here today in 1999. A lot of people who grew up in the '80's didn't think we'd make it. Ronald Reagan said, "This is the generation that may face Armageddon," and he meant it. "The Day After" never happened; nonetheless, each year seems to bring a new Nostradamus theory or bible prophecy about the planets lining up and comets hitting the Earth, and world wars that start in the Middle East. Each one seems to carry with it its own phenomenal weariness, as if they're saying, deep down, that we know the world just can't keep on like this. But here we are.

There was once a 50's Science Fiction version of the future, an IBM future of laser guns, robot slaves, and computers that filled whole rooms. But, looking at the canal today, with shopping carts from stores long out of business poking through the surface, I can't help but think, "This is what the future REALLY looks like...

Pier 7

Part 5: San Francisco

The City of San Francisco's official fishing pier is Pier 7, downtown. Every morning, the benches at the end of the pier fill up with Asian guys who come down the hill from Chinatown and spend all day there on the pier, doing some of the most breathtaking, artful fishing I've ever seen. With absolute concentration, never saying a word, they race back and forth between three or four poles, as the catch slowly fills their buckets. The stocks are trading a couple of blocks away in the Financial District, and cars and crowds of tourists race by on the Embarcadero, but at the end of the pier, all is quiet. It's almost as if the fishermen themselves CREATE silence. The fishermen seem so out of place in today's downtown San Francisco that it almost seems like they've been patiently fishing on the spot for centuries, while the City's great buildings rose and fell arounds them, like the tides.

The other day, I went down to the pier in the late afternoon. I watched one guy who hadn't made a catch all day. Even so, when his line finally pulled tight, you barely knew he had one. Almost imperceptibly, he started working it. His face was as calm and distant as a large ship on the horizon. Suddenly, he stood up and, with a flourish, reeled it in: a small, two-foot shark. it went into the empty bucket.

In the buildings all around us, this decade's fabeled economic boom shone in concrete and glass, but the fisherman's near-empty bucket suggested that there are some who will remember this time differently. As he leaned his arm back for another cast of the line, the TransAmerica Pyramid stood directly behind him, confident in its own indestructibility, seeming to say, the Big One will never come. These buildings will always grow taller and the fisherman's bucket will always be empty. But, as the late afternoon fog surrounded us, and the line hit the water, you couldn't help but think to yourself that anything could happen.

THE END

Letter From

Seattle...

Dear Iggy:

Sorry I haven't written in a bit, but I'm in JAIL in Seattle, and we don't have paper, or, mostly, pencils, unfortunately. It sucks; I came in with Claire and Cinque and Billy, but I haven't seen Cinque and Billy since 20 hours in, and now were at...uh, 55? Its been nuts. You may have heard. Its big news. After they arrested us, we were on a city bus with about 70 people for 15 very tense hours. Luckily, one of the punks figured out how to undo the temporary cuffs with a safety pin. Unluckily, there were only about 7 punks and 60 others, singing hippie songs and having endless collective style meetings, and trying, endlessly to reach consensus about the same shit over and over. Thank God I was with the kids!

Ah, Iggy, you should've been here! Not for the jail part, because this is so awful, but for the TAKING OVER THE STREETS!!! It was amazing. We held downtown ALL DAY! They had to call in the National Guard and it DIDN'T WORK! With 600 of us in jail, they're still under siege! But, yeah, I want out so bad. Tuesday was amazing, and now I'm missing everything. Tuesday is worth a whole other letter. Ivy and Jimmy made it up, bringing Cinque and Billy, and they did a generator show in the street at the protest! That night, we roamed the streets, aimlessly, drinking beer. Jimmy was off somewhere and we went to find him but Capitol Hill was totally under siege! Tear gas, lines of cops, and we were a ways behind cop lines, wearing our masks, cause of the gas, just listening to sirens and explosions (gas canisters and rubber bullets) and helicopters... It was the most surreal fucking thing! This was in the middle of normal Tuesday night life. The bars were full of folks who were stuck inside and getting gassed anyways and shit like that.

There's an International Day Of Action for us tomorrow. God, I wish I could watch, hear, or read the news, for real, though we, at least, get constant updates and, sometimes ARE the news. I've been in cells while interviews over the phone were conducted with ABC, CBC, and other places.

There's massive protests outside the jail. Last night, the protesters negotiated with the mayor and got our lawyers in. Tonight, people are locked to the front door demanding release for everyone (well, only the protesters, not EVERYONE...)

So, what happened was they arrested us everyone marching on Wednesday (after Tuesday they were scared) loaded us onto busses and drove us out to the old Navy base that they'd decided was going to be the processing center. They parked in the lot next to another bus full of protesters, and there we stayed for over 15 hours. Finally, they pulled the bus around to the back of the building (away from the TV cameras) and got on in full riot gear and started pepper spraying and pulling people off the bus by their ears, noses, cuffed hands, hair...We were in the building in this big concrete room. Around 5 or 6 AM we were shackled and moved to the jail. Everyone here is refusing to give names or any info., dmenading to be released with no charges. People who give their names, however, can be cited out BUT are ditching all the others, including some with felony charges and some who are in solitary experiencing some fucked up abuse and who will have to go to court and get god knows how screwed.

We just learned that there's 5,000 people out front and they're gassing them! Still! Even after the mayor called for the police chief's resignation! Maybe he just doesn't care anymore... Well, I hope I can get this out with me and I hope I get out soon!
XXOO,
Anandi

TAPE REVIEW:

LIFE DURING WARTIME #5: This is the latest issue of Erin's audio zine from Portland, and this is probably the best one I've heard yet. The tapes are somewhat like radio shows, with a theme, interviews with people on the theme and related punk music. This one's about the WTO protests in Seattle in December, and has lots of great sound right from the streets! It sounds great, and is definately the best produced issue yet, with all the people being interviewed actually being able to be understood clearly by the listener. Good job, and deserves points for actually coming out when the WTO stuff is still fresh in people's minds. 3$ from PO BOX 1113 Portland, OR 97207

MAS DAY '99

..., MY FAVORITE THING HAS JUST BEEN HANGING OUT IN THE TRAIN [YARD]. I LIKE TO GO DOWN THERE AND WALK AROUND, SPRAYPAINTING [MES]SAGES ON THE TRAINS FOR MY FRIENDS IN OTHER CITIES. THE THING [IS,] THEY ALWAYS GET 'EM, TOO. MY GRAFFITI, SOMEHOW GETS WHERE IT NEEDS [T]O GO. I REMEMBER BRAD AND MIKE TELLING ABOUT SITTING IN THE YARD IN RICHMOND, ON THEIR WAY DOWN TO MIAMI, WATCHING CAR AFTER CAR OF MY TAGS GO BY. OR THE TIME I WENT ON A DATE IN THE ALAMEDA TUNNEL AND [L]ATER, THE GIRL SAW THE BOXCAR WITH "I LEFT MY HEART IN THE ALAMEDA TUNNEL" ON IT. OR THE TIME ANANDI WAS HOPPING OUT OF PORTLAND, WORKING ON A LETTER TO ME, AND THE OPEN BOXCAR THAT SAID "SCAM PUNKS" WENT BY. SHE SHOULD HAVE PUT THE LETTER IN IT! BUT, I LIKE GOING DOWN THERE TO MISS EVERYBODY IN THE OTHER TOWNS, MY FRIENDS OUT THERE ON THE ROAD, TOO. AND TO HEAR THE BALL RATTLE IN THE CAN IN THE QUIET YARD, AND SAVOR THE "END OF THE WORLD", NO ONE ELSE AROUND FEELING.

ON CHRISTMAS, IVY AND IAN HAD THIS COOL PARTY. THEY PUT OUT FLYERS [T]HAT SAID, "FUCK CHRISTMAS! LET'S PAINT!" AND DIRECTED EVERYONE TO JUST [S]HOW UP AT THIS WALL DOWN IN THE ABANDONED, RUNDOWN WAREHOUSE DISTRICT BY THE PORT TO PAINT MURALS. THEY HAD TONS OF STOLEN AND DONATED PAINT [A]ND FOOD AND A BAR-B-Q TO COOK UP THE VEGGIE DOGS. JIMMY BROUGHT THE GENERATOR, OF COURSE, AND A STEREO, AND TRACY BROUGHT A COUPLE CRATES OF RECORDS! SINCE IT WAS X-MAS, THE WHOLE CITY WAS DESERTED, AND WE TRULY [OW]NED THE STREETS. SOON, THERE WERE 10, OR 15 PEOPLE PAINTING, RECORDS B[ROAD]CASTING, AND FOOD COOKING.

AS THE MURALS GOT MORE ELABORATE, WE STARTED ADDING TO OUR PARTY. ANANDI [AN]D I FOUND A COUCH AND DRAGGED IT OVER AND PUT IT IN THE MIDDLE OF THE STREET. THEN, WE FOUND SOME ORANGE CONES AND PUT THEM AROUND US TO MAKE IT [L]OOK OFFICIAL. WHEN CARS CAME, THEY HAD TO GO AROUND.

AFTER AWHILE I SET OUT TO EXPLORE THE PORT. IT WAS X-MAS, SO THERE [WE]RE ALL THESE PLACES YOU COULD GO, WHERE YOU NORMALLY COULDN'T. I [W]ALKED ALL AROUND THERE, THEN WENT INTO THE NEIGHBORING JUNKYARD AND [C]LIMBED TO THE TOP OF THAT HUGE 5-STORY CRANE WITH THE GRAFFITI ALL [O]VER IT. I'D ALWAYS WANTED TO GO UP THERE.

LOOKING DOWN TOWARDS THE PARTY, I COULD WATCH THE WALLS SLOWLY FILL UP [W]ITH PICTURES AND LOOK OUT AT THE WHOLE CITY AT THE SAME TIME. IN A COUPLE [D]AYS, SUPPOSEDLY, THE COMPUTERS WOULD ALL SHUT DOWN AND THE WORLD WOULD END [AN]D ALL THAT. I DIDN'T REALLY THINK ANYTHING WOULD HAPPEN, BUT I WAS REALLY HOPING IT WOULD. I COULD USE A COUPLE WEEKS MORE LIKE THIS DAY.

BUT WHAT WILL WE DO WHEN NOTHING HAPPENS? IT SEEMS LIKE, MY WHOLE LIFE, PEOPLE HAVE BEEN WAITING FOR SOME BIG EVENT — THE END OF THE WORLD, THE REVOLUTION. [I]N S.F. NOW, PEOPLE EVEN TALK OPENLY OF WAITING FOR A HUGE EARTHQUAKE TO COME SCARE OFF THE YUPPIES AND DESTROY ALL THE BANKS. WHAT IF YOU JUST LIVED HOW YOU WANTED TO, INSTEAD OF WAITING? WHAT IF WE WANTED "THE BEGINNING" INSTEAD OF THE END?

I LEFT THE CRANE AND HEADED BACK TO THE PARTY. IT WAS GETTING DARK. I FIGURED IF WE JUST STARTED SOME TRASH CAN FIRES IN THE STREET AND HAD A FEW BEERS WE'D REALLY BE SET...

THE  END

4/00

SCAM PUNKS

ABOUT THE AUTHOR

THE AUTHOR, PICTURED HERE PUSHING A XEROX MACHINE UP MISSION STREET, S.F., SUMMER 2001.

ERICK LYLE GAVE UP THE NAME "IGGY SCAM" IN 2004 BUT IS STILL THE EDITOR OF SCAM ZINE, NOW IN ITS 19TH YEAR. HE IS A FREQUENT CONTRIBUTOR TO NOSEDIVE AND RICE HARVESTER AND HIS WORK HAS ALSO APPEARED ON NPR'S THIS AMERICAN LIFE, THE SAN FRANCISCO BAY GUARDIAN, THE BROOKLYN RAIL, AND RARITAN. HE IS THE AUTHOR OF THE BOOK "ON THE LOWER FREQUENCIES: A SECRET HISTORY OF THE CITY" AND HIS NEXT BOOK WILL APPEAR ON SOFT SKULL PRESS, SPRING 2011. CURRENTLY, LYLE PLAYS IN BLACK RAINBOW, ONION FLAVORED RINGS, AND, PROBABLY, SHOTWELL. HE LIVES IN BROOKLYN, NY.

AUTHOR PHOTO BY CAROLINE PAQUITA. "BISCAYNE BOULEVARD" ORIGINALLY APPEARED IN STARFUCKER #4, "SO MILLION" IN MAXIMUM ROCKNROLL #205, AND "SAFE SEX GET PAID" IN DESPERATE LIVING #8. THANKS TO JOHN DANIA, ICKY, ERIN YANKE, JEFF MILLER, AND JOSH MACPHEE FOR HELP THIS TIME!